'THE INFIDEL WITHIN'

HUMAYUN ANSARI

'The Infidel Within'

Muslims in Britain since 1800

OXFORD
UNIVERSITY PRESS

OXFORD
UNIVERSITY PRESS

Oxford University Press is a department of the
University of Oxford. It furthers the University's objective
of excellence in research, scholarship, and education
by publishing worldwide.

Oxford   New York

Auckland   Cape Town   Dar es Salaam   Hong Kong   Karachi
Kuala Lumpur   Madrid   Melbourne   Mexico City   Nairobi
New Delhi   Shanghai   Taipei   Toronto

With offices in

Argentina   Austria   Brazil   Chile   Czech Republic   France   Greece
Guatemala   Hungary   Italy   Japan   Poland   Portugal   Singapore
South Korea   Switzerland   Thailand   Turkey   Ukraine   Vietnam

Oxford is a registered trade mark of Oxford University Press
in the UK and certain other countries.

Published in the United States of America by
Oxford University Press
198 Madison Avenue, New York, NY 10016

Library of Congress Cataloging-in-Publication Data is available
Humayun Ansari.
'The Infidel Within': Muslims in Britain since 1800.
ISBN: 9780190909772

Printed in India on acid-free paper

CONTENTS

CONTENTS

CONTENTS

LIST OF MAPS AND DIAGRAMS

Maps

Diagrams

GLOSSARY

alim	Islamic theologian, jurist, religious teacher
ayah	nanny, lady's maid
bhangra	Punjabi folk music/dance
batin	'inner', esoteric meaning
biradari	family, clan-like, connections
burqa	complete covering for the female body
dar al-ahd	house or land of pact
dar al-ahl al-kitab	house or land of the People of the Book
dar al-aman	house or land of peace
dar al-harb	house or land of war
dar al-kufr	house or land of unbelief
dar al-sulh	house or land of truce
dar al-ulum	house of knowledge and learning; religious seminary; school
dargah	shrine
darura	doctrine of necessity that allows for concession and transgression of religious prescriptions under conditions of absolute need
dawa	preaching, to invite non-believers to Islam
dhikr	a remembrance of God
dossandh	religious tithe paid annually to the Imam by Ismailis
dupatta	scarf
Eid al-Adha	Feast of Sacrifice celebrating the end of the annual pilgrimage to Makkah

GLOSSARY

Eid al-Fitr	Feast marking the end of Ramadan (the Muslim month of fasting)
farman	Imam's edict
fatwa	expert advice of a jurist on a specific legal problem
fez	brimless male headcovering, usually red
fiqh	technical juristic elaboration of detailed content
gaddi	position of *pir*, literally seat upon which he sits
ghee	clarified butter
Hadith	Traditions of the Prophet Muhammad
hajj	pilgrimage, annually to Mecca and Medina
halal	permitted or sanctioned within Islam
haram	prohibited or unsanctioned within Islam
haya	modesty
hijab	headscarf
hutbe	sermon
ibadah	worship
idda	period of three months in which the paternity of an unborn child can be determined
ijma	consensus of opinion
ijtema	large congregation
ijtihad	the exercise of human reason
ikhtilaf	differences of opinion in respect of *fiqh* (Islamic legal science)
imam	religious leader, one who leads prayers in the mosque; title by which the Ismaili leader, the Aga Khan, is known
istihsan	method of reasoning employed in the absence of textual precedent; to make a particular interpretation of the law as a result of one's own deliberation
istislah	reasoning based on search for the common good
izzat	honour
jalabiyya	headcovering
jalsa	large congregation
jamaat-khana	Ismaili assembly and prayer hall
jihad	struggle, strenuous effort; the greater *jihad* is

	considered to be the struggle to overcome inner personal weaknesses while the armed struggle or 'holy war' is the lesser *jihad*
kafir	one who is ungrateful to God, unbeliever
kamadia mukhi's	deputy
khilafah	global Islamic state
khula	a legal process under Islamic law which allows women to seek divorce independently of their husband's wishes
Koola-Izzat	hat of honour
kufr	system of unbelief
lascar	maritime worker
lillah	for God
madrassa	religious school
mahr	dower
mahrem	a close relative with whom marriage is prohibited
masjid	mosque
Milad-i Nabi	the Prophet Muhammad's birthday
Mirza	a prefix adopted by scribes, secretaries and other educated men; as a suffix it denoted 'prince'
moulvi	title used by an alim
muallam	Muslim high priest
muballighin	voluntary preachers
mudaraba	a contract of joint partnership
muezzin	one who gives a call to a congregational prayer
mufti	specialist on Islamic law
mujahideen	those who wage *jihad*, holy warriors
mukhi (female: *mukhiani*)	official of the Ismaili *jamaat-khana*
mullah	title often used by South Asian Muslims for a Muslim religious man, often a leader
munshi	clerical official
muqaddam	literally one who commands a troop or a ship; similar to *serang*
murabaha	instalment sale contract
murid	disciple, follower of a Sufi *pir*
murshid	spiritual guide

GLOSSARY

naat	devotional poem
nashids	a form of vocal music in praise of God
Nawab	title for Indian Muslim prince or noble
pir	spiritual guide, often a Sufi leader
purdah	female seclusion
qawwali	rhythmic group (usually devotional) singing
qiyas	reasoning by analogy, analogical deduction
Quran	Islam's Holy Book, revealed to the Prophet Muhammad
qurbani	sacrifice
Ramadan	Muslim month of fasting
sadaqah	religious voluntary alms or donation
sajjada-nashin	literally 'one who sits on the carpet', head of *pir* family
salah	prayer
salam	praising Muhammad by Barelwis
serang (ghat serang)	labour agent, money lender and lodging-house keeper rolled into one
Sharia	the path to be followed; Islamic law
Shia	Those belonging to the Party of Ali; general name for all those Muslims who regard Ali, son-in-law and cousin of the Prophet Muhammad, and his descendants, as the only legitimate leaders of the Muslim community after Muhammad's death
silsila	Sufi order
Sufism (Sufi)	Islamic mysticism
Sunna	'the trodden path'; the practice and example of the Prophet Muhammad which Muslims should follow in order to live a correct life
Sunni	literally 'one who follows the trodden path'; the majority community within Islam
tabligh	preaching
talaq	divorce
taqwa	piety
tariqa	Sufi (Muslim mystic) order
tawil	allegorical interpretation
tawiz	amulets

GLOSSARY

topi	hat, head covering
ulama	plural of *alim*
umma	world-wide community of Muslims
urs	annual commemoration of the death of a Sufi saint or *pir*, often the occasion for a pilgrimage to his tomb
zahir	superficial, exoteric meaning
zakat	religious tax
zawiya	literally a corner or nook; a centre of social and religious activity in Sufi Islam
zikr	the remembrance of Allah through repetitive ritual chanting of divine names or religious verses intended to cultivate religious experience in Sufi circles

PREFACE TO THE NEW EDITION

Since this book was first published, life in the UK for Muslims has grown more precarious: their 'othering' has become much more acute. British Muslims have increasingly come to represent the ultimate stranger in the British imaginary, their bodies often the site of anti-Muslim racism and xenophobia. Identified as an 'outsider inside' and marked by name, religion, skin colour, dress and language, they have been perpetually at risk of stigmatisation.[1] The increased mobilisation of Muslims across transnational space—the so-called Muslim invasion—has only served to entrench the view of Muslims as a dangerous, socio-cultural threat. Terrorist attacks since 9/11 have undeniably resurrected latent stereotypes of Islam as an anachronism, a civilisation trapped in a time warp, and 'the Muslims' as irrational, fanatical, intolerant, misogynistic and violent 'folk devils', constituting a constant danger to public order. Against the backdrop of heightened securitisation, they have been re-framed as a problematic outsider or, even worse, the enemy within. Being born, bred and raised in Britain has not guaranteed automatic membership of the British nation. Instead, a performative belonging has been demanded through articulations and practices of 'proper' political and cultural behaviour.

Since the first edition of this book in 2004, there has been a surge of interest in the life and experience of Muslims in British society. Published ahead of the London bombings in July 2005, *The Infidel Within* anticipated a growing socio-political crisis that since then has steadily deepened. London's terrorist attacks since 7/7 reignited the debate about the putatively malign presence of Muslims in Britain. Since then, the lives of

British Muslims have become increasingly on edge. A high degree of mutual distrust, resentment and even hostility was stoked between British Muslims and the majority population, as the former increasingly came under political, media and policy scrutiny, with a focus on immigration, securitisation, integration and citizenship. Events since 7/7 have further fed the securitisation narrative, ratcheting up anti-Muslim tension. In the wake of the 2017 Westminster, Manchester and London Bridge attacks, shrill calls for internment, Muslim bans, treason charges and even an end to Islam in Britain were raised.[2] The perception that the British society and state are pitted against an alien, antagonistic religious minority has intensified in many quarters; in the British imaginary, Muslims have become the ultimate threatening Other.[3] What is the context in which this has happened?

This new preface seeks to scrutinise these shifts by providing a nuanced assessment of British Muslim experience since the beginning of the twenty-first century. It looks at changes in the profile of British Muslims and the resultant impact on the perceptions, attitudes and behaviours of both Muslims themselves and the wider British population. It explores and challenges the dominant discourses on Muslim identities, and the conceptual shifts surrounding 'the Muslim community' in the twenty-first century UK.

First, a few updated facts and figures. Since 2001, the Muslim socio-economic profile has undergone significant changes. According to an analysis from the Office for National Statistics, in 2014 there were 3,114,992 Muslims in the UK (excluding Northern Ireland), compared with 2.71 million in 2011 and 1.55 million in 2001. With 1,554,022 (a shade under 50%) born overseas, they made up 5.4% of the population of England and Wales (4.8% in 2011 and 3% in 2001).[4] Many Britons have felt that the growth of Britain's Muslim population presents a threat to national identity.[5] Negative perceptions in wider society concerning Muslim residential concentration in separate communities have heightened tensions and perpetuated the stigmatisation of British Muslims. The reality, however, is more complex. On the one hand, British Muslims have spread out into more mixed areas and mingled with the rest of the population:[6] so while Tower Hamlets' Muslim population (34.5%) grew 19% over the decade to 2011, that was far slower than the UK growth of 75%, or even London's figure of

35%. At the same time, and on the other hand, they have formed bigger clusters in particular areas. For Muslims, the 'index of dissimilarity' (a measure of integration) has gone down from 56% in 2001 to 54% in 2011, meaning that over the ten-year period there was a slight shift towards greater integration. By comparison, in 2011 Sikhs were slightly less integrated (61%) and Hindus slightly more (52%). And surprisingly, the only religious group to have increased its separation during the last decade is the relatively small Jewish population (63%), the most separated of all religions in the 2011 Census.[7]

More significantly, though, Muslims have remained disproportionately concentrated in areas of deprivation (for instance, Tower Hamlets and Newham in London). Measured against all other religious groups, they had the highest level of household overcrowding, with more than four times the national figure.[8]

Research has shown that socio-economic constraints, individual and group choices, 'white flight', and institutionally discriminatory policies and practices from local authorities to estate agents had all contributed substantially to the formation of segregated communities.[9] In 2016, while numerically Muslim communities still remain largely concentrated in the areas in which they settled from the 1960s, the picture appears to be more complex. Professor Ted Cantle, who inquired into the 'race riots' of 2001, accepted that 'there is more mixing in some parts of our society. But there is also undoubtedly more segregation in residential areas, more segregation in schools and more segregation in workplaces …'[10] In his 2016 study, 'Is segregation on the increase in the UK?', however, he cites other research, which concluded that 'while mixing between all minority ethnic groups is growing, as ethnic minorities disperse out of their historic concentration, it is also the case that the minorities, when grouped as a whole, are in most cases becoming more isolated from White British people in urban areas'.[11]

Be that as it may, the 10% of council wards that count as the most deprived parts of the country were, in 2011, home to 1.22 million Muslims: around 46% of their total, compared with 10% of the overall population. Only 1.7% lived in the 10% least deprived local authority areas in England, compared with 10% of the whole.[12] 28% of Muslim households lived in social housing as compared to 17% of overall households. A much smaller proportion of Muslim households still owned their own property outright as compared to the overall population (15% versus 31% overall). A much greater proportion of Muslims continued to live in privately rented accommodation (30% of Muslim households as compared to 18% overall).[13] Neighbourhood deprivation and low family income have been shown to have had a disproportionately deleterious impact on their health and educational achievement.

While successful business ventures in property, food, services, and fashion have emerged and, for younger Muslims with higher qualifications and a wider range of skills, social mobility has increased, they remain on the whole more likely than members of other faith communities to be economically inactive. According to the 2011 census, 21.3% of British Muslims had never worked, compared with 4.3% of the UK as a whole. The rate of unemployment among British Muslims (12.8%, of which 65% were women) was over twice that of the population as a whole (5.4%).[14] 19.8% of the Muslim population was in full-time employment, compared to 34.9% in the overall population.[15] While the higher levels of unemployment compared to the overall population have been the outcome of numerous factors, there is now enough evidence to suggest that they face the double penalty of racial discrimination as well as Islamophobia in entering the labour market.[16] In terms of occupational status, while in the higher managerial and professional groups Muslims are only slightly under-represented, moving lower down the scale they represent just 10% of those employed in lower managerial, administrative and professional occupations, compared with 20% overall. However, on a more positive note, recent research shows that the number of British Muslim millionaires had doubled from 5,000 in 2002[17] to 10,000 in 2013.[18]

Research shows that British Muslim women still face multiple discrimination in the shape of 'the triple whammy' of gender, ethnicity and religion, facing prejudice when searching for employment, in career progression, and in gender-based pay equity. They are much less likely to have a graduate level job than Christian women with exactly the same qualifications and are also less likely to receive replies to job applications.[19] A combination of factors is likely to account for their less favourable outcomes in the labour market. For instance, 18% of Muslim women in the 16–74 age band are 'looking after home or family', compared to 6% in the general population. While 44% of the

Muslim women surveyed were reluctant to go out to work because of their domestic obligations, 25% of the employers admitted to being reluctant to recruit Muslim women due to concerns that they would put family commitments and caring duties above their professional duties: British Pakistani women, it would seem, were more likely to be asked whether they had plans to get married or have children, with 1 in 8 being asked, compared to 1 in 30 white women.[20]

Muslim communities in the UK in 2011 were comparatively better educated than in 2001: 'the proportion of Muslims with no qualifications [had] fallen from 39% to 26%; however, it still [remained] above the population as a whole, where the figure [was] 23%'. While 26% of Muslims had no qualifications, the percentages for Hindus and Sikhs were 13.2% and 19.4% respectively. The reasons for many young British Muslim males doing worse than their peers included 'overcrowded housing, the relative absence of parental English language skills in some Muslim communities, low level parental engagement with mainstream schools, low teacher expectations, the curricular removal of Islam from the school learning environment, racism and anti-Muslim prejudice'.[21] Moreover, the growth of widespread anti-Muslim prejudice and discrimination in the wake of the so-called 'War on Terror' has made a negative impact on young Muslims' education through the pathologised framing of Muslim pupils in the implementation of certain strands of the PREVENT policies in schools.[22] This environment has had an alienating and potentially provocative effect on an increasingly frustrated Muslim youth.

While the number of Muslims with degrees rose from 20.6% to 24%, over the same period the educational level of the overall population accelerated faster: the share of British adults with degrees went from 19.8% to 27.2%. Other religious groups have also outperformed British Muslims: 30.1% of Sikhs and 44.6% of Hindus had degrees. Muslim underperformance at the level of higher education was at least partly down to gender dynamics. In the population as a whole, young women were more likely to go to university than young men. But among British Muslims, the pattern was reversed, with three Muslim boys going on to higher education for every two girls. And when British Muslims did go on to university, some studies suggest they were less likely than other groups to attend the best institutions.[23]

PREFACE TO THE NEW EDITION

Over the last decade and a half there has been a demonstrable rise in Islamophobia. This went hand in hand with a wider backlash against multiculturalism. Detractors argued that instead of being an effective strategy for managing an increasingly ethnically and religiously plural Britain, multiculturalism encouraged 'cultural apartheid' by elevating difference and acceptance of distinct identities. It was blamed for 'perverting young Muslims', and fanning 'the flames of Islamic extremism'. British Islamist terrorists were, it was alleged, a 'consequence of a misguided and catastrophic pursuit of multiculturalism'.[24] To the liberal columnist Yasmin Alibhai-Brown, the discourse of multiculturalism no longer offered a shared narrative of who the British were. For the conservative philosopher Roger Scruton, 'multiculturalism [was] a recipe for disintegration'.[25] For its critics, the government's multiculturalist doctrine had facilitated Islamic extremism, as these policies (often perhaps unwittingly) imposed Islamist leadership upon Britain's Muslim communities. When David Cameron, in his speech at the Munich Security Conference in February 2011, suggested that 'under the doctrine of state multiculturalism, we have encouraged different cultures to live separate lives, apart from each other and the mainstream [and that] we have even tolerated these segregated communities behaving in ways that run counter to our values', it was clear that his target was primarily British Muslims.[26] Recurrent Islamist terrorist attacks, combined with on-going conflicts in Libya, Syria and Iraq, the rise of ISIS and security fears generated by the arrival in Europe of thousands of refugees from the war-ravaged zones, further heightened antipathy towards Muslims. Negative coverage and opinions in the media, comments from political circles, and the drip feed of policy related announcements in these contexts have further deepened an increasingly anti-Muslim climate.

Sustained by the relentless negative media coverage and vitriolic political rhetoric, Islamophobia moved beyond small fringe far right groups to circulate instead within broad sections of the population. Already in 2011, the then Co-Chairman of the Conservative Party Baroness Sayeeda Warsi's declaration that Islamophobia had crossed the threshold of middle class respectability and 'passed the dinner-table test', suggested its extensive permeation within British society. Anti-Muslim bigotry, she surmised, was accepted as normal and uncontroversial.[27] Since then, an extensive range of people and social groups—politicians, judges, journalists, intellectuals, universities, middle and working classes, even members of the communities under suspicion themselves—have felt sufficiently persuaded to be co-opted into the process of detecting, monitoring and reporting 'suspect' Muslim individuals and behaviours. This response has been found in official policy documents, and heard in voices of state institutions and of those holding authoritative positions. In millions of daily speeches and acts it became increasingly normalised. Thus, a broad undercurrent of secular polemics against Islam and Muslims as a focus for wider opposition to organised religion provided credibility and authority to the Islamophobic discourse.

Arguably, a key player in the normalisation and intensification of Islamophobia in Britain was the media. During the early decades of the twenty-first century, as research amply demonstrated, anti-Muslim sentiments became increasingly prevalent, conspicuous and explicit in the British media.[28] Evidence supported the existence of widespread and systematic discriminatory practices in reporting on Muslims and Islam, with a trend towards disproportionately negative, distorted and even fabricated coverage.[29] These helped to reinforce wider popular beliefs that Muslims, as a supposedly violent and intolerant people, were prone to extremist behaviour and actions, and possessed the potential for undermining social and political cohesion.

Cultural controversies highlighted in the mass media, such as so-called 'honour killings', female genital mutilation, and the grooming for sex and sexual abuse of young white girls by Muslim men, further exacerbated this negative image. Through their exaggerated and sensationalised take on oft-repeated news stories, the tabloids in particular increased such fears, threats, and suspicions by disproportionately reporting on the growth and vociferousness of fringe Muslim groups possessing anti-western and isolationist ideologies. This, in turn, went some way towards both shaping and simultaneously reaffirming public anxieties that were subsequently—and quite inappropriately—attributed indiscriminately to all Muslims.

The public, in effect, was fed messages regarding Muslims' inherent difference and incompatibility with 'normal' values and 'normal' ways of life, which were then offered as reason enough to view 'anti-Muslimism' as acceptable and justified. For instance, a 2008 analysis of newspaper coverage of Muslims revealed that four of the five most common discourses used about Muslims in the British press associated Islam/ Muslims with threats, problems or in opposition to dominant British values. By contrast, only 2% of stories contained the proposition that Muslims supported dominant moral values. The Cardiff School of Journalism, Media and Cultural Studies, commissioned by Channel 4 to examine reporting of Muslim issues, found that of the 974 stories it analysed approximately two-thirds of all 'news hooks' for stories about Muslims involved either terrorism, religious issues such as Sharia law, highlighting cultural differences between British Muslims and others, or Muslim extremism, concerning figures such as preacher Abu Hamza.[30] These stories all portrayed Muslims as a source of trouble. By contrast, only 5% of stories were based on problems facing British Muslims. Hence, while different sections of the press participated in the construction of Muslim communities as 'suspect' in public discourse, to varying degrees and in divergent ways, the broad tendency was to magnify and extend the perceived threat posed by Muslims to entire communities.[31] Similarly, in the aftermath of the murder of soldier Lee Rigby in 2013 by Islamic extremists in London, Michael Adebolajo and Michael Adebowale, and that of Mohammed Saleem by a far right extremist, Pavlo Lapshyn in Birmingham, an analysis of over 1,022 UK newspaper articles showed that 'news coverage had generalised about Muslims … in an overtly prejudicial way'.[32]

Moreover, it revealed apparent double standards regarding media reporting on terrorism. For instance, the Islamist extremist motivation of the murder of the off-duty soldier Lee Rigby contrasted with that of eighty-two-year-old Mohammed Saleem. Member of Parliament Jo Cox's murderer, Thomas Mair, who is alleged to have said 'Britain first', 'this is for Britain', 'Britain always comes first' and 'keep Britain independent' as he attacked the MP, and who in court gave his name as 'death to traitors, freedom for Britain', was described as a 'helpful and polite loner with mental health issues'.[33] The Finsbury Park Mosque attacker of Muslims in London in June 2017, Darren Osborne, who was heard shouting, 'I'm going to kill all Muslims', was reported as a 'complex … troubled man' on medication but 'no terrorist' according to his family.[34] By contrast, Lee Rigby's murderers were cast as 'butchering', 'depraved', 'Islamist fanatics'.[35]

Beyond the popular manifestations of Islamophobia, a wide body of research now suggests that the phenomenon has become more systemic and increasingly institutionalised since 7/7, though, in March 2005 (before 7/7), Hazel Blears, the minister responsible for counter-terrorism, was already reflecting the official construction of Muslims as 'suspect'. Addressing the Commons Home Affairs Committee inquiry into the impact of anti-terrorist measures on community relations, she declared that Muslims had to accept as a 'reality' that they would be stopped and searched by the police more often than the rest of the population because 'if a threat is from a particular place then our action is going to be targeted at that area ... It means that some of our counter-terrorism powers will be disproportionately experienced by the Muslim community'.[36] Since then, a further range of anti-terrorism measures has subjected Muslims to disproportionate surveillance, detention, and deportation. In the assessment offered by a 2011 report comparing the construction of the Irish and Muslims as suspect communities in the last 40 years, substantial evidence showed that the laws of 2000, 2001, 2005, 2006, 2012, and 2015 were underpinned by an anti-Muslim official discourse, and expanded the offence of terrorism in a way that meant that anything (even remotely) associated with Muslims and possible dissent could potentially become an object of suspicion.[3738]

The argument that anti-terrorist laws may have played a significant role in producing greater suspicion of Muslims received further empirical support by a May 2011 report that Britons of South Asian descent, predominantly Muslims, were over forty-two times more likely than white people to be the target of a counter-terrorism power that allowed for the stopping and searching of individuals.[39] The impact of these measures was a sharp increase in the number of Muslim internees from the turn of the twenty-first century: the UK's Muslim prison population increased from 5,502 (7.7%) to 12,225 by December 2014 (over 14%), while 97% of all those serving time for terrorism offences were Muslims.[40]

A particularly controversial example of what came to be characterised as institutional Islamophobia was the PREVENT Programme. In the wake of the 7/7 bombings, the Labour Government launched the programme in 2006, with the aim of intercepting people whose activities, behaviours, and beliefs were not criminal but, according to government officials, indicative of extremism. All the same, it is worth noting that at this stage, extremism had not been officially defined. In his speech, Blair referred alternatively to 'radical Islam', a 'politicised view of Islam', 'Sunni and Shia extremism', 'religious extremism' and the 'Islamist ideology', but admitted that 'one of the frustrating things about this debate is the inadequacy of the terminology and the tendency for any short hand to be capable of misinterpretation, so that you can appear to elide those who support the Islamist ideology with all Muslims'.[41] In 2015, however, a specific definition of extremism, though still no less problematic, was given statutory status.[42]

At its very inception, PREVENT was concerned primarily with what it termed as Islamic radicalism and the 'hatred and violence [conducted] in the name of Islam'. In 2007, a new Preventing Extremism Pathfinder Fund of £6 million was made available to support 'priority local authorities' in taking forward a programme of activities 'to tackle violent extremism at a local level'.[43] These areas were notably, as highlighted by Kundnani, defined by the size of their Muslim population. Ninety-four local authority areas with more than 2,000 resident Muslims (2001 census) were targeted for PREVENT intervention, with funding allocated in direct proportion to the number of Muslims present in each area, rather than 'according to identifiable risk of violent extremism'.[44] In this regard, it seems that the government used the size of local Muslim populations as proxies for risk [i.e., degree of vulnerability-threat] of radicalisation.

At the heart of the PREVENT programme lay a particular conceptualisation of the notion of 'radicalisation', which was most powerfully drawn upon in PREVENT's analysis of the causes of terrorism. Whereas before 9/11, the term 'radicalisation' had been used in academic literature to refer to a shift towards more radical, usually secular, politics, by the mid-2000s the term had acquired its new meaning of a psychological or theological process by which Muslims moved towards extremist views. This understanding of radicalisation was underpinned by a particular analysis that suggested Islamic culture was anti-modern and totalitarian. It largely ignored the role of social, economic, and political factors as significant sources of political violence, or the view that an extreme ideology becomes appealing when social, economic and political grievances give it legitimacy. Rather, it contended that religious ideology was the primary driving factor for terrorism and that some extremist versions of Islam—usually defined as 'Islamism' or 'Salafism'—were on their own capable of capturing the minds of Muslims and turning them into terrorists. Hooked on sociopsychological theories for their understanding of radicalisation, policymakers now dismissed addressing wider social and political issues.

The challenge for the state in putting a stop to terrorism was how to understand the process by which extremist religious ideology took hold among Muslims. A number of theorisations fortified this thinking: first, that there existed a much larger pool of people negatively predisposed towards Britain in which the terrorists swam, and PREVENT was about reaching that group and challenging and changing their beliefs and attitudes; second, that entry into this wider pool of extremists could be predicted by individual or group psychological or theological factors; and third, that knowledge of these factors would lead to government policies that would reduce the risk of terrorism. Despite much academically rigorous and incisive criticism of this 'conveyor belt' theory, the notion of a clear process, from initial influence by 'non-violent extremists' to the embrace of violent methods, became the key feature of official thinking that underpinned much early twenty-first century counter-terrorism policy-making.[45] Indeed, a 2011 review re-affirmed the link between religious conservatism and terrorism, and the government pursued PREVENT, if anything, even more robustly than before. In the context of securitisation, a host of measures (including legislation) aimed at stemming 'extremism' at its source were introduced.

In 2014, following the 'Trojan Horse' allegations of an Islamist conspiracy to take over schools in Birmingham and promote their agenda (no evidence of terrorism, radicalisation or violent extremism ever came to light), the Conservative-Liberal Democrat coalition government issued advice on the 'Promotion of British Values', ostensibly under the PREVENT scheme.[46] The July 2015 Counter-Terrorism and Security Act (the seventh such piece of legislation in fourteen years) provided more stringent guidance stipulating that 'being drawn into terrorism includes not just violent extremism but also non-violent extremism which can create an atmosphere conducive to terrorism and

can popularise views which terrorists then exploit'.[47] That it disproportionately targeted Muslims could be gauged from the exponential
rise in the number of referrals to the Channel programme[48] incorporated within the PREVENT strategy: from 5 in 2006–7 to 1,281 in
2013–14[49] to 4,611 people—including more than 2,000 children and
teenagers—in the year ending in June 2016 (a 75% rise on the previous year).[50] The number of referrals to PREVENT reached a record
8,000 in the year to April 2016.[51]

While there has been no wholesale rejection of state-led counter-
terrorism intervention (and nor has this been viewed incompatible
with Muslim communities' own efforts to tackle terrorist attacks)
there remained substantial unease with the official definition of extremism. Many Muslims cited the PREVENT programme as a significant
source of fear, anxiety and tension among their communities.[52] They
argued that it was a significant factor in the rise of 'street level' hostility
against those perceived as Muslim, as well as normalising differential
treatment of communities on the basis of their putative lack of commitment to British values and community cohesion. Some British
Muslims, insisting that PREVENT made things worse, launched their
own alternative grassroots-led initiatives, which, rather than challenging extremist ideology, focused solely on a total rejection of violence.[53]
Despite trenchant criticism from across the political and academic
spectrum, successive governments stubbornly remained wedded to the
programme, though Andy Burnham, who was elected Mayor of
Greater Manchester in 2017, took note and pledged to replace it with
a new scheme that, in his view, had to command the confidence of the
region's Muslim communities through local involvement.[54]

The impact of the rising curve of Islamophobia on Muslim communities has been extensive. While terrorist attacks inevitably provoked periodic spikes in Islamophobic attacks, the trend in religious
hate crime, according to London's Metropolitan Police, rose sharply
after 2013, with a further 41% rise following the EU referendum.[55]
When the perceptions of British Muslims are compared with those in
the country at large, the gap is striking. On the one hand, Muslims have
been accused of resisting integration; on the other hand, many Muslims
view British society as increasingly antagonistic towards them.
Regarding the former accusation, as one Birmingham Muslim MP

insisted in his Foreword to a 2017 Policy Exchange report, 'British Muslims are amongst the country's most loyal, patriotic and law-abiding citizens ... it cannot be stressed enough that most British Muslims want to integrate with their non-Muslim neighbours'.[56] There was a lot of evidence to corroborate his conclusion. In 2007, a Gallup poll, for instance, revealed that though religion was said to be an important part of Muslim identity (88% in London) in contrast to the wider population (36%), the overwhelming majority of Muslim residents maintained that they were loyal to the country in which they lived.[57] In 2009, another Gallup survey found that 'more Muslims identify themselves with being British [77%] than the rest of the population [50%] and most have far more confidence than the general public in courts, fair elections, financial institutions and the media'.[58] A YouGov poll for Demos in 2011 similarly found that Muslims were more patriotic than Britons as a whole, with 83% of Muslims agreeing with the statement 'I am proud to be a British citizen' as compared to 79% among the general population.[59] In 2015, a BBC survey disclosed that almost all Muslims living in Britain felt a loyalty to the country (95%): nine in ten (93%) believed that they should always obey British laws, with only 11% feeling sympathetic towards people who wanted to fight against western interests.[60] Additionally, British Muslims were more likely, as a group, to condemn various acts of political violence (and even non-violent political protest) than the UK population as a whole.[61] All the same, the perception of the majority population regarding British Muslim incompatibility with the established norms, as well as a perceived proclivity to intolerance and violence, has showed no signs of abating. In 2015, a YouGov survey found that 55% thought that 'there is a fundamental clash between Islam and the values of British society', as opposed to 22% who agreed that Islam and British values were 'generally compatible'.[62] By 2016, only 28% agreed that Islam was compatible with British values, 72% had a negative view of Islam, and a third saw it as promoting acts of violence in the country.[63] Yet, despite growing manifestations of anti-Muslim bigotry and prejudice, British Muslims continued overwhelmingly to believe that Britain was a good place in which to practise their religion. 91% felt able to follow Islam in Britain entirely freely; only 2% said they could not practise it at all. And they tended to be among Britain's more socially and politically engaged citizens.[64]

PREFACE TO THE NEW EDITION

The fact that, in a number of respects, Muslim values and traditions have been perceived to be incompatible with the established norms of the majority population and its institutions has made the task facing British Muslim communities in the new millennium a challenging one. Nevertheless, in the main they have navigated resiliently the actual and perceived demands and values of British society, and the needs, beliefs and practices of different Muslims themselves. The range of heterogeneous Muslim organisations equipped and able to represent the interests of their particular communities compared with the past has expanded, as has the infrastructure aimed at sustaining the Islamic faith among future generations. By the early twenty-first century, an estimated 1,700 mosques served a variety of religious, educational, social and cultural functions. They engaged with institutions of wider society, local government, national policy structures, and other areas of public life more confidently and robustly than ever before.

Notwithstanding setbacks such as the marginalisation of representative bodies, including the Muslim Council of Britain, by the Conservative-Liberal Democrat coalition government of 2010–15, British Muslims on the whole continued to regard formal political mechanisms as an effective way of getting their problems addressed, if not solved. The proportion of Muslims as active participants in national and local politics—as voters, as members of mainstream parties, and as candidates for election—continued to grow steadily. The number of Muslim MPs doubled from four in 2005 to eight in 2010, and then nearly doubled again to fourteen in the 2017 general election, including eight women. Similar proportions of Muslims sit in the House of Lords. In contrast, their representation in local government seems to have been at a standstill in the five years leading up to 2017, despite the fact that Sadiq Khan was elected London's first ever Muslim mayor in 2016.

This pattern, however, should not hide the fact that substantial numbers of British Muslims have often felt ignored by mainstream political parties. Disillusioned, they have shifted to non-parliamentary political action; they have pursued the politics of the street, confronting the power of the state through direct and disruptive collective action. Among them, a tiny socially-alienated and marginalised minority, harbouring a mixture of resentment, anger, and despair, have resorted to jihadi terrorism. But this spontaneous and relatively unorganised political response has proved hugely counter-productive and damaging for relations between Muslims and wider society, even when it is over-whelmingly and unequivocally rejected by the members of most Muslim communities across the country. A powerful example in this regard was the refusal of 'at least 500 imams and religious leaders to perform funeral prayers for the London Bridge attackers in condemnation of the "vile murderers"'.[65]

Among young British Muslims, the critical questioning of their elders' norms and values has continued to take place, combined with increasing participation in the cultural practices of the majority population, some innovatively experimenting with hybrid fusions of cultural forms. Nadiya Hussain, the 2015 winner of BBC's hugely popular cookery contest 'The Great British Bake Off', was subsequently invited to produce a cake for Queen Elizabeth's 90th birthday celebrations. In 2016, cricketers Moeen Ali, Adil Rashid, Zafar Ansari and Haseeb Hameed were selected to represent England against Bangladesh and India. In 2017, Saliha Mahmood-Ahmed, a doctor, won the BBC's 'Masterchef' competition, with a menu of 'East meets West' dishes inspired by her Pakistani heritage.

Contrary to enduring popular depictions of Muslim women as passive and docile, compliant and unreflective, and subject to patriarchal traditions, research instead pointed to their increasingly active agency. Among younger women there was greater questioning of the traditional male-dominated community leadership and of wider double standards in gender relations. In order to address their own collective needs and concerns, British Muslim women have made considerable progress in building, managing and operating women-led organisations. Some have challenged the inferior position of women in Muslim communities by referring back to Islam. They have rejected Islamist agendas, which they regard as inherently opposed to female liberty and equality, by participating in activities that resist traditional male authority. A small but growing group of Muslim feminists have defied the mindset that has traditionally discouraged if not excluded women from leadership roles within the mosque. In 2015, the Muslim Women's Council announced plans to create a women-led mosque, open to both women and men of all denominations.[66] The Muslim Women's Network UK, led by Shaista Gohir, served as a link between Muslim women and the government, providing myriad resources for Muslim women on issues such as forced marriage and domestic violence.[67] Big Sister was another organisation dedicated to the promotion of female Muslim role models. Younger Somali women, in particular, took an active role in campaigns against practice of female infibulation and circumcision.[68] However, while education and financial independence enabled a growing number of Muslim women to lead more independent lives than had been the case for previous generations, compared with the majority of British women they remained relatively more constrained in their public and private lives.

To conclude, in the years following 2005, the 'Muslim Question' acquired increased political saliency as the British state focused on securitisation and border control alongside issues of social cohesion and citizenship. The Casey Review of 2016, commissioned by the then prime minister, David Cameron, tackled community cohesion.[69] But rather than acknowledging that social and economic factors combined with discrimination were arguably the key to understanding (any) community segregation, it pointed to British Muslims as predominantly isolationist and prone to self-segregation. Hence, its recommendations included an 'integration oath' to encourage immigrants to embrace British values, and greater focus on promoting the English language.[70] The Review's author Louise Casey highlighted what she considered to be the 'problems' among British Muslims, though she admitted that there was a 'vicious circle' in which Muslims felt they were being blamed for terrorism and extremism, leading to suspicion, mistrust and hostility. In her view, in order to help bridge divides in the UK, the British government had to act to end the 'misogyny and patriarchy' in some Muslim communities and to secure 'women's emancipation in communities where they are being held back by regressive cultural practices'.[71]

A wide cross-section of commentators and observers on the Casey Review held that it damaged rather than improved community relations, thanks to its official focus on Muslims as the sources of and obstacles to community cohesion, and the absence of any serious recognition of anti-Muslim prejudice, or the way in which the perpetration and condoning of hatred formed a significant obstacle to integration and participation.[72] The fundamental impact of spatial segregation, socio-economic disadvantages and discrimination as obstacles to integration, to limiting opportunities, networks, confidence and capacity, its critics argued, had been disingenuously down-played.[73] Muslims, from their perspective, continued to be essentialised, exceptionalised and pathologised across a wide cross-section of British society, despite, as research findings in 2013 highlighted, the fact that when socio-economic disadvantage and high religiosity (both of which predict social conservatism among all Britons) were taken into account, British Muslims' attitudes were relatively similar to those of non-Muslims.[74]

The complexities, nuances and diversity of identities among Muslims in Britain thus need to be understood at multiple levels, from transnational connections, to national representations and local formations of Muslim life in the context of the precariousness of their citizenship. British 'Muslim-ness' more than ever needs to be understood as a dynamic process shaped by their diverse and ever-changing experiences—the interactions between new migrants and settled communities, and among a range of ethnic and national origins across and within generations and gender. The changing permutations of these experiences (interlaced with differentiated education and socio-economic status)—of upward mobility versus marginalisation, of the greater likelihood of being unemployed than the population generally, of a growing concentration in some inner-city areas alongside a growing spreading out of the Muslim population across suburban Britain—have continued to shape the contours of British Muslim identifications. These identifications are being buffeted by battles taking place within British Muslim communities against regressive religious forces that seek to dissolve women's basic human rights under the guise of religious expression and tradition.[75] Large numbers of British Muslim women have challenged normalised patriarchal traditions and structures,[76] arguing and organising in pursuit of gender rights and against aspects of systematic gender discrimination and inequality.[77]

As *The Infidel Within* concluded in 2004, the result of the fluidity and multiplex nature of these experiences (now a fact of British life) is not one single, neatly identifiable British Muslim identity but, instead, a range of identifications, expressed in different dispositions with regard to changing social and cultural trends. Through these complex processes, Muslims continue to address the challenges and dilemmas involved in living in the UK in a rapidly globalising context and to respond to them in diverse ways. While degrees of social conservatism among layers of British Muslims continue to be reflected in comparatively high levels of support for gender segregation, the *hijab*, supposed 'traditional' clothing and certain elements of Sharia law, the vast majority of British Muslims, in their concerns, lifestyles and approaches to everyday issues—earning a living, apprehension for the plight of others here and elsewhere, the challenges facing the young, the old, the sick, the disadvantaged—lead essentially secular lives, and so are little different from their non-Muslim counterparts:[78] 'British Muslims are, on a whole range of matters, no different in their views and priorities than their non-Muslim neighbours. In response to the question regarding the most important issues facing Britain today (2017), the most likely answer was NHS/hospitals/healthcare (36%), followed by unemployment (32%) and then immigration (30%)'.[79]

Undoubtedly, over the course of the early twenty-first century, British Muslim identities showed signs of becoming increasingly politicised, in part as a reaction to widely-experienced shared grievances based on the interaction of domestic discrimination and deprivation, and connected to the international threats that faced Muslim communities around the world. Neither Islam nor its purported 'culture' alone explains this politicisation. The greater awareness of a British Muslim collective identity and the power struggles that underlie this have unfolded as a sequence of politicising events that have gradually transformed British Muslim relationships with the broader social environment. The mainstreaming of an essentialising, rejectionist anti-Muslim rhetoric, and the exaggerated media and political attention that this has received, have forced and forged a more consciously collective formulation of the role of the broader Muslim community in British society by British Muslims themselves. An aspect of identity formation that is rarely recognised, but should be viewed as a factor in the politicisation of a collective British Muslim identity, is the internal politics of Islam within the global context. As political, sectarian conflicts around the world become increasingly intensified, this has been mirrored in Britain by the construction of 'internal others' amongst British Muslims.

More importantly, British Muslims have been 'othered' within and by British society in a variety of ways, with individuals and communities the targets of state and neighbourhood surveillance, securitisation and sanctions. They have been subject to tailored forms of legal constraints, forms of civil society exclusion, restriction of movement, and an elite and corporate driven negative media onslaught. But 'othering' is always a multifaceted process that includes not only suspicion by insiders, but equally the negotiation of identity by those considered 'the other'. In multiple ways, as developments in the early decades of the twenty-first century have demonstrated, British Muslims have contested their 'othering' through practices of assimilation, integration and hybridisation, and in so doing they continue to highlight their complex, modern and shifting identities, reflecting the multidimensionality of their individual and collective experiences.

Humayun Ansari   March, 2018

1

IS THERE A BRITISH MUSLIM IDENTITY?

An issue that has generated great interest in recent times is identity. This is partly due to political developments in Europe, where national solidarities, especially in the Balkans, have come to be challenged by powerful forces of ethnic assertion. In Britain the 1980s saw the rise of populist 'English' nationalism in the rhetoric of the New Right, which contributed to the marginalisation of minority ethnic people through its racialised constructions of national belonging. Within identity discourses the meaning of who British Muslims were came under severe scrutiny, especially at key moments such as the Honeyford affair in the mid-1980s and *The Satanic Verses* controversy and the Gulf War in the late 1980s and early 1990s. Muslims, more than ever, came to be imagined as 'outsiders', excluded from the essential notions of 'Britishness' which, steeped in nostalgia, continued to be perceived as homogeneous, Christian, white and rooted in past centuries.

In the 1980s, however, British Muslims began confronting this established notion of identity through the celebration of difference and the construction of new so-called hybrid identities. Their ways of imagining identity involved challenging the reductionist explanations of community belonging apparent in discourses on 'Britishness' and in equally homogeneous imaginings of 'the Muslim community'. British Muslims thus started to offer a contrasting view of belonging which questioned, locally but in a global context, notions of national cultural 'British' hegemony.

This introductory chapter seeks to provide an assessment of the possibilities for the emergence of British Muslim identities within a range of historical perspectives. Therefore, in exploring themes concerning the relationships between British Muslim communities and the wider society, it questions presuppositions about Muslims and their identity, and so contributes to debates on what it meant to be Muslim in Britain at the end of the twentieth century. It looks at the sources of the construction of British Muslim identities—the ethno-religious culture of migrant Muslims, the changing context of British society, the changing global context, the changing profile of British Muslim communities and the dynamic interaction among them.

The context

According to current estimates there are over 1.5 million Muslims living in Britain.[1] They are more numerous than Jews, and numerically second only to members of the Church of England in terms of active religious observance. But while British Muslims have acquired a relatively high profile in the media only recently, they have been part of the British social, religious and cultural landscape for almost a century and a half. Although Muslims in Britain are associated first and foremost with a South Asian background, a Moroccan merchant community was already well established by the end of the nineteenth century with its own *halal* butchers and places of worship, and by that time Somalis and Yemenis had also begun to form distinct Muslim communities in Cardiff and South Shields.[2] Also, no later than the end of the nineteenth century there were a small number of white people who converted to Islam.[3] Clearly, then, Muslims in Britain can trace their origins to diverse historical settings with distinct cultures and languages, even coming from places that at times have been politically antagonistic to Britain.

As a result of this diversity, British Muslims at the start of the twenty-first century are neither ethnically nor ideologically homogeneous. Yet generalisations about Muslim communities have tended to rely heavily on the experience of South Asian Muslims, who have come predominantly from Pakistan and Bangladesh, bringing with them particular socio-economic characteristics, rural origins and religious beliefs and practices heavily infused with mystical and magical features.

Their often socially conservative ways differ greatly from the more puritanical and legalistic strands followed by the geographically and educationally distinct Indian Muslims, let alone Muslims from other parts of the world. Thus any presumptions of Muslim homogeneity and coherence which claim to override the differences between rural and urban, rich and poor, educated and illiterate, do not necessarily correspond to social reality. A Sylheti from Bangladesh, apart from some tenets of faith, is likely to have little in common with a Mirpuri from Pakistan, let alone a Somali or a Bosnian Muslim. Values, symbols and aspirations, approaches to issues of identity, strength of adherence to ritual and loyalty to kin networks, and the form and nature of institutions are likely to be extremely varied, making Muslims in Britain a very heterogeneous population. As Halliday has pointed out regarding the Yemenis, even ethnically homogeneous Muslim communities can be 'internally fissured'.[4] Predominantly British citizens, they are both connected and separated by a multitude of intersecting variables—ethnicity, kinship, tribe, nationality, geographical and regional location and doctrinal and sectarian traditions, practices and interpretations. In the past these Muslims have attached as much importance to these forms of identification as to religion.

Among the Arab communities in Britain, a collective Arab identity, leaving aside the Muslim one, remains a potent complex of common features and divisions shaped by many social variables. For instance, middle- and upper-middle-class Jordanians, Lebanese, Palestinians and Syrians appear to possess more multiplex relations with each other than with their own working-class compatriots. However, these ties are mostly regionally bound and do not, for example, extend to middle- and upper-middle-class Algerians, Moroccans or Tunisians or Gulf Arabs, who have their own social networks, which in turn are influenced by their own circumstances of settlement.

Furthermore, anecdotal evidence suggests that social ties between Muslim working-class Egyptians and Moroccans tend to be minimal, even when they pray in the same mosque. Nor does the common bond of Islam seem to have fostered particularly meaningful connections between working-class Bangladeshis and Somalis settled in the East End of London. The middle-class Iraqi Shia and Iraqi Sunni Kurds seeking asylum in Britain also appear to have little social interaction.

The existence of a whole range of voluntary associations—The Arab Club of Britain, the Arab Women's Association, the Moroccan Information and Advice Centre and the Al-Hassaniyya Women's Centre (both of which serve the Moroccan working-class community but are ideologically more or less opposed over gender issues), the Egyptian Community Association, the Iraqi Community Association and Ahl al-Bayt (a mainly Iraqi Shia association, where sectarian affiliations may override class considerations)—to name only a few—provide ample testimony to the diversity among British Muslims.[5] In this heavy ethnic mix, religious affiliations intersect in many ways with age-group, gender and socio-economic status, as well as with the specific circumstances of immigrant settlement experience in Britain. Thus in reality tensions persist between belief in the unity of the Muslim *umma* and the conflicting ties that distinguish these communities. When material self-interest and competition for scarce resources, are at stake, the common bond of Islam often becomes irrelevant, as can been seen in the resentment of Somalis towards Bangladeshis in Tower Hamlets in east London. Thus, given the diversity of ethnic backgrounds (in London alone there are Muslims from over fifty ethnic backgrounds), British Muslims have seldom viewed Islam as the sole form of social and political identification, and usually it is not even the primary one. Indeed, as Nielsen has pointed out, 'the experience of meeting other modes of Islamic cultural expression with equally strong claims to validity as one's own raises questions as to the exclusive legitimacy of any one particular mode'.[6]

The experiences of migration and exile have also played their part in constructing new identities. For many economic Muslim migrants 'the myth of return' has until quite recently sustained a degree of uncertainty about where they belonged, and for refugees and political exiles from Africa and the Middle East emotional attachment to their homelands has been even stronger. With time these emotional ties have slowly receded, but continuing links with their homelands still sustain past affiliations.[7] In these circumstances Muslim identity, itself diverse and changing, can provide only a partial picture of how British Muslims live and see the world.[8] Still, there have been occasions in Britain's recent past, rare though they might be, when 'Islam' has become the main or even the sole identity for many British Muslims, particularly when they have been criticised or attacked by others on the basis of their religion.

But despite tensions such as these, Islam is seen by many of its adherents as a common source of moral values that plays some role at least in shaping appropriate behaviour. Indeed, a view appears to have emerged that enough of a common experience and context exists for some Muslims to regard themselves as a distinct community in Britain, with a degree of underlying unity and coherence in the structures of public life and in terms of the character of Muslim communities.[9] Associations have been established that provide meeting-points and common forums for Muslims from varied ethnic backgrounds, fostering a specifically Muslim consciousness in different ways. For instance, the chairman of the Council of Imams and Mosques, Dr Zaki Badawi, who is also director of the Muslim College in London, is Egyptian, as is Hesham El Essawy, head of the Islamic Society for the Promotion of Religious Tolerance in the United Kingdom. Muslims from different parts of the world fill leading roles in diverse but influential and symbolically pivotal institutions, such as the Sharia Council, the Central Mosque at Regent's Park in London, the Muslim Council of Britain and the Federation of Students' Islamic Societies. Notable among these is Yusuf Bhailok, general secretary of the Muslim Council of Britain, an umbrella organisation with 300 Muslim organisations affiliated to it; he, like his predecessor Iqbal Sacranie, is of Indian Gujarati background.[10] Moreover, the more extreme organisations, such as Hizb-ut-Tahrir and Al-Muhajiroun, which have support among young Muslims from many backgrounds, especially those of South Asian origin, are also led by Arabs of different persuasions.

This coming together of particular British Muslims, whether for reasons of faith or to satisfy shared social and cultural needs, does not necessarily eliminate the divisions among them. For as long as there has been a Muslim presence in the British Isles Muslims have had to face dilemmas (concerned with personal morality, codes of behaviour, types of education, forms of religious practice and cultural identity) which they have approached within differing Muslim perspectives but which they have also perceived that they partly share. From within these perspectives a continuous dynamic engagement has evolved with the British social, economic, cultural and political environment. Crucial questions are the challenge of secularism and modernity, responses to the narrower issue of racism and its impact on politicisation, and who should set the so-called 'Muslim agenda'. Different groups of Muslims—migrants, youth, women, converts—have striven to engage with these questions, and their various perspectives have made it difficult to establish a unity of views and approaches to a whole range of moral and practical concerns.

The issues

Identity has been one of the key issues for Muslims in Britain. In contrast to past thinking on the subject, which saw it in relatively fixed and settled terms, the current view is of something malleable and constantly shaped by the changing context. Its various aspects—religion, ethnicity, custom, class—are thought to be susceptible to historical processes, and it is seen as being constantly refashioned and reimagined in accordance with internal and external social forces. The broadly secular and plural character of British society is seen as generating an array of competing identities. Many Muslims settled in Britain have had to reconcile their ethnic, religious and other affiliations at community and individual levels with the claims of class and gender. All have been buffeted, to some degree at least, by rapid social and cultural change in the late twentieth century, compelling them to adapt and negotiate, consciously and unconsciously. As the influence of the societies and cultures from which they originated on attitudes and behaviour has faded with the emergence of a larger number of British-born and -educated Muslims (around 70% of all British Muslims are under 25),[11] they have come increasingly to identify common features, as reflected in their exhibition of greater solidarity across linguistic and regional differences. In Scantlebury's examination of Manchester Muslims in 1995 there was a recollection of Muslim unity at the Central Mosque, reflecting the ideal of the *umma*, epitomised by the multi-ethnic constitution of the committee that ran the mosque's affairs: 'The first headmaster of the Sunday School was a Nigerian, the Mosque President a Syrian who was later succeeded by a Mauritian. The Imam was a Pakistani and the Vice-President was a Turk, the Secretary an Egyptian and the youth were organised by an Iraqi.'[12] Such groups of Muslims

6

are much more exercised today than earlier by their experience of British society and how they can respond to the issues of greatest concern to them.

The behaviour of many of these Muslims is governed by their perception that they are part of a worldwide community which does not recognise national or racial differences—what Muslims call the *umma*. Closely linked to this idea is their belief in the supremacy of the 'God-given code' enshrined in the Quran and the Sunna (despite there having arguably been no time in Muslim history when all life was subject to divine law). Islamic law, contrary to ideological and political pretensions, has historically been open to disputation, and its mutability in changing circumstances has generally been accepted.[13] Both these apparently unchanging ideals of the Islamist strand of thinking challenge Western secular concepts of national sovereignty and law and bring them into potential conflict with notions of popular will and democracy.

Such a basic conflict might be expected to pose problems for Muslims living as minorities in non-Muslim societies under secular or quasi-secular systems of law. Many so-called Islamists have a sense of being a beleaguered minority: they find they have no clear guidelines, although they have invoked historical precedents to make sense of their situation. One way out of these apparently irreconcilable contradictions has been to argue that minority status can only be conceived as a 'transitory phase' on the way to their becoming the majority and so able to lead their lives according to 'correct' Islamic prescriptions. Khurram Murad, sometime leader of a strand of British Islamism, saw nothing to be gained by establishing Islam in Britain with the status of a minority subculture 'grudgingly accepted' by the wider society, and suggested the creation of 'a potent counter-culture'; mere survival was not a realistic option since 'intrusion and encroachment of the hegemonic culture [was] inevitable'.[14] Kalim Siddiqi, founder of the Muslim Parliament, likewise envisaged a Muslim community that would act as a beacon to the rest of British society and persuade the majority population to accept Islam; this would lead to the establishment of an Islamic state out of *dar al-kufr* (the house of unbelief), and thus bring Muslims—eventually—to numerical power. In this design 'plugging into the global Islamic grid' and at the same time asserting one's 'Muslimness' in opposition to the national British identity clearly signalled loyalty to a supranational entity and undermined the 'British' credentials of such Muslims in the eyes of the country's majority community.[15] Nevertheless, with time British Muslims of migrant heritage have gained in confidence, and challenged with some success the attitudes, policies and concerns of the majority social order as part of the process of re-evaluating their treatment by wider British society. This increase in confidence has also encouraged certain Muslims to move from a defensive position to a proselytising one in the hope of winning new converts to Islam.

However, *dawa* (the invitation to convert) is not a newly-discovered impulse among Muslims in Britain. Converts to Islam in the nineteenth century were driven by similar aspirations, although their goals were modest and purely religious, as opposed to the more political motivation of present-day Islamic groups. Even so, most Muslim communities in Britain in the last century have been primarily concerned to survive, and beyond that to preserve the essential elements of their faith by transmitting them to future generations. For much of this period they have sought to adjust and accommodate to existing institutions and practices, so long as these have not been viewed as undermining core-values. In other words, they have responded in a variety of ways to achieve the best possible conditions for the maintenance of their beliefs and traditions. It might therefore be argued that over-concentration on the Islamist perspective, widely accepted as hegemonic, downplays the diversity which persists among British Muslims, offering only a partial understanding of the range of beliefs, practices, issues, developments and movements to be found among Muslims who have settled and emerged in Britain over the last two centuries.

Indeed interpretations of Islam that portray it as irreducible, impermeable and undifferentiated, and immune to processes of economic, social, ideological and political change, have long obscured the complexities of the historical experience of Muslims in different societies. They have also prevented meaningful exploration of, on the one hand, the existence of alternative interpretations which may have had the potential for development, and on the other hand the reasons why they have not prospered. Western 'orientalists' and Islamists alike have tended to emphasise what distinguishes Islam from the West and have thus presented it as the 'Other'.[16] The West has constructed and stigmatised an Islam with little resemblance to anything that is of value in ordinary Muslim lives. Islam has been conjured up as a danger to be kept at a distance and as a potent force—irrational, fanatical and violent—that requires tight control. More recently the imagery of the Iranian revolution and Ayatallah Khomeini, the public burning of Salman Rushdie's *The Satanic Verses* and the hysteria orchestrated before and after Saddam Hussein's invasion of Kuwait and the subsequent Gulf War have reinforced an antipathy towards Islam in the Western popular mind. But while many in the West continue to demonise Islam and Muslims in particular, on the Islamist side visible boundaries have been consciously erected to create a sense of religious exclusivity. A past has been reimagined, new sensibilities have been discovered and particularist institutions established. Thus Muslim identity in Britain is being constructed very much against a background of negative perceptions about who and what Muslims are. It is evolving as an identity of 'unbelonging' in a 'culture of resistance' and in contest with hegemonic British identity.

Until the 1980s Muslims were generally subsumed within ethnic categories and as part of the discussion of race relations. The Muslim identity of those studied was considered of secondary importance. Ethnic identifications—black, Asian, Pakistani, Arab—which determined language, colour, race and nationality rather than religion were recognised in society as the key signifiers of individual and collective difference. But structural changes in British politics during the 1980s had a major impact on the race-relations discourse and created a context in which Muslim identification gained prominence. The New Right, pursuing a largely exclusionary and culturally essentialist agenda, unleashed a virulent assault on local government autonomy and policy, reducing the power of the ethnic minority leaderships that had gained considerable influence on the basis of community support in local politics. The attack on multiculturalism and its replacement by a pluralism in which separatism deterred cultural pollution and encouraged cultural exclusivity compelled some in the ethnic minorities to use a religious vocabulary in their quest to address social problems. This New Right discourse had added appeal to a Muslim consciousness which rejected skin colour as a form of core identification and emphasised cultural and religious heritage. Made to feel different and excluded, many British Muslims, especially the youth, found a valuable resource and alternative forms of identification in 'religion'. There was a conscious effort to move away from ethnic and national identifications towards being defined first and foremost as Muslims. The projection of this identification grew in response to the local, national and global issues in which Islam was seen as to be centre-stage, as well as to increasing anti-Muslim sentiment in Britain reflected in antipathy locally and nationally.

One of the earliest signs of the emergence of British Muslim consciousness was the struggle over Muslim schools. The demand for these institutions was seen by the British establishment as an attempt to create 'pockets of pure Islamic culture sealed off from the influence of the majority culture of Western Europe'[17] where Muslim pupils could be 'diverted into some isolated and possibly militant tributary'.[18] Muslims in this construction came to be seen as 'outsiders' and their affiliation to Islam as threatening to the majority culture. In contrast, multicultural education was approved of by the British establishment, but while it was perceived as meeting some of the needs of Muslim pupils, for many British Muslims it had not been successful in protecting and developing their children's distinctive religious identity, or given them the 'cultural strength' to challenge their experience of racism. Muslim schools rather than multicultural education were seen as a way of combating discrimination since it was primarily the religious dimension in which they felt their disadvantage most keenly, and from which they derived their 'greatest collective psychological strength'.[19] Muslims who campaigned for separate schools with a Muslim ethos saw this as symbolic of the challenge to the hegemonic culture. The more the campaign was resisted, the more British Muslims saw it as a denial of their equal citizenship and of their very identity since in their view Muslim schools were precisely where a distinct sense of Muslim identity could be constructed.

The Rushdie affair and the Gulf War were a watershed in the formation of British Muslim identities, causing the question of what it meant to be a British Muslim to be debated with much intensity. The secular liberal establishment raised serious doubts about whether one could be British and Muslim simultaneously. Their scepticism was based on the supposedly homogeneous character of 'British culture', and a similar construction of the nature of British Muslims. The Conservative Home Affairs Minister, John Patten, saw British citizenship as a combination of legal rights and obligations and shared 'British' values. For him it was a matter not merely of paying taxes, using state welfare services and being subject to the laws of the land, but one of essential sentiments and loyalties and cultural norms established over centuries by the majority community. Muslims in Britain could not 'be British' as long as they pursued a separatist agenda, owing allegiance to Islam and threatening to destabilise a cultural hierarchy organised around an essential 'Englishness' that defined British identity. Being British had to do with those things that were held in common—'our democracy, our laws, the English language, and the history that has shaped Britain'. For Patten 'Britain's part in world history' was a settled matter that could not be contested. Diversity was tolerable so long as it did not conflict with British identity. As he declared, 'one cannot be British on one's exclusive terms or on a selective basis, nor is there room for dual loyalties where those loyalties openly contradict one another.' A choice had to be made, and loyalties had to be given only to Britain. Participation in the 'British way of life' required 'forgetting one's cultural roots', and if Muslims brought new beliefs, practices and traditions to Britain, they would remain external to an essential 'authentic', 'unchangeable' Britishness of which they could never become an intrinsic part.[20]

It was in response to these attacks on Islam from the establishment that British Muslim identities took shape and religious consciousness increasingly acquired significance. Indeed, in the Fourth Policy Studies Institute Survey of 1994, 74% of the Muslims interviewed considered Islam a very important influence in their daily lives. By contrast only 43% of Hindus and 46% of Sikhs considered their religion 'very important'.[21] While these data tended to conceal the diversity of responses across age, class, gender and ethnic groups, the relative strength of views on religious belief and practice was illuminating. The hold of religion on a relatively large proportion of Muslims in Britain was reflected in the concerted efforts undertaken by their communities since the 1970s to institutionalise Islam, and the mushrooming of mosques and other religious organisations across Britain testify to their commitment.[22] The role of Muslim institutions, particularly the mosque, in reinforcing Muslim identities has been significant. These institutions established a cultural infrastructure enabling the reproduction of religious beliefs and practices and helping Muslim children to be consciously socialised to imbibe the norms and values of their parents' generation. A dialectic clearly operated here: the institutionalisation of Islam contributed to the formation and shaping of Muslim identities, and they in turn sustained the institutions.

As noted earlier, Muslims in Britain represent a diverse population in their ethnic, linguistic and social constitution. This immense variation creates problems about how to define these Muslims officially. For statistical purposes, family background has been thought most relevant, and the term 'Muslim' has been applied to those for whom Islam is considered to have some significance in the ordering of their daily lives. But, as Nielsen tells us, 'it is necessary to be aware of the differing factors (social, economic, cultural and generational) which may contribute to vary the application of ideas of Islam to the ordering of that daily life, at both the individual and the collective level.'[23] For many of Modood's respondents Islam was 'a core identity, meaning not that it is always the most prominent aspect in all contexts, but, rather all other significant identities and identity-shaping practices must not be incompatible with it ... [although] what Islam means will be subject to debate and creative interpretation'.[24] As a seventeen-year-old boy in Kucukcan's study of young Turks in London explained, 'you cannot be a proper Turk without being a Muslim'.[25] Halliday, however, has provided a different emphasis. For him, the commonalities of faith, practice and solidarity are not the whole story: 'Islam may, in some contexts, be the prime form of political and social identity, *but* it is never the sole form and is often not the primary one within Muslim societies and "communities", divisions of ethnicity matter as much and often more than a shared religious identity, and this is equally so in emigration.'[26] To ethnicity must be added identities of location, class, gender and so on. Halliday suggests that there may be occasions when Islam is the main or sole identity, not least when people are attacked on that basis, but such occasions are rare—and Islam subsumes other identifications so long as it is mobilising the 'community' against exclusionism. And, as Samad has argued, as soon as 'business as usual resumes', the salience of 'British Muslim identification' returns to competing with other forms of identification. Even in 'crisis' situations such as the Rushdie affair and the Gulf War, Muslim solidarity was frequently contested.[27]

But these descriptions do not adequately define Muslims and Muslim identity in Britain, for there are also those who identify with a Muslim tradition but do not necessarily possess cultural competence in things Islamic or conscious attitudes towards Islam as a political or religious system. Nor do they necessarily view Islam as a religious system or adhere to a specific form of religious practice. For them Muslim identification is a matter of family origin and heritage. In Knott and Khokher's research, Yasmin encapsulated this view: 'Why am I Muslim? I don't know. Because that's my origin ... And I've been taught that I am a Muslim because my parents are Muslim. I might not follow their traditions, but I am Muslim ... like a lot of English girls say 'I'm Christian', but they won't go to church.'[28] Support for Palestine, denunciations of Western hegemony and the oil market, solidarity with Iraq, protests at 'double standards' on human rights—these are all part of the Muslim indictment of the West, but are not necessarily religious in content. Much of this has little to do with belief and a lot to do with secular (often nationalistic) protest against political power and dominance. For example, to understand British Muslim responses to Britain's involvement in the Gulf War it is necessary to appreciate the Muslim sense of political impotence and alienation in British society. In the context of British society, Muslim social and economic grievances have tended to be expressed in a 'religious' idiom.

Other British Muslims have been socialised into a Muslim cultural tradition and to a certain degree have internalised it. For them Islam serves as a frame of reference—a pattern of thought and communication—and gives meaning to their condition and behaviour. These Muslims may also have very diverse attitudes towards Islam and its practice. But what they do have in common is knowledge of Islam, on which they draw while engaging in a discourse so that they can communicate meaningfully and with relevance. In the study by Modood *et al*. one glimpses a range of approaches towards religion. For one respondent Islam 'provides a sense of identity. It teaches us what is right and wrong.' Another strongly propounded an 'ethical' Islam; religion could not be just a set of petty rules but was a body of ethical principles that had to be engaged with and newly interpreted in

13

changing circumstances. She saw Islam as 'an inspiration ... and a source of a sense of ... decency and civilised behaviour ... as a guidance on how I live my life'. Still others professed specific beliefs, participated in religious rituals and other practices, and adhered to Islamic principles of piety as they understood them. A fourth significant group of British Muslims held specific ideas about the place and function of religion in society, claiming Islam to be a political and social phenomenon. For them establishing the sovereignty of God through the implementation of the Sharia represented an article of faith; Islam was a complete way of life, which could only be fully achieved in a state run under Islamic law. 'Islam', according to one, 'influences the way I relate to the family, ... at work. My behaviour is influenced through the *Sharia* ... in every situation.'[29]

So while these different varieties of Muslims are to be found in Britain, all have had to face the reality of living as a minority under non-Muslim rule, and have had to construct different strategies with two objectives: to transmit this identity to their children and to create the best possible conditions to survive with their identity intact. This has involved processes of negotiation between themselves and the wider society, and how this is done has depended on the character of the Muslims and the context in which they find themselves. There is a contrast between converts and migrant Muslims. The 'problem' is that the vast majority of Muslims, being from outside Britain, have not been seen primarily as members of a religious minority but, in terms of their culture and ethnic background, as 'outsiders' rather than as authentically British. Being mainly from countries formerly ruled by Britain, they and their religion have usually been regarded as 'inferior'. As a result, they have had to establish their credentials and prove that they do indeed belong to British society. This has not been easy since a suspicion lingers in the mind of the majority population that they do not and perhaps cannot fully understand that society and its norms, values and institutions. Since the power to decide policy, distribute resources and arrange the various affairs of society rests with the majority community, these Muslims have suffered disadvantage and exclusion, and consequently their identity has been shaped by negative interactions with this society.

IS THERE A BRITISH MUSLIM IDENTITY?

Muslim identity and 'native' British converts to Islam

The experiences outlined above cannot be said to be shared by white British converts—who, while not numerous (between 5,000 and 10,000, according to Modood),[30] have a tradition dating back to the late nineteenth century. Beginning as members of Britain's majority community they have chosen, at some point in adult life, to take on a Muslim religious identity.[31] In the context of current debates about negotiating a British Muslim identity it is clearly interesting to explore how converts, presumably more firmly rooted in British society, have tried to effect a working balance between the 'British' and the 'Muslim' aspects of their identities.

When we look at these efforts, we see that for these converts it has not been a question of simply making Islam indigenous but, more urgently, of reconfiguring Islamic ideas to make meaningful connections between Islam and British religious norms. During the late Victorian, Edwardian and interwar eras, Muslims, whether converts or from outside Britain, looked for similarities between Islam and Christianity and tried to disturb cultural practices as little as possible by a deliberate building of bridges. Jesus was acknowledged as a prophet of God, and no distinction was made between him and the prophet Muhammad as deliverers of the divine message.[32] Indeed being a Muslim was presented as being a 'better Christian'. The Woking Mission established at the Woking Mosque (built in 1889) was often referred to as a 'Muslim church',[33] and those running it often presented Islam as compatible with being 'British' and 'Western'. Thus it delivered its message in a vocabulary familiar to English ears. Since the Second World War converts to Islam have represented a small but significant group among British Muslims. Depending on their view of British society, they have adopted diverse strategies to sustain themselves. For some conversion has meant a radical and profound break with previous beliefs and practices and indeed identities. Many have idealised the apparent stability of Muslim family life, the absence of alcohol, drugs and sexual 'excesses', and the sense of 'discipline' and order in individual Muslim lives, and tended to move consciously away from the materialism and secularism of the wider society.

Conversion, however, has usually not led to a complete rupture with the past or 'a total renunciation of their former religious traditions'.

Some have even discovered that what they learned from their previous religion helped them to understand Islam, and have believed that Jesus and Muhammad had essentially the same mission. Islam has meant finding the end of the line started by Abraham, and a culmination of the Judaeo-Christian tradition; these converts display no hostility towards practising Christians or Jews. Indeed Kose's research tells us that many ordinary converts, like their British-born counterparts of migrant heritage, have been fairly selective in how they incorporate Islam into their identities. Most retain their British names, exchange Christmas presents with their parents, and are not actively 'puritan' in their outlook.[34] Most male converts do not change their dress at all, and although 'all the women converts wore clothes which covered their bodies, about a third of the women did not wear a scarf'.[35] A significant minority of converts seem more at ease with the 'don'ts' rather than the 'do's' of Islamic religious prescriptions. They adhere to prohibitions on alcohol, eating pork and sex outside marriage, but can find difficulty in praying (51%) and fasting (27%) regularly.[36] It appears that for many of these converts religion as such is taken much more seriously than accompanying cultural traditions, whether Arab or South Asian. Thus these Muslim Britons seem to be seeking ways of retaining their Britishness in combination with aspects of their new religious identity. Daoud Owen, president of the Association of British Muslims, which represents the majority of converts, suggests that a typical convert is 'steeped in British culture' and, in contrast to the more ritualistically and indeed politically inclined strands of South Asian Islam, shows much greater involvement in 'genuine mystic paths and masters'.[37] Most of Kose's respondents did not seem to have changed culturally to any great degree either and saw little conflict between 'following British culture and adopting the religion of Islam'. Being a British Muslim for them was just as valid as being a Nigerian Muslim or an Egyptian Muslim.[38]

The converts' way of being Muslim in Britain, therefore, has tended to be different from that of Muslims of migrant origins. Instead of associating with a specific Muslim community, the converts interviewed by Kose had a sense of belonging to the greater Muslim community—the *umma*. They were not at ease with the culture of Muslim communities around them, which they felt immigrant Muslims confused with their religion. Discussing Islam in Bradford, Lewis similarly drew attention to the difficulty that prominent converts, such as Rashid Skinner and Sufyan Gent, found in relating to South Asian religiosity and culture, which they viewed as narrow and intolerant in that it denounced those not in agreement as 'enemies of Islam'.[39]

By the end of the twentieth century a convergence was perhaps taking place between the convert approach and the that of some Muslims of migrant heritage, in particular those of the second generation and beyond, who now shared much of the world-view and values of wider British society. The new generation had come to recognise the cultural specificity of the migrant generation's religious behaviour and to question the need to retain emotional links with their non-British past. For example, they increasingly criticised the reluctance of Muslims to use any language except Arabic for religious worship, but any attempts to move away from what Akhtar calls Islam's traditional 'Arab linguistic imperialism' or 'Arabolatry' have been strongly resisted. Any attempt to question, let alone rupture, this link with Arab culture and language is liable to be denounced as heresy.[40] This present-day challenge to established convention meshes with the unsuccessful attempts by British Muslim converts in the past—to cut the umbilical cord that has kept Islam tied closely to its Arab origins and so free Islam from its dominant cultural moorings. In the process, this would assert the universality of Islam while enabling it to connect more organically with particular local cultural traditions.

Young British Muslims

Young Muslims in Britain hold a range of beliefs about their different identities, with much heart-searching about whether they belong in Britain or in an Islamic community. Out of these reflections they have formed differing perceptions of national, ethnic and religious belonging, which they see as facets of belonging interdependently, while at the same time placing them in some order in their self-conception. Jabida, a respondent in Eade's study in 1994, declared: 'If you had to go on a scale of one to ten of who you are, what you are, it [goes] Muslim, Bengali and then British … If you take the top two away, that wouldn't be me. If you take the British away, I think that would still be me.'[41] Jahanara also asserted her Muslim identity above others: 'If somebody comes up to me and said "What are you?", first I would say "A Muslim". Then ... "Yes ... I am British".'[42] Even those who did not identify with Islam felt unable to jettison it totally—because of being seen as such by others, because of their Muslim family background, because of their Muslim name and because of their origins in a predominantly Muslim country.

The identification with 'Britishness' is usually pragmatic. While many young Muslims do think of themselves as on the whole culturally and socially British, there is some reluctance to assert Britishness in terms that might suggest anything more than legal entitlement. Their awareness of the appropriation of that concept by racists as exclusively denoting white skin colour and 'indigenous' culture tends to create a psychological distance from the majority population. As Azad says, 'belonging [means] something that is catching, holding on to and I don't think the English society holds on to me ... I don't really belong here. There is nothing I don't like about being here, but I don't see this country's people actually accepting us, which makes you feel uncomfortable.'[43] Hence Britishness is often described in terms of citizenship, a birthright, but not really a deeply-held emotional and cultural bond shared with the white, secular or Christian majority.

However, the weakness of their identification with Britishness still does not necessarily rekindle great interest in ethnic affiliations. Indeed, as Gardner and Shakur discovered in their study in 1993, while 'Bangladeshiness' was important to some extent to almost all British Bengalis, 'the country itself is a largely alien world'.[44] They had begun to see their parents' homelands as an ideological and geographical 'Other' and perceived the beliefs, morals and practices of those countries unfavourably.[45] This view caused many to be highly critical of their parents and to shed the 'cultural baggage' they feel has little relevance in Britain. It is Islam, they assert, that plays the most important part in their lives. Vertovec too discovered in his research on young people of Pakistani origin that identification with Islam was more important than being Pakistani, although this did not imply any keen interest in the practice of Islam.[46] Saeed et al. found in Scotland that a Muslim identity was chosen by double the number of those who chose the Pakistani alternative. Many respondents claimed that this was because they found

18

the Muslim identity empowering in an environment where they saw themselves as part of a maligned minority. By identifying with global Islam they were able to see themselves as part of a potentially powerful community. This provided a sense of stability rooted in historical continuity stretching back over centuries,[47] and the symbolic language in which they could express their highest ideals. They were able to transcend the negative particularistic ethnic attributions heaped upon them by the majority by positively reasserting a universal heritage, while at the same time it gave them a sense of belonging akin to being part of an ethnic group. The attachment of the migrant generation of Muslims to their ethnic and cultural past has been replaced not by feelings of belonging to the British way of life, from which they still feel excluded and alienated, but by Islamic values and practices which they feel are generic, adaptable and relevant to any social environment, including the British. By relinquishing their ethnic identification these young people have tried to counter their definition by the indigenous population as being from somewhere else, while by adopting a Muslim identification they have challenged traditional notions of Britishness. This kind of self-consciousness helps young British Muslims to cope with the ambiguities and contradictions they experience in British society.

Young British Muslims have been helped to move away from their parents' way of seeing themselves by participation and socialisation in a number of contrasting cultural arenas—the home, where norms and moral values from another world are inculcated and where different migrant cultures and traditions are reproduced in varying degrees; the school with its individualistic, questioning and largely secular ethos (99% of British Muslims attend state schools); and the authoritarian and traditional religious instruction in community-based schools. Beyond this immediate social experience, the lives of these young British Muslims are being shaped by local geography, state institutions, class dynamics and racism. The result is that there now seems to be a greater propensity to associate with the culture of the indigenous white majority and adopt many of its traits. Young Muslims have come to feel that while the religious element in their identities remains relatively stable, the ethnic boundaries are malleable and permeable, and have the potential for intermingling and change. This trend was particularly apparent in the findings of Jacobson's study of British Pakistanis in

1997, in which many respondents, while regarding Pakistan as an 'exciting and interesting place to go on holiday and something with which they have close ties, [nevertheless] at the same time, they felt strongly that Britain was the country in which they were "most comfortable and at home"'. While many of these young people could reach a level of mutual understanding with Pakistani or Asian friends which was difficult with whites or Afro-Caribbeans, they still enjoyed to socialise in mixed friendship groups. They tended to converse in Urdu or Punjabi with their parents, but almost invariably in English with members of their own peer generation. Many found Indian music and female dress appealing and interesting, but felt that interest in those aspects of South Asian culture did not preclude a liking for 'British', 'Western' or other 'ethnic' alternatives.[48] Lewis's study of South Asian Muslims in Bradford also discovered an emerging Muslim youth culture expressed in musically hybrid fusions of South Asian and British forms. Following the Rushdie affair the band Fun-da-mental articulated Islamist ideas in its songs, which supported Khomeini's *fatwa* pronouncing a death sentence on the author. Young Muslims UK produced music cassettes such as 'Lost Identity' and 'The Hour' to express similar sentiments. Magazines such as *Trends, Sultan* and *Q-News* provided space to explore British Muslim identities with positive images of Islam and critiques of sectarianism, mosque politics and the *ulama*. *Q-News* in particular encouraged exploration of British Muslim identities by initiating discussions on how Muslims could come to grips with some of the key issues in their domestic and public lives within a rapidly changing environment. With the twenty-first century approaching, it wanted to move the debate on Muslim identity 'beyond beards, scarves and *halal* meat'.[49]

However, the shaping of self-identity of young Muslims through a blending of culture between the white majority and the Muslim minorities has been circumscribed by racist notions of difference in the former and this looks set to continue. Moreover, the sense of 'Muslimness' and detachment from non-Muslim society is reinforced by the behaviour required of members of a Muslim community. Even many less religiously oriented young British Muslims feel the need to show some commitment to the religious community, expressing their distinctiveness symbolically through, for instance, observance of dietary restraints or participation in collective worship. Nevertheless, younger Muslims of both sexes seem less willing to accept their parents' rejection of British cultural styles. Nor are they willing to accept the unquestioned beliefs and assumptions of their parents, particularly since their education encourages them to demand rational explanations for everything. Many question the meaning and relevance of elaborate rituals, the segregation of sexes and the minutiae of dietary restrictions.

The challenging of received wisdom is well illustrated in the letter pages of *Q-News*. For instance, a lengthy and cogently argued letter from Tanya Hussein, one of its regular readers, expressed real anger about two articles in previous issues, 'Is Kosher Halal?' and 'Muslim Women and Sports'. Both these articles were, in her view, 'presented as the authoritative, Islamic perspective on the issues' whereas she felt that they 'were only opinions from Muslim individuals'. Instead of their 'simplistic' and 'naive' views, which presented Islam as either *halal* or *haram*, and a 'do' and 'don't' religion, she suggested that there were a lot of complex areas in life for which 'Islam provides a guide'. Moving away from the inflexibility reflected in these articles, she proposed a more contextualised exploration of issues within religious parameters. On *halal* meat she invoked the sacred texts to counter (and implicitly reject) the opinion offered in the article that kosher was not *halal* by asking: 'And how come Kosher is not halal when Allah says in the Quran we can eat the food of the people of the Book? Doesn't this opinion [therefore] abrogate the Quran?'[50] Yet, while moving resiliently in a variety of cultural contexts, the majority of young Muslims of migrant heritage still feel that their roots lie in the resources of their parents' traditions, where they still feel generally, and at least emotionally, more secure.

While this description is a fair representation of South Asian Muslim attitudes, the process of re-evaluation of parental and community attitudes has perhaps been more radical among other Muslim ethnic communities. Many young Turkish Cypriots still express a desire to preserve their parents' values, but in a number of crucial areas—marriage, social relations and sexuality—they have tended to move closer to the mainstream values of their British peers. This is nothing new. Indeed, the movement away from the traditions, customs and practices of their homelands began decades ago. Ladbury, in the late 1970s, noted that 'only a tiny minority of Turkish Cypriots in London, men and women, make any concession to formal religion, either by attending a mosque or by making namaz [prayer] in their homes'.[51] In Kucukcan's 1998 survey arranged marriage, especially among girls, was the practice that younger Turks most often wanted to see abandoned: 54% approved of premarital male–female social meetings, while 43% approved of pre-marital sexual relationships.[52]

But even among younger British Muslims identities are being con-structed in different ways, shaped largely by gender and reflected in a questioning of the traditional male-dominated order within Muslim communities. Some young women have become aware of the double standards they see in the freedoms and opportunities accessible to men and not to women. They resist the claim of young Muslim men to represent their interests adequately, as became apparent in women's reactions to the Bradford troubles in 1995,[53] and argue that the sociali-sation of Muslim boys into traditional patriarchal roles leads men to believe that they are more important than women and to assume a right to represent their interests and control them in the name of fam-ily honour. In their view, the result has been the construction of a par-ticular male Muslim identity, suffused with a macho religio-cultural ideology, which is used to maintain power over them. They point to the involvement of young Muslim men in 'discos, drink, drugs and white women' in contravention of cultural and religious codes and, at the same time, to male insistence that their own female relatives stay at home and behave as 'good' Muslim women—proof of the contradic-tory character of these identities.[54] These women say that Islam is used to legitimate male control by asserting the importance of appropriate gender roles, codes of dress and family honour in religious terms. It is also used to justify the harassment of the women and violence more generally, through organisations such as Hizb-ut-Tahrir. Some women are challenging these constructions of Muslim male identity, which continue to shape gender relations in British Muslim communities,[55] and rejecting the system of 'community leadership'—overwhelmingly male—as outdated, and are demanding a voice in their communities.

'The Infidel Within' approaches the issues raised here by examining the Muslim presence in Britain within a historical perspective. Part I,

'Arriving', considers the 150 years or so up to 1945 during which Muslims from many different parts of the world arrived in Britain in small but still significant numbers. While not all stayed, they established a Muslim presence in Britain that laid the foundations for larger-scale migration later. Part II, 'Staying', covers the period since the 1945 watershed when Muslims from different countries arrived in larger numbers and chose to make Britain their permanent home. Migration, settlement, engagement with the wider society, the role of women and the family, attitudes to education, the changing role of organisations— all are key elements of British Muslim identity as it had emerged and evolved by the start of the twenty-first century.

PART I

ARRIVING, 1800–1945

2

MUSLIM MIGRATION AND SETTLEMENT
IN BRITAIN BEFORE 1945

As we saw in Chapter 1, perhaps the most striking aspect of the Muslims living in Britain today is their diversity, as reflected in their wide range of ethnic backgrounds. This is directly related to the importance of Muslim migration to Britain from many parts of the world since the early nineteenth century. For most British Muslim communities migration is a process which they have shared, but it has not been identical for all concerned. Being a Muslim nowadays increasingly challenges ethnicity and culture as the basis for self-identification, but this does not mean that Muslims can be described as a single homogeneous community; ethnic and cultural loyalties remain the main practical determinant of day-to-day social behaviour. So to appreciate the variety of the Muslim experience in Britain, we must first examine the history of their migration before large numbers of Muslims made Britain their permanent home.

Many of the people and communities investigated in this chapter did not publicly act under the label 'Muslim' and were not even necessarily perceived as such by wider society, but on the whole in broader racial terms. Extracting and assembling information about the migration and settlement of Muslims before 1945 therefore involves some labelling of people with identities that were not uppermost or particularly relevant at the time. It was mostly material circumstance that determined when and why they arrived in Britain. Nevertheless, this was when Muslims from a range of social, economic and ethnic backgrounds made an impact on British society and the ways in which they did so were influenced to varying degrees by their religious identity.

Muslim migration to Britain leading to the evolution of 'settler' communities of significant size can be traced back to the mid-nineteenth century, when the first relatively permanent Muslim populations were established in Manchester, Cardiff, Liverpool, South Shields and the East End of London. These consisted primarily of sailors but were joined by merchants, itinerant entertainers, servants, princes, students and a sprinkling of people from the professional classes. While their migration was due largely to economic reasons, a combination of complex factors led individuals to leave their homes and families and finally settle in Britain. The vast majority were in some way connected with the Empire and so came from the colonies or protected territories, such as the Aden hinterland, British Somaliland, Malaya and the Yemen. Indeed, Muslims arriving before 1945 came from diverse backgrounds with distinct cultures, languages and political traditions.

Inward and outward migration has been a major aspect of Britain's social development for centuries. Historians have argued that its present population has evolved as a result of a complex process by which people from overseas have arrived and settled here: 'All our ancestral stocks came from somewhere else.'[1] There have been few periods in British history without some immigration—through invasions, influx of refugees and trade and commerce—from different parts of Europe, Africa and Asia. From the nineteenth century Britain, like other European empires, established wide-ranging connections with different regions of the Muslim world, and with industrial expansion fuelling the demand for labour a pattern of migration involving Muslims took shape, contributing one stream to the many migratory flows that have criss-crossed the globe over the last two centuries. The forces, both personal and impersonal, which produced this movement, appear not to have been very different from those that stimulated the migrations of other groups. But it was in this way that Muslims developed a significant presence in Britain as in many West European countries, contributing to the expanding cultural and religious diversity of these societies.

The pattern of Muslim arrival in Britain did not follow a uniformly rising curve. Periods of most intense activity coincided with the consolidation of Britain's position as a leading imperial and industrialised country at the turn of the twentieth century, with the First World War stimulating migration to meet the demands of the war effort. In contrast the interwar years, with economic stagnation and high levels of unemployment, inhibited the flow of new arrivals. Thus in practice, Muslim movement to Britain went through peaks, troughs and disjunctures caused by the material and ideological circumstances of individual migrants and the societies from which they came.

Early Muslim migration to Britain: visitors, sailors and settlers

People in Britain knew of Islam almost from its inception in the seventh century, mainly because of the Muslim incursions into Europe, with Arabs coming as close to England as Poitiers in France in 732. Once Muslims had firmly established their hegemony over Spain and Sicily, they were perceived as a major threat to Christendom in Europe. The Crusades of the early Middle Ages were one response to a military and ideological enemy, with the military contingent led by Richard I of England (the Lion-heart) representing his country's robust contribution to the campaign. The Crusades seemed to blunt the Muslim assault on Europe, with the exception of Spain and southern Italy where Muslim rule was already well established. There is only sporadic evidence of Muslim visits to England in this period; Al-Idrisi (1100 66), the North African Arab scholar patronised by Sicilian kings, travelled to the west of England[2] and North African pirates were occasionally reported to be operating in English waters. The first Persian emissary arrived in 1238 with a plea—which failed to move Henry III—for help against the Mongol threat to Ala ud-Din's kingdom.[3] Little communication between Persia and Britain was recorded until the next Persian ambassador Naqd Ali Beg arrived in February 1626 in one of the East India Company's ships.

The Muslim advance across Europe resumed with the defeat of the Byzantine Empire in 1453, by the Ottomans who subsequently swept through the Balkans, besieging Vienna in 1529. With these conquests the Ottomans became an acknowledged power in Europe, and the recognition of their strength culminated with Elizabeth I's offer in 1588 to enter an alliance with Murad III (1546–95), 'a fellow monotheist', to bring about the downfall of the papist and 'idolatrous' King of Spain.[4] In this period the Ottomans and the British developed collaboration in various ways—as trading partners and as military allies to thwart European rivals, in particular putative Russian expansionism. Travel and commerce between the two countries led to more substantial interactions. There is evidence of a Muslim presence in Britain under the Tudors and the Stuarts.[5] Two groups in particular were found in England: freed slaves and traders. Merchants were also supported with stipends to promote British interests in Muslim lands. In the 1620s a number of Muslims were gaoled in Launceston, Plymouth, Exeter and Bristol in retaliation for English pirates and traders captured off North Africa, and some of these escaped to London. In 1627 nearly forty 'Turks' were said to be living in England as tailors, shoemakers and menders and button makers, and one even as a notary.[6] A 1641 document confirms the presence in London of a sect 'with a certaine foolish beliefe of Mahomet'.[7] Indeed there is ample evidence that hundreds of Muslims visited England, although no more than a few score lived in the country at any one time, primarily in southern England where they interacted with the English 'in the market and in gaol, at royal residences and in seaside towns, in ships and on the streets, in Hyde Parke and in Whitehall, in the Levant merchant offices and in the courts of law'. Muslims were 'traded and feasted with, admired and feared, understood and misunderstood, gaoled and tried and hanged... By 1725 English society was "pretty well accustomed" to them.'[8]

Ottoman Muslims travelled to England from the end of the sixteenth century. Ahmet Efendi, a merchant accompanied by one Niqula, was believed to be the first Turk to arrive in England.[9] Samuel Pepys in 1662 mentioned 'a little Turke' whom the Earl of Sandwich brought as a present for his daughter, and a Turkish bath, opened in 1679, further testifies to the presence of Turks in London at that time.[10] Ottoman ambassadors were appointed in the seventeenth and eighteenth centuries, and diplomatic exchanges between the court of James I and the Sublime Porte came to be conducted by a 'Ledger Embassadour';[11] inevitably their staffs and servants accompanied them, and merchants and travellers followed. However, although a permanent Ottoman embassy was established in the latter part of the eighteenth century, it is uncertain whether any of these representatives or their retinues ever settled in Britain.

Imperial connections. The carve-up of Africa and Asia left few Muslim countries outside Europe's sphere of influence. British ascendancy in India was established by the mid-eighteenth century, and Napoleon's invasion of Egypt in 1798 led to a tightening of the European stranglehold over the Muslim world. By 1818 Britain was recognised as the paramount power in India, and it soon extended control over those Muslim lands that it felt were strategically important for securing India, its most valuable possession. Britain spread its domination in the Persian Gulf, and after the opening of the Suez Canal in 1869, and in competition with other European powers, it acquired huge Muslim territories in the Middle East and Africa. In 1882 it occupied Egypt and then instituted an Anglo Egyptian 'Condominium' over Sudan in 1898. In East Africa it shared Zanzibar and Somaliland with other European powers, and acquired the key port of Aden on the Arabian Peninsula. Persia, meanwhile, was already being divided into spheres of influence, with Russia annexing Muslim central Asia. Although the French swept through most of Muslim North and West Africa, Britain absorbed the Muslim sultanate of Sokoto within its Nigerian colony. In South East Asia the Dutch took Indonesia, leaving Britain to establish its hegemony over the sultans of the Malay states. For much of the nineteenth century the Ottoman Empire, the only significant centre of Muslim power, lost ground to Europe, and its defeat at the end of the First World War meant relinquishing control over the Balkan Muslims and the sharing-out of its Arab territories between Britain and France. By 1919 only Afghanistan, the Yemen (excluding Aden), and Hejaz and Nejd on the Arabian peninsula retained any semblance of independence.

The rise of the West had a far-reaching impact. With economic and political subordination, Muslims generally no longer controlled their own material resources. With the creation of colonial relationships ensuring economic dependence, a yawning gap developed between the level of prosperity enjoyed in Britain and the impoverishment of the Muslim world. People living in many Muslim societies had to fashion strategies to survive and pursue their own interests in circumstances largely circumscribed by the strategic and material interests of the British government and major British business interests. Consequently, whenever a demand for cheap labour appeared in any part of the British Empire, labourers—many from places under British rule— were exported to work on terms that offered a choice only between great hardship abroad and bare subsistence at home. Hence early Indian Muslim migration to Britain can be seen as an offshoot of the mainstream of migration which took thousands of Indians as indentured labour to the British colonies to escape the hunger, poverty and disease produced by periodic crises such as flooding, famine (particularly serious in the late 1870s and late 1890s) and debt. In Punjab, one of India's most fertile regions, the *per capita* acreage dropped from 0.95 in 1848 to 0.59 by 1891, and as conditions worsened many drifted off to the towns in search of employment and so a pool of casual labour accumulated in cities such as Calcutta and Bombay. There were already traditions of labouring far from home and leaving families behind, but now the further they went in search of work, the less likely it became that they would return.

Increasingly Muslim frameworks of law and philosophy, systems of values and organisation of society were also challenged by the secular, rationalist and scientific traditions of Europe. Most crucial of all, Muslims had to come to terms with the power of the European imperial state, through which material and human resources were harnessed to the needs of the European empires. European ideas began to shape institutions and channel energies, bending existing systems in the Muslim world to Western interests; more specifically, British laws and policies began to transform many societies that came under British control. Existing institutions were brought under the sway of British overall stewardship and new state machinery and structures that were thought suitable for its purposes were transplanted. Thus the British empire created systems that incorporated and transformed previously established Islamic frameworks.

The technological and other developments imported from Europe compelled a growing number of Muslims to consider the possibility of their extinction if they did not in some way compromise in the face of the overwhelming power of European ideas. Engagement with the framework established by British authority increasingly appeared a necessary precondition for any future progress. Muslims had to acquire a 'modern' outlook and come to terms with the 'modern' world. Indeed, many of those not moved by economic need were genuinely impressed by the power of Western ideas. Even the more sceptical members of local Muslim élites believed that their future would be jeopardised if they did not to some extent acquiesce in the assimilative cultural process, even though they might not necessarily identify with it in any fundamental way. And where better to pursue these objectives than at the heart of Europe itself? Hence, by the nineteenth century the traffic in Muslims making their way to Europe under different guises had begun in earnest.

By the end of the eighteenth century, a combination of external factors had compelled Turkey and Britain to forge a close commercial, political and military relationship, encouraging a wide range of interactions and visits by Ottoman subjects to Britain. Ottoman sailors and traders visited British ports more often and for longer during the nineteenth century, with some taking up permanent residence. According to the 1881 census, there were eight Egyptians and forty-four Turks living in Merseyside.[12] Salter's *Sketches of Sixteen Years' Work among Orientals*, published in 1868, gave a vivid account of the transient Muslim population in the ports and urban centres of Britain; he recorded the visits to Liverpool, among other ports, of Arab sailors on trading vessels and warships of the Ottoman navy. He reported a brig called *Syar Bahakt* undergoing major repairs in the Graving Dock, 'manned entirely by Arabs, thirty-eight in number', and in 1866 a frigate, *Ruseed*, with 450 Egyptians on board. Salter visited the graves of thirty Ottoman sailors buried in a Liverpool cemetery, met the Arab Ziad, one of 'the many Eastern celebrities at Liverpool', and attempted to rescue from 'the chill winds of the winter an entire crew [of Arabs which] had deserted a ship at Liverpool'.[13]

Political push factors also encouraged secularising intellectuals to leave Turkey in the second half of the nineteenth century. As the weakened Ottoman Empire retreated in the face of European assault, the sultans attempted to resist this challenge by opening up their society to many of the secular systems of thought which they believed had made the Europeans powerful. However, having set off modernising reforms in law, education, military know-how and other major institutions of the state, they were unable to make any fundamental changes to the absolutist character of a political regime still struggling to come to terms with a constitution infused with the Islamic principles of state. Such a repressive environment was clearly at odds with the aspirations of many intellectuals, who felt that only by going into exile in a country that had developed a strong tradition of individual and political liberty could they voice their opposition to the suppression of what they believed were fundamental human rights without fear of persecution. Britain—fast developing into what seemed a liberal democracy, embracing freedom of expression, association and the press—was seen as an attractive destination by many of the émigrés who hoped to continue their campaigns from a safe distance. Closer Ottoman–British relations during the nineteenth century and a greater knowledge of the liberties Britain offered further encouraged some of the Turkish opposition to move to Britain.

The first influx of Turkish political refugees came to Britain in the reign of Sultan Abdulmecit (1823–76): in 1867 exiles such as Namik Kemal, Ziya Pasha, Ali Suavi and Sinasi escaped to London, where they brought out broadsheets such as *Hurriyet* (Freedom) protesting at the Sultan's tyranny. A second wave came during the rule of Sultan Abdul Hamid II (1876–1918), who was perceived by many of the republican intellectuals as politically repressive. The Young Turks added to this growing exodus, following their revolutionary attempt in July 1908 to overthrow the Ottoman Caliphate. A trickle of Muslim migrants also arrived from Cyprus once Britain had taken control of the island in 1878 Some of these came as students, but then married and settled in Britain; others came seeking adventure, and still others came primarily to escape the harsh realities of economic life in Cyprus.[14] But the majority left Cyprus to discover new places or to break away from the constraints of their social environment and shape their own destinies.

Likewise sojourners from India, driven by wanderlust, had started to make their way to the British Isles by the end of the eighteenth century. The East India Company had stimulated interest among some Indians, especially its employees, to experience a culture, glimpses of which promised riches and sophistication. As early as 1777 Monshee Mahomet Saeed from Bengal was advertising for pupils in London;

another who acquired prominence was Sake Dean Mahomed, who came with Captain Baker of the East India Regiment in 1784 and was among the first to settle permanently in England. He wrote *The Travels of Dean Mahomet*, the first work published in English by a Muslim in Britain, and set up an 'Indian Vapour Bath and Shampooing Establishment' in Brighton. While he was already popular with the public, his success was assured when he was appointed 'Shampooing Surgeon to His Majesty George IV'.[15]

So from the early nineteenth century Indian Muslims visited Britain, but their numbers remained small, partly because of the practical difficulties of travelling. Prominent visitors were Mirza Abu Talib, Lutfullah, Mirza Ihtisamuddin and Sayyid Ahmed Khan, members of India's professional and wealthy élites, already closely associated with British authority. Personal considerations, rather than economic motivation, clearly made them decide to travel. The pull of Western systems of thought and knowledge was strong on these professional Muslim families who had traditionally enjoyed a privileged position in society and exercised considerable power. Since it seemed to many of them that British rule was in India to stay, then a Western education offered the best credentials for participating in running the colonial system. Thus the 1840s saw the start of an inflow of Indian students of the upper and middle classes to study law at the Inns of Court and other 'useful' subjects at reputable English and Scottish universities. From a mere four in 1845 their numbers steadily rose to 207 in the 1890s and 700 by 1910. Syed Ameer Ali, a Shia Muslim from Calcutta who came to study law in 1873, returned to Britain at the turn of the century and after marrying into an English family, settled permanently. He was later appointed a Privy Councillor, with Muslim issues as his central concern. Muhammad Ali Jinnah, who became leader of the Muslim League and founding father of Pakistan, came as a student in 1892 and was called to the Bar at Lincoln's Inn. In 1930 he returned and practised law in England till 1934. Muhammad Iqbal, revered as the interpreter of Muslim nationhood in India, arrived in 1905, studied at Cambridge and qualified as a barrister, returning home in 1908. Indeed, scions of leading north Indian Muslim families formed a sizeable proportion of the transient Muslim student population in Britain by the early twentieth century.[16]

Scottish universities were especially popular, perhaps because of the disproportionately large number of Scottish teachers in India. These institutions gained a high reputation, particularly in engineering and medicine. The first Indian student in Scotland was probably Wazir Beg from Bombay, who was recorded as a second-year medical student at the University of Edinburgh in 1858–9. From then on there was a steady trickle until the 1880s when greater involvement in running the machinery of state and the various institutions of society brought over much larger numbers. The Edinburgh Indian Association, formed in 1883 by six students, had 200 members by the turn of the century.[17] Personal circumstances and an evaluation of the costs and benefits— emotional, social and economic—of returning to India or staying meant that some of these students eventually settled in Britain.

A more motley crew of Muslims came in search of adventure and opportunities. Apart from the 'young men of wealthy patronage study- ing', there were 'wealthy merchants' and 'learned Moulvies, the expositors of Mohammedan law and faith'.[18] There were also scholars of languages, such as Professor Syed Abdoolah, who taught Hindustani at University College London in the late 1860s. Merchants and traders, many involved in peddling and some with a flair for enterprise, arrived in the nineteenth century as employees of British Indian firms and proceeded to establish their own small businesses. There were street hawkers and musicians, itinerant surgeons, and ear and eye doctors. In addition a petitioner class, mainly of small-scale farmers from Punjab, came to pursue land claims. Higher up the social scale visiting Muslims included nawabs with their retinues. Nawab Nazim of Bengal, who arrived in 1870, became a favourite of Queen Victoria but fell out with the Government of India for apparently leading 'a life of debauchery' and marrying an 'English woman of low extraction'. Mir Jafar Ali of Surat and his entourage settled in Paddington,[19] and 'the Mohammedan Queen' of Oudh and her 130 followers made an extended stay in London. These members of the 'native' élites, with their exotic life- styles and forms of dress, stirred the popular imagination; many col- umn-inches were devoted to them in court circulars and society maga- zines, creating an image of opulence and luxury.

A far cry from the Ottoman representatives, who enjoyed diplo- matic status, and the privileged few from India were those Muslims who arrived in Britain as servants of returning East India Company employees. From the end of the eighteenth century an increasing number had been brought over to work in various roles. Some had served their masters loyally for years and so could not easily be left behind; others were kept as virtual pets; and yet others accompanied children with parents in India who were sent to England for education. It also became fashionable to employ Indians as footmen and valets. Many employees of East India Company, especially those who had made enough money in India to go on living in the style they had become accustomed to there, brought back their servants and *ayahs* (nannies or ladies' maids).[20]

The most famous example was Munshi Abdul Karim, who arrived soon after Queen Victoria's Golden Jubilee in 1887, and as a favourite of the Queen taught her Hindustani and rose to become her 'Indian Secretary'. But most of these servants were involuntary migrants, and in practice they were little different from slaves, since they were effectively bought and sold in the market. Once in Britain some were maltreated and cases of cruelty were not unknown. Many eventually ran away, and some who could not find alternative employment drifted into criminal activity. Those who were discharged and left without means of livelihood when their employers failed to honour promises of their safe return to India lived in extreme poverty and overcrowding, eking out a miserable existence as street herbalists, sellers of rhubarb, spices and religious tracts, tom-tom players and crossing-sweepers, and even as beggars.[21]

This practice of bringing over servants continued after the British government took direct control of Indian affairs in 1858. Indeed, with improvement in communications, the flow of traffic between Britain and India increased, and with it the size of the pool of Indian servants. These were more likely to be Muslims than Hindus, since Hindus were more reluctant to travel overseas as a result of caste taboos associated with notions of the 'black water' and pollution.[22] As the number of servants rose, so did that of destitutes, and their presence caused enough concern in London for an Ayahs' Home to be set up in East London in 1890 to accommodate around 100 maidservants annually.[23]

As already pointed out, England had a growing reputation during this period as a place of opportunity. Among the men of enterprise who gravitated to its industrial and commercial centres to further their ambitions were Moroccan and other Arab merchants lured by, *inter alia*, Manchester's position as the textile-manufacturing capital of the world. The signing of the Anglo-Ottoman Commercial Treaty at Balta-Liman in 1838 directly facilitated a large increase in the volume of textiles exported to many Ottoman dominions and considerably improved the prospects for transit trade to India, China and beyond. By the mid-nineteenth century 'the Sultan's dominions were taking more Manchester piece goods than all European countries put together'.[24] The opening of the Suez Canal at the end of the 1860s further expanded commerce, which continued to grow for the rest of the century. Arabs were obviously well placed to benefit from the profitable opportunities offered by Manchester's leading position; they established trading houses there to export cotton goods back to their home countries, and traders from various parts of the Middle East and North Africa settled in the city from the 1830s. One Abdoullah Yadlibi set up the first trading house in 1833, and by the mid-1860s there were over thirty such establishments, of which the majority were apparently 'Turkish' (a description used of anyone thought to have originated in the Ottoman provinces). By the end of the century the number of Middle Eastern merchant houses had grown to 150, of which several dozen were 'Arab', including some from what later became Syria as well as merchants with their families from the Moroccan city of Fez. Towards the end of nineteenth century, with increased competition from France and Japan, Manchester's domination of Middle Eastern markets gradually declined and had finally ended by the beginning of the First World War. Arab merchant communities in the city waned too, and finally disappeared almost completely by the late 1930s.

Seafaring sojourners. A particularly significant group of migrants to arrive in Britain during the nineteenth century were maritime workers or lascars. Once the East India Company established its factories in some of the key coastal centres of India in the late eighteenth century, their chartered ships plying between there and Britain increasingly recruited Indian sailors as cheap labour. These sailors were also taken on to overcome the labour shortage created on trading vessels by the induction of British seamen into the navy for war service against France from the 1760s onwards, as well as by British seamen deserting at Indian ports. So substantial was their recruitment that during the Napoleonic wars over 1,000 lascars were reported to be arriving in British ports every year.[25] The majority were Muslim, referred to in more virulent Evangelical circles as 'the deluded followers of the licentious doctrines of a false prophet'.[26] Provision for their upkeep on shore between voyages was the responsibility of the East India Company, but by 1782 there were reports of lascars being cast adrift in European ports. Greatly distressed, they demanded relief,[27] but with only the barest food rations and accommodation available winters took a heavy toll, and it was conservatively estimated that over 100 died each year.[28] Nevertheless, the number of lascars in Britain increased rapidly from 470 in 1804 to 1,336 in 1813.[29] Some 3,000 arrived in 1842 and, according to one estimate, 10,000–12,000 in 1855.[30] Their number grew throughout the century, the majority undoubtedly Muslim. Salter calculated that of the 3,271 lascars from forty ships arriving in 1873, 1,653 were Muslims from India, Egypt, Malaya and Turkey. Of the 7,814 lascars surveyed in 1874, 4,685 came from India and 1,440 were Arabs, 225 Turks and 85 Malays.[31]

As a receiving country Britain in the nineteenth century was already a relatively rich industrial society attracting migrants from other parts of Europe. There were long periods of economic growth in this period that helped to create a perception of England as a land of 'milk and honey', and this was an era when movement across countries was relatively free and migrants entered at will. For Indian migrants a big attraction of working in Britain was that wages there were much higher than for a comparable job in India.[32] There was also rising demand for lascar labour because the former reservations of shipowners and masters regarding Indian seamen's physical capacity and ability to withstand the cold were overcome. In addition, these employers were prepared to tolerate the relatively high cost of their upkeep because of their much lower wages—between one-sixth and one-seventh of those received by white seamen.[33] Bombay was the port where Pathan and Mirpuri lascars were taken on for labouring jobs as donkey-men and firemen in the British merchant navy.

However, despite the better wages there is evidence that many of these Indian Muslim sailors were brutally treated on ships, which compelled many to try to escape such harrowing ordeals. One entire crew of Muslims deserted when their ship docked in the Thames after some had reportedly been 'hung with weights tied to their feet, flogged with a rope' and forced to eat pork, 'the insult carried further by violently ramming the tail of a pig into their mouths and twisting the entrails of a pig round their necks'. One lascar jumped overboard and drowned. Another, called Abdullah, died after being flogged, tied to the windlass and doused with salt water. It was little wonder that an increasing number jumped ship, and took their chances in London's East End.[34]

Away from London, in Cardiff the vast majority (95%) of Muslims were concentrated in the dock area with a handful in the city centre and other working-class districts. A significant proportion of seamen originating in different parts of the British empire with predominantly Muslim populations—Yemen, Somaliland, Malaya and India—put down roots there in the last quarter of the nineteenth century. By 1881 they were numerous enough to warrant the establishment of a so-called Home for Coloured Seamen. Accurate figures are hard to come by, but one contemporary estimate put the permanently settled coloured population at around 700 (the majority probably Muslim) on the basis of the 1911 census.[35]

Similarly, from the middle of the nineteenth century a number of Indian Muslim seamen could be found in Scotland. Glasgow was by now the 'Second City of Empire'; production of heavy capital goods ensured that it was a major port, causing Muslim seamen recruited as lascars eventually to congregate there. Dundee, with its import of raw jute from Bengal and export of jute products, attracted Indian sailors from Bengal. Salter mentioned Ben Lomond, Aberdeen, Dumbarton and Clydebank among the provincial towns where 'these disciples of the prophet of Mecca wander'. At the turn of the century Hammerton also remarked on the presence of Indian seamen in Glasgow, 'coolies' working for a miserable pittance. Further confirmation of the presence of Muslim lascars can be found in the records of the Glasgow Sailors' Home, opened in 1857. Its 1903 report noted that nearly one-third (around 5,500) of the annual number of nightly boarders were lascars.[36]

As the British empire expanded in the nineteenth century, so too did the volume of passenger and cargo sea traffic with the colonies and the rest of the world. The shipping industry grew at an unprecedented rate. The number of seamen employed on British merchant ships alone rose rapidly to 240,480 in 1891 and 295,652 on the eve of the First World War. Of these, 24,037 (10%) and 51,616 (16%) were classified as lascars, and 30,267 and 31,396 as 'foreign', many of whom would have been black undocumented British subjects.[37] Among these lascars were Yemenis and Somalis who, from as early as the 1850s, were recruited on steamers as firemen and stokers. In the East End of London, apart from Indian lascar communities, Yemeni and Somali seamen together with Ottoman Turks represented some of the earliest Muslim communities in Britain, who started arriving particularly after the opening of the Suez Canal in 1869. Apart from London, many settled in Cardiff and South Shields, with smaller communities in Liverpool and Hull.

The social, economic and political push factors that contributed to the uprooting of Yemeni peasants and turned them into seamen were in many ways similar to those experienced in India. Many Yemeni men were drawn to working on ships by a series of droughts followed by famines in the latter half of the nineteenth century: the interminable struggle to produce enough food from insufficient plots of land forced people to leave their villages in search of alternative livelihoods. However, the vital link in Yemeni emigration to Britain was the port of Aden. Annexed by Britain in 1839, it rapidly became a crucial refuelling station for steamships *en route* to East Africa, India, East Asia and Australasia. As the flow of traffic in the Indian Ocean increased, so did Aden's prosperity. Major shipping companies set up coaling depots there, and the various port activities expanded the scope of and prospects for employment. Migrants poured in from India, Somalia and the surrounding areas. A population of 2,000 at the time of the British take-over increased sharply in the second half of the century to between 40,000 and 50,000 by 1900. Foreign remittances helped to support families, especially in the periodic crises caused by drought and crop failure, and their increasing affluence visibly demonstrated the benefits of migration and thus encouraged others. With savings in their pockets, men returned home to rest, and meanwhile were replaced in their jobs by nominated relatives or kinsmen.

Once migration had started, other factors strengthened the ties of prospective workers from these regions of the Muslim world with seafaring as an occupation. One was the system of indirect recruitment, which meant obtaining employment 'through a combination of family contacts and professional intermediaries'. *Serangs* and *ghat serangs*—labour agents, moneylenders and lodging house-keepers rolled into one (and therefore very powerful men)—were already well established in Calcutta and Bombay. They were encouraged to seek out their relatives and fellow-villagers and present them at the head of the recruitment queues. In this way peasants from north-east and north-west India followed one another on to ships, to foreign lands and eventually to Britain in search of riches.[38] Yemeni and Somali maritime employment was organised and controlled in a similar way: *muqaddams* (similar to the *serangs*) were charged with supplying labour from their own tribe and negotiating contracts to the best advantage of the shipping companies and themselves. The abundance of coolies from the southern highlands of Yemen enabled *muqaddams* to drive down the wages and so give Aden a competitive edge over other bunkering stations. Yemeni crew members in this category were hired ahead of other groups and many worked on ships arriving at British ports. Those discharged in Europe did not always return to Aden, and so pioneered the Muslim settlements of the late nineteenth century, mainly in Cardiff and South Shields, but also in Liverpool and London. With the introduction of steam, shipping companies relied even more on lascars since, coming from tropical and hot climates, they were presumed to be able to adapt to the furnace-like atmosphere in the engine-rooms below the steel decks—lascars labouring in these roles comprised nearly half the crew afloat, and their work, usually the shovelling of coal into the furnace, was 'arduous, hot and dirty'. Clearly, however, it was usually economic necessity rather than any ability to cope with intense heat that forced them to accept these strenuous and life-threatening duties. The incentive to work and live away from home for prolonged periods was therefore closely linked to the lure of better wages offered by jobs on British ships.

With ships criss-crossing the globe as frequently as they now did, British seaports expanded to cater for the enormous growth in exports and accommodate the rising demand for maritime facilities. London, Southampton and the Bristol Channel ports of Cardiff, Newport, Barry and Bristol, as well as Liverpool, Tyneside, Hull and Glasgow, all scaled new heights and at the turn of the twentieth century were at their peak. Cardiff's prosperity was founded on being the primary outlet for coal from the South Wales valleys after 1850, and in 1900 it was the world's largest exporter of coal. Its population grew from 1,000 in 1801 to 10,000 in 1838 and 182,259 in 1911,[39] and the net registered tonnage of vessels cleared by the port increased from 1 million tons in 1857 to a massive 12.6 million tons on the eve of the First World War, second only to London.[40] Similarly, Tyneside expanded to become the fourth largest shipping centre in Britain after London, Cardiff and Liverpool. It regularly produced 10% of the world's merchant shipping. Engineering flourished, and Armstrong's became a world leader in armaments production; by 1894 it employed 13,000 men at its Elswick (Tyneside) plant alone. By 1906 wages there were as high as anywhere in England except London.[41] Its exports in 1909 exceeded those of Liverpool, with Tyne Dock alone shipping 6 million tons of coal and coke annually (the largest quantity exported from any one dock in the world). With the development of trade and commerce facilitated by a river improvement scheme, the population of South Shields had its most rapid growth in the second half of the nineteenth century and was acknowledged as the most important port in northeast England.

Liverpool was also one of the busiest ports in Britain, and the turn of the century represented the high noon of its affluence. Shipping grew from the mid-nineteenth century onwards at an impressive annual rate of 2.6%. In 1914 over 15,000 ships, with a tonnage of 15 million, docked there. The city owed its prosperity to the docks, shipping repairs and the export of manufactured goods from Lancashire. As trade and shipping with the Middle East and East Asia grew, it attracted people from every corner of the empire as well as other parts of the world in search of opportunities.[42] Likewise, in both Cardiff and South Shields, Muslim communities took shape in the late nineteenth century and at the beginning of the First World War were the two largest identifiable Muslim settlements in Britain.

Thus by the early twentieth century Muslim seamen formed a substantial section of the 'visible' migrant population in Britain.[43] This was largely the result of the evolving economic and political relationship between Britain and its colonies, which encouraged both visitors and those in search of employment. However, Muslims were not affected in any way differently from other communities in these parts of the world. Indian Muslims who came to Britain, for instance, did not all come from all the regions of the subcontinent populated by Muslims or even from places where they might have known similar circumstances. Instead a combination of factors persuaded particular groups of workers to explore possibilities far from home, and then the financial resources they accumulated emboldened others to venture abroad and seek richer prizes in places such as Britain, thus adding to Britain's migrant, and Muslim, communities.

Muslim migration to Britain, 1914–45

During the First World War migration from those parts of the empire that had traditionally provided cheap labour accelerated. This initial burst quickly dried up after 1918 and a virtual labour drought followed. Thus the period between the wars saw a relative downturn in the migration of Muslims to Britain. Numbers only picked up again in the late 1930s and the Second World War, and then developed into mass migration in the period of postwar reconstruction. These migratory peaks and troughs between 1914 and 1945 broadly coincided with periods of economic growth and labour shortage on the one hand, and of recession and unemployment on the other. However, refugees also arrived as a result of political repression. The years 1914–45 therefore formed the immediate background to arrivals on a much larger scale after the Second World War.

Fluctuating fortunes. The First World War resulted in an enormous demand for labour to replace men called up for war service. This was met partly by importing labour, largely from the colonies. In consequence the number of Muslim seamen increased greatly in all British ports. On Tyneside the 'black' population increased fourfold,[44] while in Cardiff it rose from around 700 in 1914 to 3,000 by April 1919[45]— more than fourfold.[46] Their numbers were augmented by stranded crews of ships requisitioned for transport troops brought to Britain from the European battle-fronts for convalescence and recuperation, and those demobilised there. There were also individual Muslims who came to cities such as Manchester to work in the munitions and chemical plants, while other unskilled shore jobs (such as ships' runners, shipbrokers and labourers in auxiliary industries such as timber yards), which were in plentiful supply, were also filled by non-indigenous labour that included a large Muslim component.

Thus the increase in the size of Muslim communities, especially in Cardiff, Newport, Barry, Liverpool, Tyneside, London and Glasgow, was directly produced by the impact of the war on the shipping industry. The shortage of seamen was felt immediately. Within forty-eight hours of the declaration of war, 8,000 British merchant seamen had joined the armed forces and 9,000 enemy seamen serving on British ships had lost their jobs. The resulting vacuum was filled primarily by lascars. Seafaring became more attractive for them as wages rose and the demand for their services grew. There were also even better opportunities for work on land in wartime industries. But despite a grudging recognition of their contribution to the war effort, questions were raised even in this period of high demand about the surfeit of 'alien seamen' in British ports. In 1916 the *South Wales Daily News* expressed concern at the 'large influx of native races'. It stated that whereas the number of Arabs 'before the war … had been reduced … today there are more Arabs … entering Cardiff than ever before'.[47] There were also complaints about 'Arab seamen' discharged in Marseilles and drifting to South Shields.

However, the mini-boom created by the exceptional circumstances of the war could not reverse the long-term stagnation of the economy in Britain as in the rest of the industrialised world, which started in 1913 and continued, with fluctuations of various lengths, till 1938. The immediate postwar boom, which had brought in yet another fresh influx of seamen from India, Yemen and British Somaliland, collapsed in 1920. Thereafter economic growth in general and particularly in older export industries—coal, steel, shipbuilding, cotton and jute textiles—slowed and almost came to a halt.[48] In both Cardiff and South Shields, the coal trade was dislocated by the 1914–18 war and exports declined sharply after the restoration of peace, which had a negative effect on the demand for shipping and shipping services.[49] Indeed world trade, which recovered to the pre First World War levels in the 1920s, fell again during the Great Depression of 1929–33 and did not surpass the 1913 volume until the Second World War. Unemployment rose sharply and remained above 10% for much of the next decade. The slump struck particularly hard in those regions of Britain where Muslims had congregated in significant numbers, with a devastating all-round effect. Unemployment in north-east England averaged over 28% in industry as a whole in 1928–32, and in shipbuilding it rocketed to 70% in 1931. The shipping tonnage at Tyneside, which had broken all records in 1906 with over 1 million tons launched, fell to a mere 37,419 tons in 1933.[50]

The economic downturn which started after the First World War and developed momentum in the 1920s had negative consequences for Muslims in Britain, which in turn discouraged potential immigrants. While jobs were generally still plentiful in 1919, the transition from military service to civilian occupations meant that many demobilised soldiers were out of work. They demanded preference over 'aliens' who, they argued, should be deported or repatriated to make space in the labour market for men returning from the war. These tensions exploded into race riots in 1919, with white mobs violently attacking black and coloured people and demanding their expulsion from Britain. Although many migrants acquiesced and returned home, others protested and warned that 'the Moslems all over the world will require an explanation of why their brothers in Cardiff ... should have been treated in the scandalous manner they have by an unruly mob'.[51]

The British government, though well aware of the lascars' invaluable wartime contribution, felt unable to respond favourably to anti-alien protests during the war itself. However, once the war was over and with lascars now surplus to requirements, official steps were taken to stop the flow. It was asked in Parliament why the government had not addressed the issue of lascar employment which, as was simplistically alleged, 'kept our men walking the street'.[52] As a result the Alien Restriction (Amendment) Bill was introduced in early 1919, and controls were further strengthened through the Aliens Order of 1920. With 30% of those engaged in shipping services unemployed in 1921, the government and employers heeded demands for restrictions and introduced numerous policies and practices that excluded 'aliens' from the available job opportunities. Joynson-Hicks, the Conservative Home Secretary in 1924–9 and a prominent 'anti-alien' politician in the agitation of 1905–6, accordingly brought in the 1925 Special Restrictions Order to stop England being 'flooded with the whole of alien refuse from every country in the world'.[53] This was not revoked till 1943, when once again a manpower shortage caused by war compelled the government to lift the restrictions.[54]

Buckling under pressure from white workers, many of whom refused to work with Arabs and other 'aliens', employers likewise decided to carry out wholesale sacking of 'coloured' employees. In Cardiff over 1,000 'coloured' seamen were replaced by white men, mostly unskilled, returning from service in the navy and auxiliary services.[55] By mid-September 1921, 500 Adeni men had been repatriated from Cardiff.[56] In Liverpool 120 were laid off by one factory alone. A typical letter of dismissal from one employer to his Indian employee read: 'You were quite efficient but there are 11,000 demobilised soldiers to be reinstated and they must have first chance. The unions insist on it.'[57] The Aliens Order of 1920 was used to penalise undocumented Arab seamen and by the autumn of 1921 hundreds had been deported.[58]

One indication of the impact of these discriminatory policies was that unemployment among Muslim and other 'coloured' sailors became disproportionately high, reflecting the National Union of Seamen's explicit campaign for all white seamen to be accommodated before 'Arabs' could be considered. At the same time there was concern that the Muslim and 'coloured' population had stabilised, contrary to the hope that the wide range of stringent measures would have reduced it. Loopholes in the system and illegal immigration were blamed for allowing migrants to continue arriving albeit in reduced numbers.[59]

As economic conditions worsened in the early 1930s, a further set of procedures was proposed to stop white seamen being displaced by migrants. A discriminatory rota system was introduced in several seaports with high numbers of Muslim and other coloured seamen. Re-registration, the deportation of those deemed to have entered illegally, strict language tests, tight monitoring and control of boarding-houses and cafés, and fingerprints and photographs in discharge books were demanded. Some of these steps, together with strong action by police in combination with immigration officers, including prosecution and deportation, did stem the flow of migrants to ports such as Cardiff by early 1930.[60] At the same time, unemployment among the 'coloured' population increased further. The number of Arabs and Somalis out of work, estimated by the police at 600 in 1919, rose to 2,000 by 1930.[61] By the summer of 1930 many Arabs in British ports were virtually starving. Some were deported and, despite the recovery in shipping in the late 1930s, non-white seamen continued to suffer disproportionately high levels of unemployment.[62] Out of the 690 unemployed seamen on the Cardiff Dock Register on 1 June 1936, 599 were 'coloured'.[63] The meagre relief available, even in the early 1920s, to only a few 'alien' unemployed was gradually reduced to a pittance by 1937. The 1935 Maritime Assistance Act excluded 'coloured aliens' from receiving help from public funds.

Once news circulated of the ill-treatment of their compatriots, either through newspapers in India and various colonies or brought back by repatriated and returning migrants, potential migrants felt discouraged from embarking on a journey to a land where they could expect nothing more than an unwelcoming reception and violent opposition to their presence. As a result, migrant and settled Muslim communities in Britain fell. For instance, the chairman of the Public Assistance Committee estimated that there were only 563 Arabs, Somalis and Indians in South Shields in 1930, of whom only ninety were permanent residents. Numbers here continued to drop throughout the 1930s till 1944, when police records showed sixty-eight permanent residents and 139 on ships. Elsewhere there is evidence that, with the rise in demand for shipping during the late 1930s and the Second World War, the Muslim seafaring population significantly increased. However, a survey by Muslims themselves estimated that only 850 (including white wives and children) lived in South Shields in 1948.[64] The aggregated population of Arabs, Somalis, Indians, Malays and Egyptians in Cardiff, overwhelmingly Muslim, was estimated to be just over 1,800 in 1930.[65] By the early 1940s it had risen to 2,500–3,000.

A much smaller stream of migrants, which laid the foundation for a larger movement after the Second World War, had its source in British-controlled Cyprus. With the outbreak of war in 1914 when the Ottomans joined the German side, Britain quickly annexed Cyprus, which meant that Cypriots became British subjects. The facility to enter Britain unhindered by immigration legislation, combined with military service during the war and awareness of opportunities abroad acquired through travel and interaction with other soldiers, led to a growing number of Cypriots migrating at the end of the war. The flow continued throughout the 1920s and 1930s. The 1921 census indicated the presence of 80–100 Cypriots in Britain. These included students and some professionals, but there were also Cypriot seamen in the dockland areas of the major ports—Stepney in London, the south side of Liverpool and Tiger Bay in Cardiff. The Cypriot migrant population increased further when the economy picked up in 1927 and although most suffered considerable hardship during the Depression of the early 1930s, the short-term push factors in Cyprus and positive perception of opportunities in Britain were sufficiently strong to persuade at least some Cypriots to migrate. Among the push factors were the depressed condition of agriculture created by drought in the 1930s and the repressive policies imposed by the colonial administration in the aftermath of the 1931 Greek-led riots.[66]

In general, the situation in Cyprus—the absence of good economic prospects, pressure on agricultural land because of population growth, encouragement to travel and increasing availability of affordable transport—acted primarily as factors that predisposed individuals to migrate. A personal desire to discover a new world, together with the perception of Britain as a modern society at the leading edge of scientific and cultural advance, perhaps carried more weight than pure economic need; there was a feeling that even starting from small beginnings one could aspire to great things. With that hope about 200 Cypriots arrived in England in 1930, mostly to work as waiters or take up menial jobs in hotels and restaurants in the West End of London.[67] Others engaged in hawking and street selling. However, with economic recession at its deepest, many were forced to resort to the dole while others turned to criminal activities. These various motivations and preoccupations were remarkably similar to those of Asian migrants, as also were the varying degrees of hostility—with demands for immigration control or repatriation—which they experienced from sections of the indigenous white population. Despite these barriers, cafés slowly appeared which provided employment for the newcomers and by the early 1930s perhaps 1,000 Cypriots were living in Britain; in 1939 the official estimate was of 8,000 Cypriots settled in London. Many were ethnically Greek, but there is evidence that many Turkish Cypriots came too, migrating for similar reasons and entering similar occupations once in Britain. Like other Muslim communities of this period, they acted as a nucleus for the much bigger migration of the 1950s and the early 1960s.[68]

One group that remained relatively unaffected by the steep downturn in the global economy was that of students from an élite Indian Muslim background. Until difficulties of transport during the Second World War put a virtual stop to their sojourns in Britain, a steadily expanding stream arrived from India. They did so for quite straightforward materialistic reasons. By the 1920s they could be found not only at such traditionally prestigious universities as Oxford and Cambridge but also those of London, Birmingham, Manchester, Bristol, Liverpool, Leeds, Sheffield and Wales (at Aberystwyth). In 1921–2 there were 450 at London University, 140 at Edinburgh and 647 at the four Inns of Court.[69] By 1927 there were around 1,700 Indian students at British institutions.[70] Many who came to study medicine and engineering decided to settle in Britain, and around 1,000 Indian medical doctors were in practice, with 100 in London alone. Other professionals put down roots, such as R.B. Jillani, who qualified as a civil engineer in London in 1935, secured a job on his professor's recommendation, and like many other Indian professionals contributed to the war effort.[71] Yusuf Ali, a former Indian civil servant whose translation and exegesis of the Quran commanded great respect, was another Indian Muslim who settled in Britain during this period and made important contributions to its religious, political and intellectual life.

New opportunities. Another reason why Muslim migrants along with others from the colonies continued to drop anchor in Britain was the opportunities on offer, for although the interwar years were a time of mass unemployment and economic gloom, the overall picture was much more complex, and infact there were many real advances. While older export industries declined, new industries such as car manufacturing, chemicals, and electrical and consumer goods were growing in regions such as the Midlands, creating many job opportunities and raising the living standards of most of the population. The prosperous regions of southern England and the Midlands—contrasted with the north, Wales and Scotland which were experiencing decay. Because of these developments, cities such as Birmingham began to attract Muslim and other 'coloured' migrants from other parts of Britain where structural unemployment, particularly among the unskilled (seamen, coalminers and dock labourers), was high.[72]

The fact that lascar contracts were so much worse than those for European sailors meant that there was strong motivation for lascars to jump ship and escape inland in search of more lucrative work.[73] Since mainstream unemployment persisted during the early 1930s, these men had to use all their inventiveness to make ends meet. Some struggled by hawking on the margins—selling chocolate surreptitiously in public houses, and concocting 'oriental fragrances' and exotic perfumes in boarding-houses and offering them to young women who were happy to indulge in a little luxury at affordable prices.

By the time the Second World War began, Muslim migrants from middling Indian rural backgrounds had taken up petty trading and other entrepreneurial activities, particularly as pedlars. During the late 1930s a number had gravitated to the Midlands, the north and even Scotland, encouraged by the many stories which circulated among migrants about the economic success of earlier pioneers, especially in the 'door business' (door-to-door selling). Among these success stories was Nathoo Mohammed, who came to Britain as a lascar in 1919, started peddling clothes and in due course became a successful wholesaler. In 1924 he summoned his two younger brothers, who were then joined by relatives and friends. Ata Mohammed Ashraf and his cousin, close relatives of Nathoo, arrived in 1926. According to Ashraf:

> there were about 40 to 45 Indians in Glasgow, all living in Anderton and Port Dundass districts. They were mostly illiterate peasant farmers from villages in the Nakodar and Jagraon areas of District Jullandhar. There were also two or three Pathans, from the North West Frontier Province, a similar number of lascars from Mirpur in Kashmir, and Bengal. Many of these people were ex-seamen who had jumped ship ... two or three ex-soldiers who were in this country during the war and had come back here after getting demobbed in India. All were engaged in selling door-to-door out of bags.[74]

What all these pioneers had in common was that they came from a petty farming background, from villages within a few miles of each other. They had left their villages in search of opportunities through which they hoped to escape the trap of bare subsistence inherent in small landholdings. As they themselves became established they called their kin over and helped them to get started. From 1927, as the news of how well many of the migrants were doing got around, the number of Indian Muslims multiplied. Since the majority were engaged in peddling, that market soon became saturated and, as sales declined, it became much harder to earn even a modest living. Many decided to disperse to other parts of Scotland—Dundee, Aberdeen and Edinburgh— in search of new openings for trading, with some success. Thus, there was just enough incentive for the trickle of migrants to continue. The Depression years of the early 1930s spelt short-term disaster for these peddling communities; the demand for their goods dried up and many found survival extremely difficult. Finding the prospects hopeless, some returned to their villages in India, but others, more adventurous and determined, took the initiative of leaving the familiar streets of Glasgow to try their hand in more remote villages. Their enterprise and perseverance paid off, and when the economy had picked up again after 1933 they capitalised on the niches they had created. As they began to prosper, they realised that further growth depended on a fresh supply of labour and this gave new impetus to immigration in the last years of the decade. More kinsmen were summoned, with the result that the number of Muslim migrants, still from within a ten mile radius of Nathoo Mohammed's village Tando Badal Khan, rose dramatically and, by 1940, over 400 had settled in Glasgow, especially in the Gorbals neighbourhood, and also in other cities as well as the more outlying areas such as the Highlands and Islands and the north-east. It was in this way that the 300-strong Muslim community on the Hebridean island of Lewis (mainly in its only town, Stornoway) evolved. Similarly the earliest Muslims arrived in Manchester from east Punjab in the 1920s and 1930s and although they struggled for many years as pedlars, they laid the foundations of the thriving clothing and garment trade, subsequently developed by some of those who from the 1960s went on to wholesaling and manufacturing. Various reasons have been advanced for the tenacity of these men in sticking with these occupations in extremely trying circumstances. But peddling—credit drapery, humping suitcases full of socks, handkerchiefs, shirts, clothes, 'this and that', doing the rounds of villages and knocking on doors—was one of the few occupations open to them at the time, and it is striking how many felt that they should try their luck in this kind of trading. Apparently 'once they had saved up enough, they opened fish and chips shops ... They would also have stalls in markets and then they moved on to shops.'[75]

An important factor in this success, especially in north-eastern England, given that few indigenous people had any particularly positive perceptions of them, was the tradition of tallying and check selling, which had already been made popular by English and Jewish salesmen in pit villages of the region. The familiarity of this business approach, adopted with minor modifications by Asians, helped them establish their credentials with their potential customers. Perhaps another factor was their determination to achieve the aspirations for which they had left their families and homes behind: to save and return to their villages to live in comfort, with their status and prestige enhanced. This goal, they must have felt, was only attainable if they could accumulate more and more capital for investment in bigger and bigger enterprises. An ordinary labouring job in a factory would not have been enough. These early entrepreneurs were at the starting end of migratory chains, which developed on a mass scale from the late 1950s in the major industrial cities such as London, Birmingham, Manchester, Bradford, Newcastle, Glasgow and Oxford, where they laid the foundations of future Muslim communities. In the south, particularly in London, Muslims adopted a number of different approaches to making a living. Already by the 1920s individual seamen were selling exotica bought in Aden or Alexandria. Others had renewed the tradition of setting up lodging-houses to cater for lascars in London. A few went on to set up coffee shops after working as kitchen porters or peeling potatoes and washing dishes in hotels and restaurants in the West End; or they established profitable businesses catering for seamen on shore leave or in between ships. The more enterprising felt confident enough to try on a wider clientele the Indian cuisine, which for years they had prepared for their fellow seamen on ships and in ports. The first two restaurants were established in the late 1920s, and their success attracted others to the catering trade so that by 1946 the number of Indian, mainly Sylheti-owned, restaurants in London had risen to twenty. Some of them acted as 'clearing-houses', meeting a variety of migrant needs, including accommodation, meeting and contact points, hubs of networks and provision of advice and guidance on jobs and other opportunities.[76] Thus, with communications and social networks already in place, these various economic activities drew an increasing stream of migrants to the employment opportunities which they generated.

The looming clouds of the Second World War in the late 1930s gave a further, albeit perverse, fillip to the growth industries of the interwar period, many now converted to the manufacture of essential wartime products. With demand for war materials rocketing, migrants, particularly those unable easily to find work, were directed by the authorities to factories in cities such as Bradford, Leeds, Birmingham and Coventry. The new prospects for relatively well-paid skilled and unskilled work—as blacksmiths or, say, as porters and sweepers in aircraft factories—offered opportunities to, among others, the small numbers of Indian, Arab and Somali seamen who became stranded without employment because of the war.[77] Indeed it was some of these ex-seamen who first settled in Bradford during 1941; by 1944–5 a nucleus of some thirty Muslims from the subcontinent, all former seamen, were living and working in the city.[78] Moreover, the Indian population of Birmingham, estimated at only 100 in 1939, had increased to 1,000 by 1945.[79] Among the new arrivals there in early 1940 were around thirty merchant seamen, including Muslims from Indian and Yemeni backgrounds, who were instructed to go to the city by the Ministry of Labour and work in factories producing war materials. At first they lodged with Turkish Cypriots already settled in the city, but later began to buy up property for their own use as well as to let out to tenants.[80]

Compared with the mass migration that soon followed, Muslim settlement in Britain remained limited immediately after the Second World War. While there are no definite figures, a range of estimates exists which allow for a tentative idea of the numbers of people involved. For the end of the 1940s Dilip Hiro produced an overall figure of 8,000 Indians scattered around Britain, of whom a significant proportion would undoubtedly have been Muslims, but this is lower than other contemporary estimates.[81] For instance, Banton, writing in the early

1950s, stated that there were 2,000 to 3,000 Muslims in East London, mainly Pakistanis, but also—East Africans, Somalis and others;[82] he added that 'in the same year as the census [1951] it was authoritatively estimated that there were about 30,000 Pakistanis in the country, but I am inclined to consider this figure too high', although he was prepared to concede that the overall 'coloured' population, including a substantial proportion likely to be Muslim from a range of ethnic backgrounds, could be as high as about 80,000.[83] His caution was not echoed by Hunter, who argued somewhat later that 'by the end of the last war, the number of Indian Muslims [alone] in Britain had exceeded 30,000'.[84] Clearly by this time Britain's Muslim population in Britain had grown sufficiently to exceed the numbers present in the period before the First World War. While by no means on the same scale as the migration of Muslims from the 1950s onwards, it formed the basis of subsequent migratory processes. Just as push and pull factors operated before 1950, they also played a crucial part in attracting new Muslim migrants to Britain. What made these pioneering settlers all the more important was the groundwork they carried out, forging links in the chain which would come to connect earlier and later generations of Muslims migrating to Britain. Most important, however, was the extent to which the migration of these earlier Muslims was motivated by their material circumstances. Their religious affiliation was often largely irrelevant.

3

MUSLIM ENGAGEMENT WITH BRITISH SOCIETY
UP TO THE FIRST WORLD WAR

This chapter examines the wide range of interactions and relations that evolved between Muslims and the indigenous population and institutions of Britain in the period leading up to the First World War. It looks at the reactions and responses of different groups of Muslims to their social, economic and cultural circumstances, and at the different strategies that they formulated to negotiate survival in their new environment. As we have seen, Muslims who came to Britain did so for varying periods of time, and the duration of their stay shaped the nature of their relations with the wider society: the more transient their situation, the less committed and participatory they seemed to be. In addition many were not regarded as Muslims *per se* but in terms of their racial or ethnic back-ground. Within the framework of the British Empire, with few restrictions on the travel and settlement of imperial subjects, permanent settlement in Britain was an option that only a small number exercised, in the process forming small embryonic communities contesting the material, moral and cultural space that comprised British society at that time. However, the sheer imbalance of the numbers and power relationships involved meant that their struggles to sustain distinct identities proved largely unsuccessful, and that many of these groups of Muslims became so culturally diluted that they virtually disappeared from the social landscape as separate communities.

The engagement that did take place was to a great extent shaped by the dominance over the Muslim world by Britain and its subordination to British interests. This unequal relationship produced images of a 'subject people', many of them Muslims, which led in general to negative evaluations with discriminatory effects for individual Muslims in key spheres of their lives. Within these parameters Muslims from different social backgrounds, with varying levels of skills and knowledge of British society, strove to achieve different kinds of engagement with that society in order to retain some measure of control over their lives. It is the extent to which Muslims succeeded in achieving their individual and collective goals that we investigate here.

Contact, channels of communication and early arrivals in Britain

As Chapter 2 showed, the growing presence of Muslims in Britain from the late eighteenth century owed its character and timing to the contacts between Britain and the outside world developing at this time and intensifying the channels of communication in the decades that followed. By the beginning of the nineteenth century the major stimulus for the growing movement of Muslims to Britain was trade in various forms. And the slave trade, which had flourished and was only just beginning to flounder, had led to a variety of contacts between Muslims and the British. Thus as British influence grew and Muslim power waned, British perceptions of Muslims, from having recognised a fair degree of equality between them, began to exhibit clear signs of superiority and hence a shift in the reception accorded to people from Muslim lands. Nevertheless, until the mid-nineteenth century interaction between the British and those Muslims who arrived in their country was shaped by the social status possessed or claimed by the visitors and, on the other hand, the status accorded to them. During the late eighteenth century Muslims were an important part of the 'permanent' black population of Britain, conservatively put at 10,000 and mostly concentrated in London.[1] Many worked as domestic servants, with a status often no higher than slaves. King George I's servants Mustapha and Mahomet, brought to England from Hanover in 1714, were undoubtedly the most prominent.[2] However, these ascriptions of status were not always fixed. Indeed, some who had been sold into slavery claimed to belong to families of substantial status in their native lands.

The examples of two Muslim slaves illustrate this dramatically. Ayuba Suleiman Diallo (b. 1701), son of a Muslim *muallam* (a high priest) of Bondou, a Fula principality (Gambia), was captured in 1731, ironically while himself on a slave-trading mission, sold off and shipped across the Atlantic to Maryland. Later Diallo was recognised by his owner as being from a higher class, and the philanthropist and deputy governor of the Royal African Company James Oglethorpe, once aware of his erudition and scholarship, had him set free. Diallo arrived in England in 1733 as a guest of the Royal African Company and was soon 'enthralling the gentry of Cheshunt, Hertfordshire, and the London merchants who had their country houses there with his tales of adventure and accounts of life and customs of his homeland'. Having written out the Quran from memory while in England, he impressed

> the group of scholars and virtuosi around Sir Hans Sloane, the famous naturalist and collector, for whom he translated several Arabic manuscripts. He received the Duke of Montagu's patronage and was elected an honorary member of the [distinguished antiquarians'] Gentleman's Society of Spalding ... and was presented to the king and queen receiving from the latter the present of 'a rich gold watch'. Once his merchant and slave-trading economic and social antecedents were established he was received by English merchants, gentry and nobility not merely as exotica from a far off land but as very much their equal.[3]

Job ben Solomon, son of a Muslim *imam* of royal lineage, enslaved and brought to England from Maryland, America, in 1733, was likewise 'lionized and feted by polite society, treated as an equal by some of the country's greatest scholars and heeded by the nation's elite'.[4] Towards the end of the eighteenth century another Muslim slave, called Mohammed, similarly impressed his owner with his knowledge of the Quran and scholarship in Arabic literature. He too was freed by his owner to return to Africa after a short stay in Liverpool in 1811.[5]

It is noteworthy that despite apparently widespread hostility to Islam in Britain in the eighteenth century, the devotion to their faith displayed by both Diallo and Mohammed greatly impressed their benefactors, the respect for their spiritual commitment which this engendered seemingly contributed to the decision to grant them their freedom.[6] But many other Muslims were less fortunate. In due course slaves from Senegambia and Guinea arrived in Britain, and remained mere chattels; they experienced harsh treatment and penury, and starved to death, utterly destitute.[7] This is not to say that they all accepted their unfree condition meekly. In the second half of the eighteenth century many fled their owners and became active agents in transforming their social status and claiming their legal rights. There is evidence that late in the century slaves were becoming increasingly insubordinate, treacherous, 'intoxicated with liberty', expecting 'wages according to their own opinion of their merits', and refusing to put up with inequality of treatment. The fugitives entered into associations and made it their 'business to corrupt and dissatisfy the minds of every fresh black servant who comes to England'.[8]

Other domestic servants, unable to tolerate the cruelty meted out to them, also ran away, prompting their employers to advertise in the press for their return. An example was the notice printed in the *Morning Chronicle* in 1795 on behalf of Mrs Ramus requesting the recovery of her absconding Bengali servant boy Hyder. Those who escaped capture or were discharged on arrival in England without any recompense eked out a living as musicians, street hawkers or beggars. Homeless and verging on starvation, many were reluctantly supported by the workhouses. This motley assortment of the colonial poor congregated in places frequented by their indigenous peers. 'The wonted haunts of Moormen [Muslims] and Gentoos [Hindus]' organised elaborate musical and dance gatherings at 'fashionable clubs and routs'. In their struggle to escape their unfree condition they were supported by the English working people, known pejoratively as the 'Mob', who often befriended runaways and defended them against bounty hunters. According to Henry Fielding, a magistrate sympathetic to the British slave-owners and also a famous novelist, these 'vicious white servants, and abandoned prostitutes of the town' corrupted the morals of the slaves, encouraged them in crime and made them 'ashamed or afraid to return to their masters'.[9]

Interactions between Muslims and British society were largely shaped by contemporary popular views regarding their position in the human hierarchy relative to degrees of civilisation. These views were complicated by the juxtaposition of race with religion. As non-European 'races' became subordinated to the British, those from Muslim lands were evaluated disparagingly. Negative images were reinforced by the collective memory acquired over the centuries since the Crusades. But social status also affected the way these visiting Muslims were received. Some Indian Muslims who travelled to Britain towards the end of the eighteenth century suffered from hardly any sense of inferiority and found they were able to interact with their British hosts without experiencing any patronising attitudes or condescension. Undoubtedly their class, together with awareness of India's own long and complex civilisation, made their acceptance into British society easier. Their descriptions of these interactions manifested confidence in their own culture and religion, and a measure of social equality. Hence the accounts of Muslim travellers such as the Indians Mirza Abu Talib and Mirza Ihtisamuddin, and the Egyptian scholar Rifa al-Tahtawi a little later suggest that, far from being treated as members of an inferior and defeated race, they were welcomed and fêted—not as curiosities but for the intellectual and social enrichment they offered British élite circles.

Through these travellers' writings one glimpses the attitudes that shaped social intercourse between particular strata of British society and individual Muslims. Abu Talib detected the intolerance of the English, the 'obstinacy and prejudice' of the British, their 'contempt for the customs of other nations, and the preference they give to their own, although theirs in fact may be much inferior'. He wrote of his chagrin at being attacked for the 'unreasonableness and childishness of some of the Mohammedan customs'; and hearing 'the ceremonies used by the pilgrims on their arrival at Mecca' ridiculed.[10] But he was not discouraged from forming a quite positive perception of the élite Britons he encountered. His narrative conveys a sense of considerable mutual goodwill. He described vividly the warmth and hospitality he received; he was lavishly entertained, his society was 'courted' and his 'wit and repartees, with some impromptu application of oriental poetry, were the subject of conversation in the politest circles'. Abu Talib seemed perfectly at ease in such circles, enjoying 'every luxury my heart could desire', drinking 'exquisite' wines and visiting operas in the company of 'ladies of quality'; indeed he was quite taken by the beauty of the women and their grace in dancing, his sense being 'charmed' by their music, and was 'so exhilarated by the coolness of the climate and so devoid of all care' that he gave himself up 'to love and gaiety'.[11] Through much of the eighteenth century there was still curiosity and fascination with the strange and exotic that was not much influenced by racial or religious prejudices.

The Persian 'Envoy Extraordinary' Mirza Abul Hasan Shirazi, who travelled to England with his party in 1809, certainly impressed the upper classes. The attraction between the English, their society and the Mirza was mutual, his positive view of the country was partly due to the warm reception he received. He praised English civility, admired the monarchy and was impressed by the institutions catering for soldiers, sailors and poor children. Similarly, his admirers found his manners 'truly captivating, graceful' and commanding respect. He charmed the English ladies with his good looks and attentive manners, and he in turn found them 'very handsome; very beautiful'. He admired their freedom and independence, and wished that 'the women in Iran could be more like the women of England' who were chaste by choice, unlike Iranian women, who had no choice in the matter, being compelled to remain secluded from men. All in all, the Mirza was a major draw for leading hostesses and organisers of charity benefits. As with Abu Talib, a major reason for his popularity was that he mingled with important people with unselfconscious ease and had similar interests. He went to the opera and theatre, rode daily and quickly became fluent enough in English to converse on topics of the day: 'On Sundays he walked with the fashionable in Kensington Gardens, where his fine presence and colourful Persian attire attracted much attention'.[12] In contrast to Abu Talib, who had declined to join the Freemasons in spite of finding many of their customs 'praiseworthy', especially their non-interference 'with any man's religion', Abul Hasan was happy to be initiated into the Craft by Lord Moira in 1810 on the proposal of Sir Gore Ouseley, then acting as Abul Hasan's host. This tradition of embracing Freemasonry was continued by some of the early Persian students sent to England by Crown Prince Abbas Mirza in 1815 and the Qajar princes, who arrived in the 1830s. It seemed particularly to intrigue those Persians who tended towards Sufism and freethinking in religion. Perhaps too they believed that those who belonged to the Society possessed 'mystical and supernatural knowledge'.[13]

Carving out a niche: interaction during the early nineteenth century

Thus by the beginning of the nineteenth century there was a range of interaction and contact operating within British society. Despite the inequalities connected to slavery and servitude, the kind of mixing that could take place in England at this time also generated respect based on social status. There was much less of the condescension and patronising arrogance that characterised contact between the colonisers and the colonised from the middle of the nineteenth century. Among the lower classes issues such as colour and country of origin presented relatively few barriers to free mixing, although incidents of prejudice still occurred.[14] In relation to marriage, for instance, income was often more significant than colour or even religious origins.

A notable Muslim whose career illustrated what could be achieved under the right circumstances was Sake Dean Mahomed, who accompanied Captain Baker, under whom he had served in the army in India, to Ireland in 1784. He improved his English at a local school, eloped with and married a 'pretty' Irish girl from a 'respectable family', and finally settled in the increasingly fashionable health resort of Brighton at the turn of the nineteenth century. Although the shampooing and herbal vapour-baths business which he established eventually became a roaring success, he initially experienced difficulties due to suspicion caused by 'prejudice against his race' and partly from scepticism regarding the efficacy of the seemingly exotic remedies which he suggested. Nevertheless, the fact that his reputation spread throughout Britain indicates that the obstacles of race and religion were not insurmountable. As with other classes of Muslims who settled in Britain, it appears that his white wife 'Mrs Mahomed' served as an effective conduit for dissolving residual antipathy and developing goodwill and trust with the clientele. With her understanding of the customers' social and cultural world, she helped greatly in running the business, providing appropriately packaged care for the patients. However, intermarriage in this case, given Dean's religious isolation, also speeded up the process of acculturation of the family into British society. While a surviving portrait of Dean Mahomed, showing him in Indian clothes, suggests that he held on to symbolic features of Indian culture, they may well have been used to enhance the uniqueness of his trade. His children's names—Rosanna, Henry, Horatio, Frederick and Arthur—perhaps more significantly reflected their mixed ethnic and religious origin and the shift towards acceptance of English identity. When his internationally known grandson, the physician Frederick Akbar Mahomed, died in 1884, an obituary notice stated that he had 'English parents'.[15] The completeness of the religious absorption of Dean's descendants was sealed by the appointment of the Rev. James Kerriman Mahomed, another of Dean's grandsons, as vicar of Hove, Sussex, later in the nineteenth century.

Interracial sexual relations and mixed marriages were not uncommon, although they were generally disapproved of, especially by those who had constructed a racial pecking order. Such relationships were perhaps inevitable with women belonging to the same community in such short supply. *Ayahs* had been recruited for some time, but few seem to have married. Although instances of 'Hindoostany ladies' accompanying British officers back to England could be found, they were very rare. Among only two or three whom Abu Talib met was Noor Begum, said to be the daughter of a Persian colonel. Married to a General de Boigne, she came to live in London in 1797. They had a son and daughter, Ali Bux and Banu, but her husband eventually deserted her for a Frenchwoman.

By the end of the Napoleonic wars in 1815, Britain's naval supremacy was firmly established. It was the world's leading industrial power and its imperial position seemed unassailable. With this dominance came a rapid increased share of international trade and shipping. As we saw in Chapter 2, these conditions encouraged Muslim seamen from British possessions, particularly India, to seek work as lascars on British ships. As mainly transient workers, they lived in lodging-houses set up by English people, but in time their own countrymen took on this role and capitalised on their greater ability to identify their clients and so provide appropriate services. Given the language difficulties and problems over dealings with the various institutions of British society, it was inevitable that a class of intermediaries should have emerged to advise these seamen and mediate with the local community. To be effective, these mediators either already possessed or came to acquire skills that made their interactions with the wider society fruitful. A key factor was that they often entered into marriages, formal and informal, with white women who adopted the names of their lodging-house keepers, such as Mrs Mohammed, Mrs Peroo and Mrs Janoo, and their mode of life. Over time these relationships gained these men local acceptance. The women were also helpful on a practical level. For instance, men with a poor grasp of English could use their wives or mistresses to communicate their own and their clients' needs to the authorities. And since they were conversant with the 'oriental vernacular', they acted as interpreters at police courts 'when the oft-repeated quarrels of Asiatics ... brought them into trouble'.[16]

Changing British attitudes towards Muslims

The attitude towards Muslims in Britain which saw them as forming part of the non-European and non-Christian world went through major transformations in the decades after the French Revolution. In the eighteenth century Indians and Egyptians had been respected as inheritors of ancient civilisations, but by the early nineteenth century a new sense of cultural superiority had emerged. The European fear of the Ottomans had gone and the Turks, with their turbans and tunics, had become innocuous objects of amusement and caricature at fancy-dress balls. This great Muslim power seemed exhausted while British élites saw their nation as vibrant and expanding. The roots of this sense of superiority lay partly in the expansion and consolidation of European influence over Muslim territories, partly in the stereotypes formed by travellers, missionaries, administrators and merchants in their brief interactions with local people, and partly in awareness and admiration of the technological achievement behind British dominance. Thus by the beginning of the nineteenth century, popular prejudice against non-Europeans and Christian hostility towards 'heathens' in Britain had gained considerable currency; colour was the outer reflection of mental and moral inferiority.

All this significantly affected how Muslims were received by British society. Indians, once considered gentle and cultured, were being described in 1792 as 'a race of men mentally degenerate and base, retaining but a feeble sense of moral obligation'.[17] The generation of Clive and Warren Hastings, less self-righteous and more appreciative of the value of other cultures, gave way to one with overtly condescending imperial attitudes. Burke's respect for Muslim institutions expressed so eloquently during the impeachment proceedings against Hastings was superseded by assumptions of 'native inferiority'. The sympathy publicly expressed for lascars as 'a race of human beings, who, though different in colour, religion, and country from ourselves, are still our fellow-creatures' was increasingly drowned out by accusations of laziness and stupidity, and by exhortation to self-help as the right way out of their misery.[18] In addition, the pre-Victorian period of Evangelicalism, utilitarianism and reformism put paid to the still paternalistic philanthropy that had characterised abolitionist sentiment. Imperial trusteeship implied imbibing the 'civilising', evangelising mission, nobly diffusing 'the laws of Alfred, the language of Shakespeare, and that Christian religion, the last great heritage of man' over a newly-created world. The empire was believed to be 'an instrument put into our hands by Providence for the working out some great purpose of His government...'.[19] Thus any underlying belief in the homogeneity of human beings and respect for oriental civilisations was largely eroded away between 1790 and 1840.

By the mid-nineteenth century many Christian evangelists were convinced that their religion was the only path to salvation and that the followers of all the other faiths were doomed to eternal damnation. Macaulay, in his well-known 1835 'Minute on Education', had demanded total assimilation to English 'taste, opinions, morals and intellect' if Indians were ever to become civilised. Disillusionment with the idea of 'improving' the 'native' accumulated as experience of governing and converting offered little encouragement for the achievement of the humanitarian endeavour. In Britain certain politicians touted the belief that Christian missions and national interests went hand in hand; certainly Lord Palmerston supported the promotion of Christianity as part of national duty. The Church Missionary Society received support from high-ranking evangelical Christian officials such as William Muir. When the so-called Indian Mutiny occurred in 1857, it was seen as due to the inability of Indian minds to accept moral and intellectual uplift, a more progressive system of administration, and modernisation. To the British, who had expected gratitude for their beneficence, the uprising was an act of betrayal. Muslims in particular were blamed for having inspired and led it and thus became the main focus of English bitterness. Sensationalised stories of Muslim cruelty and rapacity added fuel to the fire. Muir wrote his *Life of Mahomet* during this period of crisis and concluded that 'the sword of Mahomet, and the Coran are the most fatal enemies of Civilization, Liberty and the Truth which the world has yet known'.[20] In his view, Islam was a false religion which kept Muslims 'in a backward and in some respects barbarous state'. While 'conciliatory' themes represented by scholars such as Bosworth Smith were concurrent with the 'confrontational', they dismissed Islam as a wholly false and evil doctrine. By the 1860s negative images of Islam and Muslims were embraced in the hardening religious and racial prejudices that were beginning to be articulated in the form of pseudo-scientific theories of race in Britain.

The relatively large number of Muslim lascars found in Britain by this time were directly affected by this shift in British outlook. While lascars had attracted the attention of Christian philanthropists such as Wilberforce at the beginning of the nineteenth century and Thomas Clarkson a little later, the idea of some sort of moral obligation towards the 'backward races' gave way to the notion of Britain's civilising mission. From about 1812 there seemed to be attempts to convert them to Christianity while at the same time teaching them English: missionaries perhaps felt that this combination was the most effective way for these 'depraved' mendicants to be helped to adapt to their new environment. In any event, they were passionately devoted to civilising and Christianising the lascars, especially 'the Mohammedans' among them, and all the resources they deployed and the relationships they constructed tended to that end. Whether standing surety for those convicted of petty crime, exercising influence with magistrates on behalf of those needing good character references, or meeting their 'temporal' needs in hospitals and prisons, the beneficiaries were always reminded that their rescue from distress was the work of Jesus, to whom they ought to submit. Despite this fairly unremitting proselytisation, the missionaries had to admit that Muslims, including educated Indians such as apothecaries and interpreters, were extremely resistant to their message. They had 'a decided dislike to attend Christian services, and when invited, they ran away from fear of Christian influence or refused to attend out of prejudice'. All were denounced as infidels and spiritually ignorant: the numerous Arabs who refused to have any truck with the missionary and boldly expressed their conviction of achieving salvation through Islam were denounced as 'deluded'. Even those who refused to adopt an adversarial and confrontational stance were not spared; for instance, a practising Muslim from Calcutta was said to be deluded because his view that 'God had provided salvation for every one in the world, but each must seek it through the medium of their respective prophet' did not accord with the dogmatic approach of the missionaries.[21]

Many Muslim sailors were forced by their vulnerable financial circumstances to 'go about the streets' playing drums, singing and posing as models for artists. Islam, with its restrictions on diet and restraints on forms of social mixing, also shaped their mode of interaction. Some of these Muslims, unable to meet Islamic obligations and reliant on charity, converted to Christianity out of what may well have been sheer necessity. Usef Asman and his cousin 'Peter' typified this response. As Usef said,

> We are all turned Christians now; we go to school every Sunday ... and always to chapel ... We were forced to become Christians when we came here. Of course a true Mussulman won't take anything to eat that has been touched by other people's hands ... The beasts were slaughtered by other people and we wanted meat to eat. The bread too was made by Christians. The school-teacher used to come to father. We remained Mussulmen as long as we could, but when winter came on, and we had no money, we was obliged to eat food from other people's hands.[22]

However, not all those who claimed to be Christians had really converted. Some gave the impression of having converted to Christianity without actually doing so in order to earn a living. Jan Meer, for instance, bought a board with a printed statement to that effect which he hung round his neck inviting Christian sympathy and charity. Apparently he had no knowledge of what was on the board, and did not care either. All that concerned him was that he was able to make a good living by doing so. Other Muslims, less willing to convert but aware of the material benefits accruing from an overt declaration of conversion, also publicly renounced Islam. Zaid, an Arab from Liverpool, converted on the grounds that his Christian wife would otherwise have refused to marry him—and as soon as his wife died he rejected Christianity.[23] Jumal Deen epitomised the most cynical form of conversion, saying to a missionary: 'Padre, I am a Christian now; I have been in England fifteen years, married an Englishwoman, and I eat pork and drink beer when I can get it.' Later, when the marriage broke up, he reverted to Islam. Many others came under similar pressure from their white wives to change their religion. Among the converts some must have been sincere, but the material rewards were the crucial factor for the vast majority who did convert. They were often persuaded that 'it was no good looking to Mohammed here in London, ... no hope for them in Mohammed now, but there might be some in the Christian's Saviour'.[24]

Muslims formed a significant part of the 'black' presence in Britain. It mattered little whether they were Malays, Indians, Somalis or Arabs, since non-Europeans generally came to be described as 'black', and since the majority of blacks had either been slaves or were domestic servants or casual workers, most belonged to the poorest class of society and as such were treated with the same contempt as whites in the same predicament by those higher up the social scale. This suggests that sometimes their mistreatment may have had little to do with prejudice against them on account of their religion, colour or race. Indeed, for much of the eighteenth century black people in Britain had experienced little racial or religious hostility because their subordinate and submissive status did not pose a social or economic threat. However, by the late eighteenth and early nineteenth century the increasing pace of industrialisation and the progressive abolition of slavery altered their social status and the nature of their relationship with the indigenous population. Elites who had once given protection and patronage now declined to do so, leaving their non-white servants more exposed to the vicissitudes of everyday life.

As indicated in Chapter 2, lascars by now formed an integral part of the casual poor of Britain, excluded from the 'respectable classes' of society, although it was difficult at times to distinguish where one class began and the other ended. They mingled without much difficulty among this 'residuum', and were found in the public houses, theatres and music-halls of London's East End. Here 'colour or country [was] considered no obstacle ... Everybody free and easy—lascars, blacks, jack tars, coal-heavers, dustmen, women of colour, old and young, and a sprinkling of remnants of once fine girls ... were all jigging together.'[25] No doubt colour prejudice did exist on the streets of London in the mid-Victorian period. 'Darkies' were considered troublesome and pestering even by the workhouses and were never treated 'too kindly, for they don't understand it'. The workhouse master who made this statement had probably understated the abuse suffered by the Muslim poor. As one Muslim-turned-Christian beggar explained, he had had to put up with many insults and with violent assaults in the street. He had been called 'black dis or de oder'.[26]

Such instances, however, need to be balanced against evidence that the indigenous poor seemed on the whole racially tolerant. As in the eighteenth century, black servants, sailors, casual labourers and indigents mixed freely with their white counterparts and, despite opposition from many in the 'respectable classes' to cohabiting and miscegenation, found Englishwomen quite willing to consort with them and marry without any feeling of shame or degradation. A member of the London Mission Society observed 'how extensively these dark classes are tincturing the colour of the rising race of children in the lowest haunts of this locality … It is an instance of depraved taste, that many of our fallen ones prefer devoting themselves entirely to the dark race of men, and some who are to them [sic] have infants by them.'[27] Reports on the parlous condition of the Scottish poor referred to Asians masquerading as destitutes, 'accompanied with the appropriate set of groans', in the streets of Edinburgh while in private they 'spoke fluent English'.[28] Still language and religion as well as race left many isolated and neglected. Some succumbed to the underworld of brothels, gambling rooms and opium dens, acquiring a notoriety that was sweepingly and undeservedly applied to their compatriots as a whole. Henry Mayhew, a keen observer of the London poor in the 1850s, considered these 'spare, snake-eyed Asiatics' sly and cunning, while the missionary Joseph Salter's view that these 'cringing mendicants of the sunny land' lived by 'artifice and deception' confirmed a certain Christian view of lascars as 'practically and abominably wicked' and 'extremely depraved'.[29] What both men failed to appreciate was that it was precisely the application of resourcefulness, resilience and wits that enabled these people to survive in their hostile environment. Pretending to be converts to Christianity in order to evoke sympathy among the more charitably minded, sitting as models for artists, displaying colourful dresses and playing unusual music all formed part of the repertoire of novel and distinctive skills which they deployed in their daily struggle. Even Mayhew and Salter had to acknowledge that the majority were more than willing to earn an honest living if it was available, even when deplorably underpaid. Salter described the lascars as 'sons of honest toil' arriving with substantial savings but soon to be found destitute in the streets 'seeking the beggar's pittance'.[30] Mayhew reported a Bengali Mussulman who came to Scotland 'as servant to military officer'. Left stranded, he moved South and, like many of his countrymen, survived by 'playing and begging in the streets of London'. His parents were Muslim but he had become a Christian and was married to an Englishwoman. He had been a servant but was now out of work, and despite his precarious situation was prepared to do 'anything for honest bread'. Similarly, according to him, most of the lascars escaping the brutal treatment on the ships would beg or sweep but 'dey are never pickpocket'.[31]

Until the late nineteenth century, therefore, class rather than colour tended to determine the experiences encountered by Muslims in Britain. But the identification of the 'coloured' races with the 'residuum' increasingly solidified in assumptions of the superiority of 'civilised whites'. The darker the complexion, the lower the status. For nineteenth-century Muslim Arabs and Indians, lack of familiarity with the English language and customs increased their isolation and alienation and could compound their problems, leaving them to eke out only the barest subsistence. They lived in the cheapest and usually the worst lodging-houses, where there was almost total disregard for hygiene and overcrowding was intolerable. Many ended up in prison convicted of vagrancy and some were found dead in the streets of the metropolis, killed by starvation, disease and exposure. With lascars ill-fed and clothed in rags, the death rates, especially in winter, were inevitably high.[32]

Measures to administer relief to 'deserving cases'

The position of the lascars and other working-class Muslims deteriorated progressively throughout the first half of the nineteenth century. As early as 1814 William Allen and Thomas Clarkson, the abolitionist, investigated their plight and wrote to the then Secretary of State about the horrific treatment they received in the East India Company barracks in Wapping, but apparently these letters evoked no response. The Society for the Protection of Asiatic Sailors similarly highlighted the lascars' deplorable circumstances, and this finally yielded a parliamentary inquiry, which concluded that the sailors were indeed 'grossly neglected'. Despite some measures recommended by the inquiry, however, there was little significant change in their situation. In 1842 letters in the *Sailors' Magazine* and the *Evangelical Magazine* again highlighted their wretched state. With scores of lascars dying in the 1850s and with twenty-seven inquests in the winters of 1854–5 and 1856–7 alone, matters once more came to a head, but again, even though the coroner wrote to Lord Palmerston, the Home Secretary, the East and West India Dock Companies and the local marine boards, there is no record of any tangible action being taken by any of these authorities. It seemed that once the East India Company barracks had closed down after the grant of a new charter to the Company in 1833, no one was prepared to take any responsibility for the lascars' welfare while on shore and they were left to fend for themselves.

By the mid-nineteenth century Christian philanthropists were perturbed that little had been done 'to save the heathens in our midst' when thousands of pounds were being spent on foreign missions. The desolate condition of the lascars aroused concern also because of the revival in religious enthusiasm, which turned people's attention back to the home missions. Evangelical paternalism reasserted itself. Since 'the heathens of the heathen land associate here with the heathens of Christian London' and conversion was viewed as one of the highest forms of Christian service, arduous efforts to save the downfallen were encouraged. The English were concerned that the lascars did not see them as civilised and Christian but 'as vicious or even worse than their own countrymen'. Indeed, it dawned on them that the lascars possessed 'the very reverse of a favourable impression of the Christian religion',[33] and that 'in this professedly Christian country' these 'heathens' received no instruction in 'the saving truths of Christianity'. Instead 'they were allowed to leave [its] shores and return home as heathens, perhaps more corrupt and depraved than when they left their native land'.

The initial impetus to end this 'shameful neglect' came from an aristocratic Indian, Maharajah Duleep Singh: well aware of the distress of the Indian poor in Britain, he reminded the Church Missionary Society that no provision existed for his destitute countrymen needing asylum here. Various missionary societies then deliberated and reached a collective decision to establish a home for this class of people. Donations came from a broad spectrum of English people with a philanthropic and evangelical outlook. While there included aristocrats and radical workers, the backbone of those interested in the welfare of the non-white poor in Britain was provided by the evangelising or nonconformist middle classes, who were actively involved in organising charitable works. The Strangers' Home for Asiatics, Africans and South Sea Islanders, the first of its kind, was opened with great pomp and show by Prince Albert in 1857, and under its royal patronage came to symbolise the relationship between Britain and its poorer colonial subjects. The people for whose benefit the institution had been built had little say in how it was set up and operated. In planning and organising its functions its Board of Management kept in view the 'temporal and moral destitution' of the wandering blacks. As a charitable institution it provided board and lodging at an economical rate, along with interpreters, information and advice. It acted as 'clearing-house' for the recruitment of seamen on departing ships, but above all the administrators saw it as a centre for the propagation of Christianity to those of non-Christian faiths, especially Muslims. The heathen mind was thought to be dark and 'the vices of the heathen systems in which the Asiatic is brought up' formed part of his superstitious nature. Because the 'Natives of the East' possessed 'prejudices', the directors felt that their Christian duty required that the gospel be set plainly before them. The Bible translated into their own language was given to those who could read and a scripture reader was appointed. So certain were they of their belief and so contemptuous of other faiths that those who stayed at 'the Home' were force-fed with scripture whether they were 'willing to listen' or not; perhaps these recipients of Christian charity knew that it was the price to be paid for whatever help they received. However, serious complaints of religious interference were raised. Cama & Co., a Parsee firm, when offering to pay off the mortgage of the Home, stipulated that the first rule in its trust deed, that Christian instruction be given to those needing its protection and assistance, had to be abolished. The company stated that its objection was based on information from a variety of sources, but the Home's directors refused to make such an undertaking.[34]

On the practical level, however, the inauguration of the Strangers' Home had a positive impact on the lives of the Muslim poor with many tangible results. Undoubtedly lives were saved, thousands of pounds worth of savings were protected and secured, and people who might have previously got sucked into the twilight world of gambling, opium-smoking and petty crime were happy instead to go shopping and spend their leisure time at fêtes and 'places of art and amusement'.[35] Those who found their well-established lucrative but illicit businesses wither-ing and ruined by the alternative services offered at the Strangers' Home were persuaded either to act as recruiting agents for shipping firms or to work on ships again themselves. For the vast majority of the Muslim poor the saying that 'beggars can't be choosers' was wholly applicable, and their well-being was almost totally dependent on those from the wider society who chose to be involved in their affairs.

Muslim life in late Victorian Britain

Despite their often precarious state, Muslims in late Victorian Britain held fast to many of their religious values and were critical of those they encountered in the indigenous population. Respect for parents, highly regarded among them, was just one such value they found lack-ing among the English. As one Usef Asman said, 'My father has often called shame on the laws of this country, to hear the children abusing their parents.' That he accepted this view was illustrated in the example that he gave of his thirty-year-old brother, a seaman, accepting 'a side slap on the chops' for 'back-chatting' and disobeying his father. The Muslim poor also continued to live in their own groups in East London localities such as Shadwell and Wapping, inhabiting the 'Oriental quar-ter' probably because of religious prohibitions and out of a sense of communal solidarity. While disease, criminal activity or the need for shelter and food meant that the Muslim poor were often strongly rep-resented in all the typical institutions of vagrant life such as prisons, workhouses and hospitals, according to Salter 'they would rather huddle twenty or thirty together in a small house, where they can cook and eat and drink and smoke, *à la mode Orientale*, amid the fumes of opium and jogree, each defraying his own small portion of the rent'.[36]

But the approach to culture, custom and religion of those Muslims who formed part of the 'residuum' was on the whole entirely pragmatic. Given the limited intellectual rigour they were capable of bringing to bear on the challenges to their faith by such missionaries as Salter, they continued to excuse their adherence to Islam as the religion with which they had very close associations and in which their forefathers had died. However, when they felt that their needs were in conflict with tradition governing such matters as social and sexual relations, then they were quite willing to alter their practices sufficiently to achieve workable compromises with their cultural and economic environment. One, Shaik Hammed from the Dudley Refuge for the Destitute, who acted for Muslims as the link between those who were servants of the nobility and their more settled counterparts, having received 'spiritual attention', apparently got married in the same way that many other English, Irish and 'Oriental' vagrants did: 'They got some gin and some beer, a fiddle, and a broom; we drank the gin and the beer, and jumped over the broom, sang, and played the fiddle, and I was married!'[37]

By the mid-nineteenth century an increasing number of Muslims of more substantial means could also be found in London. According to Salter, they formed 'an attractive element in London life: their means and position placing all amusements and social enjoyment ... within their reach'.[38] More transient Muslims from the upper echelons of society such as the nobility were more confident in their social dealings with the British, and so had less cause to alter their behaviour than members of their retinues such as their secretaries, interpreters and personal attendants. In effect they could come and go in terms of their interactions with British culture. They continued to use spices and *ghee* (clarified butter) in their cooking and to eat sweetmeats for pudding. The ladies in the party of Oude's 'Mohammedan Queen', clad in their saris 'thrown over their heads and drawn tightly round their faces so as to leave little more than their eyes visible', observed *purdah*.[39] Even the 'frank open-hearted and liberal' Nawab of Surat, Mir Jafar Ali, who lavishly entertained the English aristocracy, 'did not partake of European food' though always present at his own table.[40]

This is not to say that no inconsistent behaviour occurred among these Muslims. Salter, who developed close connections with some of them, rebuked them for praying five times a day and then immediately paying a 'sinful' visit to the racecourse or the theatre, but the objects of his criticism saw no hypocrisy in setting aside spiritual concerns while enjoying more worldly pleasures and yet performing their religious duties. So, like many Victorians already applying British standards to measure the worth and rank of others in the scale of civilisation, Salter reached a low opinion of these high-born Muslims:

> The morals of these people were very low, and their temper savage, cruel, and disdainful, with very little regard for one another ... Their claims to civilisation, and their position in the social scale of life, may be estimated from the fact, that chairs and tables, knives and forks, shoes and stockings, were luxuries, the use of which they had never learnt.[41]

Even the Shah of Persia was declared uncouth.[42] However, most Muslims from the upper classes saw these practices as culture-specific and rejected any claim that British ways were superior. The servants of the Muslim nobility resident in London also often continued to observe many of the rituals of their faith, such as abstaining from eating pork and strictly observing Ramadan. Yet they too could be inconsistent, and Salter found some of the servants of the Queen of Oude at Abdool Rhemon's lodging-house enjoying opium, a smoke and a drink in the holy month of Ramadan.[43]

Other groups of Muslims in late Victorian Britain were perhaps more reluctant to embrace local customs and social norms. By the second half of the nineteenth century Arab merchants had become a permanent feature of Manchester life and created a separate enclave in which they successfully retained some of the key features of their culture—language, customs, dress, diet and religion. As distinct communities they lasted well into the interwar period. At first, like Indian travellers in the eighteenth and nineteenth centuries, these 'white turbaned individuals ... in Moorish garb' might produce a smile in the street but with increasing numbers they 'ceased to be a wonder, and so they go to and fro and do their business in their usual quiet way, and make their purchases at the shops without more than perhaps a casual glance from the passers by'. They conducted most of their business and correspondence from their homes in Arabic, and their dress was distinctive—a red fez worn with a long overcoat. They had large families. 'The womenfolk—mostly black women some of whom had been previously purchased in the slave market, married and brought to England—in a short time mastered the language, much quicker than their lords and masters.' These Moroccans seemed to adhere strictly to their Muslim religious practices: for example, before arrangements could be made for *halal* meat, a ruling was requested regarding eating of meat slaughtered by non-Muslims from the Islamic reformer Muhammad Abduh, and this allowed for kosher meat to be purchased from a Jewish butcher. Subsequently:

> one of the gentlemen undertook to see that the meat was provided in accordance with the Mohammedan rites. A butcher had the monopoly of supplying Welsh lamb, having in his yard a small abattoir, and each morning this gentleman proceeded with the killing of the required number of sheep. This same gentleman also led them to prayer every Friday, the service of which was held in a house in Parkfield Street.

At home too there were few adjustments. They ate highly spiced food and 'oriental sweets' and drank 'green tea served with mint'. The women ate after the men and separately from them.[44]

Despite these distinctions, some accounts of Moroccan life in Manchester suggest that some outward adjustment to mainstream English life could not be avoided. The second generation, while still familiar with Arabic, adopted English as their first language. Similarly, their appearance changed sufficiently for their dress and 'long hair' to be viewed back in Morocco as 'Christian'. Some of those who settled permanently anglicised their names. However, engagement with the British society was selective and largely in the context of the working environment with little social mixing involved, hence adaptations to English life were kept to the minimum. The lack of social contact was partly caused by the suspicion towards Arabs that surfaced from time to time—children met with hostility at school and were sometimes excluded from them as foreigners.

As a community these North African Arab Muslims retained links with their homelands. This was reflected in the material help they provided for their families and villages, the wives they acquired there, and the political initiatives they took to accelerate the process of their countries' independence from Ottoman rule. Yet this commitment was not perceived negatively by the wider society, partly at least because their activities harmonised easily with British imperial interests in the Middle East. As hostility towards the Ottomans resurfaced, the welcoming of the Young Turk revolt by, among others, the 'Mussulmans ... of Manchester' in 1908 was received approvingly by the establishment. The Manchester Syrian Association, formed during the First World War 'to help the allies in freeing their Country from the blasting rule of the Turks' and which included many Muslims, was enthusiastically supported by senior British officials such as Sir Mark Sykes. The Arabs reciprocated, and the sons of some merchants joined the army as officers and interpreters as the British encouraged the Arab revolt. The Syrians publicly supported the claims of Britain's ally Sharif Hussain of Mecca, and worked closely with Amir Faisal on the diplomatic front. Finally, they congratulated the British for defeating the Ottoman 'forces of barbarism' in 1918 and hoped that in consequence of the British victory 'Syria, Mesopotamia and Arabia' would be liberated. Such demonstrable commitment to British policy and collaboration in its implementation brought them public goodwill too strong to be undermined by lack of assimilation.[45]

The second half of the nineteenth century increasingly saw the arrival of Indian Muslims with landed connections, who accepted the reality of British dominance. One such was Lutfullah, who believed that British rule represented divine providence. So Muslims like him sought to bolster their influential social positions by accepting British superiority in scientific education and industrial technology. They acknowledged the framework of empire, wanted to make it work, and were keen to show loyalty to its rulers, hoping that cooperation would secure patronage and opportunities and open up processes through which they could carve out places for themselves in the new imperial dispensation. Lutfullah, Mirza Abu Talib and Sayyid Ahmed Khan—travellers to Britain in quest of the secret of British dominance that they wished to emulate—all came from this kind of Indian Muslim background. Abu Talib, in many ways a forerunner of Sayyid Ahmed Khan, expressed the hope that many of 'the customs, inventions, sciences, and ordinances of Europe, the good effects of which are apparent in their countries, might with great advantage be initiated by Mohammedans'.[46]

These Muslims, instead of shunning British education, became familiar with Western language, literature, philosophy and science and were keen to integrate rationalist methods with Quranic explanations. They still believed that European concepts and methods could be adopted without necessarily accepting Western social morality; indeed Abu Talib was critical of the British 'want of chastity', their 'want of faith in religion', their arrogance and passion for wealth and their pre-occupation with worldly affairs. Similarly, Lutfullah remained unconvinced of the propriety of men and women mixing in public, which he believed would lead to immorality. In his view women in Britain were 'uncontrolled' and immodest and he cited statistics to prove his view that this freedom led to widespread prostitution. Instead, he recommended Muslim seclusion. Yet many of these men mixed freely with Englishwomen of different classes and enthusiastically attended functions where women appeared in 'indecent' dress. Sayyid Ahmed Khan, for instance, held both upper-class and working-class Englishwomen in high regard. He was impressed by their standard of education and interest in public and current affairs, and thought them cultured, considerate and appropriately respectful, fine qualities that Indian Muslim women lacked. Given this kind of admiration, it is not surprising that many individuals from this background who settled in Britain wished to assimilate. They mixed socially and Professor Syed Abdoolah, Syed Ameer Ali and Abdullah Yusuf Ali all married Englishwomen. They were therefore receptive to some of the values and ideas of the West, but awareness of the shortcomings of British society also confirmed them in their Islamic faith and some of their traditions. While they experienced contempt and rudeness in their encounters with the English, they put these attitudes down to a lack of understanding.[47]

Thus while these Muslims accepted the hegemony of British values, they also wanted to push at the boundaries of social and political discourse to create more space for Muslim concerns. Using modernist methods, they defended Islam against aggressive British and Christian official 'cataloguers' and 'interpreters', such as William Muir. Mir Aulad Ali (d. 1898), professor at Trinity College, Dublin, used rationalist arguments to condemn as false the charge that polygamy and slavery are core practices in Islam. Syed Ameer Ali wrote a major work presenting Islam as a progressive faith amenable to the growth of human intellect. Sayyid Ahmed Khan sponsored and supported writers on Islam such as Bosworth Smith, who adopted a conciliatory approach, and in 1870 while in London he published (at substantial cost to himself) *A Series of Essays on the Life of Muhammad*, which questioned and rebutted many of Muir's claims. The late Victorians' response to the Muslims among them thus varied according to their own class as well as the social background from which the Muslims in question came. British upper classes treated their Muslim counterparts on equal terms with due regard for each other's status, while the lower middle and working classes were suitably obsequious. Sayyid Ahmed Khan thought that the maidservants employed to serve him had polite manners, liked the respectful way they addressed him as 'sir', and appreciated the 'careful attention' they paid to all his comforts.[48]

Encounters with the opposite sex

In public the anonymity of the crowd tended to encourage relatively inhospitable behaviour towards exotic foreigners, betraying attitudes possibly acquired as the offshoot of caricatures in newspapers, popular magazines and the music hall. Muslim visitors certainly reported harassment in the form of jeering street urchins and the polite but intrusive curiosity of young ladies. The latter encounters were particularly fraught by the different perceptions regarding the relationships that were possible between Englishwomen and men of colour. On the whole sexual relations between Muslims and white women were rejected because they closed the social gap between the ruler and the ruled that was considered essential if belief in the superiority of the British race and imperial domination was to be maintained. Social distance was necessary to sustain the charisma of British character and its resulting prestige and authority in the minds of subjugated people, which familiarity would dissipate.

Among the many ways assembled to prevent such interactions had been the use of images of sexual licence in popular literature such as the novel *The Lustful Turk* or the horror stories of their behaviour fabricated after the 'Mutiny' of 1857. It was widely believed that Muslims had 'inflammable' minds; they were presumed to lust after white women, who were thus at risk and therefore in need of protection from them. British colonial officials held firmly to the view that Muslims, especially from India, lacked 'self-control' in sexual matters and found white women 'almost irresistible'. At the turn of the twentieth century Indian students, who were coming to Britain in growing numbers, were described as 'raw youths' who were in 'no way fitted to encounter the temptations to which many of them succumb'.[49] Some of the officials who made arrangements for them thought that the life they led in Britain was a 'scandal'. Perhaps some of these Indian Muslims were excessively self-indulgent and given to fast living. But for others exposure to new kinds of social and sexual relations triggered processes of self-discovery. Sayyid Ahmad Khan's son Sayyid Mahmud, who studied law at Lincoln's Inn, wrote: 'After my arrival in London I became a true and faithful Muslim.'[50]

Even so, in spite of contradictory evidence many influential British people continued to believe in stereotypes associated with Islam. When wounded Indian soldiers were brought to the south coast of England for convalescence during the First World War, the mail censor noted deprecatingly the crude ideas that 'Orientals' had about European women, commenting: 'They cannot understand the freedom with which the sexes mingle.' The War Office believed that this kind of mingling was not part of their culture and that 'the ill-advised conduct of the women of the town [Brighton], though partly innocent in intention, was bound to result in the gravest scandals.' So, in order to prevent Indian soldiers from gaining wrong ideas and impressions, their movements and liaisons with white women were severely restricted. It was feared that if they were allowed to 'conceive a wrong idea of the "izzat" of English women', then it 'would be most detrimental to the prestige and spirit of European rule in India'. Draconian measures were taken to prevent Indian soldiers mixing with white women. At the sign of the flimsiest contact, for example a nurse having her photograph taken with Mir Dast, an Indian Muslim soldier awarded the Victoria Cross, instructions came from the top prohibiting all such association. No females were allowed to work in any capacity at the Kitchener Hospital, reserved for Indian soldiers, in Brighton: 'If anyone is seen talking to a woman, young or old, he is severely punished.'[51]

However, perceptions of Muslims craving for sexual contact with white women did not seem to accord with the readiness of white women to fuss over these men. Even at the height of imperial power, some people felt that an attraction for 'Oriental' men 'pervaded' ladies of 'all classes of society'—from 'the smartest peeresses' to 'English women of the housemaid class'. The guardians of empire viewed this with some trepidation. Lord Curzon, Viceroy of India between 1899 and 1905, expressed concern that 'at home every man with a turban, a sufficient number of jewels and a black skin is mistaken for a miniature Akbar, and becomes the darling of drawing rooms, the honoured guest of municipalities and the hero of newspapers'.[52] The racial and social hierarchy so carefully cultivated in the colonies appeared to be under threat back in the mother country, and instances of overfamiliarity between the rulers and the ruled was seen as subverting the relations underpinning imperial domination. As a result, campaigns were organised to instill imperial propriety in interracial sexual relations. In turn-of-the-century Britain, with sexual respectability increasingly sanctified and imperial supremacy believed to be founded on racial qualities, people were earnestly cautioned against 'sexual pollution', which they were told would lead to racial degeneration. This, it was argued, had to be prevented in order to avert social chaos and imperial decline. The imperial order would be safeguarded if social distance were maintained between the ruling race and the subjugated races, and that would be impossible if the ruled developed intimate relations with European women and came to be accepted as equals. But all this propaganda had little effect. For while the Indians on the whole 'behaved with great self-restraint and propriety', a Secretary of State for India at the end of the nineteenth century admitted that it was proving extremely difficult to dissuade white women from having relationships with them, given their apparent 'craze for running after' them.[53]

Under these circumstances, with the British establishment so strongly disapproving of interaction between men of the subject races and white women, it was not easy for Muslims, whatever their class, to navigate amid mixed company. Among Muslims of the upper classes, especially those still imbued with traditional social values and accustomed to segregation of men and women both in public and in private, encounters with women in public could be unnerving. Like Lutfullah earlier in the nineteenth century, many associated 'mischief' with the freedom granted to womankind in this country and thought it 'most deplorable'. 'Women in public' were viewed as 'uncontrolled' with a licence to enjoy the society of men. There was, in their opinion, no better way than the Muslim practice of seclusion to protect female virtue from male intrigues. Not that the sense of 'modesty' was regarded as less important among English ladies. Victorians were equally inimical towards sexualised encounters in public. English-women sometimes went to great lengths to avoid public spaces where large numbers of men were present. Middle-class Victorians had also firmly defined distinct domains for men and women: as a general rule, the external world was open to men while women were confined to the domestic sphere. But physical proximity between the sexes in social encounters—long a British cultural norm—threw many of these Muslims off balance. The mere act of entering the public domain trans-formed all Englishwomen in their eyes into the wrong kind of woman. A woman elbowing and pushing past in the street or leaning against them inside a bus generated embarrassment and discomfiture and, often, misunderstandings. In 1890, M.H. Khan, later Chief Justice of Hyderabad, described an encounter that illustrated this dilemma: he took a woman's innocent interest in him as solicitation, and she was then horrified for being thought a prostitute.[54] Thus gender relations between Muslims and white women were differentiated by social and cultural perceptions which in turn were influenced by the notions of racial superiority and class respectability.

The class factor: the case of Munshi and the Court

Attempts by the colonial élite to prevent social and sexual mixing between black and 'Oriental' men and white women had to contend with changes taking place within British society itself. While British society seemed entrenched in ideas of moral supremacy and sexual respectability, industrialisation produced from the 1880s onwards an increase in waged work for women which thus, brought about changes in their economic position, emancipation from domestic obligations and significant freedom of social movement. Gaining in self-confidence, some young women began to challenge existing conventions of public respectability and to question racist and masculine disapproval of inter-racial sexual relationships. They fought the popular view that preference for dark-skinned men was a sign of 'depraved tastes' and resisted their treatment as 'fallen', impure and socially or sexually deviant, unable to exercise self-restraint and to strive for a supposedly more spiritual sexuality.

Yet for many British people sexual relations between women of the ruling race and colonial subjects threatened the racial hierarchy and narrowed the social distance on which the imperial order rested. What concerned the official establishment was that, in Britain, class mattered far more than racial or cultural differences. While poorer Muslims had to contend with the heightened sense of social and class distinction that combined with their racial differences in the late Victorian period to reinforce their association with the servile status of the lower orders, aristocrats from India were regarded in the highest circles as members of the ruling class and treated as honoured guests. What also rankled with colonial officials was that, while Indian princes were received at Buckingham Palace, Windsor and Sandringham and danced with ador-ing duchesses, they, who had lived as virtual aristocrats in India, now joined the common ranks of the middle classes at home. All this clashed with the belief that the superiority of some classes over others was part of the natural order. Just as the poor were 'a caste apart', a 'race' of whom the upper classes 'knew nothing' and with whom there 'was no point of contact', so people with different physical and cultural traits occupied lower rungs on the social ladder. Racial divisions, seen as similar to the pervasive and enduring distinctions of class, attributed to Muslims generally the characteristics of the labouring poor as ignorant, uncivilised and stupid. Thus class attitudes were in the process of being transformed into racial attitudes lodged in an imperial setting. Racial feelings became more explicit and aggressive and reached their peak in the aftermath of the Queen's Diamond Jubilee in 1897. Tension grew as British colonial élites found more and more difficulty in asserting their claim to power on grounds of knowledge or intellectual ability, and so resorted instead to notions of racial superiority.

An interesting example of this interplay between race and class was the relationship between Queen Victoria's Muslim servant Munshi Abdul Karim, the court and the official establishment in Britain and India. In the eyes of many British observers, this man moved too close to the seat of power, and came to be suspected of pursuing interests other than those of Britain, with the result that his loyalty was constantly questioned.

The Munshi, one of the Queen's two Indian attendants, arrived in Britain in 1887 not long after the Golden Jubilee in 1887. He soon rose in the Queen's estimation and moved from waiting at her table to being entrusted, in 1889, with the task of teaching her Hindustani and informing her about Indian people and their religions and cultures. So pleased was she with him that she wrote to Lord Lansdowne, then Viceroy of India, asking for a grant of land for her 'exemplary and excellent munshi'. In the years that followed his promotion continued. In 1890 he was painted by von Angeli, and in 1894 the Queen appointed him as her 'Indian Secretary' bestowing on him the honour of Companion of the Order of the Indian Empire. As Karim climbed up the court hierarchy and his influence with the Queen increased, he generated jealousy and hostility among her courtiers and officials in the India Office, who became determined to pull him down. They believed that his social origins were doubtful and that if they could demonstrate this his influence with the Queen would be diminished. In their efforts to malign Karim, they used all the resources they could muster— reports on his father's occupation, his own qualifications and the character of his contacts and friends. In their view and that of the India Office, and contrary to the Queen's own perception, the Munshi was not a gentleman, and they felt no qualms in snubbing and scorning him whenever occasion arose. These instances multiplied as he enjoyed the monarch's increasing patronage. In 1890 the Queen's son, Duke of Connaught spotted him mingling with the gentry at the Braemar games and complained to Sir Henry Ponsonby, her private secretary. Karim was deliberately seated among the dressers at theatres until he made a scene and stomped out; Ponsonby had to promise the Queen that nothing like this would happen again. Although he was grudgingly accommodated between the Viceroy's staff and the 'distinguished guests' at the Durbar in November 1890, his father was excluded as being of insufficient social standing. Sir Fleetwood Edwards, an equerry, would not take tea with him and Dr Reid, another of the Queen's courtiers, declined to show him round the London hospitals. The royal household refused to countenance the possibility of eating with Karim when the Queen wished to take him to Ciminez in France in her entourage, and when he arrived there uninvited with his friend 'the untrustworthy adventurer' Rafiuddin Ahmed, he was humiliated by the household when Rafiuddin was ordered to leave at short notice.[55]

Throughout the Munshi's career with the Queen, her household staff and government officials resented the 'social and official position accorded to him in Court Circulars and in all occasions by the Queen'. They denigrated him as a 'thoroughly stupid and uneducated' man who 'on that account may become a tool in the hands of other abler men', and were convinced that he was passing state secrets through Rafiuddin, a law student, 'who supplied the brains that were deficient in the mun-shi'. While courtiers denounced him as politically dangerous and a spy on behalf of Afghanistan, the ministers considered him a 'bore' and certainly not as dangerous as some assumed; nevertheless they were suspicious enough to have him watched. Eventually the concerted pres-sure of the 'old India officers in her Court' began to tell on the Queen, and she was apparently persuaded to reduce his position. She assured the Prime Minister, Lord Salisbury, that 'no political papers of any kind are ever in the Munshi's hands, even in her presence'.[56]

The episode revealed the degree of intrigue to which the British establishment would resort in order to exclude the 'inferior races' from progressing to high office in the imperial power structure and decision-making process. The Queen realised that class and race preju-dice was furiously at work in the efforts to undermine the Munshi and did all in her power to resist it. When reminded of his lowly origins, she lashed out against the 'division of classes' as 'most ... dangerous and reprehensible'; the scheming against Karim in which the court was so deeply involved was based on 'race prejudice'. However, for all the Queen's efforts the long-term impact of her interventions was mini-mal. After her death, her officials took their revenge: on their advice King Edward VII ordered two bonfires of all Karim's papers, and only a few letters from the Queen were left to his widow as a memento.[57]

Nevertheless, Muslims who succeeded in developing relationships and credibility within establishment circles found that in a modest way they could influence official thinking and policy on some of the issues of concern or interest to them. Rafiuddin, 'a leader of the Mohammedan community in London', was able to glean information from the Munshi about British government policies towards the Muslim world, which he used when trying to mobilise opinion in its favour. He also influenced the Queen's perception of the mood of Muslims in Britain. For instance, Rafiuddin was able through his friend to get her to read Wilfred Scawen Blunt's protest against the massacre of Omdurman published in *The Times*.[58] Indeed many of the Queen's close advisers believed her to be favourably inclined towards Muslims and anxious to see improved relations with the Ottomans brought about through British Muslim mediation.

Perfidious Turks and despotic Orientals

Lord Salisbury and members of his government, however, blocked all initiatives to promote these Muslims. This was partly because there were powerful political and religious forces within Britain ranged against the terminally sick Ottoman Sultanate. Intensified economic rivalry among European powers made a scramble for new territory inevitable, and this included much that had formed part of the Turkish domain. Imperial expansionism at the end of the nineteenth century was revitalised and bounced back to regain its declining popularity, but this time infused with a new moral purpose. The 'Turkish tyrant'— 'brutal, barbarous, perfidious'—was viewed as the enemy of 'domestic happiness, of Christianity and civilisation'.[59] The Muslim mind was considered incapable of rational modern thought and as such unable to effect change, since Islam reformed was Islam no longer.[60] In the opinion of many, it would have to be cast aside before Muslim countries could hope to make progress.

Pronouncements made at regular intervals by giants of the Liberal Party in the late Victorian and Edwardian period were vehement against Islam and the Ottoman Turks. W.E. Gladstone expressed his deeply-rooted suspicion of Islam, which he thought 'radically incapable of establishing a good and tolerable government over civilised and Christian races'.[61] In a public speech he asserted that for as long as there were followers of 'that accursed book' (the Quran), Europe would know no peace. In his view Europe—in other words Christendom—should have united to impose its will. Only over 'lesser' peoples such as the so-called 'Orientals' and 'Mahomedans', where there was no 'complication of blood, of religion, or tradition, or speech', did Gladstone accept the Turks' ability to provide imperial rule. So firm was his belief in the reality of Muslims' fanaticism and their capacity to commit atrocities against Christians that he completely accepted Bulgarian allegations of massacres in 1876 and reports of Armenian persecution in the 1890s, ignoring any evidence that pointed to similar acts committed against the Turks. Consequently his passionate and immensely popular pamphlet, *The Bulgarian Horrors, or The Question of the East*, reinforced British perceptions of Muslims as an 'anti-human specimen of humanity'. Not surprisingly such rhetoric encouraged an outpouring of anti-Turkish emotion and agitation. Fed on partisan yet plausible information by the popular media, it became overwhelmingly an expression of the high Victorian moral conscience, whipping up indignation and guilt feelings over the government's, in many people's view, unprincipled pro-Turkish stance, which was prepared to sacrifice liberty and justice in pursuit of narrow and selfish national interests. Some of the clergy further raised the temperature by drawing attention to 'those unspeakable hotbeds of vice—the harems of dissolute Turks', and denouncing Islam as that 'most nauseous abomination'.[62]

These opinions reflected more general perceptions of Muslim despotism, corruption, religious fanaticism, sexual depravity and inequality depicted in literature, painting and travel writing. They were further accentuated by reports of major policy decisions, diplomatic initiatives and military expeditions undertaken around the world in pursuit of imperial interests—'the Eastern Question', 'the Occupation of Egypt', 'the Conquest of Sudan' and so on. They were reproduced in accessible and popular forms such as newspaper cartoons, music-hall songs, novels and religious journals, and then from the beginning of the twentieth century in photographs and cinema. These themes and images came to inform popular attitudes towards the small but growing Muslim population in Britain. The British establishment was more divided over what the correct policy should be towards Muslims, and especially the Ottoman Caliphate. The Armenian Question in the 1890s provoked widespread indignation. Peers, politicians, clergy and 'leaders of thought in every department of life' denounced the Ottomans in speeches and writings. Respectable journals and newspapers such as *The Times*, *The Contemporary Review* and *The Nineteenth Century* published diatribes condemning the Ottoman empire as, in the words of one commentator, the 'great anti-Christian and anti-social power … founded on slavery and polygamy and operating by massacre and rape'.[63]

Islam was identified as the ultimate source of all wickedness: a religion that regarded the 'killing and plunder of infidels' as being 'as much an act of worship as prayer'. The Sultan was portrayed in *Punch* as 'the unspeakable Turk'. In 1896 Gladstone, now aged and infirm, was once again sufficiently moved to fulminate against 'the Great Assassin', 'that wretched Sultan, whom God has given as a curse to mankind'. Too old to lead a new Crusade himself, he nevertheless zealously supported the powerful Armenian lobby in Britain, which demanded military intervention from the British government as its Christian duty. At the other end of the spectrum the Queen, more sympathetic to Muslim sensibilities, denounced 'the impolitic half-mad attitude of Gladstone' and recommended that Rafiuddin Ahmed should become an attaché to the British Embassy in Constantinople in order to assuage the rising tide of anti-British feeling among Indian Muslims. Lord Salisbury, the newly-elected Conservative Prime Minister, was rather more pragmatic and tried to placate the widespread antagonism against the Turks being generated in England at the time through diplomatic efforts, viewing the use of force as unlikely to help the Armenian cause. Salisbury was not lacking in Christian conviction and had in the past expressed a 'distaste for the Turks'; he once described the Sultan as 'sickly, sensual, terrified and fickle'. Indeed, in 1895 he had toyed with the idea of dismembering the Ottoman Empire but, after consulting the other European powers, realised that armed intervention was unlikely to succeed. Given that British strategic interests were not coterminous with those of the Armenians, he was not prepared to involve Britain in any action that, in his view, increased the risk of a Europe-wide conflict. Even if he had wanted to do so, he was anyway doubtful that Britain had the resources to occupy and hold large parts of the Ottoman Empire for a prolonged period. He then redressed the balance a little by questioning the accusation that the Turks alone were to blame for the massacres, thus undermining the justification for such extreme action.[64]

Nevertheless, the negative views of Islam and Muslims generally continued to generate hostility and resentment towards Muslims in Britain, particularly during those periods of rising tension such as the mid-1890s when they challenged the accepted view of events or rejected the validity of arguments justifying a particular policy or ideology. The behaviour of non-Muslims towards a small community of Muslim converts in Liverpool demonstrates the impact of these attitudes on their mutual relationships.

Quilliam's Liverpool Muslim congregation

The Liverpool Muslim congregation in question was set up by a prosperous solicitor from the Isle of Man, Quilliam, who converted to Islam in 1887 after a trip to Morocco, and was immediately stigmatised, 'looked upon as a species of monomaniac'. At first he was insulted and ridiculed; this system of religious belief was pronounced absurd and ridiculous—'with some good points' it was deemed to be 'blended with so much unmitigated nonsense and it is a belief so foreign to western minds, that its chances of success here are evanescent. It is an exotic.' The old clichés about Islam—its fatalism adapted for the indolent races of the South but unsuited to the energetic people of the North, the promise of a sensual paradise, its lack of progressive capacity, institutionalisation of the inferiority of women, its repugnant practice of polygamy—flooded back in articles and newspaper columns.

With such propaganda it was not long before some Christian zealots lost patience with those espousing an 'un-English religion'. 'The muezzin's call to prayer ... aroused the mob's active antagonism for such a glaring advertisement in England.' Several hundred assembled in front of the mosque and greeted the *muezzin* with 'discordant yells and loud execrations', pelted him with mud, stones and filth; and also pelted worshippers leaving the mosque. Several of the congregation were struck and hurt. Eventually the police appeared and the mob dispersed. Justifying the mob's violence, a local newspaper commented:

> To hear the muezzin here it is most incongruous, unusual, silly and unwelcome, and the man who stands howling on the first floor of a balcony in such a fashion is certain to collect a ribald crowd, anxious to offer a copper or two to go into the next street, or even ready to respond to his invitation with something more than jeers.[65]

This violent opposition was taken as proof that England and Liverpudlians 'detested' Mohammed's creed, 'this Eastern humbug' which, as history proved, had been 'hand in glove with cruelty, murder, moral and imperial decay, and barbarous ferocity'. 'How, then, can any Mohammedan,' it was asked, 'however earnest or enthusiastic, *dare* to force his objectionable creed upon the notice of a mixed crowd in a Christian country?'[66]

Such comment, an amalgam of bigotry and intolerance, fed by inaccurate and misleading history, relied on the folk memory of the Crusades and the charge of Muhammad's imposture to give them the moral rectitude to justify lawlessness and disorder, which in other circumstances would be deplored. With feelings so inflamed, Quillium decided that if he were to induce people to discuss the relative merits of Christianity and Islam with equanimity, then it was advisable to 'promulgate the tenets of Islam in an indirect way'. For instance, in talking about temperance he might refer to the insistence on total abstinence from intoxicating drink, thus opening the way for further inquiries about Islam. However, in spite of this change in strategy Muslims in Liverpool continued to be criticised by local Christians. In January 1895 the Muslim Institute's weekly journal *The Crescent* reported that 'furious Christians threatened to burn Sheikh Quillium alive', and in October there was a 'dastardly attempt to maim Muslims' when a wire was placed across the mosque's entrance.[67]

The attitudes revealed in this example of British society reacting to the presence of Muslims within it continued largely unaltered into the 1890s, when foreign policy decisions and the stands taken by the governments further boosted anti-Muslim sentiment. Quilliam persisted in making statements in reaction to events that challenged many of the British people's perceptions and assumptions on the question of their identity—and not surprisingly drew antagonistic responses. By calling on Muslims not to fight fellow-Muslims on behalf of the British in Sudan, he indirectly called into question the ability of Muslims to be loyal to both Britain and their religion. While for Quilliam and his supporters his statements were logical, to those less sympathetic they were dangerous and to be vigorously rejected. On the Armenian Question too, when Gladstone tried to mobilise mass support for his demand that the government should take punitive measures against Turkey, Quilliam pre-empted his speech in Liverpool by calling a meeting of his congregation to redress the balance. He talked of England blinded by religious bigotry and horror-struck with tales of alleged Armenian massacres 'practically preaching a new crusade against Islam', but hypocritically ignoring 'Christian atrocities' elsewhere. His warning that such a crusade might be answered with a *jihad* was immediately dismissed in the press as a hollow threat. When in 1903 Quilliam spoke out against Western condemnation of atrocities in Macedonia as unfair to Turkey because it failed to take account of similar actions by other governments, the press response was again to reject such criticism as 'un-British'.

Pan-Islam and the First World War

By the early twentieth century the politics of pan-Islamism, together with Muslim modernism, formed the twin pillars on which Muslims from Western-educated classes of Indian society—administrators, merchants and professionals—built strategies to pursue their individual interests as well as the interests of their community. While they may have been seen as self-appointed spokesmen of the British Muslim community, their challenges to policies regarding the Muslim world were thought sufficiently in tune with the sentiments of those they claimed to represent for the British authorities to feel compelled to step back and reflect on the implications before reaching any final policy decisions. As British foreign policy began to move away from support for the Ottomans at the turn of the century, several strands of pan-Islam emerged. The older generation of 'Empire-loyalists', led by stalwarts such as Syed Ameer Ali, continued to influence British policy towards the Muslim world through constitutional means within the framework of the empire, but attacks against the Ottomans increased its unease, and many younger Muslims took a more challenging stance. Influenced by Jamal-al-din al-Afghani's proto-nationalist ideas, they favoured an anti-British pan-Islamic struggle to achieve freedom for the Muslim world from Western dominance. Among them were Munshi Abdul Karim's friend Rafiuddin Ahmed, Mushir Hussain Kidwai, Syed Mahmud and Nasir-ud-din from India, and Bedr-ud-din from Egypt. These men were all convinced that the true interests of Muslims could only be secured through total political independence from Britain and the forging of greater unity among Muslim countries, not necessarily by constitutional means. They set about organising activists in Britain with a view to supporting pan-Islamic and nationalist forces in Turkey, Egypt and India. Moreover, Kidwai, together with another Indian Muslim, Barkatullah, was particularly influenced by the Bolshevik ideas emanating from Russia in the early twentieth-century, and so advocated revolutionary socialism as compatible with the achievement of Muslim aims. Consequently, he worked hard to bring about a closer relationship between the Bolsheviks and the Ottoman Caliphate, Afghanistan and Persia, the only independent Muslim states left with any hope of withstanding the onslaught of the West.

Because of these developments, a range of political societies were set up that shared the broad aim of stemming the decline of the *umma* by pursuing pan-Islamic objectives. The Pan-Islamic Society founded in 1903 with Abdullah Al-Mamoon Suhrawardy, a graduate of Edinburgh University and a barrister, and Mushir Hussain Kidwai as its President and Secretary respectively had its antecedents in the Anjuman-i-Islam of 1886. Kidwai, writing in the Society's organ *Pan-Islam*, rebutted accusations that the pan-Islamic movement was in any way either fanatical or secretive, and asserted that it was dedicated to defending Islam against Christian misrepresentations. In response to the rising tide of pan-Islamic sentiment from 1908 onwards, he renamed the organisation the 'Central Islamic Society' in 1910: its stated objectives were to remove 'misconceptions prevailing among non-Muslims regarding Islam and Muslims', disseminate information on Muslim issues, and involve powerful British people to influence in positive ways both public perceptions and official policy regarding the Muslim world. The Society's president, vice-presidents, managing committee and other officials offered an impressive array of activists in London from different parts of the Muslim world, including a number of leading white British converts. They established links with those in ruling circles of the empire who expressed sympathy—some lukewarm but others more passionate—for their cause.

Among this charmed circle of allies the most prominent was a member of the English upper class, Wilfrid Scawen Blunt (1840–1922). At the time of the British occupation of Egypt, which he opposed, he had become interested in Islam and Muslim affairs, and was closely associated with modernists such as Muhammad Abduh, a disciple of Afghani, and Muslims in Britain with similar views. He was especially impressed by ideas to reform and modernise the Muslim world which the Persian Ambassador Mirza Malkum Khan and the Egyptian Louis Sabunji, both converts to Islam, articulated in their journals *Qanun* (Law) and *El Nakleh* (The Bee), published in London in the last quarter of the nineteenth century. He had become so closely identified with the beliefs and struggles of Muslims that 'more than once in the succeeding years' he was on the verge of 'making the required profession, but somehow the incredulity [of his] reason [had] at the last proved too strong', preventing him from converting formally to Islam.[68] While Blunt was an ardent supporter of Muslim nationalism in Egypt between 1905 and 1913, he remained firmly of the belief that British rule benefited India and that 'an imperial government and an imperial army will remain a necessity for India'.[69] Moreover, though accused of disloyalty for championing the pan-Islamic cause, he was very much a conservative in domestic politics. Well connected in establishment circles, he provided advice on what tactics and strategies were likely to be the most effective.[70]

However, the British establishment never felt confident enough to allow Muslims under their tutelage to play any significant role in policy-making. As we have seen, ideological developments at the beginning of the twentieth century had begun to justify the subordination of non-European people in racial terms. Eugenicist theories combined with social Darwinism were conscripted to rationalise their exclusion from the imperial power structures by suggesting not only that certain classes and races lacked the capacity for sound judgement but also policies to maintain the superiority of the British race by preventing its contamination should receive particular attention. The increasing links between the Ottoman government, revolutionary nationalists and some of the Muslim activists in Britain therefore reinforced suspicions within British official circles. Muslim students, now quite numerous in Britain, were developing close contacts with other radical nationalists and becoming active in campaigns for home rule back in India.[71] When the Italians invaded Tripolitania—then under Ottoman control—in 1911, pan-Islamic sentiment, simmering since 1908, boiled over and a spate of newspaper articles, petitions and manifestos poured out of London. Agitation and protest meetings were organised with the help and support of prominent Britons, and great disappointment was expressed at the British unwillingness to intervene against the Italian military invasion. Empire-loyalists could not but be caught up too in the turmoil. In 1912 Syed Ameer Ali, undeterred by the lack of official response, set up the Red Crescent Society to channel funds and provisions to help the Turks. However, he had already paid for his pan-Islamic sympathies: his nomination for membership of the Privy Council in 1909 was opposed by the King on the grounds that no matter how 'clever the Native might be and however loyal you or your Council might consider him to be, you never could be certain that he might not prove to be a very dangerous element'.[72] More outspoken activists, such as Rafiuddin Ahmed, argued that Islamic sentiment towards England was changing for the worse and that this would prove harmful to British interests since the British Empire represented 'the greatest Muslim power on earth'; it had 'intricate political and commercial relations with all Moslem states' and its strategic position was exposed in Asia to her dangerous rival Russia.[73]

Early in the twentieth century, therefore, a significant cluster of Muslim activists with the intellectual capacity to articulate the concerns and discontents of their co-religionists had gathered in London. This group was perhaps most clearly epitomised by Duse Muhammad Ali, an Egyptian who became politically active after a career as an actor. In 1913 he was suspected of collecting funds in England and sending them to Tripoli to arm the Arabs. Much of his work was carried out clandestinely. He established contact with the Young Turks and Nationalist Socialists in Egypt, and in London became connected with a number of pressure groups through whose journals and seemingly innocuous charities appeals he reached respectable and influential figures in the upper echelons of British society. He wrote articles in the liberal magazine *New Age* which were highly critical of Western values and civilisation and *The African Times and Orient Review*, which began publication in July 1912 under his editorship with a circulation mainly 'among Mohemaddans', became a powerful vehicle for his views. The fact that the authorities viewed the latter as 'a notorious disseminator of sedition' caused it to be banned in India and Africa and closed in September 1914. It reappeared in January 1917 and was published intermittently until its final demise in December 1920. The journal dealt with a bewildering array of issues and supported a wide range of causes. Nevertheless, all were underpinned by a coherent principle that opposition to imperialism and to the domination of the African and Asian peoples the struggle for freedom, required solidarity with the few remaining non-European independent powers. Among these the Ottoman Empire was pre-eminent, but Duse felt that its defence could only be mounted under the guise of pan-Islamism, and so his efforts were geared to increasing this solidarity. The channels of support in which he was involved included not only existing ones such as the Islamic Society but others, such as the Albanian and Ottoman Committees, which he helped to create and which were able to attract sufficient patronage within the British élite to make official establishment feel uncomfortable.[74] Duse managed to mobilise considerable support among the 'political Mohammedans' from 'the Gold Coast and many parts of the world', while always maintaining a non-sectarian position. He was ably assisted in his efforts by the Indian Muslim missionary Khawaja Kamaluddin, who arrived in Britain in 1912 and established the Muslim Mission at the Woking Mosque, in whose journal *The Islamic Review* Duse also wrote articles.

By the outbreak of war in 1914 Duse's reputation stood high within the multinational Islamic community of London and this gained him a measure of respectability. As a result his network of contacts within the British élite widened, and for his political work he was able to use respected British public figures as virtual 'front men' (who themselves thought involvement in the pan-Islamic bodies an effective way to keep 'native' susceptibilities in check). In this way he could keep suspicious officials at bay. In 1915, when British public opinion against Islamic Turkey—allied to the principal enemy, Germany—was running high, he shrewdly launched through the Islamic Society a charity called the Indian Muslim Soldiers' Widows and Orphans War Fund, apparently without raising suspicions. Indeed many powerful figures, some as highly regarded as the Earl of Cromer, were persuaded to support it without realising that they were thereby helping Duse to pursue his broader anti-colonial objectives. Though hardly a financial success, the appeal for funds was cleverly used to present a robust defence of the Turkish Caliphate 'as the sole remnant of Muslim political advancement'. He warned of the turmoil felt by the '100,000,000 Muslims of the British Empire', torn between their sympathy for Turkey and their loyalty to the British empire, especially Muslim soldiers who were fighting against the Ottoman Sultan. At the same time the stinginess of the British public—altogether only a paltry sum around £2,000 was collected—made it clear to the Muslims that while influential people in Britain were willing appeal for help for the families of 'our gallant Muslim soldiers' who had fallen in battle fighting for the imperial cause, the British were, seemingly, in less than generous mood when it came to actually loosening their pursestrings.[75]

Duse and others involved in these activities were therefore able to convey to Muslims in the British Empire the realisation that, regardless of official platitudes, they were being used as cannon-fodder. Although the British authorities attempted to undermine him by engineering splits in the organisations in which he was involved, he emerged relatively unscathed, and unsubstantiated smears brought against him by government collaborators and erstwhile colleagues, such as Abdul Majid, the President of the Central Islamic Society, failed to dent his reputation and influence. Indeed he continued to play a prominent part as Vice-President for Egypt in that Society during and after the war. Through the columns of *The African Times and Orient Review* he pressed home the message that the sacrifices of Muslims for the British cause should not go unrewarded and that a just settlement must include full recognition of their rights. He emerged as one of the leaders of an activist group of articulate and well-connected British Muslims who saw a convergence in Afro-Asian and Islamic politics after the war and began to call on 'the coloured people of the world to show a solid front'. Viewed as an 'agitator', he was kept under surveillance. His close connections with 'political malcontents' such as Ihsan al-Bakri, 'a keen member of the Anglo-Ottoman Society' and the Egyptian Association of Great Britain, who was considered 'frankly hostile to British rule in Egypt', were closely monitored.[76]

However, British Muslims were greatly affected by the First World War. Turkey's involvement on the side of Germany created immediate doubts about the loyalty of all classes of Muslims within the empire, which reinforced perceptions that Muslims were essentially 'un-British'. In the war atmosphere that hung over British society for four years, perceptions of national identity and loyalty to that identity were intensified. Leading politicians such as David Lloyd George (Prime

Minister 1916–22), in order to heighten hostility to the 'enemy', unleashed a barrage of hostile rhetoric against Islam and the Turks. Lloyd George largely typified the politician of his time. However, there was a close similarity between the sentiments expressed by him and those of his nineteenth-century predecessors. In many ways his utterances after Turkey's defeat in 1918 reflected the low opinion of Muslims and hostility towards them still prevalent in Britain. By the early twentieth century British politicians had learned the importance of knowing and appealing to the voters who would return them and their parties to parliamentary power. Extensions to the franchise meant that all adult male householders could vote, and so more than ever before rhetoric had political value. Lloyd George thus whipped up anti-Muslim feeling during and immediately after the war; he called the military operations in Palestine 'the British crusade' and described the conquest of Turkey as 'the achievement of Great Britain'. He characterised the Allied intervention in Turkey (spearheaded by the Greeks, who suffered a catastrophic defeat in the process) as 'the burden of civilisation' and 'the emancipation of vast territory ... from the blighting influence of the Turks as one of the finest tasks for civilisation' upon which Britain had ever embarked. Echoing late-nineteenth-century imperial pretensions Lloyd George declared in 1919:

> We are undertaking a great civilising duty ... a mission, which Providence had assigned our race, which we are discharging to people living under the shadow of great tyranny for centuries, trembling with fear, appealing with uplifted hands for protection. Turkish misgovernment ... shall come to an end now that Britain and the Allies have triumphed.[77]

By the time that Duse's *The African Times and Orient Review* had ceased its erratic publication in 1920 it, together with the efforts of other Muslim activists, had succeeded in giving a voice to those colonial subjects who were striving to establish pride in a separate non-Christian identity in Britain. As attacks against Islam and Muslim Turkey increased during and after the war, there was also an intensification of awareness of Muslim concerns among Muslims in Britain. Nevertheless, by recognising that all non-Europeans were labelled 'niggers' by Europeans, Duse reflected the awareness of many British Muslims that, without wider cooperation with other non-Europeans in the face of racism in various parts of Britain, and dialogue with a range of local and national British institutions, further progress would be impossible. Muslims were urged to combine on the basis of their common colonial history in the struggle against their racial subordination.

The First World War created circumstances in which more Muslims than ever before formed part of the fabric of British society. Some remained essentially 'sojourners' in the sense that their stay was usually transient, connected to employment opportunities, engagement in the war effort or the pursuit of education. However, sizeable numbers had become more or less permanent residents. While Muslims had been engaging in various ways with British society since the early nineteenth century, the nature of this interaction continued to be affected by their uncertain status as far as being British was concerned. Few would have tried to claim that they were British Muslims—rather than Muslims living in Britain. Being Muslim in these circumstances during the early twentieth century was not easy, as Chapter 4 explores.

4

'BEING MUSLIM' IN EARLY
TWENTIETH-CENTURY BRITAIN

As we have seen, Muslims who came to Britain and settled there in the nineteenth and early twentieth centuries formed a highly differentiated population in ethnic and class terms. As a result, the approaches they adopted to sustain themselves in an environment that saw them as threatening 'aliens' and 'outsiders' varied widely and depended on the different attitudes and behaviour of the local white population. These different groups of Muslims experienced British society at a time when the country's imperial power was at its peak and colonial subjects were viewed as inferiors who deserved to be treated less than equally. Consequently they often suffered the full force of discrimination, especially when they came into competition with their white counterparts over jobs, housing or relationships with white women. This exclusion did not go uncontested, and Muslims resisted their subordination with much ingenuity and determination. They did ultimately gain a measure of acceptance in their localities, but this occurred largely at times when their contribution was needed to resolve a national crisis, as in the two world wars. At other times they suffered enormous hardship and survived mainly by relying on their own cultural and religious resources and indomitable spirit. Often Muslims were not seen primarily in terms of their religious identity. Their ethnicity or colour was crucial in defining how they were seen and the treatment they received. All the

101

same their Muslim origins could at times be a marker to be used by both themselves and the wider society. Religion, ethnicity and colour all formed strands that together made up the fabric of their identities. This chapter considers the pressures experienced by Muslims who were in the process of putting down roots in Britain in the period up to 1945.

Social engagement during the interwar years

By the early twentieth century social Darwinism, the doctrine of 'survival of the fittest', together with Eugenicist theories, had taken root in the popular mind and resonated right across the political spectrum. During the interwar years they influenced the ways in which Muslims were perceived by the British public and provided an ideological framework which helped to shape policy. For much of the British population the superiority of the white race had become entrenched, and their prejudices were based on a confusion of cultural and biological evidence. They viewed sexual mixing between Muslim men—indeed 'coloured' men in general—and white women as biologically and socially disastrous; 'pollution' of the white race lowered social status. Despite the outrage generated by Nazi racial philosophy in the 1930s, the 'science' of phrenology and Jung's ideas on inherited 'racial consciousness' were widely disseminated and accepted. Genetic explanations of the criminal type and moral traits formed part of popular opinion. Both the national and the local press carried scare stories. Misconceptions about the consequences of sexual mixing aroused passion and were used to discourage white girls from forming relationships with Muslim men. In 1929 the following headline appeared in the labour newspaper, the *Daily Herald*: 'Black men and white girls—seaport problems of mixed marriage—Café menace'.[1] Captain A. Richardson's report, echoing that of Muriel Fletcher portraying the black population as a 'shiftless, immoral, disease-ridden, uncivilised community' casting off its 'mixed-breeds', was given much prominence.[2] Hostility to intermarriage reached its height in the interwar period when any form of intimate relationship between Muslims and white women was regarded as offensive. Sexual jealousy and moral outrage were combined when Arabs were been consorting freely with white women. Cardiff's mayor was quoted as saying that 'the most difficult problem is that of the coloured sailor who settles down and intermarries'.[3] White girls who mixed with Muslims were denounced as 'shameless' and put under immense pressure by families, friends and workmates to break off such relationships. The police, in particular, felt it their moral duty to try and halt such liaisons; like other sections of society, they perceived them as immoral, and 'half-caste' children as the product of depravity. The view of the so-called 'half-caste' population as 'alien in sentiment and habits to the native white population', and the culturally transmitted notions about the 'dangers' and harmful effects of hybridisation, led to calls for a ban on 'the breeding of such children', by legislation if necessary. In 1935 Richardson, in his report for the British Hygiene Council and the British Council for the Welfare of Mercantile Marine, characterised Arabs along with other coloured people as 'a social problem' with 'immorality' rooted in their culture. Their 'standard of civilisation' was questionable, their moral codes were different, and they had not 'assimilated our conventions of life'. Having come 'into intimate contact with white women ... of loose character', they had produced a 'half-caste' population with inherited social flaws. The half-caste girl, according to Richardson, was 'disinclined to discipline and routine work'. Letters to the editor expressed the sexual fears of ordinary white people and cautioned Members of Parliament to wake up to the menace of black (largely Muslim) and white marriages or cohabitation.[4]

These attacks made no serious impression on the formation of relationships between Muslim men and white women, temporary or permanent. The reasons were to be found partly in the social circumstances at the end of the First World War. The loss of life in the war had left a huge surplus of women of marriageable age in Britain, while Muslim seamen in British ports were either single or had left their wives at home. So both Muslim men and white women had the opportunity and relative social freedom to become intimate. Relationships between white women from lower-middle-class 'respectable' backgrounds and Muslim men tended to be less common since there were few places apart from cafés and lodging-houses where contacts could be made. For Muslims from this—low—stratum (perhaps the lowest) of the working population the choice of spouses or partners was severely restricted by their social milieu. The girls that Arab, Somali and Indian seamen were liable to meet were predominantly from difficult working-class backgrounds lacking in family stability, and had in some cases suffered personal rejection. With their social status damaged or completely lost, they were often seeking security, material and emotional. At the same time most of the seamen were transients, waiting to take the next ship out of the port. Not surprisingly under these circumstances many of the arrangements between them and the white women were temporary and the rate of marriage failure was quite high. Since cohabitation was socially acceptable in these mixed communities, an increasing number of 'half-caste' and illegitimate children appeared, whom many in authority and among the white local population considered a social menace. Even the National Union of Seamen, to which the vast majority of Muslim seamen belonged, attacked them as 'dole aspirants', potentially unemployable, whose education was a burden on the taxpayer.[5]

A widespread objection to this mingling was apparently connected to the perception that women in Muslim societies enjoyed a low status. A woman writing in the *Spectator* in 1931 asserted that while she did not suffer from colour prejudice, she strongly objected to the treatment of her sex by the majority of coloured people. Presumably regarding Muslim men as the main culprits, she wrote: 'When I see a veiled woman, it is as if she shouted at me "My menfolk are barbarians"'.[6] It presumably followed that an Englishwoman, once married to a Muslim, would find herself in the same subservient position, and this had to be avoided. However, these perceptions were considerably off the mark. A growing body of evidence suggested—and white women married to Muslims often confirmed—that Arab husbands often treated their wives better than white men did, spent much time at home and took a great deal of interest in the upbringing of their children, who were clean and well-fed. It was also acknowledged that the children were generally well behaved and disciplined.

Racist views, which were widespread in British society, did not go unchallenged. In South Shields there were rebuttals of these condemnations from the Arabs themselves, their wives and a number of liberals within the white population. Ali Said, a leader of the Arab community, repudiated the charges of the white councillors that the Arabs in the town were a 'menace'; he contended that since they paid their taxes and rates like any other citizen, and indeed spent much of their hard-earned money in England, they and their families were fully entitled to the services offered by the state.[7] The white wives also put up a spirited defence of their Arab husbands, whom they found 'kind and gentle'; many talked of 'happiness and comfort' in their relationships. They denied the routine accusations of Arab promiscuity or that their 'half-caste' children were any less well looked after or disciplined than their white peers.[8]

But racially prejudiced attitudes influenced not only the emotive issue of inter-marriage, but also behaviour in a wide range of other interactions between Muslims and the institutions where contact was relatively impersonal. Besides 'genetic inferiority', antipathy towards Muslims was explained more in terms of 'innate' differences in habits and customs. It was believed that 'man' possessed some instinct of clannishness which it was claimed was the 'incipient stage of specific aversion'; thus prejudice against people not of 'their own kind' was 'natural'. Based on these premises, Muslims were deemed 'uncivilised', and were to be avoided because of their 'smell' or just because they looked different. Muslims were portrayed as strangers and intruders, bearers of an alien and polluting culture, and white antipathy towards them was depicted as a natural and justifiable response to 'other-ness', deviancy and 'pathological' practices. 'Half-caste' boys and girls were rejected because of their background and had little prospect of absorption within the wider society. For the girls the situation was worse than for the boys; while some of the boys, at least, had the possibility of going to sea like their fathers, most of the girls could only count on menial domestic service—or work in light industries, but only with difficulty since employers were reluctant to take them on, claiming that they were shunned by the white workers.

In the immediate postwar period, British society seemed particularly sensitive to the issue of who was and who was not 'an alien'—who had the right to be in Britain and who ought to be compelled to leave. This crystallised in 1919 in a series of riots, mainly in Liverpool, South Shields and various ports in South Wales, in which white protesters targeted those they perceived as unwelcome aliens. The riots were ostensibly inflamed by the issue of race, but the way they were perceived and dealt with reveals a more complicated set of factors at work. To appreciate these we should look at the broader context of these events and how it influenced popular attitudes.

The end of the First World War ushered in a period of considerable social crisis. The postwar economic boom, which largely bypassed the port industries, ended quickly, with the loss of many jobs. The unemployment was aggravated by the demobilisation of a vast number of servicemen and women, who could not be readily absorbed in the jobs available. The war had also brought about an expansion of the communities of black and Arab seamen in British ports. They had replaced indigenous workers, who were absent on war service, both in the merchant navy and in certain shore jobs, but with the downturn in the shipping industry due to intensified international competition, even the seamen found themselves out of work. Resentment against an 'alien' population grew rapidly and demands for their exclusion from jobs and homes became more intense. Informal procedures were instituted by employers giving preference to white job-seekers, but apart from this the notion of 'Britishness' was invoked to legitimise exclusion. During the war appeals had been made to patriotism, exhorting shipowners 'not to engage an Arab whilst there was a Britisher wanting a job'—the former were after all 'aliens' and therefore naturally less deserving.[9] There was also always a sneaking suspicion that 'some of these men's relatives may be conspiring against our own lads in the desert at the present time'.[10]

Much of this perception had no foundation in fact and betrayed only prejudice and ignorance. Arab seamen had not taken white jobs; most were British subjects and had contributed significantly to the British war effort. Still, hostility towards Arabs, blatantly and virulently fuelled by the National Sailors' and Firemen's Union throughout the war, resulted in the more general demand for restriction of Arab entry to Britain and repatriation of those already here. After the war, when there was felt to be much less need for them, the Home Office submitted to pressure from white sailors and the Board of Trade, and introduced the Aliens Order and other legislation effectively reclassifying Arabs as 'coloured aliens'. Those who claimed to be British subjects found their status repeatedly questioned, and the racist definition of 'Britishness' was reconfirmed. Loyalty to the Crown was not enough;

Arabs, it was asserted, could never be British—something which only white people could claim to be—and should therefore be repatriated. Justification for the Arabs' social and economic exclusion relied on assumptions of their inferiority, and also brought into play other traits in their character that were perceived to be negative and thus to disqualify them from equal treatment with whites. They were accused of cowardice during the war, and were thought to be indolent, inefficient and unhygienic. They were criticised for being prepared to work for lower pay, undercutting white men's wages. It was claimed that Arabs had done well out of the war and achieved prosperity at the white man's expense. Even the 1919 riots themselves were blamed on them. Dubbed the 'Arab Riot' by the *South Shields Gazette*, it reported 'gangs of Arabs' attacking 'the crowd indiscriminately' and 'in their state of frenzied excitement' discharging their weapons 'wildly'.[11]

It is noteworthy that while there is evidence that religious practice formed part of many seamen's daily lives, Yemeni and Somali seafarers in South Wales, Liverpool and South Shields made few references to their Muslim identity in public dealings. Dr Abdul Majid, the Muslim barrister who defended a number of them during the 1919 riots, argued that 'they have adopted European life and customs to a large extent and in sympathy, and in their domestic life they are English'. During his visit to South Shields he established a branch of the Islamic Society, with himself as president, with the aim of looking after the economic, moral and religious welfare of Muslims in the town. Thus it was Majid who encouraged the South Shields Arabs to become more publicly conscious of their Islamic identity, and there is nothing in the records to indicate that the attitudes of the white population towards them up to this point had in any way been shaped by the fact that they were Muslim. This is generally true also of how these communities were viewed in South Wales and Liverpool.

The other crucial factor that contributed to the violence in 1919 was moral panic as a result of sexual relations between non-white men and white women. A set of racial stereotypes already existed on which popular views were based. While assumptions about the moral conduct of Muslims in general may have overlapped with those about Arabs in particular, the language used at the time emphasised above all the 'Arabness' and colour of the men involved. There seemed to be a widespread horror at the thought of marriages between Arab men and white women, with moralists (springing into action) to defend the endangered purity of the white race. At the peak of the riots a letter to *The Times* expressed these sentiments with some intensity: 'It is an instinctive certainty that sexual relations between white women and coloured men revolt our very nature ... What blame ... to those white men who, seeing these conditions and loathing them, resort to violence.'[12] The *Western Mail* likewise commented that 'such consorting is ill-assorting; it exhibits either a depravity or a squalid infatuation; it is repugnant to our finer instincts in which pride of race occupies a just and inevitable place'.[13] In South Shields the association of Arabs with white women produced something approaching hysteria, and official voices joined in exploiting widespread fears of the moral danger posed by 'the Arab menace'. In Cardiff the Chief Constable called for legislation to make sexual relations between coloured seamen and white women a criminal offence. The children of these unions possessed 'the vicious hereditary taint of their parents',[14] and were alleged 'to inherit the worst characteristics of each race'. They were seen as 'outcastes' and unemployable; 'no mixed breed child was as good as a child of white parents', and so on.[15] In the aftermath of a protracted war to defend and enhance what was deemed to be special about Britain it was obviously too much for many white people to contemplate losing the fight for British women to men perceived not merely as outsiders but as inferior. Here, as in other settings, women came to symbolise the honour and identity of the wider community—they were the weakest link in its chain of defence, and so their protection, and that of British society with them, demanded more than just words.

Muslim communities that developed in the interwar period continued to respond to the antipathy they encountered according to their class backgrounds, cultures and traditions, and conversely their approaches to the wider society were shaped by the social and economic forces then operating in British society. These forces tended either to separate them from white people, encapsulating them into distinct groups, or to integrate them with indigenous local communities, dissolving the ties that bound them together. As Chapter 2 indicated, there was a substantial rise in the Muslim population of Cardiff, Liverpool and South Shields immediately after the First World War mainly due to the influx of seamen attracted by the labour shortage produced by the economic boom. More permanent settlers, including lodging-housekeepers and owners of cafés and market stalls, provided services for the transient population. In the absence of female company within their own communities, Muslim men turned to white women, mainly from the lower classes, for sexual or more permanent relationships. The integrative influence of mixed marriages was reflected in the fact that white women enjoyed stronger connections with British society than their husbands, and were therefore able in many instances to obtain material concessions for their spouses—in council housing and by interceding on their behalf and acting as interpreters with employers. [16]

Processes of integration were also at work in the evolution of religious practices among the different ethnic groups that formed the Muslim communities. Male migrants from Aden, Yemen, Somaliland, Malaya and the Indian subcontinent, with the exception of on-shore permanent settlers, had relatively little social contact with whites. Much of their working lives was spent on ships away from their seaport bases, with the result that they developed few contacts in the dock areas they shared with white men when they returned from work. Given the barriers caused by difficulties of communication and different dietary habits, they inevitably mingled with the indigenous population only when no other options were available. Thus they continued to re-create an environment with which they were familiar and in which they felt comfortable. Pork, lard and alcoholic drinks were prohibited. Marriages within the community were encouraged as far as possible, as was segregation of the sexes in the religious and, as far as possible, the economic domains. Married women were rarely allowed to work except assisting their husbands. The conditions for unmarried Muslim girls were slightly more relaxed: if necessary, they could seek employment. Marriage with white women—the situation of most Yemeni, Malayan and Egyptian men—was preferably conducted under Muslim rites and was commonly accorded the same status in the community as the British, although some women understandably considered these ceremonies, which lacked legal recognition, less secure for themselves and their children. The marriage of Sheikh Abdullah Ali al-Hakimi, the religious head of the Yemeni community in South Shields in 1936–8 and in Cardiff thereafter, to a 'half-caste' girl and his success in securing the custody of her two children from a children's home immediately raised their prestige. Bonds of clan loyalty and mutual obligations further reinforced the construction of these groupings. Degrees of involvement with the white community were also shaped by the attitudes that particular ethnic groups adopted towards the indigenous population. Somalis, generally mixed less than Yemenis; fewer married white women, a fact influenced by their perception that the exclusively domestic role they expected of their wives and daughters was likely to be at variance with the relative freedom of white women in the social and economic spheres.[17]

Many Muslim migrants during this period therefore maintained a degree of segregation, partly because they found some features of British society undesirable and partly because greater interaction with white women tended to create sexual jealousies and friction with white males. Their daily routines were still to some degree regulated by religious prescriptions, which excluded members of other communities, and their white wives, through conversion and their enthusiasm for Islamic practices, could become estranged from their own relatives and friends. This suggests that Muslims settling in Britain during this period were in various ways concerned to retain Muslim values themselves and to secure their transmission to future generations. White mothers, on the whole, cooperated with their husbands' wishes, subordinating their own religious position and adhering to Muslim traditions regarding food and drink. Their children were taught prayers and verses from the Quran; they attended the religious festivals, and in their fathers' absence their mothers ensured that their lives were managed in line with the norms of the local Muslim community. In practice, however, Anglo-Muslims—the second generation—showed certain signs of erosion in their social and cultural behaviour. Over time fewer of them, and less often, were seen in the cafés frequented by their communities, and they were less inclined to participate in religious gatherings and functions. Their preference for 'English lifestyles' was shown by their involvement, with their white peers, in such leisure activities as cinema-going, drinking and dancing.

By 1945 the processes taking place within Britain's Muslim communities that began immediately after the First World War had gone a long way towards weakening the cohesion and distinctiveness of these communities. Arabs married to white women gained entry into the primary groups of the host communities, and became increasingly integrated into local kin networks; social barriers were eroded and they accumulated resources that could be used in times of need. This intermingling reduced prejudice, despite underlying sexual jealousies, and with a foothold thus secured and increased support from within local white society, the balance of power within communities also changed a little in favour of the immigrants. Muslims' obligations to their new families began to grow and their loyalty to pre-migration ties declined correspondingly. With further adjustments to new conditions the differences between their households and those in the white community decreased too, and over time there were few ways in which immigrants' households looked dissimilar to the English ones around them. Younger Anglo-Arabs strove for social adaptation because they realised that only through assimilation rather than accommodation were they likely to escape the limitations imposed on their parents' social and economic opportunities by prejudice and discrimination. As the older generation died out, the religious outlook of the younger elements also weakened and their enthusiasm waned. Their participation in the 1939–45 war effort had enhanced their prestige and status in the white communities, and at the same time encouraged the view that Islam was 'old stuff' that could not be reconciled with the modern world. Al-Hakimi had already sensed the wind of change, and gradually developed a more liberal religious position, suggesting to Muslims that they needed to learn from British society and its values. He pursued his Sufi vocation by calling in 1938, when he had established his credentials in Cardiff, for the reform of Islam and unification of all religions. These radical ideas aroused some opposition from within the Muslim community but there was no total rejection.[18]

Contacts with whites were generally limited. Often they were with people in various official capacities or providing services. Being in positions of power *vis-à-vis* the Muslims, their approach tended to be at best patronising, and at worst they applied overt or subtle forms of discrimination, leaving little scope for friendship, intimacy or even mutual respect to develop. As one Englishwoman remarked, 'the impression we were given at school, and also in church, was that they were alright as a people to preach religion to, or to have as servants, but companions—it wasn't done'.[19] At the institutional level, there is evidence that for many Muslims it was difficult to find lodgings and work. They, like other 'visible' minority groups, adopted a wide range of strategies to overcome the 'colour bar' in Britain, some attempting to escape 'the domination of aliens' by acquiring the refined tastes of the 'dominating natives'.

Such attitudes and behaviour were epitomised by Muslims such as Abdullah Yusuf Ali, a member of that group of Indian Muslims from professional families concerned with rank and status who aspired to influence under the British. Deference, if not outright obsequiousness, was a central feature of their relationship with the British. Having won a scholarship to St Johns College, Cambridge, Yusuf Ali was called to the bar in the 1890s and selected to serve in the élite Indian Civil Service. During the formative phase of his life, when he mixed mainly in the upper circles of British society, crude racial prejudice surfaced only rarely. He was particularly impressed by his mentors and by the refined behaviour and cordiality of people with whom he associated, and as a result became ineradicably Anglophile and made enormous efforts to ingratiate himself with the establishment. He was keen to present what he thought were the interests of the Muslim élite in a form that would appeal to the British, whom he deeply admired. He trusted that 'British people were willing and anxious to understand Indian needs and Indian aspirations, and to do justice to India'. His marriage to Teresa Shalders according to the Anglican rite, his active membership of the National Liberal Club and his hosting of receptions for the great and the good were attempts to assimilate into British society. For a while he lived at Cromer House in Norfolk, indicating connections with members of the aristocracy; he had contacts with leading Liberal politicians, such as Lord Morley, sometime Secretary of State for India; he acquired a taste for Greek artefacts and culture and a fascination for Greek heroes; he commended Freemasonry in India as a way to bridge the racial and social divide; and he advocated the dissemination of rationalist and modernist thought through secular education on the Oxbridge model. For him the Anglo-Saxons' love of organisation and discipline put them at the head of human progress; with these qualities they had achieved major advances, and thus membership of the British Empire with its liberal vision was to be greatly prized.[20]

112

Yusuf Ali was thus consistently loyal to the British Empire and cherished the sovereign; for him the imperial connection was inviolable, with the monarch serving as a precious example of virtue and purity, and he aligned himself with the English in believing that India formed an integral part within this firmament. Consistent with the British view, he considered Indian Muslim society, in both social and religious terms, to be decaying, corrupt and archaic and in urgent need of reform. Hence in the First World War he volunteered his services to the Crown. At a time when many Muslims in Britain felt unease in supporting the war effort against the Ottoman Empire, Yusuf Ali declared unequivocal backing for Britain's cause and expressed his unshakeable faith in and loyalty to the British in frankly jingoistic articles and public speeches (his rhetoric was described as 'cringing' and 'sycophantic'), in which he spoke of India's readiness 'to die for country, Padishah, flag and Empire'.

Yusuf Ali was equally content to further British interests in the Second World War, and continued to write propaganda pieces and participate in operations abroad on their behalf. Even in 1940 he rejected the idea of Indian independence, reassuring the British that Muslims in India remained loyal. Until the end of the war he continued to enthuse about the British Empire, and predictably the government regarded him as the pre-eminent Muslim spokesman in Britain. His Islamic scholarship was widely recognised, but in order to reconcile his political leanings with his religious thought, he tried to 'depoliticise' Islam. In his personal conduct Yusuf Ali scrupulously adhered to the religious ritual, attending prayers and festivals as required, but his acceptance of British hegemony may have been rationalised as part of Providence's scheme on earth. He led the *Eid al-Fitr* congregation at the Shah Jahan Mosque in Woking, of which he was a trustee, in February 1943, and maintained close ties with the small but growing British Muslim community in London, of among whom almost all the converts belonged to white middle-class British families. Through their activities he attempted to change the widespread negative perceptions about Islam. However, his loyalty to the Empire drove him to use all his intellectual powers to attack pan-Islam as a political movement and to relentlessly pursue arguments that tried to show that religion dealt only with 'an inner world'. He desperately wanted to bring about a marriage of what, in his view, was best in the East and the West, and wrote a series of 'Progressive Islam' pamphlets in which he attempted to demonstrate that Islam could make a useful contribution to Western civilisation. In his struggle for reconciliation between Islam and Western philosophy, he argued that the religion of all thinking men was essentially the same. That in 1936 he preached a sermon at the Unitarian Church in Cheltenham to a packed congregation is a testimony to his conviction in the basic unity underlying all religions. Having been closely associated with interfaith dialogue, he was one of the key speakers at many of the World Congress of Faiths conferences, including one during the Second World War at Oxford in 1941, and frequently gave papers on Indian culture and Islam at the Royal Society of Arts.[21]

Yusuf Ali's services, especially as a publicist, were much appreciated by the British government and he was duly rewarded. Even before the First World War he had received flattering notices in the élite press. *The Times* in 1907 had already described him as 'a very talented member of the Indian Civil Service and a representative of the great Muhammadan community'. In 1917 he was awarded the CBE for his services to the Empire and secured an entry in *Who's Who*, he was one of the advisers to the Indian delegation at the Paris Peace Conference in 1919, and in 1928 he represented India in the assembly of the League of Nations in Geneva. In 1929 he was elected a Fellow of the Royal Empire Society, which boasted many members from the élite of the British establishment, and during the Second World War his advice continued to be sought and heeded by the Ministry of Information. As with many Muslims from his background, the British establishment, still full of the self-confidence and arrogance born of a sense of superiority, treated him on occasion with patronising and condescending disdain.[22] Still, for much of his life he gained a limited acceptance among the kind of British people whom he regarded as his equals. The circumstances of his death rather shattered this image: inspite of all the services he had given, he died 'abandoned' both by his family, from whom he apparently became alienated, and the establishment, which had 'lost track' of him. Indeed, it could be argued that his trust in the British had been misplaced. While he might have expected that his loyalty and espousal of British values would gain him acceptance, he found himself very much alone in old age, with his mental faculties deteriorating and desperately needing proper care. The lack of interest in him was such that his funeral was arranged by the Pakistan High Commission. Yusuf Ali endeavoured to mould himself in the British image and at the same time retain a spiritual vision that Muslims would share some of their own religious values within a universalistic framework. In this way he hoped to be accepted in the élite circles of British society on the basis of genuine respect and equality. His chances of success were of course limited by the realities of his time, and it is unlikely that he would have regarded his efforts as very successful compared to his high expectations.

The strategy pursued by Yusuf Ali was only open to a small group of Muslims in Britain. Most of the settled Muslim population, especially in cities such as London, Cardiff and South Shields, carried on living in virtually segregated localities, not dissimilar to ghettos, in response to the refusal of white communities to have any kind of close physical or social contact with them. This antipathy was given formal expression by many city councils in their housing policies.[23] Proximity was deemed to lower social status; antipathy was deepened by Muslim seamen being perceived as men of low-status occupations living in areas associated with crime and violence.[24] Tiger Bay in Cardiff, where Muslims were largely concentrated, was viewed by the rest of the city as 'unsavoury' and 'disreputable'; its residents were seen as 'undesirable',[25] and their cafés and boarding-houses as centres of organised prostitution.[26] As men of low moral standards, they were best kept at a distance and tolerated only in the docks, the dumping-ground for the dregs of society. Isolation from the white population was also necessary because of the danger of contracting venereal disease and tuberculosis, of which they were perceived to be the main source.[27]

Individual segregation was underpinned by the refusal of white people to take them in as tenants or lodgers, forcing them to rely on their kin or fellow-countrymen and to live in overcrowded conditions. Even here the local authorities would not allow lodging-houses to be established in white areas. Estate agents in South Shields confirmed racial prejudice against coloured seamen, reporting that white tenants 'objected to coloured people living in the same building. If landlords agreed to a coloured tenant occupying the premises, the white tenants ... would state their intention of leaving.'[28] Most hostels and boarding-houses refused to accommodate them—not, they insisted, because they themselves were prejudiced, but because other white boarders would object. Landlords and house-agents were disapproved of for letting property to coloured people, since it was believed that Muslim tenants would lower property values. Public opposition to 'respectable houses' in the Riverside district of Cardiff being occupied by 'coloured' people was reported in the *Western Mail*. It was based on the image of Muslims variously as 'turbulent' and 'excitable' (Arabs) and 'truculent' and 'vicious' (Somalis) by nature,—people who 'constituted a menace to peace at times of rioting'.[29]

Segregation had increased after the First World War when the 1919 riots had discouraged Muslims from using facilities in the town centre for fear of attack. The police also maintained a more stringent style of surveillance over them, discouraging them from venturing too far from home. In Cardiff they retreated to the safety of Bute Town. The closing down of the wartime industries and the rapid decline in other forms of employment meant that Muslims returned to those areas where there were still some opportunities in the traditional occupation of seafaring. This process contributed further to the formation of the Muslim quarters in ports such as London, Glasgow, Cardiff, Liverpool and South Shields.

The concentration of the Muslim population in docks areas around the country also developed out of the desire of Muslims to remain in close contact with people from their own communities and was partly due to the need to be in close proximity with their seafaring occupation. They were seen by the wider society as figures low in the social scale and relatively isolated. In South Shields, from 1929 onwards, comments began to appear about the 'Arab invasion' of the town. The impression, albeit quite mistaken, had been created that the Arabs were 'descending' upon the town 'in hordes'. Given that in 1930 there were only forty to fifty Arab settlers and a further 'floating population' of around 250, these claims were wildly exaggerated. Nevertheless, because of the association of Arabs with overcrowding, slums, disease and death in the imagination of the white population, there were calls for them to be corralled in particular areas and kept under close watch. In the City Council Housing Committee discussions in South Shields, demands were made that Arabs live 'in a colony by themselves and not mixed up with white people'. They seemed to be reflecting the opposition of the white community generally to living with Arabs, especially the 'danger of their penetrating good class residential areas'. When the City Council initiated the scheme to rehouse the Arabs as part of slum clearance in the mid-1930s, white residents petitioned to be given the first choice of the newly-constructed houses. The mayor also supported segregation because it would allow better control over the Arabs. The Housing Committee willingly acceded, paying little heed to the Arabs' resentment at being 'put on one side as if we were lions or tigers or horses'. White wives also preferred dispersal to segregation. However, once they had sensed that their presence was not welcomed by their white neighbours, they actively sought housing in their own locality. A deputation of women from the Muslim community saw the mayor and asked for separate housing, arguing that their children faced racial antipathy from white children. Religious leaders and Arab men actively sought segregation in order to maintain their cultural and religious traditions.[30]

In Cardiff too the City Council pursued a policy of segregating Muslims. The *Western Mail* confirmed in 1936 that 'it had always been the aim of the corporation to segregate the cosmopolitan area covered by Bute Street from the city itself'; also, businesses in that area were 'opposed to any of the coloured population encroaching on the city end of Bute Street'.[31] When the Council put through proposals to rehouse a few coloured residents from Bute Town, with very minor adjustments to the boundary of the coloured settlement, petitions were immediately sent protesting at the move, and letters appeared in the press claiming that by encroaching on areas close to the city centre the coloured people would lower its tone. The Council began to buckle under the pressure, but as the war approached the plan was put in abeyance. Instead it amended by-laws to keep Muslims confined to Bute Town so that they could be closely supervised, and those who attempted to escape were made to feel uncomfortable. Thus Muslims were forced to live in deprived areas and then blamed for creating the miserable conditions.

The authorities went further and asserted that Muslims themselves wished to stay in these areas to be with their kinsmen, and certainly it was easier there to get a job on a ship. Given the level of discrimination they experienced, this was probably true. While segregation created social distance and prevented Muslims from engaging with the white community, it allowed them to 'be themselves' and establish communities with a distinctive identity in which they could take some pride. A substantial majority, afraid of being humiliated and anxious to preserve their self-respect, limited their interactions with the indigenous population to the minimum and only when it could not be avoided, especially with the lower class, who were perceived as more prejudiced and overtly hostile than the 'better-class people' with whom they much preferred to deal. Therefore in order to avoid conflict Muslim communities adopted voluntary separation, and acquiesced in their subordinate position by accepting roles which the host society considered appropriate for them and which did not cause them to compete with the white population. Most, with their sojourner mentality, did not agitate for change in their conditions for fear of being labelled as 'troublemakers'.[32] They shunned mixed social gatherings, preferring to congregate in cafés and lodging-houses in their own localities, run by people from their own ethnic and religious background. They rarely went to the shops, cinemas and other public places frequented by white people.[33]

Within these broad patterns of interaction between Muslims and the wider communities there were always variations, some quite complex in character and open to a range of explanations. The degree of segregation between Muslims from the dock communities varied on between ethnic groups. Given the social and cultural impediments experienced by Muslim seamen, contacts with white women mostly took place in lodging-houses where the women might be employed as domestics or at the home of a kinsman or friend who already had connections in the white community. Much leisure time was spent in mutual visiting. Yemenis, while of the view that the less they were noticed the more they would benefit, established rather closer ties with white people than some other Muslim groups. Somalis and Indians apparently mixed less easily with the local white population, at least partly because, in addition to the dietary taboos common to most Muslims, their own traditions regarding sexual relations and the 'home orientation' exercised a greater pull, making more permanent connections less feasible. Thus, adherence to religious codes of conduct was important in maintaining separation from the local people.

Muslim communities during the interwar years therefore evolved in ways in which their own traditional social practices and the 'British way of life' were mixed. For instance, the Tyneside Muslim community of South Shields adapted to the new environment. In their religious practice they generally became quite relaxed, and many of the 'pioneers' were criticised for drinking, gambling and indulging in 'illicit' sex.[34] To have and show off British education and middle-class social etiquette were seen as deserving of approval and emulation, but fraternisation remained variable, especially between white women married to Muslim men and unrelated males. Religion seemed the primary source of identity among Muslims generally and for many was more important than their racial origin: Islam continued to shape their behaviour. Their religious practice was undoubtedly stronger than that of their offspring, whose interest in the Muslim way of life became increasingly diluted, finding it difficult to sustain it beyond adolescence. The migrants remained tenacious in their efforts to preserve certain traditions that they saw as central to the maintenance of the Muslim character of their communities. They persisted in keeping marriages endogamous, although this applied much more to girls than to boys. Muslims regarded marriages of their daughters to Englishmen as almost inconceivable, even if this self-limitation might have been partly due to the rejection of 'half-caste' girls by white men. That attitudes to skin colour were significant in the way white people interacted with Muslims meant that, while they might have few qualms about inviting them to tea, they would rarely allow their daughters to go out with them.[35] Arabs seemed little troubled by the implications of colour and countered it through their cultural pride and religious solidarity. While they seemed to suffer less prejudice because of their lighter skins, in general, they were treated no differently from other 'black' people by whites, who simply lumped them all together. Muslims therefore realised that despite their differences from other 'black' people they needed to unite in their opposition to racial discrimination, especially in employment and housing, and therefore developed organisations to pursue their common objectives more systematically.

Relations in the workplace

The gulf that developed between Muslims and local white communities during the interwar years was reflected at work too. Relations between

Muslim seamen and white workers throughout this period were strained. Language difficulties, cultural differences and ignorance of the function of trade unions hampered communication and generated negative feelings, and misplaced sexual jealousies and competition were transferred to the workplace. Contacts with employers and white fellow workers did result in a degree of familiarity, but the scope was limited and the relationships were unequal. Much of this inequality was, organised through the institutions of the state or by white workers themselves through their unions. Both the Aliens Order of 1925 and the British Shipping (Assistance) Act of 1935 had an exclusionary impact on all 'coloured' seamen.

The National Union of Seamen (NUS) was vitriolic and often racist in its attacks on Arabs in the interwar period, in particular after the death of its long-serving General Secretary Havelock Wilson in 1929,[36] and collaborated with other authorities in their efforts to regulate the employment of Muslim seamen. The NUS's own newspaper, *The Seaman*, while agreeing that the Aliens Order had resulted in many injustices, continued to provide at least passive support for its operation. In support of the British Shipping (Assistance) Act, the main impact of which was to exclude Muslim seamen from subsidised ships, the union's officials actively intervened against the engagement of 'coloured' seamen. Working with the Shipping Federation early in 1930, the NUS instituted the 'rota system', whereby registered 'alien' seamen (most not alien but British Protected Persons from Yemen and Somaliland) had to accept whatever job was offered to them once they reached the top of the rota. More informally, ships' officers were pressed to employ white crew, and where Muslims had to be taken on, they were given heavier duties; segregated crews were condoned, and bribery was rife. As one Muslim who served on a ship said, 'you were in a slave labour market and you had no protection whatever'.[37]

Muslim seamen around the country reacted strongly to this discriminatory attack on their livelihood, and despite the strenuous efforts of the NUS to persuade them to accept the rota system as in their best interest, they refused to register. In Cardiff and the other Bristol Channel ports many Arabs and Somalis were deeply opposed to the scheme and protested violently against its implementation. Feelings against those who complied with the scheme ran so high that the agitators threatened to 'kill' anyone who did and confronted those who broke ranks with sticks and umbrellas. Although the police generally kept them apart, violence erupted several times and led to many arrests and harsh sentences. These Muslim seamen continued to withhold support for the resolutions passed in favour of the rota system at their local union branches. There was equally vigorous resistance to the scheme in South Shields, although they began their protest first by picketing the shipping office peacefully for a fortnight. When this action failed, more strong-arm tactics were applied, ending in scuffles between the Arabs on the one side and white seamen and police on the other. A number of Arabs were arrested, charged with obstructing the police and rioting, sentenced to hard labour and deported. Thereafter resistance to the scheme collapsed. Many of the unregistered seamen were deported and the rest resorted to more individual tactics to escape penury; the unemployed members of the Somali Warsangeli tribe were supported by a fund established from voluntary contributions (£1 per person per voyage) by returning seamen.[38]

Muslim responses to their circumstances and discriminatory treatment from the wider society varied. Sometimes they came together in social and self-help groups, often retaining ethnic and religious boundaries to enhance their pride and give their lives a semblance of dignity. At other times, they joined more comprehensive organisations to assert their rights, claim their entitlements and struggle more effectively against discrimination and prejudice from employers, unions, city authorities and the state. Whenever appropriate and feasible they sought support from other organisations. The women did not get involved in the campaigns and were not encouraged to do so by their husbands, given their customs, but behind the scenes their role was crucial in maintaining cohesion within the community—they would do the catering for meetings, often held in their homes.

The level of organisation among Muslims continued to increase throughout the interwar period and they became more effective as they learned from past mistakes and gained experience. However, given the huge odds against them, it is no surprise that their achievements were relatively modest. As early as December 1924 the Cardiff Adenese Club and Association was established to protect the Yemenis from charges of 'crimping' and bribery[39]—allegations that did not go away and later re-appeared to devastating effect. It would be more accurate to say that Muslim organisation probably delivered as much in the purely religious domain and in building self-esteem and confidence as it did in the resolution of practical concerns, if not more.

Believing that class solidarity would protect them in their struggle for jobs, Arabs had been among the first members and usually many of the strongest supporters of the seafarers' union—indeed Wilson taunted the white seamen that their union subscriptions kept the NUS going.[40] However, this strong support for the NUS from Muslim seamen seemed to count for little when it came to addressing issues of exclusion and discrimination in employment. Union leaders were ambivalent and often antagonistic towards their Muslim members, but on occasions came to their defence. Within the union the relative status of black and white seamen as well as who was rightfully British was constantly contested. Race rhetoric in *The Seaman* resumed against the 'alien Arab'. Constant requests by Muslim seamen for a voice and representation were rebuffed and the paternalistic approach of the union leadership towards their concerns continued. Yet with few effective options open to them, they continued to pursue union membership and agitate from within for equal and democratic representation, albeit with little success. While they persisted in laying claims on the union's leadership, they were still marginalised and silenced. The union's policies of racial divisiveness continued into the 1940s, and if anything, its attitude to hardened as employment opportunities for seamen contracted in the late 1920s and the 1930s. In agreement with the objectives of the Shipping Federation to exclude Muslim and other 'coloured' seamen from marine jobs, it mounted campaign against the Arabs in 1929–30, rather than seeking to organise them. Deputations were sent to relevant government departments demanding restriction on Arab seamen entering British ports and the deportation of 'alien' seamen already there. The union moved resolutions at the Trades Union Congress, attacking them in *The Seaman* and vilifying Arabs in a series of articles that were little less than diatribes. Negative racial and cultural images and colonial sexual taboos were conjured up to inflame popular prejudice. The main focus of these tirades were the Muslim communities and families in the dockland areas: they were denounced in general for their mixed racial and cultural character, and more specifically those who ran boarding-houses were condemned as exploiters and criminals.[41]

With the NUS doing little to represent their interests, Muslim seamen faced the painful choice of either joining and supporting an organisation that subordinated and excluded them or remaining even more vulnerable outside it. Their reactions varied. Individuals responded to the restrictions imposed by the British authorities by making a rush for naturalisation to bypass the legislation directed against them; for instance, in 1931 the South Shields Corporation demanded the deportation of Arab claimants of relief on the grounds that as 'aliens' they were ineligible. By 1938, 2,000 'coloured' seamen had acquired British citizenship.[42] Other strategies for survival were used too. After the passing of the Shipping Act in 1935, unemployed Arabs applied for relief since many were left destitute in the wake of the reduced job opportunities. In South Shields, where assistance from the state was not readily forthcoming, they either had to rely on their own resources or were sustained by advances from the boarding-house masters at considerable cost to themselves. Collectively, their attempts ranged from developing alliances with the more sympathetic and radical wings of the labour movement to withdrawing from the NUS and setting up their own unions. As the economic situation worsened in the early 1930s, they participated increasingly in the more politicised mainstream workers' struggles. In South Shields a substantial number of the Arabs united with the radical Seamen's Minority Movement (SMM) in opposition to the rota system. Ali Said, a powerful figure among them, argued passionately on behalf of Arab seamen and defended their right to employment on equal terms with white sailors. In Cardiff the seamen's union was equally unresponsive to the needs of Muslim seamen, and the General Secretary of its Cardiff branch even called for the repatriation of the '8,000 to 9,000' seamen brought there by the shipping companies since they would be a burden on the ratepayers once they were discharged. Muslim members were so dismayed by the union's attitude towards them that they decided to join the Cardiff Coloured Seamen's Committee, which tried to expose the NUS's racist attitude and called for black and white workers to unite to demand equal protection for equal contributions and equal pay for equal work. It called for solidarity between all seamen, black and white. In the

wake of the British Shipping (Assistance) Act of 1935 a defence committee including Malays, Somalis and Arabs was formed in Cardiff to
resist it, and in the late 1930s the Islamia Allawia Friendly Society was
set up for the 'purpose of providing a meeting place for Moslem seamen ... [and] aims at uniting all members of the Moslem community
in the port'.[43]

As the situation in Cardiff deteriorated, 'black' activists tried to
organise resistance. The South Wales Association for the Welfare of
Coloured People, the British Somali Society (BSS) and the Somali Youth
League were formed in the mid-1930s, with links to a parent organisa-
tion in British Somaliland and to other branches in Britain. In 1937 all
these associations came together as the Somali Association of Great
Britain and, realising that there were many socio-economic issues on
which common cause could be made with other 'coloured' people in
Britain, it took part in the annual conference of the League of Coloured
Peoples. Key members of the BSS, Mohamed Siad and Duallah
Mohamed, collaborated closely with the local Communist Party. The
Somalis also sought the assistance of sympathetic organisations such as
the League Against Imperialism (LAI) and the National Council for
Civil Liberties; they lobbied MPs and with their support attempted to
squeeze concessions out of the government, but the changes they
achieved were only cosmetic. The Somali organisation also dealt with
welfare matters—their people had the problem of being separated by
language from some ethnic groups and by religion from others.
Religion remained a key organising principle for many of these groups,
and thus the Islamia Allawia Friendly Society was formed in part to
give expression to this feeling. From time to time the sheer struggle to
earn a living caused religious and colour differences to be set aside, and
'coloured' workers were driven into a common course of action. This
in turn led to the United Committee of Coloured and Colonial
Organisations (UCCCO) being set up in the early 1940s. It kept a low
profile in the early years of its existence, but was propelled into action
in 1944 by the local authorities' renewal of plans for segregated housing and social facilities first proposed in the late 1930s. The Committee
obtained the support of the Labour Party. The Muslim youth leader
H. Hasan protested that the people whom he represented should not
be treated like pariahs: 'We were born in this country and we expect

to enjoy all the privileges afforded other British youth and are opposed to discrimination on account of colour or race.' Public meetings were held to mobilise the community and walls were plastered with posters protesting against segregation.[44]

While this campaign persuaded the authorities to shelve the housing plan, the efforts of these bodies proved relatively ineffective, partly because the Muslims remained faction-ridden. Divisions were exacerbated by interventions from organisations that claimed to represent specifically Muslim interests, but many Muslims had been persuaded to join these pressure groups with specifically Muslim identities partly because they had been initiated by Muslim professionals with access to higher levels of national government, and it was felt that they stood a better chance of having the Muslims' demands met. However, this analysis seems to have been flawed. Dr Abdul Majid and Khalid Sheldrake, who led some of these Islamic organisations (the Islamic Society established in 1919 and the Western Islamic Association established in 1929), might have had influence with the relevant authorities, but they were also suspected of being paid agents of the government who, while attempting to persuade Muslims of the effectiveness of their strategies, also had to demonstrate that these interests did not conflict with government aims. So in the disturbances in South Shields in 1930 Sheldrake, as President of the Western Islamic Association, strongly criticised the NUS for its opposition to its Arab section, but also opposed the mobilisation of the SMM against the rota system and continued to urge support for the government, which he thought was doing all it could at a time of recession and mass unemployment. Indeed, he exhorted the Muslim seamen of South Shields to accept the rota system—advice heeded by many, but which proved of no more benefit than many of the other approaches. Resistance to the rota system subsided quite rapidly, and yet the social and economic problems of the Muslim seamen received no more consideration from the authorities than before.[45]

The Arabs of South Shields realised they had been defeated. They had no choice but to accept the resultant suffering stoically, and for the rest of the decade they remained 'well-behaved, law-abiding' and broadly peaceful. Having been excluded from job opportunities, the unemployed coped in a variety of ways. In Cardiff, they fell back on poor relief, which the local Public Assistance Committee (PAC) finally agreed to provide after months of prevarication. In South Shields, however, the PAC denied them outdoor relief. Some, especially those who were unregistered and therefore ineligible for work, sought indoor relief *en masse* to make their plight better known. In this they were encouraged by the boarding-house owners faced with the prospect of having to support them indefinitely. This went down badly with the white population, and when in late September 1930, reeling from the effects of the depression and of the rota system, ninety-seven Yemenis entered Harton Institution (the local work-house), this immediately triggered widespread protests in the press from local ratepayers.[46] Wild stories circulated about Arabs invading the work-houses and being 'fed on mutton, poultry, pancakes' instead of their staple diet of 'melon husk'.[47] Offered such 'luxury' they were likely to become permanent residents. In fact these protests were misplaced because the burden of caring for the majority of Muslims in need had not shifted to the rate-payers; as before, they relied on mutual aid, for Somalis organised through tribal networks and most of the seamen were still looked after by the boarding-housekeepers. However, the widespread calls for their repatriation did have almost immediate effect on the destitute Arabs: by 3 October 1930, within four days of having sought refuge, all the jobless Arabs had left Harton. Hence this move, launched as a form of protest by the unemployed Muslim seamen in South Shields to high-light their desperate situation, ultimately backfired. Thirty-eight of those who were shown to have received poor relief recently, being in the 'alien' category and therefore ineligible for work, were deported.[48] New restrictions in the mid-1930s resulted in further bouts of pro-longed unemployment, leaving many Arabs indigent and homeless. In 1936, having been refused assistance by the PAC, some, as Muslims, requested financial help from the Nizam of Hyderabad and the Aga Khan, who sent £100! With over sixty Arabs deemed eligible for assis-tance the amounts distributed were negligible, and most of it went to boarding-housekeepers who had been responsible for the seamen's maintenance from their own resources.[49] They also had to rely on the Unemployment Assistance Boards (UABs) for more regular help, but even here they suffered discrimination, since the UABs paid them less than the basic rates administered to the jobless whites, arguing that they needed less. Stung by this palpable unfairness, Muslims along with other unemployed 'black' workers made strong representations to the authorities. Their lobbying achieved some success in 1938 when the UAB set up a Special Scheme for Assistance of Colonials (SSAC) to supplement their meagre UAB payments.[50]

While Muslims were able to gain some improvement in their circumstances through a combination of individual initiatives, mutual help and collective action, on the whole their efforts had only limited effect. Muslim organisation was weakened by the transience of most of the seamen, combined with their diverse ethnic, tribal, cultural and linguistic affiliations. This was reflected in the sprouting of a whole array of societies, such as the Somali Club and the Arab Club. They themselves recognised this and the settlers among them challenged this distinction between the residents and transients deliberately created by the institutions of the wider society for their own purposes. For instance, in 1935, the Jumait-ul-Muslimin in the East End of London tried to keep the Strangers' Home open, signalling that Asian seamen, even if they lived in a hostel, were accepted as part of the larger Asian community with overlapping allegiances and identities.

Thus Muslims in Britain found themselves forming part of a broader multicultural identity, which coexisted with and sometimes transcended religion. As workers they were drawn into setting up separate trade unions and other pressure groups in response to trade union discrimination to strengthen their negotiating position. In 1938 Akbar Khan, together with two Sikhs, founded the Indian Workers Association (IWA) which consisted mainly of Punjabi pedlars and factory workers in Coventry. In the mid-1930s Surat Ally, a skilful Indian labour organiser, founded the Colonial Seamen's Association of which he became its first secretary, and later used wartime rhetoric to win concessions for colonial seamen. He continued to organise them in Britain in the 1940s, and in September 1943 formed the All-India Union of Seamen (AIUS). It was centred in Liverpool, and branches were soon opened in Glasgow and London. Steeped in the idea of class struggle, the main theme of AIUS was salvation through unity between black and white workers. The All-India Seamen's Federation (AISF) was another trade union established to pursue the interests of colonial, mainly Indian, workers. At first it was virtually a one-man band, dependent on Aftab

Ali, but as the Second World War approached it was noticed increasingly within British establishment circles as they realised the potential contribution of the mercantile marine to the war effort. Lascars based in London, Glasgow, Liverpool and other British ports, many of them Muslims, also became more aware of their own worth, and went on strike in support of their entirely economic demands. The strike was settled in December 1939 with the AISF wringing concessions from a British government acutely aware of the contribution to the war effort that would be needed.[51]

Demanding the rights of citizenship

Muslim seamen had given enormous service during the First World War and had felt entitled to recompense for their sacrifices. Although employers, the state and the seamen's union sought periodically between the wars to bar them from Britain, Muslim seamen continued to migrate and settle in dockside neighbourhoods, forming social networks and institutions and marrying into local white families. As they became more established and began to challenge their subordination, they increasingly became the focus of racial hysteria, expressed in various ways—social exclusion, negative newspaper comments, and refusal to serve them in bars and restaurants or admit them to dancehalls and hotels. Local and national institutions responded to the demands of the local white population by bringing in measures that reduced the meagre resources and opportunities still available to Muslims settling in Britain. By the mid-1920s the state had successfully redefined racial and national categories in response to competing pressures from employers, unions, local and national government, and resistance by Muslim seamen and their advocates. The 1920 Aliens Order and the Special Restrictions (Coloured Alien Seamen) Order of 1925 implicitly codified racial difference itself. The Colonial Office, using its many bureaucratic ruses, created difficulties for 'coloured' seamen wanting to obtain passports. The Home Office thereafter supported projects for the deportation of unemployed Muslim seamen, and local authorities and police, often influenced by images of colonised peoples' irrationality and volatility, as well as class-based hostility to workers in general, increasingly viewed local Muslims as potential criminals. The Chief Constable of Cardiff, James A. Wilson, considered 'African men', among them many Somalis, to have 'a very low standard of morality'. Harassment of Muslim residents in British seaports such as Barry (South Wales), Cardiff and South Shields became widespread. Moses Hassan, a leader of the Muslim community in Cardiff, described how Arabs found out in the town after dark would be questioned, provoked and arrested. Many Muslims were arbitrarily registered as 'aliens' and threatened with deportation. Others saw their passports and other documents confiscated or altered by the police. An example of the arbitrary application of the 1925 Order was the registration of sixty-three Indian pedlars—neither seamen nor aliens—by the Glasgow police.[52]

The most powerful force that modified, moulded and undermined official policy was the resistance of the Muslims themselves. Throughout the interwar years they struggled to preserve their livelihood through collective and individual protest. The ambiguity of Muslim seamen's nationality, of which British authorities took ample advantage during the 1914–18 war (wooing Arabs from the Turks), now become a weapon used against them, and instead of being welcomed as valued contributors to Britain's seafaring force, they were presumed to be aliens illegally in Britain. Muslims responded to these attacks by reasserting their right to live and work in Britain unmolested on the basis of their British citizenship and their participation in the war. The repatriation campaign initiated at popular demand failed as the overwhelming majority of seamen refused to depart. Even the experience of white violence, destitution and the slender hope of employment did not persuade them to leave. Between 1925 and 1937 only 178 of the thousands of Muslims and other 'coloured' settlers in Cardiff took up the offer of repatriation.[53]

This pattern of resistance continued throughout the 1920s and 1930s, often in individualistic, uncoordinated and spontaneous ways. As the Muslims' circumstances deteriorated between 1925 and 1932 they resisted the effects of economic decline and political subterfuge. These forms of resistance ranged from simple evasion to collective petitioning of state institutions and concerted public protest. They appropriated the British imperial rhetoric of fair play, claiming that their service and sacrifices during the First World War entailed reciprocal obligations. They felt that they were entitled to jobs, and could justly lay claim to British resources and to pursue their rights as British subjects. Fraternisation and comradeship during the war had eroded 'the mystique of invincibility' and any belief in superiority predicated on racial differences. However, prejudices still endured and, as the depression deepened in the early 1930s, the fact that Muslims were citizens of the Empire and had done 'fine work in the war' merited little consideration in the allocation of rights and resources.

The conflicts during the interwar period emanated largely from the Muslims' sense of betrayal at Britain not honouring its part of the bargain—accepting them as legitimate imperial subjects with equal claims to resources—once they had done their duty. These protests showed that Muslims felt sufficiently empowered to pursue their rights as British subjects and still assert their legitimacy as imperial subjects by acquiring passports, by making trouble on board ships, by 'wandering away' in search of better jobs and better lives, and by establishing and defending their families and settlements in Britain. To challenge the mechanisms of exclusion applied by the Home Office, the Colonial Office, the India Office and the seamen's unions they used other means too such as legal action, appeals to ministries, and direct action. The Cardiff Adenese Association, for instance, submitted a number of objections to the change in their status through its solicitor, Willett, who argued that they considered themselves 'very much British indeed', and having served in the war under the British flag, were greatly offended by the term 'alien'.[54] Indians too, as subjects of a multicultural empire, mobilised opinion against attacks on their rights as British citizens. After the rounding-up of the pedlars in January 1926 the Indian Union of Glasgow contacted the India Office, the Indian Legislative Assembly and the Indian press on their behalf. Protests continued in Britain. On May Day 1927 a 'mass protest of Indians' in Liverpool denounced the use of aliens' certificates for Indians, calling on the Indian National Congress to investigate their complaints and assist in their redress. Faced with this resistance the Home Office at first retreated, but ultimately it defined nationality on racial lines.[55] The principal method of resistance was to obtain passports and other credentials, legally or illegally, identifying them as British.

The 1925 Order continued to be applied for the rest of the interwar years, being renewed in 1938 and again in 1942, but the shortage of manpower during the Second World War forced the government to abolish it and to make 'British Protected Persons' eligible for conscription. The subsequent record of the Arab and Indian seamen and their sons during the Second World War was crucial in getting them accepted on relatively equal terms. They suffered heavy losses in the merchant navy, and this sacrifice was acknowledged and thus helped the process of subsequent assimilation.[56]

In many ways the engagement of Muslims with British society during this period was a dialectical process, in which those who succeeded, at least individually, did so at the cost of giving up some portions of their cultures, traditions and values, which eventually led to their becoming diluted and invisible communities.[57] As Muslims adjusted to the realities of British society in the first half of the twentieth century, some did become more like their white counterparts and less like members of their communities of origin. But the more Muslims attempted to maintain their distinct community identities during this period, the less they seemed to be accepted by the society as a whole. Being Muslim in Britain during these years was not easy: it involved trying, in an atmosphere of racial hostility, to claim the rights that went with being British while still hanging on to what distinguished these communities from those around them. To a great extent Muslim communities succeeded in both endeavours, but their successes were won in the face of resentment from sections of the wider society, which resisted their presence for economic as well as social reasons.

5

'WEAVING THE CULTURAL STRANDS TOGETHER'

INSTITUTIONALISING ISLAM
IN EARLY TWENTIETH-CENTURY BRITAIN

Wherever Muslims have established relatively long-term communities in the non-Muslim world, they have tried to preserve the essential elements of their faith for present and future generations. As we have seen, for much of the period of their presence in Britain in the nineteenth and early twentieth centuries, many Muslims sought to adjust and accommodate to existing institutions and practices. This required experimentation and negotiation between the actual and perceived demands and values of British culture and society and the needs, beliefs and practices of the Muslims themselves. The fact that in many ways their identities and values were—or were perceived to be—in conflict with the established norms of the majority population made the task facing Muslim communities in Britain difficult. This chapter investigates how the increasingly diverse localised Muslim communities established from the late nineteenth century sought to institutionalise Islam in the British context. It explores the gradual emergence of organisations created to sustain Muslim identities that now formed a part, albeit a small one, of the British social and political landscape.

Quilliam and the Liverpool Mosque and Institute

The earliest example of institution-building in the late nineteenth century seems to have been the Liverpool Muslim congregation founded by William H. Quilliam, which was mentioned in Chapter 3. He set out his religious views in a pamphlet published the same year, entitled *The Faith of Islam*. However, the timing of his endeavour was not particularly good, because the ongoing conflict with the 'Mad Mahdi' in Sudan meant that the very mention of Islam in Britain was like a red rag to a bull. Indeed Quilliam was evicted from the house in Mount Vernon Street which he was using as a mosque because the landlord 'would not have any person occupying his premises who did not believe and preach the saving efficacy of Christ Jesus' blood'.[1] Consequently he moved to Brougham Terrace in West Derby Road, where he established the Liverpool Mosque and Institute (LMI) in 1891.

Within a few years these latter premises were enlarged, and by the mid-1890s the LMI consisted of a mosque, a *madrassa*, a library and reading-room, a printing-press, a museum, a boys' boarding- and day-school, a girls' day-school, a hostel for Muslims and an office for a literary society. Quilliam and his adherents also established a home for unwanted children. The LMI conducted Friday congregational prayers and celebrated the many annual Muslim festivals. The first funeral prayer according to Muslim custom was said at the Institute in 1891, and many weddings thereafter were solemnised in the Islamic tradition. At the core of LMI's ethos was a sense of belonging to a global Muslim community; Quilliam believed in the 'complete union of Islam and of Muslim peoples', and worked hard towards the accomplishment of this goal. 'Here within the walls of this institution', he declared, 'who knows but that the scattered cords may not be able to be gathered together and woven into a strong rope?'[2]

Quilliam adopted various approaches to achieve this objective. He was aware of the power of the press and was keen to utilise it for the benefit of the LMI's cause; the press in Liverpool gave the activities of the LMI extensive coverage. The Muslims' eagerness both to counteract hostile opinions and to encourage favourable ones resulted in several open debates in the columns of local newspapers. The LMI also brought out two journals of its own to publicise its views and activities. *The Crescent*, with eight pages, first published in 1893 and appearing weekly till 1908, dealt primarily with the concerns of Muslims in Britain, providing local news relevant to their concerns and reporting LMI activities. The Islamic World, a 32-page monthly publication, dealt with matters that affected Muslims 'throughout the globe'. Lengthy reports and features dealt with aspects of the tenets of Islam and with the politics of Muslim countries. It also published articles on topics as diverse as 'Lord Byron from an Islamic Point of View', 'Islam, Science and Speculation', 'Saracenic Architecture', 'Muslim Precepts upon Hygiene' and 'Freemasonry and Islam', and often provided the material for weekly public meetings and lectures. Both journals seem to have had a wide circulation through subscription. By 1899 demand for The Crescent in Liverpool was such that it was sold through five newsagents. There were subscribers all over the world, including India, Turkey, China, the United States, Egypt, Morocco, Switzerland, West Africa, New Zealand, Germany, Afghanistan, Iran, Syria, Australia and Canada. In addition, these publications were on the exchange list of around 100 foreign journals, which Quilliam regarded as 'one of the most important features of our work', since potentially it enabled the LMI to reach hundreds of thousands of people every week. He compared the effectiveness of this with his lectures which, despite their success in arousing the interest of non-Muslims, could not be read, re-read and reflected upon later.[3]

Quilliam travelled widely and built up important contacts in the Muslim world. He met the Shah of Persia when that potentate visited Liverpool in 1889: the Shah congratulated him on his conversion and presented him with a gold pin. The importance of the Liverpool community was recognised in the 'Muslim world' when the title of Sheikh al-Islam of the British Isles was conferred on Quilliam in 1894 by the Ottoman ruler and the Amir of Afghanistan, and the Shah appointed him Persian consul in Liverpool. Further recognition came with the visit in 1895 of the Amir of Afghanistan's son with a personal gift of £2,500 and the Koola-Izzat (hat of honour); the money was spent on improving and extending the Institute and its facilities.[4] The Institute aimed at establishing conditions that could best ensure the survival of the embryonic Muslim community. It had a written constitution and was managed by a committee elected at its annual general meeting. Members of the congregation reviewed the previous year's work and suggested ways forward. Current issues and concerns were discussed and decisions taken on matters needing both practical action and intellectual responses. The education of the community's children was given much attention; a 'Muslim College' was established which offered the children of Muslim parents in Britain and abroad an English education without exposing them to the influence of Christian missionaries and the 'vices of so-called Western civilisation'.[5] Among the courses offered included one that prepared pupils for bar examinations.

The over-arching aspiration of the Institute was to convert the British nation to Islam: responsibility for this rested, in Quilliam's words, 'upon not one but all of us'.[6] Liverpool's Muslims were encouraged to exemplify 'true' Islam in their daily practice and act with discretion in their management of the Institute. To advance this ambition several projects were developed. The Muslim community undertook social work; the 'Medina Home for Children' was founded as a refuge for unwanted children, who were cared for and brought up as Muslims. Another example of the Institute's concern with the people in its locality was its annual celebration of Christmas Day from 1888 by entertaining and providing meals for hundreds of the poor. The Liverpool Muslim view was that, although they did not accept the divinity of Jesus, they honoured and respected his memory as a prophet. They also sought to show 'in a most practicable manner that the religion of Islam inculcates almsgiving to the deserving poor and the needy as one of the pillars of the faith'. Thus it was their duty to feed the 'poor ill-clad Christians in a Christian city neglected by the followers of their own creed'.[7]

Despite the sensitivity of his approach to the wider society in promoting Islam, Quilliam met with intense opposition.[8] Thus, it was perhaps surprising that he gained as many converts as he did—they came at first from among friends and acquaintances in organisations in which he was involved, such as the Freemasons, the Temperance League and the Manx Clubs. The rate at which people converted to Islam was significant. According to *The Islamic World*, there were twenty conversions in 1896 alone,[9] and over the next twenty years a steady trickle of people—some 600 in all, mainly from the professional middle classes—followed. This was regarded by the LMI as a considerable success. The reasons for it were to be found in the changes in people's thinking reflecting changes in British society as a whole from the mid nineteenth century. During the last quarter of the century the religious views of a large segment of the population had been transformed by scientific developments, and a new approach to apprehending and structuring the universe had emerged. Doubt and speculation had undermined the certainties of religious belief and created thought-processes in which the supernatural and miraculous were increasingly believed to be irrelevant. Rationalism as a method of understanding nature and society was rapidly gaining in acceptance, with the Unitarian and deist trends having advanced among sections of the middle classes in particular. A high proportion of professional people were attracted to these Nonconformist Christian denominations. Liberal thinkers, convinced of the scientific method as a way of demystifying the cosmos, searched for ways of reembodying faith in a believable form. Unitarianism had proved particularly attractive to them since it made reason the ultimate test even for the scriptures, and Islam seemed to others to be a religion that encouraged inquiry through reason—something that harmonised with the emerging values of moderation, balance, self-development and progress through public service. Quilliam adopted a strategy for propagating Islam that seemed in line with these values, and used an idiom that his audience could readily understand. So, bearing in mind the social and intellectual environment in which the LMI was doing its missionary work, he mainly addressed the people he already knew and whose concerns he had shared and championed for years, such as his 'old temperance friends'. He was English and therefore the majority population could not dismiss his views as 'alien' so easily as if they came from someone of a different ethnic origin or culture.

Quilliam's careful and subtle approach can be gauged from the way in which he introduced Islam in his lecture 'Fanatics and Fanaticism', delivered at Liverpool's Vernon Temperance Hall.[10] The first two-thirds of the lecture did not refer to Islam at all; fanatics and fanaticism, he argued, were terms used by some to persecute all who did not conform to their own beliefs. He gave examples of men denounced as 'fanatical' in the past—such as Granville Sharp, Thomas Clarkson and William Wilber-force—but to whom 'the very nation who traduced them has since raised statues of honour'. Having established a connection with the British heroic tradition, Quilliam then introduced Muhammad, and even then only allusively, drawing parallels between the 'noble band of emancipators' and 'benefactors of mankind' who had once been stigmatised in Britain, and the earlier years when the Prophet had been persecuted. At this stage he mentioned that Muhammad was 'a total abstainer from alcohol and gave that law to his followers', thus pointing out that the audience's own convictions coincided with those of Islam. Thus Quilliam was attempting to found an indigenous tradition that would be able to connect with the religious practices of potential converts and so create a sense of receptive familiarity. For example, many of the LMI's activities were similar to the 'good works' being vigorously carried out by nonconformist Christians, especially the Unitarians. The LMI also made contact with interested Christians by adopting a form of ritual they were accustomed to: morning and evening services were organised on Sundays, where hymns were sung, many of them taken from the Christian tradition and adapted by Quilliam to Islamic beliefs and 'suitable for English-speaking Muslim congregations'.[11]

With Quilliam's departure overseas in 1908 the thriving Muslim community of Liverpool, lacking the direction and determination of its founder, declined sharply. Nevertheless, there is evidence that a community of about 200 survived for some years and continued to conduct its business quietly and unostentatiously with the LMI as its institutional focus.[12]

The Woking Mosque and the Muslim Mission

The LMI's public activities ceased as relations with Turkey deteriorated before the First World War. But with its demise another Islamic mission took shape, this time centred around the Muslim population in London. Dr G.W. Leitner, an ex-Registrar at the University of Punjab in Lahore, had already established in 1889 the first purpose-built mosque in Britain in Woking, with substantial financial help from the female ruler of the Indian princely state of Bhopal, Shah Jahan Begum. However, his attitude towards South Asian Muslims was patronising. In his view the mosque had been built to provide a place where Muslims of 'good family' could practise their faith; it was not to be used 'for the purposes of converting Englishmen to Islam, or to introduce new doctrines into that faith, or to promote religious and political propaganda, or to celebrate the generally unhappy marriages between Mahommedans and English-women'.[13] In short, only those deemed fit by Leitner were allowed in.

For many Muslims these strictures went against the grain of 'correct' Muslim behaviour, in which the upholding and transmission of Islamic values were vital. Consequently, his conditions for the use of the Mosque did not go unchallenged by London-based Muslim societies, mainly of students from the Indian subcontinent. After his death the site fell into disuse until Khwaja Kamaluddin, a barrister from Lahore, established the Woking Muslim Mission on it in 1912. Kamaluddin was at the centre of a group of South Asian Muslims who arrived in Britain at the turn of the century and proceeded to consolidate a distinct Islamic presence. Significantly the concerns of these Muslims were in many ways little different from those that preoccupied British Muslims in the second half of the twentieth century, but the their strategies appear quite dissimilar.

These South Asian Muslims in Britain,[14] observing the crises through which the Muslim world was passing, strove hard to defend their heritageand did what they could under the circumstances, constrained as they were by their subordinate position and imperial tutelage. They pursued their objectives with remarkable vigour considering their low numbers. The main thrust of this engagement with British society was towards acculturation—demonstrating the similarities between Islamic and Christian beliefs and values. Islamic thought was reinterpreted to make it more conducive to the British environment where rational debate was firmly established as one of the main vehicles for intellectual development. 'Religious' practice also became somewhat modified to take account of the non-Muslim British context.

Of course, the kinds of activities these Muslims pursued had a strong élite bias. This was perhaps to be expected since they were frequently leading lights of the emerging Indian professional upper middle and landed classes and therefore concerned to represent the interests of this particular Muslim segment without seeming to challenge the imperial *status quo*—an enterprise in which they saw themselves as junior partners. The socio-economic and cultural world of these

Edwardian Muslims and their class and education shaped very directly the ways in which they responded to their new environment. Khwaja Kamaluddin, Abdullah Yusuf Ali and Syed Ameer Ali were three of the leading lights of the Woking Mission, and as Chapter 3 showed they moved in élite circles while in England, having adopted much of their lifestyle. They worked closely with the British imperial establishment even if they fell a little way short of becoming part of it. Yet they understood that Islam had been maligned for centuries and that this had generated intense hostility towards its perceived values and its adherents. On the political front Turkey was increasingly the object of trenchant criticism, with its miserable, backward and uncivilised state being blamed by Western critics squarely on the Islamic ideology of its rulers and its people.

Indeed, with Turkey ranged against Britain in the First World War, any political intervention on its behalf was likely to cause sharp controversy. Loyalty to Britain was demanded, but it was emotionally impossible for such Muslims to oppose the Ottoman Caliphate, the most important symbol of the worldwide Muslim community. Many of them could not avoid being concerned at the hostility being expressed in official circles as well as the press, and in response they articulated their thoughts publicly. What is more noteworthy still is the intensity of their feelings and commitment, which led them to take considerable risks and to expend much energy and personal resources trying to defend the integrity of the Ottoman Empire. Indeed it could be argued that the campaigns these Muslims conducted on behalf of the Ottoman Empire at this time helped to give Islam in Britain a more organised shape. That such a small group of Muslims could make its voice heard at the highest political level says much for their understanding of the workings of British society and its institutions. To argue their case they were able to line up an impressive cast of tactically valuable British establishment 'front men', including Lords Mowbray, Morley, Lamington and Newton, who for whatever reasons were prepared to support them. They also created a web of pressure-groups in the attempt to influence government policy. When war was declared between Turkey and Britain, the Anglo-Ottoman Society, founded in January 1914 and run almost single-handedly by Marmaduke Pickthall, lobbied vigorously on Turkey's behalf. Similarly the Central Islamic

Society[15] organised public meetings concerning the Ottoman Empire, wrote letters to *The Times*, sent petitions and memorials to the Prime Minister, and after the end of the war issued a number of bulletins to counter what it perceived as anti-Turkish propaganda.[16]

In Britain during this period public perceptions of Muslims fluctuated from extreme distrust to acknowledgement of the valuable contribution of Indian Muslim soldiers to the war effort. At a time when Turkey was clearly one of Britain's main enemies, any deviation from explicit loyalty to the British Empire was naturally suspect, hence many Muslims were kept under surveillance. The paranoid public view of them was reflected in the Foreign Office's description of Syed Ameer Ali and Dr Abdul Majid as 'fanatics'—both were close to the British establishment and untiring in their declarations of loyalty. When the more radical Secretary of the Pan-Islamic Society, Mushir Hussain Kidwai, was questioned by the police about his Turkish sympathies, he replied, flabbergasted: 'Could I or can I deny that?'[17] Ultimately they were kept out of trouble by their political skill and influential friends. On a less individual level, the government recognised the services of Indian Muslims by approving the establishment of a Muslim cemetery at Horsell near the Woking Mosque for the burial of Muslim soldiers.[18]

Small though they were in number, these South Asian Muslims began the task of creating an institutional base and intellectual space for Islam in Britain by establishing some consonance between it and the native religion, Christianity. In this they continued the work begun by Quilliam and his supporters in Liverpool. Their strategy was broadly assimilationist. One of the Woking Mission's objectives was to build a viable Muslim community in Britain, partly at least through conversion, and if this was to come about Islam needed to be made indigenous, as it had been elsewhere. It could not expand if it was perceived as an 'alien' and 'exotic' religion practised by people whose traits the majority population regarded as inferior. These Muslims trod delicately. Belonging to the élite themselves, they could make contacts in the middle classes and the aristocracy with relative ease. From these beginnings they were able to develop good connections and so tried to influence views and policies relating primarily to South Asian Muslim concerns.

Like Quilliam, they realised very soon that if they were to make any headway on conversion they would have to adopt an approach with which their audience was familiar. The Woking Mission did not seek to be 'antagonistic or hostile' towards Christianity, but rather to contest its popular version, which, it was claimed, little resembled its original form. In keeping with well-established traditions of discussion and persuasion, they applied rational methods to explain the practice and social positions they believed were intrinsic to Islam. Weekly lectures on different topics were conducted at the Mosque and later at the Prayer House established in London. Questions from the audience—consisting of both Muslims and non-Muslims—were encouraged. 'At-homes' were arranged with a similar purpose, but in more relaxed and informal settings.

Through its journal the *Islamic Review* (distributed widely and free of charge), the Woking Mission's leading lights elaborated their views on the position of women in Islam, polygamy, the drinking of alcohol and eating of pork, usury, gambling, circumcision, fasting, *zakat* and prayer, and many other issues which aroused controversy or seemed at variance with Christian practice. Rather than highlighting the differences between Christianity and Islam, they emphasised the Abrahamic tradition, which, they claimed, formed an important part of the two religions, together with Judaism. They acknowledged and respected Jesus as a true messenger of God no different from Muhammad: indeed, they claimed that he was a Muslim, since in their view 'true' Christianity and Islam were identical. Quoting from the Quran, they affirmed that, unlike any other religion, Islam recognised that 'every nation has an apostle'. Invoking the Quran they preached tolerance, stating that there was no compulsion in religion. Even the terminology they used in their publicity materials—such as 'the Muslim Bible' for the Quran and 'the Muslim Church' for the Mosque and Prayer House—was meant to show maximum affinity.

A parallel organisation, the British Muslim Society (BMS), was set up in December 1914 under Lord Headley, an influential convert, with the object of bringing Muslims and interested non-Muslims together. Many who joined were from the middle classes and aristocracy, with experience of the 'Muslim world', but most were South Asian Muslim students. Also among its members were eminent figures of British Islam such as Marmaduke Pickthall and Syed Ameer Ali. The Society met regularly for Friday prayers and Sunday services, and Islamic literature was distributed at its public meetings. Every year it celebrated Muhammad's birthday at one of London's best hotels. On one such occasion Maulvi Inayat Khan, a newly arrived Sufi, presented a rendition of Indian classical music on the sitar, and a number of English ladies performed on the piano and violin.[19] Lectures by eminent speakers on the life of the Prophet were also usually followed by refreshments and music. A Muslim Literary Society (MLS) was established with Abdullah Yusuf Ali as its president. Thus much of the work of these Muslims was conducted with a light touch in a convivial atmosphere with due regard for the social etiquette, conventions and customs, and adopting British cultural forms to give as little sense of 'strangeness' as possible.

Khalid Sheldrake, an early convert to Islam, shed light on the uncertain attempts of 'a few pioneers of the Pan-Islamic movement' to institutionalise Islam in Britain during this period. Writing in the *Islamic Review and Muslim India* in 1914, he reminisced about the resuscitation of the Islamic Society in 1904:

> I remember Dr Suhrawardy when the Pan Islamic Society was formed ... The Islamic Society held the *namaz* at Caxton Hall [London], and the worshippers were Ottomans, Indians and Egyptians, myself the only Englishmen. Lectures were held and offices opened in Green Street, Leicester Square. Inquirers were many; and the 'Light of the World', our little magazine, was eagerly subscribed to by all kinds of people. Opposition was very keen in those days and many obstacles were placed in our path. Dr Abdullah Suhrawardy published many pamphlets and many letters to the press. A mass meeting was held in Leicester Square Gardens ... We held several open air meetings on Peckham Rye which were very well attended. Suhrawardy returned to India [but] the principal events of our faith continued to be celebrated and a splendid library of Islamic Literature was collected.[20]

Likewise, a congregation was organised 'in [the] pouring rain, surrounded by a numerous audience, and in full gaze of the cameras, in the Hyde Park of London, near the Marble Arch'.[21] Sheldrake epitomised the type of white Briton to whom Islam appealed during this period. Born in 1888, the son of a pickle manufacturer, in the 'unpretentious South London Suburb of Forest Hill' he was drawn towards Islam early in the twentieth century, and became actively involved in the Muslim societies and clubs that had emerged in London around the turn of the century. After the First World War, in which he seems that he served in the army, he played a significant role in the Islamic Society.[22]

Muslims involved in both the Woking Mission and the BMS were convinced that Islam would have to be presented in a modernist fashion to appeal to British people. The success of this approach was confirmed by a steady stream of conversions—regularly announced in the Mission's journal—during the interwar years. Among these converts, apart from Lord Headley and Marmaduke Pickthall, were the President of the Selsey (Sussex) Conservative Association and Deputy Surgeon-General in the Royal Navy, Sir Archibald Hamilton; a barrister, Sir Lauder Brunton, and Lady Evelyn Cobbold, probably the first Englishwoman to set foot in Mecca, whose vivid account of her travels in the Libyan desert and of the *hajj* (pilgrimage) itself excited much interest at the time. One reason why such apparently staunch figures of the British establishment should have found Islam attractive, given that it had been under attack for so long, could be the disillusionment and despair caused by the slaughter of millions during the First World War, which Christianity had been powerless to prevent. Furthermore, as already discussed in relation to the Liverpool Muslims, those who became interested in Islam already possessed Unitarian tendencies and so did not find the move theologically difficult. Finally, many had spent lengthy periods of time in Muslim societies and reacted positively to the Muslims with whom they interacted.

The persuasiveness of the leading Muslims at the Woking Mission in their debates with Christians is clear from the testimonies of converts. They consciously tried to obtain respect for Islam by presenting it as a progressive moral force. Even more important, they were able to suggest that Islam could be relevant to people living in Britain and was no more an alien presence than Christianity itself. The Mission was at pains to display flexibility and patience towards new Muslims who strove to give up the values and habits of their pre-Muslim lives. Some converts, felt that insistence on strict observance of certain practices would lay Muslims open to the same criticisms that they made against Christians who gave ritual a central place in their faith. For instance, Lord Headley found giving up alcoholic drinks extremely difficult and it was several years after his conversion before he could do so completely. He also felt that 'the busy city man' could not be asked to pray five times a day and thought that 'sending up the silent prayer' was sufficient.[23] Marmaduke Pickthall was aware of the challenge that conversion to Islam posed to the British way of life. He likened the British Muslim community to the early adherents of Islam in Mecca and exhorted them to draw inspiration from their sacrifices in an equally hostile environment. At the same time he recognised the difficulties experienced by converts in following practices such as fasting in the month of Ramadan, and suggested a gradual move to total abstinence.[24]

On some of the fundamental issues too—apostasy and the punishment for it, *purdah* and women's position in Islam, slavery, *halal* food and approaches to music and art—they defended their positions with rational arguments. On the question of apostasy they absolutely denied that the punishment for it was death. The Quran and the Hadith were invoked to demonstrate the validity of their position. They declared that Islam respected individual freedom of religion and conscience, but they acknowledged too that 'fanatics' existed in all religions and might insist on capital punishment for apostasy. They felt unhappy about the blasphemy law in England which only provided protection for 'a state religion', and called for the Anglican Church to be disestablished. *Purdah* was deemed quite impracticable in the British environment, and British women who converted were never asked to use the veil. Indeed, the frontispieces in the *Islamic Review* show no departure from Western dress for both men and women. Public gatherings organised by the Mission and its offshoots were generally mixed, as were religious festivals and the bigger congregations. On the question of *halal* meat, the *fatwa* of Muhammad Abduh permitting meat which had not been ritually slaughtered was accepted as lawful for Muslims under particular circumstances. Music was not thought to be 'in the bad books of Islam'; it was a fine art and, outside the confines of religion, might be 'a real blessing for humanity'.[25] Similarly, any strictures against art were aimed at killing polytheistic propensities and not at discouraging art itself.

Thus throughout the interwar period modernist Islam was in the ascendant, in contrast to the much more ritualised, albeit disparate, Islamic practices of South Asia which later came to dominate the British scene. AbdullahYusuf Ali was one Muslim of that time who wrote pamphlets trying to establish a depoliticised progressive terrain for discourse on religion. By joining such institutions as the World Congress of Faiths (1936) these Muslims developed the notion not just of inter-faith dialogue but also that the religion of all reasonable people was basically the same. Muslims involved in the work of the Woking Mission were prepared to enter into rational debate with those of other persuasions whenever the occasion demanded. They accepted the intellectual traditions and conventions of British society and conveyed their ideas in that mode. The local and national press was used to good effect; lectures and talks were given; public meetings were addressed; non-Muslims were invited to visit the Mosque and engage in constructive and reasoned dialogue. The broadest possible definition of 'Muslim' was used. Converts were accepted as Muslims if they declared their belief in the prophethood of Muhammad alongside Abraham, Moses and Jesus.

Even more important was the emergence of the Woking Mosque as a symbol of the worldwide Muslim community in Britain. This gave South Asian Muslims a high place and considerable influence in the Muslim world and greater exposure to British society. Muslim dignitaries made a point of attending the Mosque on their visits to Britain. Implicit in the visits by prominent figures from so many different denominational backgrounds was acceptance of the non-sectarian character of the Mission. The head of the Ismaili sect was welcomed with the same dignity and warmth as Amir Faisal of Saudi Arabia or King Faruq of Egypt. Tribal chiefs came from Kano in Nigeria, as did the Grand Mufti of Palestine or the minister from Java, and all were treated with the respect due to them.

Thus these groups of Muslims in early twentieth-century Britain developed an ongoing engagement with the wider society. Their aim was to integrate Islam and Muslims into the fabric of British society. Perhaps the Mission, relatively isolated as it was, had little choice but to develop connections further afield, especially in London, if it was to have any impact. It had to engage with British élites on the theological plane, and remove misunderstandings about Islam that had damaged relations between Muslims and Christians in Britain for centuries. However, the Mission would have had little chance of success if the indigenous communities had had any notion of the sectarian divisions that had come to bedevil Islam on the Indian subcontinent. Hence, the Mission remained utterly non-sectarian, and its leading members gave many warnings of the damage that sectarianism would wreak. Headley, in a lecture to the British Muslim Society, criticised the so-called 'Qadianis' (or Ahmadis) for creating divisions within the Muslim community by denouncing as *kafirs* those who did not believe in Mirza Ghulam Ahmad as the Messiah, but showed a spirit of tolerance by refusing to cast them out of the Muslim community for holding such beliefs.[26] Aware of the dangers inherent in allegations of any kind of doctrinal bias, Kamaluddin and later *imams* deliberately rotated those who led the congregations. Thus the official *imam* did not always conduct the prayers at the Woking Mosque. Often members of the congregation from a diversity of Muslim countries and followers of different schools of thought were invited to lead, demonstrating a fundamental unity and their acceptability to all those who attended.

While the Woking Mosque during and after the First World War became the hub of Muslim activity in Britain, there was a need as London's Muslim population increased to establish an Islamic centre in the capital itself. This aspiration was given further impetus by the construction of the Central Mosque in Paris in 1926, built in recognition of the contribution of North African Muslims to the war effort. Lord Headley and Kamaluddin canvassed the British government vigorously for support for a similar project in London, and Syed Ameer Ali with other leading Muslims in London established a trust fund to finance construction of the mosque, and prominent Muslims were approached with some success. In 1926, as a temporary measure three houses in Stepney were converted into a mosque, then in 1928 the Nizamiah Mosque Trust was set up and a site in Kensington was bought with the help of a large donation—some £60,000—from the Nizam of Hyderabad. In 1930 plans for a complex were announced, and the foundation-stone was laid in 1937,[27] but the project failed to come to fulfilment because its moving spirits, Headley and Kamaluddin, had died in the early 1930s. A new committee took over the Mission, and the Woking Mosque remained the focus of Muslim activity until well after the Second World War. Its recognition as the centre of Islam in Britain was reflected, as ever, in its regular stream of visits by dignitaries from all over the Muslim world. However, after the war its influence and importance declined although the Mission continued to disseminate information on Islam through its organ the *Islamic Review*. The East London Mosque was inaugurated in August 1941, and the Islamic Cultural Centre, precursor of the Central London Mosque in Regent's Park, with strong support from several Muslim countries, became recognised as the central religious institution of the diverse Muslim communities in Britain.

Process of institutionalisation among the Muslim communities of Cardiff and South Shields

Muslim communities outside London developed somewhat different institutions in this period. We have seen that from the mid-nineteenth century, especially after the opening of the Suez Canal, Muslims established significant communities in British port cities—Cardiff and South Shields—with Yemeni and Somali sailor settlers the most numerous element. Seamen from West Africa were common in Liverpool and migrants from South Asia in London. Many married locally and, concentrated in particular parts of neighbourhoods, their families evolved into cultural communities with traditions, sentiments, attitudes and memories in common with the local white population but distinct from it. Like the earlier Manchester community of Moroccan and Middle Eastern merchants, Islam was pivotal—like kinship, nationality, common locality and friendship—in sustaining cohesion within these communities. Being to some extent physically and socially segregated from the white population and living mainly among other 'coloured' seamen and their families, these groups secured social cohesiveness by reproducing and re-imagining Muslim ways of living. Hence they observed religious rituals and obligations, celebrated Ramadan and other festivals and observed the various Islamic prohibitions. In South Shields documentation of Muslim burial practices dates back to 1916 if not earlier. Yet living and working in Britain made some degree of adaptation and acculturation necessary; for example, no marriages appear to have been conducted according to Muslim law in South Shields till the 1930s. Presumably Muslims married in local register offices. Further, while many probably preferred common-law marriages, evidence exists of marriages between Arabs and local women being celebrated at both local Anglican and Roman Catholic churches.[28]

While at first no purpose-built mosques were built by these communities, collective worship was regularly performed in specially allocated rooms in the Arab boarding-houses. Eventually *zawiyas* (centres of religious activity) were founded to give an organised shape to social and religious life where basic Islamic instruction and facilities for worship were provided and Arabic was taught. Here Muslim marriage ceremonies were conducted, newly converted wives and their offspring were given religious instruction, and rituals were carried out, such as male circumcision which initiated newborn males into the Muslim community. While in many ways the Islamic dimension predominated in defining Yemeni and Somali community life, it was also shaped by its own social, linguistic and ethnic features and religious and cultural practices, which distinguished it from others. For instance, *zawiyas* were specifically created by the Alawi sufi order to give institutional expression to its particular religious practices, which did not necessarily have the same resonance among Muslims from other parts of the world.[29]

Other forms of organisation had developed after the First World War when, as Chapter 4 showed, Arab sailors operating from British ports became the target of a rising tide of racial hostility.[30] Discrimination in jobs and calls for tough immigration controls and repatriation generated a will to resist. In the early stages this resistance was not formally organised and so remained divided and relatively weak. After the 1919 'riots' in South Shields involving white ex-soldiers and sailors and Arabs, Dr Abdul Majid, President of the Islamic Society, established a branch there with a membership that included boarding-housekeepers and representatives of seamen from different parts of the Muslim world. Majid's primary aim was to create a better feel in the town by arguing for equal entitlement and rights as loyal British subjects who had risked their lives in the First World War and had contributed to Britain's prosperity.[31] However, these efforts at reconciliation made little progress. In the circumstances of economic depression and unemployment, popular hostility towards Arab and Somali communities continued throughout the 1920s and 1930s. Muslims resisted the attacks through a variety of organisations—some secular, others based on their religion. Majid's colleague Khalid Sheldrake set up a branch of the Western Islamic Association (WIA) in South Shields in 1929–30,[32] and in spite of being obscure it was clearly connected with the Islamic Society, the British Muslim Society and the Woking Mission. It was keen to unify the Arabs as a socioreligious community with the construction of a mosque, a Quran school and a Muslim cemetery and by representing their interests with the British establishment. It was willing to defend the material rights of Arab seamen, but although it fiercely attacked the National Union of Seamen, it was reluctant to criticise the British government's discriminatory policy towards Arabs and urged acceptance of the iniquitous government-backed rota system. This proved to be deeply divisive because many of the Arab sailors opposed it. Indeed, in strong opposition to the WIA, they continued to organise under the Communist-dominated Seamen's Minority Movement, which had condemned the rota system as the 'slave ticket'. After the Mill Dam disturbances in August 1930[33] the WIA in South Shields declined and played only a minor role in the affairs of the Arabs there. Hassan Mohamed, secretary of the South Shields branch, left for France in 1932, and the Association more or less disappeared as a living body.[34]

There were doubtless several reasons for the demise of the Islamic Society and the WIA. Both organisations consisted of London-based professionals, far removed in social class and education from the constituencies they sought to represent. While their connections in the British establishment equipped them well for a role as buffer and broker between these evolving Muslim communities and the wider society, they scarcely empathised with the conditions of their lives. Unwilling and lacking the strength to disturb the *status quo*, they were unfitted to represent those whose needs and interests brought them into direct conflict with the institutions of British society.

Sheikh Abdullah Ali al-Hakimi and the Alawi tariqa

The next important phase in the development of Muslim organisation in England and Wales outside London began in 1936 with the arrival in South Shields of Sheikh Abdullah Ali al-Hakimi, who founded the Alawi order in that year and called it the Zaouia Islamia Allawouia Religious Society of the United Kingdom, with *zawiyas* in Cardiff, South Shields, Hull and Liverpool. The order felt that Muslim communities in many of the sea ports of Europe were moving away from their religious and cultural roots—partly because of mixed marriages, which in any case were not being conducted according to Muslim law—and therefore needed to be reintroduced to proper Islamic practices. It was particularly concerned about the religious education of the children in these communities. Al-Hakimi was appointed by Sheikh al-Alawi, leader of the Moroccan *al-Shadhali* order, to work among his compatriots, and his background made him particularly suitable for religious service among Arab sailors in England. His origins are not entirely clear, but he was known to be well-educated, and with business interests and good connections in Aden's trading community. Before his arrival in England he had lived and done religious work in the Arab communities of Marseilles and Rotterdam, earning his living as a sailor. The Alawi order was virtually unknown in Yemen, but it had acquired a following in some of the ports in Europe, partly because of the Yemenis' general inclination towards sufi Islam and partly because of al-Hakimi's powers of persuasion.[35] Thus the impetus for organising the religious life of these communities came first from a sense of mission elsewhere rather than the communities' perception of their own needs. However, once the initiative had been taken, the further development of organised religious life was driven by awareness among these communities themselves of their specific religious and material needs.

Al-Hakimi's Zaouia Islamia Allawouia was notably successful in institutionalising the religious activities of the Yemeni and Somali Muslim communities in England and Wales. Its aims were imparting Islamic education to young Muslims of both sexes, publication of Islamic literature; improving health and initiating social reform among the Muslims in Britain; strengthening cultural and social bonds between Muslims and non-Muslims; strengthening communications between Muslims in Britain and outside; exchanging Islamic knowledge and sending groups of students abroad to study at Islamic universities; and these were largely achieved. Through the Society al-Hakimi formalised the long-established system of voluntary offerings within the Arab community; these funds, managed by a local committee, were used for welfare purposes, such as payment for the repatriation of the bodies of seamen who had died in poverty and monetary assistance for unemployed sailors. Religious teachers in other towns were paid from this fund, as were scholarships to outstanding students.[36]

Funds were collected in various ways but their primary source was donations from within the communities themselves. As for the construction of *zawiyas* and mosques, al-Hakimi's efforts bore fruit only in Cardiff, where the Nur al-Islam Mosque was built in 1947, the makeshift building in which it had been housed since the 1930s having been destroyed during the Second World War. A printing-press was established on the same premises and an Arabic fortnightly paper, *Al-Salam*, disseminated al-Hakimi's views on religion and politics.

On al-Hakimi's arrival in South Shields in November 1936, after a stop in Cardiff, he set about organising the religious life of the Muslim community, predominantly Yemeni and Somali. While there had already been some community organisation, religious observance had largely taken place in private. Boarding-houses catering for Arabs had rooms reserved for prayers, daily and during Ramadan, but congregations were not organised in a regular way, although for some time a large room in a boarding-house was used for gatherings at annual festivals. Al-Hakimi set about putting formalising these arrangements, and quickly established a new *zawiya* in a converted public house with accommodation for a prayer room, a bathroom for ablutions with changing facilities and a residential section for himself. As al-Hakimi hinted in a letter written to the Governor of Aden in the late 1930s, the existence of such institutions was important for ensuring the survival of the communities in Cardiff and South Shields:

> There are a large number of Moslems resident in Cardiff, and many of us have become citizens, married, and have familys [*sic*], and we are very anxious that our children shall be given the opportunity of being educated, and in this connection we hope to have your able assistance in raising the necessary £ 4,000 so that the Mosque and school can be built.[37]

The new *zawiya* rapidly became the hub of a variety of religious and educational activities. Scores of Muslim children were given weekly instruction in the Quran, as were many of the white wives of Arabs who had converted to Islam. Ceremonies marking circumcision were also conducted there. Festivals were regularly celebrated, with processions involving hundreds from all over Britain reflecting a strong and distinct Muslim identity that was both audible and visible. The *Shields Gazette and Shipping Telegraph* provided a glimpse of life in this community in 1937. Reporting on *Eid al-Adha*, it estimated that over 200 had marched through the town. Alawi *nashids* (praises of God) were sung and banners bearing the Arabic words *la ilaha il allah* (There is only one God) headed the procession. According to the *Shields Gazette*, 'The different racial types and their strange headgear gave the festival a cosmopolitan flavour rarely found in an English town.' The congregational prayers were followed by a ceremonial feast to which all the participants and guests were invited.[38] With al-Hakimi installed as a permanent *imam*, daily congregational prayers were now conducted at the *zawiya* and in line with Sufi practice new rituals such as *zikr* were introduced.

The success of al Hakimi's institutionalising impulses can be gauged from the observations of Kenneth Little, who visited and researched the Cardiff community during the 1940s, and noted that most of the children and many of the white wives who had married Muslim men had been 'islamized'.[39] Local Muslims

> not only carry out their ritual and religious obligations with vastly more fervour and enthusiasm than the rest of the community, but are correspondingly surer both of themselves and their own way of life. The principal injunctions of Islam are fulfilled assiduously, and the various prohibitions enjoined by the Prophet are on the whole rigorously observed, as are Ramadan and other fasts and festivals, in celebrating which Arab dress is worn by most of the Arabs. This constant display of devotion is regarded by the rest of the community with a certain amount respect and even a little admiration.[40]

Central to the institutionalisation of Islam in the locality was the existence of a temporary *zawiya*, through which Muslim children continued to be educated. Little noted:

> This is an ordinary house whose rooms have been converted for religious purposes. The front portion is used for prayer; behind is a cleansing room containing wash bowls and shower baths. Here clothes are changed and footwear removed, and a number of pads for the feet lead directly into the prayer room so that devotees will not collect dirt on the way. Another room, constructed rather like a 'pen', serves as a school, where the young Moslem boys are given instruction in the Koran, repeating its verses after their Somali teacher. On feasts and other notable dates in the Mohammedan calendar the green crescent flag of Islam is flown outside this establishment from the flagstaff.[41]

As Little observed of Cardiff after the Second World War, local Muslim communities there, despite their relative social isolation sought to engage with their social as well as material environment. Most notably he found that 'apart from their prominent share in the commercial life of the community, the Arabs take a keen interest in certain social affairs, such as ARP [Air Raid Precautions—during the war] duties, and although comment in this respect is based on a small number of cases, their sense of social responsibility is possibly more marked than that of other sections.'[42] Further, the relative permanence of the Muslim communities necessitated interaction with the institutions of the non-Muslim surrounding society around them. As awareness grew that there were areas of life—education, health, social welfare, employment—which affected them significantly but which were beyond their control, the need to organise the Arab community to gain at least some influence over them became apparent. Collective action would be needed to persuade the institutions of the wider society to allow some space for Muslim living, such as access to *halal* food and approved burial grounds, and Al-Hakimi became a key figure in the attempts of the South Shields and Cardiff Muslim communities to negotiate on those matters with the local authorities. In his efforts to achieve a firm basis for Muslim community life, al-Hakimi painstakingly cultivated connections with local officials such as the mayor, town councillors and the Chief Constable. For their part, the local authorities seemed to welcome the establishment of the order in these towns, since by strengthening the religious organisation of the community it provided a useful means of controlling the behaviour of its members and exerting social discipline. This was thought especially important given the potential for social disruption as economic depression took its toll with high unemployment among Arab seamen. Since the order did not question the existing situation and encouraged self-control, it acted to some degree as an instrument of social control. Indeed, one of the rules of the Society was that 'in the event of any member getting into trouble of his own making, the Society shall take no part in any of his affairs.' However, 'if there was evidence of a miscarriage of justice, then the Society would help, in so far as the committee thinks fit.'[43] In return the town council was prepared to treat sympathetically al-Hakimi's request for a small part of the cemetery to be set aside for use by the

Muslim community. But when al-Hakimi started conducting marriage ceremonies according to Islamic law, as he insisted he was authorised to do by the Alawi *tariqa*, he came into conflict with the town council, which viewed such marriages as illegal.

While al-Hakimi's charisma earned him the devotion of the Arab communities in a number of British ports, his modernising impulses provoked opposition. For instance, the Sheikh favoured the idea of mixing the sexes in a religious setting, and as a concession to local ritual custom but in contrast to the Yemeni tradition, he accepted the presence of Englishwomen at their wedding ceremonies with the bride and groom 'clasping hands'. He therefore felt little hesitation in sanctioning the sharing of the prayer room by men and women. While this was well received by many of the English wives of Muslims and restored their sense of dignity and confidence, it was opposed as a deviation by most of the men; the conservative faction, led by Sheikh Hasan Ismail in Cardiff and his supporters, barred women from using the *zawiyas* for worship or education. In South Shields their participation in the celebratory or funeral processions was stopped, turning them into passive onlookers. When al-Hakimi tried to combine nationalist politics with religious organisation, he was again opposed by large sections of the traditionally disposed Yemeni community, who found it impossible to shift their allegiance away from the ruling Yemeni *imam*. So with al-Hakimi's departure traditional religious structures were re-created and these Muslim communities reverted to the familiar religious practices they had assimilated in their homeland and in which they found comfort and refuge from an alien environment.

The fissures within British Muslim communities resulting partly from the diversity of social, linguistic and ethnic backgrounds and partly from ideological differences and political rivalries between tribes tended to weaken them organisationally. On al-Hakimi's return after the Second World War the Nur al-Islam Mosque reverted to his control, but most of the Yemenis, both in Cardiff and South Shields, refused to support his campaign in favour of the 'Free Yemenis' because of their reverence for the status of the *imam*. Al-Hakimi effectively failed to sustain his religious authority and legitimacy among the Yemeni seamen who belonged to the loyalist Shamiri tribe, whose leader Hasan Ismail tried to oust him from the Mosque—the threat of a physical clash between the rival groupings brought the police to the location several times. In 1951 Hasan Ismail withdrew and set up his own separate *zawiya*. After al-Hakimi's own departure to the Middle East in 1952 the Alawi Society he had established survived and continued to provide aid for the sick, buy property as a trust investment, and settle disputes among its members according to Islamic as opposed to English law. The Nur al-Islam Mosque in Cardiff likewise continued to function as a social and cultural centre. In the late 1950s Hasan Ismail returned to Yemen whereupon his supporters—comprising by now most of the Yemeni community in Cardiff—turned for leadership to Sheikh Said, a Muslim of mixed Yemeni and Welsh antecedents.[44]

Historically Muslims living in Britain before 1945 sought to sustain at least the essential features of their faith and cultural life, whereas political commitment to the institutionalisation of Islam was almost entirely lacking. Still, the case-studies of developments in Liverpool, London, Woking, Cardiff and South Shields reveal the many ways in which various Muslim communities organised themselves as Muslims during this period. As the communities expanded, individuals identified what they perceived as the 'Islamic' requirements necessary for their survival, and this resulted in more formal institutionalisation. In all these cities and towns, physical bricks-and-mortar institutions were established to organise Muslims according to recognised 'religious' and material needs—and to formalise and develop Islam in the British context. As the experience of the embryonic migrant communities in South Shields and Cardiff show, the institutionalisation processes of these migrants to Britain were fairly instinctive. In contrast to the indigenous British Islam being forged by converts such as Quilliam in Liverpool, the intention of Muslim communities mainly of migrants from overseas was to reproduce expressions of Islamic practices and requirements with their original roots in their homelands. This is not to deny the acculturation that took place within these communities, and indeed, some adaptation of values and practices inevitably occurred through mixed marriages. More precisely, several charismatic community leaders—most notably Quilliam, Kamaluddin and al-Hakimi—tried to ensure that the kind of Islam with which they identified would engage with the wider material environment in which they and their communities operated. In Liverpool and Woking especially, efforts were made to build bridges with the non-Muslim majority population, largely through dialogue and by embracing 'native' British converts to Islam. Leading late Victorian and Edwardian Muslims had a strong conviction that the British establishment would view their attitudes and activities as conflicting with the national interest: however, they were prepared to take risks such as (in Woking) defending the integrity of the Ottoman Empire before, during and after the First World War. Hence, through to the Second World War the institutionalisation of Islam proceeded in these communities with an eye to events in the wider world, connected to the overwhelming power of the West, but it was influenced above all, by the actual situation of the Muslims in Britain themselves.

All the Muslim communities examined in this chapter were small and operated in a relatively hostile environment. Hence, all needed to adjust and to some extent make accommodations with the wider society—more than was the case with the predominantly migrant Muslim communities that settled in Britain after 1945. Religious institutions in this period therefore gave expression to cultural and ethnic identities and community life, which was particularly important in the socially segregated migrant communities in ports such as Cardiff and South Shields. After the Second World War Muslim communities, swollen in particular by migrants from the Indian subcontinent, drew on the achievements of these embryonic communities and the institutions they established.

PART II

STAYING—1945 ONWARDS

6

MUSLIM MIGRATION TO BRITAIN
AFTER THE SECOND WORLD WAR

Since the Second World War Muslims have migrated to Britain in much large numbers than before 1945, with the majority still coming from South Asia, parts of the Middle East, Africa and Cyprus. This migration differs in scale and composition from those that took place earlier—not only did its volume shoot up, but its character changed. Once the flow of primary newcomers was more or less halted by the mid-1970s, migrants already in Britain were joined by their families as well as by growing numbers of political refugees. The circumstances and timing of these patterns of migration were influenced by the broader economic context of the time, and formed part of a bigger global movement of labour from poor countries to rich industrialised societies. The period of rapid post-war growth in Europe stimulated the movement of migrant workers on a scale not seen since the First World War. Involved in all this were both pull and push factors that often operated in tandem. Either way, processes of chain migration and the presence of pioneers influenced the patterns of migration and settlement that now developed. What also affected them were the various pieces of immigration legislation passed by postwar British governments.

Phases of postwar migration

The post-1945 migration of Muslims to Britain can be divided into two main phases: from 1945 to the early 1970s, and from 1973 to the present time. In the first phase the economic strategy of capital investment and expansion of production in Britain called for a large number of migrant workers from 'less-developed' countries, many of them Muslim. This first phase ended and the second began with the oil crisis of 1973–4. The ensuing recession led to the restructuring of the world economy, investment in other areas, the introduction of new technologies and an altered pattern of world trade. This, in turn, caused reorganisation of the labour process, resulting in higher unemployment, especially in industries where migrant workers were concentrated. Technological innovation—micro-electronics and automation—also reduced the need for manual labour in manufacturing, and traditional manual skills were eroded. At the same time the services sector, with its growing demand for both highly skilled and unskilled workers, flourished. The informal sectors of the economy also expanded, leading to casualisation and differentiation of the labour force. All these developments had a negative effect on the demand for migrant labour, and so from the early 1970s any organised form of recruitment of migrant workers, particularly from the New Commonwealth, ceased.

Yet in these same decades after 1973 many countries in the developing world and also in the then Soviet bloc went through economic, social and political upheavals, starting new and more complex patterns of migration. Improved transport and communications, together with internationalisation of production, trade and finance, led to greater mobility of highly skilled and qualified technicians, professionals and executives. Migration was thus due less to poverty than to the desire to work in more stimulating environments and for greater intellectual and financial rewards. One consequence of the dramatic rise in the oil price in 1973 was that it facilitated the arrival in Britain of an élite group of Arabs, many of whom were flush with enormous capital seeking a home for investment. As political instability in their home countries continued, some of them—Syrians, Lebanese, Egyptians, Palestinians and Jordanians—decided to establish their businesses in Britain where they felt that their investments would be more secure and less vulnerable to unpredictable political developments. Saudi and

Gulf Arabs, though transient, established a more permanent base in Britain and cautiously invested capital in what they perceived as a less financially risky market. By 1988, Kuwaitis had invested some £55 billion in Britain,[1] and Saudis acquired businesses, banks and hospitals, and invested handsomely in property. Owners of stud-farms and race-horses from the Gulf states such as Dubai, Qatar and Oman started spending much of their time in Britain supervising their investments.

One common feature of the 1945–73 migratory movements had been the predominance of economic motivation on the part of migrants, employers and governments, although the expulsion of Asians from East Africa in the early 1970s was clearly political. Muslim workers, often following lines of communication built up in the colonial period, arrived in response to the rising demand for cheap labour, as reconstruction and advances in technology led to re-emergence of the economic pull factors and disappearance of the mass unemployment of the interwar period. In the 1950s and 1960s they formed part of the broader migration from the former colonies to satisfy the need for replacement labour, both in growth industries, where a labour shortage had developed, and in declining ones which were in the process of being deserted by indigenous workers because of the low pay and poor conditions, and which therefore came to rely on immigrant labour. Trades using 'sweated labour', such as garment manufacture and shoemaking, were labour-intensive and operated in a niche market, and hence maintained their competitiveness mainly by employing migrants. They did this on a large scale and paid low wages, which was made possible through homeworking, outworking, freelancing and even illegal immigration. The relatively protected restaurant environment was an ideal conduit for illegal immigrants. Immigrants from the Indian subcontinent (especially Sylhet in East Bengal), as well as from Cyprus and Morocco, played an important part in these trades and represented a growing migrant presence in catering, notably in establishing and staffing 'ethnic' restaurants. In 1971, 14% of all hotel workers and 25% of restaurant workers in Britain were born abroad.[2] Indeed, granting work permits for hotels and catering continued till 1979, and it was Muslims—Sylhetis, Pakistanis and Turkish Cypriots as proprietors and staff and Moroccans mainly in menial roles—who appropriated a large share of this market.

As less desirable unskilled jobs were vacated by indigenous workers who moved into the 'primary' advantaged sector with attractive pay, security of employment and pleasanter conditions of work, the low-paid, less skilled and less secure jobs, often requiring work at unsocial hours, were increasingly filled by migrants. Many were concentrated in the cleaning services and transport. Similarly, the enormous expansion in medical services after the Second World War would not have been economically feasible without the influx of a wide range of health professionals and workers from India, Pakistan, Bangladesh, Morocco and the Middle East. These included doctors, nurses and unskilled and semi-skilled ancillary staff—porters, attendants, cleaners, laundry and canteen workers, drivers and maintenance staff. All, with the exception of doctors, were concentrated in the more poorly-paid sectors of the health service.

Despite these trends the flow of migrants from Muslim countries remained low in the 1950s and largely corresponded to the demand for labour at that time. None the less, migration from the former colonies was already causing anxiety to the British government as relations between sections of the indigenous population and migrant groups showed signs of strain. Under British government pressure, India and Pakistan introduced voluntary controls up to 1959 to keep the migratory flows in check. As news of the impending Commonwealth Immigrants Act spread, the rate of immigration rose dramatically in 1961, and stayed relatively high in the 1960s and early 1970s. While it later tailed off as a result of further immigration legislation, the reuniting of the families and movement of refugees and asylum-seekers has seen Britain's migrant population continuing to increase in the 1980s and 1990s, despite the virtual halting of primary migration and even some movement back to migrants' countries of origin.[3]

Chain migration and the role of pioneers

The migration processes after the Second World War need to be seen in relation to social developments both in the countries from which migrants came and in Britain. One must also take account of the aspirations and practices of prospective migrants which had evolved in historically specific circumstances and which influenced their decision to uproot themselves. Furthermore, until the early 1970s the bulk of Muslim migration to Britain was motivated by socio-economic factors, as well as the material resources of potential migrants and personal and family calculations. As we have seen, sending people away from home in search of work for extended periods was a practice that had evolved in various Muslim societies into a tradition with positive values, making emigration an indicator of affluence and status, so that individuals and families competed to outdo each other in their capacity to emigrate. Migration thus became 'a system, a style, an established pattern, an example of collective behaviour'.[4] But this 'culture of migration' was solidly based on positive conceptions of material achievement and improvement, particularly among those from middling backgrounds who believed that effort and enterprise would bring them wealth and social prestige. Their assumptions were confirmed by the reception accorded to returning migrants, whose success was embodied in displays of goods, conspicuous consumption at celebrations, and purchase of property and land. These success stories aroused curiosity and jealousy, and a desire among others to emulate them. They also presented a challenge to those who, though better educated and previously higher in the social hierarchy, now found that they were no longer held in the same esteem as in the past.

The choice of locality for recruitment made by employers' agents made the source of migrants highly specific. Almost invariably migrants were deliberately recruited in response to a specific demand from employers for workers. From the employers' point of view, utilising people of one origin had certain advantages—it was thought that communication was made easier by the use of a common language and organising social events which fitted a common culture. Agents and brokers were often the essential link between supply and demand, scouting villages and providing transport to the migrants' destination, arranging board and lodging, advising and guiding, and as a target for recruitment their first port of call was usually their own villages and districts of origin.

The same was true, at least initially, of the migrants' destinations in Britain. Here the links were not simply social. Migrants moved in order to work and indeed their movement itself showed where the demand for their labour was strongest. So, not surprisingly, they headed for some of the main industrial conurbations—Greater London, the South-East, the West Midlands, Yorkshire and Lancashire in England, central Clydeside in Scotland, the ports of South Wales, and Belfast in Northern Ireland. The structures created by chain migration of this kind provided useful knowledge of the environment to which migration was envisaged, and the security and support networks in the receiving society that motivated prospective migrants to take the risks involved. Thus pioneers were the hub for the later growth in migration.

The flow of knowledge from pioneers in the form of letters and visits home, the tangible manifestation of their success in the form of remittances, and often their role as employers' agents stimulated further migratory movements. Sponsorship and patronage provided by well-established migrants helped overcome practical difficulties and led to 'chains' of migration based on kinship and friendship. Of course, this process was not culture- or context-specific. Chain migration was also said to explain Italian migration to the United States. In the British context again it showed, at least in part, why half of the 8,000 Italian brickmakers in Bedfordshire in the period immediately after the Second World War came from just four villages in southern Italy. Among Muslims this chain mechanism was used by Turkish Cypriots, Moroccans, Yemenis and South Asian Muslims; once the bridgehead had been established by pioneers, whether before or after the Second World War, migration grew, propelled by both push and pull factors.

The movement of Pakistani Muslims to Manchester illustrates the process in all its complexity because of its broad historical sweep and the cross-section of social and economic background of the migrants involved. Punjabi Muslims migrated to Manchester in three distinct phases. The first pioneers—largely from small, farming, relatively educated families—arrived in the 1930s and 1940s. As we saw in Chapter 2, they worked in factories for as long as it took them to save enough capital to set up in trading. They originated in particular districts of east and west Punjab and were interconnected through *biradaris* or family clan-like connections. Many already had family members who had migrated to other parts of the subcontinent or further afield to the Far East, East Africa and Britain, where they gained experience in trading. Their movement had been facilitated by their links with the British, serving either in the merchant navy or with the army in trades such as tailoring. Having been caught up in the upheavals of migration resulting from the partition of British India in 1947, they were more susceptible than most to the possibilities on offer in Britain. In the postwar period, therefore, those who came built their businesses up steadily from peddling, market trading and shopkeeping into wholesaling and manufacturing in clothing and garments. From the 1950s they were joined by a small group of students, many of whom had kin ties with the trader migrants from Punjab. Some returned home after acquiring qualifications, but others, tempted by lucrative opportunities in the professions in the 1960s, stayed and as doctors, accountants and solicitors became part of Manchester's multicultural landscape, largely serving the city's wider Muslim community. In due course both sets of migrants were joined by their families.

A third group, numerically by far the largest and comprising mainly young bachelor men from small landowning backgrounds, began to arrive in the late 1950s and 1960s. In contrast to their predecessors, they were not related to refugee families from east Punjab but instead were connected with villages in the Gujrat and Jhelum districts of west Punjab. While they were relatively well educated, members of their families had traditionally gone into wage-earning service occupations such as the army and police. With few skills relevant to the context of postwar Britain, most joined the unskilled and semi-skilled industrial workforce, especially in textile factories and public transport. As they became more established, they called their male relatives to join them, and later other family members followed. Thus, as many micro-studies of Muslim communities around Britain have demonstrated convincingly, prospective migrants in all three of these groups learnt of opportunities, were provided with transportation and had initial accommodation and employment arranged through links with previous migrants, or chain migration.[5]

The case of Turkish Cypriots moving to Britain in the 1950s and early 1960s confirms the generic nature of chain migration. During the Second World War demand in the catering trade grew and the number of Turkish-run cafés increased from twenty in 1939 to 200 in 1945. As the trade flourished, so did the need for Cypriot labour. To feed this demand a pattern of sponsorship based on kin and village connections developed, which became crucial in the process of migration. Similarly many Moroccans came to work specifically in Arab-owned casinos and nightclubs in London. Arab cultural and linguistic proximity probably featured in the employers' decision to import cheap Moroccan labour since it was rare for migrant workers to be recruited from countries with which Britain had had no colonial connections. This was another classic case of the chain migration of cheap unskilled labour. In no way connected with the nineteenth-century Manchester community which had disappeared by the 1930s, these Moroccans began to trickle in during the 1960s and in larger numbers by the early 1970s. Like other economic migrants, they mainly took low-paid, unskilled jobs in the hotel and catering trade and to a minor extent in the National Health Service as ancillary workers doing menial jobs with little career mobility. As with their South Asian counterparts, growing restrictions on immigration in the 1960s and 1970s encouraged them to bring over their families, at the same time as the cost of travel made periodical trips 'home' impractical. Long-term if not permanent settlement in Britain seemed the only viable alternative, and they gradually saw themselves no longer as transient workers. Not surprisingly, in view of the way the mechanisms of chain migration operate, the majority of these Moroccans originated from one northern coastal town, Larouche, and its surrounding villages. As a result of these connections the total size of the Moroccan community in London had grown to between 5,000 and 10,000 by the early 1990s.[6] The compact concentration of localities from which this kind of migration arose is seen too in the case of South Asian Muslims: 95% of Bangladeshi migrants were from Sylhet district; the majority of Pakistanis originally belonged to the Mirpur and Cambellpur (now Attock) districts; and in India the pioneers and their kin and friends who later joined them came only from the districts of Jullundhar and Ludhiana in east Punjab.

Social networks also helped migrants find work in the wider society and cushioned the loss of earnings by sharing the burden of expenditure. Chain migration and patronage ensured that the newcomer had shelter, and access to employment was secured by personal contact, recommendations and even bribes to foremen. For many, jobs had been arranged by contacts already in Britain; this in itself did not prevent unemployment but, given the information and contacts made available to them, they were often better placed to obtain jobs than they would otherwise have been.[7]

'Push' factors

It seemed, that Muslim migrants, like many of their non-Muslim counterparts, were willing to take undesirable, low-skill and low-waged jobs with poor conditions primarily because they could earn more in Britain than back home. 'Wages for labouring jobs in Britain in the early 1960s were over thirty times those offered for similar jobs in Pakistan' and generally much higher than even those paid to professionals such as teachers.[8] In Mirpur in Pakistan the average weekly wage was equivalent to approximately £0.37. In Birmingham a Pakistani's average weekly wage was £13, while the annual *per capita* income in Pakistan in the same period was just £30.[9] With much higher incomes in Britain individuals could realistically hope to save and remit substantial sums to their families back home.

The building of the Mangla dam near Mirpur in 1960 also had a marked impact on the migration of Mirpuris to Britain. The lake it created submerged 250 villages, with consequent difficulties for the livelihood of people in the area, thus adding practical urgency to the idea of migration from the region. The building of the dam displaced some 100,000 people who had to be rehabilitated either by land grants elsewhere or with monetary awards. Since the project acted as a push factor for Mirpuris who might previously have been hesitant about migrating, the Pakistani government issued 5,000 passports to prospective migrants from this area.

The partition of India in 1947 and, to a lesser degree, that of Cyprus in 1974 had major repercussions for the migration of Muslims to Britain. Many of those who had to move from Indian Punjab—Julludhar, Ludhiana and Hoshiarpur—to Pakistan felt that migrating to Britain was probably one of the more desirable ways of recouping their losses. Similarly Bengali Muslim peasants, who had moved from Sylhet to Assam to take advantage of the more favourable land-tenure system introduced in the British period, returned to their home districts as refugees without land once Assam became a province of the new India at Partition. Those who had contacts with earlier migrants in Britain decided that the opportunities that Britain offered more than compensated for the emotional, social or financial price of migration. The significant point is that although economic considerations were important in making individuals decide to migrate, it was push factors that made them feel they had little choice but to leave their homeland.

As the independence of Cyprus approached in 1960, Turkish Cypriots felt a somewhat similar vulnerability to that of Muslims living as a minority in India at the time of Partition. They too had cause for concern about their future and many were forced to think of the possibility of migration. Under British rule in Cyprus the privileges and influence the Ottomans had bestowed on the ethnically Turkish population of Cyprus had gradually been eroded. Social systems were redefined and reinterpreted in such a way as to magnify the differences between the two communities, as well as shifting the balance of power in favour of the majority Greek Cypriots. A policy of compulsory education also helped the much more urban Greek Cypriot communities, and Islamic family law came under increasing pressure from the colonial authorities' secularising policies.[10] The economic gap between the two communities widened, with Greek Cypriots increasingly taking control of the country's major institutions. Distrust between them reached such a point that the EOKA insurgency against the British from the mid-1950s, led by the Greek General Grivas, was perceived by Turkish Cypriots—correctly—as an attempt to establish Greek Cypriot hegemony on the island with the ultimate aim of achieving Enosis—union with Greece. This was anathema to them and they opposed it vehemently, strongly asserting their Muslim and Turkish identities. The two communities became progressively polarised, as was reflected in the drop in the proportion of mixed urban centres. While in 1881, 346 of the 702 population centres were mixed, by 1970 their number had fallen to only 46 out of 602.[11] Thus social and economic mingling became minimal. After independence the political temperature rose further and violent clashes took place between Greek and Turkish Cypriots after President Makarios tried to change the constitutionally agreed power-sharing arrangements between the two communities in November 1963. Many from both sides of the divide felt vulnerable as minorities in mixed villages, and took refuge within their own communities. Some of them, with relatives already established in Britain, could secure patronage and job-sponsorship there and those who could afford to travel decided to make the journey in search of a more stable and secure existence. These groups, together with the more economically motivated migrants, continued to arrive till the mid-1960s—the fear of immigration controls accelerating the inflow dramatically between 1960 and 1962. So while Britain's prewar Turkish Cypriot population laid the basis for the pattern of migration, most of the expansion and consolidation of Turkish Cypriot communities took place between the late 1940s and the mid-1960s, except for an influx of about 3,000—resulting from the partition of Cyprus in 1974. By 1958 it was estimated that as a result of developments in Cyprus there were 8,500 Turkish Cypriots in Britain.[12]

Thus the South Asian and Cypriot Muslims who moved to Britain during this period had many similar motives for migrating. In both cases few were driven to leave by poverty alone. Many members of both communities migrated with the aim of profiting from opportunities in Britain and accumulating enough savings to return home with enhanced status, to retire in dignity and in comfort. For a significant number this 'home orientation' or 'myth of return' was an enduring aspiration, but for others it was neither the sole nor even the most important objective. Some wanted access to better education for their children, and a few had political and personal motives—to live in a more stimulating 'modern' environment, to strive for self-improvement, and to break away from communal and family obligations.

Turkish Cypriot migration also resembled the chain process prevalent among Muslims from the Indian subcontinent. They too made use of kin networks and contacts to locate or create opportunities, building a social context within which migration and settlement could materialise.[13] However, it was different in one significant way, in that the phase of males arriving first and then being joined by their families was telescoped for many Cypriots into a period of just a few months, in contrast to several years as for the majority of South Asian Muslims. Their experience was therefore analogous to that of East African Asians obliged to leave Kenya and Uganda in the late 1960s and early 1970s who found that they too had to telescope all the stages of chain migration into a short time-span due to factors beyond their control. Moreover, for most Turkish Cypriots, unlike the majority of South

Asian Muslims, leaving family and village was not a collective decision to support relatives by remittance and invest resources in improvements back home but essentially a matter of individual choice. Differences such as these had implications for the way South Asian and Cypriot Muslims were to engage with British society.

Data examined by Robinson suggest that unemployment in Britain significantly reduced Indian and Pakistani migration but that the demand for labour was by no means the only factor influencing net migration flow.[14] Migration from Bangladesh increased in the 1970s and 1980s when it was declining from other South Asian countries. The general material conditions in Bangladesh as well as the needs and circumstances of the potential migrants (e.g. an improved quality of life, better education for children, substantial social security, housing and health provisions) were perhaps equally relevant. For the rest of the decade after gaining independence in 1971, Bangladesh went through political instability and considerable economic turmoil, and these pressures combined with natural disasters such as floods and cyclones to create immense hardship for the rural population. Hence those who could manage it felt that their families had a better chance of survival, even living in run-down tenements and squalid 'bed and breakfasts' accommodation in Britain than by remaining in Bangladesh. After weighing up the costs and benefits of their decision against the possible attendant hardships, many Bangladeshis moved to Britain even when the prospects for employment were extremely poor. Without jobs they were even less able to support families back home in Bangladesh or afford to make periodic trips there to maintain the necessary links. It has been shown that there was a perverse positive correlation between the rate of Bangladeshi migration and the overall rates of unemployment in Britain:[15] between 1980 and 1988, when unemployment in Britain was at its peak, Bangladeshis arrived in larger numbers than ever before.[16]

The case of postwar Yemeni settlers

The experience of Yemeni migrants to Britain typifies much of the experience encountered by other Muslims, even though in detail they are not identical. Following the Second World War, the ports that had flourished in the past and the shipping services on which the Yemeni sailors had relied went into terminal decline and with them Arab communities, which had been sustained by the demand for labour, aged and withered too. Yemeni seamen, tired of waiting to 'sign on', sought onshore employment. With full employment in Britain these workers were paid better wages, and with overtime and bonuses enjoyed a level of prosperity and job security rarely attained by earlier migrants. As work in the factories decreased in the 1950s, many found jobs in the service sector and some opened shops, largely to cater to the embryonic Yemeni communities in Birmingham, Sheffield and South Shields. From the early 1960s, like the mass of migrants from the British colonies and ex-colonies, they gravitated towards industrial centres where cheap and unskilled labour was scarce. In Liverpool a distinct Yemeni community had emerged by the mid-1970s, at first no more than about 100 and only tenuously connected with the slowly disappearing seafaring settlements of the past, but its size grew as out-of-work Yemenis arrived in a steady stream from the stagnating ports of Cardiff, South Shields, Hull, Glasgow and East London and from 'de-industrialising' towns. By 1992, in sharp contrast to the Arab communities of other prewar maritime centres—Cardiff and South Shields—Liverpool's Yemeni community flourished, and with about 3,500 members was perhaps the largest such settlement in Britain.[17]

Other settlements of Yemeni migrants developed during this period, as in Sheffield where they worked for British Steel. From the employers' point of view, donkey-men used to stoking ships' steam engines were eminently suitable for the job of firing steel furnaces. This Yemeni Sheffield community had grown by the late 1970s to 2,000, but with steel manufacture devastated by the recession of the early 1980s, most were made redundant and some returned to Yemen.[18] Meanwhile others coming directly from Yemen had linked up with groups of earlier migrants. These particular Yemenis, mainly from a peasant background with a small number belonging to the religious élite, went to Birmingham, Brighouse and Scunthorpe, where they found work in engineering and metal-working factories. In the early 1960s there were estimated to be about 12,000 Yemenis in Britain: by the mid-1970s there were around 2,000 of the first generation in Birmingham alone, the vast majority in unskilled and semi-skilled manual labour, although a few with skills and professional qualifications were able to move into white-collar work.[19]

However, 'home orientation' was more evident among Yemenis than among South Asian Muslims and chain migration was only tenuous, partly due to the absence of women in the migratory process. In the pre-Second World War migration those Yemeni seamen who had settled in British ports frequently married local women, producing future generations of mixed Yemeni and English or Welsh background. In the post-1945 period, although a much smaller proportion of Yemeni migrants married locally, only a few brought their families over (in contrast to the South Asians especially). Consequently, a large number of Yemenis continued to live in Britain as transient residents, at least mentally locked into Yemeni society. For many of them the idea of a return to Yemen was not just a myth, and periodic trips home remained very much a part of their calendar. However, the experience of Yemeni migrants showed the crucial role of the demand for labour in Britain in attracting peasants, not necessarily suffering serious deprivation, from places with imperial connections to Britain. The decline of the older maritime Yemeni communities demonstrated the power of economic demand as the engine of labour migration, and at the same time as the determinant of its character and direction. It is highly unlikely that chain migration, the key mechanism activating movement from many parts of the Muslim world after 1945, would have acquired the mass proportions that it did if the hopeful postwar economic context in Britain had not emerged to attract migrants to its shores.

Government intervention and immigration controls

Migratory movements, as we have seen, arose from the existence of prior links between sending and receiving societies based on colonisation, political influence, trade, investment and cultural ties. But in certain ways non-economic and political forces, especially government policies in the sending societies as well as in Britain, had just as great an impact on the pattern of migration as the periodic rise and fall in the demand for labour. From 1962 these forces influenced immigration into Britain more strongly, and from the late 1970s it was government policy, together with largely non-economic factors and political crises, that shaped the patterns of migration to Britain. Government policies, both in Britain and in the migrants' countries of origin, reflecting public opinion on migration issues, played an important part in these patterns. While the flow of migration in the 1950s from the Indian subcontinent was modest in absolute numbers as well as compared with that from the West Indies and Cyprus,[20] racial tension had started to cause the British government considerable anxiety. Consequently, Indian and Pakistani governments, responding to pressure from the British authorities over the increasing rate of migration from the subcontinent, applied 'voluntary' restrictions on emigration by introducing controls on the issuing of passports, medical checks, language tests and financial guarantees. These measures led to massive forging of passports and other irregularities, and failed to stem the flow significantly. Indeed, once the Indian and Pakistani governments found themselves unable to deal effectively with their own worsening economic conditions and correspondingly high levels of unemployment and tensions, they relaxed restrictions on travel abroad to alleviate their own mounting problems.[21] However, Cypriot immigration remained subject to tight local administrative controls, right through to the beginning of the 1960s; financial guarantees, language tests and affidavits of support were all standard requirements. The stringency and effectiveness of these conditions of immigration were shown when the affidavit system was abolished in 1959 and an immediate influx of 25,000 Cypriots took place in 1960–1.[22] The numbers then quickly declined under the impact of the voucher system. None of these fluctuations, however, was determined by the state of the economy in Britain.[23]

Under these circumstances the announcement in 1961 of the forthcoming Commonwealth Immigrants Act triggered an enormous rush to 'beat the ban'. The rate of immigration from India, Pakistan and Cyprus rose sharply and at first had the opposite effect to that intended by the legislation.[24] By removing the right to come and go freely, the 1962 Act transformed what had in the past been temporary movements from the New Commonwealth into the permanent settlement of migrants and their families, and in the process did away with the relatively flexible reserve of labour hitherto available. Also, it disrupted the link between the supply of and demand for migrant labour and the self-regulating patterns of migration—single men periodically replaced by relatives and others—which had traditionally maintained a fairly stable balance between the rates of in- and out-migration. The inflow of families and dependants now began substantially to outpace the number of primary migrants and shifted the balance from the economically active to the economically inactive, which in turn exacerbated the very problems which the Act had been brought in to resolve. The objective of return receded; remittances that had previously supported family members in sending countries were gradually reduced as they were increasingly needed to meet the needs of those who had joined their menfolk in Britain. Connections with home villages weakened as immediate settlement became the norm.

However, the employment-voucher system, a central feature of this legislation that was designed to limit and regulate labour migration in tune with the needs of the market, continued to allow entry to people recruited to specific jobs in services such as catering, transport and health, skilled and white-collar professional occupations such as medicine and those too with no definite employment prospects or specific skills and qualifications. Since Bengalis had already established a toe-hold in the growing 'ethnic' catering trade, category 'A' vouchers were used by them to import Sylheti labour for a variety of tasks in Bengali restaurants. As for category 'C' vouchers, while the unskilled and those without any training or qualifications were eligible to apply, preference was given to those who had worked with the armed services in the Second World War or later. As a result, over 40,000 holders of vouchers in this category from India and Pakistan entered Britain between 1962 and 1967, many of them Muslims. The overall effect of this system also reinforced the established patterns of migration from exactly those areas where people already knew of the opportunities in Britain and had some experience of the benefits of working abroad.

The 1970s onwards

From the 1970s a different kind of migration phenomenon gathered momentum. Large numbers of people from the so-called Third World began to arrive as a result of involuntary or coerced migration. At first these inflows received little attention, partly because the numbers were small and partly because providing a haven for refugees had been viewed in Britain as a proud tradition stretching back centuries.[25] But the number of refugees grew rapidly from the mid-1970s responding to crises produced by ethno-religious and communal conflict, famines and natural disasters, and oppression by various political regimes. Certainly the demarcation between 'economic migrants' and 'refugees' has often been blurred; the choices facing a displaced peasant and his family on the one hand, and a political or religious dissident on the other, may not be very different in their consequences. In both cases the options available are limited and relatively unpalatable, involving loss of control over one's life. Between rational, well-informed decisions calculated to maximise personal advantage and panic reactions to a crisis or an intolerable threat there are innumerable alternatives to which individuals and groups respond, and Muslims have been no different from other people in these positions. Often as economic migrants they have been affected as much by political repression as by diminishing material opportunities and deprivation; for instance Muslim refugees from Somalia in the 1980s and 1990s can be seen as attempting to escape clan warfare as well as the massive economic dislocation that resulted.

However, personal factors such as individual resources and knowledge of the options—such as those available to middle-class professionals with high qualifications and skills from countries such as Afghanistan, Iran, Somalia and Iraq—helped to determine the decision to move, its timing and the choice of destination. The needs that many of these migrants have striven to satisfy went beyond the basic need for physical survival. Lack of material and intellectual fulfilment and a sense of alienation from the operations of the newly-emerging society were often more important in prompting these Muslims to migrate. Indeed, since the Second World War, socially and politically determined needs have brought a stream of Muslims from countries in Africa and Asia to Britain. After the creation of Israel in 1948 some Palestinians who had previously worked for the British were given citizenship so that they could move to Britain if they felt unable to live under Israeli rule, and many exercised this option. Similarly, East African Asians with British passports, nearly a quarter of whom were estimated to be Muslims, felt compelled to leave as a result of pressure from some of the governments of newly-independent East African states, and as a result began arriving in Britain from the mid-1960s. The Lebanese, well established in professions, commerce and the media since the 1970s, similarly chose 'exile' in Britain, not just because of the violent breakdown of civic life in Beirut but because they saw a realistic chance turning their skills and resources to advantage. The largest Arab community in Britain by the 1970s consisted of Egyptians; they had arrived in significant numbers since the 1950s, and by 1991 were estimated to number between 23,000 and 90,000.[26] In contrast to some of the other Arab migrant communities, it represented a wide social cross-section, and included both the skilled—doctors, teachers and academics—and the semi-skilled, and former students who had decided to stay on in Britain after qualifying.

By the 1970s Arabs coming to Britain not only increased substantially, but also seemed to come from more diverse national and class backgrounds. Writers, poets and journalists, living in exile after having escaped the censorship in much of the Arab world and challenging it from a safe haven such as London, proceeded to form an important part of a culturally variegated and intellectually polymorphic community. For most Arabs, therefore, movements away from their homes since the 1970s were mainly caused by a series of political conflicts, although it would be difficult in most cases to separate political from economic determinants. Nevertheless, it was a feeling of political or religious persecution that compelled many of them to migrate—Iraqis, Algerians, Somalis, Turkish Kurds, Libyans, Egyptians, Palestinians and Iranians. Only for a minority were economic pull factors, such as investment opportunities and the demand for professionals and technical experts, or the political pull of individual and political freedoms, strong enough incentives on their own. Among the refugees of Middle Eastern origin who found sanctuary in Britain from the late 1970s were some 20,000 from Iran, including supporters of the Shah who were out of favour with the new regime, and moderate as well as revolutionary Muslims opposed to the clerical political system brought into existence by the 1979 Iranian revolution. Kurds suffering abuses to their human rights in Iran, as well as in Iraq and Turkey, also entered Britain during the 1980s and 1990s.

In the late 1980s and early 1990s, with the global economic crisis deepening, postcolonial states struggled to establish social and political authority and many began to disintegrate under the weight of their own ethnic contradictions. Unable to cobble together consensus on core social and political issues and fearful of losing control, some of them embarked on violent suppression, denying basic protection and liberties to dissenters. Consequently, the number of asylum-seekers from countries where Muslims have lived for centuries, like Somalia, Eritrea, Afghanistan, Kurdistan, Algeria, Iran and Bosnia, rapidly increased. Thus one state from which a large number of Muslims have arrived is Somalia. From the mid-1980s over 15,000 Somalis arrived as refugees, most from the north and east of Somalia resulting from the civil war and famine. Britain was seen as an appropriate destination because of the colonial links and the well-established Somali communities there which might provide social and material support. This second wave of Somalis, particularly from the Darood and Issaq clans, represented the hub of the main opposition movement in Somalia and their fear of persecution by the Siad Barre regime caused them to seek asylum in Britain. Many were from urban, relatively prosperous and professional backgrounds. As civil strife intensified after 1988, the flow of refugees increased, and the overthrow of the Barre regime in 1991 did not stop the internecine violence, and the stream of Somali refugees continued through the 1990s.

In many of these cases, therefore, it was neither purely sociopolitical nor economic circumstances alone that drove Muslims to migrate, but usually a combination of factors some of which proved to be 'the last straw'. Few of them could be categorised as refugees according to the United Nations Convention definition, but nor were they pure 'economic migrants'. Since the Second World War, Iraq has had a longer history of driving out its citizens for political dissent than most other Middle Eastern states. First the monarchist regime banned all political parties, which led to a small number of political migrants, including liberal and radical intellectuals who had become dissatisfied with that regime and opted for exile in Britain in the late 1940s and 1950s. When the monarchy was overthrown in 1958 many of its supporters and associates—officials, diplomats, army top brass, civil servants and especially wealthy landowners—fled in fear of political and economic reprisals as well as social exclusion. Most had already established good connections with Britain through the British control of Iraq after the First World War, and having transferred their capital to Britain were able to settle in relative comfort. Many professionals and merchants, some of whom had already experienced life in Britain either as students or on business trips, also left Iraq unable to tolerate restrictions on their freedom to hold and express dissenting views. A distinct Iraqi presence took shape in Britain in the 1960s as political freedoms were further curtailed by the new Iraqi authorities. In the 1970s and 1980s an intensification of political and religious repression led to a bigger inflow of refugees, in particular Kurds, whose cultural and ethnic identity was being brutally suppressed. When the Iran–Iraq war broke out in the 1980s, thousands of Shia Muslims were deported to Iran, and some travelled on and sought asylum in Britain. These refugees included merchants stripped of their assets, professionals who had lost their jobs for allegedly siding with the enemy, and displaced unskilled and semi-skilled workers. Madawi Al-Rasheed has stated that by the early 1990s 'an estimate of the Iraqi community cannot exceed 70–80,000, fifty per cent of which were believed to be resident in London'.[27] The majority of those living in London belonged to the middle classes—professionals such as doctors, teachers, engineers, journalists, writers and artists, also self-employed merchants and business people. The majority were not strictly asylum-seekers or refugees according to the UN Convention definition, since they had not arrived in Britain explicitly claiming that status; most continued to hold Iraqi passports and did not seek employment for extended periods, surviving on their savings. They often entered Britain as visitors or students and then gradually won the right to 'permanent stay' on the grounds of potential persecution due to their vocal opposition to the Iraqi regime. Others who had been more passive and left Iraq because of their dissatisfaction with the social and political climate also came within this category: they were not individually under immediate threat of persecution or torture, but given the Saddam Hussain regime's all-pervading control and surveillance over its citizens, the possibility of severe punishment for those seen to transgress was indeed real. The 9,000 or so Iraqis who came to Britain in the 1990s thus seemed to fall much more clearly into the category of political refugees. The majority were Kurds, although some Marsh Arabs also escaped the religious and political persecution after the

Gulf War in 1991. Similarly, of the 15,000 people from Turkey who arrived in Britain in the 1980s and 1990s, 95% were Kurds fleeing human-rights violations, including detention and torture, which they had suffered increasingly since 1978 at the hands of the Turkish army. They were later joined by Alavis, a minority Muslim religious sect with unorthodox practices, who were under increasing pressure to abandon their homes in Turkey for exile abroad.

Similar to the fate of these groups of refugees was that of many thousands of Muslims who were 'victims of generalised violence' rather than necessarily having experienced direct persecution themselves. About 3,000 Afghans came to Britain from the early 1970s, finding the conditions of life in Afghanistan too insecure, and while some left in fear of sanctions after the 1973 coup, the majority fled the 1979 Russian invasion and the prolonged civil war that followed it. They no doubt chose Britain as a place of refuge because of the West's support for the resistance movement against the Russians, although they could not be described as supporters of the dominant Islamist factions that became locked in the power struggles of the 1990s. Many of these Afghan refugees were of liberal political persuasion or belonged to more moderate tendencies within Islam, perhaps fearing the Islamist groups as much as the Russians. Likewise Eritreans, mostly located in central London, and several thousand Muslims from Ethiopia went to Britain to escape political repression associated with the military dictatorship, the ensuing civil war and periodic droughts and famines. Since the possession of financial resources was a prerequisite of migration—to pay for the passage and other needs—most refugees of this kind belonged to the middle-class, and were from relatively prosperous, professional or merchant, and well-educated urban backgrounds. The case of Algerian Islamic 'fundamentalists' in the early 1990s could perhaps be viewed as a more severe example of violent state repression, and leaving the country was the only way for opponents to escape incarceration and death. Indeed, many left Algeria owing to a well-founded fear of persecution for their religious activism and political dissidence. They were targeted for mobilising mass popular support in favour of an Islamist programme and in opposition to the existing secular regime, which was trying to impose its own brand of social and political unity on the country. The irony was that the Algerian and

Egyptian Islamists (as did Iran's Ayatallah Khomeini) took refuge in precisely those European countries such as Britain whose values and 'godless' systems they utterly and sometimes violently opposed.

Migration by Muslims since the Second World War helped to produce the heterogeneous mix of communities in contemporary Britain. While the detail varied from case to case, they were mainly influenced in their decision to migrate by similar combinations of factors: push factors encouraging them to leave their original homes, and pull factors drawing them to the various opportunities on offer in Britain; processes of chain migration that facilitated their arrival; and the presence of pioneers whose experience encouraged them to accept the same challenge themselves. At first it tended to be young single males who came in search of opportunities and employment. They remained transient workers, shuttling between their countries of origin and Britain, maintaining social and cultural continuity and struggling not to expose their families to an alien environment, until British immigration legislation forced them to opt for permanent settlement and bring over their families. Thus with the exception of Turkish Cypriots, for whom the period between the arrival of migrants and reunion with their families was relatively short, mostly women, children and other dependants arrived over a more extended period. However, where ideological factors came into play whole families have eventually moved—this was the case with Afghan refugees after the Russian invasion—although individual Muslim refugees have often sought sanctuary in Britain.

These patterns of migration to Britain since 1945 suggest that the changing material circumstances of Muslim peoples from a variety of social and cultural environments have influenced their decisions to move much more than any particular aspect of their religious identity or life. Of course this may have been partly due to the way people and groups arrive at their choices, which are neither wholly rational nor completely determined by their own situations. In this sense Muslims migrating to Britain since the Second World War have behaved no differently from any other groups of migrants, although how they viewed themselves as communities had implications for their subsequent engagement with British society. Kalim Siddiqi, looking back in the late 1980s, regarded Muslim migration as a socio-economic and cultural consequence of imperialist devastation.[28]

7

CONTOURS OF MUSLIM LIFE IN BRITAIN SINCE 1945

Britain's Muslim population has undergone massive changes since the Second World War. As a result of migration patterns a patchwork of communities emerged in England and to a smaller extent, in Scotland, Wales and Northern Ireland. As we saw in Chapter 6, the immigrants have come from all over the Muslim world and represent a microcosm of its global variety. And behind some appearance of religious homogeneity, they have distributed themselves into ethnically distinct communities upholding a broad range of sectarian allegiances.

Given the complex character of these communities, one might ask to what degree Islam has influenced the configuration of the British Muslim population and how significant religion has been in the rapidly changing realities it has experienced since 1945. Religion has had little to do with shaping their material circumstances beyond the prejudice they may have encountered as Muslims. Instead the changing material circumstances of British Muslims have been shaped much more by interactions with the wider society and the options available to them regarding their place in British society. This chapter maps the contours of Britain's Muslim population that have evolved since the Second World War. It analyses the facts of life of British Muslim communities in the second half of the twentieth century, and argues that these have largely been determined by socio-economic factors. In more recent years Muslim refugees and asylum-seekers, compelled to leave their

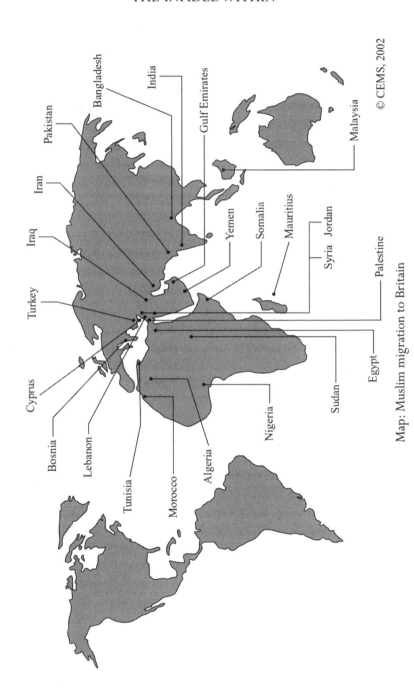

Map: Muslim migration to Britain

© CEMS, 2002

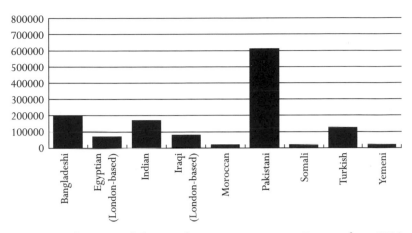

Countries of origin of the Muslim communities in Britain, late 1990s (estimated)

homelands for political and non-economic reasons, have been consciously consigned to particular parts of Britain as government policy has responded to 'public opinion' and broader political imperatives. However, the settlement patterns of most Muslim migrants were influenced above all by their need for suitable work and cheap housing. Religion, initially at least, appears to have played little part in their decisions either to migrate or to settle, and there is little evidence that it influenced the way they organised their lives in Britain.

The size of the British Muslim population

The size and composition of the British Muslim population have been debated ever since Muslims first made their presence felt, and especially from the early 1970s. No reliable nation-wide statistics exist for religious affiliation, although a religious question was included for the first time in the 2001 census. Before the 1991 census estimates drew on relatively large surveys (the PSI data and the Labour Force Surveys), which based their conclusions on inferences drawn from other available, seemingly helpful information such as ethnic origin or country of birth. For South Asians the extrapolation from ethnic origin to religion was relatively straightforward since almost all Pakistanis and Bangladeshis were Muslims. This was difficult in the case of Muslims from, say, India, Cyprus and Malaysia since the populations of these countries are not overwhelmingly Muslim. To these one could add Turkish refugees and asylum-seekers from mainland Turkey (Turkish Cypriots are deemed to be ethnic Turks); according to the 1991 census the Turkish-born population of Britain was 26,597, almost all Muslim.[1] This figure was probably an underestimate since it did not take account of those born in Britain. Furthermore, there was uncertainty over 15,000 Turkish Kurds who arrived after 1980 as asylum-seekers, since few of them were granted refugee status, especially after the Immigration and Asylum Act was introduced in 1993. Many were either detained or deported. While some found casual work around London, where they are concentrated, almost 90% were unemployed. There remains no consensus on the size of Britain's 'Turkish' population: Kucukcan estimated it in 1996 at 'around 125,000'.[2]

The overall size of the heterogeneous Arab population in Britain, besides that of each 'ethnic' group within it, is even more subject to speculation. The uncertainty about the size of the Arab/Middle Eastern Muslim community in Britain is related to questions about whether they can be properly defined as 'settled' or whether they remain 'transient'. Lewis differentiated between Middle Eastern Muslim *residents*—political refugees, entrepreneurs and those motivated by personal, domestic and recreational considerations—and those who 'form genuine communities' (as defined by Halliday). The latter will have worked as opposed to merely residing in Britain, and remained in contact with each other as fellow-emigrants from a particular country through residence in a particular urban area. They will also work in a similar branch of economic activity and have created some kind of communal organisation.[3] In Lewis's view, 'according to such criteria the large number of Arabs who have congregated in and around London are residents rather than part of cohesive communities. Their main country of residence and work remains the Middle East. The exceptions are communities of Egyptians [doctors, teachers and academics], Iraqis, Moroccans [hotel and catering staff], Palestinians [business people] and Yemenis [workers in manufacturing industries]', who have settled in Britain and work in services and professions as well as manufacturing industry.[4] Consequently there are many different estimates, based on a variety of empirical data. In 1992

Nielsen, using the 1981 census data, arrived at figures of 50,000 Arabs and 20,000 Iranians out of a total of 690,000 Muslims in Britain. He also quoted a 'private survey conducted in 1986', which advanced the figure for Iranians to 50,000 and for all Muslims to 936,000.[5] The 1981 census put the number of Arab-born residents in England at 76,563, with over 30,000 concentrated in London. These figures were inferred from 'the birthplace of the head of the household' data, and fell far short of the claims of the Arab–British Chamber of Commerce, or the 500,000 quoted in *The Economist* at the end of the 1980s— embracing, among the main Arab communities, 50,000 Moroccans, 'somewhere between 90,000 and 120,000' Egyptians, 100,000 Iraqis and 20,000 Palestinians.[6] Halliday in the early 1990s estimated that perhaps 15,000 Yemenis were living in settled communities in Britain.[7] El-Solh stated that Moroccan and Somali claims of over 15,000 for their communities and Egyptian and Iraqi estimates of 60,000 and 70,000, respectively, in London alone were realistic. Similarly, thousands of Iranians also arrived as economic and political migrants from the late 1970s, as did significant numbers of Jordanians, Lebanese, Palestinians, Sudanese, Syrians, Tunisians, Algerians, Mauritanians and nationals of the Gulf Emirates. Weighing up all the official evidence in combination with data from the other available sources, El-Solh concluded 'that by the end of the 1980s Arabs settled in Britain might well have numbered around 250,000.'[8] Later Al-Rasheed, analysing the 1991 census data, arrived at a similar figure.[9]

The Muslim population of Indian and Turkish Cypriot origin should be added to the above estimates. The 1982 PSI survey suggested that Muslims formed 16% of the Indian population in Britain or, on the basis of the 1991 data, 134,000 people. In the 1990s researchers such as Anwar and Peach evaluated the latest surveys available to establish more accurate estimates of Britain's Muslim population. Peach's estimate of approximately 1,000,000 in the early 1990s relied on 1991 census data and drew somewhat conservative conclusions from it. Anwar, making not unreasonable assumptions also largely from the 1991 census, suggested 1,500,000.[10] More recent surveys have suggested a considerable increase in the Muslim population of Britain by the end of the 1990s. The Pakistani/Bangladeshi population alone had grown by 36% from 640,000 in 1991 to around 1,000,000.[11] Hence it is reasonable to suggest that since Anwar and Peach made their calculations, the number of Muslims in Britain has risen nearer to 2,000,000.[12]

While the vast majority live in England, there are also sizeable communities in other parts of the British Isles. In Scotland the 1991 census estimated its total ethnic minority population at 62,000, of whom just over 21,000 were Pakistani, over 10,000 Indian and over 1,000 Bangladeshi. A survey by the Scottish Office revealed that 61% of Scotland's ethnic minority population, or about 38,000, were Muslim at the time of the 1991 census.[13] To this figure could be added the diverse Muslim population of Wales, which the *Guardian* estimated at around 50,000 in 2002, and Northern Ireland, which had apparently increased from the 1991 figure of 952, the vast majority of whom seemed to be of South Asian, particularly Pakistani, origin, to around 4,000.[14]

Geographical distribution

Migrant Muslims to Britain have shown strong tendencies to form communities along ethnic lines, which have become concentrated in different parts of the British Isles. The 1991 census shows that while more than half of the Bangladeshis lived in Greater London (53%), nearly half (43%) of these were resident in just one borough, Tower Hamlets (23% of the total Bangladeshi population of Britain). Their level of segregation is extremely high.[15] Given that they arrived relatively recently, have younger and larger extended families, and find themselves in poorer economic circumstances, their quick dispersal into the broader community appears unlikely. While Pakistanis are also substantially segregated in communities across the United Kingdom, a relatively smaller proportion live in London (18.4%).[16] Nevertheless, much bigger concentrations of Pakistanis have emerged in the industrial West Midlands, the 'mill towns' of Lancashire, Greater Manchester and West Yorkshire. In the south-east of England, Pakistanis are mainly located in north-east and west London, Slough, Buckinghamshire and Oxford. They also form sizeable communities in Lanarkshire and some other Scottish urban centres such as Glasgow, Edinburgh and Dundee; most of the Muslim population of Scotland is settled in the Strathclyde region, followed by Lothian, Tayside, Grampian, Fife and the central region. The majority of the Muslim population of Scotland are Pakistanis, with small numbers

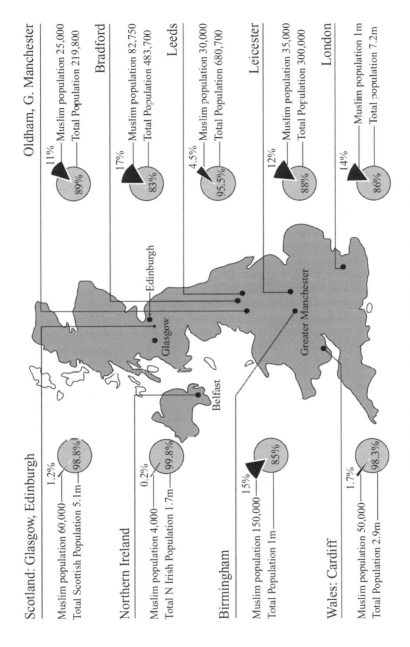

Oldham, G. Manchester
11% — Muslim population 25,000
89% — Total Population 219,800

Bradford
17% — Muslim population 82,750
83% — Total Population 483,700

Leeds
4.5% — Muslim population 30,000
95.5% — Total Population 680,700

Leicester
12% — Muslim population 35,000
88% — Total Population 300,000

London
14% — Muslim population 1m
86% — Total population 7.2m

Scotland: Glasgow, Edinburgh
1.2% — Muslim population 60,000
98.8% — Total Scottish Population 5.1m

Northern Ireland
0.2% — Muslim population 4,000
99.8% — Total N Irish Population 1.7m

Birmingham
15% — Muslim population 150,000
85% — Total Population 1m

Wales: Cardiff
1.7% — Muslim population 50,000
98.3% — Total Population 2.9m

Edinburgh
Glasgow
Greater Manchester
Belfast

Map: Muslim population in Britain by regions and cities

of Arabs, Turks and Iranians in the larger cities and Dundee, as well as in Newport and Cardiff in South Wales.[17]

Turkish Cypriots have tended to be even more spatially concentrated. Just a few boroughs of London contain around 90% of their total population in Britain. While the pre-war immigrants lived in lodging-houses in London's West End near the hotels and restaurants where they worked, costs have become increasingly prohibitive, particularly after the arrival of families, and there has been a movement to the cheaper parts of the outer London boroughs where financial circumstances have permitted such an undertaking. They are evenly distributed north and south of the River Thames—Enfield, Haringey, Barnet, Islington, Hackney, Southwark, Lewisham, Waltham Forest, the City of Westminster and Kensington and Chelsea. Oakley noted that Camden Town was called 'Little Cyprus'. A number of small Turkish Cypriot communities have also been established in the Home Counties and at Luton, Birmingham, Liverpool, Manchester, Newcastle, Nottingham, Derby, Southend-on-Sea and Brighton, amounting to about 5,000 in all.[18]

Between 1981 and 1991 urban concentrations of Muslims seem to have become even stronger. However, while largely concentrated in particular areas, Muslims do not form the majority of the population there. Only 20% of Pakistanis and Bangladeshis live in wards where the majority of residents are from ethnic minorities. The inner metropolitan areas seemed to have the highest concentrations of Muslim residents and in some inner London wards the average proportion of Pakistanis and Bangladeshis was over 40%. The most marked concentration of all has occurred in metropolitan areas outside London. The Fourth PSI Survey disclosed that in other inner metropolitan areas— Birmingham, Manchester, Sheffield, Leeds, Liverpool, Newcastle— the proportion of Pakistani (15%) and Bangladeshi (13%) respondents was quite high. It was even higher for Pakistanis (36%) in the areas away from London—Tyne and Wear, Merseyside, Greater Manchester, West Yorkshire, South Yorkshire, West Midlands—and only slightly less for Bangladeshis (11%). The proportion of Pakistanis and Bangladeshis living in non-metropolitan areas is also substantial: 33% and 22% respectively.[19]

Muslims from the Middle East have in some ways similar and in others different settlement patterns in Britain. Like other Muslim ethnic groups, a substantial minority (41%) is located, in roughly equal proportions, in some of the inner and outer boroughs of London. Just over one-sixth live in south-east England, followed by the West Midlands and the northwest. However, over 25% of this group are dispersed in the remainder of the country. Unlike other Muslim ethnic groups, many of them reside in the more affluent boroughs of inner London, such as Westminster and the Borough of Kensington and Chelsea.[20] However, Middle Eastern Muslim communities of poorer migrants also live in the less prosperous boroughs of Hackney and Tower Hamlets, as do Somalis.[21] Away from London, Yemenis and Somalis were to be found in Cardiff, Birmingham, Liverpool, Sheffield and South Shields.[22] However, the concentration of these Muslims is nowhere as dense as that of some of their South Asian counterparts.

A combination of factors is usually responsible for producing these kinds of patterns of concentration and segregation. Cheap housing and availability of jobs requiring particular skills and experience initially attracted many Muslim migrants to certain areas, but as they have become more established, settlement is explained in terms of 'choice' and 'constraint'. Those who lean towards 'choice' suggest that migrants prefer to reside within their own groups for reasons of social support, and shared linguistic, cultural and religious traditions. Dahya and Robinson in their studies of South Asian Muslim populations in Bradford and Blackburn gave prominence to the 'internal' reasons, such as savings through investment in cheap housing, for their concentration in 'slums of the inner wards of British industrial cities', as against 'external' factors, such as racial discrimination or structural constraints, for the formation of immigrant Muslim areas.[23] This argument has been shown to have some validity, at least in regard to some Muslim groups. For instance, Dokur-Gryskiewicz found that 54% of her Turkish respondents in London preferred living with Turkish neighbours. The existence of social networks and institutional structures, kinship ties and patronage contributed to the attraction of such communities.[24] Proponents of the 'constraint' model, on the other hand, have argued that it is external factors, such as economic position, lack of information regarding housing opportunities and discriminatory and exclusionary practices on the part of the majority population, which have prevented minorities from moving out.

The more recent explanations suggest a more dynamic interplay between choices that individuals make and socio-economic circumstances that constrain choices. Evidence now available tends to support this explanation. Muslim migrants have preferred to live in communities of their own ethnic group so long as this does not disadvantage them in other ways. Indeed, Unsworth's study of the spatial distribution of Pakistanis in Slough in the mid-1980s found that, while there were greater concentrations of Pakistanis in the older parts of the town, housing decisions were made 'according to what was available, given the constraints of their financial position, lack of prospects, housing needs and the restricted opportunities in the local housing system, not according to priority of living amongst their own people'. As a result of these centrifugal forces, trends emerged 'both towards dispersal and towards the "in-filling" of earlier areas of settlement' as households divided.[25] Both Unsworth, using her Slough data, and Werbner, researching the Pakistani community in Manchester, have suggested that Pakistanis with more money at their disposal were likely to move out from the older, central urban areas of immigrant settlement.[26] Werbner argued that the dispersal from the Pakistani enclave in Manchester is not unique but formed part of a pattern that had emerged more generally among migrant Muslims across the whole of the country. She asserted that 'movement rather than stability' was the distinctive feature of Pakistani immigrants' settlement patterns in Manchester. When circumstances allowed, they have looked for more valuable and advantageous properties in better neighbourhoods. Successful Muslims, even in the 1970s and especially more recently, sought accommodation in superior housing to match their improved position.[27] The decision regarding the area to which they move seems to be shaped more by social and financial requirements than by religion or ethnicity. For example, successful Muslim businessmen have moved into inner suburban neighbourhoods where other businessmen live. Many former factory workers who had become largely self-employed, those involved in public services and professionals, on the other hand, lived in medium-priced houses in areas closer to their workplace. They did not have the same degree of dependency on the areas where immigrants had initially formed clusters because, having worked with white people over time, they had acquired knowledge of English and the

British ways of life, giving them the confidence and independence needed to live with neighbours in non-immigrant areas. That said, there have been some distinct features of these Muslims' dispersal. Many of them have tended to follow their relatives and friends into new areas of settlement. Others have moved close to immigrant areas with convenient access to culturally sanctioned necessities and religious facilities. As a result, new clusters formed with infrastructures and Muslim institutions appropriate to their needs. They came to resemble, albeit in a modified shape, the immigrant communities from which these Muslims had originally moved.

Thus the picture that had emerged by the 1990s of the geographical distribution of British Muslims is full of complexity and shaped largely by the material changes experienced by Muslims since the Second World War in the conditions and circumstances of their lives. Across the Pennines, from Oldham, Burnley, Accrington, Blackburn and Preston to Dewsbury, Keighley, Bradford and Leeds, a string of Pakistani and Bangladeshi communities have survived the enormous impact of socio-economic restructuring. The collapse of the cotton and woollen industries in the 1980s led to segregation of white and Muslim populations. Depressed inner-city areas, lined with old 'two-up, two-down' terraced houses built for mill-worker families, were abandoned by those white people who could afford to move out to the suburbs, but as in other cities it was not only the whites who left the inner cities; upwardly mobile or middle-class Pakistanis and Bangladeshis have shifted as well. Moreover, those whites who could not afford to buy themselves out took advantage of discriminatory council-housing policies that allocated whites to new housing estates cut off from Asian areas.[28] With whites in a rush to flee the 'ghettos', prices were kept low, further encouraging Muslims to buy cheap homes in these areas. This 'white flight', to some degree enabled by the local council, has turned many British towns and cities, into a mosaic of mutually exclusive areas.

For many in the second generation, while they are close to their families, jobs and better housing take precedence over living in areas with a concentration of their own ethnic group. Those who have acquired higher qualifications and access to opportunities in professional careers have left the areas of social stress and poverty. Only those young Muslims remain who have few or no qualifications and are unemployed largely because they are considered unfit for lawful work.[29] They continue to be greatly disadvantaged because of their residence in multiply deprived areas—precisely the ones where they are most likely to suffer from environmental and social problems such as vermin infestation, graffiti, vandalism and higher levels of personal and property crime and harassment. Such areas are the least attractive to inward investment or amenable to regeneration.

Households and housing

The 1991 census revealed that Pakistani and Bangladeshi households, compared with other ethnic groups, had quite a different configuration. They tended to be much larger (Bangladeshis 5.34, Pakistanis 4.81, Indians 3.80 and whites 2.43) and much more concentrated in the 'nuclear family' category (Bangladeshi 63.6%, Pakistanis 58.3%, Indians 49.7% and whites 21.8%).[30] Because of the ageing population and the increase in single-parent families and cohabiting couples, the nuclear family is much less prevalent in the white population than it was in the 1950s and 1960s. This might suggest that both these groups of South Asian Muslims have moved towards what used to be the 'indigenous' ideal. However, a look at the proportion of extended families in these groups reveals that traditional patterns of kinship, while becoming modified, are being eroded less rapidly.

In fact, the choice of housing for Muslims has been diverse and constrained by a range of factors. Most South Asian Muslims come from cultural traditions that place a high value on extended families, and so personal considerations have been important in their choices of where to live. Along with these factors, perhaps a more important element in their decision-making was the shape, size and cost of the housing stock. According to the 1991 census data, the vast majority of Pakistanis lived in cheap terraced houses (41.6%) which they owned (77%), with a much smaller proportion living in public housing. In contrast, only 45% of Bangladeshis were owner-occupiers,[31] and depended much more on social housing, with 43% living in council or housing association properties—50% higher than the national average.[32] However, the situation was not static. Between 1982 and 1994, according to a survey in the mid-1990s, while owner-occupation had gone up among most ethnic groups, among Pakistanis there had been little change or even a small decline. Bangladeshis, on the other hand, starting from a very low base, saw the largest increase in owner-occupation. These changes, however, did not alter the broad patterns of tenure in each ethnic group. While Pakistanis remained one of the highest owner-occupiers, Bangladeshis were at the other end of the spectrum. They not only lacked the financial resources, a prerequisite for access to better-quality housing, but suffered from institutional discrimination at the local level. For instance, in the London borough of Tower Hamlets, to which a large proportion of the Bangladeshi families migrated, the Liberal Democrat-controlled council passed legislation that excluded newly arrived families in the late 1980s and the '90s from local-authority housing on the grounds that they had made themselves 'intentionally homeless'.[33] As a consequence many of them remained trapped in decrepit and overcrowded 'bedsits' and flats or were left to fend for themselves. Pakistanis too were still concentrated in cheaper terraced poor-quality housing (41.6%) compared with the white population (28.6%).[34] Further, the census data revealed that they live in relatively overcrowded conditions,[35] and in this Pakistanis and Bangladeshis find themselves at the bottom of the ethnic pile.[36] For example, in the Manningham district in Bradford a report in the mid-1990s found overcrowding in 14% of households, rising to 35% where there were dependent children, compared with 4% in the district of Bradford as a whole.[37]

A smaller proportion of Muslims from the Middle East than the total population were owner-occupiers (54% as opposed to 64%). As would be expected of a recently arrived group of migrants, a much higher proportion of these Muslims, though somewhat less than the total population (21.4%), lived in publicly and cooperatively provided rented accommodation. Many businessmen and professionals viewed their stay in Britain as temporary and, being 'in exile', perhaps felt less encouragement to seek permanent accommodation. In terms of amenities (sharing baths or showers: 3% compared with 1.3%) or absence of central heating (16.7% against 18.9%), there appeared to be no noticeable difference between what these Muslims enjoyed and what was available to the white population.[38]

Differences in tenure distribution among these Muslim groups reflected to some degree their historical and socio-economic circumstances, although high owner-occupation among Pakistanis, despite their relatively low income levels, made the validity of such explanations questionable. That said, the property they owned was likely to be at the lower end of the market. Compared with Indians, Pakistanis owned poorer-quality houses, and Bangladeshis were even worse off. While Indians had come to occupy detached and semi-detached houses (55%) in a similar proportion to whites (56%), many more Pakistanis resided in terraced houses (64%) and Bangladeshis were largely flat-dwellers (37%). Both these Muslim groups were also more likely to own properties that lacked central heating, bathrooms and inside toilets—three of the measures normally used to assess the quality of housing.[39]

Demographic characteristics: age and gender distribution

The 1991 census findings underlined the fact that Britain's Muslim population, in particular its South Asian component, remains much younger than the white majority, and Bangladeshis and Pakistanis had an even younger age profile than the rest of the Muslim ethnic groups. Compared with 19% of whites, 43% and 47% of Pakistanis and Bangladeshis, respectively, were aged under sixteen years. Conversely, only 2% of Pakistanis and 1% of Bangladeshis, compared with 17% of whites, were over sixty-five. The age structure of the North African and Middle Eastern Muslim groups was similar to that of the other Muslim ethnic groups in Britain, in that they also presented a much younger profile than the 'indigenous' population.[40]

Natural population growth (births minus deaths) among South Asian Muslims, especially Bangladeshis and Pakistanis, was higher than among other Muslim ethnic groups (which had more net migration). Bangladeshis were one of the fastest-growing groups in Britain.[41] Since the South Asian Muslim population had a much younger profile than the white population, the fertility rate, while declining, remained much higher than the average for the whole population. Pakistanis and Bangladeshis started their families earlier than other ethnic groups, completed them later and had more children than was now typical in Britain. Consequently they continued to produce larger families, with

33% and 42% of them, respectively, having four or more children and many having six or more.[42] There was a reduction in the average size of Pakistani households, but the average family size for Bangladeshis held steady. In the decade 1984–94, the structure of households in all ethnic groups in Britain began to change. Partly this was also because they had not been fully able to escape the traditional mindset that children—especially males—are a potential asset to the family. As migration slowed, the proportion of the British-born Muslim population increased rapidly. According to the 1994 Fourth PSI Survey, 52% of Pakistanis and 44% of the Bangladeshis were born in Britain; thus the substantial proportion of South Asian Muslims of working age born abroad was evened out by the overwhelming majority of the children born in Britain.[43]

By 1991 the gender imbalance within the Pakistani population had virtually disappeared.[44] On the other hand, the distribution across the age spectrum remained sharply skewed but generally in line with what would be expected among those who have migrated relatively recently and possess a high fertility rate. The proportion of the South Asian Muslim population in the youngest age-groups was much larger than average. In Bradford, where Muslims formed approximately 15% of the total population, it was estimated that by the year 2000 they would form 50% of the school rolls. Only a very small proportion of the Bangladeshis and Pakistanis had reached retirement age.[45]

Among the Middle Eastern Muslim groups in Britain sex distribution was much more skewed in favour of males than among, say, the Turkish Cypriots or Pakistanis, although Bangladeshis (who were still being joined by large numbers of migrants) had a ratio of males to females comparable to the relatively more recently established Muslim communities.[46] There were high variations among Muslims from various North African and other Middle Eastern Muslim countries. Algerians (65.4%), Iraqis (60.3%) and Jordanians (63.6%) had a pronounced male bias. Many of these men had arrived without their families as political migrants or refugees. While 46.5% were married, a substantial minority, around a third, had no families in Britain. The proportion with extended families was negligible.[47] On the other hand, Egyptians (53%) and Saudis (52.8%) were more family-based, and as a result their distribution seemed less unbalanced.[48]

Education, qualifications and skills background

As in other areas of social life, a great diversity had emerged in the education, qualifications and skills profile of British Muslims. Historical, social, economic and cultural factors have largely contributed to the differential social and economic trajectories of Britain's various Muslim communities. If we assume fluency in English to contribute towards economic advancement, then the 1974 and 1982 PSI surveys revealed that relatively few Pakistanis and Bangladeshis, coming from non- or semi-literate rural environments, spoke English well or even fairly well. By 1994, however, the proportions of Muslims with adequate competence in English had increased greatly (78% Pakistani men and 45% women; 75% Bangladeshi men and 40% women). This progression suggested that fluency in English developed over time and was strongly linked to age as well as sex. According to the 1994 survey, young men in all ethnic groups spoke English well, whereas only about half of Pakistani and a quarter of Bangladeshi women aged between twenty-five and forty-four were as competent. The lower level of language facility among older Muslim women and to some extent men suggests the combined effect of both age at the time of arrival and length of residence in Britain. Only 4% of Bangladeshi women between forty-five and sixty-five spoke English well, but 60% of those who had been in Britain for twenty-five years or more spoke it well. More recently, one factor that had affected the acquisition of fluency in English was the taking of marriage partners from South Asia—the marriage between a Muslim born in Britain and a spouse from the subcontinent. Since the home language in these 'international marriages' was likely to be an Asian one, the children of such marriages would be likely to have limited English skills before starting school. Institutional support for these children, it was reported, was inadequate.[49] The initial factors determining fluency in English by the 1990s, were age at arrival and sex rather than length of residence. Among both men and women, those who arrived in Britain after the age of twenty-five were least likely to be competent in English, regardless of their age.[50] Moreover, there was apparently a clear pattern that those who lived with more people from their ethnic group were progressively less likely to speak English fluently or fairly well.[51] While people were aware that English-language skills were an obvious necessity for taking a full part in most aspects of life in Britain, they also realised that the acquisition of language was a complex social process on which community and personal beliefs, values and practices impinge, and which required not only an effort on the part of Muslim communities but also appropriate action from the institutions of the wider society. Moreover, these were precisely the communities in which educational resources and opportunities for language acquisition were limited and where socio-economic circumstances and their associated health and housing conditions made the remedying of these deficiencies difficult.

Given that initially, because of difficulties with English, many Muslim children could not access the curriculum properly, that they were likely to come from deprived and overcrowded backgrounds and that many local education authorities (LEAs) continued to pursue discriminatory policies and practices in the allocation of schools, it was not surprising that educational achievement among British Muslims was on average lower than among other ethnic groups. The educational disadvantage experienced by these Muslim children was exacerbated by the social class to which the majority of Pakistani and Bangladeshi migrants belonged: their families were usually not well educated, and many of the more recent arrivals had little familiarity with the British educational system.

This pattern of disadvantage was rooted in the history of post-Second World War Muslim, especially South Asian, migration. Among South Asian Muslim migrants, only a few had recognised formal qualifications. Bangladeshis had the fewest, with 75% with none or below O-level, although their situation was broadly comparable with that of Pakistanis, who had 63% in the same category. Women were less likely to be qualified than their male counterparts. Of the migrant Pakistani and Bangladeshi men 15% had degrees, compared with 5% and 3% respectively, of the women. A much greater proportion of Indian (33% men and 25% women) and African Asian (50% men and 50% women) migrants, held degree-level qualifications. Compared with whites too, they were proportionally as highly qualified or more so.[52] That historical and social factors rather than cultural or religious factors were more significant was reinforced by the empirical data of successive PSI surveys from the mid-1970s, which found that while Indians and East African Asians, of whom a significant proportion were Muslims, had higher qualifications than whites, Pakistanis were less qualified (and Pakistani women were much less qualified than men). In the 1980s the Labour Force Survey data revealed that over 80% of Pakistani women aged forty-five to fifty-nine, and over 70% of Pakistani and Bangladeshi women aged twenty-five to forty-four, had no qualifications, while 57% of the former and 25% of the latter age-groups had never been to school.[53]

The situation in this respect had changed little by the 1980s, when it was reported that more than half of the Pakistanis and Bangladeshis still had no qualifications. On the other hand, 'Indian and African Asian men were half as likely again as whites to have a degree'. Again, among women there was a marked difference between those who migrated to Britain aged sixteen or over from Pakistan and Bangladesh, and African Asians. While 12% of African Asian women possessed degrees, only 1% of Pakistani and Bangladeshi women did so.[54] In contrast, the 1991 census data on the Other-Other category, to which the Arabs and Muslims from other Middle Eastern ethnic backgrounds were consigned, revealed that 'the proportion of educationally qualified in this category [was] double that of the total population' (26.0% versus 13.4%). This was also the category with a relatively small proportion of people with no qualifications (75% compared with 92% Pakistanis, 95% Bangladeshis and 85% whites), and the second highest proportion with degrees (16% compared with 6% for Pakistanis, 5% for Bangladeshis and 8% for whites). Both males and females in this category were shown to be much better qualified, especially if they were born outside Britain, than Muslims of Pakistani and Bangladeshi background.[55] Analytical data from another survey in the 1990s confirmed this finding by revealing that the proportion of those qualified who held advanced degrees was more than double that of the total population (16.6% compared with 7%), while those with first degrees and lower qualifications appear close to those for the total population. However, because these figures were expressed as percentages of those with qualifications, they were in effect twice as high as those for the total population.[56] The 1994 Fourth National Survey further confirmed these patterns, suggesting that the impact of religion on educational achievement was not necessarily significant.

Evidence from successive research data did show that differences in the educational attainment between Pakistani and Bangladeshi women and women from other ethnic backgrounds were markedly greater than those among similar categories of men. Women from these Muslim ethnic groups were much less qualified than all other women. These significantly lower levels of educational attainments, or even none at all, among a large proportion of Muslim women from rural areas of the subcontinent might have been due to cultural factors, since education was traditionally seen as far more important for men than for women.[57]

For those Pakistanis and Bangladeshis who were either born in Britain or had arrived by the age of fifteen, or were second generation in the twenty-five to forty-four age range, the situation, according to data collected in 1994, had not changed significantly when compared with the older migrant generation. The proportion without qualifications remained almost as high as for the latter group (54% Pakistanis and 70% Bangladeshis). More encouragingly, the proportion of Pakistanis in this category with higher British qualifications had risen substantially (by 50%), for women in particular; their Bangladeshi counterparts seemed to have made much less progress (with only 2% with degrees), perhaps reflecting their more recent entry into Britain as well as the poor quality of educational provision in the localities they inhabit. Indians and African Asians had taken the biggest strides, with nearly a quarter of the latter holding British degrees. Indeed African Asian women were more likely than women of any other ethnic group to possess such qualifications. The slow pace of progress among Pakistanis and Bangladeshis perhaps reflected the impact, on younger people from these ethnic backgrounds, of their parents' relative lack of competence in English, of recognisable qualifications and of familiarity with British culture. Anwar reported that his data revealed 'class differences which perhaps are producing differential success rates for Pakistani pupils'. He offered as evidence in support of his explanation the fact that 'the majority of Pakistanis belong to the working class (over 70% in manual occupations) compared with, for example, Indians (57% in manual occupations)'.[58]

As the influence of the British educational system took hold on migrants, the rate and level of educational attainment even among those from the most deprived Muslim ethnic groups rose significantly. Analysis of the 1991 census data revealed that in the sixteen to twenty-four age group, most of whom would have been born in Britain (some even with parents born in Britain), there were far fewer with qualifications below GCSE level or with no qualifications at all.[59] Still, there were twice as many from Pakistani and Bangladeshi communities in this category of low attainment as Indians and African Asians. They continued to acquire fewer degrees, and Pakistani and Bangladeshi women continued to be considerably less qualified than their male counterparts.[60]

The progress that was taking place was reflected in the highest participation rates of Muslim ethnic groups in post-compulsory education. In the 1990s the proportion of Pakistani and Bangladeshi and of white young people aged sixteen to twenty-four entering post-compulsory education was similar (54% Pakistanis/Bangladeshis compared with 56% whites), many more than for twenty- to twenty-four-years-olds. It was striking that while social class differentials might have had a considerable impact on these rates of participation, research revealed a weaker relationship between social class and staying on among South Asian Muslim communities than in the white population. While participation rates for each ethnic group were higher the further up the social class ladder they were, the rates of participation among Pakistanis and Bangladeshis were proportionally much higher (35% and 46%) than respectively among whites (20%) in the partly skilled and unskilled categories. Among whites, according to the 1991 census, many more (63%) from professional and managerial home backgrounds stayed on in post-compulsory education compared with those from partly skilled and unskilled ones (30%). For Pakistanis and Bangladeshis the comparable figures were 70% and 88% respectively, for the sixteen- to nineteen-year-olds from professional and managerial families and 55% each for those from partly skilled and unskilled backgrounds.[61] The relative length of stay in Britain of many groups of Muslim migrants, their greater motivation to do well and higher levels of youth unemployment must be taken into account as factors contributing to these higher rates of participation.

Jobs: employment patterns

When we consider the employment situation of British Muslims in the post-Second World War period, since the vast majority of these

Muslims possessed migrant origins their employment patterns in many ways replicated those of other migrants and were largely shaped by the changing economic and social imperatives in Britain. As Chapter 6 showed, post-war economic reconstruction and technological advances created a demand for labour in many sectors of industry that could not be satisfied domestically. Hence migrant Muslim workers from South Asia, Yemen and Cyprus replaced indigenous labour in a wide range of low-paid and unskilled or semi skilled manual jobs, with the result that Pakistani and Indian Muslims became concentrated in woollen and cotton textiles and heavy engineering in the north of England, Yemenis in iron and steel works in the north-east of England, and Turkish Cypriots in clothing and catering in London and the south-east of England. For a large majority of these Muslim migrants, their lack of proficiency in English and of technical skills and industrial experience kept them at the bottom of the labour market, but widespread racial discrimination also meant that their existing qualifications frequently counted for little and they were restricted to a few sectors of the economy with a severe labour shortage.

British Muslims have generally occupied a relatively poor economic position, with Pakistanis and Bangladeshis perhaps the worst off. In the early 1970s their male employment participation rates, compared with

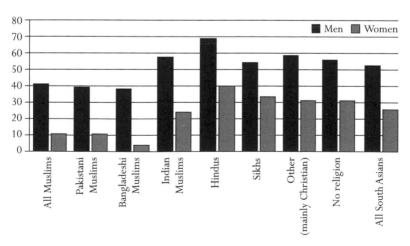

Working-age adults in fulltime work, by religion (%)

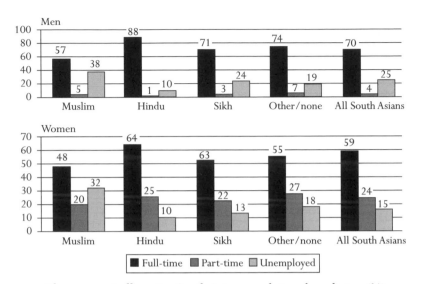

The economically active South Asian population, by religion (%).

Based on data from the 1994 National Survey of Ethnic Minorities as analysed by Mark S. Brown, 'Religion and economic activity in the South Asian population', *Ethnic and Racial Studies*, 23,6 (November 2000), p. 1045.

the white population, were high (92% for Pakistanis compared with 81% for the total population),[62] but by the end of the '80s participation rates among Pakistani and Bangladeshi men, compared with their white, Based on data from the 1994 National Survey of Ethnic Minorities as analysed by Mark S. Brown, 'Religion and economic activity in the South Asian population', *Ethnic and Racial Studies*, 23,6 (November 2000), p. 1045.

Indian and African-Asian counterparts, had dropped significantly (77% and 79% compared with 89%, 84% and 89% respectively).[63] By 1991 their rate of economic activity had declined even further (73.3%) although it was now in line with the national average (73.3%).[64] The much lower levels of participation among Pakistanis and Bangladeshis[65] were partly explained by the continually low rate of participation of South Asian Muslim women in the formal labour market—22% of Bangladeshi and 27% of the Pakistani women over sixteen were economically active compared with the national average of 50%,[66] but this seemed more a characteristic of the Pakistani and Bangladeshi populations than of, say, African Asians or Indians.[67] Modood *et al.* explained the low level of economic activity of Pakistani and Bangladeshi women as 'partly a feature of Asian Muslims' and suggested that 'the small number of Muslim women from Indian or African-Asian backgrounds were much less likely to have jobs than Hindu, Sikh, or Christian or non-religious women from India or East Africa; on the other hand, Muslim women from India (coming from relatively more urbanised backgrounds) were more likely to enter the labour market than Pakistani or Bangladeshi women. [...] The cultural norms of Pakistanis and Bangladeshis may have been a factor.'[68] These findings were further supported by the contrasting tendency among Muslim women from other ethnic groups to be as active as the majority population. Not only was a higher proportion (75.4%) of men from the Middle Eastern, predominantly Muslim, groups more economically active than white males, but the percentage of economically participating females from this group was higher than for their white counterparts (54% compared to 50%).[69] Thus socio-economic factors rather than religion seemed more relevant in these patterns.

However, patterns of employment have changed greatly since large numbers of Muslims first arrived in Britain in the 1950s and early 1960s. Then the different proportions of the major Muslim ethnic groups in various occupations reflected the differential skills each group possessed on arrival in Britain, their knowledge of English, their educational qualifications and their commitment to upward social mobility in the new context. Proportionally Indians and African Asians—groups that contained sizeable Muslim populations—were more highly educated, possessed better professional qualifications and were more commercially experienced than their Bangladeshi and Pakistani counterparts. Consequently, while some among the latter groups sought out top-category jobs like their Indian and African-Asian counterparts, realistically, in keeping with their capabilities, most tended to work lower down the labour ladder. Thus the vast majority of Pakistanis were involved in manual work (82.34%) on low earnings with long working hours.[70] The pattern changed little in the 1980s, with 70% of Pakistani men working in manufacturing industries compared to 41% of white men.[71]

The movement of Pakistanis out of the kinds of occupations which they had largely entered on arrival in Britain reflected changes brought about by the radical restructuring of the British economy and labour market from the end of the 1970s. The labour-intensive and undercapitalised manufacturing industries—textiles and heavy engineering—where they overwhelmingly worked were hit extremely hard, resulting in huge job losses among the less skilled. Consequently, towards the end of the 1980s and the beginning of the 1990s many of them had moved into jobs in the service industries, especially distribution, catering and transport.[72] Bangladeshis became even more concentrated in hotels and catering,[73] while men and women from Middle Eastern backgrounds were represented more in white-collar occupations, and correspondingly less in manual work.[74] For Pakistanis and Bangladeshis the range of occupations remained generally much narrower than for the white population. Even compared with Muslims from other ethnic groups, Pakistanis still remain over-represented in manufacturing.[75]

All of this did not amount to a radical reconfiguring of Muslim patterns of employment. The Political and Economic Planning (PEP) and PSI surveys of 1974 and 1982 showed that South Asian men held relatively poor position in the labour market. Then the Labour Force Survey (LFS) revealed that by 1990 African Asians and Indians had achieved parity with whites; that participation of Pakistani and Bangladeshi women, which were extremely low in 1982, had improved a little; and that ethnic minorities had entered the service sector faster than whites, with Bangladeshi men in services advancing from 37% in 1982 to 75% in 1989[76] and the proportions of Pakistanis and Bangladeshis doubling in the 'other non-manual' category. But the polarisation in job levels among Pakistanis and Bangladeshis continued. In the 1980s they made hardly any progress in the top category of jobs (professional, managerial and administrative). While the proportion of whites increased in this category from 19% in 1982 to 27% in 1988–90 and 30% in 1991, as had African Asians and Indians respectively, to 30% and 25% to achieve near-parity, Pakistanis and Bangladeshis barely increased their proportions from 10 to 12%. On the other hand, they were still concentrated much more in semi-skilled and unskilled manual work, with Bangladeshis, unchanged from 1982, at 70% in 1988–90, compared with 19% of whites.[77] Thus the 1991 census data revealed no radical reshaping of Muslim patterns of employment, but showed that economically active South Asian Muslim men, especially those in employment, continued to be strongly represented in the manual (73% of the Bangladeshis and 60% of the Pakistanis compared with 54% for the total male population) and distribution sectors. The majority of the Pakistanis were still in those manufacturing industries (30% in textiles, 11.5% in engineering, 10% in clothing and 16% in transport and communication), even though some of them have been decimated since the early 1980s. The proportion of Middle Eastern Muslims was much lower in the manual categories (39%), suggesting that religion was not a determinant of the level of work which Muslim men had been able to find.[78] Muslim women had established a different and more diverse employment profile from Muslim men. While a significant proportion of Pakistani women were still in clothing and footwear manufacture, they also acquired a presence in retail distribution, public administration, education and 'other services'. Large numbers of African-Asian women are in retail distribution and banking and finance. A smaller proportion of Muslim women seem to be engaged in manual work than their male counterparts (39% Bangladeshis, 41% Pakistanis and 26% Middle Eastern).[79]

At the other end of the spectrum, only 14% of Bangladeshi men were engaged in professional and managerial occupations (socio-economic classes I and II), i.e. less than half of the national average of 34% and the lowest of all the ethnic groups. Their Pakistani counterparts were better represented (26%), and the proportion of Muslim men from the Middle East in top jobs seemed even higher (45%) than that of the total population. Muslim women, strikingly, did not show such variations: 25% of Bangladeshi and Pakistani and 35% of Middle Eastern women belonged to the top two economic categories.[80]

Similarly, the 1991 census data revealed a significant movement away from industrial employment to services, technical and office work among many younger Muslims, particularly of South Asian origin. Their involvement in manufacturing had dropped to 30% among all age-groups except the oldest. Younger Pakistanis had found employment in distribution, catering and transport. Among Pakistani males, for instance, compared with the thirty- to forty-four- and forty-five- to fifty-year-olds, there were many more eighteen- to twenty-nine-year-olds in sales and services (17.2% as opposed to 9.1% and 6.7% respectively), although there was no increase in the proportion of younger professionals relative to the older groups.[81] Except for transport, younger South Asian Muslim women were even more concentrated in other services and distribution. However, the proportion of Pakistanis, but not of Bangladeshis, in each age of the above groups involved in industrial work was still much higher than for whites or even Indians.[82] On the other hand, in more prosperous categories younger Pakistanis seemed less far behind other ethnic groups. South Asian Muslims were also making headway among small-scale employers in non-professional areas such as taxi-driving and the restaurant trade.[83] Notably, there is little difference between the proportion of younger white and Pakistani women still concentrated in junior non-manual jobs, but the gap widens in semi-skilled work. Younger Pakistani women seem to be achieving relatively greater success than their Bangladeshi counterparts. Indeed they seemed better able to gain access to professional occupations even than white women of a similar age.[84] Having started out on the lowest rung of the employment ladder (as do most migrants), younger Pakistanis seemed to have achieved considerable social mobility, and were increasingly establishing patterns of class hierarchy not dissimilar to the white majority.[85]

One of the most dynamic features of employment in the restructuring of the labour market was the growth of self-employment among all ethnic groups—the number of self-employed rose by 49% between 1971 and 1992, mostly between 1980 and 1991. The proportion of self-employed among Muslims, particularly from a South Asian background, was much higher than for white and black ethnic groups (23.9% of the Pakistanis and 18.6% of the Bangladeshis in work). In the 1990s the proportion of each ethnic group in self-employment declined to some extent.[86] There was local variation, with self-employment more prevalent among Muslims in Greater Manchester than in Greater London. In the latter local variations were striking: in Brent 22.7% of the Bangladeshis were self-employed, compared with only 4.2% in Tower Hamlets[87]—differences partly owing to the origins and social and economic circumstances of each local Muslim community. Tower Hamlets is an economically deprived area, and Bangladeshis there are from low-skill, less-educated peasant backgrounds and have been confined to low-skill, low-wage jobs. Most have lacked the capacity to accumulate sufficient capital to establish their own businesses, and the 'cultural capital' to acquire relevant skills to run a business successfully, hence their low level of entrepreneurship.

The Pakistani community in the Greater Manchester area is similarly varied, with 33% of the population of Trafford self-employed as opposed to 17% in Oldham.[88] Werbner's research on Pakistanis in Manchester has shown that many migrants from Punjab who began arriving from the late 1940s tended to work for short periods in factories—long enough to repay their fares and accumulate initial capital (often a very small sum) to start trading. Thus, immediately after arriving, they entered different sectors of the clothing and garment trade in which most became market traders and later wholesalers. Some subsequently grew into the largest wholesalers and manufacturers in the city. Others became established in shopkeeping and catering. Most of these families were literate and educated up to high school and college levels, and many held university degrees. Beyond these Punjabi families, some students—Urdu- and Gujarati-speakers from Karachi—also settled in the city and made the most of their trading connections in Pakistan. Finally, there were the worker migrants, some of whom have also moved into self-employment. In the late 1950s and 1960s young bachelor men began to arrive from West Punjab—primarily from the Gujrat and Jhelum districts. They belonged to smallholder families and *biradaris*, with deep and extensive roots in their village localities. Traditionally, they came from police and army backgrounds, and were relatively well educated but with no tradition of trading. They came to Manchester to work in local factories or in public transport (buses and trains). Most remained wage earners, but some entered trading and laid the foundation for this group's entry into business in the 1980s. Although they are the most recent migrants, they appear to be the largest group numerically. However, most Pakistanis in the city were still in the food, services and fashion industries or professionals—doctors, accountants and solicitors. Other immigrant business enclaves had started to emerge in relation to property, hotels and taxi-driving.[89]

It seems that there was generally a greater involvement of Muslims in Britain, both men and women, in self-employment. The trend was equally marked among Pakistani women, particularly those originally from the urban South Asian Muslim élite or older women from rural areas who avoided overt economic activity and the local labour market.

However, research suggests that economic and cultural factors have combined in different ways to drive the movement into self-employment. Pakistanis, for example, have been pushed into self-employment more by poor prospects of waged employment and racial discrimination than African Asians, who have viewed their earnings and skill development before self-employment more positively. Rather than using self-employment as an escape from racism, Indians have seen it more as a way of increasing their incomes and independence, although for Pakistanis acquisition of higher status has also been an important motivator. In contrast to Indians, lack of initial capital outlay was a constraint for Pakistanis, who usually started from scratch and relied more on their own savings, partly because of the difficulty of obtaining finance from bank managers with negative stereotypes of Muslim entrepreneurs compared to people from other faith and ethnic groups.

However, religion may sometimes have acted as a constraint on Muslim business development, influencing the choice of business and the goods and services provided. For example, handling alcohol—not a constraint for non-Muslims—would be frowned upon among Muslims on religious grounds. In some cases the lack of sufficient initial and follow-up investment was due partly to Muslim reluctance to seek certain kinds of interest-based loans, again on religious grounds. However, these limitations have not always prevented the success of Muslim entrepreneurial activity. Werbner described the strategies that some Pakistanis in Manchester pursued in the 1970s and 1980s to go from 'rags to riches'.[90] They did so by identifying and addressing demand in what Rafiq has called 'under-served and abandoned' markets.[91] They penetrated the cheap end of the 'rag trade' and gained competitive advantage by using low-paid ethnic labour, cutting overheads and operating on small profit margins. Entrepreneurs from many migrant Muslim communities have been able to gain an advantage over their white counterparts by using the cheap labour of their women, who had little chance to work elsewhere. The ideology of the extended family and ethnic loyalty proved ideal for recruiting a docile, cheap—and overwhelmingly female—labour force.[92] So while formal records suggested a comparatively low level of Muslim female economic activity, in reality, as Brah argues, 'homeworking' and other forms of informal labour 'not accessible to statistical collation' enabled Muslim women to contribute much more to entrepreneurial development than was first thought.[93]

Muslim enterprises, like those set up by other migrants from the sub-continent, seemed also to benefit from other cultural practices. Drawing on their experience of trade back home, they were able to raise and accumulate capital for additional growth from informal sources such as family and friends on a mutual-aid basis and by offering 'ethnic credit' in the style of Asian bazaars. However, research from the mid-1990s supported the view that the cultural factors which caused the low participation of Muslim women in the labour market are likely to have had a negative effect on Muslim enterprises (relative to non-Muslim ethnic groups). In the 1990s the PSI suggested that Pakistani men, much more than their Indian or African Asian counterparts, preferred their married women 'to spend their time looking after the home' rather than doing paid work.[94] They wanted wives and daughters to work in businesses that employed only women. The research concluded:

> Gender played a critical role in the types of workplaces that the Pakistani respondents wished their daughters to work in, and it was within such a context that cultural factors such as religion may have potentially acted as a constraint on maximising opportunities in the labour market. The issues for them were clearly to do with the separation of the sexes, rather than ethnic or religious exclusivity.[95]

The negative impact was also suggested by the smaller incomes that accrued to Muslims in self-employment than to their non-Muslim counterparts. The stated earnings of the respondents in the Fourth National Survey showed that non-Muslims earned much more than Muslims.[96] However, while cultural and religious factors cannot be overlooked, the main reasons for these disparities appeared to be much more connected with the different histories and social and material backgrounds of individuals.

Muslims in Britain have usually had to set up businesses with little start-up capital and with less business acumen and experience than non-Muslims. Research comparing Muslim and non-Muslim businesses has also suggested that Asian Muslim businesses have done less well because they were established primarily to meet the demand for ethnic goods and services in the inner-city areas with high levels of economic and social deprivation.[97] Hence their turnover and profitability have

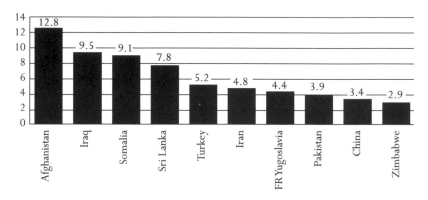

Asylum in Britain: total applications, 2001.

been low, relying on a customer base with limited financial and consumption capacity. Non-Muslim businesses have been much more involved in providing non-specialist goods and services in suburban areas with a small density of ethnic minority population.[98]

The 1991 census comparative ethnic data also revealed that in almost all occupational sectors unemployment rates were much higher among Bangladeshis and Pakistanis of all ages who were still connected with 'old' types of industrial work, especially if they had particular skills in those sectors. In the 'new' sectors of the economy their unemployment levels were lower, the lowest being in those sectors which offer greater opportunities for self-employment. According to the census data, unemployment was the highest among Bangladeshis (31% men and 35% women) of all ethnic groups.[99] Pakistanis had only a marginally lower rate of unemployment (28.5%).[100] A more recent survey suggests an even higher rate of unemployment. According to the Fourth National Survey, even more Pakistani and Bangladeshi were unemployed: 38% and 42% respectively, compared with 15% for whites and 19% for Indians.[101] The generally higher proportion of Muslims unemployed was reflected among Britain's Middle Eastern Muslims (19.5%), although this was much lower than that for Pakistanis and Bangladeshis.[102] Paradoxically, a higher proportion of Middle Eastern Muslims than whites (45% compared with 34.3% for men and 35.3% compared with 27.6% for women) were in the top

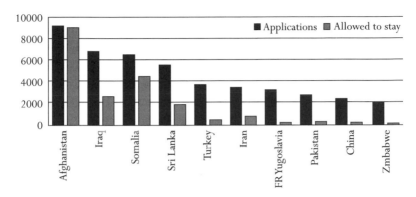

Asylum in Britain: applications from the top ten nationalities, 2001: success and failure.

two occupational categories.[103] This could be partly due to the more mixed socio-economic composition of Middle Eastern Muslims, among whom are affluent groups as well as the poorer old-established urban and port communities, and more recently-arrived refugees and asylum-seekers.

Local variations have been striking. According to the 1991 census, while 11.8% of Bangladeshis were unemployed in Brent, a colossal 47.3% were out of work in Tower Hamlets.[104] These differences may reflect the more working-class or underclass character of Tower Hamlets Bangladeshis compared with their more middle-class counterparts in parts of Brent, but they may also reflect the variations in unemployment rates in the various London boroughs, as they would across the country. The Inner London and West Midlands conurbations that have had the highest rates of unemployment in the country are also those with some of the biggest concentrations of Muslims. Recent Pakistani and Bangladeshi migrants were more likely to be unemployed than others of their age and education who had arrived in Britain before the age of sixteen, suggesting that migration did affect employment prospects.

Educational variations between Muslim and non-Muslim ethnic groups also seemed to have influenced employment patterns. In 1988–90 and 1990 the estimated unemployment rate among white men was 12% for those with no qualifications and 3% for those with a degree or equivalent. For Pakistanis the corresponding figures were 24% and 9%.[105] But while Pakistani and Bangladeshi men had fewer degrees than their white and Indian counterparts and were more than twice as likely to be without any qualifications, they showed considerable improvement by the 1990s in obtaining higher qualifications.

Thus the initial concentration of migrant Muslims, particularly of South Asian origin, in particular categories of jobs, does much to explain their subsequent employment experience. The restructuring and decline of manufacturing in the 1980s, particularly textiles and steel, affected them disproportionately. Unemployment among them increased rapidly, though 'hypercyclically'.[106] Periodic surveys since 1968 have highlighted that, despite some progress in relative job levels and earnings among non-white Britons, and therefore the majority of Muslims, they continued to suffer from disproportionately high unemployment, although many had moved into self-employment after giving up on prospects of any kind of waged work. Consequently, in many ways the employment situation for Muslim workers by the 1990s had not changed significantly, although differences related to class and gender had become apparent between and within various ethnic groups.[107]

Problems of discrimination

While socio-economic disadvantage has undoubtedly held the vast majority of Muslims back, ethno-religious discrimination has also affected them adversely. In the early postwar decades discrimination tended to take an ethnic and racial form. Along with other ethnic minority groups, Muslims, especially of South Asian origin, were discriminated against in various spheres: housing, education, employment, social and welfare services, the media and public life. There is now evidence that Muslims have also experienced more specifically religious discrimination, direct and indirect. The nature, level of seriousness and frequency of this kind of discrimination was identified by the Home Office in its report, *Muslims and Religious Discrimination in England and Wales*, which highlighted education, employment and the media as the areas where it was most likely to occur.[108] Among the issues that resulted in discriminatory treatment or exclusion were the availability of *halal* food, time off for prayers and religious festivals, inadequate prayer facilities and dress and language in many settings—schools and colleges, prisons, and private and public organisations.[109] In housing the unfair treatment of Muslims identified in Weller's study stemmed from interactions with the staff of housing associations, local councils and estate agents or with local residents,[110] which meant that on occasion planning permission was refused for mosques, schools and burial sites.[111] In employment, discrimination was identified in relation to acceptable dress codes, lack of respect for and ignorance of religious customs, and recruitment and selection practices.[112] The wearing of the *hijab* has proved problematic in schools and the workplace; while a number of bodies have taken steps to reach acceptable compromises on this, others have been known to discriminate against Muslim women wishing to wear it.[113] Beards have also sometimes caused problems, with instances of Muslim boys not being allowed in to school unless they shave.[114] Taking time off (even out of earned holiday entitlement) for Muslim religious festivals seemed at times to be resented by employers,[115] and although *halal* food has become more widely available, the response from institutions to this Muslim need is still inconsistent.[116] Thus, hostility to Muslims has taken a variety of forms, from discriminatory treatment to abuse and outright physical violence—assaults on individuals, desecration of graves and attacks on mosques and other Muslim community buildings and centres.[117] These acts reached various levels of intensity in the changing context of the 1980s and 1990s.[118]

Beyond disadvantage and discrimination, evidence accumulated in the 1990s revealed patterns of exclusion of Muslims from public life, broadly in form of a lack of representation and visibility at high-profile public events.[119] Muslim involvement at the level of national government, if it existed at all, remained more or less invisible, and this was reinforced by a perceived lack of consultation with Muslims at this level. And individual Muslims were being excluded in more subtle ways.[120]

But despite considerable impediments and still facing resistance, a small minority of Muslims in Britain did make encouraging, albeit slow and patchy, progress in different walks of life during the 1990s. This was due to increasing acceptance both of their particular concerns and of their contribution to British society among sections of the British establishment and institutions. Consequently some were awarded honours. At a more practical level, positive action was taken by an ever wider range of institutions which recognised the benefits of overcoming exclusion of Muslims, both in service delivery and in organisational life. The Ford Motor Company in Dagenham made provisions for members of minority religions to take some of their annual holiday entitlement as occasional days off to coincide with major religious festivals;[121] the Safeways store in Manchester allowed a sales assistant to wear a headscarf;[122] and the armed forces introduced measures to cater for Muslim needs, such as ration-packs that included *halal* food, and allowed Muslims to fast and pray five times a day unless it was impossible for operational or 'practical' environmental reasons.[123]

Nevertheless, the overall situation of British Muslims remained bleak. Looking at the 1990s, most of the evidence suggested that Islamophobia[124] was widespread and manifested in prejudicial views, discriminatory policies and practices, social exclusion, and different forms of violence. Under these circumstances many British Muslims felt a mixture of resentment, anger and despair, and not surprisingly remained alienated from the mainstream of British society. The circumstances that had shaped their lives and caused disaffection in the 1960s remained essentially unaltered.[125]

From when Muslims began to arrive in large numbers in the early 1960s, significant changes took place in their socio-economic circumstances and conditions of life. Starting off in the inner cities of Britain, many have progressed economically, become more affluent and dispersed to suburbia. 'White flight', which initially referred to the movement of white people out of areas with large concentrations of ethnic minorities, has expanded to include upwardly mobile Muslims who want to distance themselves from declining educational provision, scarce job opportunities and the run-down image of these areas. However, most of the Muslims living in these multiply deprived areas are in no position to take advantage of this movement. Given their limited opportunities, lack of educational qualifications and low level of acquired skills, they find themselves unemployed or on low wages and consequently cannot escape the 'ghetto'. Therefore the contours of Muslim life in Britain continue to be shaped largely by socio-economic factors, even though discrimination has added to their difficulties.

8

ASSIMILATION, INTEGRATION, ACCOMMODATION

ASPECTS OF MUSLIM ENGAGEMENT
WITH BRITISH SOCIETY SINCE 1945

As Chapter 6 showed, since 1945 a growing number of Muslims in Britain have come to perceive themselves not as temporary migrants but as permanent settlers. This produced challenges—not least the fact that few guidelines exist in Muslim history for living permanently in a society with a large non-Muslim majority and in which non-Muslim law, government and institutions predominate. Those Muslims who have chosen to settle in Britain have therefore had to resort to some degree of experimentation to negotiate in pragmatic ways how to live with the non-Muslim majority. As Muslim communities from around the world confronted complex issues in a new environment, they have inevitably done so in diverse ways and with different perspectives.

British Muslims have presented and attempted a range of prescriptions and strategies. Some believe that the only rationale for settlement in Britain, a non-Muslim state, is for purposes of *dawa*, to bring the non-believers to Islam. Others, such as Kalim Siddiqi, founder of the Muslim Parliament in 1990, took this idea a step further: denouncing the West as morally bankrupt, he urged his supporters to draw inspiration from the Prophet Muhammad who 'showed us how to generate the political power of Islam in a minority situation and how to nurse it

... until the creation of an Islamic state and the victory of Islam over all its opponents'.[1] But the majority of Muslims in Britain seem to be much more pragmatic. Ishtiaq Ahmed at the Bradford Council for Mosques in the 1990s entertained 'no such illusions'. British Muslims had arrived as 'economic migrants in order to escape the harsh socio-economic realities in their countries of origin ... in search of a better economic deal and improved life opportunities'; thus, in contrast to the Islamist view, British Muslims were not 'on a mass conversion spree'. Nor did they seek 'to dismantle the political, socio-economic fabric of this society. We have no grand hidden ambition or grand plan.'[2] Shabbir Akhtar, a key figure in the Salman Rushdie protest of the late 1980s, likewise developed a position that radically challenged the 'Islamic chauvinism' that refused to engage with the intellectual and social realities of British society. Instead of viewing Britain as *dar al-kufr* (house of unbelief), he asserted that 'the freest Muslims live in the West ... Everywhere else, Islam is an outlawed political force.'[3] So these are some of the voices of Islam heard in Britain by the 1990s, but how accurately did they reflect the impulses of British Muslims more generally? To understand these discourses we need to look at the contexts in which Muslims have formed communities and engaged with British society since 1945.

Patterns and processes of interaction

Most of the Muslim migrants who arrived in Britain in the 1950s were young men. They lived in inner-cities in dormitory houses, which they shared with male relatives or friends, working day and night shifts. Their social life revolved around a few local cafés, with traditional food, music and other pastimes. Religious observance tended to be relatively lax—drinking and pre- or extramarital sex were frequent, and caused only momentary anxiety, if that. The subsequent arrival of families, women and children, compelled these migrants to think of a longer and more permanent stay in Britain, being settlers rather than sojourners. As such, they wanted to pass on their Islamic traditions to their children and grandchildren. The rapid creation of religious and cultural institutions, facilitated by the development of Muslim residential zones where they felt secure and could apply some social control over their communities, reflected this shift in their strategies for living in Britain.

South Asian Muslim communities strove particularly to preserve religious, cultural and linguistic distinctiveness, and a dense network of voluntary community bodies representing specific interests and issues, often with local and central government support, provided them with a measure of autonomy. From quite early in their history some migrant Muslim interaction with the institutions of wider society was inevitable. Muslim councillors began to be elected to provide representation in local government. This representation was important since it was in local government that issues relevant to Muslims, such as education, were usually processed.

The 'institutional completeness'[4] of Muslim communities of the mid-1960s was characterised by 'a separate institutional and economic infrastructure', and enhanced by the proliferation of culture-specific goods, services and organisations and an educational system which, with local authority encouragement, similarly sought to support and perpetuate rather than undermine religious norms and cultural distinctiveness.[5] Muslim institutions forming part of the structure of such communities still make explicit their 'refusal to adopt local norms or to surrender [their] ... identity', except as part of a process of local negotiation.[6] In this way Muslim communities have tended not to see cultural independence as 'a permanent barrier to participation in the outside world ... [instead] it constitutes a protection from stigma and external domination'. Processes of interaction between Muslim communities and British society have therefore resulted in 'increasing integration into wider structures' while simultaneously fostering 'a separate cultural institutional identity'.[7]

The context of majority–minority encounters

The sheer weight of increased numbers since 1945 has had significant implications for the Muslim experience in Britain. As we have seen, when numbers were smaller initiatives emphasised similarities between Muslim values and those of the wider community, and efforts were made to clarify misunderstandings and erase negative images and stereotypes. However, Muslim 'mass' migration in this period has been accompanied by social processes ranging from 'assimilation' to mere 'accommodation'. These multifaceted and dynamic processes have been shaped by highly differentiated and constantly changing life patterns, social forces and power relations within and between the groups concerned. The pace of absorption, incorporation and adjustment that minority groups experience has varied. Often the rate and nature of second-generation British Muslims' assimilation and accommodation have depended on ethnic family background, class, priorities, aspirations and reactions to and from the host society, and, while assimilation has not been total, younger British Muslims have become more assimilated in more ways than their parents: they have developed more informal contacts with the wider society. This has not necessarily meant greater engagement with British institutions, even when they have found it easier to move away from traditional observances and have less fear of the dangers of contact with Western culture.

What, in the context of Muslim engagement with British society since 1945, do the concepts of assimilation and accommodation mean? 'Assimilation' has been treated sociologically as synonymous with 'acculturation', to describe a process by which the language, customs and institutions of the adopted country become those of an immigrant or outsider group in a more thorough way than mere use implies. The group becomes indistinguishably integrated into the dominant host society. At the end of this process 'natives' accept them as their equals, in intimate social situations—as relatives by marriage or as friends. The immigrant feels at ease with the culture of the adopted land, and has internalised its values. The group has adapted to and identifies itself with the host society and been accepted by it so completely that it has merged into the whole and lost its separate identity.

'Accommodation' and 'competition' stand in contrast to 'assimilation'. Those who accommodate may be content with a minimum *modus vivendi* between themselves and the host society while remaining largely encapsulated within their own group, and adapting only slowly to the social environment. Those competing assert their own values in opposition to the mainstream. However, in a plural society such as Britain, not only are the values of the dominant group being affected by minority cultures, but dominant and subordinate groups have also striven to achieve coexistence, while continuing to adhere to their own values and traditions. Social scientists have described this process as 'integration', according to which a minority group retains its own culture and religion, but adapts itself to and is accepted as a permanent member of society in all its external aspects of association. Its members enjoy full political, civil and social rights and perform all their obligations to society as equal citizens, but may remain members of separate communities with close links between them, preserving their own language within the home and retaining certain group institutions.[8]

Distinguishing integration from assimilation, Roy Jenkins, as Home Secretary in the mid-1960s, defined it as 'not a flattening process of assimilation but as equal opportunity accompanied by cultural diversity, in an atmosphere of mutual tolerance'.[9] Where Muslims are concerned, individuals and communities may have adapted and adjusted to different degrees to various aspects of British society. For example, many older migrants assimilated to some extent in language and dress, and adapted largely to economic life, but were reluctant to accommodate to the dominant patterns of family life, leisure and recreation.

Case-studies have shown that, while the first generation of British Muslims remained relatively unassimilated, the second generation, more exposed to British culture at an earlier stage of development, have assimilated more and more. First-generation migrants were likely to reach, at most, the level of 'integration': while retaining their own culture and religion, they continued to adapt and were to some degree accepted by the majority in external aspects. Second-generation Muslims adapted partly and were partly accepted in some roles and not in others. As individuals they may have been well integrated but their communities remained detached.

From the history of first-generation post-Second World War Muslim migrants in Britain there is ample evidence that, given their personal priorities, aspirations and social and religious pressure, they were content to remain detached from the wider British society. They had come to Britain to raise their living standards, not to change their way of life. They were prepared to establish contact with British society only to the extent that it impinged on their material welfare, but wanted their value system left intact. In sustaining a traditional way of life these Muslims were encouraged by their Islamic faith through its requirement of certain modes of behaviour. It was not only South Asian

Muslims but those from many other ethnic backgrounds who succeeded in retaining many of their core cultural traditions and values. A
study of Turkish Cypriots in the 1970s, while recognising adoption of
Western dress by women, increasing female employment and greater
mixing between the sexes as signs of adaptation to British life, also
observed an ability to preserve traditions of marriage, family life, religion and community spirit.[10] Similarly, a mid-1980s study of the
Turkish Cypriot community in North London saw little evidence of
acculturation. Its members seemed to have a strong sense of difference
from what they described as 'English' culture and had no particular
desire to be like the English.[11] Arabs, especially those who came in the
1970s and 1980s as political migrants, were as little or even less disposed to interact with the British and their institutions: 'Their lives,
feelings, society, hopes and interests are firmly sited with other Arabs,
both here and in the Arab world. This lack of involvement in British
society was manifested in that many Arabs who work here are engaged
in activities that are linked to the Arab world—businesses, journalism
or the professions.'[12] This stemmed partly from the history of Arab
migration. While many Arab countries were dominated by Britain in
the late nineteenth and early twentieth century, there were not the
same colonial links as existed with the Indian subcontinent, and Arab
immigration was mainly the result of relatively open policies towards
skilled migration, students and exiles or those fleeing civil conflict.
Hence the older generation of Arab settlers maintained an awareness
of difference, and accepted exclusion from social and political life. But
younger Arabs went further in accepting Britishness as the norm, and
developed an increasing tendency to conform—relegating their culture to the 'private sphere' while accepting and adhering to the majority's values and social practices in the 'public sphere'.[13]

Muslim migrants after 1945 from diverse cultural and social environments obviously shared similar experiences of migration and settlement, but they were also imbued with a greater degree of communal
consciousness than their prewar counterparts. They tended to associate
more closely with their compatriots, although with time, as they learnt
the mores of British society, they were better able to enter its life. As
immigration into Britain accelerated, Muslim communities evolved
into substantial self-contained entities. The patterns of Muslim migra-

tion ('pioneer' versus 'mass') and settlement ('in isolation' versus 'in an area of high density of fellow-countrymen') largely determined the options that were open to migrants or were forced upon them and later their children. In the earlier phases of this migration and settlement, many, perhaps out of a sense of inferiority, were prepared to absorb British values and lifestyles. Rediscovery and re-evaluation of their own cultural features were played down by earlier migrants, who believed that this might prejudice their chances of acceptance in Britain; they accepted the assumption that cultural assimilation and abandonment of their mother tongues were the precondition for integration and upward mobility. Thus they attempted to adjust in two broad ways: first, they sought to accept the standards of the host society, and secondly they attempted to gain self-esteem through social approval. Those who did this more successfully were helped by better education, which resulted in access to more secure jobs and higher incomes. Their dispersal from inner-city migrant enclaves further facilitated their adoption of the norms of their white counterparts, and among them religious observance frequently declined.

South Asian Muslims, in particular, adopted 'accommodation' as their main strategy, and became largely a non-assimilating community rather than an adapting one. This was partly because the host community withheld its social acceptance of them, thus compelling them to create ties within their own groups to overcome social isolation, prevent demoralisation and establish structures that would enable them to pursue their interests and meet their needs. The result was cultural encapsulation and minimum involvement in British life and institutions. Participation in the host community's social, cultural and leisure life was avoided. As regards interaction, some was 'casual', 'residential' and 'occupational'; a little was 'recreational', 'civic', and 'political' contact; but none was 'religious' and 'fraternal'. Relations could be amicable in the workplace, but did not extend into leisure activities. Alcohol prohibition and limitations of language discouraged closer association. Moreover, negative perceptions of the values of white British society, especially the 'permissiveness' of the 1960s and 1970s, caused concern and, together with awareness of discrimination, precipitated reactive pride in ethnic and/or religious distinctions and further encouraged ethnocentric encapsulation. Still, there was a desire for some form of dialogue with local institutions. So, while concessions were sought, confrontation was rejected. Caution needs to be exercised in relation to invoking religion as an important feature of Muslim communities in Britain since it concealed a great deal of diversity and interlocked with other, secular, forms of identity.

Since the mid-1950s the experience of South Asian Muslim migrants in Britain can be divided into three phases. The first phase required a radical adjustment to a new environment. In the 1970s, the second phase, these migrants began to get used to the environment and to cope with everyday life. Then in the 1980s and 1990s the initial uncertainties were largely overcome and migrants were in a position to participate and to contribute to British society. They knew their rights and how to go about things. They had established cultural and religious institutions and, having achieved a measure of economic success, had acquired greater self-confidence in their dealings with the wider society.

However, the majority of Muslims remained concentrated in the inner cities and this spatial distribution largely shaped social interaction. They spent a great deal of time in the company of other Muslims of the same ethnicity and distanced themselves socially from the majority population. Muslim migrants continued to be excluded from the institutions of British society and the structure of employment encouraged segregation and exclusion. This in turn encouraged differential treatment and inhibited contact with the white population, reducing opportunities to acquire linguistic and social skills leading to greater interaction instead of further exclusion. Thus, limited interaction reinforced the tendency towards introversion, and mutual stereotyping enhanced segregation. Spatial and social segregation, produced by the desire of the first generation to congregate as well as by 'white flight' from migrant areas in towns and cities, had the effect of denying the younger generation of Muslims contact with children from other ethnic and faith backgrounds and experience of alternative cultures. Furthermore, Muslim communities were never unstratified, and continued to be shaped by ethnic, linguistic and sectarian diversity. Pakistanis and Bangladeshis usually lived separately from Yemenis even in the smaller cities of Cardiff and South Shields.

The differences between Muslim groups and their relations with white people extend to family structures, behavioural norms, cultural practices and community identity. Pakistani and Bangladeshi Muslims, while they have different family structures from the white population, have clearly been influenced by the conditions they have experienced in Britain. For instance, following the majority pattern, there has been a marked fall in the number of children in Pakistani families. Likewise, the younger arrivals and British-born are less likely to have had an 'arranged' marriage than those who were born (and perhaps married) in Pakistan and Bangladesh.[14] Another aspect of life clearly influenced by residence in Britain is the choice of white partners in cohabitation, marriage and child rearing. Modood *et al.* have shown that there is some coming-together in these areas. They have provided evidence to suggest that South Asian Muslims are slowly moving towards white British patterns: those born in Britain have slightly smaller families than those born abroad, and attitudes to marriage are becoming less 'traditional' among younger people and those born in Britain.[15]

In other ways it could be argued that Muslims have fewer contacts than before with the wider society. Data from the 1981 and 1991 censuses revealed a trend towards greater rather than less urban concentration of ethnic minority people, and an increased share of the South Asian Muslim population in its core areas. Pakistanis had become more clustered in the north-west, especially Greater Manchester, West Yorkshire and the Midlands, and Bangladeshis in inner London.[16] However, this might have been due more to higher birth rates than to lack of social mobility and dispersal.[17] Also the 1991 census revealed that the density of these Muslim communities had risen because, first, the white population had moved out of some areas of Muslim ethnic concentration; secondly, new Muslim households were forming close to existing households; and thirdly, new arrivals, either from areas of industrial decline or from abroad, were joining communities already established.[18] Nevertheless, even in areas where they were most densely concentrated, Pakistanis and Bangladeshis formed only a minor proportion (20%) of the overall population, and most resided in areas where they formed less than 10% of the population.[19]

When the focus shifted to proportions of population at ward level, there were exceptions. According to the 1991 census, almost 90% of Birmingham's Pakistanis (over 70,000) lived in only five inner-city wards, and 61% of those living in the Spitalfields ward in Tower

Hamlets, east London, were Bangladeshis (over 39,000 in the borough), rising to around 90% in the most densely populated enumeration district.[20] Similarly, Pakistanis formed 52.8% of the population of the University ward in Bradford (out of their city-wide population of over 48,000).[21] In these areas Pakistanis and Bangladeshis seemed to have evolved into ghetto-like communities[22]—figures from the 1991 census revealed Bangladeshis as the most highly segregated population, followed by Pakistanis. Significantly, these figures also demonstrated a high degree of segregation of Bangladeshis from Pakistanis, who were not only co-religionists but, up till 1971, citizens of the same country.[23] A number of factors combined to produce this residential clustering. As Modood *et al.* have suggested, while a high proportion of Pakistanis and Bangladeshis expressed no preference as to the proportion of ethnic minorities living in their neighbourhood, a similar proportion was positively disposed towards living in areas where the majority of the population comprised residents from their own group.[24] The 1991 census figures also showed that the socio-economic circumstances of South Asian Muslims have played only a small part in producing segregation.[25]

Degrees of British Muslim assimilation

British Muslim approaches to engagement with the wider society have taken several different forms, the most significant being the subcultural, the counter-cultural, the accommodationist and the assimilationist. The subcultural response entails separation from the cultural mainstream, with the desired degree of separation depending on the proponents. The counter-cultural response attempts to safeguard distinctiveness in the midst of the mainstream, and by exercising influence in favour of reform strives to win concessions from the wider society. The accommodationist response opposes withdrawal and isolation from the wider society but differs from the counter-cultural response in its positive evaluation of mainstream culture, or at least in being less dissatisfied than the other respondents. Those who hold this view fear labelling and alienation, are relatively tolerant of other faiths and ideologies, and feel that their children should avoid social and cultural conflict, if necessary by conforming to the mainstream. Indeed, those who support this position wish to be recognised as part of the mainstream, although Islamic identity for them remains paramount. The assimilationist response, while not explicitly endorsing religio-cultural absorption into the mainstream, does tend towards it quite strongly. It allows Islamic specificity to give way to the vague generalities of civil religion, with perhaps a few incidental religious or ethnic vestiges being retained. In all likelihood those Muslim parents who adopt this perspective are themselves not particularly observant; this response tends towards secularism, and has reflected the view of a substantial proportion of British Muslims.[26]

All these responses have been present to some extent among British Muslims and have been manifested in a variety of social arenas. Clothes are a visible aspect of culture and provide clues to the level of integration of a particular group. The Fourth PSI Survey in 1994 showed that only a small minority of Pakistani and Bangladeshi men always wore their traditional clothes; as many as one-third never did. However, they were more likely to wear traditional clothes than other South Asian people. Moreover, women from these groups are much more likely to wear 'Asian' clothes (79% of Pakistani and 85% of Bangladeshi women stated that they always did so). Hardly any men of Pakistani and Bangladeshi background in the sixteen to thirty-four age-group always wore traditional clothes, though 75% of their female counterparts did; the proportion of these women who never wore 'Asian' clothes was negligible. Geographically, too, traditional dress was much more prevalent in the north of England than in the south-east. These clothes were worn mainly in a domestic setting and on social occasions, though here too gender and geographical contrasts were evident. At the same time, 'Asian' clothes were worn much less by any of the Asian groups in the workplace, and those who did were concentrated in semi-skilled and unskilled manual work.[27]

Another indication of how far Muslims have moved towards absorbing the values and norms of the dominant group is the shift in their attitudes to the tradition of arranged marriage. In the mid-1980s nearly all second-generation Pakistanis who were married were found to have had the most traditional type of arranged marriage.[28] A combination of motives—close family ties, respect for parents' wishes, Muslim identity—probably explain this outcome. The Fourth PSI Survey a decade later revealed that the role of parents and other family elders in selecting and 'arranging' partners was less widespread than before; instead, while a majority of South Asians Muslims over thirty-five 'had their spouses chosen by their parents' (68% of Pakistanis and 57% of Bangladeshis), the proportion among the younger generation was 57% of Pakistanis and 45% of Bangladeshis. But Muslim parents still had the decisive role in the vast majority of their daughters' marriages (87% for the fifty-plus age-group, 78% for the thirty-fives to forty-nines and 67% for the sixteens to thirty-fours).[29] By the 1990s it was clear that at least a large minority of younger Muslims would probably have a much bigger say in the choice of their marriage partners. Parents appeared less insistent and more prepared to allow their children to make up their own minds and arrive at a compromise.

However, while many Muslim men and some Muslim women were increasingly prepared to enter into intimate relationships with non-Muslim people, intermarriage remained virtually out of bounds, and Pakistani or Muslim partners were both preferred by parents and accepted by the children, although marriage to People of the Book (Jewish and Christian) had always been religiously acceptable.[30] Hence, at the level of primary relationships little change seemed to have occurred, and the view among South Asian Muslims regarding inter-ethnic unions continued, in line with other groups, to be largely negative; 72% of Pakistani and 50% of Bangladeshi respondents felt that mixed relationships would be frowned upon in their communities, although a substantial minority among the Pakistanis (41%) and a majority among the Bangladeshis (52%) stated that they personally were not worried. Moreover, the differences in the Pakistani and Bangladeshi responses suggested that religion was not necessarily the reason for the negative view. In general, younger as opposed to older South Asian Muslims and men compared with women were less critical of mixed relationships.[31] Thus attitudes and behaviour were gradually changing, pointing to greater integration. Evidence from the 1991 census indicated that the choice of interethnic unions among South Asian Muslims was increasing—more among men than women. A much larger proportion of younger Pakistani and Bangladeshi men (sixteen- to thirty-four-year age-group compared with thirty-five- to fifty-nine-year agegroup and 'second' generation as opposed to 'first' generation) were either married to or cohabiting with white partners.[32] South Asian Muslims from urban backgrounds and in professions and management, as well as in higher education, were more likely to enter partnerships with whites than their working-class counterparts.[33] So findings from the 1990s pointed to the conclusion that younger Muslims were definitely becoming more assimilated than their parents. While their decisions and plans were very much in accord with family priorities, they, like other young adults in British society, also did so on the basis of their own skills, aspirations and potential. Increasingly, material as much as, if not more than, cultural factors were shaping their decisions.

The generation gap: British Muslims and youth culture

By the 1990s there was also plenty of evidence that divisions had begun to emerge along generation and gender lines as ever more young Muslims gravitated towards popular culture. The clash between the values of the older and younger generations was creating some tension, with traditional male hegemony within the family and the community challenged more often. It has been argued that lack of mutual understanding due to inadequate communication, which was thought to have become endemic within the white population, is increasingly occurring in Muslim communities, sometimes leading to violence.[34] Inevitably younger people in any community will have different ideas from their elders about how to deal with life, but in the absence of any indication of a full-scale rebellion developing, loyalty to and respect for the traditional values and their upholders are still much in evidence. But it is noticeable that younger Muslims feel that they have a stake in Britain and therefore want to assert their rights in ways that their parents felt unable to do. This difference in approach is sometimes mistaken as a clash between generations. While continuing to hold their immediate families in high esteem, young Muslims do feel that the views of their parents and grandparents are increasingly out of touch with British society: the extended social networks based on caste, clan and tribal and regional loyalties, which loom so large in the perceptions of the older generations, have little relevance for them in the British context. Their expectations are similar to those of their white counterparts and have redefined their cultural and religious values in relation to standards and values emerging in the environment with which they interact in their daily lives. So in reality most young Muslims have striven to steer a course between several sets of expectations emanating from home, the community, the 'majority British culture' and the mass media.

This has not prevented an antisocial street culture, little different in nature from that endemic in white society, from developing among some Muslim youth, involving truanting, vandalism, drug-trafficking, crime and gang violence. In the Muslim 'ghettos' of Bradford, Birmingham and Oldham, amid unemployment, urban decay and allegations of corruption in the communities, young Muslims have broken away from family clans, resorted to militancy or found refuge in the Quran. In local amusement arcades, in ragga clothes and with razor-cut hair, they while away their time on slot-machines and video games. Drug dealers, in their Reeboks and with mobile phones, do their business selling an assortment of drugs—whiz, crack, smack, skunk—on street corners. Others 'flog stolen gear' such as car radios and mobile phones.[35] Consequently Muslim prison inmates doubled in the 1990s, with a quarter convicted of crimes related to drug pushing or drug use. Over 65% of Muslim prisoners were young men between the ages of eighteen and thirty. According to police figures for the London Borough of Tower Hamlets, 50% of drug offenders were young Bangladeshi men, and while there are no official statistics available for women, cannabis use was increasing among them as well.[36]

The emergence of this kind of Muslim youth reflected their alienation from parents and disaffection with the communities in which they often felt 'imprisoned', and the leaders who claimed to represent them between whose values and those of the wider society there was a clear contradiction. Many of them consequently found Islam 'drab and boring', lacking in 'fun and laughter',[37] and in their frustration they formed gangs and engaged in violent turf wars. The deepening gulf between them and the older generation, their alienation and the lack of strategy to cope with their rapidly changing environment were well articulated in a letter that appeared in the Muslim magazine *Q-News*:

> Yes, you have set up a system of *halal* meat. Yes you have built Mosques. Yes you have taught us Urdu … But you have also … built Mosques that were alien, hostile and irrelevant to our needs and requirements. Mosques that are full of squabbles and fights. Not love and compassion.

Mosques full of notices of 'don't' do this and 'don't' do that. Mosques whose doors are closed to the destitute, the poor, the orphans.

How then, the letter asked, could the young face the forces of the outside world, which were 'bad for your mind, body and soul'? How could they cope in a world where 'pornography awaits you at every other shelf, pubs confront you at every next corner and the behaviour of most Muslims you come across sends you reeling back'? For these young Muslims the future looked bleak since they could see 'no role models, nobody to admire up and down the street, and nothing to aspire to'.[38]

Thus by the 1990s it had become clear that a gap had developed between the perspectives of the older and younger generations of British Muslims.

> Parents were at a loss to understand their children because they have given up speaking in their mother tongue, practising their religion and were becoming disrespectful and arrogant to their parents ... their children soon begin to adopt English standards and ideas. They start to question not only traditional customs but also religious ideas which seem largely alien to life in a Western materialistic society.[39]

On the other hand their children also seemed to be experiencing their own dilemmas. Here is a succinct expression of the difficulties facing Muslim youth in Britain in the 1990s from a Muslim journalist:

> It is a confusing time to be young, Muslim and British... The Muslim leadership in Britain is bankrupt of ideas. It is the difficulties of living a religious life in a secular society which should be addressed. Youngsters continue to learn the Koran in Arabic, which they do not understand. There is a communication gap between the elders and the young... The Koran says we are the caretakers of the world. We should be involved in Green politics. We are not taking part in our host country enough.[40]

In their efforts to come to grips with life in the British environment, the majority of young Muslims have struggled to reconcile and synthesise inputs from three distinct spheres of their lives—the 'individualistic and critical ethos' of the secular state education system; the prescriptive teachings, largely by rote, of traditional Islam at the mosque; and 'the home, where after mosque school the young are exposed to South Asian videos, with their beguiling world of music, drama and dance'. For many this has meant that Islam simply becomes 'but one component in an inherited culture, of declining significance and relevance'.[41]

However, the cultural and leisure arenas are where British Muslims have been confronted most acutely with moral choices. Increasingly it has been local youth clubs, rather than community or religious institutions catering for Muslim youth, where a social space has been created for them to develop and enjoy a distinctive and usually unselfconsciously Islamic youth culture. Young Muslims have inevitably been drawn in a variety of ways towards music, now recognised as one of the central components of British youth culture. In pursuing their interests in music and dance, they have faced opposition from the religious establishment within their communities; in Bradford community leaders complained of the corrosive and subversive effect that *bhangra* music and discos were having on younger Muslims. The president of the Council for Mosques declared that disco dancing was 'sexually suggestive' and therefore 'banned by the Islamic faith'. In his opinion 'exposing the body of a male or female in such a way as to attract the opposite sex is forbidden',[42] but harsh criticism of this kind has not prevented the growing involvement of young Muslims in the performing arts. 'Asian' bands have appeared on the scene, which have attracted a popular following. Asian Dub Foundation, Kaliphz, Naseeb and Fun-da-mental made their mark on 'pop' music more broadly during the 1990s, but were able to escape religious objections to musical production and enjoyment. In response young Muslims, while unwilling to withdraw from participating in the broader youth culture, have tried to meet their elders' objections sensitively and thoughtfully. Aki Nawaz, Fun-da-mental's lead singer, while acknowledging that there could be conflict between Islam and music, denied that all music was prohibited to Muslims. In the context of a normal meat-market, condom-culture club where the masses go and where music has no artistic purpose but is simply about sex, drugs and rock 'n' roll, he could 'appreciate how that is in conflict with Islam'. But he could find no fault with 'Muslim classical music' as a form of *zikr*.[43] For Aki Nawaz music was an effective means of questioning established norms and ideas. It was also a means of expressing resistance, protest and disillusionment over contemporary issues through modern musical techniques and genres in combination with traditional forms.[44] It is with this understanding of music and its relation with Islam that he has applied Islamic chanting and extracts from the Quran to articulate politically controversial Islamic sentiments, as with his group's support for Khomeini's *fatwa* against Salman Rushdie in their album 'Righteous Preacher'.[45] Nawaz's view that the lyrical and poetic expression of mystical thought in *qawwalis* was hugely educational brought criticism from Islamic purists, who saw little spiritual value, for instance, in the contribution of Nusrat Fateh Ali Khan (1948–97), a global figure in the world of *qawwali*, to several popular sound tracks, which they believed had compromised *qawwali*'s religious value.[46]

Indeed, the view that Islam frowns upon most forms of music remained widespread and continued to over shadow the engagement of young Muslims with British youth culture. The impact of this view was felt most dramatically in the abrupt halt in musical creativity brought about by the conversion to Islam of Cat Stevens (Yusuf Islam). After being an extremely popular singer in the 1960s and 1970s, he abandoned the lifestyle of a pop icon in 1976 and, after briefly attempting to combine music with his new faith, gave up recording and performing completely. His return to music in the mid-1990s was rationalised along the lines that Islam did not prohibit it as such but only the use of instruments and music for entertainment. Hence it was permissible to create and participate in music so long as it furthered the cause of Allah.[47] Similar issues have been raised regarding the fine arts, which have been the subject of intense discussion among British Muslims. Even relatively moderate Muslims, such as Professor Dawud Noibi of the Iqra Trust, argued that art forms such as sculpture could lead to worship of images and were therefore forbidden. The religious establishment took a broadly negative view especially of figurative painting and sculpture. But more militant Muslims of the younger generation accepted the view that Islam rejects all modern forms of artistic production and that consequently it is legitimate for them to dissuade their co-religionists from artistic activity.[48] Nevertheless, many Muslims have interpreted Islamic treatises on art differently and have developed a much more intimate association with Western art.

There are a number of positions, each with its own sources of legitimacy and rationale, within British Islam regarding musical and artistic production, which suggests that the debate among British Muslims has moved beyond the *halal–haram* (permitted–prohibited) dichotomy. The Islamist strand asserts that both the playing of musical instruments and listening to music is forbidden, implicitly in the Quran and explicitly in the Hadith. A variation on the theme is the view that 'music is a dangerous activity, with the potential to lead the believers astray from the true path and to lull them into a state where their passions dominate their reason', and therefore ought to be discouraged. A third, widely-held perception among ordinary British Muslims is that musical activity has little intrinsic or utilitarian value and is therefore unworthy of any attention. A fourth position on music offers an essentially Sufi perspective, whereby music is understood as a spiritual experience with the sole purpose of getting close to and knowing God. Many converts to Islam in Britain have been attracted by this approach and applied it to their newly-acquired religious life. Finally, the idea that music is 'one of the instinctive pleasures in life, given by Allah to provide human beings with necessary refreshment and relaxation', and that its enjoyment should be welcomed, appears to be gaining ground among the younger generation of British Muslims. It has aroused interest in certain kinds of music, such as rap, especially when fused with traditional Punjabi, Gujarati or Bengali forms.[49]

Similar debates have taken place regarding art and architecture, reflecting the evolving relations between British Muslims and wider artistic creativity as well as the influence of Western art on their artistic production. With such a broad range of ideas there is no consensus on the kind of art allowed by Islam, nor is it clear what constitutes Islamic art—between its traditional and modern forms and the distinction between sacred and profane.[50] Yasmin Alibhai-Brown has written of a renaissance among Muslim artists in Britain, and the range of artistic production emanating from them is impressive. Not all devote their art to God, but most give short shrift to the notion of art for art's sake and 'sheep in formaldehyde'.[51] The institution of Visual Islamic and Traditional Arts (VITA) in London (the Prince of Wales is its president) offers an environment and resources for students in the midst of a modern, secular, commercial world where the 'sacred Islamic arts' are learned and practised at the highest level by graduates from around the world. The work produced is grounded in Islamic aesthetics, inspired by a desire for spiritual uplift: 'each piece is a *dhikr*—a remembrance of God'.[52] Ali Omar Ermes, who presented the Prime Minister Tony Blair with one of his paintings at the beginning of 2001, is also traditional in his belief. Like VITA students, he rejects replication of nature in figurative painting as against Islamic injunctions, and insists on discovering 'new shapes' and 'modes of reflecting the spiritual'.[53] This suggests that in art British Muslims respond in several distinct ways. Some have begun to produce devotional work of high quality, others have moved beyond the boundaries of the traditional forms of Islamic art, and use their creativity to make sense of their lived experience. For Alibhai-Brown they are 'the reclaimers, the rebels, and the people who are trying to make new artistic settlements with their adoptive country'.[54] Reclaimers would include Ermes, but not necessarily exclude Fatima Zahrah Hassan who paints miniatures in the Mogul style; these may express her own individual values, but also clearly stem from the Muslim artistic tradition. The rebels see reclaimers as fossils stuck in the past when what is needed is art that expresses their struggle with modernity from a secular angle. A third group of Muslim artists, including those associated with the Al Furqan Centre, wishes to develop a synthesis of Islamic and Western traditions. It rejects simplistic distinctions between Islamic and other art and questions disengagement from the Western artistic imagination. Instead, they have striven hard to develop a productive exchange between modern Islamic art and Western aesthetics. Vaseem Mohammed's paintings, which have been appreciated by a varied public, exemplify this attempt at a fusion between Islamic inspiration and Western sensibilities. Similarly the King Fahd Mosque in Edinburgh, which used Scottish stone and slate to represent both modern-day Islam and Scottish nationhood, blends well in Scotland's capital city.

Beyond visual art, Muslim engagement with British culture is growing steadily, whether in theatre, cinema, television or the novel. Playwrights such as Ayub Khan-Din have challenged traditional values while producing work to wide critical acclaim.[55] More recently, Shazia Mirza, a practising Muslim woman comic, has won plaudits for her 'great routines', which expose Muslim culture in Britain, as well as the myths and false perceptions that surround it.[56] Novelists such as Hanif Kureshi and Ahdaf Soueif (her novel *A Map of Love* was shortlisted for the Booker Prize in 1999) have sought to engage with a complex range of embattled Muslim experiences in the modern British cultural arena even at the risk of harsh strictures from their communities.

At a more popular level the fusion of artistic expression can be seen in fashion. While, as some Muslim women believe, Islam demands that they wear the *hijab*, fashion requires that they wear designer *jalabiyyas*. Chanel scarves, Gucci turbans and Versace *topis* are among the sought-after brands among devout Muslim women. While headscarves signal their Muslim faith, short-sleeved blouses and leg-revealing slits in their dresses show their allegiance to fashion. Hafsa Garwatuk wearing a beautiful *hijab* on the cover of *Elle* magazine represented a powerful image of what it could mean to be a European Muslim woman.[57] But some Muslim women have completely broken with Muslim dress codes and their associated values. Safira Afzal, one of a handful of Muslim models in Britain, left home when she was eighteen and has since broken almost every religious taboo, drinking alcohol and living with her Australian Jewish boyfriend. But she still admitted to the need to say her prayers before going to sleep.

Segregated leisure and sport?

Sport is another major aspect of British culture. Historically modern sport first developed in Britain and both national and local government, acknowledging its potential to contribute to healthier communities, have been prepared to invest large resources in its promotion. Sport, together with physical education, has long been a compulsory part of school curricula, and young Muslims and their counterparts from other ethnic groups have shown great interest in it. Muslim boys and men have participated enthusiastically in many sports, some with great distinction; one need only think of Naseem Hamed in boxing; Nasser Hussain, Aftab Habib and Usman Afzaal in cricket; and Muzzy Izzet in football. A survey in 1991 showed that more Bengali boys (60%) played football than the English (47%), and Pakistanis (42%) were not far behind.[58] Muslim girls and young women have also shown a positive attitude towards sport, but participation has been much greater in other faith and ethnic groups; theirs continues to be circumscribed by cultural and religious traditions of modesty and patriarchally prescribed gender roles. This disparity is often explained by the Islamic rules regarding female seclusion, segregation of sexes, dress regulations and women's generally subordinate status. These limitations seem to have prevented Muslim women from participating in outdoor activities and particularly in leisure pursuits. While the majority of Muslims in Britain would accept these strictures as part of their faith, an increasing number are coming to challenge them as cultural impositions, arguing that men and women alike need exercise and that the Prophet Muhammad was at ease with women's participation in competitive sport, as confirmed by a Hadith in which he asserted that physical activity was a right of both boys and girls.[59]

While there has been much intermingling in sport between Muslims and others, the continuing segregation of the communities has meant that leisure activities and team sports have tended to develop separately. White prejudice and bias in organised sports have discouraged Muslim participation;[60] the bigotry and discrimination they have experienced from administrators, coaches, players and spectators have caused Muslims to withdraw from multicultural interaction and move away from playing in mixed teams. They have organised Muslim-only teams with Muslim names, and compete in tournaments with teams from their own faith.[61] In Yorkshire, one of the heartlands of English cricket, hundreds of Pakistani players, having experienced racism in various forms, have opted out of the county's major leagues, competing instead in the largely segregated, marginalised and ignored Quaid-i-Azam League, which affords little opportunity to progress higher within the sport.[62]

Young Muslim women have even fewer opportunities than the men to share leisure activities with the majority population, since they have to contend not only with the negative stereotypes of the wider society but with the restrictive patriarchal control of their families. But since the younger Muslim women have usually been through the education system in Britain with compulsory sport, they have become increasingly aware of the need for sport and exercise as an enjoyable and beneficial leisure activity. Some have begun to challenge their isolation even when faced with opposition and restrictions from their families and communities. When criticised for wearing sports clothing, such as shorts, T-shirts, leotards and swimming costumes, as exhibiting immodest behaviour, especially in the presence of men, younger Muslim women have attempted to get round these kinds of objections in a variety of imaginative ways while at the same time continuing to assert their Muslim identity. Ameena Mohammed, aged twenty-four, the first female British Muslim Thai boxer and previously a bus driver, argued that she did not want to be dependent on her husband for protection and had therefore taken up martial-arts training to protect herself, often training with men and quite comfortable doing so. While she wore the *hijab*, she again saw it as a form of protection and not oppression. In spite of contending that being physically fit is an integral part of the Islamic way of life, Ameena was criticised by no less a religious authority than Dr Zaki Badawi: there was nothing intrinsically wrong with self-defence or sports for women, he said, but 'fighting in a ring with spectators cheering you on is clearly not acceptable in Islam'.[63]

Matters of law

Whenever Muslim engagement with British society and its institutions is discussed, the place of Islamic religious law has been to the fore. Since increasing numbers of Muslims arrived from the 1960s onwards, the central importance to them of these laws has been reflected in various ways. The issue of *halal* food has been a consistent source of controversy; the education system has had to take account of Muslim concerns over dress and over religious and sex education; local authorities have had to deal with requests for planning permission for mosques and forms of burial agreeable to Muslims; and employers have had to meet Muslim demands on dress codes, for prayers at set times and for time off to celebrate religious festivals. Muslims also wish to have the family laws based on Islamic traditions incorporated in the British legal system.

For many Muslims in Britain adherence to Islamic law is part of living in accordance with God's will. Two kinds of human behaviour are regarded by Muslims as subject to the Sharia: individual duties towards God and individual duties towards society. The former are based on articles of faith and are primarily devotional by nature—such as the five pillars of Islam—while the latter are social rules regulating behaviour with other human beings. The dilemma for many Muslims is that a non-Muslim society may not have made legal provision for their practice. Both kinds of human behaviour are further divided into five categories—forbidden, rejectable, permitted, recommendable, and obligatory. The areas of life not covered by distinct codes fall into the very large neutral category—which can be governed by secular laws. *Darura* (the principle of necessity) allows Muslims to engage with wider society: it authorises and justifies an accommodation enabling the faithful settled in a non-Muslim society to break the letter of certain rules and to partake of some things that are in principle forbidden while still continuing to be recognised as Muslims.

However, law for the regulation of human life can require elaboration and development. Muslim jurists developed the content of Islamic law on the basis of methodological principles applied to scriptural sources, the core of which was the Quran and then the Hadith—the model set by the Prophet Muhammad himself. Three further methods were used when an Islamic rule could not be worked out on the basis of these two sources: (1) *ijtihad*, the exercise of human reason, the application of which could only be by reference to relevant texts; (2) reasoning by *qiyas* (analogy); and (3) *ijma* (consensus) of the Prophet's companions on a particular case, which became the final authoritative source of Sharia. Much of the construction of Islamic law took place under the Ummayad and Abbasid caliphates where Muslim power prevailed.

However, there is no clear-cut guidance or direction available in the *fiqh* (the technical juristic elaboration of detailed content) about how permanently settled Muslims should live in a quasi-secular non-Muslim state such as Britain; historically English law provided no safeguard for non-Christian faiths other than that their followers were free to practise them. The net effect for Muslims of the traditional common law environment has been that it creates practical constraints in the form of a legal framework which has been perceived as indifferent to their religious needs. In the culturally diverse and plural society that Britain has become, many Muslims feel that this framework does not offer equality of treatment in terms of available legal remedies, and that many aspects of Islamic law are not covered by English law. Indeed, some elements of English law—e.g. those relating to usury, abortion, homosexuality, gambling, the sale and consumption of alcohol, and the absence of capital punishment—might even appear to conflict with Islamic principles. Individually and collectively British Muslims have developed a variety of responses to these legal realities. Since a substantial majority of them do not consider Britain to be *dar al-kufr* (the house of unbelief) but rather *dar al-ahd* (the land of pact), *dar al-sulh* (the land of truce), *dar al-aman* (the land of peace) or *dar al-ahl al-kitab* (the land of the People of the Book), they have not regarded non-compliance with English law as an appropriate response. Even separatist strands among British Muslims—represented by, among others, the Muslim Parliament—have accepted obedience to the laws of a non-Muslim state in return for 'protection of life, property, and liberty ... as long as such obedience does not conflict with their commitment to Islam and the Ummah'. The Muslim minority has promised qualified cooperation with the British state in the maintenance of law and order, demanding in return protection from 'gratuitous obscenity and abuse', as well as serving notice that insult and abuse on the grounds of religion, culture and traditions would not be tolerated. Thus it reserved the right to reject 'any part of a legal and social agenda which ... flagrantly violates the law of nature as well as of God'.[64] The perception among these Muslims is that they cannot rely on the structures of British society to identify and support Muslim interests. Hence they have suggested the construction of separate structures in education, publishing and various areas of economic, professional and welfare activity.[65]

Justification for accepting the provisions of English law has been derived from Islamic principles, which require a Muslim minority to submit to a state in which it has taken up residence. In the period soon after the arrival of Muslim migrants in Britain, *ijtihad* was used to ascertain what the rights and responsibilities of Muslims were in a secular non-Muslim state. *Ijtihad* allowed British Muslims to explore the limits and relevance of the Sharia for Muslims living under particular circumstances, at the same time preserving in all cases the spirit of the Quran and Sunna. However, with the arrival of Muslim migrants of whom the majority had been socialised into subcontinental Sunni beliefs and practices, more orthodox views based on the four widely recognised schools of Islamic law—Hanafi, Maliki, Shafi and Hanbali—became ever more dominant through the 1960s and 1970s. Social and legal obstacles to a whole host of religious practices and the compatibility of the faith and ceremonies of Islam with the secularised situation in Britain came to be identified, and they in turn led to negotiation for the provision of legal space at local and national levels. While Muslims accepted the necessity to obey the law of the land, they also tried to use the opportunities offered by the liberal and flexible principles of English law to harmonise it with their values and traditions. In two specific areas of English criminal law Parliament legislated to exempt Muslims from certain statutory provisions   shops could be opened on Sundays without any breach of trading laws, and Muslims could slaughter in abattoirs according to their religious methods. Thus, beyond obtaining these kinds of legal concessions, three types of approaches have been adopted by those Muslims who have believed that acceptance of British laws is obligatory and that partial integration of Islamic law in this system is feasible—acceptance of the legal *status quo*, manipulation of the legal system to suit their purposes, and pursuing the possibilities of legal reform.

Elements of Muslim family law have come into conflict with aspects of English law, obliging British Muslims to look for ways of reconciling the two. On the one hand they may be in conflict with laws that have been promulgated by the state, but on the other the law of the land may not consider certain forms of behaviour or human interactions to be criminal—such as fornication, adultery, homosexuality, consumption of alcohol and usury. Some interactions, such as adoption or fostering, may not be recognised by Islamic law. Other forms of behaviour or interaction that are permitted under Islamic law may be expressly forbidden under state law or may not be recognised by the state— polygamy, procedure for divorce, and stipulation regarding inheritance. Still others, notably blasphemy and incitement to religious hatred, may be declared as criminal by the state only in specific instances. Muslims in Britain have had to come to terms with a complex legal situation. Islamists, by contrast, have decried the preoccupation of the majority of Muslims with attempts to gain 'little rights as a minority'—an approach that, in their view, has inevitably led to compromises. In their view, Muslims should not look for remedy through legal measures but seek to build an alternative system of power and economic cooperation, to engage with the wider society and to organise its internal affairs. Kalim Siddiqi, a strong proponent of this strand of thought, condemned those seeking accommodation and compromise with British society.[66] He favoured the establishment of a Muslim Law Commission, which would be competent to decide on matters of marriage, divorce, custody of children and inheritance on the basis of Islamic law and 'decide cases that may then be recognised as valid in British law'.[67] This demand represented nothing new; at a conference in 1977 the Union of Muslim Organisations of the UK and Eire (UMO) sought the 'domestication' of Islamic family law in Britain,[68] but there has been little evidence of the popularity of this demand. When Dr Zaki Badawi tested support for its implementation regarding inheritance in 1975 by proposing a form of will, executable under English law, whereby it would be possible to dispose of property according to Islamic law, there was apparently no take-up.[69]

By the 1990s there was indirect evidence that the practice of paying *mahr* (dower) continued to be widespread and that the demand for an Islamic dissolution of marriage to accompany a divorce secured in a British lawcourt was growing. The lack of more extensive lobbying on these matters may be partly because common ground has been found between the essential features of English law on marriage and divorce and Islamic principles on those issues. Moreover, the liberal principles of the English legal system—'everything is permitted except what is expressly forbidden'[70]—have enabled Muslims to resolve many of their concerns regarding family law according to Islamic principles within the framework of English law (arranged and cousin marriages, payment of *mahr*, the use of mosques for weddings). The freedom allowed under English law to settle disputes out of court by agreements negotiated with the help of lawyers or third-party mediators and conciliators has led to disputes between Muslims themselves in the area of family law being resolved by reference to religious principles and values without resorting to the English judicial system. In addition, the evolving and flexible nature of English law has given it the potential and space to recognise and grapple with Britain's multi-faith diversity by applying the test of 'reasonableness'. There has also always been room for reform since unsatisfactory laws can be challenged, especially with the incorporation of the European Convention on Human Rights. Legal change can be influenced through the Law Commission or through direct approaches to the government.[71]

This has meant that Muslims in Britain have largely come to accept that neither a separate legal system nor even separate legislation is necessary to meet most specific Muslim needs in the area of family law. Even on those points where Muslims believe that English law is incompatible with Islamic law, they have found little difficulty in living with the strictures of English law over such matters as the minimum age of marriage, the non-recognition of *talaq* (divorce) except through a British court, the continuation of maintenance beyond the *idda* period (three months in which the paternity of an unborn child can be determined), access to and custody of children, and the ban on polygamy. This is partly because no consensus on some of these issues exists among Muslims themselves, and partly because they are not considered obligatory from a religious point of view.[72] Furthermore, British Muslims' wide acceptance of the English legal system in this area reflects a shift away from prescriptions of classical jurisprudence towards preparedness to exercise personal judgement over current problems, and also a lack of willingness on the part of the British legislature, influenced as it has been by anti-Muslim trends in public opinion, to view Muslim demands favourably. Because of the reluctance of the British state to concede Muslim demands, a parallel set of institutions has gradually been created to provide religious legitimacy for individual actions. The UK Islamic Shariah Council, consisting of religious scholars, gives guidance and advice, mainly on marital matters, on the basis of their understanding of Islamic law. The advice of such bodies is being accepted by individuals and parties on a strictly voluntary basis. For instance, a panel at the Central Birmingham Mosque issues certificates to Muslim women wishing to secure religious recognition of their divorce in addition to the legal form obtained through the courts, through *khula* (a legal process under Islamic law allowing women to seek divorce independently of their husband's wishes).[73]

Many mosques have also obtained the services of *muftis*, specialists on Islamic law, to issue *fatwas* (expert advice of a jurist on a specific legal problem) on personal and social minutiae. Lewis refers to *fatwas* issued in Bradford on such questions as whether it is sinful for taxi-drivers to take customers to pubs and clubs where alcohol is consumed; whether contraception or abortion can take place under any circumstance; whether television, videos, cinema and theatre are *haram*; and whether mortgages can even be permitted. Guidance has been sought on issues ranging from questions about prayers, fasting, *zakat* and *hajj* to marriage, divorce, custody, inheritance, investments and professional conduct.[74]

The dilemma between owning a home and remaining faithful to the Sharia prohibition on usury has confronted many Muslims at some stage in their lives. In the absence of a *halal* financial services sector, aspiring home-buyers have been faced with either signing up for a mortgage or forgoing ownership and remaining in rented accommodation. In the 1990s that choice was made a little wider, for at least a few Muslims, with the introduction of Britain's first *halal* mortgage. The Manzil programme run by the United Bank of Kuwait through its Islamic Investment Banking Unit offered an alternative to mortgage financing in 1997. Although the bank refused to call the Manzil by this description, it was in reality a fixed-rate mortgage, which conformed to a traditional Islamic contract known as *murabaha* (instalment sale contract). In 1993 the Al-Baraka Bank's British operation also attempted to run an interest-free property-financing scheme but it quickly folded.[75] Given the paucity of such options, the majority of Muslims in Britain have continued to resort to the concession offered in the Sharia allowing those living in non-Muslim countries to take out a mortgage on the grounds of necessity. Another attempt to meet the capital investment and religious requirements has been the Halal Mutual Investment Fund. Based on the rules of a *muda-raba* contract, this transaction satisfies the Sharia stipulation that both lender and borrower share risks as well as rewards. The approval of British *ulama* such as Dr Syed al-Darsh of the UK Islamic Shariah Council and Mufti Yusuf Satha of the Institute of Islamic Jurisprudence gave the initiative legitimacy.[76] However, the vast majority of Muslims in Britain still use high-street banks and building societies to meet their financial needs, knowing full well that interest and credit are an inseparable part of their financial system.

The 1980s saw Muslims in Britain struggling for official acknowledgement of religious rights against a background of increasing anti-Muslim sentiment in the wider British society. The high point of this struggle was reached with the Rushdie affair. Outraged by what to them was the blasphemous content of Salman Rushdie's novel *The*

Satanic Verses, groups of British Muslims engaged in protests and petitioned the government to ban it. Their sometimes violent campaign suggested that they had not quite understood British cultural sensibilities and that they lacked respect for the rule of law. This general perception tended to isolate them from the rest of the population. The book-burning episode in January 1989 and the media-manufactured support for Khomeini's *fatwa* sentencing Rushdie to death alienated popular opinion already shaped by negative stereotypes and images of Muslims as intolerant and incapable of resolving disputes through peaceful and rational debate.[77] As the atmosphere polarised and became more vitriolic, the demand for the banning of the book was opposed by the majority of the establishment as well by as the public at large, who saw it as an attack on the principles of free speech, thought and expression. Muslims were condemned by the more extreme elements as 'intellectual hooligans' and their actions compared with those of the Nazis.[78]

The call for a ban on *The Satanic Verses* and a change in the blasphemy law failed because they were unable to convince the non-Muslim majority of the validity of their case in an idiom and in ways which that majority could understand. While actively seeking a more sympathetic hearing for these religious grievances, Muslims did not seem to be engaging constructively with British political, social and cultural institutions. Some even acknowledged that they had not fully understood British political and legal processes and traditions—and had therefore not gone about lobbying for wider support for their cause in the right way. Lessons were learnt, however, and, with the injection of ideas and strategies more in tune with the tenor of the wider society, greater support for change was gained among politicians and leading figures in the Church and other faith communities. As Lord Scarman put it, 'In an increasingly plural society such as that of modern Britain it is necessary not only to respect the differing religious beliefs, feelings and practices of all but to protect them from … vilification, ridicule and contempt.'[79] The Law Commission did not quite agree, and recommended the abolition rather than the extension of the blasphemy law; and the Minister for Home Affairs, John Patten, was unwilling to extend the law, even though he recognised that British Muslims were justified in their claim that the law unfairly discriminated against them on religious grounds. Thus short shrift was given to the secular principles of equality, fairness and justice and British Muslims were denied the possibility of engaging with society on the basis of mutual respect.[80]

Two further areas of British law have had a significant impact on Muslim social behaviour and engagement with society. While the Race Relations Act of 1976 made racial and ethnic discrimination unlawful in a wide area including employment, education, housing and the provision of goods, facilities and services, religious rights fell outside its purview. Hence Muslims have had no recourse to any legal remedy if denied observance of their faith (Friday and daily prayers, time off to go on a pilgrimage to Mecca, wearing of the *hijab*) by, for instance, employers. Given the terms of the Public Order Act of 1986, sacrilege and incitement to religious hatred of Muslims were even less subject to law, even though substantial anecdotal evidence exists to suggest that anti-Muslim harassment and attacks on Muslims, their property and their places of worship were on the increase. This formal exclusion inevitably produced a sense of alienation and marginalisation, making the entry of British Muslims into mainstream society somewhat problematic.[81]

Muslim political engagement in Britain

Any discussion of Muslim interaction with British society must involve an examination of Muslim engagement with wide political processes, if only because the degree of their political incorporation represents an important indicator of the wider acceptance of Muslim settlers. There is no conclusive proof that in late-twentieth-century Britain Muslims have participated in politics any more than other groups, but research indicates that their involvement is in fact greater than that of the majority population. In other words, growing numbers of Muslims have come to regard formal political mechanisms as an effective way of getting their problems addressed, if not solved. Another motive behind their involvement in British political processes has been a belief that the values of equality and justice, which are highly regarded in Islam, might be better promoted by means of democratic strategies. In negotiating their identity as members of British society they have sought, with varying degrees of inclusion and exclusion, representation and involvement in both local and national government. In the process they have developed particular party alignments and political agendas that have reflected their concerns and circumstances, which have also been changing over time. So while certain generalisations can be made about Muslim political engagement in late-twentieth-century Britain, this process has grown more complex as Muslim communities have evolved.

Since the Second World War the relationship between local and central government in Britain has changed enormously, but until the 1970s local government retained control over large areas of activity, including law and order, licensing and control of trades, social services, health, education, planning and transport. In the early phases of postwar Muslim settlement in Britain, interest among migrants was still directed towards politics in their countries of origin—for instance, many political parties in Pakistan set up branches in cities such as Bradford. But as families arrived, concern shifted to emerging local social and educational issues. In these early years it was ethnicity and culture, rather than religion, which provided the framework for these Muslims' entry into the public sphere. Even so, religion could become an issue as Muslims came up against planning laws and education policies, affecting such things as the obtaining of mosque premises and the court-matters in schools. Thus, as Muslims became more settled and confident their political involvement increased—at first locally and then on the national stage. Muslim interest in politics has taken many forms and been shaped by various factors, both internal to the Muslim communities and emanating from the wider society. It has been moulded by differing Muslim attitudes towards political participation in a society that is not only non-Muslim but also largely secular.

In the 1970s, as permanent settlement caused Muslims to relate with a broader range of institutions, they began to create organisations to pursue their interests. Each religious 'denomination' established its own local, national and indeed international organisational expression, in order to negotiate access to resources and individual welfare provision with the state. They debated policy on Muslim rights. In all this, they acted as brokers between the state and their communities, a role not dissimilar to that played by 'indigenous' leaders under colonial patronage. However, there was little penetration of mainstream institutions where real power was located; on the contrary, distinctiveness, separateness and autonomy were asserted, partly in response to exclusion and devaluation of values and norms they held dear. Broad-based alliances were eschewed. Thus the first generation of migrant Muslims during the 1960s and early 1970s worked through intermediaries between their communities and the British establishment; few joined mainstream political organisations, and so their impact on politics remained marginal.

As agendas widened in the 1980s, Muslims took a more extensive part in the public sphere but still on the basis of distinct community organisations, which sometimes received encouragement from the state as part of the desire to reflect Britain's emerging multicultural, plural society. The Bradford Council for Mosques, which was constituted in September 1981, was thus supported by the City Council through grants. Drawing strength from community support, this and other organisations used their strength in local politics to achieve agreement on specific issues through a typically British process of negotiation and compromise rather than confrontation. Muslim organisations therefore mushroomed in this period, coming together from time to time to lobby local authorities to change policy and act on particular areas of concern. At the same time they realised that with some issues local efforts were insufficient and that to make an impact they had to apply political pressure at the national level. The campaign against proposals to abolish exemptions to regulations governing slaughter of animals for food and the debate on religious matters addressed in the 1988 Education Reform Act were among the first attempts at a nationally coordinated operation.

By the mid-1980s a more active involvement in local politics began to develop as younger Muslims realised that their lack of participation had proved detrimental to Muslim interests. Their involvement in local politics grew substantially, and alliances with mainstream parties were developed on the basis of ideological understandings. For instance, young Bangladeshi activists of the influential Federation of Bangladesh Youth Organisations in the London borough of Tower Hamlets had much in common with their white counterparts. This helped them to build cross-ethnic political alliances that kept the focus on secular concerns, involving provision of resources for housing, education, employment and welfare rights, and provision of amenities.[82]

However, following the coming to power of the Conservative Party in 1979, policies became less sympathetic towards ethnic minorities and local resources began to dry up. Muslim groups that had not pre-viously relied on public funding or been closely tied into local state initiatives began to mobilise young Muslim activists on more reli-giously-oriented issues, pressing mainstream institutions for action. These groups were anxious to see issues of a more specifically reli-gious nature addressed—such as provision of *halal* food, a change in dress requirements in schools, and the extension of the blasphemy law to Islam. While these campaigns were not particularly effective, the experience gained enabled Muslim groups to unite when *The Satanic Verses* controversy erupted in the late 1980s. And, while the unity forged at this time only lasted while the issue was under the spotlight, an increasing number of Muslims realised that unity had been essential to the effectiveness of the campaign. In other words, they saw the usefulness of a broad unified alliance if Britain's normally fragmented Muslim communities were going to persuade British society as a whole to engage with any of their major concerns. At the same time, many Muslims emerged from the Rushdie protests feeling isolated; convinced that their core values had been violated, they saw little space in which to reach political accommodation with Britain's appar-ently secular establishment.

This sense of separation from society was heightened by differences in perception that emerged during the Gulf War over the winter of 1990–1. The lack of Muslim support for the position of the British government, combined with the frustration felt by many in the Muslim community at the failure of the wider society to understand their ques-tioning the wisdom of the Western intervention, fuelled a move away from political disengagement that produced the creation of the Muslim Parliament in 1992. Its supporters felt that the British establishment could only be persuaded to pay attention to specifically Muslim con-cerns through community and pressure-group politics since the main channels were proving largely ineffective. But the result was a popular perception that Muslims had distanced themselves from the rest of society and so were in conflict with its values and norms. However, the government was keen to see Muslim ethnic groups, both local and national, forging unity (similar to that achieved by the Jewish com-munity in the shape of the Board of Deputies of British Jews), with Islam as the common reference-point. Such an organisation, credibly representing Muslim interests, could link British Muslims to wider local and national political institutions. Such a degree of unity (which does not exist even among British Jews) proved unrealisable since it did not take account of ethnic, sectarian, political and historical differences among the various sections of 'the Muslim community', and was criticised as a modern form of the colonial policy of 'divide and rule'.

Muslim political participation has taken various forms, including voting, party membership and standing as candidates for election. The level of 'passive' involvement in politics can be gauged from electoral behaviour in the period 1974–2001. The first indicator of Muslims' participation in the electoral system is the extent to which they have been registered to vote. Up to the mid-1970s, their registration rate was lower than that of other groups, although there were wide variations according to area and the numbers of Muslims registered did gradually rise.[83] The number of registered voters increased from around two-thirds in the 1960s to three-quarters in the 1970s.[84] Anwar suggested several reasons for this early 'non-registration' including 'the newness of migrants, the language difficulty [which 'Asian' migrants experienced], the general alienation of some groups, and feared harassment and racial attacks' from far right groups, who could identify Asians by their names on the register. There was also 'the fear of "fishing expeditions" by immigration authorities'.[85] Husband later added to this list 'the effects of the Conservative switching of local taxes' (especially the 'poll tax'), which resulted in dramatic increases in tax bills.[86] That said, from the mid-1970s there was a steady increase in the level of Muslim registration, with a study in 1991 showing that nationally only 15% of South Asian Muslims were not registered.[87] Improved dissemination of information by administrative authorities through minority media reinforced the rising level of Muslims' awareness of the political process. By 1997 registration rates across all ethnic groups had become 'surprisingly uniform', suggesting 'a fairly buoyant level of interest in the electoral process among blacks and Asians', although registration among Pakistanis and Bangladeshis was still a little lower than for Indians and whites.[88] Correspondingly, fewer Pakistanis and Bangladeshis, the predominant Muslim groups in Britain, voted at the 1997 general election (76% and 74% respectively, compared with 82% Indians and 79% whites), perhaps indicating greater political alienation.[89] However, the turnout among South Asian Muslims reflects broadly an encouraging level of political participation. According to Anwar, surveys during various local and general elections in the 1970s and 1980s showed that on average 'Asian turnout is always higher than that of non-Asians [including white] from the same areas'.[90] An even clearer sign of the Muslims' growing interest in electoral politics has been offered by Lelohe's analysis of electoral data in Bradford, where the bulk of the Asian population is of Pakistani and Bangladeshi origin, and concluded that 'the Asian communities in Bradford ... have excellent records of electoral registration, an excellent polling-day organisation with very high turnout levels'.[91]

The available evidence suggests that on the whole British Muslims have not voted only on the basis of 'religious' allegiances. When Muslims have stood as independent candidates, they have not secured much Muslim support even when specifically Muslim issues have acquired a high profile. Muslim voting alignment has been shown to be more complex. For instance, a Muslim charter in 1984, supported by the UK Islamic Mission, Ahl-i-Hadith and Muslim Educational Trust, recommending that Muslims should vote for candidates who would be ready to meet specifically Muslim demands failed to make much impression on Muslim voting patterns in Birmingham. Successive general election results have shown that Muslims do not simply vote for Muslim candidates. For instance, Conservative Muslim candidates have not been successful in Muslim areas even against white or other non-Muslim Labour candidates. However, ethnic and/or religious affiliation was not insignificant. For instance, when in 1997 the Labour Party selected non-Muslim ethnic minority candidates in the 'safe' seats of Bradford West and, in London, Bethnal Green and Bow (in both Muslims formed an overwhelming majority of the ethnic-minority population), the Conservatives, by selecting Muslim candidates matching the respective electorate's ethnicity, were able to reduce significantly Labour's share of the Muslim vote.[92] For example, in the 2001 general election the Labour candidate in Bradford West, Marsha Singh, increased his share of the vote by a greater margin (6.5%) than that of his Conservative opponent, Mohammed Riaz (4.1%).[93] Against this, Riaz argued that Singh's gains did not necessarily show greater support among Muslims, but could have resulted from shifts among other communities. He claimed, on the contrary, to have made substantial inroads into Singh's Muslim support, winning '70% of the Muslim vote' and that his gains would have been much bigger had traditional Conservative voters not stayed at home. All this remained conjecture, given that Singh was himself selected by a Muslim-dominated constituency Labour Party.[94] Rashid Skinner, a convert to Islam standing as a Conservative candidate in Pendle against Reg Prentice, made significant gains, but it would be difficult to prove that the increase in his vote (3.6%) was religiously motivated. In Birmingham's Perry Barr constituency, a Labour stronghold with a substantial Muslim population where the MP up till the 2001 general election was a government minister, Jeff Rooker, there was almost a 9% swing against Khalid Mahmood, a Kashmiri Muslim, although this might have been partly due to Mahmood's selection being opposed by an influential section of the constituency Labour Party.[95]

Information on voting patterns from 1974 onwards reveals that the majority of British Muslims have supported the Labour Party, since they have perceived it to be more sympathetic to their concerns than the Conservatives: 'Muslims are loyal to the Labour Party because they believe it to be for the working class, and also the Labour Party is far less racist in both attitude and practice than the other parties, particularly the Conservative party'.[96] Labour policies on employment and services have resonated with Muslim ideas on these issues. Nevertheless, while the data are not clear-cut, Anwar's 'detailed analysis of results from some areas shows that Pakistani support for the Labour Party has come down from over 80% in the 1970s to over 60% in the 1980s and to just over 50% in the 1990s.'[97] In the 1987 general election, a significant proportion of Asians, among them many Muslims, transferred their support to the Conservatives. Some previously Labour-supporting prosperous traders switched their allegiance, as did many Ismailis and other Muslims from East Africa with professional and business backgrounds.[98] More generally, as Anwar has pointed out, an emphasis on the importance of self-employment, home ownership and family life has been viewed, particularly by many first-generation Muslims, as more in tune with the philosophy of the Conservative Party. They owned their own businesses, of which the Conservative Party was viewed as being traditionally more supportive. The attraction of the Conservative Party also developed as Muslims became more disenchanted with Labour's failure to represent their interests and respond to their demands, and to support their protests against *The Satanic Verses* and against religious discrimination. A number of Labour Party MPs were likewise targeted for their support of Israel.[99] Thus it should perhaps have come as no surprise that in the 2001 general election, given a national swing to the Conservatives of 1.8%, only one of the seven Muslim Labour candidates made any gains, whereas five of the eight Muslim Conservatives improved their vote. However, the Labour Party maintained its privileged position among British Muslim communities and, despite the erosion of support for Labour, the number of Muslims supporting the Conservatives remained relatively small. In areas of high Muslim concentration, for instance, Muslims are a majority of the local Labour Party membership, and by the late 1990s 'an estimated 90% of Muslim political party membership [was] in the Labour Party'.[100]

Thus, empirical evidence confirms the impression that British Muslim participation in national mainstream politics has steadily grown since the 1970s. A record fifty-three Muslim candidates stood in the 2001 general election, a great change from the 1970s and 1980s[101] and even over the 1990s.[102] For the first time a Muslim, Muhammad Sarwar, standing on the Labour Party platform was elected from a Scottish constituency at the 1997 general election, and was returned in the 2001 general election with increased support. And Khalid Mahmood, representing the Labour Party (as mentioned above), was elected from a Birmingham constituency in 2001. In 1999 Bashir Khanbhai was elected to the European Parliament as a Conservative. Meanwhile Muslims have been appointed as peers to sit in the House of Lords—Lord Nazir Ahmed of Rotherham, Baroness Pola Uddin of Bethnal Green, Lord Waheed Alli and Lord Adam Patel of Blackburn are all Labour peers. A recent Muslim appointment to the House of Lords is that of Amirali Bhatia, a businessman originally from Tanzania.[103] However, Abdul Matin Pelham, the eighth Earl of Yarborough, a Conservative hereditary peer, had to relinquish his seat as a result of reform of the House of Lords. Meanwhile, the political establishment has come to acknowledge the Muslim presence by giving *Eid* parties for British Muslims at the House of Commons and in Downing Street.[104]

Participation in local politics expanded even more sharply: 160 Muslim local councillors (153 Labour, six Liberal Democrat and one Conservative) were elected in 1996; by 2001 the figure was 217. However, a significant change of party affiliations has occurred. While the number of Labour councillors increased by only eight the Liberal Democrat ranks had been swelled by twenty-one and the Conservative by twenty-two. These councillors represented areas of high Muslim concentration and were predominantly male. The relatively steep rise in Muslim involvement in local mainstream politics has been particularly notable in cities with high Muslim concentrations, such as London, Birmingham and Bradford. By 1996 London alone had forty-nine Muslim councillors, though in areas with significant Muslim concentrations, such as Newham (eleven), Tower Hamlets (ten) and Waltham Forest (seven).[105] By 2001 this figure stood at sixty-three.[106]

In Britain as a whole the rate of growth has been slower and more erratic, with something of a breakthrough in the late 1980s and 1990s. While Bashir Maan was the first Pakistani councillor to be elected anywhere in Britain (from a ward in Glasgow) as far back as 1970, only in 1982 did Birmingham, with the largest Muslim population apart from London, have its first Muslim councillor. By 1987, of the fourteen ethnic minority councillors in the city, six were Muslim (all Labour); by 1996–7 there were thirteen.[107] In Bradford only three of the ninety city councillors in 1981 were Muslims. A decade later their number had trebled, and by 1996 there were eleven,[108] testifying to their rapidly increasing involvement and influence in local mainstream politics towards the end of the twentieth century.[109]

However, while Muslim influence and involvement at the grass-roots level gradually increased within mainstream parties, Muslim politicians largely remained sidelined in terms of power: there have been no Muslim leaders of local councils and only a handful of deputy leaders. Some councillors have been fobbed off with high-profile but largely ceremonial roles, such as mayor.[110] Others, as secretaries and vice-chairs, have occupied positions arguably with little real power, despite considerable experience of local politics.[111] This exclusion of Muslim politicians from rising in the main parties' hierarchy is due to a number of reasons. Discriminatory attitudes have been blamed for this: 'Muslims are allowed to join the Labour Party but are not allowed to influence policies. If the local party allows access, the National Executive steps in to control anything it does not like through suspension and exclusion. The old colonialism is still in place.'[112] They have faced resistance in the selection process because of the negative stereotypes of Muslims, including lack of professionalism and ideological commitment to democratic practices (Muslim networking has been seen as undemocratic). They have been accused of opportunism, illegal recruiting practices, bribery, corruption and using politics for personal gain, despite little evidence to show that the conduct of Muslim politicians is open to any more suspicion than that of their white counterparts.

Clearly, even at this local level, let alone nationally, Muslim politicians have not been a homogeneous group in terms of countries of origin, generation, ideological tendencies and attitudes towards 'Muslim' demands. Hence Muslims have not always presented a unified political stand. While all Muslim councillors have deplored clientelism, many Muslim politicians have operated within their own communities along client–patron lines. Increasingly, however, young Muslims have dissociated themselves from this type of politics. Khalid Mahmood, MP for Birmingham's Perry Barr constituency, thus stated that he was 'first and foremost' a representative of the people. While admitting that he would look 'especially at the underachievement of ethnic minority children in the education system' as well as 'speaking out on human rights issues ... in Palestine, Kashmir, Bosnia, Chechnya', he insisted that his focus would be not only on Muslim issues but on the concerns of all his constituents.[113]

In many ways, therefore, Muslim councillors have been typical of politicians in Britain as a whole. They have been predominantly middle-aged and male, and belonged to economic, occupational and educational élites, thus bringing a wide range of professional experience and skills to their elected political role.[114] While Muslim councillors have varied in the profession of their faith and the significance of religious practice in their lives, many have described themselves as 'secular Muslims':[115] formal religion was part of their private lives and not a defining characteristic in their professions. They rarely went to the mosque, certainly much less than recent estimates for the wider Muslim community, perhaps reflecting a desire to move the communal focus away from the mosque to wider institutions in society.[116]

Meanwhile, the main British political parties have been reluctant to advance ethnic minority (including Muslim) participation beyond certain 'acceptable limits'. They have certainly acknowledged that Muslims have the potential to influence electoral outcomes in a number of constituencies but fear of a 'white backlash' has often discouraged these parties from selecting Muslim parliamentary candidates. None was selected in any of the four general elections held in the 1970s. A sprinkling appeared in the 1980s and the trend continued in the 1990s, but they remain under-represented. Out of seventy-seven minority candidates in the 2001 general elections, twenty-four were Muslim, mostly in unwinnable constituencies,[117] and of the thirteen ethnic minority candidates elected only two were Muslim, both from constituencies with large Muslim concentrations, thus reinforcing the appearance of 'political ghettoisation'.[118] Yet in spite of these hurdles British Muslims still seem convinced that one of the most effective ways of influencing policies and institutions is through mainstream political action. Consequently, the drive to become involved in the main parties acquired momentum throughout the 1990s. Muslim membership of all those parties, especially in constituencies with high Muslim populations, seems to be increasing.

Thus the potential impact of what could be achieved locally through effective use of voting power has been apparent for some time. Muslims were aware of their electoral muscle as early as the 1970s, when the Pakistan Welfare Association supported the Liberals in local elections in Rochdale. While their choice was probably due to the Liberals having nominated three Pakistanis for the district elections, one winning a ward where 30% of its total electorate were immigrants,[119] this success emphasised that political mobilisation as an ethnic (as opposed to religious) group at this stage of Muslim settlement brought some political influence—more at the local than at the national level—and this influence was accentuated by the fact that in the past Asians had been 'twice as likely to turn out to vote in council elections as white voters'.[120] Muslim communities around Britain have subsequently become even more aware of the pressure they can exert on politicians, especially in constituencies where they have the potential to alter the balance of power. In the 1997 general election Iqbal Sacranie, for the UK Action Committee on Islamic Affairs (UKACIA) spokesman, estimated that there were about twenty constituencies where the total of Muslim voters exceeded the majority of the sitting MP. The lobbying group Muslim Election 1997 disseminated information on the main candidates in forty marginal seats where Muslim voters could affect the outcome. In many of these constituencies UKACIA called on 'the Muslim community to exert its numerical significance by extracting promises from candidates'.[121] Similar strategies were suggested by Muslim Election 2001. Extensive lobbying was organised, candidates from the major parties took part in discussions on Muslim issues, and campaigns were organised against MPs perceived as being 'anti-Muslim'.[122]

This growth of Muslim participation in mainstream British politics is connected to the accumulation of sufficient economic resources to build a political organisation and carry out political action. The need for the mainstreaming of political action has come to be felt more strongly, and Muslims have decided that they need to engage with wider institutions to secure the rights of themselves and their families. As their ability to communicate effectively has improved, they have become more confident about engaging with the British political system and, by working within it, have learned to bend it to serve their interests. Large numbers of Muslims have deliberately and successfully penetrated the British political establishment, becoming active in secular politics and in effect accepting its 'ungodly' character. They have recognised that as members of secular political parties they need to adopt, as a minimum, an acquiescent approach to non-Islamic ideologies, and their freedom to speak up on Muslim issues has been limited by party discipline. They have represented in the first instance their parties' policies and the views of all their constituents—not just Islam and Muslims—on such issues as abortion, homo-sexuality and Israel. Their loyalty was first to the party and then to their religion. Thus, though religious and cultural matters were articulated more often by those Muslims engaged in formal politics than by their white counterparts, most of their activities concerned normal 'interest politics', responding to routine issues as and when they develop, such as access to local services (youth facilities, accommodation for the elderly, homelessness), road safety, street lighting, refuse collection, small-business policies and Housing Renovation Grants, none of which is a uniquely Muslim issue. Nevertheless, their greater reliance on their

Muslim electorates has meant giving more attention to Muslim agendas, and this has tended to marginalise their work as representatives of a broader, non-Muslim constituency.

While many British Muslims have demonstrated commitment to the principles of a democratic, pluralist and secular state and society, others have supported 'withdrawal into cultural ghettos', and still others are keen to initiate mass conversion to Islam and have the Sharia incorporated into the legal framework for Muslims in British society. In the early 1990s the Muslim Parliament—according to Kalim Siddiqi, 'a minority political system for Muslims of Britain'—suggested the creation of a separate political system parallel to the dominant one. Its view was that 'nothing can be achieved with democratic politics'. Hence, Siddiqi called for a collective Muslim voice outside the mainstream political systems, which would always be dominated by non-Muslims and anti-Islamic interest; any attempt to work through, within or in cooperation with the establishment was bound to fail in the long run even though it might be rewarded with minor, short-term gains.[123] More specifically, Jahangir Mohammed, the deputy leader of the Muslim Parliament at the time of the general election in 1997, advised Muslims not to vote, arguing that 'politics is about power ... Parliament merely reflects the existing balance of power in society. If we do not have organised power outside Parliament, we will not have influence inside it ... It is only by generating power ourselves that we will change our condition. It is only organisation and financial muscle that will give us this power.' Muslims should remain a separate community, and say 'yes to interaction, no to integration'.[124]

The Muslim Parliament, which many Muslims considered too radical and too separatist even at its height, attracted only a small minority of support among Britain's Muslims. Hizb-ut-Tahrir (the Liberation Party) and Al-Muhajiroun (the Emigrants), again with only marginal support, are religio-political organisations that have gone further in their aims. Their key objective is:

> to change the current corrupt society and transform it ... by establishing an Islamic state (not just in Britain but all over the world, the Khilafah would be a Global Islamic State under one Khalifah with the Ummah united under it) in which the Sharia would be implemented in its entirety. In such a state there would be no place for human beings to enact laws to organise their relations.

According to them, since the democratic system is 'a system of Kufr [unbelief], based on the creed of separating religion from life', a system in which people enact the laws, it is un-Islamic.[125] Hence, voting and political participation in a democratic but non-Islamic state should be forbidden to Muslims. For both organisations 'everything is *haram* until we have a caliph'.[126]

British Muslims aligned with the Islamic Party of Britain (IPB) found themselves criticised both by those who were calling for full electoral participation and by the 'separatist' stand for compromising their principles, on the one hand, and for wasting their energy by staying outside the political arena on the other. The IPB has rejected these accusations, arguing that participation in election campaigns enables the party to 'put forward meaningful alternatives' to a system 'built on falsehood, oppression and ignorance'.[127] Iqbal Sacranie, former secretary-general of the Muslim Council of Britain—an organisation regarded, at least by many in the British political establishment, as moderate and much more representative—argued that Muslims had a duty to vote. In 1997, as UKACIA convener, he exhorted Muslims to vote for the following reasons:

We are not and cannot be a ghetto community … We believe it is necessary for us to relate to the wider society, to understand our neighbours and to let them understand us … We need to interact with people—people of other faiths and no faith, people who have a mutual interest in human welfare and even those who may have an unfriendly agenda … Muslims should not opt out of the political life of the country and voluntarily give up their social and political rights. Neither should they surrender their duty to make their opinions and advice known on matters of concern to themselves and wider society. This is what the electoral process, voting and political representation is about … It is therefore only appropriate that Muslims take full part in the political process.[128]

The UKACIA's manifesto, *Elections 1997 and the British Muslims: for a Fair and Caring Society*, urged them to exercise their right to vote in the general elections, but at the same time counselled Muslims to press prospective parliamentary candidates on issues of specific concern to them; they should extract promises from candidates in constituencies where Muslims could alter the balance of power, and cast their votes having carefully assessed the candidates' responses.[129] In the 2001 general election the Muslim Council of Britain (a development of UKACIA) expanded on ideas presented in the 1997 election in its document *Electing to Listen*. It did this by suggesting an agenda which it felt the Muslim community would wish Parliament to address and by placing pressure on MPs in constituencies where Muslims had the capacity to exercise influence to declare their positions on issues of concern to Muslims.[130]

The different strategies and stances taken by Muslims over political participation have been connected largely to their differing views on British society. Four main positions have been identified as relevant to these patterns. First, there is the traditionalist view, which defines Britain as *dar al-harb* (house or territory of war), in which Muslims are required to have minimal contact with society, and no political engagement. Second, there is the pragmatic view, according to which Britain is not perceived as *dar al-kufr* (house or territory of unbelief) since Muslims are allowed to 'enjoin good' and 'forbid evil', and therefore have a responsibility to do so through politics as much as in other ways. Third, there is the transnational view, articulated by Kalim Siddiqi, of Muslims in Britain as part of the worldwide Islamic community; rather than participating in mainstream British politics, they should try to create a unified and well-organised community of Muslims within but separate from non-Muslim Britain. Fourth, there is a diffuse strand of Muslims who have attempted to reinterpret the Islamic tradition regarding political participation in light of modern developments. They should not view Britain as *dar al-kufr*; Muslims in Britain enjoy religious liberty, are free to practise religious rites, to create religious institutions, and to preach and convert. Hence, in the absence of any impediments, Muslims should participate fully in political activities in Britain.

To understand South Asian Muslim political behaviour in Britain, one must consider the approaches of the various strands of South Asian Islam regarding the political participation of Muslims in elections and their membership of secular political organisations. Broadly, there appears to be no objection to such participation in the political life of a non-Muslim country so long as those Muslims who participate as elected members endorse no measures that are forbidden by Islam or against Muslim interests.[131] For instance, Deobandis, while remaining fairly withdrawn from politics, do not perceive Britain as *dar al-kufr* and therefore see 'no problem for Muslims participating in politics … Muslims should vote and take interest in what is going on around them'. Barelwis too have seen no 'prohibition to Muslims taking part in political activity providing that it [does] not conflict with the basic beliefs of the faith'. They regard religious and political activities as separate, and political engagement as a duty to wider society. The Ahl-i-Hadith and the UK Islamic Mission (UKIM) have both made public relations and political pressure part of their overall strategy. Andrews in his study of Muslim political attitudes in Leicester quotes a member of the UKIM articulating its position on political participation in Britain: 'Although Muslims desire an Islamic state, this applies to countries that have a Muslim majority. It is the duty of Muslims in the UK to abide by the laws of the country, and seek to achieve Muslim interests through making representation to local and national politicians.' Muslims should not join British political parties, but rather support whichever party is prepared to meet 'Muslim demands'.[132] Sufi groups meanwhile have pursued individual tactics, participating in inner-city mainstream politics. Individual mosques have also developed wide-ranging contacts with local councillors and MPs.

With the exception of the Deobandis, all these groups seem to agree that Muslims must participate in British political life and that the actual election of Muslims is a positive achievement. M.S. Raza, a scholar and director of the Islamic Centre in Leicester, considered political participation desirable even if its only purpose was to fight the state. It was 'essential for the survival of Muslims in Britain' since it would enable them to gain the necessary power and influence over matters of specific interest and concern to them.[133] In short, while many Muslims may have rationalised their approach to political participation in the British system on religious grounds, the end result is that few have felt disinclined to take part in mainstream politics. Instead, British Muslims have become progressively more involved in constitutional politics through membership and support of mainstream political parties.

Thus Muslims have engaged politically with British society in various ways and perhaps more actively than most other ethnic or faith groups. They have operated both inside the political system and beyond it, and the diversity of their political responses reflects the differentiated char-

acter of Muslim communities in Britain as well as the range of interpretations of Islam, continually contested and negotiated, that Muslims
invoke to justify and construct particular political strategies. However,
economic deprivation and social exclusion have caused some British
Muslims to see mainstream politics as an ideological betrayal and as
part of the process of cultural homogenisation. Alienated, disaffected,
frustrated and resentful, they have lost faith in the wider, formal political structures. They therefore reject them and pursue the politics of the
street, confronting the power of the state through direct and disruptive
collective action. But this spontaneous and relatively unorganised
political response by certain groups of British Muslims has produced
few positive results and a considerable negative backlash from the
wider society. Meanwhile the majority of British Muslims have
patiently carried on attempting to penetrate political institutions that
have the power to make policies and allocate resources. The fact that
incorporation of British Muslims in the formal political system has
grown steadily suggests that they are increasingly accepted by the
wider society as part of it.

More broadly, the engagement of younger British Muslims can be
better understood by bringing together the concepts of 'assimilation'
and 'integration' with the notion of 'enculturation'—an idea first
mooted by Herskovits in his paper on Afro-Americans.[134] Mead
explained enculturation 'as the process of learning culture in all its
uniqueness and particularity'.[135] Weinreih developed the concept further, describing enculturation as 'a process whereby individuals experiment with various roles, try them on for fit, reject some components
and accept others. They formulate their own points of view on a range
of topics, such as dress, music, boy and girl friends, and begin to scrutinise given moral imperatives.'[136] Through this process people may
identify with certain characteristics of another group without forgoing
their own ethnic group allegiance, and thereby redefine or update conceptions of their own ethnicity. It is viewed as change through the
incorporation of cultural elements, as opposed to acculturation, which
is seen as change towards the dominant culture. Finally, Nasreen Ali has
summarised enculturation as

> a process of adaptation and transformation in which both the ethni-
> cised minorities and the so-called host society exchange cultural

tokens and in the process transform their identities. In some ways the notion of enculturation points towards the way in which syncretic and hybridised forms of identification are the norm rather than the preserve of an *avant-garde*. This banalisation (or normalisation) of syncretic and hybrid subjectivities is called enculturation ... In other words it is the process by which collective identities (which are internally divided and intrinsically fuzzy) maintain their stability while undergoing radical transformations.[137]

Enculturation for her is 'a process by which, coming from a specific culture one becomes part of another culture'. One can see this process at work in the way that many young British Muslim women have transformed Western dress by wearing it in combination with their own ethnic forms of clothing, filling it with a different significance. It is also apparent in a variety of contemporary British Asian musical productions.

Hence, we can see that younger generations of Muslims are engaging with British culture, the political system, educational institutions and the media more extensively and in more creative ways than their parents and grandparents. This is perhaps to be expected since they have undergone more far-reaching processes of socialisation. Indeed, while maintaining particular religious values, they have absorbed many British political values, such as the notions of democracy and freedom of speech. For them 'love' marriages are no longer a specifically British cultural practice towards which they are moving, but just one of the many ways that marriages take place in contemporary society. Viewed in this way, there is no loss of self-esteem, no sense of inferiority and much more reaching out for a vibrant and positive synthesis that enables an increasing number of Muslims to live relatively easily within British society.

9

MUSLIM WOMEN AND FAMILIES IN BRITAIN

The dominant Western picture of Muslim women is as passive and docile, subject to patriarchal traditions and lacking any active agency to change their condition; also as exotic, ruthlessly oppressed victims of religion. Invisible in the public domain and trapped within the family framework, their lives are seen as unfree and exposed to domestic exploitation. Socially and sexually controlled in their male-dominated communities, they are presumed to have few opportunities to find fulfilment.

This picture is misleading, and far removed from the lived experience of most Muslim women in Britain. No discourse on British Muslim women can ignore the heterogeneous nature of their background. The different communities of which they are part have built their own systems of gender relations underpinned by their own interpretations of patriarchal religious ideology. It must also be remembered that historically not all Muslim women have been migrants, and so their status in and experience of British society was not always that of the 'Other'. Furthermore, Muslim women who arrived in Britain as migrants after the Second World War were themselves socially, culturally and educationally differentiated. The timing and circumstances of their arrival in Britain and the specific issues they encountered were diverse, although they undoubtedly shared some of the experiences of all other women regardless of origin.

The life experiences of British Muslim women and their families can only be understood by examining the complex processes and structures that have been so crucial to in gender relations within British Muslim communities and in their interaction with the wider society. They need to be analysed in the historical context of the rapidly changing social relations—including gender relations—in post-imperial British society with all its ideological baggage, and the transformation being brought about by the newly-emerging global economic realities and division of labour. Account also has to be taken of the debates about the sources of women's oppression. The Muslim family has been seen by Western feminists as a key element in this, whereas it is held by Muslim communities, maledominated as they are, to be a source of emotional strength and a haven of spiritual and moral safety from the perceived assault of British society and its unwelcome values.

The impact of migration

Muslims have lived in established communities in Britain since the end of the nineteenth century, but mass migration after the Second World War resulted in significantly larger Muslim settlements. Initially these Muslim migrants, except for Turkish Cypriots and East African Asians, rarely arrived as extended or nuclear families. Whether migration was voluntary or coerced, they were usually at least temporarily split from their families. Those who arrived in Britain after 1945 were rarely willing to marry local women, given their obligations and loyalties to their extended families back home and the belief that their stay in Britain would be transitory. Nevertheless, once chain migration and the arrival of families led to Muslim communities emerging in which ethnic institutions could be built, the norms of their home societies could be reintroduced and the traditional values and practices could be sustained and transmitted through families to their children.

The circumstances surrounding the migration of Muslim women had far-reaching implications for their futures in Britain. Take the experience of those from South Asia, who form the largest proportion of the Muslim female population in Britain. For various reasons there were few in the first wave[1] since the joint family largely determined that sons and fathers could leave their wives and children in the family home. The 1961 census revealed that in Bradford there were only eighty-one women compared with 3,376 men, mostly young and unmarried.[2] This resulted partly from the practice of seclusion of Muslim women on the Indian subcontinent. There was reluctance to expose women to a society where the observance of *purdah*, considered a religious requirement especially by rural Muslim migrants from South Asia, would present practical difficulties and where interaction of women with unrelated men would be more likely. However, as immigration controls put a brake on primary migration of men from 1962 onwards, migration was no longer seen as temporary. Much bigger numbers of fiancées, wives and daughters arrived as the process of family reunion accelerated. In addition, as decisions about permanent stay in Britain became firmer, reports of lone males being 'corrupted' by Western culture and moving away from kin loyalty and family obligations quickly led to women being sent over in an attempt to rein in potentially or actually wayward men. However, as Shaw suggested in her study of Oxford's Pakistanis, the women's arrival was not just a way of tying the migrant men into kin obligations. These women also realised that they needed to take the initiative to protect their threatened personal interests.[3] Between 1962 and 1967, 13,600 women and 29,800 children arrived from Pakistan alone, and many more women and girls arrived in the 1970s and 1980s. With ever tighter controls on primary immigration, sex ratios gradually equalised, the proportion of Pakistani males dropping from 86% in 1966 to 65% in 1974 and 58% in 1982. By 1991 there was virtual parity between males and females among the Pakistanis and Bangladeshis in Britain. According to the 1991 census the ratio of Pakistani males at just over 51.5% resembled very closely that of the other minorities and was only a shade higher than that for the white population (48%).[4]

When wives eventually arrived, their presence strengthened both family ties, with joint families and kin at home, and religious observance. It reinforced South Asian Muslim culture by carrying the traditions and taboos of the joint family over into the small nuclear household typical of Britain. In the 1960s and 1970s, Muslim families generally began to be reconstituted on patterns to similar family arrangements in South Asia. The process of chain migration thus helped to reproduce communities with kin networks and extended families with gender relationships broadly similar to those found in their home villages. Great efforts were made to sustain the unity of families, both because this proved an excellent way of coping with economic circumstances and because the family was seen as an effective bastion against the corrosive influence of British culture. While some splitting of households on the marriage of children did take place, many adapted housing in Britain so that they could continue to live as joint families even at the risk of overcrowding. Studying Muslims in Coventry, Ellis encountered one extended family living in four adjacent houses in one street in the Foleshill area and another with family members living in ten separate houses in the same immediate area.[5] The character of South Asian Muslim families remained largely intact because many of the social factors that sustained families in South Asia were relevant in Britain. The family system provided security, especially in times of unemployment and against racist attacks. One of Shaw's respondents articulated her reasons for joint living simply but convincingly:

> I could not leave my mother-in-law, not now that her health is bad and I would miss Yacoub's sisters. And I need their help with my children, especially now that there is a baby as well. I don't speak enough English to manage alone, and Yacoub often isn't at home and works on night shifts every two weeks. And there are only three houses of our own people on that street. I would be frightened; you know what can happen if you move away from your Pakistani neighbours.[6]

Shaw's view was that many Pakistani women actually chose to accept the traditional forms of their own societies. Conditions that an outsider might consider oppressive did not appear in that way to the women themselves.

Variations on this theme existed among other migrant Muslim families as culturally diverse as the Turkish Cypriots, Somalis and Moroccans. The Turkish Cypriots, highly concentrated in certain London boroughs, were also able to re-create their male-dominated family-centred communities, with minor modifications. Kinship ties were re-formed and the system of patronage and mutual obligations was sustained. The family retained much of the importance it had possessed in Cyprus and the commitment to traditional social values, in terms of both life-style and patterns of social relationships, has hardly diminished. The resulting community encapsulation fostered conditions that supported men's control of women and, through moral and social pressure, imposed the observance of traditional behaviour norms on women. Wives were expected to obey their husbands and defer to them in public. They continued to be restricted mainly to the domestic sphere, and most accepted their traditional roles.[7] Similarly, Somali refugees reconstructed their communities, which continued to rely on traditional clan loyalties and family values.[8]

But one should not compare too closely the experiences of South Asian Muslim women and women of other Muslim ethnic communities. The cultural differences among these various communities are significant and over time, in the British context, have generated a wide range of responses among women with regard to their family relationships and interactions with the wider society. Differences in Turkish Cypriot and South Asian migratory patterns produced more evenly balanced sex ratios among the former and by the early 1960s British-style nuclear families and relationships were becoming common among them. Another contrast with South Asian Muslims was that family life among Turkish Cypriots in Britain was established with little assistance from Cyprus and became self-sustaining, thus weakening kinship ties and the expectations of the joint family. Those who migrated felt under less moral obligation than South Asians to provide financial help for the extended family back in Cyprus. Money was not widely or regularly remitted even to aged parents in Cyprus.[9] Thus, Turkish Cypriot families in Britain could invest more resources into bettering their material conditions than was possible for South Asian Muslims, and were thus able to adapt, outwardly at least, more to the social norms and lifestyles of the white population.

Whether there were more men or more women in a Muslim community had important implications for family formation and the evolution of gender relations in the British context.[10] For Turkish Cypriots, compared with South Asian Muslims at the same point in their migration cycle, a much closer balance in the sex ratio was achieved since primary migration among them, given their family structures and expectations, was less male-dominated. The vast imbalance among Pakistanis in the late 1950s and 1960s meant that the small number of Muslim women and girls who had migrated to Britain entered a predominantly male environment, thus intensifying the pressure for strict seclusion; the trend had been set for women's segregation both inside and outside the communities. The more balanced sex ratio among the Turkish Cypriots allowed them to build the traditional nuclear family, sovereign and self-reliant, more or less from the beginning. This set the tone for women, who were adapting to the urban environment in Britain and with their increasing economic influence, to assimilate many white cultural norms. Awareness of the changing gender roles in British society, and confidence in their ability to change their own position in the household, enabled them increasingly to push through changes in the family authority structure. Thus they gradually became more involved in decision-making and interacted more freely with men outside the home.

There were also many more single Cypriot women compared with the other Muslim ethnic groups in the first wave of migrants; 40% of them were not married,[11] and indeed most had come primarily with marriage in view. But some had been attracted by the possibilities of relatively more independent living and of economic advancement.[12] Their more adventurous outlook soon made them less reserved in social interaction than they would have been in Cyprus. While their conduct was circumscribed by Cypriot cultural values of modesty, relative seclusion and family honour, most were able to enjoy a modicum of individual freedom once they entered paid employment, albeit usually in an appropriately supervised workplace. Young Cypriot girls, most of whom had arrived by the mid-1960s as part of young families, were brought up in Britain and experienced domestic arrangements and relationships that had largely keen modified by the London urban context and were more in tune with Western norms, although the core Cypriot values still restricted women's roles outside the domestic sphere.

In contrast to South Asian Muslims, Turkish Cypriot marriages in the 1970s were no longer routinely arranged, although in the earlier phase they did still take place. While Cypriot women rarely married outside the community, intermarriage between Turkish Cypriot men and white women, though not favoured, was not as uncommon as among South Asians. These marriages were contracted more often with white women in the period after the Second World War, although even then they formed only around 4% of the total. The 1966 census showed that a significant minority (14%) married outside the Cypriot community. Consequently integration into the mainstream of British society was further eased as the umbilical cord tying the migrants to the village, kin and family was severed at the most emotionally intimate level, leaving migrant Turkish Cypriot families to become much more organically connected with the norms of British society. Even those who married Turkish Cypriots preferred to marry someone brought up in Britain, since this was thought to avoid cultural and linguistic difficulties and achieve a better understanding. Moreover, by the 1980s young Turkish Cypriots were increasingly choosing their own marriage partners, although formally there matches were still presented as arranged, with the parents' right to discuss it being conceded.[13] South Asian Muslims looked for spouses among kin and relatives back home, on the assumption that they would be more suitable for their domestic roles, although by the late 1980s the pragmatic advantages of a British-reared spouse were recognised even among South Asians.[14]

So, depending on a range of factors—cultural traditions and the degree and nature of interaction with the wider society (itself influenced by the time communities had been settled in Britain)—family relationships in different Muslim communities evolved along different lines as migration turned into permanent settlement.

Muslim women and family relationships

Migration influenced in many ways the nature of relationships within families and hence the lives of Muslim women. Many women from rural backgrounds in Pakistan and Bangladesh had played little or no part in the decision-making that had uprooted them from their homes, and were ill-prepared for the transition from a rural agricultural environment to an urban industrial one in a country with an alien language and culture. Within their families they were compelled to make major adjustments; they often lacked companionship of other females in the extended family, and were unable to find alternative sources of support in the wider community, with language, racism and *purdah* restrictions presenting prohibitive obstacles. The emotional and physical support system they had been used to in a joint family household at home was also mostly absent. All these factors made them more dependent on the men in their families.

However, in the absence of the extended family and in-laws, migrant wives did acquire more private time with their husbands as well as a greater say in managing their households, but even as many migrant women found that their domestic space had expanded, the absence of kin who would have traditionally provided them with emotional support placed new kinds of pressure on these relationships.

For many Muslim women coming to Britain was the first encounter with urban life in another culture. The instability and insecurity of a new physical and social environment, combined with the vastly different climate and living conditions, exacerbated uncertainty and anxiety, and lack of social and linguistic skills restricted interaction with the wider society and so increased their isolation.[15] Thus migration could bring emotional stress and a sense of loss of culture and identity.[16] Domestic isolation could be made worse by the racism of the 'host' community, since terror of racial attacks caused many women to spend their lives virtually imprisoned in their homes. In the absence of their husbands, out at work for long stretches of time and frequently at night, those used to living in joint families suffered most.[17] Isolation caused cultural shock, withdrawal and sometimes depression.[18] In the absence of family support, pregnant women in particular suffered from postnatal depression, some becoming mentally disturbed.[19] Among the Moroccan women in North Kensington, London who arrived in the 1970s isolation bred a high rate of depression and anxiety.[20] Those who accompanied or followed political migrants and asylum-seekers were more socially and emotionally vulnerable. Iraqi women entering Britain as 'displaced persons' or political refugees found themselves in a state of limbo; isolated and marginalised, they questioned the meaning and purpose of their lives. Exile brought insecurity, threatening the stability of family life and relations, and compounded by unemployment, low-grade housing and living on social-security benefits. Often living on their own with their children, they felt unprotected and came under strong pressure from their communities to conform to norms imported from the homelands, such as not socialising with unrelated men.[21] Similarly, Somali women found themselves on the fringes of British society; the persecution and torture from which they had fled exacerbated their emotional and psychological stress. Indoor life in London contrasted with the active outdoor social life they had enjoyed in Somalia. Their health deteriorated, and with stress and depression came mental illness and suicide—a phenomenon virtually unknown in Somali culture. The separation from the family took its toll as mothers and children had to fend for themselves; lone parenthood with its attendant difficulties became widespread. However, on the positive side, these women have become resourceful and pragmatic and found new ways of coping with the challenges of their harsh situations.[22]

Whether migration led to losses or gains in the status of Muslim women within the family depended on the changes in the distribution of power, which were determined to some extent by the immigrant's context and cultural background. In some cases new economic and social respon-sibilities were the basis of a Muslim woman's increasing importance in the family. The role of others, especially non-working women, was undermined as they became isolated from an extended-family network. The loss of help in domestic work and child rearing added to their burden. Daughters, especially the eldest, were asked to do much of housework and care for the younger children, thus reducing their opportunities of education and recreation. At the same time their increasing domestic responsibilities added to their stress.[23] Thus it would be difficult to say whether on balance the position of Pakistani women was weakened or strengthened by the process of migration.

In many formerly rural households *purdah* continued to operate as an instrument of social control, regulating relationships between the sexes. However, the extent and manner of *purdah* as practised among South Asian Muslims in Britain depended on the particular family and the personalities involved. The more rural households were stricter than the urban ones, and Pathan women were more restricted than those from the Mirpur area in Pakistan, although many of the latter rarely left the house except in the company of close male relatives, and thus had to rely heavily on men or the children to do the shopping and run errands. However, *purdah* in its extreme form is not prevalent even across Muslim communities in South Asia and, in contrast to communities of rural origin, had already been modified or abandoned by others, notably Pakistanis from the professional and educated urban middle class. Moreover, as daughters grew up in the British environment, *purdah* restrictions had to be relaxed for them to interact with the institutions of the wider society.

Even where *purdah* was strictly observed distancing from the joint and extended family as a result of migration transformed the relationship between husband and wife. When South Asian Muslim women final migrated to Britain, the male and female worlds had traditionally been deemed separate, and companionship between husband and wife was generally not expected. Husbands looked for company outside the home; women did not go out alone, and there were no segregated leisure activities available to them. Emotions had played a relatively secondary part in these marriages, and as roles within the family were clearly defined according to age and sex, there was little scope for individual inclinations and initiatives. In the context of Britain, a closer bond and emotional dependence developed between husband and wife as more time and privacy became available and as demands from other close relatives receded. In the absence of older women, wives also acquired greater control over the socialisation of children and the running of their homes.

The position of migrant Muslim women in Britain has also been closely connected to patterns and principles of family organisation in response to new social and economic circumstances, including the size and quality of housing in Britain. Increasingly it became impractical to accommodate extended families in relatively small houses, and therefore South Asian Muslim migrant families have moved to conjugal households of single married couples with children. As a result, women's independence was enhanced, and because of their isolation they began setting up new networks of communication and support. Conflict in marriage increased, but a new tolerance within families also appeared, and some renegotiating of relationships seemed to have occurred.[24] The absence of hierarchical joint family structures enabled Muslim women to escape some aspects of subordination. Outside the home they struggled to communicate with limited English and therefore had to depend on their husbands and other male relatives or children, but from within their communities and house-holds their position might be strengthened by their arrival in Britain. They became key players in the transmission and maintenance of cultural and religious values, shielding their families from 'undesirable' Western influences. By drawing more and more on newly-constituted networks of kinsfolk and friends, they began to give their communities a sense of cohesion, and it is in the shaping of community structures and social life that they exercised influence.[25]

However, the changes in the lives of Muslim women in Britain were related to changes in the family in British society as a whole.[26] Compared to the changes in families in Britain since the 1960s, those in the Muslim patterns of family formation and structure have been much less dramatic. In 1993 the social trends 'snapshot' produced by the Central Statistical Office suggested that Muslim marriages were generally more stable than white ones. Whereas in the population as a whole only 25% families had both parents living with their children, the proportion of such families among Muslims was 70%. Likewise births outside wedlock stood at 1.2% among Muslims compared to the general figure of 32%.[27] In 1994 a survey showed that while 59% of single white adults without children live with their parents, 87% of Pakistanis and Bangladeshis did so. While the great majority of whites ceased to live with their parents as soon as they had their own families, over 20% of South Asian married couples lived with parents (generally the husband's following tradition), underlining the durability of the joint-family system.[28] The majority (two-thirds) of Pakistani and Bangladeshi elders over the age of sixty lived in the same household as an adult child and were cared for primarily by the women in the family.[29]

Nevertheless, the process of family formation in other Muslim migrant ethnic groups has differed from the South Asian pattern according to their particular traditions. For instance, as Cypriots adjusted to life in Britain the extended family lost its force, in common with the overall population. As early as 1966 over two-thirds of Cypriots in London lived in nuclear families: 67.1% were of the 'one-family' type compared to 74.0% of all households in Greater London, the proportion (73%) being even higher outside the capital.[30] In Greater London 5% of Cypriot households were of the multiple/extended-family type, compared with 2% of the overall population of Greater London, and 90% of Cypriot children lived in nuclear family units.[31] Even during the five-year period 1961–6 when migration was at its height, the change in the direction of the nuclear family was noticeable, the proportion of households consisting of more than a nuclear family dropping by one-third, from 33 to 22%.[32] With greater prosperity and absorption of British norms over time, Cypriot families became smaller. Whereas in 1961 37% of Cypriots lived in households of six persons or more, by 1966 this had fallen to 30%. In 1966 the average Cypriot family had 2.13 children compared with 2.30 among Pakistanis and 1.85 among white families. In London the average was 1.6 children per Cypriot family, and for nuclear families 2.0.[33] The mean size of the Cypriot household came down from 4.1 in 1961 to 3.9 in 1966. The downward trend continued in the next three decades, declining from 3.74 in 1971 to 3.34 in 1981 and 3.04 in 1991.[34] Given that fertility rates began to come down and the proportion of larger Cypriot families also declined, Turkish Cypriot households in the 1990s were closer to white households (2.67 and 2.43) much more than either Pakistani (4.95 and 4.81) or Bangladeshi (4.90 and 5.36) households.[35] Thus, among Muslim communities Turkish Cypriots came closest to resembling the white population in age structure, sex ratio and family formation—marital status, family structure and size, but the family still remained of paramount importance for them, undergoing structural change only gradually.

In contrast to other ethnic groups, the almost universal practice of marriage among Muslim communities continued into the 1990s, although again patterns varied between different ethnic groups. In 1991 South Asian Muslims were still more likely to be married, and to have married earlier, than Turkish Cypriot or whites. Berrington analysed the 1991 census data and concluded that 'the singulate mean age at marriage (the average number of years spent single by those who marry) … is much lower' among the Pakistani and Bangladeshi population (22.3 years and 21.2 years, respectively, for women) compared to the Indian ethnic minority (23.7) or the white population (26.7).[36] While 55% of white women had a partner by the age of twenty-five, 78% of Pakistani women and 71% of Bangladeshi women had one; and the latter were more likely to be formally married as opposed to being involved in 'living as married' relationships, which was increasingly the case among younger white females.[37] Of Pakistani and Bangladeshi women in the twenty-five to twenty-nine age group 90% were formally married, compared to 80% of Indians and 60% of whites.[38] That said, the trend among South Asian Muslim women, especially those with higher educational qualifications who had entered employment and were engaged in professional careers, was towards later marriage.

When Berrington compared the proportion of those who were single in 1981 with 1991 by sex, age and country of birth, she found that, while women in all ethnic groups had 'seen a significant increase in the proportions remaining single by their mid- and late-twenties, the relative change is particularly great among Bangladeshi-born women in their early twenties.'[39] Among Pakistanis in the corresponding category, the change was much less, but by the time women reached their late twenties, the trend seemed to be reversed, with Pakistanis showing an increase and Bangladeshis declining slightly. Even so, many fewer Pakistanis than white women remained single.[40] In this, cultural and religious traditions appear to have been modified by educational and socio-economic opportunities and individual circumstances.

However, other structural changes in the family patterns of Muslims have been more gradual. According to the 1991 census, over 83% of Pakistanis and Bangladeshis were still living in 'traditional' families, compared with 65% whites and 66% of all ethnic minorities.[41] South Asian Muslim women appeared to start producing children earlier and to stop later, resulting in larger families. The data revealed an exceptionally high proportion of Pakistani and Bangladeshi women in their fifties and even sixties with dependent children—four times that of white families.[42] However, while Pakistanis on average had more children than any other ethnic group except Bangladeshis, they had fewer than in the 1980s.[43]

Marital breakdown, separation and divorce seemed less frequent among South Asian, Turkish and Cypriot immigrants than in the white population. The 1981 census data showed that only 3.0% of Turkish-born and 3.9% of Cyprus-born women were divorced.[44] In the 1994 PSI survey, whereas 9% of the white people who were 'ever married' said they had got divorced, 4% of South Asians were in this category.[45] The 1991 census data, showed the proportion of divorced white women as several times higher than that for Pakistani and Bangladeshi women.[46] Among the latter intermarriage remained the exception, as in the 1970s.[47] By 1994 few Pakistanis and Bangladeshis had white partners and two-thirds of South Asians in mixed relationships were men.[48] Cohabitation rates among Muslim women compared with their white counterparts were negligible, although the 1989–91 Labour Force Survey suggested that a growing number of Arab women (4.2%)

277

were living with partners outside marriage.[49] So while some changes have taken place in the pattern of family formation and structure since the 1960s, on the whole Muslim families have been able to preserve and maintain their 'traditional character' far more than their white counterparts. At the same time, the second generation of Muslim women has undergone a number of changes in their attitudes and behaviour towards the family; their marriage patterns hover some-where between those of first-generation South Asians and the white population. While 62% of second-generation Indian and Pakistani women in their early twenties were single in 1991, only 28% of Indian and 18% of Pakistani first-generation women were in that category.[50] Thus they seemed to be marrying later, though still earlier than their white counterparts. Muslims from South Asia still had larger families than any other ethnic group in Britain, although the general trend was towards fewer children as women increasingly went to work.[51] Divorce rates like-wise have risen among second-generation Muslims, though still much lower than for whites. The overall patterns suggests that Muslim women together with their families are moving gradually towards the norms of the white population although cultural traditions and religion have applied a brake on the rate of change.

Migration, Muslim women and waged work

The timing of migration, economic change, immigration control and racism all had an impact on patterns of employment among Muslim women. As migrants, usually dark-skinned, and female, they were per-ceived negatively by employers: racism limited the forms of employ-ment open to them, as did notions that their femininity made them a passive and docile workforce. While all Muslim women had to some extent to cope with such disadvantages, their different cultural back-grounds meant that their engagement with the labour market evolved differently. For instance, Turkish Cypriot women had a rather different experience from South Asians. While seclusion remained important to Turkish Cypriots, they adapted and applied it in the urban context of Britain with relative flexibility.

The primary motive for migration, that of achieving and sustaining a better standard of living, helped to overcome some of the cultural constraints within Muslim communities. In the case of Turkish Cypriots, in contrast to Cyprus, where those entering the job market were few and usually urban-educated, and where women were mainly involved in house-work and the subsistence village economy, the economic pressures of life in Britain persuaded them to take up waged work. The abundance of work in the 1950s and 1960s, when traditional skills such as sewing could be turned to material gain, provided further incentive. As early as 1966, 45% of Turkish Cypriot women were economically active in Greater London, more than for the population as a whole (42.4%). Expanding employment opportunities in the public and services sector widened the scope of their involvement in mainstream British life. While 64.5% of Cypriot women in Greater London were still engaged in the narrower ethnically dominated and gender-segregated piece-work of the clothing industry, a further 13.6% worked more diversely in the broad-based service, sport and recreation sectors, 8.1% in clerical work and 3.3% in sales.[52]

By contrast, in the West Midlands, where substantial Pakistani communities of rural origin became established in the 1960s, the proportion of economically active females was much lower, at 16%, probably because of the greater reluctance of husbands to allow their wives to go out to work because of religious belief and custom.[53] Comparisons with other ethnic groups in the 1971 census gave an early indication of the poor situation of South Asian Muslim women in the labour market. 40.8% of Indian, largely Hindu, women were in waged labour, compared to only 20.7% of Pakistani women. The 1974 PSI Survey confirmed that, compared with Asian women generally (45%), the employment rate of Muslim women was low (17%).[54] According to a 1982 PSI survey, while 59% of Hindu, 54% of Sikh and 46% of white women were active in the labour market, only 18% of Muslim women were employed.[55] Similar trends were shown by the Labour Force Survey in 1989–91, which reported that only 20% of Pakistani and 10% of Bangladeshi women were in either paid employment or seeking work compared with 66% of Indians. By 1994 the overall gap between levels of economic activity between Muslim and non-Muslim women had been only marginally reduced. White women (72%) were still much more active in the labour market than South Asian women, and even among South Asians a much higher proportion of Indian women

(61%) were engaged in economic activity than their Pakistani (28%) or Bangladeshi (15%) women.[56]

Muslim women seem also to have suffered the most from unemployment. For instance, the 1982 PSI survey showed that, while 10% of white, 18% of Hindu and 22% of Sikh women were unemployed, the rate for Muslim women was 31%.[57] A decade later, the situation had improved little: 11% of Indian and 7% of white women were out of work, compared to 29% of Pakistani and Bangladeshi women.[58] The fourth PSI survey revealed that, while 12% of Indian and 9% of white women were unemployed, the figures for Pakistani and Bangladeshi women were 39% and 40% respectively.[59] Thus the differentials in employment patterns between Muslim and non-Muslim women have changed little in thirty years and continue to reflect significant inequalities in the labour market.

In the 1960s and 1970s the low rate of economic activity among Muslim women and them low position in the labour market were seen primarily in terms of male opposition justified through Islamic patriarchal culture. For example, taking little account of the differences of region, cultural and religious traditions within the Muslim communities, both Dahya and Khan characterised Pakistani women as docile, static and incapable of changing their conditions of existence.[60] Brah has argued that these 'culturalist' explanations of Muslim women's disinclination to seek work outside the home were inadequate and took little account of the great burden of domestic duties borne by most of them compared to some of the other ethnic groups. Migrant women did not always see paid work as a boon, once they realised it was always accompanied by the 'double shift' of domestic chores. She suggested instead that the relatively large number of young children in Muslim households and the lack of labour-saving household appliances, which the families could not afford, discouraged the desire for paid work, especially among those with few qualifications and skills, who found that their opportunities were limited, the quality of work available poor, the wages offered low and their exploitation worse.[61]

These earlier analyses suffered from other shortcomings. First, there were always many more Muslim women in paid work than officially estimated, since surveys tended to under estimate the vast numbers employed in the informal sector. Secondly, while religious factors constrained Muslim women from taking outside employment where they might have had to mix with strange men, there were more important material factors limiting their choice to homeworking. The end of male immigration by the early 1970s and the continuing demand for unskilled and semi-skilled labour resulted in many Muslim women being recruited into factory production. However, with changes in the structure of British manufacturing industry, which had previously provided unskilled and semi-skilled employment for the majority of Muslim men and women, came substantial redundancies. Economic restructuring based on technological advances and a shift away from manufacturing to services, plus the powerful bargaining position of trade unions, led employers to decentralise and casualise production. Homeworking, with minimal overheads and investment in human capital, fitted well into the strategies of business expansion. In the early 1980s, a period of economic contraction, unemployment rose sharply, especially in unskilled and semi-skilled occupations. Sweated labour increased rapidly as employers sought to increase their profit margins through a more flexible, easily disposable and cheap labour force, of which Muslim women formed a significant part, and as racial tensions grew, traditional employment options, especially segregated home-based work, became preferable in some areas as families sought to shield themselves against the most virulent forms of racism. Sheer economic necessity drew Muslim women into waged work to ameliorate their families' precarious circumstances, but the fear of abuse, violence and harassment on the street and in the workplace discouraged many of them from leaving home. They felt compelled to seek invisibility and were dissuaded from looking for outside jobs.[62] As one Bangladeshi homeworker put it, 'When you live in Newham [London], you have little choice … Burning down of an Asian home does not even make news any longer. The police are no help; they would not admit that the attacks on Asian homes are from the racists. How can I look for a job outside my home in such a situation?'[63]

Throughout the 1980s and 1990s Muslim women continued to be pushed into the more informal sectors of the labour market, and working for entrepreneurs from their own communities meant that they were less exposed to racial discrimination. At the same time, they were caught up in kinship and community ties and so became susceptible to even greater exploitation than they might have encountered with a white employer.[64] Mitter's research in the early 1980s highlighted their dilemma succinctly. She wrote of Bangladeshis in London's East End that 'the informal structure of organisation [in sweatshops] made it possible to recruit at will, keep average costs to a minimum and allow the community to earn their livelihood in a racist society which made it difficult to find jobs in other areas'.[65] At the same time, whether they worked or stayed at home depended to some extent on local labour market conditions and available employment opportunities, which were themselves influenced by these women's age, level of education and social and linguistic skills. The factor of age would determine the extent to which they might have domestic responsibilities, for example, looking after young children. The availability of child care acquired considerable significance, as did the much higher rate of unemployment among the men, since the wife's earnings had a detrimental effect on the means-tested social-security benefits granted to the family.

Thus the low participation of Muslim women in paid work was due to a range of factors, among which culture was just one. Others included gender, race and class biases, a lack of proficiency in English and individual circumstances. It was the complex interaction of these factors combined with family and labour-market conditions and the working patterns of both wives and husbands that shaped the economic activities of Muslim women.[66] However, the most significant factor influencing whether Muslim women took up employment or not was economic need—when economic advantage was seen to be greater than the social costs to which patriarchal Islamic ideology contributed. Working from home was often seen as the safest option since working hours were usually flexible and there was no threat to the husband's self-esteem as the principal wage-earner. However, it did mean that women remained isolated with few opportunities to develop abilities that would make them more effective in their economic interactions with the wider society.

By the 1990s much evidence had been collected to suggest that it was the racist assumptions permeating British society, together with everyday and institutional forms of racism, which produced much of Muslim women's disadvantage: abuse and humiliation in the processes of immigration and discrimination in social and economic life. As indicated by a steady stream of discrimination cases, employers' antipathy towards Islam affected many Muslim women in the workplace. Even the British-educated professionally qualified younger women did not escape discrimination of a distinctly religious character, from which other faith communities appeared exempt. The most overt form of religious discrimination was the penalising of Muslim women by a range of employers—from estate agents to car manufacturers—for wearing the *hijab*.[67]

However, when Muslim women did not try to assert their Muslim identity overtly, and where the educational attainments of Muslim and non-Muslim young women converged, it was apparent that the differences between them in employment profiles had narrowed considerably. Indeed, as early as the 1982 PSI survey, data indicated that in the sixteen to nineteen age-group there were more Muslim women (42%) in the labour market than other Asian women (36%) although this trend was not replicated among the older age-groups.[68] The fourth PSI survey in the mid-1990s showed no marked differences between the employment aspirations of young Muslim and non-Muslim women. As young Muslim women's qualifications and language skills have improved, so has their relative participation in the labour market. Among Pakistani and Bangladeshi women with A-levels or degrees the proportion in the labour market appeared higher (74%) than in other ethnic groups (65% each for Indians/African Asians and whites).[69] Thus, while the influence of cultural tradition in producing the gap between Muslim and non-Muslim women could not be dismissed completely, the changing employment patterns suggest that many non-religious factors are as important, if not more so in determining Muslim women's employment outcomes.[70]

The impact of paid work on the status of migrant Muslim women within the family appears contradictory. Migrant women's roles largely remained subordinate. Migration and access to employment did not guarantee improvement in their status nor did it give them the opportunity to develop more equal gender relations in the family. Since much of the employment was low-paid, low-skilled, all-female homeworking, usually labelled as 'women's work', the ideological boundaries of the private sphere were merely redrawn to make paid work an extension of the domestic role and not in conflict with the women's cultural definition as mothers and wives. Waged work did not necessarily free them economically or socially, since the generally meagre wages limited their ability to bargain with their families. The interplay of religious and cultural forces and the segregation of the labour market by gender and race restricted Muslim women's occupational choices and tended to sustain their economic dependence on the male members of their families.[71] Fathers and husbands or in-laws continued to control the sexuality, physical movement, social interaction and domestic labour of the women in their households, and to make the final decision regarding children's education and careers. In the majority of households, especially where income was low and women were supplementary earners, the males continued to control their income and domestic expenditure, leaving their traditional role and position within the family more or less unaltered.[72] The decision whether Muslim women did or did not work still often rested with fathers, husbands or in-laws, which meant that only when economic necessity demanded were they encouraged to go into whatever occupations were available. The majority fitted in with their husbands' careers, accepting jobs for which they were grossly overqualified, and those who worked in factories did so with family members and neighbours, providing an element of 'supervision'. Unlike men, these women were not the untrammelled owners of their labour power. While husbands' resistance to women taking up paid employment was being gradually eroded, the options available, especially to the older women, were constrained by poor education and language skills and above all by their heavy domestic responsibilities.

Surveys in the early 1990s suggested that males continued to exercise control over the females' earnings although the trend seemed to be downwards, especially among the younger generation, where educational and occupational profiles were increasingly coming to resemble those of white women. In one study the majority of South Asian women respondents had their own bank accounts, although a substantial minority still did not. However, regardless of religion, better educated women retained greater control over their earnings, allowing them more leverage in decisions about the family and negotiating the allocation of household resources. In lower-income households it was definitely the men who controlled the purse-strings.[73] On the other hand, the situation of women working outside the home, particularly the younger more educated ones involved in professional careers, has gradually changed.[74] But even for the less educated and less skilled, entry into any one of a variety of occupations away from home had important consequences domestically. First, many were no longer only wives, mothers and housekeepers; while still having to perform many of these functions, as wage-earners, their newly-acquired economic muscle enhanced their decision-making power within the family—such as their capacity to fight for their daughters' education when faced with opposition from their husbands and indeed for their own right to work outside the home. Economic empowerment also enabled them to be less tolerant of their husbands' misdemeanours and to challenge more robustly the inappropriate and inadequate responses to their needs of the institutions of wider society. Secondly, as these women left home for work, they had to mix with unrelated men. Given the necessity to supplement the family budget and achieve a better standard of living, fathers and husbands gradually yielded and withdrew their objection to such interactions. The result was that these women's social behaviour underwent considerable change, moving it closer to the norms operating in the wider society. These trends were reflected in the way women increasingly and more overtly adopted forms of British dress, albeit eclectically, and the confidence they began to show in their working environment. These patterns of behaviour, which had first taken shape among Turkish Cypriots in the 1960s, were being adopted and consolidated by other Muslim women towards the end of the twentieth century.

So paid work has had a positive impact on the role and status of many Muslim women within their families. By forcing changes in behaviour, the new patterns of employment have produced new definitions of what is acceptable and respectable. Women's wages began to contribute substantially to the household budget, and have thus had an impact both on the negotiation of power and the allocation of household resources within the domestic sphere, and on traditional patterns of behaviour within the family.[75] In Turkish Cypriot and Somali Muslim communities relations have taken on a more equal character as women have become involved in the process of production beyond the household: they seem able to exert more influence in family decision-making. Financial independence has given many Somali women greater freedom relative to their families, and the social security safety-net further empowers the unemployed against their husbands' domestic authority by providing material support.

However, the experience of the wider society has continued to limit their scope for individual freedom, which many have to sacrifice in exchange for the emotional security provided by family and kin.[76] Thus the tension caused by Muslim women's increasing participation in the sphere of work, between adhering to cultural and religious expectations and the quest for greater gender equality, has remained largely unresolved. Patriarchal notions, with their specifically Islamic character, have endured among Turkish Cypriots and Somalis as well as among South Asian Muslim communities. Consequently, a general division of labour continues to exist between males and females, based on an ideology that continues to assert the essentially different character and temperament of men and women; women's complementarity and submissiveness in relation to men have been constantly reaffirmed. The key purpose of women's existence for many British Muslims remains child-rearing and motherhood. Wives' wages are usually supplementary to those of their husbands, and their patterns of employment have not challenged the men's position as bread-winners or the belief that women are primarily wives and mothers. Home-working, in particular, did not contravene cultural definitions of a 'good' wife and mother, or damage their sexual reputation. In reality many Muslim households rely heavily on women's income, although it has often been insufficient for them to maintain an independent existence. Nevertheless, waged work seems to have freed many Muslim women from total monetary dependence on the males of the family. It has also made them aware that in cases of divorce, widowhood, separation, desertion or domestic violence, paid work can help them to find other alternatives for survival than total reliance on and submission to the males of the family.

Thus, however imperceptibly, gender equality for Muslim women is increasing, more in some Muslim ethnic groups, less in others, partly as a result of the changes generated by interaction with the wider society in employment. But the extent to which participation in different kinds of paid work has helped Muslim women achieve personal autonomy has been partly determined by the continuing traditions of their communities and partly by their own levels of education and skills. A comparison of Somali and Bangladeshi women in London illuminates the relative empowerment for women brought by paid work. By the early 1990s Somali women appeared to have acquired more control of their lives than Bangladeshis, but especially by comparison with older migrant women, with their low literacy and few marketable skills. For the younger women more highly paid work has offered a way to break the mould of the ideology of domesticity, and so they have generally come to enjoy more independence relative to Somali men. But even some older migrant Somali women in London could become to some extent financially independent of their seamen husbands by working as hospital cleaners and factory workers, occupations that gave them immediate contact with the white community and thus a much greater opportunity to acquire linguistic and social skills, and so advance their career aspirations and life chances. By contrast, the majority of first-generation Bangladeshi women, with their lack of formal education and inability to communicate in English, spent most of their lives within the confines of their homes, where the most they did was piece-work in relative isolation. Living in seclusion, they were socially and linguistically ill-equipped to find waged work which might have secured them economic independence.[77]

Consequently, while both Somali and Bangladeshi women living in Britain are Muslim, paid work has had a very different impact on their lives, especially those of the older migrant generation, and their responses, shaped by different patterns of family organisation and cultural expectations, have produced different outcomes. Somali women in pursuit of greater personal freedom were helped by having been brought up to participate in the traditional subsistence economy outside the home, which eased adaptation to the urban economy in Britain. They were less encumbered by the rigid Islamic traditions of gender interaction applied by the Bangladeshis, and often shrugged off *purdah* as alien to their culture since the Somali notion of sexual modesty, for example, covering the hair and even the upper arms, is much more casual than the Bangladeshi. Compared with Bangladeshis and to a lesser extent Pakistanis, greater flexibility in dress and codes of modesty, mixing with unrelated men and growing participation in economic activity outside the home have all enabled Somali women in Britain to achieve greater autonomy.

The economic separation of husband and wife has also been important in Somali women's independence and sense of control over their

287

lives, making divorce a realistic means of dealing with a dysfunctional marriage. Paid work outside the community's domination has given them a degree of independence within the home, whereas housebound Bangladeshi women could not contemplate any viable alternative to even the most oppressive family life. Furthermore, work and shopping have encouraged the migrant Somali women to learn English. The result has been that the proficiency of older Somali women in English was usually much greater than that of their Bangladeshi counterparts and therefore the former have been able to take on jobs that were better paid, if not more satisfying, than those available to women engaged in homeworking—a form of employment much more prevalent among Bangladeshis. Consequently, the quality of life and health enjoyed by Somali women has usually been better, something reflected in their suffering less from depression than their South Asian counterparts.[78]

Changing dynamics in British Muslim families

Among the factors that have affected the dynamics of the Muslim family and the changes in Muslim women's roles and status in Britain, the patriarchal systems of the societies from which they originated have been highly significant. The values they inculcate regarding gender relationships have influenced British Muslim attitudes, male and female, over a wide area: relationships within the family, the socialisation of females, marriage practices, female education, the domestic division of labour, female sexuality and participation in economic life and the public domain. Central to these changes has been the interaction of attitudes between people who arrived in Britain several decades ago and the wider society in which they have settled. The main issues have been the degree of freedom Muslim women have attained relative to the men in their families and communities, and how they have responded to the oppression which they are perceived to have suffered. It is the movement away from these attitudes and behaviour regarding family relationships and women's participation in society that could indicate how far the character of the Muslim family and the status of women within it might have changed.

Since the 1960s the norms of the patriarchal cultures from which Muslim migrants came have continued to influence the attitudes of

Muslim communities towards their female members. A struggle has taken place between those British Muslim families and communities who have held fast to the traditional roles ascribed to women and those who have responded to their changed circumstances by adopting attitudes that offer women opportunities to enjoy freer and more fulfilled lives. The vast majority of Muslim migrants in Britain, especially the first generation, still held the orthodox view that there are fundamental differences between males and females, with deep implications for their attitudes and functions.[79] Men and women in this traditional view have different, divinely-ordained gender roles and it continued to be asserted authoritatively, even in the 1990s, that ideally there should be no deviation from them.[80] Muslim male-dominated communities in Britain have sought to apply their interpretations of Islamic texts to perpetuate asymmetrical gender roles. Many in these communities have continued to believe that females have a lower status than males and that it is fitting for the latter to be their legal and moral guardians. Indeed, women have been deemed to be men's property, which required their protection in order that they might not become 'damaged goods' which would lose much of their value. For these Muslims sexual relations can only take place within marriage; a woman's virginity is therefore highly prized and jealously guarded and its loss brings public shame on her family as well as potentially making the woman unmarriageable. Thus the defence of family honour (*izzat*) has acquired great significance, and Muslim men have gone to great lengths to restrict their wives, daughters or sisters from any interactions with unrelated males. For many Muslims *izzat* also constitutes an emotional attachment to the values and priorities of life in their countries of origin, and women have accepted the validity of these ideas through processes of socialisation. Indeed, the notion of *izzat* is so deeply ingrained in women that they have themselves felt a sense of guilt about interaction with strange men, however innocent. The power of this patriarchal ideology has resulted in double standards regarding social behaviour across Muslim communities by men and tolerated by women: while segregation is prescribed for women and imposed on them, men have few reservations about attending mixed gatherings. An example has been the demand for single-sex Muslim schools for girls as an antidote to the mixing of the sexes. The absence of a similar demand for Muslim boys indicates persistence of double standards. Similarly, 'illicit' sex has not invited the same degree of disapproval for males as for females, and the rules of propriety have been much more lax for boys than for girls. There is no word for male virginity among Turkish Cypriots.

The institution of marriage has remained central to the structure of the Muslim family and has probably been least subject to change; and in contrast to the trend of increasing family breakdown in the white population, family life among Muslim groups in Britain has remained relatively solid. The debates in the broader society around gender inequality, individual and group rights and power and authority in the household have not had a great impact on the attitudes of most Muslims. Increasing long-term cohabitation and births out of wedlock, one-parent families and a rapidly rising divorce rate, threatening the very future of marriage, have had much less effect on Muslims, for whom the family has mostly remained a fundamental unit of society and essential to the stability of the social order. Their perception of the changes in British society seems to have been that the family is in a process of decay and dissolution primarily due to the moral laxity brought about by secular developments and a materialistic outlook—a trend they have sought to resist through family cohesion. This does not mean that traditional forms of the family have remained completely intact. Breakdown of extended families among Muslims from many parts of the world has occurred to a certain extent, partly as a result of the migration of individual family members and the enforcement of British immigration restrictions. However, recent evidence suggests that, while the organisation of joint and extended families has been much weakened because of housing difficulties and much greater mobility, the family has remained a focal point for the vast majority of Muslims, South Asian or otherwise, in Britain. Muslim women are still much more predisposed to traditional family formation than any other ethnic group in Britain: all the women in Afshar's sample in 1989 saw marriage as 'inevitable and desirable' and felt that parents should have a say in it.[81] Brah's survey in the 1980s showed that the majority of Muslim adolescents expected their marriages to be arranged and accepted them, though not always with complete equanimity.[82] However, change was also discernible. Stopes and Cochrane showed parents' and children's attitudes to be out of step—25% of second-generation Muslims wanted a less traditional arrangement.[83] In a survey of university students in 1994, Francome found that only a minority of Muslim women would seek arranged marriages, that 36% of them would consider having sex before marriage and that 58% felt that there were major differences in attitude to relationships, sex and marriage between themselves and their parents.[84] However, contrary to the stereotype of Muslim parents forcing their children into unwanted marriages, many of them were explicit that they would not go against their children's wishes and saw marriage as a joint undertaking between themselves and their children.

How parents and children responded to the issue of arranged marriage has depended on a range of community and background factors. Arranged marriages have been more prevalent among South Asian Muslim communities than among other Muslim ethnic groups, such as Turkish Cypriots or Somalis. Even among the South Asians there were variations, with those families with low levels of education being more in favour of arranged marriage. Higher education helped women to move higher in the labour market, to remain single and independent, and to be free to choose their own partners and even cohabit with them if they wished.[85] In these cases the patriarchal attitudes of parents were beginning to be eroded by the changes in women's own experience.[86] But arranged marriages did hinder women's participation in higher education and careers and thus affected the amount of freedom they enjoyed, since they resulted in their greater dependence on males and limited their economic resources and opportunities and access to power. However, Pakistani girls with higher qualifications were increasingly able to combine a career with an arranged marriage,[87] although such girls were more vocal in asserting their choice of a marriage partner than those who were housebound. There was also less support among second-generation Pakistani women for arranged marriages compared with the first generation, and among paid workers than the unpaid ones.[88]

The degree of consultation allowed in the marriage process varied from one Muslim community to another and within each community from family to family. Among Pakistanis there appeared less consultation among families with strong rural ties than in urban ones. Children of the more liberal-minded Muslim parents were allowed more free-dom in choosing marriage partners, although parental consent was still expected. Children were willing to accept their parents' decision but did not hesitate to indicate their personal preferences. Mutual consent was approved of; differences in attitude towards dating and marriage emerged between British-born and South Asian-born children, the former giving high importance to 'love' over other considerations. Among young Turkish Cypriots arranged marriages in the strict sense became a statistically insignificant minority. However, a love marriage was presented as an arrangement between two families, sometimes because parents were either ignorant of the couple's courtship or pre-ferred to turn a blind eye to it. Formally, the young people were con-tent to go through the traditional procedures of marriage, although they dismissed these ceremonies as a mere formality or 'a farce', but they did at least concede to their parents, 'out of respect', the formal right to discuss the marriage; so strong is the hold of the arranged marriage that even elopements were converted into 'normal mar-riages'.[89] However, there was still the perception in the older genera-tion that 'choice' marriages were 'deviant', and many young people eventually bowed to parental pressure and gave up their individual choice of partner and/or agreed with little enthusiasm to an arranged match.[90] Cohabitation continued to be disapproved of both among the majority of second-generation Muslims and overwhelmingly among their parents' generation, although the incidence of even this form of relationship was steadily rising.[91]

This does not mean that there were no intransigent parents deter-mined to impose their authority, that contradictory and conflicting emotions were not felt by many Muslim adolescents about arranged marriages, or that no serious disagreement ever occurred in Muslim households over the question of marriage. Indeed, differences between the views of Muslim parents and their children about marriage had emerged by the mid-1970s. For example, while most South Asian Muslim parents in 1976 favoured endogamy, a quarter of the adoles-cents in Anwar's survey were opposed to it and there was great opposi-tion in the second generation to returning girls to the subcontinent to marry.[92] The 1984 follow-up survey revealed a substantial gap between the parents' and the young people's views on arranged marriage. While

81% of Muslim parents supported the idea, only 58% of the second generation did so, though Stopes-Roe and Cochrane suggested that conflict between first and second generations seemed far less endemic than had been supposed.[93] Their research revealed that 'more than three-quarters of both generations expected that an arranged marriage, even if somewhat modified, would take place.'[94] The older generation remained sceptical about romantic love and the Western style of marriage, but gradually they had to concede the prerogative of individual choice to their children. Increasingly, when differences of view between parents and young people have emerged, it was usually possible for their views to be reconciled through negotiations.[95]

The widening gap between the views of parents and children obviously caused some distress to both sides. Given their emotional and psychological attachment to family, children often did not wish to 'let the family down'. Yet they also could not bring themselves to surrender their right of choice in this most important personal matter. Generally though, when it came to the crunch, they 'valued their kin and culture more than the freedoms which are supposed to be so desirable'.[96] In some cases where a peaceful resolution was not possible, the media were presented with wonderful opportunities for a sensational portrayal of Muslim families as pathological and oppressive to women. Stories of girls brought up in Britain being forced into marriages with suitors from their families' home-lands hit the headlines.[97] Instances of this were the teenaged sisters Zana and Nadia Muhsen 'sold' into marriage by their Yemeni father;[98] the alleged abduction and forced marriage of Nazia (13) and Rifat (20) by their father in Pakistan;[99] and Yasmin Ahmed 'forced to marry a total stranger from Pakistan'.[100] But extreme measures have usually not had to be taken by young Muslim women resisting the imposition of forced marriages. More recently, considerable evidence of parental willingness to compromise and adapt has emerged.[101] Even among South Asian Muslims, for whom the system of arranged marriage has been of great importance, it is increasingly a halfway house between the 'forced' variety, in which the children had no say at all, and 'love' marriage, where parents have been completely excluded from decision-making. Negotiated change in the distribution of influence and power in arranged marriages as a decision-making process has begun.[102] Even parents' strictures about mixed marriages are being questioned; the children legitimise their challenge to endogamy by pointing to the Islamic rejection of notions of racial and ethnic superiority and the absence of caste, class and colour distinctions in social interactions and the construction of personal relationships.[103] Within religious limits, they are seeking to capture the major role in the process of selecting their marriage partners.[104]

Thus the broad picture emerging with regard to marriage customs among British Muslim communities is one of much greater variety: from parentally arranged to free and unguided; from not meeting till the wedding day—and no voice in the matter, (now increasingly rare)—to a liaison set-up about which nobody is informed, much less consulted, and no ceremony enacted. There are arranged marriages that are seen as a joint venture by parents and children, there are others where the task is delegated to parents and then there are still others where the individuals plan it by themselves—all can be found among Muslims in Britain. A large majority of marriages among South Asian Muslims are still arranged, have a great measure of support, and show few signs of breaking down, although the balance is beginning to shift towards more individual choice for the potential spouses. Among Turkish Cypriots, at the other end of the spectrum, the pendulum has firmly swung in favour of individual choice as the younger generation bring the full weight of their own predilections to bear.

Muslim women resist sources of oppression

Since the late 1970s the responses of Muslim girls and women have evolved, straining to keep pace with the changing social and cultural context as well as with the changes in their own family and personal circumstances. Their changing orientation and responses in relation to home, education, work, religion, leisure, marriage and family relationships have reflected, to some degree, the changes in their experience during this period.[105]

In the 1970s the younger generation of Muslims were struggling to make sense of their lives caught between the radically different environments at home and at school. By the 1980s they had achieved more control and begun to juggle identities more expertly, synthesising cultural elements from a variety of sources; they stressed reconciliation rather than conflict. By the 1990s an alternative approach had been adopted which relied not on cultural 'switching' or 'blending' but on articulating their situation within an Islamic perspective. This religious-identity strategy was in many ways a new departure, reflecting a self-conscious exploration of religion. Indeed, challenging many of their parents' assumptions from within the parameters of Islam often helped Muslim women to renegotiate their aspirations in education, employment, choice of marriage partners and participation in public life. By drawing on religious texts they began to succeed in subverting the traditions that were inhibiting their lives.

In response to their complex experience Muslim women have adopted a variety of strategies to resist their subordination. These have ranged from uncomplaining acquiescence to individual acts of defiance, including cohabiting and intermarriage, and from totally rejecting their families' lifestyles to operating a double standard, restricting their own freedom of movement and exercising self-imposed separatism. Elopement, running away, suicide and marrying without parental consent all became more frequent. Many such girls ended up living a 'double life', conforming to peer-group pressure at school and to traditional customs at home. A survey by Sharif in 1985 showed that Muslim girls regarded lying to parents as a normal survival technique. Many, feeling guilty at having failed in their traditional role, suffer in silence, neither retaliating nor protesting. Fearing punitive sanctions by their menfolk, they have accepted their word as law and been reluctant to bring family problems out into the open lest they incur the wrath of the whole community.[106]

For the many of the younger generation of Muslim women the strain of accommodating multiple and sometimes contradictory identities—in private at home and in public at school and with friends—has sometimes been almost intolerable and resulted in a painful breakdown of family relationships. They have found it difficult to go along with their parents wishes; they have disagreed with strict rules on dress and expect that traditional values will gradually be abandoned and that family patterns will change and increasingly follow wider social trends. As one of Ellis's respondents put it baldly, 'the urge among young people is to be English.'[107] In the late 1980s she found that among Muslims in Coventry daughters were no longer satisfied with a domestic role, the more Westernised among them perhaps feeling the most frustrated. Similarly, Shaw referred to several cases of Pakistani girls in Oxford attempting to escape arranged marriages by eloping with their lovers.[108] The daughters of the well-off who had been raised primarily in the dominant culture showed more signs of rebelliousness as they became identified culturally with their white peers and unable to accept the more demanding family relations imposed by traditional parents.[109] As one respondent in Afshar's sample, who ran away with a white man, put it, 'we never had to follow any traditional rituals, we never wore shelvar kemiz, covered our hair ... we had white friends and Pakistani friends. Then suddenly I could not marry a white man, suddenly this izzat was brought out ... So I just decided to leave home ... and then the roof fell in.'[110] While university education and a high-status occupation tended to free these women of many of the tangible aspects of material oppression and enhanced their sense of individuality and independence, they did not always feel able to reject their own belief in filial duty and feelings about it, making them emotionally vulnerable and guilt-ridden.

Suicide attempts by teenage girls and young wives have not been uncommon, usually as a result of violence and conflicting expectations at home, while running away from home has often resulted from the frustration caused by the constraints of life there. Figures provided by the North Thames Regional Health Authority suggested that suicide was three times higher among Asian women than in the white population.[111] Another study revealed that 67% of the women suffering from domestic violence had contemplated suicide and 13% had actually attempted it.[112] A 1998 report suggested that the number of suicide attempts among young Asian women had soared.[113] Some girls have 'defected', and in the process 'lost face' and 'dishonoured their families'. Apparently in reaction to the restrictions they have experienced on reaching puberty, when many parents, fearful of 'undesirable' influences, have denied their children the freedom routinely enjoyed by white teenagers. For instance, daughters from middle-class liberal families who had happily been swimming or attending Brownies, and ballet or gymnastics classes, have had such participation abruptly halted after leaving primary school, and contact with white friends, especially boys, has had to lapse. These daughters, identifying more strongly with non-Muslim British culture and less receptive to traditional parental expectations, have become increasingly likely to cause disruption in their families. They have insisted on wearing Western clothes and engaging in leisure activities such as going to discos and parties.[114]

The changing character of at least some younger Muslim women's behaviour has been greatly influenced by alienation, which in its extreme form results in daughters running away to escape the oppressive relationships within their families.[115] In 1997, in Bradford alone 200 cases were reported to the police of girls who had fled their homes to escape the pressures of arranged marriage; but 150 girls were sent back to Pakistan.[116] In 1990 the police dealt with only seven such cases, and the increase indicated a quantum shift in the scale of the problem.[117] A few of the girls who left home took refuge in women's centres, but with no means of support most felt compelled to return to their families.[118] Some women who decided to marry without parental consent and/or outside their communities were treated harshly. In the 1990s there were a number of highprofile cases of women being kidnapped and even murdered by their male family members for daring to enter into such relationships.[119] Bhopal's research suggested that this situation had not changed much by the late 1990s. She recalled the case of one woman, Nasreen, who was encouraged by her parents to study for a degree. At university she enjoyed new freedoms and relationships, and subsequently her parents and brothers tried to persuade her to have an arranged marriage; having become involved in a relationship with a white man she refused, and the resulting tensions within the family remained unresolved.[120] Her findings contrasted with those of Basit, who suggested that young Muslim women brought up in relatively traditional working-class Muslim families did not see parental views and wishes as oppressive and were quite happy to negotiate a middle path between their own aspirations and their parents' wishes.[121]

Collectively Muslim women have made noticeable strides in addressing their specific needs and concerns. Locked out of the male-dominated community arenas of broad social interest, they have had to build and operate all-women political and non-political organisations for these purposes.[122] The Muslim Women's Institute, while tied to the male-dominated Muslim Parliament, considered issues ranging from underachievement in education to the plight of Muslims in Bosnia, and discussed setting up an advisory service for fostering and adoption, child-care provision, and to meet the needs of Muslim women in prison.[123] Young Muslim women have also become interested in pursuing their future through religious organisations, and a growing number have become active in the Sisters' Section of Young Muslims UK (YMSS).[124] Muslim women have established local and community-based organisations with a welfare orientation, and many have become active in women's groups such as Al-Nisa, founded in 1985, where, while the ethos has remained Islamic, the range of recreational and educational activities, from keep-fit classes to language courses and computing, in an all-female, 'safe', environment has been broad-based. In the 1990s other bodies were set up to help Muslim women cope with conflict within the family. The defensiveness of earlier years declined and there was less anxiety about 'washing dirty linen in public'. Problems that were previously swept under the carpet were more widely recognised within the Muslim communities together with a new willingness to address their causes. The Muslim Helpline, a voluntary body set up in London in 1987 to provide community service—counselling and welfare—for Muslim women epitomised this development. Its 1994 report revealed a doubling of its call-up rate since the previous year. In the next three years demand for the Helpline's services doubled again, with the number of calls received annually rising to over 2,000 in 1996–7; these ranged from simple queries to desperate pleas for help. In this period the nature of the issues raised by callers changed. In 1997 there was a noticeable increase in cases of emotional and physical abuse and of conflict within 'mixed marriages', when British-born Muslim women found difficulty in coping with a newly-arrived husband from overseas because of a severe 'culture clash'. Many of the problems to do with marriage and family relations highlighted in 1994 also rose. That younger women were more prepared to seek guidance in these matters was underlined by the fact that 52% of the calls to the Helpline were from women aged twenty-one to forty.[125] Recognising that Muslim women suffered from domestic violence, leading to marriage breakdowns and the need for secure refuges, the women's sections of organisations such as the UK Islamic Mission intensified their efforts to set up such institutions.[126]

Muslim women also made efforts to address the rising demand for services in other areas of their social needs by setting up facilities to cater for them. The range of services on offer widened rapidly. In 1997 the Muslim Women's Centre in Nottingham received lottery funding to provide a day-care service for frail, elderly and disabled women,[127] as did the Disabled Muslim Women's Association in Redbridge. The Jamait-al-Nissa Muslim Women's Group of Wood Green, London, offered training in business skills, information technology, literacy and language, while the Muslim Women's Organisation of Radford introduced welfare sessions.[128] The Asian Women's Association for Awareness and Support was a self-help group formed in Watford to provide a comfortable meeting-place where women could feel safe to discuss health and family issues: their programme of education and information dissemination includes practical guidance on exercise and parenting skills.[129] Muslim women have also sought to build alliances outside their immediate communities. With help from local government, they have established services for women specifically to combat domestic violence;[130] for instance, the refuge workers from Welsh Women's Aid helped to bring back a woman from Bangladesh where her parents had taken her against her will and attempted to force her to marry, and the Black Association of Women Step Out supported her when she started to live with her boyfriend.[131] Younger Somali women were active in campaigns against female genital mutilation—infibulation and circumcision—by highlighting the cruelty and suffering involved in this practice, by emphasising that it has no basis in Islam, and by participating in the activities of broader organisations, such as the London-based Foundation for Women's Health Research and Development (FORWARD) and the Women's Action Group—Female Excision and Infibulation (WAGFEI).[132]

Building institutional support has not been easy. In the 1980s the multi-cultural agenda that had been accepted as part of the broad liberal consensus in Britain came under sustained assault from the political Right. A combination of privatisation policies, erosion of social services and heightened anti-Muslim 'racism' created a sense of deprivation. With the Honeyford controversy, the Rushdie affair and the Gulf War, young Muslim women were forced to reassess their opinion of the 'host' society. Assimilation and racial discrimination understandably led them, like other Muslims, to feel defensive—one available option being to reinterpret existing 'inferior' characteristics as positively valued distinctiveness. A sizeable number have started to deal with their concerns by asserting their Muslim identity—a movement led, ironically, by women who have benefited most from British secularism—young professionals educated in British schools and universities. This educated élite questioned the inferior position of women in Muslim society by referring back to the scriptures and traditions, at the same time applying the method of *ijtihad* to fashion arguments in pursuit of their agendas. On the one hand, they were made more conscious of their Islamic heritage by global events while, on the other, they became increasingly aware of prejudices that were having a detrimental effect on their lives. Juggling the values imbibed at home with those received at school was a challenging prospect, and many returned to the fold of their *biradaris* and clans to defend Islam and its honour with pride. Yet even those who, in their desire for self-fulfilment, wanted to break away from their communities or wished to be more enterprising in exploring the cultures of the wider community remained uncertain about venturing forth, since wider society, despite beckoning them to break free of their social and cultural controls, offered no guarantee of acceptance or alternative support systems. Indeed the Islamic strategy has been relatively successful not only in undermining Muslim communities' demands for adherence to their customs and traditions on gender issues but also in helping young women to broaden the scope for personal choice.

Somali women have deployed the strategy quite imaginatively to challenge patriarchal control, at the same time as maintaining credibility within their communities, and in this way younger women have successfully resisted community and family pressure in some core areas of their personal lives. While they have tended to show some interest in Islam, they have stretched the flexibility of culturally permissible behaviour further than the previous generation, at least through their refusal of arranged marriage, let alone a polygamous one. In the context of Britain they have abandoned traditional female dress, and many have attempted to have their infibulation reversed, even at the risk of alienation from the family, by arguing that it has nothing to do with Islam. El-Solh provided vivid examples of such Somali women. One, a migrant from Aden aged twenty-two, travelled to Britain on her own and found accommodation in a bed-and-breakfast establishment.

Separated from her family and kin, she was able to escape the social pressure of her community; the novelty of being independent was exhilarating, and with like-minded newcomers she was able to explore improving her English and employment opportunities without risking accusations of being 'untrue to her culture'. She became financially independent and her uncontrolled physical mobility increased her personal autonomy. While the public expression of her identity as a Muslim and attendance at Friday prayers in the Central London Mosque pacified her detractors and undermined criticism of her behaviour, these symbolic acts of cultural loyalty gave her space to be critical of those women who dressed in line with fundamentalist interpretations of women's gender roles. While she saw marriage and motherhood as an important part of her gender role, she continued to evade her family's pressure to marry since she was determined to acquire first an education and training, which she considered equally valuable.[133]

The popularity of the *hijab* among young economically active women has symbolised the assertion of female Muslim identity. It has been perceived as defending the uniqueness of Muslim culture and as resistance against the conformist pressure of Western dress, which the dominant culture was attempting to impose upon them. Some Muslim women have used the *hijab* as a way to loosen the bonds of patriarchy, resist cultural practices such as arranged marriage, or continue education away from home without alienating their parents and communities; also as an instrument of mediation between Muslim minority cultures and those of the host society. It has become part of a coping strategy to pacify their parents and reassure them that they will not be corrupted by the public culture of the school, college or university or the workplace. For others it helps to reshape their cultural space by indicating to young Muslim men how they wish to be treated—with respect. As Alibhai-Brown has commented, to see the *hijab* 'merely as a symbol of subordination would be to miss the subtle dialect of cultural negotiation'.[134] When Muslim students and young working women in Britain have voluntarily adopted the veil, ironically in combination with forms of Western dress such as blouses, shirts and trousers, they have done so primarily as a response to and defence against changes in gender roles and sexual identity that are occurring in Muslim communities in Britain. Adopting the *hijab* has gained them

community esteem and been rewarded with a small measure of autonomy and individual rights. Since the veil has advertised cultural loyalty,
it has engendered trust and confidence and so been used, like other
cultural practices, to help remove the constraints placed on young
women by the family, who might have doubted their commitment to
traditional values.[135] So by this symbolic moral gesture they have
increased their chances to pursue their educational or career goals and
choose their husbands. It has allowed various groups of young Muslim
women to participate more easily in public life and in political, economic and educational pursuits. It has given greater access to material
resources and enabled them to argue more effectively for their rights,
health care and control over their bodies. As Muslim women have
moved into the public world, some have turned away from what they
perceive as the seductive and therefore disempowering character of
Western dress and have adopted the *hijab* to asexualise, de-objectify
and so empower themselves.

Not all Muslim women have become convinced of the liberating
qualities of *hijab*, a perception that has by no means gone uncontested.
Many of the respondents in Mirza's study of young Muslim women in
Bradford felt that wearing a *burqa* (a more complete covering for the
female body) in a European country attracted more, rather than less,
attention, and that *purdah* lay 'in the eyes and hearts of every man and
woman'.[136] Muslim feminists have argued that the rhetoric of the *hijab*
assumes that women should ideally be inconspicuous and excluded
from the public domain, which is defined by men as theirs; that they
should be locked indoors so as not to seduce men; that they should
not go out to work; and that their rightful place is in the home as
wives and mothers, not as waged workers. While the *hijab* may have
allowed women to 'invade' the public space, they argue that it has also
legitimised and strengthened those very boundaries, and symbolically
reaffirmed that for women the proper space is in the home and that
they work only out of necessity, preferably in 'respectable' professions, and once at work should minimise their contact with men. This
approach seriously affects women's career prospects,[137] and therefore
these more secular-minded Muslim women have organised against
their oppression differently—not in separate Islamic groupings but as
part of the wider movement against women's inequality. As part of the

Southall Black Sisters (SBS) they became involved at the end of the 1980s in campaigns against abuse of women in the home, providing guidance and counselling for victims. They successfully highlighted the experiences of women forced into marriages and suffering at the hands of their male relatives and in-laws. From campaigning on these specific issues of women's oppression, SBS broadened its sphere of activity to oppose the less tangible ideological underpinning of the subordination of women on a much wider scale. Their vehicle for these campaigns was Women against Fundamentalism (WAF), a network which they established in 1989 to oppose religious fundamentalism for its rejection of the autonomy of women and children, whom the fundamentalists regarded as communal property needing protection, particularly in the sexual sphere, from unholy outsiders. This, WAF asserted, enhanced the status of women and children but also reduced it—hence the ambiguous nature of their gratitude to their protectors. WAF went further in its opposition to the Islamist agenda, which they saw as inherently and broadly against women's liberty and equality, by participating in activities designed to resist the control of traditional male authority in British Muslim communities. It issued a defiant statement in defence of Rushdie, asserting that 'our voices will not be defined by community [male] leaders'.[138] Forty of its members, including many Muslim women, confronted the emotionally charged and almost hysterical Muslim anti-Rushdie march at its peak in London on 27 May 1989. Excited young men turned on them in fury, conveniently setting aside their traditional obligation to provide protection for women and children.

WAF also opposed separate Muslim schools, which it considered were being set up for girls in an effort to police female sexuality and reinforce their religiously defined roles as future wives and mothers. The basic objection arose from their conviction that 'at the heart of the fundamentalist agenda is the control of women's minds and bodies';[139] they argued that Muslim fundamentalists' reaffirmation of women as the guardians of the home, the private domain, was an attempt to curb their aspirations and to create 'a monolithic and homogeneous Muslim community that was easier to control and discipline'.[140] WAF believed that Islamist arguments for the need to maintain a separate Muslim identity and culture had been co-opted to pursue this 'hidden' agenda.

The representation of WAF's argument in anti-Islamic terms by the media made the support for it much more ambivalent.[141] While Muslim women members of the movement felt that aspects of Islamic culture such as arranged marriages were a form of control over women's sexuality, leaving them only a limited choice as to whom and when to marry and no choice not to marry at all, this was not directed specifically at Islamic practices but formed part of their wider discussion of marriage as an oppressive institution.

Nevertheless, in the context of the late 1980s the focus of their opposition was the so-called Muslim fundamentalist agenda regarding the status of women, which defined the parameters of the Islamic community in terms of sexual differentiation of social and familial roles. So, in contrast to Kabbani's argument that the *hijab* was a positive aspect of the Islamic tradition because it had become a symbol of resistance against the Christian forces of the West, and protected women from being regarded as sexual objects, Hannana Siddiqui contended that it denied choice to Muslim women and that many feared the imposition of the *hijab* precisely because it denied their sexuality and was 'part and parcel of a wider process of male control'.[142] She echoed the argument strongly presented by secular Western feminists that in Muslim communities the way a woman dressed and behaved had heavy sexual signification, that she was constantly subjected to the test of 'honour' and reputation, and that her sense of disempowerment stemmed from 'the terror exercised over her body'.[143] In her view, working-class women had even more restricted choices since they were likely to have less resources for opting out and escaping the pressures to conform. Both Kabbani and Siddiqui were responding to the behaviour of some young Muslim women who had taken up the *hijab* after the Rushdie affair to assert their Muslim identity and, in Siddiqui's view, had thus made alliances with 'the forces of patriarchy, conservatism and fundamentalism within our communities'.[144]

Notwithstanding this secular critique, the association of cultural and religious renewal and the importance of women's behaviour and appearance in the reconstruction of the moral order have become very much part of the Islamist political project. This has been welcomed by some Muslim women as a sign of elevated status, and it was this view which the Muslim women involved in WAF found unacceptable and felt they had to confront. WAF's view largely stems from the Western feminist model, with which many Muslim women have considerable difficulty: they have not agreed with the WAF's claim that waged work necessarily liberates women, that family and kinship are intrinsically a hindrance to their liberation, and that religion is always a problem. On the contrary, they argue that recovering practices such as *hijab* facilitates Muslim women's independent participation in public life and makes resistance to patriarchal attitudes possible without compromising their religious and cultural values.[145] Many Muslim women have continued to think that to contribute their labour and their income to the family without any material *quid pro quo* is 'natural'. The sense of familial obligation is shared with pride; they have not seen family as a place of oppression; most have remained committed to supposedly traditional values; even those who have run away or 'lived in sin' tend to see marriage and motherhood as a natural progression and work as a secondary objective. For these women employment has to be compatible with marriage and, for those with children, with child-rearing. In many ways all this was not very different from the experience of their white counterparts, and for women, Muslim or otherwise, patriarchal ideology has remained important in shaping their gender roles.

The changing position of Muslim women in British society

Thus changes in the position of Muslim women living in Britain are apparent in several aspects of life—home, work and the public domain. At home relations between husbands and wives have become more egalitarian—sharing of domestic tasks, participation in decision-making, companionship, leisure, control of expenditure. For daughters too freedom has increased, more encouragement from parents for them to participate in education, careers and social activities. The vast majority of females experience the British school system, and proportionally many more than in the past progress into higher education. The proportion working outside the home has increased, although older migrant women often work within the home in order to preserve the family name and honour. More young Muslim women are moving into higher-level and better-paid employment. They may still face discrimination on religious as well as racial grounds, but they have become increasingly confident and able to challenge and combat it.

In the public domain Muslim women are increasingly involved in local politics and voluntary work and holding public office. Their achievements cover a wide range of public arenas: politics, public service, the media, culture and art. Mrs Lily Khan has long served the Asian community in Surrey. Najma Hafeez, Labour councillor, was elected chair of the Birmingham Council's Education, Social Services and Community Departments.[146] Pola Manzil Uddin rose rapidly in local politics and became the deputy leader of the Tower Hamlets Council; a professional social worker, she remains passionately concerned about the contribution women can make to political life[147] and has been made a member of the House of Lords. The 1990s saw a clutch of Muslim women elected as mayors in London: in 1994 one was elected mayor of Waltham Forest, apparently in the teeth of opposition from Muslim men in her community;[148] later Shama Ahmed was elected mayor of Newham and Fokia Hayee of Lewisham. Muslim women have begun to contribute to the dispensation of justice, with the appointment of a number of Justices of the Peace 'magistrates', including Naveed Bokhari in Essex,[149] Kauser Mirza in the London south-east division[150] and Mariame Saleh, a Liverpool woman of Somali origin.[151] Britain's first woman judge from an Asian Muslim family, Nazreen Pearce, took the oath on the Quran in January 1994.[152]

In the media, Lisa Aziz and Zainab Badawi have succeeded as television newscasters and a number of other British Muslim women have made their names in broadcasting, including television writer and reporter Belkis Beghani, a Muslim Gujrati originally from Uganda. Shama Habibullah has worked on films such as *A Passage to India, Gandhi* and *Heat and Dust*. Yasmin Hosain has presented a weekly programme for the BBC World Service. Likewise, in the world of art and culture, Naseem Khan has become a writer of stature. Nasreen 'Munni' Kabir from an Indian family has been a consultant on Indian cinema to Channel 4 and the Director of the Minorities' Arts Advisory Service; she coordinated the 'Festival of India-in-Britain' and has written on Indian classical dance. Katy Mirza, born in Aden, worked as a model before studying graphic design and becoming involved in social and charity work as well as acting on television. In business Muslim women are similarly making significant progress. Gulshan Jaffer, born into an Ismaili family of Madagascar, runs her own group of hotels and properties in central London. Syeda Jalali won the 'Business Woman of the Year' award from the *Sunday Express* in the 1990s. Farida Mazhar, whose family came from India, joined the Bank of England after taking an economics degree and then worked for the *Financial Times*, Lloyds Bank with responsibility for Middle East and North African business, and the French Banque Paribas in London.[153]

Some Muslim women have come to see themselves in explicitly secular and modernist ways. Mirza revealed in the late 1980s that eight in a sample of ten women, all in their twenties, enjoyed considerable freedom. Their lifestyles—at ease in the company of strange men, 'mouthy', out-spoken and 'give as good as we get', short hair and trousers—resembled their counterparts from other ethnic groups. Parents, moving with the times to maintain family unity, were conceding many of their daughters' social demands.[154] Halima, one of Alibhai Brown's respondents, said: 'I am twenty two, I have talents, feelings, poetry in my heart ... a young woman ... a Muslim ... profoundly changed in the years we have been living here ... I want to share my life and my dreams with this, my country.'[155] Nadima, whom Alibhai Brown described as 'a young Muslim woman ... hell-bent on working in the City, with dreams of making her first million by the age of thirty', said: 'I may be Muslim and Pakistani by origin. But I am British. I want money, the good life, the works. I hate being seen as deprived. I hate the poverty in Pakistan ... I love the west, the freedoms and the lack of hypocrisy.'[156] All this suggests that Muslim women in Britain had acquired a greater propensity to exercise choice and achieve a degree of 'self-actualisation', albeit still circumscribed by historically constituted material and cultural conditions.

This said, it still seems that these changes have brought about no radical breakdown of established traditions; Muslim families have largely, retained their integrity,[157] and sustained internal cooperation and loyalty, with no significant erosion of obligations and reciprocities or respect for elders despite revised expectations about roles and relationships. The family thus remains a central point of reference for Muslim youth in Britain, although for many it is more the immediate rather than the extended family. However, boys and girls continue to be treated differently, in part reflecting concern for the girls' reputation which still exists among both the first and second generations of

Muslims, who are largely imbued with the traditional idea that it is appropriate for communities to be vigilant in enforcing social control over women's and girls' behaviour. Consequently, girls in many Muslim communities have found their circle of friends limited to kin as they grow beyond puberty, and little variety allowed in their leisure activities. These Muslim girls are aware that they have less freedom than their white counterparts, and while many have expressed reservations about the unbridled nature of that freedom, most would probably prefer some relaxation of restrictions on their movements.

It is therefore arguable that despite access to better educational facilities and careers many younger Muslim women have not fared much better than those of the first generation. The cultural ties and family bonds have proved remarkably firm, and maintained a degree of control, despite the relative wealth and economic independence of the younger generation. But to suggest that cultural constraints are the main impediment to Muslim women's integration into mainstream society, as Western commentators have tended to do, is an oversimplification. The situation has always been relatively fluid in this respect. Families have become increasingly flexible about women holding jobs, some parents being actively supportive of daughters' education and career ambitions. But other parents, husbands and in-laws have not allowed women from their families to work, on cultural and religious grounds—even, as Rafiq in his study of small businesses in Bradford showed, when it was a family retail outlet and this resulted in loss of income.[158]

By the end of the twentieth century the pattern of gender relations among younger Muslim women seemed neither to follow parental norms nor to amount to a wholesale adoption of Western standards. Considerable social control is still exercised over them; their movements are monitored closely by their own families themselves and by their communities. A premium is still attached to a girl's reputation, although attitudes to gender segregation are becoming more relaxed. Intermarriage or even marriage outside the community still causes distress to parents and can lead to girls being ostracised. But the first signs of mixed marriages between Western men and Muslim women (in spite of hostility on occasion from families and communities) indicate a weakening of the traditional concept of the Muslim immigrant family.[159]

Thus, instead of being instruments for the continuation and reproduction of old 'traditional' structures, women are now gradually becoming the protagonists of change. A general picture of controlled acculturation or, put another way, of change with resistance has emerged. Traditional patterns have been retained but they are being fused, at least partly and in new combinations, with British customs and conventions. The once rigid constraints on young girls are shifting.

Yet the vast majority of British Muslim women, when judged according to Western concepts of sexual equality, remain restricted in their public and private lives, even though much of their oppression is one not so much due to Islam as to the patriarchy they have experienced and shared with women in other ethnic groups. These women's level of education and their position in the labour force have influenced the form this patriarchal control has taken. Those with lower levels of educational attainment have generally worked in less valued, often sexually segregated occupations, defined as having some structural resemblance to their family role of nurturing, teaching, caring, social and health work—usually at the less skilled end of the job market. Largely dependent on the men in their families, they still experience patriarchy through arranged marriages, dowries, domestic labour and unequal control of finances. At the same time, those Muslim women with higher education and professional training have become relatively independent. But while education and financial independence have helped them, like other British women, to lead more independent lives, less subordinated to the demands of family and community, they remain vulnerable to the various forms of discrimination and oppression that exist more widely in British society.

10

BRITISH MUSLIMS AND EDUCATION

ISSUES AND PROSPECTS

Education represents for British Muslims a major area of struggle for equality of opportunity and the assertion of a distinct identity. It was over education that Muslims became increasingly vocal in raising their demands from the early 1980s, and it is where they have succeeded best in having many of their needs recognised in the face of controversy and opposition from broad sections of British society. This chapter examines within a historical perspective how Muslims in Britain have engaged with the educational system in a changing society. This engagement has been predicated on a range of cross-cutting factors connected to the circumstances of Muslim parents, such as motivation for migration, social class, geographical origins, gender, educational background, competence in English and the time of arrival in Britain, as well as age at the time of entering the educational system. Clearly Muslims from different parts of the world have come to relate with the British educational system in a great variety of ways, and their diverse responses have been shaped not only by their individual circumstances but also by their collective social and cultural experiences.

Early history

Muslim children first came to be a significant proportion of pupils in schools in industrial towns and cities—Glasgow in Scotland, Newcastle, Manchester and Bradford in the north of England, Birmingham, Nottingham and Leicester in the Midlands, Greater London, Slough, Oxford and Bristol in the south.[1] State school provision in the 1960s was entirely geared to the needs of 'indigenous' pupils, albeit in many areas quite inadequately: deficiencies in the system had affected opportunities for all children in deprived areas. As a result, concerns were being raised about the unequal distribution of resources among the inner-city areas, which had already been shown to have distorted equality of educational opportunity for the children schooled there. Government research in the 1960s highlighted social disadvantage as a key determinant in shaping these children's educational opportunities. Working-class children living in areas of urban decay were badly affected by the deficiencies and inequalities afflicting the school system—overcrowded classrooms, crumbling buildings, inadequate facilities and equipment, teachers overloaded with responsibilities and high staff turnover. Girls were at an even greater disadvantage than boys.[2]

This disadvantage was further accentuated for Muslim children, most of whom lived in the same neighbourhoods as their working-class white counterparts. Newly arriving Muslim children, often with little proficiency in English, suffered from the neglect of their particular social needs, and as a result became victims of discriminatory behaviour in schools. Not only was it assumed that Muslim immigrant children would be working-class and thus exposed to obstacles similar to those of their white peers, but it was also expected that the policies being considered as appropriate to address the specific educational 'deficit' of white working-class pupils would apply equally and automatically to Muslim children. The monocultural character of education—which, as was found later, had begun to be detrimental for their educational advancement—was not questioned. Thus the view of the educational establishment was that the few children who had arrived by the early 1960s could be absorbed with little disruption to existing teaching approaches and organisational structures. Given that little preparation had taken place to accommodate the rapid influx of

Muslims into the inner-city areas of Britain shortly before and after the 1962 Commonwealth Immigrants Act, the difficulties faced by schools already struggling to cope with the endemic scarcity of resources in the inner-city areas were intensified, causing greater discontent among white parents.

As the concentration of Muslim children increased, schools in many of these areas tended to generate educational provision 'on the hoof'.[3] Since local authorities, schools and teachers retained a great deal of discretion and autonomy over curriculum and organisation, practices in areas with large Muslim intakes varied considerably. But despite ad hoc, *laissez-faire* and uncoordinated provision, the education system throughout the 1960s reflected the assimilationist assumptions of the establishment, which believed that for society to remain socially cohesive immigrants and their children needed to accept existing norms and values. In 1964 the Commonwealth Immigrants Advisory Council (CIAC), reflecting government policy, stated that 'a national system cannot be expected to perpetuate the different values of immigrant groups'.[4] In its view immigrant children, with their different outlook and way of life, presented a special challenge to teachers; according to this assimilation model, there was little room for cultural variety since differences were seen as disruptive and harmful to education. Thus schools were assigned an important role in minimising the potential for disorder. Ethnic and religious identities were to be suppressed and even deprecated. Schools were supposed instead to facilitate the transmission of 'British' culture and resocialisation of the immigrant child.[5] Politicians exhorted immigrant parents to 'encourage their children to give up ... their religion and their dietary laws ... If they [immigrants] refused,' one said, 'then we must be tough. It should be a condition of being given National Insurance that they attend English classes.'[6] None of the prevailing educational, curricular or organisational strategies was questioned: the existing provision was assumed to be intrinsically valuable and appropriate for all children, and those who deviated from the norm were deemed to be in need of further socialisation through English tuition and greater contact and communication with their white peers. In this scheme the dispersal of Muslim pupils (in cities such as Birmingham and Bradford) to predominantly white schools was presented as a solution, not only to the emerging problems of these children's under-achievement, but also, and more important for politicians, as a way of preventing protests from white parents who believed (contrary to any existing research evidence) that immigrant children retarded the progress of their own children due to the perceived 'undue preoccupation of the teaching staff' with their linguistic and other difficulties.[7]

In the framing of these policies Muslim parents were not consulted about how they wished their children to be educated, and so their rights concerning their children's religious and cultural needs, enshrined in the 1944 Education Act, were ignored. Nor was there evidence that dispersal helped with language acquisition or with 'integration'; in any case, only about a quarter of the local authorities in England and Wales introduced 'bussing' due to practical difficulties. Ironically, the policy of dispersal actually made it less likely that Muslim needs would be taken into consideration. Indeed, research published in 1972 suggested that schools with large numbers of Muslim children were much more inclined to attend to their social and cultural needs than those where a smaller intake required a much greater allocation of special resources.[8] However, at first there was little opposition from Muslim parents to this provision, not least because they were unfamiliar with the system and knew little about how to make demands of the relevant institutions. The fact that many of them were themselves nonspeakers and writers of English meant that their contact with their children's schools was minimal, and this was accentuated by the policy of dispersal. Consequently, they could not evaluate the impact on their children of what was provided, and so acquiesced in whatever education was being offered.

There were other reasons too for the acceptance of the assimilationist agenda. It was not surprising that Muslims from South Asia should have been convinced that the quality of education that had enabled the British to establish a worldwide empire and sustain a dominant position was desirable for their own children. Therefore, when their offspring had begun to arrive in Britain from the early 1960s, they were content to accept the existing system in the hope that it would help them to socialise and integrate into the wider society and give them access to opportunities for a better future. Consequently, during the 1960s and early 1970s most British Muslims were happy for the education authorities to overcome the putative 'cultural deficit'.

Muslims and 'underperformance' in education

The assimilationist policies tried for much of the 1960s did not work. The academic attainment levels of many Muslim children remained unacceptably low and their general progress was unsatisfactory. Evidence suggested that they generally lagged behind their white peers and indeed many other immigrant minorities, especially Hindus and Sikhs. Difficulties with English and inadequate testing techniques meant that a disproportionate number were channelled into educational provision of low academic quality. In 1963 Kawwa found that in Islington Cypriot boys and girls were concentrated in the lower streams,[9] and there were far fewer Turkish Cypriots in grammar schools—0.2% in Haringey in 1967 compared with 16.8% of Indians and Pakistanis and 41.1% of whites.[10] In the 1970s Turkish Cypriots were also found to be over-represented in the centres for the educationally subnormal (ESN), partly as a result of inadequate testing methods. Yule similarly revealed that the Turkish children's mean reading scores were much lower than those of their white peers (86.5 to 94.8). However, the British-born Turkish Cypriots fared as well as whites, while immigrant Turkish Cypriots did much worse. Pakistanis did little better.[11] In 1970 Townsend showed that only 2.5% of Pakistanis were selected for entry to grammar schools, compared to 20% of indigenous pupils.[12] A national survey by Townsend and Brittan in 1971–2, provided a more optimistic picture, but confirmed the previous trends, while a Department of Education and Science analysis showed that, compared with 42% of white pupils who took GCE O-level examinations in the fifth form, only 6% of Pakistanis did so. Similarly, 32% of the latter, compared with 3% of the former, were placed in non-examination streams.[13]

Attempted solutions to improve the academic performance of Muslim immigrant children, such as withdrawing them from mainstream schooling for separate language tuition, proved largely counter-productive; they tended to generate feelings of superiority among white children and of inadequacy among Muslim children, thus de-motivating them. They also reinforced negative stereotypes among teachers about Muslim children's abilities. Similarly dispersal, which was only patchily applied by local authorities, far from creating cross-cultural understanding, generated opposition among both white and

Muslim parents. White parents objected to their children being 'bussed' to overcrowded and under-resourced 'immigrant schools'; Muslim children were denied the benefits of neighbourhood schools, making it difficult for parents to establish and maintain contact with their children's school, and indeed preventing children from growing up and developing healthy interactions with their white peers in schools as well as outside school hours. Given that it was Muslim children who were at the receiving end of this experiment and thus seen as 'the problem', these policies tended to strengthen hostility in the dominant white population towards them, and the expectation that they would lead to rapid absorption and acceptance of Muslim communities into the indigenous majority, resulting in equal citizenship, was exposed as wholly unrealistic by the rising tide of racism during the 1960s. For Muslim parents even the pragmatic and secular purposes which they had been persuaded to believe would be achieved by the monocultural approach were not being realised.

In the early 1970s research still indicated that, in some schools at least, Muslim children from a variety of ethnic backgrounds performed less well than whites. This was put down to a combination of factors that had nothing to do with religion, although most of the earlier explanations referred to cultural and linguistic 'deficit'. On the other hand, some research suggested cultural bias in selection tests as possible causes for the gap between Muslim and white achievement levels.[14] Underachievement was also attributed to Muslim parents' low status, lack of education, limited aspirations and poorly-paid employment. The role of parents in the success or otherwise of their children was highlighted. Anwar found that the low achievers were children of those Pakistanis who worked long hours and night shifts and so were unable to pay much attention to their children's schooling needs.[15]

By the late 1970s there was a growing consensus that the 'immigrant' effect had begun to recede. The 1981 Inner London Education Authority (ILEA) census found only six Turkish Cypriots out of 640 secondary pupils in ESN centres. Martineau also showed that Cypriots were well represented in O- and A-level entries, despite being hampered by difficulties with English. Performance was deemed to be more closely associated with social class than with ethnicity, and once that was taken into account Turkish Cypriots were found to do better than whites, with a higher proportion of entries for GCE examinations.[16] Similarly Beetlestone reported that the head teachers whom he surveyed did not perceive Turkish Cypriot pupils as doing any less well than pupils from other ethnic groups.[17] Fullerton in Derby found that 'contrary to popular belief' there was no marked difference between proportions of Muslim and white girls who took A-levels and further training.[18] Indeed, Verma and Ashworth arrived at the view that the catching-up process needed by immigrant children was almost complete by the mid-1970s, and that educational achievement had improved with the length of stay in Britain.[19]

However, research during the 1980s seemed to contradict these findings, partly as a result of the continuing inflow of children of school age with needs similar to those of their predecessors in the 1960s and 1970s. In 1983, 27% of Pakistanis and 51% of Bangladeshis possessed no formal qualifications. In 1985 the Swann Committee observed that in a majority of schools it visited 'there was a strong feeling that these pupils, as a group, were underachieving and the Turkish Cypriots were singled out as giving particular cause for concern'.[20] While it reported that South Asians were achieving similar academic examination results to those of their white peers, it failed to distinguish between different subgroups within the South Asian population. Indeed, a Home Affairs Committee looking into disadvantage among Bangladeshis found that academic attainment among pupils from this ethnic group were at the bottom in terms of academic attainment. In 1986, in the ILEA, only 16.1% of Pakistanis and 3.6% of Bangladeshis had five or more O-level passes. In an analysis of the O-level and CSE results obtained by ILEA fifth-year pupils in the summer of 1985, the average score of the highest-achieving group, Indian pupils, with 24.5%, was nearly three times that of the lowest-achieving group, Bangladeshis (8.7%). The proportion of Indian pupils obtaining five or more O-levels, A–C grades, or CSE 1 grades (26.5%) was two and a half times the ILEA average (10.2%) and ten times that of Turkish pupils (2.6%).[21] The 1988–90 LFS revealed that 60% of Pakistanis and 68% of Bangladeshis were without formal qualifications, and while 36% of Indians and 33% of whites aged sixteen to twenty-four had obtained A-level equivalent or higher, only 18% of Pakistanis and 5% of Bangladeshis had such qualifications.[22] The evidence suggested that British schooling had little impact on gender differentials in Muslim children's academic progress, as reflected in the participation rates of Muslim boys compared with girls. Most commentators explained these differences by the difference in parents' attitudes towards their sons' and daughters' education. The attitudes of Muslims boys and girls also seemed to contribute to the academic standards they achieved—their preference for education was to an extent determined by their perception of their gender roles, which depended on the kind of conditioning they received at home.[23]

The gap between Muslim pupils and the rest persisted into the 1990s. Indeed, it seems that the overall gap in educational achievements had widened between the Indians and whites, on the one hand, and Pakistanis, Bangladeshis and Afro-Caribbeans on the other. However, these general conclusions arguably presented too simplistic a picture, since in many places, such as Glasgow and London, Pakistanis were on average achieving better results than whites. While in Bradford in 1996 13% of Pakistani and 15% of Bangladeshi males, compared with 37% of Indians and 25% of whites, achieved five or more GCSE passes at grades A–C (figures for both Pakistani and Bangladeshi females were 19% compared with 44% and 33% for Indian and white females respectively), in Waltham Forest in 1994 more Pakistanis obtained O-level passes than whites (33.5% versus 29.8%), and in 1995 even Bangladeshis in the borough outperformed white pupils (30.6% versus 30.0%).[24]

In earlier research the lower scores of Muslim pupils, especially girls, had been explained away by extended visits to their home countries and social circumstances.[25] Less account was taken of the 'school effect' on their performance. Studies carried out during the 1980s and 1990s now suggested that Muslim pupils' experience within school had more impact on their academic performance than previously thought. Given the persistence of inequalities in education along ethnic lines, the immigrant/stranger theory of underachievement was gradually divested of its explanatory power.[26] The context within which the educational system operated contributed to the overall picture of disadvantage that Muslim children had come to experience. The inner-city comprehensive schools attended by the majority of Muslim children were geared to providing lower-level courses with the objective of keeping working-class children interested and under control. This kind of education hardly satisfied the distinctly middle-class aspirations of many Muslim parents.

However, the presence of Muslim children in multiply deprived environments does not fully explain their lower attainment from the 1960s to the end of the 1990s. According to Tomlinson, evidence had accumulated 'that normal school processes ... can have the effect of disadvantaging pupils from particular ethnic groups, in addition to those from lower socioeconomic groups'.[27] Research indicated that ethnic-minority pupils may have been subject to systemic discrimination within schools. Familiar patterns of discrimination and negative stereotyping by teachers were evident in the selection and allocation of courses.[28] Many schools and teachers appeared 'at best ill-informed, insensitive, frequently ethnocentric'.[29] Few non-Muslim teachers were equipped to engage adequately with issues considered important by many Muslims. In the early 1980s most teachers still talked of 'integration'. And yet the differential treatment of Muslim pupils resulted not simply from individual prejudice but also from institutional labelling. For instance, Muslim girls were perceived by many schools as submissive and likely to lack motivation after the age of fourteen: since they were supposedly awaiting marriage and therefore unlikely to pursue a career, attention devoted to them was regarded as time and effort wasted. While this attitude may have persisted among more conservative Muslim parents, by the late 1980s, contrary to these stereotypes, 'most Pakistanis were keen that their daughters should receive education, including higher education'.[30] Negative assumptions as well as low expectations also influenced teachers' and schools' perceptions of the talents and skills possessed by particular ethnic groups and the 'gender-specific' advice they offered.[31] Subject choices were typically structured by teachers' assessment of ability, presumed academic deficiencies (not all based on formal testing), motivation and behaviour. It is easy to see how this system offered scope for the operation of exclusion and thus became part of the cumulatively disadvantaging process. The attitudes, values and behaviour of teachers and schools affected the way Muslim pupils saw themselves. Lack of individual attention, minimal praise and fewer opportunities to contribute to classroom discussion undermined self-confidence and in turn adversely affected educational attainment. The evidence in the 1990s suggested that teachers' attitudes had changed little.[32]

However, it was not just the poor academic performance of their children that led to many Muslim parents regarding the British education system as a failure. They questioned the values being imparted in the state-school environment and whether there were aspects of disadvantage and discrimination that were affecting the children's capacity to build a positive sense of their identity. Evidence emerging as early as the late 1960s and 1970s indicated that social cohesion was far from being realised and that Muslim children's personal development was being neglected. For example, a National Foundation for Educational Research report on the response of the LEAs to Muslim pupils in England and Wales had referred to their religious and cultural concerns under the rubric of 'miscellaneous provisions'.[33] But measures to address these concerns in the school environment took an ad hoc form. By the early 1970s a range of identified cultural 'problem areas', including school uniforms, meals, physical education, single-sex education and extracurricular activities, were in urgent need of resolution.[34] It was acknowledged that these aspects of schooling were likely to have an adverse effect on Muslim children's self-esteem and security, and hence on their educational achievement.

In addition to these problems, the school social environment also caused concern to many Muslims, especially the harassment experienced by Muslim pupils; evidence from the late 1980s showed how this affected academic achievement. Ahmed Iqbal Ullah's murder in a Manchester school in 1986 by Darren Coulborn, who subsequently boasted 'I've killed a Paki', and the Commission for Racial Equality's investigation into racial harassment, *Learning in Terror* (1988), gave ample and dramatic illustration of the prevalence of racial abuse and violence in schools and the distress and torment it caused. It revealed too how indifferent and insensitive teachers were to the plight of their pupils, and indeed that some teachers expressed racist opinions to their white colleagues and made humiliating remarks and jokes not only to pupils in the classroom but also to their minority colleagues in the staffroom.[35] At the same time, questions were asked regarding the content and character of the existing curriculum and indeed its capacity to meet the reasonable educational needs of Muslim children. Until the early 1970s the curriculum remained consciously monocultural, in line with the educational policy of assimilating immigrants and their children into

British culture. An HM Inspectorate (HMI) survey of 1972 found that the subject content of history, geography and religious education was becoming rapidly 'out of touch with a changing world', and noted that 'very little modification of the curriculum has taken place and there is little evidence that subject departments in general have considered the curriculum critically in the light of the presence of immigrant pupils in their classes.'[36] More specifically, research suggested that the historical experience of Muslims was being ignored and devalued and what little was offered about Islam and the history of Muslim societies was presented from within a Christian/secular framework and the perspectives of European conquerors. The world of the Muslim minorities in Britain—their cultures, languages and religion—was in effect marginalised and deprecated. Ray Honeyford, headmaster till 1984 of the overwhelmingly Pakistani Drummond Middle School in Bradford, painted a picture of Pakistan as a country run by tyrants and despots, unable to 'cope with democracy', which 'despite disproportionate western aid ... remains, for most of its people, obstinately backward, [and] where corruption abounds at every level'; it was 'religiously unimaginably intolerant, barbaric and arbitrary in its dispensation of justice' and, to boot, was 'the heroin capital of the world ... a fact that is now reflected in the drug problems of English cities with Asian populations'. Honeyford implied that somehow Pakistanis in Britain had brought with them the problems that were now afflicting British cities, especially drugs, and they presumably needed to be educationall 'cleansed' of their origins to be made fit to live in British society.[37]

More generally, textbooks continued to present a broadly ethnocentric view of Islam. Partial accounts embraced in 'orientalist scholarship' within the perspective of the dominant civilisation were taught as 'balanced' history. Similarly the choice of vocabulary in descriptions of historical events such as the Crusades and accounts of the 'freedom movements' (or was it 'decolonisation'?) were also largely Eurocentric. Analysis of school textbooks on Islam, for instance, revealed that accounts could be misleading and in some cases inaccurate. Some texts asserted that conquest had on the whole brought benefits to the colonised and that 'even the most greedy exploitation of colonial territories left the "victims" somewhat better off'. European invasions of Muslim lands were justified on the basis of the superiority of Christianity and the need to convert Muslims and save them from eternal damnation.[38] The Crusades were glorified as 'Christian ardour', in contrast to 'the fanaticism of the infidel'.[39] The 1985 Swann Report revealed how Greeks and Turks had been depicted in the curriculum, with the Greeks viewed as 'the great civilisers of the world' and at the heart of the Western tradition, and the Turks as 'uncivilised and cruel "barbarians"', followers of a strange '"foreign" faith'.[40] Muslims were worried that textbooks and courses were undermining their children's identity by 'creating doubts in the minds of students about the fundamental tenets and assumptions of Islam';[41] knowledge was being selected to emphasise certain values or a certain view of the world, cutting children off from alternative perspectives, ideas and experiences, as well as confirming white children in the prejudices they picked up from the media, comics and the cinema. It became apparent to Muslims, both parents and pupils, that this ethnocentric curriculum had a negative effect on Muslim pupils' academic performance, not least by reinforcing feelings of being outsiders and 'different'. In some instances it was felt that Asian children, many of them Muslim, who had previously been doing well suffered a loss of self-esteem through the disregard and denigration of their histories and cultures. The distress caused the standard of their work to decline.[42] While policy documents at the highest level showed urgent concern to make the curriculum meaningful and relevant by changing the content to reflect the cultural mix of society, there was little evidence that curricular modifications had taken place. Indeed, only after the publication of the Swann Report in the mid-1980s were Asian history and geography given a little space in the curriculum.

The Education Reform Act of 1988, with its establishment of the National Curriculum, had a contradictory impact. While there was some room for the inclusion of Muslim perspectives in the teaching of history, British history was to be placed at the heart of the new curriculum. So, despite scope to interpret the National Curriculum guidelines in ways that allowed sympathetic schools to engage with Islamic aspects, it was possible to maintain a Eurocentric bias in subject content and to focus on values that many Muslims found contentious. Indeed, some commentators remarked that 'national curriculum documents to date, with very few exceptions, are drawn up in an assimilationist spirit.'[43] However, by the 1990s some changes were discernible.

Many offered options in Urdu and Arabic, recognising their relevance to Muslim pupils, and there were attempts to include the contribution of Muslim scholars to science, and Islamic themes in geography.

From the point of view of Muslim parents, not only had assimilationist policies prevented their children from overcoming the barriers that had prevented them from competing with their white counterparts on equal terms, but they had also exposed them to the undesirable influences of British society. Anxieties had surfaced about the qualifications and capabilities of the vast majority of teachers to provide the kind of education that would equip Muslim children with appropriate knowledge and skills. Thus a gap grew between the points of view of the British educational establishment and Muslim parents, which tended in opposite directions. More specifically, Muslim parents were increasingly concerned about the inadequacy in state schools of religious education, which many viewed as the cornerstone of any system of education. Research in 1972 had revealed that few schools made provision for even a superficial study of religions other than Christianity in their religious education (RE) curriculum.[44] Withdrawal from school assemblies and RE lessons was legally allowed but, given the ethos of many schools, few took advantage of this, although proportionately many more Muslims withdrew than other non-Christians, immigrant or otherwise.[45] In light of this 'neglect', many Muslim parents were worried about the drift away from parental authority, which they attributed to the marginalisation of religious education coupled with a lack of inculcation of discipline in state schools. To redress this deficit, therefore, religious schools were set up within communities. By 1969 children in South Asian Muslim communities were spending between 15–20 hours a week in supplementary schools affiliated to local mosques.[46]

However, throughout the 1970s many Muslim parents had serious misgivings about other aspects of schooling that they saw as un-Islamic—sex education, religious education, coeducation, dress, diet, assemblies and fund-raising activities such as raffles that involve gambling. They demanded changes with greater vigour than before. Evidence was growing that existing policies, instead of improving the situation of Muslim pupils, actually entrenched underachievement and alienation. The educational establishment acknowledged Muslim disquiet and renewed its efforts to identify the actual, rather than presumed, needs of Muslim children in order to channel appropriate resources into meeting them. The government therefore decided to ditch the policy of assimilation and move towards a multiculturalist approach, echoed in the famous words of Roy Jenkins, Home Secretary in 1966: 'equal opportunity accompanied by cultural diversity in an atmosphere of mutual tolerance'.[47]

Multicultural education and Muslims—1970 to the mid-1980s

By the early 1970s the educational establishment was convinced that the education of Muslim children, as part of the ethnic minority population of Britain, could best be embraced within a broad multicultural structure—which, it was believed, could reconcile the opposing ideologies of assimilationism and separatism by teaching about distinct cultures and religions within a liberal framework. By exploring cultural differences, it was argued, understanding and acceptance of other cultures and faiths would be enhanced, ignorance and prejudice reduced, and the possibility of achieving social justice increased. It was hoped that ultimately this model would lead to social cohesion, harmony and reduced tension in the multi-ethnic communities of Britain. Milner's research on minority children's negative self-identity and its allegedly causal links with their 'underachievement' further strengthened the case for the move away from assimilation policies.[48] Educationalists were compelled to reconsider the efficacy of monocultural education in the light of equality of opportunity and meritocratic principles—two of the cornerstones of the 1944 Education Act. Increasingly it was accepted that positive teaching about other cultures and religions would help to overcome the discrepancies in performance and alienation shown to have resulted from a poor self-image.

Equally significant in advancing Muslim pupils' interests was the emerging resistance of Muslim parents to the racist environment of state schools, together with the incipient growth of the Muslim voluntary-school movement. These provided a potent combined challenge to the credibility of assimilationist principles. Principles of multicultural education had become sufficiently widely accepted by 1975 to be given institutional backing in Lord Bullock's report. It declared that 'no child should be expected to cast off the language and culture of the home as he crosses the threshold of school', and recommended the integration of ethnic, cultural and linguistic diversity into the curriculum.[49] More specifically Muslim educationalists suggested that state schools with a significant Muslim intake should offer Arabic and community languages as an option, since Muslim children would benefit from a combination of 'greater access to their religious and cultural heritage and an enhanced sense of self-esteem and achievement'.[50]

Between the mid-1970s and the early 1980s the idea of multicultural education took firm root. It came to be assumed that learning about one's own ethnic and cultural heritage would improve equality of opportunity and educational achievement and that learning about other cultures would reduce prejudice and discrimination. All this accepted the view that racism was largely a product of ignorance, perpetuated by negative attitudes and individual prejudice, and therefore did not require structural, systemic and collective solutions. Policymakers had come round to the view that, given that Britain was increasingly a multicultural and multi-faith society, it was reasonable to modify the system of education to reflect this changed configuration. It was also felt that the changes in the curriculum would help to integrate the minorities more firmly into British society as they received greater recognition in cultural and religious terms. Over this local authorities were encouraged to take initiatives; many subjects in the school curriculum began to draw more emphatically on the minority experience, and teachers were encouraged to reflect a greater understanding of the positive features of their pupils' backgrounds. Curriculum change was most noticeable in relation to RE, where 'there seemed to be a more or less universalistic approach concerned with moral themes'.[51]

Even a time when, more and more, Muslims were discussing Islamic notions of education as an alternative to the secular assumptions of the British education system, the religious dimension still received little attention. British Muslims, however, did not wish to see RE marginalised in the curriculum, and as they became increasingly familiar with how the education system functioned, they applied pressure more effectively to have their demands met. They argued that since Britain was a pluralistic society, all major world religions should form part of the curriculum. No longer did they feel that the transmission of culture and faith was the responsibility of Muslim families and mosque schools alone. They demanded that Islam be taught adequately in RE lessons in state schools too, so that Muslim pupils did not feel that the school ethos and curriculum were in conflict with their own and their parents' deeply-held beliefs and values. Some LEAs accepted the Muslim case in general terms. For example, a committee was established in April 1970 to revise Bradford's RE syllabus to ensure that it reflected the variety of faiths in the city, but this measure did not go far enough for many of the city's Muslims, who continued to request permission for their religious teachers to provide instruction in secondary schools, as stipulated in the 1944 Education Act. Their efforts bore fruit when, in July 1972, the LEAs relented and agreed to this being done, albeit after school hours.[52] Since the official view that the teaching of Islam in state schools countered the aim of social harmony was so deeply entrenched, this 'battle' had to be fought over and over again, all the more so because of the decentralised and fragmented nature of the education system. For example, in 1974 when LEAs in other parts of West Yorkshire dragged their feet, the Union of Muslim Organisations of UK and Eire advised Muslim parents to withdraw their children from RE lessons and morning assembly. Gradually, LEAs around the country recognised the need to replace what had hitherto been largely Bible-centred 'Agreed Syllabuses' with multi-faith ones, in which religions other than Christianity were studied for their own sake and on their own terms.[53] While this decision was duly welcomed by Muslim commentators, it raised controversy over what should properly form part of RE, since the subject also included discussion of Marxism. Thus, Hampshire learned from the Birmingham experiment, consulted widely, and adopted a policy in 1978 that gained much greater acceptance and was later introduced by eleven other local authorities.[54]

However, Muslim pressure groups, which had initially welcomed such initiatives, became disenchanted and critical, chiefly because they could not accept the secular and relativistic framework within which RE was being taught. Inquiry, openness, sympathetic understanding of other faiths and respect for differences suggested that Islam was only one among many faiths, equal in status and open to questioning by rational principles. For some Muslims this approach challenged the absolute nature of their revelation and was therefore untenable to these sections of the Muslim population, for whom multicultural education sowed confusion and subverted their traditions. This was too high a price to pay for communal harmony.[55] Moreover, it did not seem to address many of Muslims' central concerns. It was steeped in a liberal tradition, and its quasi-secular approach appeared to undermine their own authority as well as that of their religion and culture: children were being taught to question the authority of religious texts and their elders. The shift from 'confessional' to 'merely informative' or 'phenomenological' teaching of RE, in which pupils were invited to 'participate imaginatively and empathetically in the "subjectivity of others"' was therefore seen by some Muslims as problematic.[56] And apart from the practical difficulties of teaching religion in a relativistic fashion, many Muslims found the relative treatment of notions of right and wrong unpalatable.

Even more important, perhaps, the mixing of sexes at school, especially at the secondary level, was seen as a major threat to the social fabric and stability of Muslim communities. This brought them into conflict with the authorities, whose attitude was that coeducation promoted the goal of gender equality and benefited all pupils, especially girls. The concerns of parents were exacerbated by the apparent challenge of state education to the values of obeisance and *haya* (modesty) inherent in their daughters' involvement in school activities that encouraged assertive and extrovert behaviour. While schools emphasised equality of opportunity and treatment, many Muslim parents wanted girls treated differently from boys, and asserted their right to choose single-sex schooling for their children.

The controversy came to a head in 1973 when Abdullah Patel decided to withdraw his daughter from a coeducational school, demanding a place in an all-girls school on religious grounds. Later that same year, Riaz Shahid in Bradford withdrew his daughter and returned her to Pakistan rather than sending her to school, as required by law, when she was refused a place in a single-sex school.[57] Both these parents came under pressure from their local authorities to conform, the justification being that comprehensive schooling was educationally sound and their decision denied their daughters equal treatment with white girls and so put them at a disadvantage. These arguments were rejected by the parents, and both received significant support from Muslim communities. Muslim pressure groups such as the UK Islamic Mission (UKIM), the Union of Muslim Organisations (UMO) and the Islamic Cultural Centre, which had been lobbying for single-sex education since the late 1960s, all supported Patel's demand. A Muslim Parents' Association (MPA) was established in January 1974 to coordinate the demands for concessions in existing Bradford schools and for the setting up of a separate school for Muslim girls.[58] While there was little support at this stage for the latter from Muslims generally, a coherent Muslim position on separate education for Muslim girls had emerged by 1975. M. Iqbal argued in his book *Islamic Education and Single-sex Schools* that males and females were fundamentally different and their natures suited them to perform different roles, with the females primarily as wives and mothers. To carry out these tasks well, girls needed different types of education from boys, which coeducation could not provide.[59]

However, Muslim parents were still strongly rebuffed by local education authorities, which caused many to doubt the sincerity and willingness of the system to understand and accept the religious needs of significant sections of the Muslim population.[60] Some Muslim groups concluded that their needs could only be met outside the state system, and therefore pressed the Department of Education and Science to consider the establishment of voluntary-aided Muslim institutions where Muslim pupils could receive schooling in harmony with their distinct beliefs and values. Throughout this period, the assimilationist imperative remained intact, but reforms were carried out as a series of palliative attempts to make minorities feel more 'confident and competent in a new society' and so draw them 'into the mainstream of ordinary life'.

The early 1970s were a watershed in the history of educational provision for ethno-religious minorities. The new perspective, a response to the disquiet and resistance being expressed with increasing intensity, shifted the emphasis from suppression of cultural differences to their recognition and celebration. Policy-makers became readier to accept Muslim campaigners' demands as consistent with the general principles that parental beliefs had priority over predominantly secular ideas, and the right of parents to make decisions affecting their own children's education took precedence over all other considerations, even if necessary over the rights of the children themselves. The minds of policymakers were further concentrated regarding the need for multicultural reforms as campaigns against 'un-Islamic' practices—the wearing of skirts, exposure of girls' bodies in physical education, swimming, dancing and showers, and fund-raising activities based on gambling—and opposition to the requirement of Muslim pupils' participation in school assemblies gathered momentum and became more coherent.[61] In the 1970s, then, some convergence developed between Muslims' views about the kind of education they wanted for their children and the cultural pluralist strategies of local education authorities. Muslims were no longer expected to accommodate entirely to existing norms, and their right to maintain their own religious identity was recognised.

However, when the impact of these changes was assessed later, the picture seemed less rosy. Many of those closely associated with implementing multicultural policies evaluated them negatively and found them to be counter-productive; from their analyses it seemed that the Muslim pupils' problems were rooted in the values and assumptions of the wider population which shaped its prejudes and discriminatory practices *vis-à-vis* Muslims—from which the educational system and its directors were themselves not immune. Thus, unless these attitudes were vigorously addressed, no amount of cultural information and knowledge about ethnic minorities, and about Muslims specifically, would make much difference. For many Muslims, therefore, multiculturalism remained a secular ideology that promoted a view of education that ran counter to Islamic values. They refused to accept that religion should be offered as only one of a range of cultural options open to their children. Because the scrutiny of Islamic texts and authorities implicit in multicultural education was perceived as subverting their most cherished values and norms, these Muslims never felt comfortable with multicultural education.

Muslim education—from the mid-1980s to 2001

With the coming to power of the Conservatives in 1979 the multicultural agenda began to be rolled back. The New Right became ideologically dominant, and its thinking found its way increasingly into government policies. A major assault was mounted on the ideological front by its leaders on the ideas of multicultural and antiracist education.[62] It was condemned as contaminating the purity of a homogeneous and monolithic British way of life and presented as an alien threat to the fundamental values of the 'indigenous' population. This attack developed into a crescendo by the mid-1980s, with philosophers and educationists of that tendency, such as Roger Scruton and Ray Honeyford, constructing elaborate though by no means original arguments challenging the idea of cultural pluralism and justifying a return to the policies of assimilation.[63] By the time the Swann Committee, which had been asked to continue the inquiry set up in the late 1970s into provision of education in multicultural Britain, published its report *Education for All* in 1985, the impetus for multicultural and antiracist education had faded away. The political climate had become much more conducive to ethnocentric and xenophobic sentiments and more dismissive, if not contemptuous, of those perceived as 'outsiders'. At the local level 'municipal socialism', which had driven the antiracist agenda, was being systematically destroyed by the Conservative government. The Swann Report was tepidly received, its recommendations accepted only in part and reluctantly. Moreover, Muslim members of the Swann Committee registered their dissent from the line taken in the Report against the establishment of 'separate' schools.[64] Increasingly Muslims were aware that the kind of values and the sort of socialisation for which they had hoped were not being provided, and growing deeply concerned about the gap that had developed between their own views on morality and those their children seemed to be acquiring through the school system.[65]

At the same time, a growing number of Muslims, after being in Britain for decades, had become more confident of their position in society, and begun to develop a degree of clarity about their rights as British citizens. They were now prepared to argue more forcibly for their children's educational needs and priorities, and having become better organised, were able to mobilise significant numbers of Muslims in largely successful campaigns on specific educational issues.

The early 1980s saw Muslim organisations increasingly active in the field of education, which in any case had moved close to the top of the national political agenda. City-wide structures were established to give their demands more force, and many of these were successful. In July 1982 the Muslim Liaison Committee (MLC) in Birmingham, which brought together over sixty Muslim organisations, presented the city's Education Committee with a fifteen-point charter of demands, which went beyond the usual practical issues—dress (school uniform, physical education (PE) and swimming), the contents of school meals and religious education—by requesting the provision of facilities for Muslim prayers and holidays, and recognition of Islam across the school curriculum. While the last point was not accepted, most of the others were agreed. The right of Muslim parents to withdraw their children from assembly was recognised, and schools were expected to create the conditions in which religious instruction could be given in a child's own faith. Head-teachers were advised to provide prayer facilities for Muslim pupils. The wearing of religious symbols and headscarves—though not the *dupatta* (scarf) for safety reasons—and of track suits during physical education lessons was permitted. A compromise was reached on the question of changing rooms and showers: while the authorities accepted that ideally these facilities should be available separately to Muslim pupils, financial constraints precluded this in practice, although head teachers were advised to consider ways of meeting such requests if practicable. They were also advised to organise separate swimming sessions and to excuse children from mixed swimming lessons if this was requested by parents. Since music, dance, drama and art were integral to the curriculum and in the view of most teachers contributed to the children's overall development, but were thought by some Muslim parents to be un-Islamic, the only way out of the impasse was to advise schools to 'play it by ear', but to ensure that dance and drama classes were not mixed. They could only consider the issues as and when they arose. The MLC also found sex education, a compulsory part of the curriculum, unacceptable, and so the authorities advised that it might be absorbed into the teaching of science subjects, such as biology, health and civic studies or ethics. Finally, the provision of *halal* food in schools was also in the process of being organised.

Negotiations continued, and in March 1985 the MLC presented a draft syllabus which resulted in the issuing of 'Guidelines on meeting the religious and cultural needs of Muslim pupils', covering a comprehensive array of their educational needs.[66] Birmingham's state schools, because of the very uneven residential concentration of Muslims within the city, represented a microcosm of the situation across the country and this was reflected in their diverse responses to Muslim demands. As a result the agreed guidelines were implemented in a patchy and uneven way, ranging from far-reaching incorporation of Muslim concerns at schools where there were many Muslim pupils, and teachers were already familiar with multicultural issues, to relative indifference tinged with veiled hostility to even the more essential needs: in the latter case teachers held the view that these needs ran counter to gender equality and the provision of as complete an education as possible. The result was that, despite constant pressure from Muslim groups, the demand for single-sex schools has met with intransigence both from local bodies and nationally. In many other cases compromises were reached. For example, where individual cubicles were not available, children were allowed to shower in swimming-costumes or trunks. Appropriate instructions were given to kitchen staff regarding *halal* food. Opposition to music, dance and drama was softened through careful explanation and patient persuasion by teachers, allowing trust to develop. Acceptance of these subjects was also brought about by the introduction of forms with which British Muslim parents were more familiar, such as Indian dancing.

This said, a wide gap between practices at individual schools remained. For example, some schools exempted their pupils from physical education (PE) in the month of Ramadan, while others refused any concessions at all. Similarly, while some schools provided prayer facilities on their premises, others remained inflexible and refused. Here there seemed to be a tension in the minds of the authorities between meeting the cultural and religious wishes of parents (both Muslim and white) and their own definition of children's educational well-being; where there was resistance to Muslim requests, this was consistent with the authorities' view that these demands would be socially divisive and could produce a backlash from white parents complaining about declining standards. They were able to derive support for many of their own attitudes from two instances, one in Dewsbury in 1987 and the other in Cleveland in 1989, where white parents refused to send their children to schools because they no longer believed that they were receiving standard education in a suitable cultural and 'Christian' environment.[67]

However, the concessions won up to this point were considered insufficient by many Muslim parents. There was particular anxiety that little account was still being taken of Islamic perspectives in religious education (RE) syllabuses. Muslim organisations put these views forcefully to the parliamentary commission set up to investigate the situation of ethnic minority children in the education system, whose 1985 report, *Education for All*, they criticised on a number of counts. A number of Muslim organisations were especially angered by its support of continuing voluntary state-aided education for those faiths which already enjoy such provision, while raising major objections to the establishment of similar schools for Muslims.[68] Their dissatisfaction with state education began to crystallise in the establishment of private Muslim schools. At the same time, demands to extend voluntary state-aided status to private Muslim schools and to apply grant-aided status and opting-out provisions to state schools with high proportions of Muslim pupils took on a more organised character.

Thus education occupied a large proportion of the energy of Muslims throughout the 1980s and 1990s. The Conservative government's determination to make wide-ranging reforms in the education system, resulting in the enactment of the 1988 Education Reform Act, opened up new opportunities for Muslim intervention: attempts were made to take advantage of the Act's grant-aided status and opting-out provisions. The New Right's call for the RE requirement in state schools to be made more explicitly Christian was accepted, but it led to objections from other faith communities at their exclusion, eliciting a compromise in the Act that reaffirmed the multi-faith character of RE through the back door. The Act thus required LEAs to establish standing advisory conferences on religious education (SACRE), on which Muslims along with representatives of other faith communities had a voice. Schools in which Muslim pupils predominated could apply for 'determination' from their SACRE, and on approval of their application conduct Muslim school assemblies. For the first time British Muslims were in a position to influence an important element of the curriculum.

In many ways developments in education at this time reflected the confrontation between the views of the establishment pursuing policies

increasingly influenced by the positions of the New Right and a significant segment of the British Muslim population, who felt stronger and
therefore more determined to demand their own cultural and religious
space. By the 1990s they had become more assertive about what they
wanted for their children from the educational system, and those disillusioned with state provision established independent Muslim schools
as a viable option. They wanted educational institutions in which religious knowledge constructed within the context of Islam, especially
the Quran, would permeate the curriculum and establish its ethos.
Increasingly guided by the philosophical framework of Islamic education as developed by periodic conferences on the 'Islamisation' of
knowledge, these parents established a number of Muslim schools in
order to incorporate the Islamic dimension while retaining the core
features of the national curriculum.[69]

However, the assault on multicultural education from the New
Right, during the 1980s and 1990s strengthened the separatist tendency among Muslims. While in the early 1980s local authorities still
found room to embrace some of the concerns of the Muslim communities, by the mid-1980s these initiatives had come under sustained attack
from the ideologues and politicians of the New Right. Although the
1985 Swann Report made a number of recommendations that supported the pluralist vision of education, it remained trapped in the
essentialist construction of 'Asian' culture and its agent the close-knit
'Asian family' as it formulated a positive evaluation of Asian pupils'
academic achievement. In arriving at these conclusions it disregarded
evidence revealing the underperformance of Bangladeshi, Mirpuri and
indeed other Muslim children and overplayed the higher attainment
levels of those from East Africa, ignoring the possible influence on
educational outcomes of such elements as social class, urban/rural
differences and varied experiences with colonial systems of education.
Ironically, the reductionist approaches adopted by the multiculturalist
and antiracist proponents of education had unwittingly prepared the
ground for the cultural essentialism that formed the basis of the New
Right's assault on pluralist conceptions of education. Ray Honeyford's
tirades in right-wing journals such as the *Salisbury Review* in the mid-
1980s were creating considerable popular hostility to the perceived
'imposition' of multiculturalism by the so-called acolytes of the 'race

relations industry' and 'half-educated' Asian parents.[70] He rejected a Muslim father's request to withdraw his daughter from swimming lessons, castigating it as a violation of '*our* principles' and contrary to the idea of equal opportunities for girls.[71] He was vigorously supported by large sections of the media, which went as far in their attack on political correctness and antiracism as to blame the racist murder of a thirteen-year-old schoolboy in Manchester on the antiracist policy of Burnage High School.[72] By the mid-1980s, therefore, the New Right was mounting a series of concerted attacks against the initiatives of a number of local education authorities. In this rapidly changing context, the clamour for a return to the policies of blending Britain's various ethnic and religious minorities into a homogeneous culture was vigorously resisted by British Muslims. However, the central government, with only minor equivocations, fell in to step with the arguments of the New Right. Consequently, as Rattansi later pointed out, 'in a series of moves capped by the Education Reform Act and proposals for a national (or, as some were quick to point out, nationalist) curriculum, the Conservative government had effectively challenged and undermined the fragile liberal consensus Swann had tried to erect in the mid-1980s.'[73]

The government set reforms in motion through the enactment of the 1988 Education Reform Act (ERA) which, informed by the New Right's ideology, had major implications for the education of Muslim children. The National Curriculum, in the view of one Muslim educationalist, was 'based on a secularist philosophy', which 'indoctrinated' children into a particular world-view and denied the God-given nature of 'the absolute and immutable values and norms'.[74] While the National Curriculum recommended to schools that they took account of ethnic and cultural diversity, the emphasis had decisively shifted to transmitting Anglocentric culture. This came to be most clearly reflected in the teaching of such subjects as music, dance, art and drama. At the same time, the continuing formal primacy given to Christianity also caused many Muslims groups[75] to see their concerns as being in conflict with the position of the state. Meanwhile, despite the strength of the New Right within the Conservative Party, pluralist arguments continued to be defended vigorously by large sections of the education community. Against this backdrop of contested policies, Muslim parents asserted their cultural rights. In late 1989 the Alavi sisters at Altrincham Grammar School, Manchester, insisted on wearing a headscarf as part of their religious obligations, and as tensions rose the school first dug its heels in and then, finding its argument weakening, relented. The assertion by the girls' father of his parental rights, reaffirmed strongly in the 1988 ERA, was conceded—in face of considerable criticism from the media.[76]

By the mid-1990s, therefore, many of the issues which had preoc-cupied Muslim communities in the 1960s and 1970s and which they had made vigorous efforts to resolve in the 1980s had re-emerged, albeit with a different emphasis. Battles had to be fought on many occa-sions, and Muslim parents generally succeeded in having their demands conceded. But these matters were by no means a thing of the past and the legitimacy of Muslim parents' wishes was still not automatically recognised.[77] Hence some Muslim parents still felt that state schools were incapable of providing a suitable education for their children. The frustration this produced, combined with the desire to educate their children in accordance with their wishes, fuelled the demand for the creation of Muslim schools in both the independent and the voluntary state-aided sectors.

The struggle for voluntary-aided Muslim schools

Beginning in the early 1970s, campaigns to establish voluntary-aided Muslim schools became more vociferous from the 1980s.[78] The reasons for this included, first, reactions to the attacks on multiculturalism. Muslim activists helped to promote awareness of the secular nature of multi-culturalism in mainstream education, with Mustaqeem Bleher, a key figure in the campaigns in Bradford during the 1980s, describing it as 'a pretence, a device for supporting the dominant culture'.[79] According to this view, multiculturalism made only superficial conces-sions to minority faiths—dietary requirements, school uniforms, the-matic approaches to religious education—but in essence sought to include Islam under a secular umbrella. Secondly, the increase in demand reflected dissatisfaction with the secular and relativist charac-ter of the existing multicultural provisions as the aims of Islamic educa-tion came to be better understood. Leading Muslim intellectuals such as Yaqub Zaki emphasised the ideological contradiction between Islamic and mainstream British education, arguing for separate Muslim schools on the grounds that these two systems mediated a different understanding of the nature and purpose of knowledge—that in the Islamic philosophy of education there was a clear distinction 'between relative and absolute knowledge—the latter being the prerogative of God' and that there was 'no question of such a thing as secular knowledge'.[80] Muslim children therefore had a right to be educated in schools that asserted the Islamic ethos. In the school curriculum and in state schools, it was argued, Islam and Muslims were inadequately portrayed and the facilities necessary for creating an atmosphere conducive to the carrying out of Islamic duties were lacking. Thirdly, Muslim parents felt that despite the concessions they had won, socialisation in state schools threatened Muslim values. They were fearful of challenges to their authority, together with Islamic principles—something especially important for their daughters who, according to custom, represented family prestige and *izzat* (honour). Finally, since Muslims contributed their full share towards state education through their taxes, they felt it was unfair that the right to voluntary-aided schools was withheld from them while under the 1944 Education Act such schools were available to members of the Church of England, Roman Catholics, Methodists and Jews.[81]

Calls for Muslim schools were occasionally used by Muslim parents and activists to put pressure on local education authorities to pay greater attention to their concerns and bring them within state provision. This was evident in the successful negotiations between representatives of Birmingham Council, head teachers and the Muslim Liaison Committee (the umbrella organisation of representatives of various mosques and Muslim associations) in 1983–6 regarding the character of the curriculum and the availability of resources and facilities.[82] More organised efforts to have Muslim needs met in state schools were based on an acknowledgement that 99% of all Muslim children attended them, and that if Muslims were to retain their religious identity, it was the character of state schools that would have to change.[83] They hoped too that this strategy would allow some of the burden of religious education and mother-tongue teaching to be transferred from the community to the state, thus resolving the difficulties of children tired by lengthy attendance at mosque schools after school hours. They achieved some success, since Islamic studies and elements of Islamic thought were increasingly incorporated in the syllabuses of individual subjects, also through revision of existing curricula.

In the eyes of some Muslim parents and educationalists, however, the British education system was still based on premises that were incompatible with Islamic ideology; state schools could not provide God-centred education and only schools in which Islam permeated all aspects of teaching would fully satisfy them. Thus from 1982, several attempts were made to establish Muslim schools. In 1983 the Muslim Parent Association of Bradford submitted an application to take over five schools, arguing that such schools would provide the kind of education that would preserve and transmit the Islamic heritage while producing citizens fit for a multi-faith, multicultural Britain. The spiritual knowledge contained in the revelation and the 'worldly knowledge' embraced by the National Curriculum would both be taught with equal commitment.[84] These attempts at separate provision were reinforced by the concern that single-sex education was being largely phased out and there were few girls' schools left to which Muslims could send their daughters (even when the policy was changed to retain the single-sex option in 1983). Many Muslim parents believed that separate schools offered the most conducive environment for their children, and were most likely to inculcate common values and respect for Islam. These schools, such as the Zakaria School for Girls, also represented the best way to avoid the wider society's presumed laxity in sexual behaviour. While the request was justified under the 1944 Education Act and supported by many prominent figures in the national Muslim community, such as Yusuf Islam (the chairman of the Islamia School Trust), it was rejected by Bradford's Education Services Committee on the grounds that it had insufficient support within the local Muslim community itself. The Committee was able to point to opposition to the proposal from the Bradford Council for Mosques, the Community Relations Council and the Asian Youth Movement, which warned against the dangers of total segregation and the 'racist backlash'.[85]

In the mid-1980s the 'Honeyford affair' had already widened support for Muslim schools as the perception took hold among Muslims that Bradford City Council was dragging its feet and deferring to the apparent hostility to Muslim concerns in the wider population. The London Borough of Brent's rejection of attempts by local Muslims to set up the voluntary-aided Islamia School caused much dissatisfaction; set up privately in 1982, it applied for state funding as part of its struggle to survive and over time it became a test case, not finally rejected until August 1993.[86] Brent took this decision in line with its radical perspective of antiracist education, which had been set within a secular framework in which Muslims were viewed as part of a shared though highly contested 'black' identity. In the furore following McGoldrick's suspension as head teacher at the predominantly Muslim Stratford School in the London Borough of Newham in 1986 for allegedly making racist remarks, Muslims felt able to contest the dominant culture in order to construct and control their own cultural and religious space. They argued that multiculturalism had created 'moral chaos' rather than healthy pluralism as claimed by the liberal establishment. In their view the only kind of multiculturalism relevant for Muslims would incorporate the religious dimension: from this position of 'cultural' strength Muslim children would be better able to resist discrimination and harassment. Some Muslims referred back to the Jewish experience in the 1930s, when separate schools were set up as a refuge from anti-semitism. Paradoxically, they received strong support from precisely those quarters that had led the campaign for the reversion to monoculturalism. Included among these were the Parents' Alliance for Choice in Education (PACE), which ironically had backed the right of white parents in Dewsbury to withdraw their children from a predominantly Asian school in 1987 on the grounds that the presence of mainly Muslim children threatened their cultural identity; these parents had exercised their choice not to accept the multicultural provision. PACE supported the demand for Muslim schools as a return to 'traditional' values. Baroness Cox, who had played a leading part in getting the clause stipulating Christian assembly as the main form of worship in state schools incorporated in the ERA of 1988, also lent her support.[87] The labelling of Muslims involved in the anti-Rushdie campaign as 'fundamentalists' further radicalised Muslim youth—which the New Right saw as further proof of the alienating effect of multicultural education. Muslims, on the other hand, accused by government ministers of 'un-British' behaviour, felt increasingly hurt and bitter and retreated further into the bunker. It was in this context that the demand for Muslim schools achieved resonance over a wider spectrum of Muslims and extended support for them beyond those who would choose such schools for their own children.

The rejection of state funding for Muslim schools and the way it was carried out, at the same time as voluntary-aided status was granted to other religious minorities such as Jews (application granted in January 1990), reflected the relationships that these groups developed with the dominant elements in society and what 'integration' meant to the establishment.[88] That the demands of other religious groups were supported while similar requests by Muslims faced strong resistance from the wider society led Muslims to believe that they were being unfairly treated. It seemed that Muslim schools were opposed because they were perceived as a threat to the dominant culture and to the notion of British identity. To be Muslim in this view was incompatible with being British. However, the underlying reason for its rejection was that LEAs such as Bradford were still committed to meeting the needs of Muslim children within a common school curriculum by ensuring, first, that schools never required Muslim pupils to act against their own or their parents' religious and cultural beliefs and practices, and second, that their religions and cultures would be treated with equal sensitivity and respect.[89] Indeed, by the 1990s the arguments against state-funded Muslim schools remained similar to those advanced in Bradford—decline in academic standards, given the lack of resources and trained teachers; benefits of social mixing with non-Muslims in order to be better prepared for adult life in Britain; and fear of even greater discrimination on being identified as a product of a Muslim school. These opinions agreed with the official view, which was reaffirmed in the Swann Report's opposition to the establishment of voluntary-aided schools for Muslim communities. They pointed to continued divisions in opinion, especially among South Asian and Turkish Cypriot Muslims, the latter opposing the setting up of voluntary-aided Muslim schools while at the same time supporting the idea of single-sex secondary schools, especially for their daughters.

The demand for single-sex schools, primarily for girls, continued unabated among large sections of the Muslim population. The decision of Labour-led councils to shift their policies towards coeducation, especially in the north of England, meant that one-third of Britain's LEAs abolished all girls' schools, leaving only 250 still functioning. Muslim parents resented this decline in provision; in April 1987 Bangladeshis mounted protests in Whitechapel, east London, at the closure of a local girls' school.[90] Two years later 'a staggering 98% of the 7,000 Muslim parents in Keighley, Yorkshire, wanted separate schools for their daughters'.[91] There was no relaxation in the 1990s, particularly in cities with large concentrations of Muslims. Actions ranged from debates on single-sex education in Birmingham to resisting attempts to convert two of the five remaining girls' schools in Manchester into coeducational schools, and Muslim parents threatening to boycott Birmingham schools when the council there failed to provide their daughters with places in the school of their choice.[92] It seemed that formal applications for voluntary-aided Muslim schools followed closures of girls-only schools and when requests by Muslim parents for such provision were not accommodated.[93]

All this meant that the demand for Muslim voluntary-aided schools steadily grew from the late 1980s. The number of independent Muslim schools expanded from 45 in 1996 to 53 in 1997 and 77 in 2002.[94] Taking advantage of the opt-out provisions in the 1988 ERA, Muslim governors have secured grant-maintained status (GMS) for schools with predominant numbers of Muslim pupils.[95] For Muslims the establishment of these schools acquired a symbolic importance in the 1990s, when the liberal idea of multicultural education was challenged and the power of local authorities to pursue pluralist initiatives was reduced. At the same time, there were more opportunities for Muslim parents to exercise choice against the secular aspects of multicultural education, allowing them some space to pursue their 'separatist' agenda. Thus the approaches to educational issues intensified during the 1990s. This was also affected by the changes in the wider Islamic world. The so-called 'Islamic resurgence' brought in its wake a reaction against assumptions associated with Western educational aims and methods, which were seen in this perspective as largely materialistic, anti-religious and, because of their Christian origin, anti-Islamic. Multiculturalism, they believed, had diluted Muslim self-identity, rather than leading to greater self-determination and empowerment for Muslim parents and pupils within the state-maintained sector. Hence the campaigns to establish Muslim voluntary-aided schools continued through the 1990s.[96]

However, these years also revealed the enormous differentiation among British Muslims. The nature of the issues raised and the way they were resolved reflects the heterogeneous character of Britain's Muslim population and their largely local organisation. Despite some well-publicised cases, most practical issues were resolved within individual schools and with local education authorities, according to understandings reached among the various negotiating parties. A pragmatic approach was usually adopted, with each case considered on its merits. Schools with a large number of Muslim pupils reviewed their resources and facilities and reallocated them to resolve Muslim needs. Areas with fewer Muslim pupils responded less systematically, dealing with individual demands by catering for the needs through exceptional arrangements when necessary while maintaining the routine for those Muslim parents who did not object. In Woking, for instance, effective accommodation was achieved in this way; for example, objections to mixed-sex swimming were resolved on an individual basis. And the attitude of local Muslims was relatively tolerant; for instance, while Muslim children taking school meals avoid pork and ham, they did not always insist on *halal* meat and vegetarian meals were offered as an alternative.

The case of RE proved more challenging since it provoked intense disagreement, mirroring the wide range of belief and increasing disbelief in British society. Schools had to cope with contrasting demands from those lobbies which tended towards a pure form of secularism in education and those who supported a religious ethos. The solutions they offered attempted to fit the context and the relative influence the different groups of campaigners were able to exercise. In Kirklees, for example, 1,500 children were withdrawn in early 1996 from schools by parents who found the multi-faith provision unacceptable. There was support from the MP for Colne Valley for Muslim demands for separate RE provision. These demands were in part triggered by innovative approaches in schools such as Birchfield in Birmingham, where Islamic worship was introduced during the week in response to the desire of Muslim parents for Muslim teachers to teach Islam from a Muslim perspective. As they occurred in 'a very delicate area', these ideas were given cautious approval by the then Secretary of State for Education, Gillian Shepherd.[97] Muslims in Bolton, on the other hand, were quite happy with existing policies and practice on teaching RE within a multi-faith framework. Similarly, there was wide consensus by schools in Cardiff on the adoption of a multi-faith approach. Other Muslims considered RE in schools irrelevant to Muslim children since they received teaching from mosques'. The time devoted to RE, it was suggested, would be more fruitfully spent teaching something more appropriate, such as computing and mathematics.[98] Indeed, RE and worship in schools emerged as key issues after the passing of the 1988 ERA, which made RE and a 'daily act of collective worship' compulsory in all schools. Both had to be 'predominantly Christian' in nature. So the pressure for separate provision continued to grow.

The issues of single-sex education and sex education were closely linked together in Muslim minds as core concerns. The perception of both among many Muslim parents was that they encouraged permissiveness and promiscuity, both of which were unacceptable. They therefore continued their rearguard action over single-sex education, conducting local campaigns throughout the 1990s and into the new millennium.[99]

The opposition to Islamic schools, especially from the political right, continued during the 1990s, but lacked consistency since the reasons given for it did not apply to the granting of voluntary-aided status to schools of other religions.[100] Hence the Muslim Parliament described this opposition as 'racist' since 'no relevant educational considerations' were produced; the Swann Report's opposition of pupils being taught exclusively by teachers of the same ethnic group was also 'racist' since it was inconsistent with the existing situation in which white pupils were taught overwhelmingly by white teachers.[101] The whole ideological construction of 'Muslims' was deeply embedded in the decision-making process. If Muslim schools were opposed on the grounds that they would impede integration, then existing faith schools negated that argument. Muslims argued that they only demanded equity. Moreover, in their view the emergence of schools with the majority of pupils from Muslim backgrounds had come about primarily because of 'white flight'. Campaigners for Muslim schools therefore rejected the accusation that they would be divisive; they would follow the National Curriculum, but by developing an Islamic ethos they would give

Muslim children a positive sense of their own identity, so important for integration within a truly multicultural society.[102] In this way these Muslims contested the understanding of how 'integration', as presented by the British establishment, might occur. Indeed, they received support from representatives of groups who already enjoyed religious schools, such as David Konstant, the Roman Catholic Bishop of Leeds. For him 'having our own school within the state system helped us to move out of our initial isolation so as to become more confident and self-assured. The effect of separate schools [had] been integration and not divisiveness.'[103] Some senior members of the established church also supported the right of Muslims to enjoy provision comparable to other denominational groups. Strangely, many of the staunchest opponents of Muslim schools have been those who supported the idea of multicultural education, albeit in a secular framework, rather than John Patten's assimilationist view, which contended that there could be no 'room for separation and segregation'.[104]

Similarly, curriculum issues continued to cause concern to Muslims supporting the idea of separate schools. The 1988 ERA reversed, to a degree, the trend towards incorporating multicultural perspectives in history and geography. Music, dance, drama and art also became more Anglocentric. The place of these subjects within Islamic notions of education and the curriculum was regarded by some Muslims as questionable anyway, strengthening the hands of those who wished to have them either largely ignored or at least marginalised.[105] Given that music is part of the National Curriculum, Muslim schools had to devise ways of meeting its requirements. For instance, when the Islamia School in Brent was made aware of this discrepancy in its syllabus, it agreed to teach musical theory and notation, which could then be applied to choral works, with computers being used to teach keyboard technique using programmes producing choral or percussive sounds.[106] Similarly, the Muslim Educational Trust considered dance to have 'no academic significance or value, nor does it contribute positively to meaningful human knowledge'. On the other hand, the Iqra Trust thought that 'some Muslims may accept folk and cultural dances taught to single-sex classes'.[107] Many schools used the scope available in the National Curriculum with flexibility to experiment with a variety of expressions, offering traditional, folk or historical dances from different countries.[108] And it has been difficult to get broad agreement on how or to what extent these compulsory subjects could be taught satisfactorily to Muslim pupils. Under these circumstances it was felt that only some form of separate schooling would give Muslims a chance of withstanding pressure to assimilate.

There was no unanimity among different Muslim groups on what was needed. Views differed right across the spectrum of issues in education—separate schools, single-sex schools and supplementary provision. Muslim parents were being compelled to choose between two seemingly irreconcilable courses: to accept what the state education system offered and struggle as best one could against the threats to their values, or find a place in one of the few existing private Muslim schools where values were upheld but the hopes of academic success were remote. How to solve this dilemma was the challenge which Muslims tried to face in the 1990s. They strove to raise the status of religious education in the state sector by raising its profile, with the object of helping children achieve awareness of the meaning and significance of religions to their adherents and respect for them. Many Muslim organisations made voluntary-aided schools their top priority, while recognising that they could serve no more than a tiny minority of Muslim pupils. In the light of these thorny issues, Muslim parents sought schools that best satisfied their ambitions for their children. Muslim schools found more takers than before, but only after they demonstrated that they could offer an education comparable in purpose and quality to that available in the state system. Others preferred schools where academic success was more likely. The influence of parents and of governing bodies became increasingly important as the provisions of the 1988 ERA took effect. Separate schools, which many Muslim parents desired but non-Muslims feared, already existed in fact in effect, with the large number of state schools with an overwhelming proportion of Muslim pupils. They did not yet have institutionalised Muslim influence, but this was beginning to come through increasing parent participation in the running of schools in the late 1990s.

Muslim education in the 1990s

More recent surveys have revealed that trends set in the 1960s continued in the 1990s, although there was some convergence of average academic achievement between the different minority groups. Pointing to the grim situation Muslim pupils still faced, the 1992 PSI survey found that the school results of Muslim Asians were the worst in the country. At the Carlton-Bolling College in Bradford in 1992, where the majority of pupils were Muslim, only 7% gained five or more GCSE O-level passes compared with the national average of 38%. At the other end of the spectrum, 22% had no qualifications compared with 9% nationally. Shocked parents (mainly Bangladeshi), outraged by the failure of the school to deliver satisfactory results, called upon the LEA to shut it down.[109] More generally, any evidence of improvement in the academic achievement of Muslim pupils is inconclusive. While the Ofsted report published in September 1996 concluded that ethnic-minority pupils were getting better exam results than ten years before, this success was unevenly distributed.[110] The report pointed out a widening gap between high-achieving and low-achieving ethnic-minority groups. Indians and whites did better than Pakistanis and significantly better than Bangladeshis. It also found significant variations in attainment patterns in different areas. In the London Borough of Tower Hamlets Bangladeshi pupils, usually with uneducated parents from rural backgrounds who were more economically disadvantaged than any other ethnic group, had unexpectedly achieved the best results, yet their attainment levels were still below the national average. Thus, while they had been able to transcend social class more successfully than their peers from other ethnic groups, their position was far from good. However, Ofsted warned against single-factor explanations of achievement and suggested that differences in attainment were caused by a combination of highly complex factors, including social class, race and gender. Another factor cited was the school environment: one piece of research on inner-London schools, in 1991, revealed that 'amongst Pakistani pupils the differences could amount to as much as two "O" level passes'.[111] The impact of schools on Muslim children's academic achievement took into account their interaction with teachers and peers, in which lower teacher expectations, their misinterpretation of difficulties with English as learning difficulties, and the disproportionate racial harassment and violence routinely directed against them were shown to be increasingly damaging.[112]

However, while Ofsted reports on Muslim schools in the early 1990s criticised their emphasis on religious teaching at the expense of secular subjects, their pupils' underachievement in areas of the National Curriculum, their neglect of creative and aesthetic development because of a scarcity of non-religious books and teaching materials, and the inadequacy of children's accommodation and health and safety arrangements. This clearly showed that Ofsted did not necessarily see Muslim schools as the answer to Muslim pupils' educational needs,[113] but a later scrutiny of Muslim schools found that many of these earlier criticisms had been properly addressed and they were achieving no worse results than those of comparable state schools in their localities.[114] Further progress in incorporating and addressing the needs of Muslim pupils was also discernible in state schools, some of which had taken substantial measures to make Muslim pupils 'comfortable'. An excellent example of this development was Cheetham Church of England Community School in Manchester, where 98% of the children were Muslim, with twenty-five different mother-tongues. Aided by the appointment of a Muslim head teacher, the school responded positively to this cultural diversity. Five of the teachers were also Muslim and between them spoke Urdu, Punjabi, Arabic and other 'Muslim' languages. Children in the reception classes were able to start their education in their mother tongue; mid-day prayers took place in the school hall and afternoon prayers in classrooms with no apparent sense of embarrassment. In addition, the school benefited from a high level of parental involvement, and local supplementary schools used its facilities for Quran classes. All in all, efforts were being made to see how teaching materials and the National Curriculum could be adapted more closely to Muslim pupils' needs.[115]

Thus progress was tangible and was translated into rising levels of achievement. Evidence by the 1990s suggested that younger generations of British Muslims were generally better qualified than their migrant predecessors. The number with qualifications had doubled and those with higher qualifications had increased by more than 50%. However, the progress of Pakistanis and Bangladeshis relative to other South Asian groups was less encouraging; they remained the least qualified, especially the Bangladeshis. On a more positive note, there was a significant increase in the proportion of Pakistani women with higher qualifications, although this improvement began from a very low starting-point. Overall it appeared that the most recent generation of

Pakistani Muslims had benefited to some extent from participation in the British education system. Young British-educated Bangladeshis did not appear to have made similar progress, although up to a point this under-achievement probably reflected their more recent arrival, since many were likely to have been only partly educated in Britain. The length of schooling in Britain, the acquisition of facility in English and an understanding of 'British' culture were clearly important in relation to levels of attainment, and this was reflected in evidence which showed that far fewer of those educated in British schools or over-whelmingly educated in Britain (16–24 year-olds), and in some cases children of those educated in Britain, were without any qualifications.[116] However, British-educated Pakistanis and Bangladeshis were still more likely than whites to be unqualified and to be less likely to have higher qualifications (although, interestingly, surveys in the mid-1990s show that women from these two groups were more likely to be graduates than white women).[117] These lower levels of academic achievement among many Muslim young people not surprisingly rein-force, the impression of a continuing failure of provision to match their specific educational needs.

At the start of the new millennium, therefore, many of the issues with which British Muslims had been grappling in the 1970s and 1980s still caused concern. Some Muslim parents remained determined to send their daughters to single-sex schools despite the steep decline in this kind of provision.[118] But with the change in expectations regarding male and female roles over the decades, a more 'feminist' position was now being articulated, with single-sex education being demanded on the grounds that it provided higher academic standards for girls than mixed schools.[119] Debate over faith schools also continued, though perhaps without any fresh injection of ideas. However, by the late 1980s Muslim schools were eliminating academic weaknesses, and a number had started to compete with the best schools in their area.

By this time, correspondingly, resistance to the establishment of Muslim schools had lessened. The Labour government, after coming to power in 1997, took a lead in initiating debate on the subject of faith schools. Its Green and White Papers on the subject highlighted the advantages and positive outcomes of faith schools, and recommended

channelling more resources into them. It therefore approved voluntary-aided status to 'Muslim' schools, but with caution, and only four
such schools were approved between 1997 and the end of 2001. Grant-
maintained status was given to Al-Furqan School, Bradford, and Islamia
School, Brent (in London), in early 1998 after much indecision by the
government. Faversham College for Girls in Bradford and Al-Hijrah
School in Birmingham were awarded the same status in the autumn of
2001.[120] But this slow progress, and the concern still felt by many
British Muslims that their children were not getting a fair deal academically, ensured that the demand for the establishment of private
Muslim schools remained strong. The Partnership Finance Initiative
(PFI) opened up one avenue for future efforts: taking advantage of it,
the Hazrat Sultan Bahu Trust embarked on establishing a large, quality
Muslim girls' school at a cost of £ 13 million.[121]

However, in light of Lord Ouseley's report on the Bradford disturbances of 2001, which suggested that segregation in schools was a
major cause of racial tension, opposition to faith schools resurfaced.[122]
The arguments were not new, with opponents still objecting to Muslim
schools as divisive and inimical to 'integration'. Bill Morris, the black
General Secretary of the Transport and General Workers Union and a
powerful figure in the British labour movement, described plans to
increase faith schools as a 'time bomb'.[123] The National Secular Society
was, of course, similarly opposed. However, Muslim groups argued for
their right to Muslim education, not only as educationally appropriate
for their children but also as reflecting the multicultural character of
British society.[124] Politicians in the mainstream parties meanwhile
pointed to Northern Ireland, alleging that schools established on
Christian sectarian lines had done enormous damage to community
relations. Phil Willis, the Liberal Democrat education spokesman, also
thought there was 'a real danger here of educational apartheid'.[125]

By the 1990s the question of state funding for Muslim schools was
being debated in the context of the Rushdie affair and the Gulf War, and
accompanying the heightened hostility towards Muslims in Britain that
had resulted from them. In these circumstances, it was difficult to generate much support for Muslim faith schools. Also for much of the
1990s Conservative education ministers had barely disguised their
hostility to the idea of state-funded Muslim schools. Towards the end

of the decade the political climate became more supportive, partly because the British public now took a more favourable view of the quality of education provided by faith schools generally and partly because of the Labour government's thinking on ways of improving all-round educational provision. But, after the September 2001 terrorist attacks in the United States and the demonstrable rise in popular hostility towards Muslims in Britain, the enthusiasm for faith schools declined once again. How great the resulting long-term impact on the education of British Muslims remained to be seen.

11

THE EVOLUTION OF MUSLIM ORGANISATION
IN BRITAIN SINCE THE SECOND WORLD WAR

Muslim communities that have emerged in late-twentieth-century Britain have articulated their specific needs in the context of external factors and constraints, such as racism and available socio-economic opportunities. Within the changing context of British politics, specific forms of organisation have developed through which Muslim communities have related to each other as well as to the rest of society and to the state. Much of this organisational machinery was initially inherited from the other parts of the world where first generation Muslim migrants had originated. Transposed into the British context, those who operated this existing machinery found that they no longer enjoyed full control over community agendas, either because of the emergence of alternative leadership or because external constraints caused alternative communal structures to develop. Consequently, new organisations emerged at the local and national levels, many the result of specific social, cultural and political concerns. Their first priority was to represent Muslim issues to both local and national institutions of the British state, and to persuade the state to accommodate aspects of personal morality and codes of behaviour, types of education and forms of religious practice and cultural identification which had not previously come into its orbit.[1] Bodies representing the interests of British-born Muslim youth and women also took shape. Some performed as local self-help groups. Others operated as umbrella organisations, embracing divergent ideological strands and interests, and seeking to act as national symbols of the British Muslim community. This they did with varying degrees of success. This chapter considers the evolution of Muslim institutionalisation in the second half of the twentieth century, and how far British Muslim organisations have succeeded in achieving their objectives.

Early history

The process of organising Muslim communities in Britain since the Second World War has historically been complex. Up till the early 1960s, when 'mass' Muslim migration to Britain started, the symbolic centre of British Islam had been the Woking Mosque. Together with its offshoot in London, the Muslim Society of Great Britain, it frequently organised what were essentially *dawa* (invitation to Islam) activities—annual and Friday congregations, lectures on religious issues, public 'at-home'-type celebrations—similar to those in the interwar period, attracting Muslims from all over Britain.[2] However, in the post-Second World War period, given the growing Muslim community in London, the need for an Islamic centre there was felt more urgently than ever before. As Chapter 5 pointed out, Khwaja Kamaluddin and Lord Headley, leaders of the Woking Mission, had been pressing the British government since the mid-1920s for a piece of land in London on which a central mosque could be built to act as a focal point for British Muslims. Eventually, in 1940, the Churchill war cabinet approved a grant of up to £100,000 for the acquisition of such a site. The plot was apparently intended as a tribute to the thousands of Indian Muslim soldiers who had died in battle for the British Empire during the First World War and whose successors were making a significant contribution to the current war effort. King George VI inaugurated the Islamic Cultural Centre in Regent's Park in November 1944, but the mosque was only completed in 1977 and only in 1994 was an educational and administrative wing added.[3] While the Central London Mosque has served the many expatriate Muslim communities living in the capital, its status as the representative of the entire British Muslim community in all its diversity, as well as a high public profile, has necessitated a non-partisan low-key approach to Muslim issues. It has been able to do this by offering its resources and facilities to all Muslim groups, as well as giving space to people engaged in dynamic debates right across the theological spectrum. Meanwhile it has served the substantial, more settled, local Arab communities concentrated around Edgware Road, regularly hosting congregations of up to 6,000 on Fridays and 60,000 for annual festivities. In the 1950s and early 1960s, however, few of the newly-arriving Muslims were to be seen at the Islamic Cultural Centre. This was related to the fact that many of them, who had come to Britain mainly for economic reasons, saw religious concerns and practices as marginal to their daily lives. Barton's study of the Bangladeshis in Bradford has suggested that 'most Bengalis suffered an almost total lapse of religious observance' once they arrived in Britain. It appears that these migrants believed that they 'lived and worked' in Britain on behalf of their families, who prayed on their behalf, and so were not unduly worried.[4] But even at this early stage Islam played a cementing role among many Muslim workers since it stimulated a sense of identity that transcended ethnic, linguistic, doctrinal and political frontiers. J.M. Ritchie, visiting South Shields in 1972, observed that Muslims from various doctrinal schools ignored their differences and all worshipped at the same centre.[5] Beyond the setting up of makeshift mosques, organisations for meeting welfare needs also gradually emerged. For instance, the East London Mosque, established in 1942, offered space to Jamiatul Muslemeen, a self-help organisation, to provide a variety of services for the local East Pakistani (later Bangladeshi) community. Another early example of collective action in was the formation in 1946 of Jamiat Ittahadul Muslimin (Society for Muslim Unity) in the Gorbals area of Glasgow, where about 100 Muslim migrants lived.[6]

In the early 1960s, as Muslim families reunited in industrial cities and towns across Britain in anticipation of stricter immigration controls, and saw themselves more as settlers than sojourners, the communities they formed began to change in character. As we have seen, the arrival of Muslim families broadened the scope of interaction with the wider society, especially over education, health and social welfare. At the same time, chain migration brought about residential clustering of Muslim populations along distinct ethnic, linguistic and regional lines, leading to the establishment of organisations as effective channels for conducting business in areas of concern. Segregation ensued, and previously ethnically mixed Muslim communities now increasingly fragmented according to village-kinship, tribal, ethnic and sectarian affiliation. Indians, Yemenis and Turkish Cypriots who had lived together in boarding-houses during and after the Second World War, sharing more or less the same religious facilities, gradually separated to form ethnic settlements that then established their own distinct institutions.[7] Mosques and religious schools also reflected this process of segmentation, and imported religious functionaries reminded Muslim settlers of their traditional values and reinforced conformity to embedded practices. These Muslim communities, close-knit and relatively self-contained though often internally divided, became, as Halliday has put it, 'urban villages' interacting with the broader society surrounding them in a selective fashion.[8] They were able to generate and sustain institutional and economic infrastructures that embodied and perpetuated specific religious and cultural norms. What emerged at the end of the 1970s was a patchwork of communities, each impressing its particular national, ethnic, linguistic and doctrinal character on the organisations it had created. These organisations were primarily concerned with the promotion of worship and religious life, the encouragement of 'fraternal' links in Muslim communities, the provision of assistance and moral support for individuals (on immigration, domestic issues and language), and the improvement of social, cultural and educational conditions through the acquisition of subsidies locally, nationally and internationally.

Laying the foundation stones: Britain's network of mosques and Muslim organisation

From the 1960s to the 1980s British governments, both local and national, saw migrants primarily in ethnic terms. Consequently, through the provision of financial and other opportunities, they encouraged processes of organisation that were ostensibly racial and ethnic. Explicitly 'Muslim' organisations remained largely peripheral in dealings between minority communities and the state, and their activities were mainly restricted to religious affairs within these communities. However, for migrant Muslims belonging to these communities there were a number of common purposes and concerns. First, they were anxious to create the best possible conditions for them to practise their faith and, second, they wanted to ensure that their faith would survive through effective transmission to future generations. The first category of issues included practical and often quite technical matters concerning access to facilities for worship, the status of Islamic law, diet, dress, health and welfare. These issues generally arose locally and at different times, and had to be resolved through local negotiation. The second group of concerns—about the survival of the faith— had to be addressed, in the first instance, through education and the development of a relationship between Muslim institutions and those of the wider society. To meet these needs groups were set up, at first in the larger Muslim communities, to establish mosques for worship and religious instruction for children. The community saw a clear distinction between this arena and the public sphere. To begin with, mosques and *madrassas* (religious schools) became the preserves of traditional religious leaders, largely imported from the migrants' countries of origin. Given their lack of familiarity with the British urban environment and understanding of it, these religious leaders—usually village *imams*—were unable to provide appropriate guidance and inevitably responded by using these institutions to preserve religio-cultural practices from another world. Still, this early process of religious institutionalisation reflected a strong determination by various Muslim communities to construct a distinct presence. At first they made conscious efforts to create facilities to resume their religious and cultural education and practice. In a non-Muslim social environment they could take nothing for granted. Facilities for prayers, Islamic instruction for children, access to *halal* food and proper burial had to be organised afresh. Much of this development was initiated locally, but access to resources, particularly funding, required a wider effort from the activists within these communities and in some cases compelled them to establish formal links with religious institutions in their countries of origin.

With the growing number of Muslim migrants a network of mosques developed, attracting ever larger and more committed congregations, and this in turn affected religious behaviour. Many Muslims found themselves under pressure to conform to the ideal norms of their particular community. Life-cycle rituals requiring religious ceremonies further reinforced the role of mosques and made them increasingly the focus of religious, social and political activity. By the mid-1980s mosques were serving a range of functions—as places of worship, as venues for the religious education of both adults and children, as centres for the publication of religious tracts, and as libraries and bookshops. They offered funeral services and advice on immigration and social security and counselling services for families. Many could obtain resources to run mother-tongue and English classes. Others tried to become effective community centres, organising activities for women, the elderly, and young people. On a wider front they campaigned for social and political changes favourable to Muslims, acting as brokers between their communities and the institutions of the wider society. As pressure groups they expressed dissatisfaction with how these institutions dealt with specific issues and campaigned for equality of religious rights. In order to perform these functions, mosques had to adapt to the new environment and establish formal structures, with boards of trustees and management committees, and staff such as teachers, librarians, clerks and counsellors. In some mosques English became the main medium of instruction: sermons began to be delivered in English, and debate on religious matters was given more encouragement than before.

However, suitably trained personnel were difficult to find, and thus the pace of change was slow. While mosques were mainly concerned with religious issues within their own communities, the more dynamic ones began to develop links with British institutions: schools, churches, prisons, hospitals, social services and the police. Here they communicated information about Islam and the needs of Muslims. In schools, they negotiated for changes in religious education and the dress code and for the provision of *halal* food. They also pursued their objections to sex education and campaigned for single-sex schools. They intervened in British social and political life, although in the early years of mass Muslim immigration the politics of their countries of origin occupied most of their attention.

Thus early Muslim organisation in Britain arose from local initiatives, partly to preserve and sustain religious practice and partly to bring problems to the notice of the authorities and so represent their communities to the wider world. They also helped individuals and families. During this phase of evolution, religious leaders were more concerned to embed the traditions and beliefs which their Muslim flock had brought with them than to encourage any significant adaptation to the new environment. The first mosques established in Britain had no obvious affiliation to any particular Islamic school of thought. Most arose out of local initiatives and were set up to serve community purposes. However, as Sher Azam, sometime president of the Bradford Council for Mosques, put it, 'whoever established [these organisations] was going to do it his own way, in his own tradition'.[9] Thus Deobandis established the Muslim Association of Bradford in 1959; a small group of professionals set up the UK Islamic Mission (an offshoot of the Jamaat-i-Islami) in 1963; and in that year too Pir Maroof Hussain Shah, a textile worker from the Punjab in Pakistan, founded the Barelwi Jamiat-i-Tabligh al-Islam (Association for the Preaching of Islam).[10]

Initially many Muslim institutions had a home orientation, but, as the 'myth of return' faded, the preservation and support of specific sectarian traditions became a prime concern, and institutions were created to give them organisational form. The growth in the number of mosques was phenomenal, but this was accompanied by sectarian fragmentation, and ideological inflexibility led to the multiplication of mosques. In Bradford the first mosque was established in 1959, and it was attended by an ethnically diverse congregation. Two years later the Gujarati community had already moved to its own mosque, and Mirpuris set up a separate one in 1966. The number of mosques in Bradford rose steadily from six in 1969 to seventeen in 1979 and thirty-four in 1989, with nine supplementary schools teaching Islam. However, while these served their particular localities, the sectarian divisions solidified: fifteen of the mosques and seven of the supplementary schools were Barelwi, while thirteen mosques and two supplementary schools belonged to the Deobandi tradition. There were two Jamaat-i-Islami, one Ahl-i-Hadith and two Shia mosques as well as an Ahmadiyya centre. While some intersection of sectarian affiliation occurred, regional loyalties largely continued to coincide with religious identification.[11] A similar situation was replicated right across Muslim Britain. Sectarian diversity became the norm in the major cities and towns of Britain, adding to the social and theological fragmentation by national origin, ethnicity, language, age, class, education, doctrine and practice that was characteristic of most British Muslim communities. Where the differences were less pronounced, it was because of lack of numbers—here, differences were subordinated to a shared Muslim identity in order to strengthen the position of Muslims in relation to the wider society.

The Islamic institutions being established in Britain at this time often had roots in the migrants' countries of origin. Among South Asian Muslims the Deobandi and Barelwi traditions had the largest followings; with several other religious tendencies, they had grown on the subcontinent during the British period as a form of defence and reassertion of a weakening Muslim way of life. The Indian religio-political environment had shaped their language and agendas, their structures and programmes. Initially they had been motivated by the need to respond to the decline of Muslim power and the rise of British power in India. Historically many of these traditions had evolved through conflict with each other, conflicts rooted in doctrinal differences dating back to the nineteenth century. The Deobandi school was identified with the more 'puritanical', 'isolationist' strands of Indian Islam, which stressed the seeking of guidance in matters of ritual, practical and social life in Islamic scriptures and the Sharia. It developed a systematic approach to these issues by establishing a tradition of formulating and recording authoritative legal opinions. Religious scholars were trained to provide guidance in different areas of Islamic knowledge. There was little engagement with the rational sciences of logic and philosophy or the social sciences. The Barelwis, on the other hand, imbued the Prophet Muhammad with almost divine status. He and the saints were believed to have the knowledge of the Unseen and the power to intercede on behalf of their followers. The Prophet's practice, as recorded in the Hadith, was presented as the model for Muslim behaviour, and saints and *pirs* (charismatic spiritual leaders) provided religious guidance that was much more ritualised than among the Deobandis. Sectarian differences of this kind were thus replicated among Muslim migrants from South Asia, with the more active establishing these traditions in Britain on a permanent organisational basis. The differences and struggles between them were also transplanted, and tended to take the form of confrontations over the control of mosques and associated resources.[12]

Among Deobandis, the Tablighi Jamaat (TJ) was an early arrival on the British scene,[13] its goal the revival of Islam through *tabligh* (preaching). However, being based on the idea of personal worship it asserted no explicit political aspirations: in its view, Muslims are obliged to live as responsible citizens of the society in which they have decided to settle. Since they aspire to build a global Muslim community, they should play down sectarian controversies. The TJ carried out its programme by organising meetings at which small roving parties of voluntary preachers (*muballighin*) delivered the Islamic message. Larger congregations (*ijtemas* and *jalsas*) were also organised for this purpose. The first recorded meeting in Britain was held on 20 January 1945 'in an Indian quarter of London'.[14] By the mid-1960s, the TJ had spread to several British cities and towns (Glasgow, Newcastle, Manchester, Birmingham, Sheffield and Liverpool) where significant communities of South Asian Muslims had settled. Soon it initiated, along with other religious organisations, 'a phase of feverish institution building in which particular importance was given to the setting up of mosques and religious schools'.[15] This phase culminated in the establishment of the seminary in Bury (1975) and subsequently the complex known as the Tablighi Markaz at Dewsbury (1982), incorporating a mosque, a seminary and the administrative centre, under an *amir* (head), with the ambition of 'winning the whole of Britain to Islam'.[16] These seminaries offered a mixture of revivalist theological activities—the ethos, syllabus and inspiration came from India, as did the traditional teaching approaches and the texts, which had often been written decades earlier and reflected the world, imagery and problems of a largely preindustrial, rural India, with arguably little relevance for English-speaking British Muslim pupils.[17]

The TJ, like other sectarian movements in Islam, appealed only to certain groups of Muslims in Britain, usually on the basis of doctrinal allegiances and styles of religious practice that have gradually come to be seen as in harmony with their interests. Undoubtedly these religious loyalties have been shaped by factors such as social class, ethnicity, gender, education and age. In Britain the TJ is much less popular among Punjabis and Sindhis from Pakistan than among Gujarati and Pathan Muslims or, to a lesser degree, among Bengalis from Sylhet. There are many reasons for the greater appeal of TJ among Gujarati Muslims: a historical link exists between the urbanising, middle-class Gujarati community and the reformist Deobandi school of thought, while the TJ's detached approach towards active political engagement has suited Gujarati trading classes wishing to avoid controversy while they quietly advance their entrepreneurial interests. Having been a minority for centuries, they realised that anything other than a 'politically quiescent sort of Islam' of the TJ variety could cause considerable discomfort. The TJ's unsophisticated, anti-intellectual and yet activist, ascetic Islamic practice, with its stress on *taqwa* (piety) and *ibadah* (worship), appealed to semi-educated and economically less privileged lower-middle-class Muslims since it opened up 'the avenue of upward social mobility through Islamization ... within the traditional hierarchy'.[18]

Other tendencies emerged with the arrival of larger numbers of migrants reflecting the diverse ethnic, class and regional characteristics of South Asian Muslim communities. The UK Islamic Mission (UKIM), generally thought to be inspired by the Jamaat-i-Islami (JI) tradition in Britain, was set up in 1963 by a small group of students and profession-als, mainly from Pakistan, with the purpose of *dawa* (invitation to Islam) and the creation of a distinct British Muslim identity. Given its reliance at its inception on a supply of personnel from Pakistan, the UKIM developed organic and ideological links with the JI in Pakistan and its structure bore the deep imprint of its Pakistani connections. The core idea of the Mission was that to safeguard a Muslim way of life in Britain it was necessary to convert the majority of the indigenous population to Islam. Its main priority was the identification and educa-tion of young leaders and the provision of appropriate literature in English. Its main texts occupy a different space from those from the Barelwi and Deobandi traditions. Written in English, they have sought to address the questions and dilemmas experienced by Muslims in Britain, assisted by periodicals such as *Paigham* (Message) and *Impact International*, which first appeared in the 1970s. The latter, produced in English, also endeavoured to cover the developments within the Islamist movement worldwide, while the youth wing, Young Muslims UK (YMUK), spread its views via its magazine *Trends*. However, since most South Asian Muslim settlers in Britain were of rural origin, they scarcely provided a natural constituency for the UKIM, which attracted most of its support among the urbanised, educated and professional strata both in Pakistan and in Britain—those who had been greatly impressed by the scathing, albeit reasoned, criticism from Syed Abu Ala Maududi (1903–79, founder of the Jamaat-i-Islami) of the ignorance and obscurantism of many traditional *ulama* and his systematic challenging of Western civilisation. For these Muslims his ideological rigour and critique of Western ideas gave plausible explanations for their own troubles and those of the Muslim world. The UKIM, given its emphasis on intellectual effort and discipline as the key requirements for members, took much longer to establish its network. Also it was unable to sustain a viable Islamic seminary, because it had not devised a distinctive curriculum and had invested more resources in engaging with the social and political dimensions of Islam than in developing its theological content.

By 1988, while its national office was established in London, the UKIM was working primarily through a network of mosques in Birmingham. Altogether it had thirty-eight branches, including twenty-two mosques and Islamic centres in different parts of the country, and its youth work had spread to seventeen cities.[19] The Mission made itself available to local officials in government, law, education and the churches for guidance on specifically Muslim matters, and was thus able to play a mediating role, which gained it a level of public standing far exceeding its popular support. To pursue its broad aims, it had established a number of important, relatively autonomous institutions related to specific purposes. The Muslim Educational Trust (MET) was set up in 1966 to promote Islamic education in Britain, and in conjunction with the British educational system offered religious instruction to Muslim pupils in state schools. Beginning in 1971, the MET pressed local authorities to allow Muslims to give religious instruction, if not during school hours then at least afterwards. Several thousand children went through this process, many becoming core members of the Mission's youth wing.[20] The Islamic Foundation, established in 1973, engaged in publishing and research from its centre in Leicester, and was a leader in producing children's reading materials, and also responded to research in the growing area of Islamic economics. The broad objectives of these organisations were derived from the explicitly political and anti-secular vision of the Jamaat-i-Islami, in which the establishment of an Islamic state founded on the Sharia has the central place. With their literalist interpretation of the Quran and Hadith, these JI-inspired organisations gathered support among disaffected university and college graduates and professional groups in Britain, who—excluded from the mainstream—found a way to express their grievances in its vocabulary of Islam—the materialistic, 'evil' and morally 'corrupt' character of Western society.

Each wave of Muslim migration since the 1960s brought with it a new determination to pass on its religious and cultural values to its children. This commitment to embedding Islam in the British environment was reflected in the increasing number of religious institutions. In 1963 there were just thirteen formally registered mosques in the whole country, but as the pace of family reunion quickened, from 1966 onwards so did the registration of mosques. And as money began to flow into Britain from the oil-rich Middle Eastern states in the 1970s and as increasing familiarity with local political and administrative processes and power structures made resources more accessible, a new phase of mosque building started. In 1975 eighteen were registered within one year. The pace quickened further in the 1980s, and by 1985 the number of registered mosques had reached 338.[21] A survey in the 1990s suggested that there were at least 839 registered and unregistered mosques and 950 other Muslim organisations across the country.[22]

But the Muslim communities of other than South Asian origins showed less tendency to organise themselves on religious as opposed to ethnic lines. Turkish Cypriots, who had arrived in Britain in the 1950s even before the majority of South Asian Muslims, and concentrated in certain London boroughs, seemed content several decades later with the use of a single converted Victorian terrace house as a mosque. In the 1950s the priorities and orientation of Turkish/Cypriot organisation were located in the sphere of welfare, education and social and cultural fields, with religious needs considered of only minor importance. Their main object was to improve the living conditions of Turkish people in Britain. The Cyprus Turkish Association, founded in 1951, ignored religion in its activities and stressed that its primary goals were to develop ethnic solidarity and integration into British society. Religion was viewed as an obstacle to adjustment in a multicultural environment. The absence of any significant growth in religious facilities until the late 1970s and the lack of regular use of the modest ones available suggested that only a minority of Turkish Cypriots had any interest in formal religion. Nevertheless, Islamic values were deeply rooted among Turks and entwined with their ethnic self-awareness, and thus continued to be significant in the construction of Turkish identity. Once firmly settled, Turks gradually became aware that although they had succeeded in retaining many aspects of their ethnic identity, lack of attention to its religious dimension had led to its being diluted in the British context. This concern over the decline of religious sensibility resulted in the foundation, in 1979, of the United Kingdom Turkish Islamic Association (UKTIA). Its aims of providing education in accordance not only with the 'tenets and doctrines of Islam' but also with the 'traditions of Turkish culture' highlighted the close connection between religion and ethnicity.[23] The establishment of the Aziziye Mosque complex as the 'Turkish Mosque' in London in 1983 also illustrated the importance of ethnic and linguistic affiliation. Turks who had felt reluctant in the past to attend a 'non-Turkish' mosque welcomed a Turkish congregation because, as one informant put it, while 'it is a good feeling being with them [Muslim brothers] you don't really enjoy the prayer because you just pray and leave. No socializing, nothing. But when I started praying with our Jama'a [congregation] I felt myself more stronger and more self-confident.'[24] This suggested that while religious commitment had increased, the institutionalisation of Islam had consolidated, if not heightened, awareness of shared ethnicity.

It is notable that the institutionalisation of Islam among Turks in Britain, once it had begun, took a quite similar direction to the processes at work among South Asian Muslims. For instance, the Aziziye Mosque started as a non-sectarian religious establishment receptive to all groups, although the *imam* was imported from Turkey. The *hutbe* (sermon) was delivered in Turkish and not English or Arabic as in non-Turkish mosques. Activities had a Turkish colouring. However, until the late 1980s the mosque was perceived within the Turkish community as an independent institution and so played a unifying role, addressing broad concerns over *halal* food and Islamic education for children. Subsequently, it changed in a way not dissimilar to that associated with institutionalisation in the South Asian communities. 'The Imam affiliated himself with a religious group in Turkey and adopted their way of practising Islam, apparently very visible in the dress code and appearance.'

His exhortations to his congregation to do likewise proved divisive, as those uncomfortable with the prescribed changes distanced themselves from the mosque and many decided to join other Turkish mosques.[25] What this demonstrates is that, even within Britain's relatively small Turkish population, religious diversity, a historic characteristic of Turkish Islam, has been reproduced in Britain.[26] By contrast, the much smaller Moroccan community in London, having migrated from villages in a chain process in the 1970s, progressed less far along the path of Islamic institutionalisation, with the establishment of only a couple of multi-purpose centres largely resourced by local government. For instance, the voluntary Moroccan Information and Advice Centre Association offered advice mainly on 'secular' welfare and social issues and ran an interpreting service. The Moroccan Women's Centre organised a support service for women and a club for the elderly and provided personal counselling and health education. For neither of these bodies was the provision of religious services a primary function.[27]

Thus smaller Muslim communities in Britain have tended to establish multi-purpose organisations, catering for their own specific religious, social, welfare and cultural needs.[28] This was connected to the lack of a sense of permanence in Britain felt by most Arab communities, with the exception of the long-established Yemenis. Rather, their preoccupation with 'taking refuge until things improve' prevented them from developing an institutional presence. Their organisations, for example the Arab Club and the King Fahd Academy, were geared instead to reinforcing values and lifestyles that would facilitate readjustment in their 'home' societies, rather than permanent settlement in Britain.

The 1980s saw a major shift in the way that Muslim organisations engaged with public life. Thatcherism dealt hammer blows to the multi-culturalism that had been at the heart of previous government policy towards ethnic minorities since the 1960s. Growing restrictions on local government support for community organisations meant that funding for ethnic organisations declined, with drastic results. Bodies with a distinct Muslim identity (which in the past had received few resources from the state and had had to rely largely on contributions from individuals and groups within their communities) were able to survive the Conservative government's onslaught on sources of support for the voluntary sector quite well, and emerged with an enhanced profile in the eyes of the authorities. Those who wished to emphasise Islamic needs found their position strengthened in schools and in mosques, prayer halls and *madrassas*. Community identity began to be defined much more strongly in terms of religious institutions, where Muslim solidarity could be publicly celebrated, and less by nationality, family, village and class. By the end of the decade, with their leaderships having accumulated considerable experience of dealing with British institutions, the religious institutions were able to engage more effectively in the public sphere: they had gained recognition alongside other special interest groups and functioned with similar agendas, their distinctness highlighted primarily by their explicit Muslim identity. The main arena of their operation was local politics, in which they developed and exercised influence, negotiating skilfully with discrete sections of the local authority, seeking compromise and reaching ad hoc deals in a typically British fashion.

For most of the 1980s Muslim organisations continued to operate locally, although a number of issues emerged which received wider attention, and the controversy they generated catapulted them on to the national stage. The mobilisation that now took place represented the earliest instance of Muslims functioning nationally. In Bradford, in 1984, they accused the headmaster of a local school with an overwhelming majority of Muslim pupils, Ray Honeyford, of racism and forced his resignation. But the view of this campaign taken by the wider British society was far from positive, and it was denounced as an attack on free speech. Muslim campaigns on the issue of *halal* meat also generated criticism. In 1983 Muslim groups had agitated against proposals to abolish religious exemptions to regulations governing the slaughter of animals for food,[29] and at the same time those in Bradford were lobbying for the introduction of *halal* meat for Muslim children in schools. Ritual sacrifice on the occasion of *Eid al-Adha* (Feast of Sacrifice) similarly became a controversial issue. However, the mobilisation of the Bradford community by Muslim organisations through public debate, big demonstrations and school strikes yielded only mixed results. While the decision on *halal* meat was not overturned by the Bradford City Council, many in the British establishment saw the controversy as further damaging relations between Muslims and the wider society. The reaction of those who opposed religious slaughter caused ripples that spread far and wide and reinforced negative perceptions of Muslims. Compassion in World Farming (CIWF) denounced demands for 'separate meat' as 'disastrous', viewing it as the thin end of the wedge that would 'be followed by facilities for separate catering, separate kitchen staff, separate swimming for girls and boys and single-sex classes', none of which, it was argued, would be conducive to 'improving race relations'—rather it was more likely to encourage 'racial segregation'.[30]

However, the impact of these criticisms was not completely negative where the process of Muslim organisation was concerned. They alerted Muslim groups to the implications of this and other relevant issues, and the need for a concerted response. So when the Farm Animal Welfare Council's (FAWC) report suggested abolition of religious slaughter in 1985, they were prepared to mount a more effective and reasoned effort than previously. They adopted a more united approach and, probably for the first time in the history of British Muslims, were able to achieve a measure of coordination on the national level.[31] Furthermore, the hostility to 'religious slaughter' heightened awareness of Islamic practice and a sense of self-identity among a growing number of British Muslims. To ensure the long-term future of this aspect of identity, it was suggested that a body of *halal* butchers should be established.[32] Eventually, in 1994, the Halal Food Authority (HFA) was set up with encouragement from the Muslim Parliament, and established a network of approved abattoirs and shops to provide the community with independently certified *halal* meat.[33]

So from the mid-1980s British Muslims became ever more effectively organised in their dealings with local government, national policy structures and other areas of public life. As they gained in confidence, they broadened their agendas to cover a widening set of social and political issues, ranging from gaining recognition of Muslim family law to political representation. These areas of concern were themselves conditioned by a changing context—the debate on multiculturalism, legislation concerning the relationship between religion and the state, national and local policies on the status of ethnic minorities, and the many different manifestations of anti-Muslim 'racism'. While in the 1960s and 1970s Muslim institutionalisation was largely driven by the needs of Muslims themselves, by the 1980s and 1990s it was being shaped and sometimes facilitated by agents and motivations which were not exclusively Muslim. The way that institutionalisation proceeded largely depended on the degree of freedom granted to Muslims to practise their faith. This suggests that official recognition of Islam was gradual and piecemeal, and reflected in amendments to rules and regulations in specific areas. Policy-makers frequently lacked commitment to the institutionalisation of Islam; their reluctance to view Muslim demands sympathetically was apparent in the battles Muslims had to fight for permission to establish mosques. Local-authority planning committees (LAPCs) were guided by such considerations as the general plan for the neighbourhood, the appearance of the building (e.g. minarets), expected problems with traffic density and loud-speakers, and the possible effect on 'racial integration' in the immediate neighbourhood.[34] The use of mosques for social and cultural purposes could also influence LAPC decision-making. Since most members of the LAPCs were not Muslims, their decisions tended to be restrictive and have only gradually become more flexible.[35]

The evolution of Sufi orders in Britain

Alongside the main sectarian organisations, many Muslims in Britain have pursued traditions within Islam that focus mainly on personal devotion and piety. Their religious and theological general approach has been contemplative, and those Muslims practising their faith in this way have reflected engagement with the many varieties of spirituality existing within the so-called Muslim world. They view Sufism as the inner part of Islam, while the outer part is maintained by adherence to the Sharia, and a commitment to both parts is generally accepted. Some, however, regard Sufism as a universal path to self-illumination.

The Sufi Order International, dating from the early twentieth century, is an example of such development. Its founder Maulvi Inayat Khan (1882–1927), a musician initiated in the Chishti tradition, came to England with an instruction from his *murshid* to 'unite East and West through the magic of [his] music'. On the basis of his belief in the fundamental oneness of all religions, he developed the Universal Worship service, comprising an invocation, a reading from each of the holy books of the world's major religions, and the lighting of a candle for each tradition. A candle was also lit for every individual or religious system (unknown or forgotten) that had inspired humankind. Any identification with Islam was tenuous, and the practice, inspired by the Chishti Sufi order, stressed the role of music in the attainment of spirituality.[36]

In addition, from the Second World War onwards growing numbers of British Muslims, mainly from a Sunni background, gradually organised themselves in Sufi orders or *tariqas*. Most of these orders were imported from abroad in ways not dissimilar to other Islamic traditions and became part of international networks with origins in the subcontinent, the Middle East and continental Europe. Their structures tended to be informal, while their leaders were essentially charismatic and attracted their followers through example and perceived qualities. Since their aims were to develop spirituality, engagement by these *tariqas* with the institutions of the wider British society was minimal. Many of them attracted a considerable number of converts to Islam. An early group, Al-Murabitun, was established around Abd al-Qadir as-Sufi, a Scottish convert who embraced Islam in Morocco in 1967 after his disillusionment with Western culture and its materialistic values. He started the North African Darqawiyyah order in 1968, and by 1976 had set up in Wood Daling Hall, near Norwich, a community, mainly of Western converts, which rejected any engagement with wider society and its institutions and strove for a high degree of autonomy.[37] Thus, to meet the needs of its members it developed institutions in isolation from the structures of British society. Its members educated their children away from the state system, organised their own family relations without reference to civil registries, and spurned the National Health Service in favour of traditional 'Islamic' medicine. According to Geaves, Abd al-Qadir also encouraged his followers not to mix or associate with Muslims originating from outside Britain since he saw their Islam as contaminated by their own culture.[38] However, its policy of isolation did not save this group from divisions, ideological disputes and, inevitably, fragmentation, although the majority of members remained loyal to their specific Sufi identity.[39]

Other converts were attracted by the charismatic Naqshbandi *pir* Shaykh Nazim, a Turkish Cypriot who first started visiting Britain in

1974. Operating from the Haqqani Islamic Priory in North London, he became his movement's 'central figure who [determined] spiritual and structural guidelines and [represented] the ultimate source of authority'.[40] His life-style, dress, habits and spiritual practices gave the group a unique character, with followers attempting to emulate their *pir*.

Since the Second World War, one of the main strands of Islam influenced by Sufism, which has won wide acceptance among South Asian Muslim communities in Britain, is what has come to be known as the Barelwi tradition. Through this tradition a wide diversity of belief and custom has been adopted as Muslim Sunni practice. Interest was generated initially among Muslim migrants by followers of the Naqshbandi, Qadri and Chishti *tariqas* working alongside them in factories. In the early 1960s Sufi Abdullah of the Naqshbandi *tariqa* and Pir Maroof of the Qadiri *tariqa* worked night shifts in Birmingham and Bradford respectively. Several *imams* of mosques in Britain's inner cities were initiated in the Chishti *tariqa*, and soon organised groups of *murids*, formed *zikr* circles and established mosques and supplementary Quran classes. In this way different forms of the subcontinental Sufi practices became institutionalised in Britain. Membership of Sufi groups with origins in the subcontinent generally overlapped with the Barelwi tradition, which in the past had embodied folk rural traditions embracing saintly lineages and shrines in their belief systems and practices. Hence membership of a Sufi order in Britain did not always result from a clear sense of spiritual direction and after could merely reflect the dominant form of Muslim faith and practice found in a particular rural area back in Pakistan or India. Thus in the British context allegiance to a regionally located *tariqa* could be closely associated with ethnicity.

The Naqshbandi *tariqa* became the most dominant Sufi order in Britain. The form of Islam that it prescribed resembled that practised by rural people in large parts of the subcontinent, involving a wide range of local customs established by oral traditions and focused around a Sufi shrine. While its adherents have not usually been active in pursuing the goal of uniting Islam in political terms, they have been aware of belonging to the wider Muslim community or *umma*. In Britain the uproar directed against *The Satanic Verses* became a focal point in the development of this awareness. Because of the Barelwi veneration for the Prophet Muhammad the book caused immense upset among them and resulted in intense public expressions of anger. Although lack of leadership meant that it was the better educated and more structured reformist groups that organised the protest, Barelwi leaders were aware of the power of unity in this campaign and subsequently made greater efforts to achieve it. In daily life, however, rites and rituals legitimised by custom continued to strengthen kinship ties and localised identity.

From the end of the 1980s the growth of Sufi activities in Britain rapidly increased. The presence of resident Sufi *pirs* resulted in buildings, parks and procession routes in inner-city Britain becoming as sacred as shrines in the subcontinent. Indeed it is not difficult to imagine a time when the places where *pirs* have died after passing their lives in Britain (like Pir Abdul Wahhab Siddiqi, whose tomb is in the grounds of Hijaz College in Nuneaton) might become shrine locations. A visiting *sajjada nashin* might also reinvigorated popular interest in his particular tradition, as in the case of the Sultan Bahu Trust. The *pir* Sultan Bahu founded the Qadiri/Sarwaryah *tariqa* in India in the seventeenth century, but his descendants later developed connections with *Naqshbandi sheikhs*, thus linking themselves to that *tariqa*. In 1980 Sultan Fiaz ul Hasan Bahu, one of those laying claim to the *gaddi* (position of *pir*—literally the seat upon which he sat) visited Britain and set up the Trust in Birmingham. He was later joined by his two brothers, and the three succeeded in establishing mosques in Bradford, Leicester and London. Groups were also established in Leeds, Newcastle and Glasgow. One of the biggest Barelwi centres in Britain was that in Birmingham: in the early 1990s a new mosque was built and the Trust spent over £350,000, collected locally, on extending the centre to include administrative offices, areas for women to pray and for the holding of supplementary classes, and a *dar al-ulum* (school) with its hostel. Barelwi practices predominated. The customary *naats, zikr, salam*, the monthly celebration of *Giarhvin Sharif*, the annual *urs*, the celebration of *Milad-i Nabi* and the use of *tawiz* (amulets) all reflected the Barelwi tradition. The Trust developed connections, both informal and formal, with various other *tariqas*, Naqshbandi and otherwise, in Birmingham and elsewhere. However, while there was considerable interaction among these Sufi orders, they mostly retained their independence and served their local communities, although the mosques affiliated to the Trust shared guidance based on the teachings of the original saint.

The Qadiri *tariqa* also made significant efforts to institutionalise its presence in Britain—dominated by one man: Pir Maroof. With his base among Mirpuris in Bradford, he formed the World Islamic Mission (WIM) in 1973 as an umbrella organisation for Barelwi mosques and organisations in Britain. In 1985 the WIM organised a national conference in the Wembley Conference Centre which 3,000 Barelwis attended. In 1987 and 1988 it organised an extensive celebration of the *Milad-i Nabi* in Hyde Park, London, attended by over 25,000 Muslims. By 1989, eight of the eleven Barelwi mosques and six of the seven schools in Bradford were the product of WIM activities.[41] Pir Maroof was able to widen the sphere of his influence beyond Bradford with branches in Sheffield and Oldham and *zikr* circles in Preston and Halifax. However, his efforts to promote a national consciousness were not wholly successful, essentially because of the localised form of organisation prevalent among Muslims from the subcontinent. Extended-family networks maintained loyalties to their villages of origin and the customs and practices associated with them, and Pir Maroof was unable to wrench these *biradaris* away from protecting their spheres of influence. Thus his promotion of *dawa* activities was hampered by the powerful ethnic networks that had become established in Britain as a result of the processes of chain migration.

While certain strands of the Naqshbandi *tariqa* put down strong roots, with a centralised formal institutional existence in Britain, the Chishti *tariqa* maintained contact with *murids* at a distance through correspondence, telephone calls and visits. There has been no permanent Chishti centre in Britain, and the issues requiring advice and guidance have been pragmatic rather than spiritual. *Murids* attend local Barelwi mosques, with *qawwali* occasions organised to promote spirituality as well as a sense of community. However, for Chishti Muslims the focus has remained on *dargahs* (shrines) back in South Asia.

Thus the organisation of these Sufi *tariqas* has taken place largely around ethnic groups. Few of the *tariqas* deriving from South Asia have been able to transcend ethnic boundaries in their attempts to promote Islam in Britain. The close association between ethnic identity and *tariqa* membership has been replicated in other Muslim communities, and so most British Muslim communities have maintained strong ethnic boundaries despite the rhetoric of unity. For instance Mirpuris and Yemenis have shared the same geographical space in Birmingham, and both have boasted of strong Sufi traditions—the Mirpuris with their Naqshbadi *tariqas* and the Yemenis with their Alawi *silsilas*; yet the two communities have maintained little contact with each other. Likewise the more recently arrived Tijaniya *tariqa*, popular among West Africans in south-east London, functions along national lines, with Nigerian, Ghanaian and Gambian followers forming largely separate groups within the order.[42]

Umbrella organisations from the 1980s onwards

The end of the 1980s saw a major change in the way in which Muslim organisations took part in public life. They became much more visible in the public sphere and more robust in their representation of wider Muslim interests. While national organisations had been set up in the 1960s and the 1970s, they had found difficulty in making headway because most decisions and policies that affected Muslims in their daily lives were taken locally and not nationally. In addition, the major Islamic movements, as they began to establish themselves, discovered that their concerns were more limited and internal to their constituencies and immediate tasks; the need to become constructively involved in the national structures of British political and social life had not yet been strongly felt. The Union of Muslim Organisations of UK and Ireland (UMO), an umbrella organisation established in 1970, had little success in securing changes in the statutory provision in a number of practical areas. Nor was it able to mobilise significant support on international issues that had agitated Muslims for some time, such as events in Palestine and Kashmir.[43] By the mid-1980s several Islamic groupings began 'to feel the need for some kind of nationwide coordination'. Muslim concerns regarding *halal* food and education highlighted the need for joint effort nationally since it was British state policies, not local government ones, that had serious implications for Muslims. At the same time the British establishment, finding it increasingly confusing and impracticable to negotiate with numerous bodies claiming to be the authentic voice of Muslims in Britain, pressed Muslim com munities to construct a unified organisation, in some ways similar to the Board of Deputies of British Jews, which could represent their interests and with which negotiations could be conducted. Attempts were made to satisfy this demand. The Council of Mosques (COM) in the United Kingdom and Ireland was set up in 1984 as a conduit for joint action, specifically to coordinate a Muslim response to the findings of the Swann Report[44] and recommendations on the education of ethnic minorities in 1985. Meanwhile a Council of Imams and Mosques (COIM) was established with its centre at the Muslim College in West London, but this failed to unite Muslims in Britain and instead became a pole of attraction for Barelwi organisations, which regarded the COM as a rival with Saudi connections.[45]

The *Satanic Verses* affair gave further impetus to the efforts being made at the end of the 1980s to create a single organisation of British Muslims. While it was recognised that British Muslims were not a homogeneous entity, the negative results of the controversy convinced many Muslims that without unity they were unlikely to win any support or effective influence 'in the seats of power, in the media or in economic circles'.[46] For unity to be achieved they had to build a national coalition on the basis of commonly agreed issues, and it was *The Satanic Verses* and agreement to mobilise protests against the book and its author that led to the founding of the UK Action Committee on Islamic Affairs (UKACIA) in October 1988. But even as it was being conceived, other Muslims such as Kalim Siddiqi were emerging to challenge its authority.

The Muslim Parliament, the brainchild of Kalim Siddiqi, was presented as an alternative to more conventional Muslim formations. It was inaugurated on 4 January 1992 after nearly eighteen months of ground-work following the publication of the *Muslim Manifesto* in 1990—regarded as its foundation document. Its establishment was closely connected to the dissatisfaction of many Muslims in Britain with the way the major institutions of British society were addressing their concerns. These Muslims were also uneasy about what they perceived as the adverse impact of Western values on coming Muslim generations. They regarded Western society as morally in a state of terminal sickness, and believed that nothing could be gained by associating with it. On the contrary, they felt that it could infect and pollute and therefore prove harmful. Thus, in this view the Muslim 'community' needed to be an exemplary one, displaying standards of behaviour that contrasted sharply with those displayed by the wider society. However, this could only happen if it isolated itself from these damaging influences, and it could only succeed if its organisation was different from that generally adopted by Muslims in the past, which had clearly failed to achieve their objectives. The main strategy of the Muslim Parliament was to generate resources internally in place of those that Muslim organisations in the past had demanded from local and national governments, so that it could pursue its aims without any external influence. Muslim minorities would have to be strong and self-sufficient and speak with a united, collective voice; and to do this they would stay outside the mainstream political systems, which would always be dominated by non-Muslims and anti-Islamic interests.

Thus the idea of a 'Muslim Parliament' germinated, first, in the frustration, anger and need for defiance against the wider society's indifference to major Muslim concerns felt by a section of Britain's Muslim communities; secondly, in resistance to the perceived onslaught on the values and aspirations of a proud religious tradition; and thirdly, in the need to re-empower Muslims by providing them with material means to re-establish their self-confidence and a measure of control over their life. Implicit within this strategy was Kalim Siddiqi's vision: 'to survive as uncontaminated as Muslims in a hostile environment and to contribute fully to the global Ummah's struggle to re-establish Islam as a civilisational force for good in the world'. Siddiqi viewed the Muslim Parliament both as a 'minority political system for Muslims in Britain' and as a 'non-territorial Islamic state'. The former was 'primarily an instrument of communication. Its role is to listen to the community, think collectively for the community, and speak on its behalf.' The latter was the 'executive arm of the community, empowered and authorised to act on its behalf—the State is the instrument by which a community can exercise its collective power.' According to this view, British Muslims had to develop separate institutions capable of meeting their needs independently of the British state or government. These institutions would need to consider among other issues: education, poverty, unemployment, anti-Muslim discrimination, the state of the community's mosques and the halal meat trade. Bodies were set up to realise this vision. The Bait al-Mal al-Islami was established in 1993 as a registered charity to finance and administer provision for deprived families and students from a poor background. Abroad, Siddiqi supported Muslims in Bosnia through his encouragement of the Arms for Bosnia Fund and its successor, the Jihad Fund, set up to help Muslim *mujahidin* in Algeria, Kashmir and other parts of the world.[47]

The experiment of the unelected Muslim Parliament largely failed. Siddiqi died in 1996, and without his vitality, passion and charisma there seemed to be no one left to provide the necessary leadership. The Parliament declined and then splintered, but even at its peak it had proved unable to mobilise sufficient support and resources among Muslims to realise its strategy to any significant extent. This may have been partly because it bypassed established Muslim organisations, hand-picking individuals to represent Muslim groups across Britain, but also because Muslim communities in Britain, in contrast to the highly successful homogeneous, disciplined and centrally-led Nation of Islam in the United States, represent a socially, ethnically and culturally diverse set of interests, and so can be regarded as too loosely structured to develop an effective self-contained existence. While in the short term Kalim Siddiqi's denunciation of Salman Rushdie brought his initiatives much popular support among sections of the Muslim community, it did not result in any significant long-term backing for his institution. Other broad-based Muslim organisations also failed to achieve their campaign goals. The demand for *The Satanic Verses* to be banned was rejected by the British government, and calls for the blasphemy law to be extended to Islam similarly met a negative response. And, as Muslim responses during the Gulf War in 1991 demonstrated, few long-term lessons about organising effectively were learned from the Rushdie affair. According to Werbner, British Pakistanis seemed, as during that affair, to set themselves 'morally apart from the wider society, denying categorically what local people would regard as moral imperatives: the defence of democratic values'.[48] While there was some veiled criticism of the Iraqi invasion of Kuwait, British Muslim organisations showed a high level of unanimity in their call for a halt to what they perceived as the Western-led alliance's aggression against Muslims. Loyalty to the Muslim *umma* came before national interests. Needless to say, talk of 'holy war' and vengeance were clearly at odds with the views of the majority of the British population, some of whom regarded it as tantamount to treason. The organisations that expressed these views and their leaders seemed naively out of touch with the political environment, and the public perception that greeted them severely damaged community relations.

In neither of these episodes, despite the relatively non-sectarian issues at stake, could organisational unity be achieved. Even within the Pakistani Muslim community sectarian tendencies resulted in different and sometimes opposing positions being taken. Barelwis at times expressed virulently anti-Saudi views, and so the critical issue of how to develop a national Muslim organisation, able to embrace and reflect the doctrinal, ethnic and linguistic diversity of British Islam without generating controversy, remained unresolved. Thus, while in the 1980s and 1990s British Muslims united on a number of occasions to combat threats and challenges to their deeply-held values, this unity has been fleeting, and once the threats have subsided, has waned. The tension between the belief in one Muslim *umma* and the reality of a multitude of ethnic communities has not been overcome. Still, while diversity continued to characterise Muslim organisation, unity remained at least an aspiration. It became clear to British Muslims in the 1990s that when dealing with the British establishment their lack of national unity impeded access to resources and representation. In March 1994 Michael Howard, the Home Secretary, told a delegation of British Muslims requesting the enactment of anti-religious-discrimination legislation to come back once they had established a unified Muslim entity which the government could recognise as representative of the Muslim community and do business with.[49]

The effort to achieve national coordination and establish an organisation which was not closely aligned to any particular tradition, and working within the mainstream of British society and its institutions, which the state would be prepared to recognise, was resumed with renewed vigour in the early 1990s. After a long period of consultation[50] this culminated in the formation of the Muslim Council of Britain (MCB) in May 1996. Its aims were

> to promote co-operation, consensus and unity on Muslim affairs in the UK; to encourage and strengthen all existing efforts being made for the benefit of the Muslim community; to work for a more enlightened

appreciation of Islam and Muslims in the wider society; to establish a position for the Muslim community within British society that is fair and based on due rights; to work for the eradication of disadvantages and forms of discrimination faced by Muslims and to foster better community relations and work for the good of society as a whole.[51]

Its structure allowed for broad representation, 'accommodating, and reflecting the variety of social and cultural backgrounds and outlook of the community', and a system of accountability and democracy along the lines of many other mainstream voluntary organisations in Britain. Its policies and decisions would be arrived at by consensus. In May 2001 its Secretary-General Yusuf Bhailok was able to claim that the MCB was 'the largest umbrella organisation of Muslim organisations' and 'a first port of call meeting requests for information, contacts and involvement with the rest of British society'; and that it had 'met with all top political leaders', represented and lobbied vigorously on home and foreign affairs, and taken part in many international conferences and forums across the Muslim world. Nevertheless, while affirming that it was 'a non-sectarian body working for the common good', the MCB also recognised the equal status of others in its desire to seek relations of goodwill and mutual respect with all Muslim organisations and not to displace, isolate or interfere with any existing Muslim work in the community. Indeed, it made no claim to be the 'sole' representative of 'true' Islam or the 'whole' of the British Muslim community. In addition, while it may have been the most successful attempt thus far to achieve organisational unity, it was predominantly Sunni, and in its quest for state recognition it may have had to tone down its criticism of government policy and society. This overt respect for the British establishment risked arousing opposition from other groups among Muslims, and thus creating disunity in the future. Moreover, the material and psychological forces producing conflict still persisted: 'Struggles for leadership, the reflex for self-defence against outside interference, fear that a rival group might enjoy more privileges from the state or other institutions', and the pressures of unemployment and discrimination in economic, social and cultural spheres' were all likely to make 'cohesion among Muslim organisations a distant goal'.[52]

Organisation of welfare, social and cultural services

As Muslim communities became more rooted in Britain, their members strove to put structures in place to enable them to live their lives according to their own understanding of Islamic practice. They were obliged to think seriously about the kinds of practical measures needed to fulfil their religious obligations as prescribed by the Sharia in relation to God, in interactions with fellow human beings, and in relation to the rest of the social and natural environment. Beyond institutionalising religious rites such as prayer and fasting and disseminating religious knowledge, they also attempted to organise *zakat* (religious tax) and practical matters associated with the performance of the *hajj* (pilgrimage to Mecca and Medina). Travel agencies fully equipped to cater for *hajj* requirements were established to offer a variety of services, from organising travel to Mecca and arranging board and lodging to hiring religious guides to take Muslims through the proper rites involved in this pilgrimage. The number of Muslim charities dedicated to providing humanitarian assistance also mushroomed from the mid-1980s. Raising monetary and material resources from donations such as *zakat, sadaqah, lillah* and *qurbani*, organisations such as Islamic Relief (founded in 1984), Muslim Aid and Muslim Hands were set up to offer help to the needy in a multitude of ways—emergency relief in the form of food, medicine and clothing, orphan sponsorship, schools, material assistance and medical care for refugees and aid to develop infrastructure in Muslim communities. Numerous social-welfare bodies emerged to cater for the needs of British Muslims, offering guidance on a wide range of social issues. For instance, the aim of the Muslim Advice and Support Service was to encourage Muslims to approach contentious social issues in a positive frame of mind and to build a rapport between the older and younger generation in all aspects of life in Britain without losing sight of Islam. To this end it provided information, support and advice for Muslim families faced with drug and alcohol problems, help with disabled children and support for Muslim girls and women suffering from emotional crises and physical, mental and sexual abuse. Similarly, the Bait al-Mal al-Islami offered financial support for students from poor backgrounds, counselling, conciliation and support for Muslim youth and parents experiencing a breakdown in their relationships, and help for the disabled, homeless and destitute.

THE EVOLUTION OF MUSLIM ORGANISATION IN BRITAIN

The number of organisations involved in *dawa* activities similarly grew enormously. The promotion of awareness about Islam through the distribution of religious literature, audiovisual material, exhibitions, talks, lectures, workshops, discussion circles and conferences reached out into wide areas of British society. Increasingly information on Islamic matters came to be disseminated using multimedia channels (including telephone and on-line question-and-answer sessions) and software. This work was carried out in a wide variety of arenas—at libraries, camps and leisure and training centres; through publishers and bookshops, such as the International Propagation Centre International (UK); and in periodicals such as *Q-News, Muslim News, Trends* and *Sultan*. Special programmes were organised during the month of Ramadan and the *hajj* period. At the same time a number of Muslim organisations, such as the Muslim Media Monitoring and Response, closely observed the media portrayal of Islam and attempted to combat misrepresentations through comments and complaints. Organisations such as the Islamic Human Rights Commission (IHRC) and the Association of Muslim Lawyers engaged increasingly in lobbying for human rights in Britain, and concerned themselves with campaigning on the provision of justice for Muslims worldwide. The IHRC, founded in 1997, helped individuals pursue 'Islamophobic' cases in employment and brought to public notice the plight of those Muslims whom it perceived had been ostracised or imprisoned for upholding their Islamic beliefs—wearing a scarf or a beard—or for activities based on their Islamic convictions.

The family has traditionally played an important role in Muslim social life, with many aspects of family life being subject to religious obligation. One of the rites of passage for a Muslim is the Abrahamic tradition of circumcision, and since this is not available on the National Health Service, clinics have been established offering a professional service. Another area in this domain where there has been extensive institutionalisation is Muslim marriage. In the 1950s Muslims usually married with a civil ceremony in register offices and Muslim formalities were performed privately elsewhere. Now about a quarter of the mosques in Britain are recognised for the holding of valid marriages, at which an official of the civil register office has to be present. A few individual mosques have gone further and obtained recognition for one of their own officials to act on behalf of the state, and in these instances a fully valid marriage can be performed by a Muslim official. Only few mosques offer this service because traditionally Muslim communities prefer not to celebrate marriages there, and the vast majority of Muslim marriages are still performed in the register office, with religious celebrations taking place elsewhere. Marriage bureaux have blossomed to facilitate arranged marriage (a practice that had to adapt as it moved from the rural locale to the global urban arena), to which large sections of, especially, the South Asian Muslim population remain attached. Then there are bodies such as Mushkil Aasaan Community Care for Families which provide crisis intervention, counselling, advocacy, family support, personal care, interpreting and purchase of social security for the elderly. The Islamic Sharia Council of UK and Eire has dealt with many cases requiring resolution of family disputes through its application of principles of Islamic jurisprudence. Many solicitors now provide specialist advice on divorce, domestic violence, child law and inheritance.

Burial was another issue that occupied the attention of Muslim communities from the early years of mass migration. Most families preferred to send the bodies of their deceased relatives back to their country of origin. While this practice has continued (and now takes place largely through Muslim undertakers), it has nonetheless declined and burial in Britain is more common than formerly. In most cities mosques have set up facilities for performing the last rites according to Islamic requirements. Cemeteries have been purchased (for instance sections within Brookwood Cemetery near Woking in Surrey), and burial societies have successfully negotiated allocation of burial areas allowing for the correct alignment of graves, interment at short notice, burial in shrouds, filling in and mounding of graves by mourners, and roofing over the coffin to prevent direct contact with the soil.[53] Institutions have also been set up independently offering comprehensive funeral services in accordance with the Sharia.[54]

Finally, as we saw in Chapter 10, education, because of its influence on the construction of moral values and social behaviour, has been one of the key areas of concern for Muslims in Britain, and unease (if not dissatisfaction) with state provision was expressed soon after the arrival of children in the 1960s. A two-pronged approach was adopted. First, supplementary schools were set up to provide religious instruction within the communities themselves, and secondly, organisations concerned only with the education of Muslims were established. These operated across a spectrum of issues, ranging from the provision of Islamic education in a variety of forms in state schools to the production of Islamic knowledge and research. Some helped to finance and manage the establishment of independent Muslim schools as an alternative to the state system, offering academic and vocational qualifications in religious and secular studies. Both the Waqf Al-Birr Educational Trust (established by Yusuf Islam) and the UK Islamic Waqf have given financial support to Muslim schools (e.g. the Brondesbury College for Boys in London) from accumulated donations. Many of these schools have been affiliated to the Association of Muslim Schools. At the tertiary level too institutions have been established offering specialist professional religious training to potential *imams*, *ulama* and *alimas*; many of these courses have been accredited by British universities as undergraduate and postgraduate qualifications, and offer certificate-, diploma-, and degree-level courses and research programmes in Islamic studies as well as in secular subjects.[55] Organisations such as the Azhar Academy have set up *madrassas* and provided teachers of the traditional Islamic sciences. The Islamic Academy in Cambridge, established in 1983, committed itself to making Islamic values the basis of education. Its activities were geared to replacing secular concepts and underpinning academic disciplines with Islamic epistemology, and it has sought to achieve this through intervention in seminars and conferences, by cooperating with non-Muslim educational institutions in research on Muslim education in Britain and on the fundamentals of Islamic education, and through the publication of philosophical, theological and educational research in its journal, the *Muslim Educational Quarterly*.[56]

Muslim youth organisation

In the early 1960s Muslim youth in Britain were mainly in Britain temporarily as students. They were concerned to maintain awareness of their Islamic identity on a collective basis, and to meet their social welfare needs as best they could. The Federation of Student Islamic

Societies (FOSIS) was formed in 1962 to support these objectives. Thereafter it gradually expanded its activities to include conferences, camps, seminars and study circles around areas of importance to Muslims at both popular and academic levels. It now provides students with management and skills training for the effective running of Islamic societies, and publishes *The Muslim: The Voice of Muslim Students*—previously *Al-Mizan* (The Balance)—a multidisciplinary biannual periodical, and a bi-termly newspaper giving news, publicising activities and providing a means of exchanging information between universities. FOSIS organises information packs for new students and maintains an extensive collection of Islamic videos and materials for display in exhibitions and for use in its library. It also arranges accommodation for male and female students in separate hostels. FOSIS needs to ensure that its leadership, which in the past has come largely from abroad, reflects the fact that the Muslim students at universities are now predominantly British.[57] Other Muslim youth organisations—the Muslim Student Society of UK and Ireland, the Muslim Youth Foundation and the Muslim Youth League—have concentrated mainly on *dawa* activities. The World Assembly of Muslim Youth (WAMY), in particular, is involved in activities aimed at strengthening Islamic consciousness in a less political way than the more radical Islamist formations. It concentrates on religious education and training to inculcate an Islamic way of living.[58]

At the beginning of the 1980s the appeal of traditional Islam in the shape of the different sects imported from the Muslim world seemed to be declining for many young members of Britain's Muslim communities. These sects appeared to lack the capacity to address the issues that agitated young minds. *Imams*, largely from abroad and barely able to speak English, lacked knowledge of the British environment and were ill-equipped to deal with the challenges it posed. Lewis reported in 1994 that of Bradford's seventy *ulama*, those with university and college degrees and *alim* qualifications from the subcontinent could be counted on the fingers of two hands and only about half a dozen spoke in English reasonably well.[59] So, while some mosque-based organisations did subsequently adapt their approaches, they still made few concessions to the new environment and failed to connect effectively with the world of young British Muslims, male or female. Music groups, even those exploring religious themes and subjects, were treated with indifference at best and antipathy at worst. A great distance remained between young people and the *ulama*. While the former wanted to debate 'customary practice' in a sexually mixed environment with English as the medium of communication, the latter absented themselves from such discussions, refused to have any intellectual engagement with them, and were denounced in consequence as 'bankrupt'.[60]

Those Muslim organisations that did recognise the existence of the world of Muslim youth still approached the anxieties and concerns of young Muslims within an orthodox perspective. The UK Islamic Mission first began to organise its youth work under the auspices of its Islamic Youth Movement (IYM) in Bradford in the 1970s. It achieved some influence through study circles, conferences and national camps, while its quarterly magazine *The Movement* (started in 1976), pursued an Islamist discourse and debated a variety of themes and subjects. The IYM realised that unquestioning obedience to an *alim* and learning the Quran by heart were no longer acceptable to the products of the British educational system, exposed to a questioning and challenging culture. It therefore gave them space to distance themselves from their parents' culture and criticise aspects of it on Islamic grounds, while enabling them to retain pride in their Muslim identity. Most of these young people came from Deobandi and Barelwi backgrounds and were attracted to an Islam which was intelligible and accessible to them through the medium of English and which gave them a feeling of being part of a worldwide Islamist movement which in their view was morally superior to the West. However, by the end of the 1970s the IYM had disappeared, its support having evaporated because to most young Muslims the idea of establishing an Islamic state in Britain seemed far-fetched. Likewise, its dismissive attitude towards the traditional values of the parents' generation appeared élitist and potentially divisive of families. There was also growing unease over the unimpeachable status accorded to the Jamaat-i-Islami founder, Maududi, whose person had come to be viewed by the movement's leaders as beyond criticism. Furthermore, the puritanical behaviour advocated by the IYM could seem exhausting, joyless and emotionally arid.

The demise of the IYM led to a reassessment, and its successor, the Young Muslims UK (YMUK), was launched in 1984, again in Bradford.

While its mode of operation did not change radically from that of the IYM, the content of its activities now tended to reflect recognition of the complex world of young British Muslims. The male and female members of YMUK still met in separate groups, but its programme of activities combined recreation with study. It attempted to create an environment in which awkward questions were not necessarily swept under the carpet, and facets of the received culture of the parents could be challenged. The YMUK produced its own music cassettes, and its magazine *Trends* tried to address many of the issues impinging on the daily lives of young Muslims. Its articles debated careers for Muslim women, arranged marriage and women's rights. However, the great majority of YMUK members, especially those in decision-making positions, are men and hence it is their perspective that remains dominant in these discussions. More generally too the YMUK is deeply indebted to UKIM for its ideology and its structure and constitution, and therefore it has faced the problem of whether the Islamist tradition has developed sufficient intellectual capacity for its followers to live imaginatively with integrity as a minority within a pluralist state, even while relatively powerless. It has not quite come to grips with Muslims permanently living as a minority in a society that allows extensive personal freedom, not least to challenge and contest religious positions: this requires a move away from its preoccupation with capturing power, which it believes is a precondition for the achievement of its ultimate aim—the establishment of a truly Islamic society in Britain. Its literature has not clearly signalled this shift, although a later initiative (albeit still within the Islamist perspective) launched in Leicester in 1990 in the form of the Islamic Society of Britain did promise to embrace 'a more creative and imaginative outlook ... [raising] the consciousness of Muslims about their contribution to British society'.[61] Its decision to conduct its business in English clearly pointed to a recognition within its leadership of the need for a more effective way of engaging with wider audiences and intellectual traditions.

Compared with the youth wings of the more traditional Muslim organisations, the YMUK has been quite successful in attracting the interest of young British Muslims. In 1994 2,000 attended its annual camp. Its appeal lay partly in the alternatives it offered compared with other mosque-based bodies; instead of learning rituals (the usual fare dispensed at mosques), YMUK groups have operated as clubs providing support and friendship and a sense of belonging. They offer the space—often away from the parochial, sectarian, ethnic, linguistic and cultural biases of many parents and elders—for the exploration of deeper concerns. Unlike the majority of mosque-based bodies, the YMUK has made serious efforts to understand the changing aspirations of young Muslims, as is shown in its use of the internet to discuss 'traditional' and contemporary topics and its tacit support of bands such as Fun-da-mental and production of its own music tapes. Even so, its goal remains the transformation of British society into an Islamic one.

Young Muslims have also responded by forming their own institutions in which their needs are more adequately considered and expressed. These have offered them a sense of identity that has evolved through the experience of living in a minority. For them the building of structures was no longer as important as organising activities of common interest and gatherings where they could discuss relevant issues collectively. These organisations have attempted to provide young Muslims with alternative lifestyles for enabling them to keep their distance from the disputes—often petty, but still damaging—that have plagued their communities, but at the same time helping them to cope with an environment in which they continue to struggle against racism and anti-Muslim prejudice. They have also tried to connect with the more intellectually grounded and in many ways less emotionally based world of young Muslims, who now have direct access to the sources of Islam in English, by engaging them in rational debate. However, even they have found it difficult to escape the assumptions that underpin their agendas and programmes and they baulk at the idea of developing a critical Islamic scholarship, a theology responsive to the intellectual challenges of a confident 'indigenous' culture that is driven by a spirit of inquiry.

At the same time a number of youth organisations, such as Hizb-ut-Tahrir (the Liberation Party or HuT, founded in 1953 in Jordan) and Al-Muhajiroun (the Migrants, which broke away from HuT in 1996), emerged on the British scene in the 1990s. These were independent of those operating as youth wings of the traditional Sunni South Asian Muslim organisations, and some observers attributed the 'success' of these politically militant organisations in colleges and mosques to their 'preying' on unsuspecting and ill-informed Muslims and convincing them of their 'Islamicity'. Others explained their appeal as a reaction to the demonisation of Islam and of British Muslims as a 'fifth column' community. Holding its meetings under the guise of the '1924 Committee' (a reference to the abolition of the Ottoman Caliphate in 1924), HuT denounced 'Jewish conspiracies' against Muslims and exposed what it regarded as 'lies about the Holocaust'. In the context of perceived assaults on Muslims around the world, the rhetoric of Omar Bakri (founder of Al-Muhajiroun) acquired resonance among certain groups of young Muslims. Support for HuT likewise grew, as reflected in the 3,000 supporters who attended its rally in August 1995.[62] These organisations stimulated an evaluation among young Muslims in light of their experience of racism that militated against any sense of being part of British society, and helped them to deal with the alienation caused by many of the traditions, customs and practices of their elders, which young Muslims now rejected as deviations from 'true' Islam. They also attempted to foster a sense of identity that rejected the standards by which the majority community measured self-worth. Instead they sought to capture and reshape the sense of 'not belonging' and disaffection from the wider society and its institutions that many young Muslims have grown up with, and were able to transform this into a collective identity that incorporated moral and spiritual wellbeing rooted in Islam. Thus substantial groups of relatively intelligent young Muslims, many at colleges and universities, were convinced by these organisations that improvement in their social and cultural status was possible only with the realisation of their political aims and 'the flag of Islam raised in 10 Downing Street'.[63]

Disillusionment with the West's involvement in the Gulf War in 1991 provided the starting-point for a rise in recruitment to extremist organisations such as HuT, and the civil wars in Bosnia, Kashmir and Chechniya, together with the West's apparent indifference to the plight of Muslims in these countries, carried on the process. Their open condemnation of Israel's occupation of Palestinian land and continuing oppression of the Palestinian people, and their ringing condemnation of Russia's destruction of Chechniya and India's military action in Kashmir, convinced many that the militant struggle advocated by these organisations for the creation of a global Islamic state (*khilafah*) through *jihad* (armed action) was the correct strategy.[64] While they did not permit terror, the hijacking of aeroplanes belonging to a country at war with Muslims, such as Israel, was allowed.[65] The perspective of both HuT and Al-Muhajiroun remained firmly Islamist, and in that essential aspect was no different from YMUK and other Islamic societies canvassing support among Muslim students. The attraction of radical Islamist organisations rather than the mosque for young Muslims therefore lies in the way they have articulated issues which others have tried to avoid, in language comprehensible to many Muslims growing up in Britain's highly urbanised and pluralistic society. Disillusioned with the level of sectarianism in their communities, many have been attracted by the rhetoric of unity, and these organisations provide them with a set of ready-made solutions to complex political issues as well as to questions of personal identity.

Organising Muslim women

Traditional Muslim organisations, particularly those with roots in South Asia, have been less adaptable when considering the role of women, their status in the family and community, and their rights. In many ways they have reflected and reinforced the patriarchal attitudes of their communities, which have greatly influenced the extent to which Muslim women have been able to carve out a space for themselves in the public sphere. Most of the South Asian Muslim organisations in Britain have accepted separation of the sexes as the natural order. Inside the institution of the mosque traditional views have rejected the very idea of Muslim women ever assuming the role of *imam*, invoking the Hadith that 'the best mosque for women is the inner part of the house'. The Deobandi text *Bihishti Zewar* counsels women to pray at home rather than venture out to the mosque. Such edicts possess considerable legitimacy in the eyes of those who follow these traditions, which have continued to be expressed in their main institutions. Compared with Sunni Muslims, Shia women have enjoyed much greater religiously sanctioned freedom of movement and interaction with men; Andrews' study of Muslim women in Leicester revealed that a large proportion of Shia women regularly attended the mosque, but no Sunni women did so.[66] Ismaili women have gone even further: their attendance (generally mixed) at the *jamaat-khana* (assembly and prayer hall) for religious and social activities has for some time been viewed as virtually a communal obligation; indeed *mukhianis*, as female counterparts of male *mukhis* (head of the *jamaat* and official of the *jamaat-khana*), are institutionally recognised, in contrast to other strands of Islam. They are representatives of Ismaili women and responsible for their activities in the *jamaat-khana*.[67]

The result of these trends is that British Muslim women have been largely absent from the administrative and decision-making structures of most traditional Sunni institutions, since unquestioning acceptance of patriarchal perspectives on women's role and status established by male scholars and leaders of these movements has prevented them from participating in the workings of these organisations. Since Muslim women have not been required to attend congregations, few facilities to cater for their needs exist at mosques, and space was neither planned nor allocated for their participation in mosque-based activities. In Basit's study Muslim adolescent girls, like their sisters or their mothers, were seen to have little contact with the mosque. Many had read the Quran at a community-based school in a mosque, but unlike boys had stopped going when they reached puberty since studying with boys beyond that age was considered improper. In some families the female members had never been to a mosque; in others mothers and their older daughters had only done so at *Eid*, and a few had only occasionally attended religious gatherings.[68] Indeed, there seems to be a large body of young Muslim women bred in the British educational system, bilingual and aware of the many attractions of British cultural life, who have remained largely content with their parents' traditions, religious values and practices.

Since the early 1990s, however, the attitudes of more traditional Islamic organisations to female participation has shown some movement. For instance, men and women shared the same platform at a conference organised by the Barelwi Muslim Youth Movement, which allowed a relatively frank debate on women's issues to take place. While Deobandis have continued to maintain segregation of the sexes, they have set up private schools for girls where pupils were apparently equipped to challenge and fight for their rights in an Islamic environment—which it was hoped would not be a threat to the community's parents and guardians. But the generation of young Muslim women who emerged in the 1980s and 1990s were not so easily satisfied by these initiatives. With their experience of British life, they had different aspirations from their mothers: they wanted the freedom and opportunity to pursue higher education and have good careers. Their marginal position within their families and communities and in the traditional religious organisations was oppressive, and so they began to distance themselves from their roots by developing an intellectual understanding of Islam based on their own reading of the sources. Indeed, Islamist organisations have often done most to address the questions to which many well-educated and professional women, rejecting the obscurantism of the mullahs, have been seeking answers.

The YMUK's sister section (YMSS) is one Islamist organisation which, since the 1980s, has been a catalyst for women to discuss their concerns, and provided a platform for them to discuss specific problems, albeit within an Islamic framework. It offers a space where like-minded Muslim women can meet in a safe environment conducive to expressing doubt, and where they can find moral and emotional support and answers to the issues that concern them. The YMSS has allowed women to apply Islamic arguments, as the ones most acceptable to their families and the custodians of their communities, to overcome traditional opposition. While accepting Islamist thinking on the nature of gender relations and maintaining segregation between the sexes in its organisational forms and social activities, the YMSS has also encouraged women to develop fresh ideas about their role in the changing context of British society. They have been prompted to challenge aspects of traditional Islam and the customs and rituals practised by their communities by arguing critically against them on the basis of teachings in the Quran and Hadith. Muslim women in the YMSS, acquainted with Western feminist ideas and with direct access to Islamic sources and scholarship in English, have been able to reject the roles traditionally prescribed for them by older generations; indeed the YMSS has constantly tried to clarify the distinction between Islamic guidance and cultural practice over the role and status of women in the pages of *Trends* and on the internet. To some extent *ijtihad* has been exercised: for instance, on the question of whether it was lawful to go out without being accompanied by a *mahrem* (a close relative with whom marriage is prohibited) the advice was that, based on the principle of the lesser of two evils and on necessity, 'women are allowed to go out for *salah* [prayer], for studies and for other lawful needs, both religious and secular, as was customary amongst the women of the Companions of the Prophet and the women of later generations.' It denied that women were prevented by Islam from having a career; they were allowed to cut their hair and wear any form of clothing within the requirements of modesty. Thus equality between men and women was asserted.[69]

The YMSS has argued that 'the essence of Islam is not patriarchal', that the participation of Muslim women in the public domain is a positive development, and that it is legitimate for men and women to interact in a variety of ways in many social, cultural, political and economic areas of life. Women should not be barred from attending mosques. However, in interaction with non-related men, YMSS has prescribed the use of the *hijab* on the grounds that it safeguards women's honour; women in the YMSS contend that it gives them freedom of movement and hence a window on the external world. Its view is that the mixing of culture and Islam had taken away some of a woman's rights; that the *ulama*, being out of touch with women's experience, were unable to meet their concerns adequately; and that the YMSS permitted Muslim women to establish some room for manoeuvre separate from the world of their parents and claustrophobic community pressures. The direct reading of scripture in study circles gave them a better understanding of their situations. Thus being associated with the YMSS could be an empowering experience giving women access to knowledge directly from the sources of Islam without the mediation of men, whose own power resided in and was legitimated by their monopoly over the reading and interpreting of these sources. Within the YMSS it has been argued that in the past religious scholars, by controlling Islamic knowledge, have established traditions detrimental to women. Muslim women could reclaim their rights by challenging and dismantling this monopoly through independent organisation. That said, it is clear that while there has been a move away from the traditional exegesis on women's status and role, the premises underpinning YMSS thinking have changed little. In this essential respect YMSS thus is still apparently trapped in a patriarchal discourse by the logic of its assumptions.[70]

Hence, in the 1980s and 1990s it was generally accepted that in traditional Muslim institutions, women had little if any representation.

At the same time, it was recognised that if the distinction between Islam and patriarchal culture were not clarified, then 'the social distance of Muslim women from the community [would] increase'. Some 'modernists' went even further and suggested that the sources of patriarchal oppression were inherent in Muslim culture itself. Shabbir Akhtar suggested that Muslim women needed 'to interpret the sacred text and question the traditional male bias that has patronised their oppression for so long'.[71] Even the *Muslim Manifesto*, prepared for the Islamist Muslim Parliament, accepted that women should establish forums and be free to develop their own agendas. Not only did the Muslim Parliament reserve a proportion of seats in its general and leadership bodies for women, but it set up the Muslim Women's Institute where women could pursue their own objectives, strategies and interests without interference or pressure from men.

Thus, during this period a body of young Muslim women born and bred in Britain, many with university degrees and professional careers, came to grips with concerns and needs that they felt were not being met by the existing institutions in their communities. They were unhappy about their lack of representation, realising that the lack of a voice on specific issues (e.g. wife-beating and domestic violence, forced marriage, polygamy, female circumcision and child abuse) and constraints on their movement outside the home and over their education and careers meant that there were few channels available to them to express dissatisfaction with the conditions of their lives in these traditional structures. These women decided to construct separate, alternative structures to express their ideas and work for the resolution of their problems independently.

Al-Nisa and the Muslim Women's Helpline are significant examples of such initiatives. Al-Nisa based its work on the premiss that the family represented the basic unit of society. A dynamic Muslim community, healthy in Islamic terms, needed support systems and infrastructures for the family to be nurtured, and to this end Al-Nisa developed strategies to empower Muslim women, holding exhibitions on specific issues and seminars that produced open and passionate discussion about contraception, abortion, adoption, rape, education, how men can be better fathers and husbands, and geopolitical and ecological problems and changes. More practically, it operated an accredited Islamic counselling course, published material on sexual health within an Islamic perspective, and intervened in debates on forced marriage. It continues to lobby for the provision of Muslim-specific and Muslim-sensitive services, and campaigns against religious discrimination in employment and Islamophobia in public arenas.

Likewise, the Muslim Women's Helpline was set up in 1990 as a result of the concerns felt by many women about the serious problems they had faced in their communities and which other organisations were not addressing: divorce, single parenthood, domestic violence, conflict between parents and children, arranged marriage, sexual abuse and incest, depression and loneliness—all came to the fore as problems demanding urgent attention. More specifically the Helpline identified the sharp increase in domestic violence, forced marriage and mental breakdown among Muslim women. Since its inauguration, it has provided emotional support, practical help and information, and increasingly face-to-face counselling for thousands of women and girls. It has liaised with statutory and voluntary organisations, held conferences and published reports and reviews, all with a view to helping distressed Muslim women to overcome their difficulties and secure better services from mainstream organisations. Its quarterly newsletter, *ASK*, contributes to discussions and debates on social issues in the Muslim community and the wider society. While the Helpline's ethos is Islamic, it has operated in a relatively non-judgemental way, promoting the progressive aspects of an Islamic lifestyle.[72]

A third organisation based in Manchester in the 1990s and now disbanded, the Al Masoom (Innocent) Foundation, was significantly different in the breadth of its objectives and its activities, and in what its members were able to achieve in terms of Muslim women's emancipation. It was described by Werbner as a charitable body run by middle-class Muslim women. It organised aid to the poor in other parts of the Muslim world, protests against human rights abuses in Kashmir and Bosnia, and the transport of medical supplies, food, clothing, bedding and children's toys to people in Bosnia and Pakistan. For their efforts these women, most of whom were devoutly religious, faced hostility from powerful men in their community, who saw their activities—their collection of aid and their lobbying on behalf of Muslims worldwide—as a threat both to their dominance and to 'their monopoly over fund-raising and charitable work'.[73] Attempts to harass and intimidate them made these women reach out and mobilise support from important activists in the wider society. Their empowerment enabled them to challenge the social control of Muslim male leaders through their alignment with powerful mainstream allies—other women, journalists, local and national politicians—and not only to win an independent collective voice but also to assert their rights as women to operate independently in the public domain.

Finally, the emergence of a number of specifically Muslim periodicals in the 1980s and 1990s also helped women explore issues in a non-traditional way. *Sultan*, edited by a young Muslim woman Irna Khan, was launched in 1989. It was written in English, and contained articles on religion and culture seen from a Muslim woman's viewpoint. One contribution asserted that an arranged marriage lacking choice and the freedom to refuse was 'void' in Islamic terms. 'Proper' Islam gave women equality, and it was wrong that 'in our male dominated society ... women hardly have a voice'.[74] Similarly *Q-News*, which began publication in 1992 and has been staffed largely by young women, applied to Muslim women's issues what in classical Islam would have been defined as the principle of *ijtihad*, but which in the late twentieth century was defined as rational enquiry. Yet despite these developments the decision-making structures and processes affecting Muslim women remained at the end of the 1990s very much at the organisational margins of Muslim community life in Britain. Men, including *ulama*, still played the decisive role, even in relation to concerns specific to women's lives.

Institutionalisation of minority Muslim sects in Britain: the Ismailis

Little attention has been paid to the settlement histories of those Muslim communities in Britain which subscribe to non-Sunni traditions. This is due largely to the 'public face' of Islam in Britain having remained almost exclusively associated with South Asian Sunni-dominated Islam, with the result that a wider understanding of what has shaped the ways in which different groups of Muslims have become institutionalised in British society is lacking. The experience of institutionalisation among some of the minority Muslim sects, such as Shia of the Ithna Ashari and Ismaili variety and the Ahmedis, as well as British converts, helps to show that, as in other religions, a range of historical, social, cultural and theological factors have determined the ways in which diverse Islamic traditions have come to terms with British society.

There have been established Ismaili communities in Britain since the 1950s, yet the history of their settlement has gone largely untold, partly because the Sunni Muslim community is numerically predominant in Britain and so its perspectives have tended to be hegemonic, and also because of the discreet nature of Ismailism, a reaction to its rejection by other Muslims who have often believed its religious practices to be 'un-Islamic'. Only by considering its fundamental religious and cultural doctrines and traditions can Ismaili institutionalisation in Britain be understood. Ismailis are a branch of the Shia minority of Islam, for whom the legitimate headship (Imamate) rightfully belongs to Ali (the Prophet Muhammad's cousin and son-in-law, and the fourth caliph). Over time Shia Muslims evolved a doctrine of divine right and the idea of the infallible Imam, who remains to this day the bearer of an esoteric wisdom that guides Shias throughout the world. For them a belief in and submission to the divinely guided and infallible Imam is the third cardinal article of faith after belief in God and the Prophet. Although bound by this fundamental belief, Shias were (and remain) divided over the persons to be identified as Imams. The Ismailis were those who recognised the sixth Imam, Jafar al-Sadiq's son Ismail, as his successor, and after him his son and descendants to the present day, with the Aga Khan occupying the position of the community's Imam. Ismaili intellectuals gradually perfected the Ismaili system of theosophy, which conferred the role of authoritative interpreter of Muslim doctrine and practice on the living Imam, who alone interprets the all-important 'inner' meaning of the Quran and the Sharia. For Ismailis the authority of the Imam became the third and most decisive foundation of law after the Quran and Sunna, instead of consensus of opinion (*ijma*) or analogical deduction (*qiyas*), the third and fourth pillars of Islamic law for Sunnis. The Shia belief that the Quran possesses an 'inner', esoteric meaning (*batin*) as well as a superficial, exoteric meaning (*zahir*) is central to the Ismaili religious system, and crucially this distinction helps to explain how the Ismailis have embraced 'modernisation'—by differentiating and yet connecting these two dimensions.

THE EVOLUTION OF MUSLIM ORGANISATION IN BRITAIN

The 'outer' mode of religious life is contingent and constantly changing, while the 'inner' remains essential and eternally unchanging. To interpret the Quran's 'hidden' meaning Shias use the exegetical tool of *tawil* (allegorical interpretation), which is exercised exclusively through the Imam's divinely granted knowledge. In theory this authoritarian aspect is important for Ismailis, for it helps to create among them unity, uniformity and unanimity. The concept of *tawil* facilitates change, but it is clearly dependent on the character and objectives of the living Imam. In contrast to Sunni Islam, which holds to a fairly literal interpretation of the Quran in which *ijtihad* has not been exercised to any great extent for centuries, Ismailism has the flexibility that has enabled it to eschew literalism and blind imitation, adjust to changing conditions, and respect the plurality of religious belief. However, because of the belief in differential human capacities, hierarchy in intellectual, spiritual and secular matters is still accepted.

Given that the Ismaili immigrants to Britain after the Second World War came from various established communities around the world, the centrality of the Imam has been crucial in sustaining their group identification through a process of institutionalised social and economic reform. An increasingly standardised community organisation is directed by the Imam. The *jamaat-khanas* (assembly and prayer halls) were all based on the same pattern, and after the Second World War their organisation was increasingly linked to the complex three-tier council system. Enshrined within their constitution has been a system of personal law through which the Imam can guide all Ismailis according to his own beliefs and values. Through the previous Imam's edicts (*farmans*) seemingly archaic practices such as segregation of the sexes and polygamy have been condemned, and Westernisation in culture, education and social and economic matters has been vigorously pursued. The present Imam has taken the Ismaili commitment to modernity a step further, mainly by developing, expanding and adapting Ismaili institutions. He has been concerned to maintain a degree of autonomy in both material and religious life for the community.

The *jamaat* (community) in Britain was officially constituted in 1954, when the London community through the Aga Khan formally acquired a *jamaat-khana*. A *mukhi* (head of the *jamaat* and official of the *jamaat-khana*) and a *kamadia* (mukhi's deputy) were appointed and a

council was created. By the early 1960s a large number of self-support-
ing students joined the few affluent London-based, East African Ismaili
families. Thus at the core of the Ismaili community in Britain by the
end of the 1960s were relatively young and independent educated,
employable Ismailis who in theory at least would be best able to help
institutionalise and adapt Ismailism to the 'secular' British context if
they wished. The Imam issued a series of guidelines reminding them of
their religious and secular individual and communal obligations in
order to maintain a distinct identity. This encouraged a lengthy process
of institutionalisation in Britain, primarily to fulfil these obligations,
alongside a degree of 'external' assimilation into a secular society. The
periodic formal decrees from the Imam provided the direction for this
institutionalisation, facilitating adaptation to life in Britain. At the
beginning of the 1970s the institutions of the British Ismaili community
were relatively little organised, with the London *jamaat-khana*
described by Clarke as 'a heterogeneous religious group with little
more than language, ritual and ramifying kinship in common',[75] still,
by 1971 it could claim a dozen provincial *jamaat-khanas*. Again, the
importance of the Imam's *farmans* and the 1962 Ismaili Constitution
should not be overlooked, for these continued to guide followers in
Britain in the absence of formal institutions. Moreover, the Ismaili
community in Britain was to a large extent socio-economically self-
sufficient with a diversity of religious commitment and practice in
which, beyond the few fundamentals of the faith, the religious side of
an individual's life is considered a relatively personal matter. The
jamaat-khana was simply not an important part of their lives. According
to Hallam, Ismailis in Britain had 'anglicised Ismailism by the purely
formal, religious role to which they [had] reduced it. It [functioned] for
them as no more than a denomination, an optional adjunct to their
lives.'[76] Many no longer gave *dossandh* (the religious tithe paid annually
to the Imam), since it seemed unnecessary in a welfare state. They
tended also not to observe Ramadan or celebrate *Eid* because it was
likely to fall on weekdays, and all assemblies took place on Saturdays
when the majority of local Ismailis were most able to attend. That said,
by the early 1970s some 65% of Ismailis in London attended the
jamaat-khana at least once a week, but they continued to regard it as a
multi-purpose community centre, where religious ritual was down-
played and worship was primarily a social function.[77]

Clearly, like many other British Muslims, Ismailis tended to adapt their religious practice to the new 'secular' environment, mainly for practical reasons. Ismaili adaptation to life in Britain and initial institutionalisation thus represented a conscious commitment to conform outwardly to secular trends and fashions in behaviour while preserving the 'private sphere' in ethical and moral standards as well as religion.[78] In the 1970s, however, this adaptation had begun to weaken commitment to the Imam. The younger generation of Ismailis increasingly questioned his authority and guidance in temporal and spiritual matters and the hierarchical nature of Ismailism, and this created anxieties for both parents and community leaders. There was real fear that the community might fragment, and thus institutionalisation became imperative, since in its absence it was difficult to see how the Islamic and Ismaili heritage and traditions could be preserved. Regarding the Imam himself,

> As the presence of the Ismailis in Britain changed from a handful of adventurous students to an increasingly large, permanently established community … the leaders and I were faced with the difficult question of determining the steps that we should take to assist the community to establish itself well and definitively in the United Kingdom. We concluded that centres of social and religious life were a condition *sine qua non* to enable the community to practice its faith, maintain its traditions and protect its identity.[79]

The National Council for the UK, according to its 1986 constitution, aimed to 'maintain and foster the unity of the Ismailis and to preserve, protect and strengthen the Islamic social and cultural heritage' and to 'seek co-operation and friendly relations with all other peoples'.[80] Among its initiatives in this regard was the English-language newsletter *UK Ismaili* (later to become *The Ismaili United Kingdom*), launched by the Ismaili Centre in August 1981, to provide information about the 'community' and its institutions, act as a channel of communication, and instill 'a sense of identity and unity'.[81] The Ismaili Centre and the Institute of Ismaili Studies (ISS) were also established. Other initiatives included preventive dental clinics (1981), nursery schools (1982), an exclusive Ismaili Cemetery in Woking, Surrey, acquired by the National Council in 1984 and opened in 1987, and a *Directory of Ismaili Businesses and Professionals in the UK*, published since

1990. Since the mid-1990s *The Ismaili United Kingdom* has published news items fostering a greater sense of the 'global *jamaat*', information pieces on community events, activities and achievements, and articles on business, health and education matters as well as a growing quantity of advertisements from Ismaili businesses, from restaurants to solicitors. The Institute of Ismaili Studies has contributed to it a series of short essays by its academic staff as part of its attempt to 'educate' the community on specifically 'religious' matters and encourage debate and contemplation—within the parameters permitted by the Imam—on issues such as the extent to which Islamic jurisprudence has responded to the 'changing exigencies of altered times'.[82]

Given the importance of education to the Aga Khan and his followers and their concern over the erosion of religious and cultural tradition, the Ismaili community in Britain has developed its own system of imparting religious education. The Ismailia Association of United Kingdom (IA) was established in 1975 to take responsibility for encouraging Ismaili religious education for young British Ismailis, and by 1986 it had set up thirty centres called *Bait al-ilm* (House of knowledge), to give religious education according to the Imam's guidelines.[83] It also trained teachers to work in the centres. However, concerns over the quality of their teaching led to the task of training teachers being transferred to the Institute of Ismaili Studies, which went on systematically to prepare and 'modernise' syllabuses, curricula and teaching materials.[84] The IIS has promoted Ismaili scholarship and learning aimed at ensuring the survival of the Ismaili cultural and literary heritage and traditions in the modern world. According to an official statement, particular attention has been given to issues of modernity that arise as Muslims seek to relate their heritage to the contemporary situation. The Institute's programmes have been informed by the full range and diversity of Islamic practice today, from the Middle East, South and Central Asia and Africa to the industrialised societies of the West, thus 'taking into consideration the full variety of contexts which shape the ideals, beliefs and practices of the faith'.[85] Given the Ismailis' tradition of encouraging women's education, it is not surprising that women have been active in the community's religious and social life. However, where equality of opportunity is concerned there remain fundamental shortcomings, since the patriarchal framework still circumscribes the role of Ismaili women. For instance, a female associate of the *mukhi*, known as the *mukhiani*, is responsible for women's activities and is a representative of women in the *jamaat-khana*, but she is not permitted to lead the ceremonies. Similarly, the Women's Organisation within the National Council 'works to strengthen the role of women as the main source of support within the family, with emphasis on the upbringing of children and the maintenance of the family unit'.[86]

In many ways, then, the institutionalisation of Ismaili Islam has gone the same way as with other Muslim denominations. However, it has developed differently in that unlike other Muslim communities, which recognise no Imamate, Ismailis in Britain continue to be held together as a community with particular doctrines, traditions and customs by the Imam's 'absolute unfettered power and authority over all religious and jamati matters'.[87] Moreover, the present Imam is a 'westernised' man who lives a fairly Western life and hence has sought to implant 'Western' values and practices in contemporary Ismaili doctrine and everyday life. No similar mechanism for institutional change exists among Britain's Sunni Muslims. However, the 'modernity' of Ismaili institutionalisation has inevitably been limited by the Imamate's 'authoritarian nature'. Nevertheless, although many Ismailis retain their spiritual and cultural identi-fications, the vast majority living in Britain's secular context do not pretend that Islam is a total way of life. The small British Ismaili community—probably numbering no more than 10,000, centred around forty-four *jamaat-khanas* nationwide—while remaining fairly 'exclusivist and secretive' has developed into 'a highly efficient, organised, independent and prosperous community'.[88]

The institutionalisation of Islam in Britain has been a complex process, reflecting the immense diversity of the Muslim communities. Since the Second World War, a range of heterogeneous Muslim organisations has emerged representing different memberships, client groups and administrative structures with functions and activities manifesting a multitude of ideologies, aspirations, purposes, strategies and priorities. These reveal converging as well as conflicting concerns, depending on their particular cultural, religious and political orientations. Institutionalisation proceeded at first in ways that gave Muslim communities some control over the ways in which they adapted to British society, offering a measure of protection from stigma and not necessarily on the terms set by the wider society. Many Muslims would claim that the goals envisaged at the beginning of the process have largely been achieved and hence that it has been effective. Facilities are now widely available enabling Muslims to practise their faith in diverse ways, and an infrastructure has been established to sustain Islam among coming generations of British Muslims. There is an extensive network of mosques providing for religious observance, and the attached Quran schools offer basic Islamic instruction to thousands of children. The intervention of organisations such as the Muslim Educational Trust has meant that Muslim pupils in state schools are offered religious educa-tion specific to their faith. Religious commitment regarding dress and diet is widely accepted, due largely to the efforts of dedicated Muslim organisations. Their local and national lobbying has caused schools to be modified to meet the wishes of Muslim parents.

There has been less progress in bringing elements of Islamic family, criminal and economic law within the orbit of the British legal system. Several Muslim organisations have lobbied about this, but with only mixed success.[89] The result is that they have tried to bypass the institu-tions of the state and set up parallel structures to resolve disputes, formally and informally. These institutions have acquired a degree of legitimacy in the eyes of some Muslim communities. Several Sharia courts have been established in England under the aegis of the Islamic Shariah Council, and concentrated their efforts on the informal settle-ment of disputes between Muslims according to Muslim law.[90]

Sectarianism with its rivalries and competing loyalties continues to be a feature of Muslim organisation in Britain, and hampers the quest for unity. Segmentation along ethnic and doctrinal lines has if anything become more institutionalised, and hence the educational and welfare work of Muslim organisations is inevitably sectarian, with doctrinal propaganda and services limited to one sect. While younger Muslims are highly critical of the traditional movements and wish to strip Islam of all cultural accretions, they are hindered by the hold which the old guard retains over religious structures. These structures have prolifer-ated and consolidated. Sectarian organisations have proved durable because of the appeal of the collective identity, rooted in the cultural and religious heritage of the society of origin which they constantly reaffirm. Strong family and community loyalties are maintained through socialisation and personal links between *imams*, religious functionaries and ordinary numbers of the communities, on the basis of old personal connections or personal charisma. The majority of first-generation South Asian Muslims in Britain remain loyal to the generation-old traditions they imbibed in their villages of origin, and disinclined to analyse or challenge them. They are happy with the version of Islam they brought with them.

The institutionalisation of Islam in Britain has been shaped to a great extent by the predominance of male leaders who see 'modernist' interpretations of the position of Muslims in Britain and discourse on Islam as a threat to their legitimacy. Muslim institutionalisation has proceeded in ways determined by the existing legal system, where the position of religious institutions has been subject to implicit and explicit regulation, depending very much on the changing context of British society. In addition, accommodation of Muslim institutions and needs, and support for Islamic ideologies in Britain, have never been forthcoming from an establishment that still harbours doubts about Islam and Muslims as un-British and therefore as alien to British culture and society.

Many Islamic organisations have remained too closely tied to distant traditions to appear organic in the British environment. Earlier emphases on preserving cultural, linguistic and ethnic identities suggested that to become a Muslim meant adopting immigrant cultures and theological doctrines, which did not necessarily connect with the concerns and experiences of the majority population. The result is that most 'indigenous' Muslims who have converted to Islam through the Sufi route have not been willing to accept the immigrant cultural baggage and have maintained separate institutions closer to their requirements. The Association of British Muslims is the foremost example of this kind of development. Nevertheless some indigenisation has taken place among Muslims of immigrant heritage—for instance, with the Islamic Society of Britain—trying to develop a religious consciousness that has little to do with ethnic solidarity.

12

CONCLUSION

BRITISH MUSLIM IDENTITIES

During the summer of 2001, a decade after the Gulf War, riots took place in the north of England, evidently provoked by the British National Party (BNP), whose targeting of Muslims in particular served to inflame antagonism and mutual distrust between Muslim and white communities.[1] In towns such as Oldham, disturbances involving mainly Muslim men of South Asian descent produced violent clashes with the local police, highlighting the considerable discontent felt within local Muslim communities. After the 11 September 2001 terrorist attacks in the United States, British Muslim anxieties increased further, stoked by a hostile media. These have not been eased by subsequent government initiatives, such as the 'anti-terrorism' legislation, which Muslims (as well as non-Muslims) have perceived as discriminating unfairly against them, infringing their civil liberties and incompatible with international standards. All these developments brought British Muslims once more under the spotlight and made them feel highly vulnerable.

However, as our study has shown, the misrepresentation, disadvantage and discrimination experienced by Muslims in late-twentieth-century Britain existed long before the well-publicised events of 2001. Indeed, the view of Islam as impermeable, undifferentiated and immune to the processes of economic, social, ideological and political

403

change has long obscured the complexities of the historical experience of Muslims in different societies. Western 'orientalists' and Islamists alike have tended to emphasise what distinguishes Islam from the West, and have presented it—along with Muslims themselves—as the 'Other' or the 'infidel within'.[2] Over the centuries the Christian/secular West has effectively constructed and stigmatised an Islam that has little resemblance to anything of value in ordinary Muslim lives. It has conjured it up as a powerful and dangerous force—irrational, violent and fanatical—and requiring tight control but also to be kept at a distance. More recently the imagery of the 1979 Iranian revolution, the public burning of Salman Rushdie's *The Satanic Verses*, the hysteria orchestrated before and after Iraq's invasion of Kuwait and the 11 September attacks have combined to confirm an antipathy in the Western popular mind towards Islam and Muslims.

Immediately after September 2001 this antipathy was expressed in a number of ways. Muslims around the world were targeted during a period of 'reprisals', and those in Britain were not exempt. Both adults and children were attacked, like the girl who had her *hijab* pulled off outside her school by a non-Muslim adult, and many who were punched, spat at, publicly doused with alcohol, pelted with rotten fruit and vegetables, or called murderers. Some were sacked from their jobs; others received death threats. Sikhs whose beards and turbans gave the impression that they were Muslims were abused. Vandals attacked mosques and Asian-run businesses around the country, and bottles of alcohol, fire-bombs and excrement were pushed through letter-boxes. Many mosques were said not to have reported attacks because of fear of reprisals.[3]

The British Prime Minister Tony Blair sought to convince the public that the events of 11 September had nothing to do with Islam or Muslims *per se* and that Muslims should not be targeted in any way. Police forces across Britain condemned the attacks and cooperated with Muslim, Hindu and Sikh communities in a renewed effort to work against ethnic and religious discrimination. Furthermore, organisations representing a range of religious denominations came together to pray for the 11 September victims. Nevertheless, the mainstream media in particular continued reproducing stereotypes of Muslims as 'fanatics'. Sections of the British press typically called for the rooting-out and bombing of Islamic 'fundamentalists' and did not distinguish between extremists and the vast majority of Muslims who were peaceful and law-abiding. In the event, only a handful of British Muslims were roused by a combination of disillusionment and anger towards Western Christian/secular countries, loyalty to the *umma*, the lure of 'martyrdom' and the 'obligation' of *jihad*, to try to assist or defend Al-Qaeda or the Taliban in Afghanistan. And only a small minority of British Muslims did not see the attacks in the United States as an act to be condemned and made that opinion public. Nevertheless, the media persisted in giving these small factions extensive coverage, although the overwhelming majority of British Muslims see their religion as a moderate one. A survey for *Eastern Eye* (Britain's biggest-selling Asian newspaper) showed that 87% of Muslims polled considered themselves loyal to Britain, even though they were generally less supportive of British military action in Afghanistan than the white majority (76% in a *Sunday Times* poll in early November 2001).[4]

By the end of the twentieth century, as we have seen, the majority of British Muslims belonged to diaspora communities from diverse back-grounds concentrated along ethnic lines in different parts of urban Britain, and their persistent physical segregation from the white population, particularly since the Second World War, greatly inhibited social interaction. Thus a degree of 'ghettoisation' evolved in several of Britain's inner cities. As the result, 'parallel communities' still exist there with different social configurations and behavioural norms and values. Indeed, the fact that they continue to experience relatively high levels of socio-economic disadvantage has reinforced patterns of exclusion in many British Muslim communities.

Muslims migrating to Britain brought their religious identity with them into a new sociocultural setting, which in turn presented them with a range of challenges. At the same time, Muslims born and raised in Britain inherited an attachment to their families' countries of origin, albeit a diminishing one, as well as the problem of securing their own place in British society. They had to work hard to sustain their religious beliefs and practices, since the quasi-secular structure of British society, far from providing confirmation for a religious world-view, tended increasingly to make it irrelevant. But the more Muslim communities became rooted in Britain, the more their members strove to put structures in place to enable them to live their lives according to their own understanding of Islamic practice. In short, space in public life during the later decades of the twentieth century has been 'stretched' to include Islam. Many facilities now exist in Britain enabling Islam to be practised in ways reflecting the diversity within the Muslim communities.

However, it could be argued that less progress has been made in incorporating elements of Islamic law in various areas of English law. Muslim organisations have long lobbied in this regard but with mixed success. The result is that, where feasible, they have tried to bypass the British state's institutions, setting up parallel structures to resolve disputes formally and informally, and these now command a degree of legitimacy in the eyes of some Muslim communities. In broader political terms, the engagement of Muslims with British society has taken different forms and they have perhaps been more active than most other minority groups, they operating both inside the political system and beyond it. Again, the range of political responses pursued has underlined the differentiated character of Muslim communities in Britain, as well as the range of interpretations of Islam—continually contested and negotiated—that they have invoked to justify and construct particular political strategies. Yet in the context of economic deprivation and social exclusion some British Muslims have regarded participation in mainstream politics as an ideological betrayal and as part of the process of cultural homogenisation. Alienated, frustrated and resentful, they have lost faith in the wider, formal political structures, and have instead pursued street politics, confronting British state power through direct and disruptive collective action. This spontaneous and relatively unorganised political response by certain groups of British Muslims has arguably produced very few positive results and much more in terms of negative backlash from the wider society. In the mean time the majority of British Muslims patiently carried on attempting to penetrate those political institutions with the power to decide policies and allocate resources. Undoubtedly their under-representation in the 'corridors of power' (e.g. appointments to public service positions) reflected a lack of recognition of their contribution to society. But the steady growth of British Muslims' incorporation in the formal political system during the late twentieth century suggests that they have in some ways been increasingly accepted as part of—and by—the wider British society.

CONCLUSION: BRITISH MUSLIM IDENTITIES

Thus, British Muslims have responded in various ways to the challenges of living in Britain. For instance, they have been particularly affected by the largely secular environment in which they live, and responsive to it. In this context new perspectives on relations with the wider society have emerged, effectively encouraging participation rather than the intro-version that is still a characteristic of Muslim migrant communities. So while many British Muslims continue to fulfil their religious obligations, some find that the rhythms and demands of contemporary life have relegated religion to the margins of their social and working lives. For many young Muslims popular Western culture holds an increasing appeal, which is reflected in their rising consumption of its material and cultural products. Secular pursuits, rather than specifically religious ones, occupy much of their lives. At the same time there have been creative attempts at synthesis, so that many British Muslims are more ready than in the past to engage with the British society and state, although some still want to distinguish themselves by offering religiously based alternatives. Taken as a whole, Muslim patterns of political and social engagement, together with their various approaches to participation in public and cultural life, have come to reflect changing attitudes to the country in which they have sought to play an increasingly active role.

Alongside the trend towards greater secularisation, some British Muslims have become firmer and more uncompromising in their religious convictions. Critical of the 'Islam of their forefathers', which they view as increasingly irrelevant to the British context, younger Muslims in particular have sought 'true' Islam through their own interpretation of religious sources. Often feeling devalued, humiliated and stigmatised by mainstream society, they started to explore strategies designed to resist the onslaught of what they perceive as a hegemonic ideology and political culture. Their reading of religious texts has led them to seek solutions in 'religious extremism'; they have been drawn by *jihad*, which they interpret as the defence of Muslims under threat. Advances in global communications have meant that British Muslims can now respond quickly to conflicts involving Muslims elsewhere in the world and can use them to publicise and win support for their own religio-political perspectives. As a result, radical Muslim organisations are in a position to offer alternative interpretations of events to those in the Western media, and to gather support among the disillusioned—hence the 'jihadist' mentality among some sections of the British Muslim population.

All the same, a range of perspectives on religion has evolved among British Muslims, linked to age, ethnic background, socio-economic circumstances, education and gender. As Muslims have acquired a more established presence in Britain, debate has intensified and produced a rethinking of Islamic issues. The freedom of thought and expression available in Britain has opened up opportunities for Muslims to reassess beliefs, traditions and practices, and the coexistence of different Muslim cultures in Britain has led to the exchange of ideas across sectarian lines.

So while there is polarisation, there are also signs of growing interaction and dialogue. The coming together of diverse groups of Muslims through migration, settlement and, to a limited extent, conversion has generated both 'fission' and 'fusion'. British Muslims are more sensitive than ever before to the differences between them over how they lead their lives and practise Islam. At times this has caused a tension, but simultaneously they are asserting the continued relevance of the Muslim *umma*, however widely dispersed and fractured, and its concerns in their lives.

These processes seem to have produced somewhat contrary effects. They have given rise to new ideas about identity and citizenship, so that many young Muslims now place the religious component of their identity above their ethnicity. They are quick to claim the entitlements of citizenship that being 'British' gives them; but while they may reject aspects of Britishness, they do not automatically see themselves as belonging somewhere else instead. British Muslim identities at the beginning of the twenty-first century have been shaped by evolving Muslim and British social history and culture. Some British Muslims are Muslims first and then British; others are the other way round. Far from there being a single, clearly defined perception of British Muslim identity, the notion is complex, diverse and equivocal. The result is not a neatly identifiable British Muslim identity but a range of identities co-existing within Britain's Muslim communities.

All these developments have taken place within Britain's undoubtedly Islamophobic environment—that contributes to and reinforces the disadvantage and discrimination experienced by many Muslims. While the 2001 riots may have hardened negative images of Britain's Muslims, they were themselves partly a reaction to anti-Muslim provocation. Government policies have also been accused of acquiescing in popular Islamophobic sentiment. Critics have seen evidence of this in the Labour government's campaign to stop so-called forced marriages, its 2002 White Paper looking at immigration and citizenship, and its reluctance to fund Muslim schools. Similarly, the Anti-Terrorism, Crime and Security Act 2001 following the events of 11 September was taken as an official reflection of popular anti-Muslim backlash. The eleven suspects interned under the Act were all Muslims. At the same time the government's failure to retain the Act's original clause against incitement to religious hatred, which was intended to contain the anti-Muslim backlash provoked by 11 September, reinforced the Muslim view that the government lacked commitment to protecting their communities.

But if Islamaphobia in Britain is nothing new, how deeply ingrained are present-day attitudes towards Islam and Muslims in Britain? Can we trace a continuous line from the Crusades through the Ottoman Empire and European colonialism to the Islamophobia of the 1990s?[5] Norman Daniel, in his introduction to the revised edition of his seminal work *Islam and the West: The Making of an Image*, tends to see this as an enduring pattern, and earliest Christian reactions to Islam as having been much the same as they were until quite recently—the tradition has been continuous and it is still alive.[6] Indeed, as our study has highlighted, it is remarkable how often in the history of the Christian–Muslim engagement the same themes and stereotypes have been used to represent Islam and Muslims in Britain and how often stories from the past are invoked to reignite fears, anxieties and animosities generated by events in the present. Since the 1980s the process of demonisation has become, if anything, 'more explicit, more extreme and more dangerous'.[7]

However, to assert that hostility to Islam is deeply ingrained in the white British psyche and relies for its justification on invoking stereotypes, images and ideas developed over centuries of encounter between Muslims and the West would appear to be somewhat simplistic and historically contentious. Fred Halliday has provided a different perspective on the issue, pointing out that there have been many periods in the past when antagonism between Muslims and the British has drawn on assumptions in which negative ideas about Islam or Muslim practices *per se* have not been spotlighted. He has argued that even in the current period when it is claimed that Islam is seen as a major threat to Western civilisation, there is no conclusive evidence for the validity of this thesis. Instances of anti-Muslim attitudes have certainly surfaced in particular conjunctures but, according to Halliday, it is not necessarily or always Islam as a creed that is being maligned. Depending on the context and the nature of the conflict, other labels such as ethnic and national origins have been selected, imbued with negative connotations and applied to people who also happen to be Muslims.[8]

There is much that makes sense in Halliday's argument: just as it is impossible to demonstrate an unbroken connection between the attitudes engendered in Europe at the time of the Crusades and those at the beginning of the third millennium, it is equally not possible to attribute antipathy towards British Muslims solely to religious difference. Other dimensions of their identity, such as the ethnic, have also affected the view taken of them by British society. But the process has been complex, since the particular aspect of Muslim identity that is reinvented and reinterpreted to justify frictions has depended on contingent material factors and the broader social and political influences in society.

The history of the Muslim presence in Britain suggests that hostility towards Muslims has taken a variety of forms, from discriminatory treatment to physical violence, that includes assaults on individuals, desecration of graves and attacks on mosques and Muslim community buildings and centres. Yet attitudes towards Muslims in Britain have varied according to contemporary circumstances, and have depended also on the kind of Muslims involved: there was a world of difference between those represented by Quilliam and the Arab seaman in the early twentieth century, and this difference had as much to do with their colour as with the way their religion influenced their lives. However, we can also see that there were persistent stereotypes about Islam that were common throughout the nineteenth and twentieth centuries and which political developments in the wider world did little to dispel.

We have highlighted the different ways, political and social, by which Muslims have tried to deal with the prevailing Islamophobic climate since the early nineteenth century. Their strategies have also been shaped by the context in which they have found themselves. At the height of the West's political and intellectual dominance, Islamic modernism associated with Sayyid Ahmed Khan and Muhammad Abduh emerged as a way of preserving a religious dimension in a world moving rapidly towards a scientific view of life. In late-nineteenth and early-twentieth-century Britain leading Muslims such as Abdullah Quilliam, Khawja Kamaluddin and Lord Headley followed in these modernists' footsteps, recognising in their thought the potential for offering Islam in an idiom that would be understood in Britain's secularising environment. After the Second World War, the context changed as decolonisation gave many in the Muslim world a greater sense of political self-determination. Britain's increasing Muslim population, made up largely of people from a rural background, settled and reproduced religio-cultural practices drawn from elsewhere, but by the early 1970s global developments had brought about a new situation, and Islamism came to be offered as a credible challenge to Western hegemony. But Islamism has arguably proved to be just as much a strategy to resist Eurocentric dominance as the Islamic modernism pursued by Muslim élites earlier in the twentieth century.

Indeed, British Muslim history tells us that, while it would appear that threats (real or perceived) to their religious values and identity have mobilised Muslims, irrespective of their background, other issues more closely related to their social conditions of life and material interests have also shaped the nature and priorities of their communities, whether in early or late-twentieth-century Britain. Just as during the First World War when Muslims in Britain agitated in support of Ottoman integrity partly to protect and enhance their own place within British society, so it is possible to interpret current Muslim activities to secure greater respect for Islam as motivated largely by the desire to secure *equal* status in the country. In both cases, there are close links between perceptions about what is happening in the wider world, connected to the power of the West, and the immediate position of Muslims living in Britain. Herein lie fundamental similarities. The main difference has hinged on the style in which this 'debate' or 'lobbying' has taken place and the strategies pursued by different groups of British Muslims at different times to promote a visible Islamic presence in Britain.

Around the middle of the twentieth century another watershed was reached when Muslims were able to draw on much greater financial and other resources to establish the kind of Islamic institutions befitting their expanding presence in Britain. The sheer growth in overall numbers was significant in this expansion, as were accompanying shifts in class, generational structure and education. The character of the Muslim presence in Britain changed greatly when a large number of rural, working-class Muslims, representing diverse strands, arrived in the 1960s and 1970s—hence the somewhat insular and tradition-bound approach of the majority of migrant Muslims as well as the more recent radical developments among younger British-born generations. It equally explains the differences between the more substantial and close-knit communities and the more marginal and dispersed ones. Where the numbers involved remain comparatively small, there is still evidence of that earlier, more relaxed approach, albeit subject to change as a result of the shifts in outlook and approach generally within Britain's Muslim communities.

Thus in the history of Muslims in Britain one can observe significant changes and continuities in their varied experiences and interactions. Muslim identities in Britain in the late nineteenth century and the first half of the twentieth were shaped by negative attitudes and assumptions to an even greater degree than a century later. This was an age when identity was hardening in Britain, and when that identity was beginning to be both enhanced and challenged by the interactions taking place between British society and peoples with other traditions and ways of life. Muslims were caught up in this process and seemed to suffer on both counts: ideologically their religious identity was regarded as antithetical to 'Britishness', and their ethnic difference was an obstacle to 'fitting in'. As for continuities, the similarities between the kinds of issues that engaged earlier generations of Muslims and those which emerged towards the end of the twentieth century are remarkable: the veil, 'swine and wine', apostasy and the blasphemy law, the privileged position of the Church of England, loyalty to the British state versus the *umma*, and the thorny question of ethnic, religious and national identity. All these issues tend to exclude and marginalise British Muslims, many of whom however have persisted in articulating their anxieties and disaffection through a religious discourse.

CONCLUSION: BRITISH MUSLIM IDENTITIES

The historical evolution of Muslim communities in Britain shows that they are above all the products of their history. It has been a dialectical process defined by the specific and relatively stable sources of Islamic identity as expressed in fundamental beliefs and ritual practices, and by the changing configuration of local, national, cultural and linguistic factors. The main difference is that, whereas in the past this configuration of the local was relatively stable, in today's continually globalising world the local/global culture is in rapid and continuous flux. Furthermore, identity, ethnicity, religion, class and gender are all susceptible to historical processes as well as to internal and external factors that have been reimagined in this context. Of course, it could be argued that in any environment the concept of Muslim identity has continuously evolved from its earliest formation and has never been static and immutable—rather, the specifically Islamic element has always synthesised with pre-existing local cultures in order to take root. The globalising world does not change this dialectical pattern, but it does radically transform the parameters of 'local' culture, with the result that now it might be said that the entire globe has become localised and thus the formal elements of a specifically Islamic identity are having to be accommodated within a much wider framework.

In these circumstances we find that the movement towards Islamic homogeneity, on the one hand, and towards fragmentation on the other, affects Muslim identity in complex ways. It could be argued that while Muslim identity has been splintered by the multiplicity of inputs from the global environment, particular modes of this identity have also become globally entrenched. But even this homogenisation, largely understood as the ideologisation of Islam, can be seen as part of the process of fragmentation, since it is only one mode of Muslim identity and not all Muslims identify with it. The homogenising aspect of globalisation, reflected in an anti-Muslim slant in the Western-dominated global media, provokes a reactive mode of identity. At the same time the globalisation of a relatively anti-Western Islamist ideology itself serves as a kind of shadow of the 'enemy'. The tension between local and global forces sets off two processes, one tending towards the homogenisation of global culture and the other towards differentiation of cultures—globally and locally.

Undoubtedly globalisation, in the form of new technology, has made the Muslim *umma* more integrated. For Muslims it has made for greater communication between them worldwide and thus brought them closer. Because of this process of compression they are more aware than ever before of their social position and their cultural and economic power around the world. Islamist resistance movements effectively transcend local boundaries, serving as mirror-images of what they oppose. They are committed to making Islamic ideology pervasive—in one interpretation, as a religious response to globalisation, multiculturalism and post-modern pluralism.[9] This reaction may be attributed to the labelling of Muslims as extremists and terrorists—thus reinforcing an Islamophobic environment, which in turn promotes extremism—and to the fact that cultural globalisation is seen as antagonistic to Islamic culture. These Islamists uphold traditional Islamic values and stress the necessity of a return to tradition, even if they do so in ways that are far from traditional. Modernists, on the other hand, seek to go into the modern world with a minimum of cultural and religious baggage, and they too do this in a globalised manner. In the former case, a radical Muslim perspective, taking advantage of global communication, presents itself in sharp contrast to the images presented by the Western-controlled media and gathers support among the most disillusioned and alienated.

The 1990s saw a vast growth in the Islamic web scene and the explosion in the number of sites and their multifaceted nature now require more searching and specialised treatment. Through computer-mediated communication, Muslim organisations, their ideas, their interpretation of religious materials and information about their offerings have become globally accessible.[10] They have acquired the capability to influence Muslims and non-Muslims in numbers larger than ever before, as they come to consider the nature of Islamic authority, the fulfilment of religious obligations and the countless issues in the 'secular' domains of British society. Many established Muslim organisations now communicate by the Internet.

In general the ideologies and objectives that Muslim organisations pursue have changed little. Their output amounts to little more than old topics and ideas in a new context. However, their practice has been transformed to some degree by the use they increasingly make of sophisticated technology to disseminate their ideas and offer their services. The transmission of religious traditions and practice through such media makes them much more accessible to their Muslim audiences in Britain; some organisations are devoting increased resources to the production of relevant material in English, making it readily accessible to younger British-educated Muslims. The oral traditions of imparting learning and knowledge are being similarly repackaged to reach a much larger public as these organisations make greater use of electronic media.

The establishment of independent Internet sites is a new departure in the institutionalisation of Islam in Britain. Muslim organisations operating solely through the Internet have widened the dissemination of Islamic information, messages and ideas very effectively. As Gary Bunt has put it:

> The spectrum of Islamic understandings and content available online within Cyber Islamic Environments ranges from: propagation-orientated *Sunni* (orthodox) and government-linked Islamic sites; through to a spectrum of *Sufi* (Muslim mystics) and *Shi'a*-related sites; and non-orthodox, so-called 'schismatic' or 'Islamic sect' sites. Common threads of Muslim beliefs, and different shades of meaning are represented on many of these sites.

Although the Internet is used to disseminate Islamic 'conventional wisdom', that is not the whole picture. These groups 'cannot be perceived as a monolithic entity, and ... generalisations cannot be made relating to a single Cyber Islamic Environment, or any shared agendas'.[11] In Bunt's view, while computer-mediated environments are still far from offering much space in which uninhibited debates among divergent viewpoints can be conducted in an atmosphere of mutual tolerance and understanding, they do now to some extent 'provide a means for diverse Muslim platforms to express their opinion on a variety of matters from sacred to profane', with the potential to make some impact. The availability of religious texts on CD-ROMs or electronically formatted Islamic materials on sites such as the Islamic Computing Centre opens up possibilities for individual independent reflection, understanding and intellectual analysis without any external influence. Consequently, while there is support and cooperation among many Islamic websites, there is also 'internecine "web war" between different ideals or methods or even theological differences', with rivals having no compunction about 'hacking' each other's computer systems to destroy or steal data or disrupt websites.[12]

Thus in some ways an electronically connected *umma* is emerging with an awareness of commonalities as well as differences. The 'virtual mosque', 'digital minbar', 'digital Islamic library' and 'digital Islamic bookshop' have been established; sermons, recitations of the Quran and prayers can be offered in 'real-time'. However, 'Cyber Islamic Environments' have also opened up possibilities for *ijtihad* and so loosened the homogenising stranglehold of 'orthodox' Islamic organisations. Indeed, there are databases on specific sites containing advice from a range of religious 'authorities'; this widens the capacity to exercise *ijtihad* and apply it with a view to making relatively informed choices. Through Multi-User Dungeons (MUDs) and 'chatrooms', computer technology has enabled people to participate in discussions, within Islamic perspectives, on contemporary issues. This does not mean that the influence of the *ulama* or the power of the oral tradition is yet in terminal decline; indeed, the new technologies of the mass media are channels for reaching Muslims at the grass-roots level and are thus increasingly important as sources of popular mobilisation.

However, there is no doubt that the Internet has also helped to increase the availability of the (many critical) Islamic perspectives and voices in all their diversity. Not only have minority Islamic sects been able to reach wider audiences through electronic media, but other alternative interpretations and expressions of Islam are discernible through the music of Yusuf Islam and Nusrat Fateh Ali Khan.[13] And the balance of power between the established Islamic movements and more peripheral ones has tended to be evened out on-line. No religious position need be accepted as universal or denounced as irredeemably blasphemous. By injecting the element of reasoning and tolerance of differences into Islamic discourse, the Internet has generally had a moderating influence on debate. However, this diversity has in some ways remained limited, partly because many sectors and platforms do not have a presence on-line. Up to the time of writing it has been predominantly the educated élite who engage with the 'digital *umma*'. Web designers and the religious authorities they offer for discussion, guidance and 'counselling' control the scope and method of presentation of information and ideas. So, for instance, Sunni-centric revivalist and reformist perspectives embodying specific interpretations based on the Quran, Hadith and *fiqh* seem to have established a pervasive presence on the Internet. Nevertheless, the Internet has allowed the creation of organisations and the expression of views that make possible the countering of enable mainstream Islamic world-views to be countered. 'Virtual' Islamic organisations, while similar to their 'real' traditional counterparts in their mission statements, structures and activities, have an approach that is more broad-based and less sectarian.

The Internet has helped to inform and potentially to empower those, Muslims, especially women, who feel marginalised and even excluded from traditional channels of self-expression. Examples of how this technology has given 'deviant' Muslims a voice of their own are the two sites, Queer Muslims and Queer Jihad, which provide space for Muslim homo-sexuals and bisexuals who are not only struggling to resolve their 'gay, lesbian, bisexual, transgendered' and Muslim identities, but also challenging the views which deny them this reconciliation.[14] Al-Fatiha is one organisation that has appeared on the scene representing gay and lesbian Muslims and engaging other Muslims in discussions on issues and views that were considered taboo till recently and have remained subject to strict censorship among traditional Muslim organisations. The Internet has thus provided platforms for dialogue and the airing of contentious issues without fear of physical attack. The absence of physical proximity and the existence of personal anonymity prevents discussions from degenerating into emotionally charged and violent confrontations. This perceived relative safety of the Internet has created a climate in which people have been encouraged to raise sensitive questions—such as the enjoyment of music, premarital sex, adultery, children born out of wedlock, homosexuality, suicide, organ transplantation, *in vitro* fertilisation, cloning and euthanasia. While much of the discussion is carried on within an 'orthodox' Islamic perspective, the communications revolution has made it possible to by-pass and even challenge traditional religious authority and so potentially undermine it by claiming validity for alternative moral and intellectual viewpoints. Thus the extensive and enduring ideological control of traditional Islamic organisations over Muslim Britain is being transcended.

All this begs the question of what impact globalisation has had on British Muslim identity.[15] For the vast majority of British Muslims it has not substantially altered the basics of faith. Satellite dishes incessantly beaming in the 'homeland' cultures have helped sustain the values, traditions and norms of their societies of origin. Islamic belief, at least regarding the raw material of traditional dogma and doctrine, does not appear to have been dislodged, although it is difficult to say what its spiritual or psychological impact has been and to what extent dogma translates into political activism. Islam has certainly remained the key determinant of identity. Where the implications of globalisation for individual and social life are concerned, there appears to be considerable variation. Here the influence of a liberal, secular and cosmopolitan local culture, greatly strengthened by the influx of similar forces from the global arena, is clearly discernible. Secularising tendencies have undoubtedly been accelerated by globalisation. People can read, watch and listen across international boundaries, and significant changes in the thought processes and ways of understanding Islam have accompanied these changes in behaviour. The main reason for changes in thinking may well be the day-to-day environment rather than careful reflection. These environments affect not only habits, images and products but also ideas, theories and ideologies; thus they influence religious orientation. So, for instance, while a life-style influenced by secularism may displace a religious practice in someone's daily life, it may also contain the politicising influence of the religious ideology that suggest combating Western imperialism with an Islamist solution, and thus offering a paradoxical 'secular/militant' Muslim identity.

Hence, enormous diversity can be discerned among British Muslims, and particularly of the younger age-groups, in religious belief, understanding and practice and in social relationships. Some believe that in order to be Muslim one need merely bear witness; others insist that Islam is a way of life. For example, Sunni modernists call for flexibility in religious thought and for a fresh interpretation of the scriptures; they favour reopening the 'gate of *ijtihad*' and do not wish to rely totally on the 'medieval synthesis' which, in their view, the four established schools of Islamic jurisprudence represent. Islamists, on the other hand, adopt a more rigid and holistic approach. Indeed the impact of globalisation on religious practice is reflected in the wide spectrum of adherence to the normative rituals, ranging from the maximalists to the minimalists to the indifferent. Here the influence of the diversification of choice is apparent, together with the secular content of much that is offered for the individual to choose from in the 'global market'. Even if most of the accessible choices are not intrinsically contrary to religion, their very diversity, volume and density constitute an implicitly secular force—that pushes religion to the margins of the field of attention.[16]

Thus, no single British Muslim identity can be clearly defined. It is largely the product of a synthesis of Muslim and British cultural dimensions (both with deep historical roots but not fixed and immutable—indeed, both have been subject to paradoxical forces of globalisation) and is still developing and crystallising. While it acknowledges British citizenship, it does not necessarily generate much sense of empathy towards the pain or problems of Britain (e.g. fighting in a war or supporting sports teams). In any case the sense of belonging and patriotism has receded with the advent of plural societies. The heterogeneity, in practice, of British Muslim identity is rooted in a clearly observed diversification of social and global environments, culture and religious tendencies, all expressed in a range of different attitudes towards Western culture. The result is several types of British Muslim identity rather than one type which is neatly identifiable. Living within one culture while belonging to another is a consequence of the global movement of people across boundaries. Muslim identity has been shown to be a complex matrix of perceptions: it is internally differentiated, and its precise nature can only emerge from empirical studies.

Over recent decades, the attraction of the *umma* conceived as a social expression of the worldwide Muslim community—with no separation between the individual and the community, the social and the spiritual, on the temporal and the eternal—has grown among sections of Britain's Muslims. Many have sought to re-establish a global Muslim *umma*, embracing the idea of unity in diversity and Durkheim's concept of 'collective consciousness', and to safeguard what is left of the fragmenting collective Muslim consciousness, through either traditional/conservative or Islamist strategies. In both a local response to the perceived global reality of a disunited and increasingly fragmented *umma* can be seen. The Westernisation of culture has meant in practice the creation of 'trans-religious' values, but while in the past the central Islamic state was viewed as the main unifying force for the community of believers, creating a homogenised consciousness, it is no longer 'a cultural entity patterned on the norms of any one dominant group or groups'. Instead it exists within and is expressed through diverse cultural groups—'diversity within unity'.[17] This has obliged Muslims to become more engaged with other peoples, nations, world-views, religions and ideologies to work for a set of moral objectives that can be defined together. It requires that the so-called *umma* of other people is respected as part of a multiracial, multi-cultural, multi-religious and pluralist society.[18]

Thus Muslims in Britain have responded to modernity and plurality over time in various ways. Some have become firm and uncompromising in their scriptural absolutism, which can be seen as a way of countering 'the pluralism and relativism engendered by modernity' and of overcoming the plurality of ideological dissonance in Britain.[19] However, they are not sure whether to detest liberal secularist modernism for its tolerance or to denounce it 'for not being tolerant enough, notably of their own intransigence'.[20] Many young British Muslims feel they have integrated to varying degrees—from those who see it within their capacity to speak fluent English and seek employment in mixed settings, to those who interact with their British counterparts but maintain close friendships within their own ethnic groups, to those who are even more assimilated.

Living in a culturally and religiously plural Britain has brought about radical changes in gender relations among Muslims. The practice of wearing the *hijab*, so closely associated with Muslim women in the popular perception, is being transformed in the British context as the influence of traditional authority and its prescriptions diminishes in this and other spheres. While some Muslim women (by no means the majority) wear the headscarf out of religious obligation, this does not prevent them or those who have adopted it more as a mark of identity from interacting socially with unrelated men or operating freely in the public sphere. It is likely that in time British Muslim women, as they pass through the educational system and become more economically engaged, will be in a better position to assert and secure their rights both within and outside their communities.

British Muslims, however, are questioning not only the West but also Islam itself. In this process they are seeking to create a kind of Islam better able to meet the dilemmas of British life in a rapidly globalising context. Living in a diaspora has compelled British Muslims to encounter alternative articulations and interpretations. They have also been encouraged, partly through the resurrection of such Islamic principles as *darura* (the doctrine of necessity that allows for concession and transgression of religious prescriptions under conditions of absolute need), *ijtihad, ikhtilaf, istihsan* and *istislah* to generate innovative critical thinking capable of producing 'a new theology' more responsive to the pressures and assumptions of a relativising post-modern and sceptical world. While the modernist reform of Islam is not yet a dominant tendency, it is undoubtedly growing. Historical investigation is helping to deconstruct hitherto immutable theology, and the question of authenticity is being vigorously debated. A large body of British Muslim opinion now agrees that it is futile to talk of Islam as undifferentiated, but it is also difficult to identify several distinct 'Islams'. In reality, the perception and practices of Islam are fluid and tend to overlap and, on one level, Muslims do have a sense of a common, integrated and identifiable world-view. For the vast majority of Muslims Islam remains and operates as the 'master signifier'.

British Muslims, therefore, are increasingly challenging the hegemony of traditional authority and its intolerance of hybridity. At the same time, they are re-examining issues of power and 'othering' within their religion. The relativistic character of their discourse means that no particular positions are being negated: 'difference is negotiated rather than eradicated'.[21] As part of this discourse, Muslims living in the beginning of twenty-first-century British transnational space are creating a range of identities that combine their consciousness of the global *umma* with their British citizenship—identities which have come over time to be constructed in terms less of ethnicity and nation than of a particular ethic.

NOTES

PREFACE TO THE NEW EDITION

1. Jack Straw (former Foreign Secretary), 'I felt uneasy talking to some-one I couldn't see', *The Guardian*, 6 October 2006; [The veil is] 'a vis-ible statement of separation and of difference', 'In quotes: Jack Straw on the veil', BBC News, http://news.bbc.co.uk/1/hi/uk_poli-tics/5413470.stm, accessed 18 July 2017.
2. For example, 'Katie Hopkins reported to police after "final solution" Manchester attack tweet', *The Guardian*, 23 May 2017, https://www.theguardian.com/uk-news/2017/may/23/manchester-attack-police-investigate-katie-hopkins-final-solution-tweet; 'Manchester attack: intern terror suspects, urges Cambridge-based writer', Cambridge News, 23 May 2017, http://www.cambridge-news.co.uk/news/cambridge-news/manchester-attack-intern-terror-suspects-13078688, accessed 18 July 2017.
3. Sayeeda Warsi, *The Enemy Within: A Tale of Muslim Britain*, London, 2017.
4. 'Number of UK Muslims exceeds three million for first time', *The Telegraph*, 31 January 2016; 'Muslims in Numbers: A Demographic, Socio-economic and Health profile of Muslims in Britain drawing on the 2011 Census', Muslim Council of Britain, January 2015, p. 16, http://www.mcb.org.uk/wp-content/uploads/2015/02/MCBCensus Report_2015.pdf, accessed 20 July 2017.
5. 'According to the British Social Attitudes (BSA) survey, in 2003, 48 per cent of Britons worried that an increase in the Muslim popula-tion threatened and would weaken Britain's national identity. By 2013, that had risen to 62 per cent', James Kirkup, 'British Muslims: integra-tion and segregation are about economics, not values', *The Telegraph*, 13 February 2015.
6. Ibid; also see 'Britain is becoming more diverse, not more segregated', The Conversation, 17 November 2016, https://theconversation.com/

britain-is-becoming-more-diverse-not-more-segregated-68610; Gemma Catney, 'The Changing Geographies of Ethnic Diversity in England and Wales, 1991–2011', *Population, Space and Place*, 22, 2016, pp. 750–765.

7. *The Telegraph*, 13 February 2015; also see 'More Segregation or More Mixing?', Centre on Dynamics of Ethnicity, University of Manchester, December 2012, p. 1, http://www.ethnicity.ac.uk/medialibrary/briefingsupdated/more-segregation-or-more-mixing.pdf., accessed 18 July 2017.

8. '32% of all Muslim households were overcrowded against a national average of 7%', Housing–Overcrowding, Policy Research Centre, http://www.policyresearch.org.uk/index.php?option=com_content&view=article&id=186&Itemid=74, accessed 20 July 2017.

9. Deborah Phillips, 'Black Minority Ethnic Concentration, Segregation and Dispersal in Britain', *Urban Studies*, 35, 10, 1998, pp. 1681–1702; https://www.theguardian.com/commentisfree/2016/nov/02/segregation-inner-cities-racism-ethnic-minority-communities-white-people, accessed 21 July 2017.

10. 'Britain becoming more segregated than 15 years ago, says race expert', *The Guardian*, 23 May 2016.

11. Ted Cantle and Eric Kauffman, 'Is segregation increasing in the UK?', Open Democracy, 2 November 2016, https://www.opendemocracy.net/wfd/ted-cantle-and-eric-kaufmann/is-segregation-on-increase-in-uk; the following offer a range of perspectives on the dynamics of this issue: 'Call for action to tackle growing ethnic segregation across UK', *The Guardian*, 1 November 2016; for a counterpoint see Ludi Simpson and Nissa Finney, 'Parallel lives and ghettos in Britain: facts or myths?', *Geography*, 95, 3, Autumn 2010, pp. 124–131; Kehinde Andrews, 'Segregation isn't the problem in Britain's inner cities—it's old-fashioned racism', *The Guardian*, 2 November 2016.

12. Aisha Gani, 'Muslim population in England and Wales nearly doubles in 10 years', *The Guardian*, 11 February 2015, https://www.theguardian.com/world/2015/feb/11/muslim-population-england-wales-nearly-doubles-10-years, accessed 21 July 2017.

13. 'British Muslims in Numbers: A Demographic, Socio-economic and Health profile of Muslims in Britain drawing on the 2011 Census', Muslim Council of Britain, January 2015, pp. 46–50, http://www.mcb.org.uk/wp-content/uploads/2015/02/MCBCensusReport_2015.pdf, accessed on 18 July 2017.

14. Siobhan Fenton, '6 charts which show the employment barriers faced by British Muslims', *The Independent*, 11 August 2016, http://www.independent.co.uk/news/uk/home-news/muslims-more-likely-to-be-

unemployed-than-any-other-social-group-in-the-uk-mps-warn-a7185451.html, accessed on 18 July 2017.

15. 'Muslims in Numbers: A Demographic, Socio-economic and Health profile of Muslims in Britain drawing on the 2011 Census', Muslim Council of Britain, January 2015, p. 58, http://www.mcb.org.uk/wp-content/uploads/2015/02/MCBCensusReport_2015.pdf, accessed 21 July 2017.

16. Elisabeth Garratt, 'Do British Muslims face employment penalties?', based on a submission made to the Women and Equalities Committee on Employment Opportunities for Muslims in the UK by Asma Mustafa and Anthony Heath, (submission MIE0008), September 2016, http://csi.nuff.ox.ac.uk/wp-content/uploads/2016/09/CSI-26-Muslim-employment.pdf.

17. '5,000 Muslims make millions', *The Guardian*, 1 February 2002.

18. 'London's Mecca rich: the rise of the Muslim multi-millionaires splashing their cash', *Evening Standard*, 30 October 2013, http://www.standard.co.uk/lifestyle/london-life/londons-mecca-rich-the-rise-of-the-muslim-multi-millionaires-splashing-their-cash-8913153.html, accessed on 18 July 2017.

19. Siobhan Fenton, 'British Muslim women face "double bind" of gender and religious discrimination, report warns', *The Independent*, 25 May 2016.

20. Siobhan Fenton, '6 charts which show the employment barriers faced by British Muslims', *The Independent*, 11 August 2016, http://www.independent.co.uk/news/uk/home-news/muslims-more-likely-to-be-unemployed-than-any-other-social-group-in-the-uk-mps-warn-a7185451.html, accessed on 18 July 2017.

21. Matthew L.N. Wilkinson, 'Helping Muslim boys succeed: the case for history education', *The Curriculum Journal*, 25, 3, p. 399.

22. Shamim Miah, 'School desegregation and the politics of "forced integration"', *Race and Class*, 54, 2, pp. 28–30.

23. 'While British Muslims are well represented within universities, they are still disproportionately under-represented within the Russell Group', 'Widening access to university', https://publications.parliament.uk/pa/cm201617/cmselect/cmwomeq/89/8907.htm; see also Vikki Bolivar, 'Exploring Ethnic Inequalities in Admission to Russell Group Universities', *Sociology*, 50, 2, pp. 247–266, 2016.

24. M. Nazir-Ali, 'Multiculturalism is to blame for perverting young Muslims', *The Telegraph*, 15 August 2006, http://www.telegraph.co.uk/comment/personal-view/3627155/Multiculturalism-is-to-blame-for-perverting-young-Muslims.html; William Pfaff, 'A monster of our own making', *The Guardian*, 21 August 2005, https://www.

theguardian.com/uk/2005/aug/21/july7.terrorism, accessed 19 July 2017.

25. 'Equality chief branded as "right wing"', *The Guardian*, 4 April 2004, https://www.theguardian.com/uk/2004/apr/04/race.britishidentity, accessed 19 July 2017.

26. David Cameron, 'Speech on radicalisation and Islamic extremism', *New Statesman*, 5 February 2011, http://www.newstatesman.com/blogs/the-staggers/2011/02/terrorism-islam-ideology, accessed 19 July 2017.

27. 'Lady Warsi claims Islamophobia is now socially acceptable in Britain', *The Guardian*, 20 January 2011, https://www.theguardian.com/uk/2011/jan/20/lady-warsi-islamophobia-muslims-prejudice, accessed 19 July 2017.

28. P.M. Thompson, 'Allen's Islamophobia and the British News Media: A critical evaluation of Islamophobia as a concept and its application to the written news media in Britain between 2001 and 2008', http://repository.uwtsd.ac.uk/354/1/Philip%20Thomson.pdf, accessed 19 July 2017.

29. Fleur Allen, 'Islamophobia in the UK: The role of British newspapers in shaping attitudes towards Islam and Muslims', http://repository.uwtsd.ac.uk/413/1/Fleur%20Allen%20new.pdf, accessed 19 July 2017.

30. Peter Oborne, 'The shameful Islamophobia at the heart of Britain's press', *The Independent*, 6 July 2008, http://www.independent.co.uk/news/media/the-shameful-islamophobia-at-the-heart-of-britains-press-861096.html, accessed 19 July 2017.

31. In January 2017, Dominic Ponsford found that Muslims comprised only 5% of the UK population, yet they appeared to account for the majority of newspaper mistakes which disparage a particular religion, for instance, the following headlines: '1 in 5 Brit Muslims' sympathy for jihadis', *The Sun*, 23 November 2015; 'One in five British Muslims has sympathy for Isis', *The Times*, 24 November 2015; 'UK mosques give cash for terror', *Daily Star*, 22 November 2015, were all found to be in breach of the IPSO code. 'No other faith or minority community is exposed to such a stream of erroneous, often malevolent misrepresentation in the national press; the use of such content by the far right BNP, EDL and Britain First in their anti-Muslim campaigns points to its inflammatory potential', Press Gazette, 27 January 2017, http://www.pressgazette.co.uk/newspaper-stories-misrepresenting-islam-would-not-be-tolerated-if-they-were-about-judaism-regulator-ipso-needs-to-step-in/, accessed 19 July 2017.

32. Imran Awan and Mohammed Rahman, 'Portrayal of Muslims Following

the Murders of Lee Rigby in Woolwich and Mohammed Saleem in Birmingham: A Content Analysis of UK Newspapers', *Journal of Muslim Minority Affairs*, 36, 1, 2016, pp. 16–31.

33. 'Jo Cox murder accused gives name as "death to traitors, freedom for Britain"', *The Guardian*, 18 June 2016, https://www.theguardian.com/uk-news/2016/jun/18/jo-cox-murder-suspect-thomas-mair-told-police-he-was-political-activist. See also *The Telegraph*, 16 June 2016, http://www.telegraph.co.uk/news/2016/06/16/jo-cox-mp-every-thing-we-know-so-far-about-thomas-mair/; *The Telegraph*, 17 June 2016, http://www.telegraph.co.uk/news/2016/06/17/jo-cox-mur-der-thomas-mair-asked-for-mental-health-treatment-day/; *The Guardian*, 17 June 2016, https://www.theguardian.com/uk-news/2016/jun/16/suspect-in-mp-killing-described-as-quiet-polite-and-reserved, accessed 19 July 2017.

34. *The Telegraph*, 21 June 2017, http://www.telegraph.co.uk/news/0/darren-osborne-everything-know-finsbury-park-mosque-suspect/, accessed 19 July 2017.

35. *The Mirror*, 19 December 2013; *The Sun*, 26 June 2017; *The Telegraph*, 19 December 2013.

36. 'Terrorism and Community Relations: Sixth Report of Session 2004–05', House of Commons Home Affairs Committee, Volume III, March 2005, p. 97, https://publications.parliament.uk/pa/cm200405/cmselect/cmhaff/165/165iii.pdf, accessed 19 July 2017.

37. Mary J. Hickman, Lyn Thomas, Sara Silvestri, Henri Nickels, 'Suspect Communities? Counter-terrorism policy, the press, and the impact on Irish and Muslim communities in Britain', London Metropolitan University, July 2011, https://www.city.ac.uk/__data/assets/pdf_file/0005/96287/suspect-communities-report-july2011.pdf, accessed 19 July 2017; in 2012, Terrorism Prevention and Investigation Measures (TPims) were introduced and in 2015, the Counter-Terrorism and Security Act was passed into law.

38. For example, a 14-year-old British Muslim, at a north London school, was questioned about the Islamic State for having referred to "*l'écoterrorisme*" while discussing environmental activism in a French lesson. After the lesson, he was taken out of the class and asked whether he was 'affiliated' with ISIS; Vikram Dodd, 'School questioned Muslim pupil about Isis after discussion on eco-activism', *The Guardian*, 22 September 2015, https://www.theguardian.com/education/2015/sep/22/school-questioned-muslim-pupil-about-isis-after-discussion-on-eco-activism, accessed 22 July 2017; also, Faizah Shaheen, a Muslim woman, was stopped after returning from her honeymoon in Turkey in August 2016 under the Terrorism Act and questioned by police

about a book on art in Syria that she was reading on the flight; Martin Bentham, 'Plane woman quizzed on Syria book', *Evening Standard*, 21 July 2017, p. 6.

39. 'Asian people 42 times more likely to be held under terror law', *The Guardian*, 23 May 2011, https://www.theguardian.com/uk/2011/may/23/counter-terror-stop-search-minorities, accessed 19 July 2017.

40. 'Why the surge in Muslim prisoners?', BBC News, 11 March 2015, http://www.bbc.co.uk/news/uk-31794599; 'Operation of police powers under the Terrorism Act 2000 and subsequent legislation: arrests, outcomes and stops and searches, Great Britain, financial year ending 31 March 2015', https://www.gov.uk/government/publications/operation-of-police-powers-under-the-terrorism-act-2000-financial-year-ending-march-2015/operation-of-police-powers-under-the-terrorism-act-2000-and-subsequent-legislation-arrests-outcomes-and-stops-and-searches-great-britain-financial#terrorist-and-extremistseparatist-prisoners-1, accessed 19 July 2017.

41. 'Why the Middle East Matters—a keynote speech by Tony Blair', 23 April 2014, http://www.tonyblairoffice.org/news/entry/why-the-middle-east-matters-keynote-speech-by-tony-blair/, accessed 19 July 2017.

42. The Government has defined extremism as: '[V]ocal or active opposition to fundamental British values, including democracy, the rule of law, individual liberty and mutual respect and tolerance of different faiths and beliefs. We also include in our definition of extremism calls for the death of members of our armed forces, whether in this country or overseas', 'Counter-extremism policy: an overview', Briefing Paper, Number 7238, 23 June 2017, p. 8.

43. Preventing violent extremism pathfinder fund 2007/08: Case studies, Department for Communities and Local Government, April 2007, p. 4, http://www.tedcantle.co.uk/publications/022%20Preventing%20violent%20extremism%20pathfinder%20fund%20case%20studie.pdf; Arun Kundnani, 'Spooked! How not to prevent violent extremism', Institute of Race Relations, 2009, p. 11, http://www.kundnani.org/wp-content/uploads/spooked.pdf, accessed 10 July 2017.

44. Ibid, pp. 12–15.

45. Marc Sageman (a forensic psychiatrist and former CIA case officer), whose work underpinned PREVENT, considered the conveyor belt theory of radicalisation flawed. Marc Sageman, *Leaderless Jihad: Terror Networks in the Twenty-First Century*, Philadelphia, 2008, p. 72. In July 2010, a confidential paper, 'Government Strategy for Extremism', prepared for coalition ministers on the Cabinet's home affairs subcommittee, concluded that it was wrong 'to regard radicalisation in this

country as a linear 'conveyor belt' moving from grievance, through radicalisation, to violence …'; Andrew Gilligan, 'Hizb ut Tahrir is not a gateway to terrorism, claims Whitehall report', *The Telegraph*, 25 July 2010, http://www.telegraph.co.uk/journalists/andrew-gilligan/790 8262/Hizb-ut-Tahrir-is-not-a-gateway-to-terrorism-claims-Whitehall-report.html, accessed 22 July 2017.

46. 'Schools should promote the fundamental British values of democracy, the rule of law, individual liberty, and mutual respect and tolerance of those with different faiths and beliefs', 'Promoting fundamental British values as part of SMSC in schools, Departmental advice for maintained schools', Department of Education, November 2014, p. 5, https://www.gov.uk/government/uploads/system/uploads/attachment_data/file/380595/SMSC_Gui dance_Maintained_Schools.pdf, accessed 19 July 2017.

47. Statutory guidance issued under section 29 of the Counter-Terrorism and Security Act 2015, Prevent duty guidance, p. 10, http://www.legislation.gov.uk/ukdsi/2015/9780111133309/pdfs/ukdsiod_9780 111133309_en.pdf., accessed 19 July 2017.

48. 'Channel is a programme which focuses on providing support at an early stage to people who are identified as being vulnerable to being drawn into terrorism', https://www.gov.uk/government/publications/channel-guidance, accessed 22 July 2017. The 'prevent duty' puts the Home Office's Channel Programme, a scheme coordinated by the Metropolitan Police in certain parts of the UK, on a national legal footing. Under the programme, individuals identified as extreme, or being 'at risk' of extremism, must be referred to Channel, which will make an assessment to determine whether the referred individual requires an intervention to de-radicalise them, and the kind of intervention they will make. See 'The Prevent Duty, Departmental advice for schools and childcare providers', Department of Education, June 2015, https://www.gov.uk/government/uploads/system/uploads/attachment_data/file/439598/prevent-duty-departmental-advice-v6.pdf, accessed 22 July 2017.

49. National Police Chiefs' Council, 'National Channel referral figures', http://www.npcc.police.uk/FreedomofInformation/National ChannelReferralFigures.aspx.

50. 'Jump in Channel referrals after duty to combat extremism introduced', http://www.aol.co.uk/news/2016/09/11/jump-in-channel-referrals-after-duty-to-combat-extremism-introduced/, accessed 22 June 2017.

51. 'Muslim Council of Britain to set up alternative counter-terror scheme', *The Guardian*, 19 October 2016, https://www.theguardian.

com/uk-news/2016/oct/19/muslim-council-britain-set-up-alternative-counter-terror-scheme, accessed 19 July 2017.

52. *The Independent*, 11 August 2016, http://www.independent.co.uk/news/uk/home-news/muslims-more-likely-to-be-unemployed-than-any-other-social-group-in-the-uk-mps-warn-a7185451.html, accessed 19 July 2017.

53. *The Guardian*, 19 October 2016, https://www.theguardian.com/uk-news/2016/oct/19/muslim-council-britain-set-up-alternative-counter-terror-scheme, accessed 19 July 2017.

54. 'Andy Burnham pledges to replace Prevent strategy in Manchester', *The Guardian*, 22 June 2017, https://www.theguardian.com/uk-news/2017/jun/22/prevent-andy-burnham-greater-manchester-muslim-communities, accessed 19 July 2017.

55. For year-on-year percentage increase in religious hate crime in England, especially London, see Sayeeda Warsi, *The Enemy Within: A Tale of Muslim Britain*, London, 2017, p. 318.

56. 'Unsettled Belonging: A survey of Britain's Muslim communities', Martyn Frampton, David Goodhart and Khalid Mahmood MP, November 2016, https://policyexchange.org.uk/wp-content/uploads/2016/12/PEXJ5037_Muslim_Communities_FINAL.pdf, accessed 19 July 2017.

57. 'European Muslims Show No Conflict Between Religious and National Identities', Gallup, http://media.gallup.com/WorldPoll/PDF/WPSRMuslimsinEurope2050707.pdf, accessed 19 July 2017.

58. 'More Muslims identify themselves as British than rest of population', *The Telegraph*, 7 May 2009, http://www.telegraph.co.uk/news/religion/5287105/More-Muslims-identify-themselves-as-British-than-rest-of-population.html, accessed 19 July 2017; 'More Muslims identify as "British" than Christians', https://mend.org.uk/news/more-muslims-identify-as-british-than-christians/, accessed, 19 July 2017.

59. 'Muslims are well-integrated in Britain—but no one seems to believe it', *The Guardian*, 3 July 2012, https://www.theguardian.com/commentisfree/belief/2012/jul/03/muslims-integrated-britain, accessed 19 July 2017.

60. '94% said, "If someone I knew from the Muslim community was planning an act of violence I would report them to the police"', ComRes BBC Radio 4 Today, Poll of 1,000 Muslims in Britain for BBC Radio 4 Today, http://www.comresglobal.com/polls/bbc-radio-4-today-muslim-poll/, accessed 19 July 2017.

61. 89% of Muslim respondents condemned the use of violence in political protest and 90% condemned terrorism; in both instances, just 2% of people expressed sympathy for such actions (for the population as

a whole, the equivalent figures were 5% and 4%). 'Unsettled Belonging: A survey of Britain's Muslim communities', Martyn Frampton, David Goodhart and Khalid Mahmood MP, November 2016, https://policyexchange.org.uk/wpcontent/uploads/2016/12/PEXJ5037_Muslim_Communities_FINAL.pdf, accessed 19 July 2017.

62. YouGov, http://cdn.yougov.com/cumulus_uploads/document/ogqzisd2xq/Islam%20and%20British%20values.pdf, accessed 19 July 2017.

63. 'UK attitudes towards Islam "concerning" after survey of 2,000 people', BBC, http://www.bbc.co.uk/newsbeat/article/36346886/uk-attitudes-towards-islam-concerning-after-survey-of-2000-people, accessed 19 July 2017.

64. 'Unsettled Belonging: A Survey of Britain's Muslim Communities', p. 8.

65. *The Independent*, 7 June 2017, http://www.independent.co.uk/news/uk/home-news/london-attack-imans-no-funeral-prayers-terrorists-refuse-500-muslim-clerics-islam-isis-burial-khuram-a7776861.html, accessed 19 July 2017.

66. 'Why I Want to Build a Women-led Mosque in Britain', Muslim Women's Council, http://www.muslimwomenscouncil.org.uk/uncategorized/why-i-want-to-build-a-women-led-mosque-in-britain/, accessed 19 July 2017.

67. Shaista Gohir: 'I wish the words shame and honour could be deleted', *The Guardian*, 19 January 2015, https://www.theguardian.com/lifeandstyle/2015/jan/19/muslim-womens-network-chair-lot-of-women-suffering-silence, accessed 19 July 2017.

68. 'British girl leads Guardian campaign to end female genital mutilation', *The Guardian*, 6 February 2014, https://www.theguardian.com/society/2014/feb/05/british-girl-guardian-campaign-end-female-genital-mutilation-fgm, accessed 19 July 2017.

69. 'The Casey Review: A review into opportunity and integration', Department for Communities and Local Government, December, 2016, https://www.gov.uk/government/uploads/system/uploads/attachment_data/file/575973/The_Casey_Review_Report.pdf, accessed 19 July 2017.

70. 'Casey review raises alarm over social integration in the UK', *The Guardian*, 5 December 2016, https://www.theguardian.com/world/2016/dec/04/social-integration-louise-casey-uk-report-condemns-failings, accessed 20 July 2016.

71. In reference to what she found in some predominantly Muslim areas, Louise Casey wrote: 'I've met far too many women who are suffering from the effects of misogyny and domestic abuse, women being subjugated by their husbands and extended families. Often, the vic-

tims are foreign-born brides brought to Britain via arranged marriages. They have poor English, little education, low confidence, and are reliant on their husbands for their income and immigration status. They don't know about their rights, or how to access support, and struggle to prepare their children effectively for school', 'The tough questions on social integration are being ducked', *The Guardian*, 4 December 2016, https://www.theguardian.com/commentisfree/2016/dec/04/tough-questions-social-integration-laws-values-every-person-britain, accessed 20 July 2017.

72. 'Casey report criticised for focus on UK Muslim communities', *The Guardian*, 5 December 2016, https://www.theguardian.com/society/2016/dec/05/casey-report-criticised-for-focus-on-uk-muslim-communities, accessed 20 July 2017.

73. This became clear when, in contrast to the representation of British Muslims' proclivity to 'lack of integration', another Commission reported encountering 'a wealth of positive community work by British Muslims at a local level, across ethnic and religious lines'. It found that the lack of integration was most apparent in areas of high deprivation; it suggested the need to address structural barriers as well as the racism and xenophobia. 'The Missing Muslims: Unlocking British Muslim Potential for the Benefit of All, a Report prepared by the Citizens Commission on Islam, Participation & Public Life', Citizen UK, London, 2017, https://d3n8a8pro7vhmx.cloudfront.net/newcitizens/pages/1261/attachments/original/1499106471/Missing_Muslims_Report_-_Electronic_copy.pdf?1499106471, accessed 19 July 2017.

74. Valerie Lewis and Ridhi Kashyap, 'Are Muslims a Distinctive Minority? An Empirical Analysis of Religiosity, Social Attitudes, and Islam', *Journal for the Scientific Study of Religion*, 52, 3, September 2013, pp. 617–626.

75. Amina Lone, 'Muslim girl power is reclaiming Islam from patriarchy, *The Times*, 13 May 2017; 'The Missing Muslims: Unlocking British Muslim Potential for the Benefit of All, a Report prepared by the Citizens Commission on Islam, Participation & Public Life', Citizen UK, London, 2017, https://d3n8a8pro7vhmx.cloudfront.net/newcitizens/pages/1261/attachments/original/1499106471/Missing_Muslims_Report_-_Electronic_copy.pdf?1499106471, accessed 19 July 2017.

76. 'Meet Bana Gora, the woman planning Britain's first female-managed mosque', *The Guardian*, 31 July 2015.

77. 'Women's rights organisation says Muslim women "blocked from seeking office by male Labour councillors"', *The Independent*, 5 February 2016.

78. 'One Day in the Life of Muslim Britain', *The Guardian*, g2, 10 November 2006.
79. 'Unsettled Belonging: A survey of Britain's Muslim communities', p. 8.

1. IS THERE A BRITISH MUSLIM IDENTITY?

1. C. Peach, 'Current estimates of the Muslim population of Great Britain' (paper presented at the Conference on Statistics and the UK Religious Communities, University of Derby, May 1994). M. Anwar, on the other hand, using a number of other factors put the figure at 1.5 million in his paper, 'Census data and Muslims in Britain', given at the same conference.
2. See R. Visram, *Ayahs, Lascars and Princes, the Story of Indians in Britain 1700–1947*, London, 1986; N. Matar, *Islam in Britain 1558–1685*, Cambridge, 1998; F. Halliday, *Arabs in Exile: Yemeni Migrants in Urban Britain*, London, 1992; R.I. Lawless, *From Ta'izz to Tyneside, an Arab Community in the North-East of England during the Early Twentieth Century*, Exeter, 1995.
3. A. Kose, 'Conversion to Islam, a study of native British converts', unpublished PhD thesis, University of London, 1994, p. 35.
4. Halliday, *Arabs in Exile*, p. x.
5. M. Al-Rasheed, 'Invisible and divided communities: Arabs in Britain', in *Arabs in Britain: Concerns and Prospects*, London, 1991, pp. 1–13. See also C.F. El-Solh, 'Arab communities in Britain: cleavages and common alities', *Islam and Christian–Muslim Relations*, 3, 2, December 1992, pp. 236–57.
6. J. Nielsen, *Muslim Immigration and Settlement in Britain*, Research Papers: Muslims in Europe, no. 21, CSIC, Birmingham, 1984, p. 16.
7. See M. Anwar, *The Myth of Return: Pakistanis in Britain*, London, 1979; M. Al-Rasheed, 'Political migration and downward socioeconomic mobility: the Iraqi community in London', *New Community*, 18, 4, pp. 537–50; D. Griffiths, 'Somali refugees in Tower Hamlets: clanship and new identities', *New Community*, 23, 1, January 1997, pp. 5–24; C.F. El-Solh, 'Somalis in London's East End: a community striving for recognition', *New Community*, 17, 4, July 1991, pp. 539–52; F. Ulug, 'A study of conflicting cultural pressures with particular attention to the Turkish Cypriot community and a small group of secondary school Turkish girls now living in North London', unpublished BEd dissertation, Middlesex Polytechnic, 1981, pp. 8, 26, 30–1; F. Halliday, *Arabs in Exile*, especially chapter 6 ('The "invisible" Arab') pp. 131–45.
8. F. Halliday, '"Islamophobia" reconsidered', *Ethnic and Racial Studies*, 22, 5, September 1999, pp. 896–7.

9. As Modood has argued, for purposes of analysis, the category 'Muslim' is no less coherent than, say, 'working class', 'woman', 'black' or 'youth'—it is susceptible to 'a dialectical tension between specificity and generality' but no different from what is found in all social categories; see T. Modood, *Muslim Identity: Real or Imagined? A Discussion by John Rex and Tariq Modood*, no. 12, CSIC, Birmingham, November 1994, p. 9.

10. *Q-News*, June 2000, p. 10.

11. Commission on British Muslims and Islamaphobia, *Islamaphobia: a Challenge for Us All*, London, 1997, p. 18.

12. E. Scantlebury, 'Muslims in Manchester: the depiction of a religious community', *New Community*, 21, 3, p. 430.

13. See F. Rahman, *Islam*, Chicago, 1979; D. Waines, *An Introduction to Islam*, Cambridge, 1995; A. al-Azmeh, *Islams and Modernities*, London, 1993.

14. K. Murad, *Muslim Youth in the West: Towards a New Education Strategy*, Leicester, 1986, p. 6.

15. K. Siddiqui, 'Generating "power" without politics', Speech at Conference on the Future of Muslims in Britain, London, 14 July 1990, p. 8. See also J.S. Nielsen, 'A Muslim agenda for Britain: some reflections', *New Community*, 17, 3, April 1991, pp. 467–75.

16. F. Halliday, 'Orientalism and its critics' in his *Islam and the Myth of Confrontation: Religion and Politics in the Middle East*, London, 1995, pp. 195–217.

17. *The Times*, editorial, 18 May 1989.

18. J. de Candole, 'The politics of Muslim schooling', *Salisbury Review*, March 1991, pp. 23–5.

19. T. Modood, 'Being somebody and being oppressed: catching up with Jesse Jackson' in his *Not Easy Being British: Colour, Culture and Citizenship*, London, 1992, p. 55.

20. See T. Asad, 'Multiculturalism and British identity in the wake of the Rushdie affair', *Politics and Society*, 18, 4, 1990, pp. 455–80.

21. T. Modood, R. Berlhand, J. Lakey, J. Mazroo, P. Smith, S. Virdee, S. Beishor, *Ethnic Minorities in Britain, Diversity and Disadvantage*, London, 1997, p. 301.

22. According to Nielsen, in 1963 there was a total of thirteen mosques registered with the Registrar General as places of worship; by the end of 1985, a total of 338 mosques had been registered; at the beginning of the 1990s, Raza estimated that over 1,000 mosques had been established. See J.S. Nielsen, *Muslims in Western Europe*, Edinburgh, 1992, p. 45, and 'Muslims in Britain: searching for an identity?', *New Community*, 13, 3, spring 1987, p. 387; and M.S. Raza, *Islam in Britain:*

Past, Present and the Future, Leicester, 1991, p. 37. A survey conducted by the Religious Resources Centre, University of Derby and the Inter-Faith Network for the UK in the mid-1990s put the number of Muslim organisations at 950; See G. Nonneman, T. Niblock and B. Szajkowski, eds, *Muslim Communities in the New Europe*, Reading, 1996, p. 175.

23. Nielsen, 'Muslims in Britain', p. 386.
24. Modood, *'Muslim Identity: Real or Imagined?'*, p. 11.
25. T. Kucukcan, 'Continuity and change: young Turks in London' in S. Vertovec and A. Rogers, eds, *Muslim European Youth: Reproducing Ethnicity, Religion, and Culture*, Aldershot, 1998, p. 119.
26. F. Halliday, '"Islamaphobia" reconsidered', p. 896.
27. Y. Samad, 'Imagining a British Muslim identification' in Vertovec and Rogers, eds, *Muslim European Youth*, p. 59.
28. Quoted in K. Knott and S. Khokher, 'Religious and ethnic identity among young Muslim women in Bradford', *New Community*, 19, 4, 1993, p. 606.
29. T. Modood, S. Beishon and S. Virdee, *Changing Ethnic Identities*, London, 1994, pp. 51–2.
30. *Ibid.*, p. 70.
31. See Matar, *Islam in Britain*, for evidence of earlier Muslim presence in Britain.
32. *Islamic Review and Muslim India*, February 1915, p. 60.
33. *Islamic Review and Muslim India*, December 1915, p. 607.
34. Most converts in Kose's study adopted an 'Islamic name, but very few [6%] changed their names legally. They did not necessarily feel comfortable with the outer trappings of Muslim lifestyle, for example clothing', see Kose, 'Conversion to Islam', p. 138.
35. *Ibid.*, p. 131.
36. *Ibid.*, p. 137.
37. *The Independent*, 26 August 1991.
38. Kose, 'Conversion to Islam', p. 142.
39. P. Lewis, *Islamic Britain: Religion, Politics and Identity among British Muslims: Bradford in the 1990s*, London, 1994, p. 201.
40. S. Akhtar, 'Ex-defender of the faith', *Times Higher Education Supplement*, London, 22 August 1997, p. 15.
41. J. Eade, 'Identity, nation and religion: educated young Bangladeshi Muslims in London's "East End"', *International Sociology*, 9, 3, September 1994, p. 386.
42. *Ibid.*, p. 387.
43. *Ibid.*, p. 390.
44. K. Gardner and A. Shukur, 'I'm Bengali, I'm Asian and I'm living here:

the changing identity of British Bengalis' in R. Ballard, ed., *Desh Pardesh: the South Asian Presence in Britain*, London, 1994, p. 158.

45. J. Jacobson, 'Religion and ethnicity: dual and alternative sources of identity among young British Pakistanis', *Ethnic and Racial Studies*, 20, 2, April 1997, p. 243.

46. See evidence of the weakening trend in J. Rex and R. Moore, *Race, Community and Conflict*, London, 1967, p. 170; M. Anwar, *Young Muslims in a Multi-cultural Society: Their Educational Needs and Policy Implications: the British Case*, Leicester, 1982, p. 17; I. Wilkinson, *Muslim Beliefs and Practices in a Non-Muslim Country: a Study of Rochdale*, Research Papers, Muslims in Europe, no. 39, CSIC, Birminghan, September 1988, p. 12; Modood *et al.*, *Changing Ethnic Identities*, p. 52.

47. A. Saeed, N. Blain and D. Forbes, 'New ethnic and national questions in Scotland: post-British identities among Glasgow Pakistani teenagers', *Ethnic and Racial Studies*, 22, 5, September 1999, pp. 826, 830.

48. Jacobson, 'Religion and ethnicity', p. 247.

49. Lewis, *Islamic Britain*, pp. 173 ff.

50. *Q-News*, December 1999, pp. 4, 23.

51. S. Ladbury, 'The Turkish Cypriots: ethnic relations in London and Cyprus' in J.L. Watson, ed., *Between Two Cultures: Migrants and Minorities in Britain*, Oxford, 1977, pp. 306–7.

52. Kucukcan, 'Continuity and change', p. 126. Regarding arranged marriages, Anwar's survey in the 1980s revealed similar tendencies among young South Asian Muslims, see *Young Muslims*, pp. 13–15, also M. Anwar, 'Religious identity in plural societies: the case of Britain', *Journal of the Institute of Muslim Minority Affairs*, 2, 2–3, 1980, pp. 110–21.

53. S. Burlet and H. Reid, 'A gendered uprising: political representation and minority ethnic communities', *Ethnic and Racial Studies*, 21, 2, March 1998, p. 283.

54. M. Macy, 'Class, gender and religious influences on changing patterns of Pakistani Muslim male violence in Bradford', *Ethnic and Racial Studies*, 22, 5, September 1998, p. 852.

55. S. Sulaimani, 'The multiple and changing identities of young Pakistani women in Woking', Safer Surrey Partnership, Woking, 2000, pp. 20–1.

2. MUSLIM MIGRATION AND SETTLEMENT IN BRITAIN BEFORE 1945

1. C. Holmes, *John Bull's Island: Immigration and British Society, 1871–1971*, Basingstoke, 1988, p. 3.

2. W.M. Watt, *The Influence of Islam on Medieval Europe*, Islamic Surveys no. 9, Edinburgh, 1972, p. 21.

3. D. Wright, *The Persians amongst the English*, London, 1985, p. 1.
4. P. Lewis, *Islamic Britain: Religion, Politics and Identity among British Muslims*, London, 1994, p. 11; M. Rodinson, *Europe and the Mystique of Islam*, London, 1991, pp. 33–7.
5. N. Matar, *Islam in Britain: 1558–1685*, Cambridge, 1998, pp. 45–9.
6. N.I. Matar, 'Muslims in seventeenth-century England', *Journal of Islamic Studies*, 8, 1, 1997, pp. 63–82.
7. Matar, *Islam in Britain*, p. 46.
8. Matar, 'Muslims in seventeenth-century England', p. 81.
9. S.R. Sonyel, *The Silent Minority: Turkish Muslim Children in British Schools*, Cambridge, 1988, p. 3.
10. *Ibid.*, p. 9.
11. *Ibid.*; N. Daniel, *Islam, Europe and Empire*, Edinburgh, 1966, p. 12.
12. D. Caradog Jones, ed., *The Social Survey of Merseyside*, Liverpool, 1934, p. 72.
13. J. Salter, *The Asiatic in England: Sketches of Sixteen Years' work Among Orientals*, London, 1873, pp. 157–61, 230–3.
14. Sonyel, *The Silent Minority*, p. 10.
15. Dean Mahomet, *The Travels of Dean Mahomet*, Cork, 1794; R. Visram, *Ayahs, Lascars and Princes: the Story of Indians in Britain 1700–1947*, London, 1986, p. 12.
16. K. Hunter, *History of Pakistanis in Britain*, Norwich, 1963, pp. 31–5.
17. R. Visram, *Asians in Britain: 400 Years of History*, London, 2002, p. 91.
18. M.M. Ally, 'History of Muslims in Britain, 1850–1980', unpubl. MA thesis, University of Birmingham, 1981, p. 23.
19. Salter, *The Asiatic in England*, p. 42.
20. P. Fryer, *Staying Power: the History of Black People in Britain*, London, 1984, p. 77.
21. Visram, *Ayahs, Lascars and Princes*, p. 17; H. Mayhew, *London Labour and the London Poor*, vol. IV, London, 1861, pp. 423–5; Greater London Council, *A History of the Black Presence in Britain*, London, 1986, pp. 38–40.
22. Visram, *Ayahs, Lascars and Princes*, p. 15; D. Hiro, *Black British, White British*, London, 1992; H. Tinker, *A New System of Slavery: the Export of Indian Labour Overseas, 1830–1920*, London, 1974, p. 46.
23. Visram, *Asians In Britain*, pp. 51–3.
24. F. Halliday, 'The *Millet* of Manchester: Arab merchants and cotton trade', *British Journal of Middle Eastern Studies*, 19, 2, 1992, p. 160.
25. C. Dixon, 'Lascars: the forgotten seamen' in R. Ommer and G. Panting, eds, *Working Men who got Wet*, Proceedings of the Fourth Conference of the Atlantic Canada Shipping Project, 24 July–26 July 1980, University of Newfoundland, St John's, 1980, p. 267.

26. Fryer, *Staying Power*, p. 549.

27. Dixon, 'Lascars: the forgotten seamen', p. 265.

28. Visram, *Ayahs, Lascars and Princes*, p. 40.

29. *Ibid.*, p. 34; Dixon, 'Lascars: the forgotten seamen', p. 267.

30. Visram, *Ayahs, Lascars and Princes*, p. 52.

31. *Ibid.*, p. 53.

32. In 1895 the estimated per capita income in Britain was £ 36.94 com-
    pared with only £2.65 in India, and, as far as business was concerned,
    the cheapness of labour from the coloniespresented a profitable oppor-
    tunity. J. Brown, *Modern India: the Origins of an Asian Democracy*,
    Oxford, 1994, p. 110.

33. Dixon, 'Lascars: the forgotten seamen', p. 266.

34. Visram, *Ayahs, Lascars and Princes*, pp. 35–6.

35. N. Evans, 'The South Wales race riots of 1919', *Llafur*, 3, 1, 1980,
    p. 6.

36. A. Dunlop, 'Lascars and labourers: reactions to the Indian presence in
    the West of Scotland during the 1920s and 1930s', *Scottish Labour
    History Society Journal*, 25, 1990, p. 43.

37. The category 'British' also included some documented 'black' British
    subjects—see Dixon, 'Lascars: the forgotten seamen', p. 281.

38. C. Adams, *Across Seven Seas and Thirteen Rivers: Life Stories of the Pioneer
    Sylheti Settlers in Britain*, London, 1987.

39. F. Halliday, *Arabs in Exile: Yemeni Migrants in Urban Britain*, London,
    1992, p. 17; Evans, 'The South Wales race riots of 1919', p. 6.

40. R. Ramdin, *The Making of the Black Working Class in Britain*, London,
    1987, p. 70.

41. J.H. Taylor, *The half-way Generation: a Study of Asian Youths in Newcastle
    upon Tyne*, Windsor, 1976, p. 28.

42. Salter, while visiting Liverpool, observed Arab, Indian and Malay sail-
    ors in the port.

43. It was estimated by one source that the migrant Muslim population
    of Britain had grown to 10,000 by the early 1920s. Additionally it was
    thought that the number of converts had risen to around 1,000. See
    Islamic Review, March 1924, p. 118.

44. Fryer, *Staying Power*, p. 299.

45. *Ibid.*, p. 304.

46. Evans, 'The South Wales Race Riots of 1919', p. 6.

47. *South Wales Daily News*, 2 September 1916.

48. E. Hobsbawn, *Age of Extremes: the Short Twentieth Century, 1914–1991*,
    London, 1994, pp. 88 ff.

49. Evans, 'The South Wales Race Riots of 1919', pp. 10–11; R.I. Lawless,
    *From Ta'izz to Tyneside: an Arab Community in the North-East of England
    during the Early Twentieth Century*, Exeter, 1995, p. 78.

50. Taylor, *The Half-way Generation*, p. 29.

51. Evans, 'The South Wales race riots of 1919', p. 20.

52. M. Sherwood, 'Race, nationality and employment among Lascar seamen, 1660 to 1945', *New Community*, 17, 2, January 1991, p. 236.

53. See D. Cesarani, 'Anti-alienism in England after the First World War', *Immigrants and Minorities*, 6, 1, March 1987, pp. 5–23.

54. Sherwood, 'Race, nationality and employment among Lascar seamen', p. 236.

55. Evans, 'The South Wales race riots of 1919', p. 12.

56. N. Evans, 'Regulating the reserve army: Arabs, blacks and the local state in Cardiff, 1919–1945', *Immigrants and Minorities*, 4, 2, July 1985, p. 76.

57. R. May and R. Cohen, 'The interaction between race and colonialism: a case study of the Liverpool race riots of 1919', *Race and Class*, XVI, 2, 1974, p. 119.

58. Evans, 'Regulating the reserve army', p. 76. See also L. Tabili, *'We Ask for British Justice': Workers and Racial Difference in Late Imperial Britain*, New York, 1994, pp. 116–119.

59. Evans, 'Regulating the reserve army', pp. 77–8.

53. See D. Cesarani, 'Anti-alienism in England after the First World War', *Immigrants and Minorities*, 6, 1, March 1987, pp. 5–23.

54. Sherwood, 'Race, nationality and employment among Lascar seamen', p. 236.

55. Evans, 'The South Wales race riots of 1919', p. 12.

56. N. Evans, 'Regulating the reserve army: Arabs, blacks and the local state in Cardiff, 1919–1945', *Immigrants and Minorities*, 4, 2, July 1985, p. 76.

57. R. May and R. Cohen, 'The interaction between race and colonialism: a case study of the Liverpool race riots of 1919', *Race and Class*, XVI, 2, 1974, p. 119.

58. Evans, 'Regulating the reserve army', p. 76. See also L. Tabili, *'We Ask for British Justice': Workers and Racial Difference in Late Imperial Britain*, New York, 1994, pp. 116–119.

59. Evans, 'Regulating the reserve army', pp. 77–8.

60. *Ibid.*, p. 86.

61. *Ibid.*, pp. 78, 84; Fryer, *Staying Power*, p. 304.

62. Evans, 'Regulating the reserve army', p. 84.

63. K. Little, *Negroes in Britain: a Study of Racial Relations in English Society*, London, 1972, p. 96.

64. D. Byrne, 'The 1930 "Arab riot" in South Shields: a race riot that never was', *Race and Class*, XVIII, 3, pp. 265, 274; S.F. Collins, '"Moslem" and "Negro" groupings on Tyneside: a comparative study of

social integration in terms of inter-group and intergroup relations', unpubl. PhD thesis, University of Edinburgh, 1952, p. 162.

65. Evans, 'Regulating the reserve army', pp. 70–1.

66. Sonyel, *The Silent Minority*, pp. 10–11.

67. R. Oakley, 'The control of Cypriot migration to Britain between the wars', *Immigrants and Minorities*, 6, 1, March 1987, p. 31.

68. R. Oakley, 'Family, kinship and patronage: the Cypriot migration to Britain' in V.S. Khan, ed., *Minority Families in Britain: Support and Stress*, London, 1979, p. 15.

69. Visram, *Ayahs, Lascars and Princes*, pp. 279–80.

70. A.K. Singh, *Indian Students in Britain: a Survey of their Adjustment and Attitudes*, Bombay, c. 1963, p. 21.

71. Hiro, *Black British, White British*, p. 111.

72. See S. Constantine, *Unemployment in Britain between the Wars*, London, 1980, pp. 8–9, 25; see also S. Constantine, *Social Conditions in Britain, 1918–1939*, London, 1983, pp. 8–13.

73. The Metropolitan and Thames Police Court records suggested that their numbers remained relatively small. See Sherwood, 'Race, nationality and employment among Lascar seamen, 1660 to 1945', p. 240.

74. B. Maan, *The New Scots: the Story of Asians in Scotland*, Edinburgh, 1992, p. 120.

75. P. Werbner, *The Migration Process: Capital, Gifts and Offerings among British Pakistanis*, Oxford, 1990, pp. 17 ff.

76. Adams, *Across Seven Seas and Thirteen Rivers*, p. 51.

77. *Ibid.*, pp. 46–7; M. Banton, *The Coloured Quarter: Negro Immigrants in an English City*, London, 1955, p. 70.

78. B. Dahya, 'The nature of Pakistani ethnicity in industrial cities in Britain' in A. Cohen, ed., *Urban Ethnicity*, London, 1974, p. 84.

79. Visram, *Ayahs, Lascars and Princes*, p. 191.

80. Dahya, 'The nature of Pakistani ethnicity in industrial cities in Britain', pp. 95–6.

81. D. Hiro, *Black British, White British: a History of Race Relations in Britain*, London, 1992, p. 111.

82. Banton, *The Coloured Quarter*, p. 224.

83. *Ibid.*, p. 68.

84. Hunter, *History of Pakistanis in Britain*, p. 17.

3. MUSLIM ENGAGEMENT WITH BRITISH SOCIETY UP TO THE FIRST WORLD WAR

1. F.O. Shyllon, *Black People in Britain, 1555–1833*, London, 1977, p. 103.

2. W.M. Thackeray, *The Four Georges*, London, 1856, pp. 38, 52.

3. P. Fryer, *Staying Power: the History of Black People in Britain*, London, 1984, pp. 421–3.

4. J. Walvin, *Black and White: the Negro and English Society, 1555–1945*, London, 1973, p. 80.

5. Shyllon, *Black People in Britain*, p. 60.

6. *Ibid.*

7. A.G.B. Fisher and H.J. Fisher, *Slavery and Muslim Society in Africa: the Institution in Saharan and Sudanic Africa, and the trans-Saharan Trade*, London, 1970, pp. 24–33.

8. Fryer, *Staying Power*, p. 71.

9. *Ibid.*, pp. 69–72.

10. C. Stewart, trans., *Travels of Mirza Abu Taleb Khan in Asia, Africa and Europe during the Years 1797 to 1803*, London, 1814, vol. 1, p. 178.

11. *Ibid.*, p. 198.

12. D. Wright, *The Persians Amongst the English: Episodes in Anglo-Persian History*, London, 1985, p. 58.

13. J.B. Fraser, *Narrative of the Residence of the Persian Princes in London in 1835 and 1836*, London, 1838, vol. 1, p. 232.

14. R. Visram, *Ayahs, Lascars And Princes: the Story of Indians in Britain 1700–1947*, London, 1986, p. 56.

15. *Ibid.*, pp. 66–70.

16. J. Salter, *The Asiatic in England: Sketches of Sixteen Years' Work among Orientals*, London, 1873, p. 27. Salter dedicated a major part of his life to this work, his memoirs, and they represent a vivid testimony to his religious, albeit prejudiced, zeal.

17. D. Hiro, *Black British, White British: a History of Race Relation in Britain*, London, 1992, p. 5.

18. *Public Advertiser*, 16 March 1785, no. 15854.

19. C.C. Eldridge, *England's Mission: the Imperial Idea in the Age of Gladstone and Disraeli, 1868–1880*, London, 1973, pp. 238–9.

20. W. Muir, *Life of Mahomet*, London, 1858–61, vol. 4, p. 322.

21. Salter, *The Asiatic in England*, pp. 136, 137.

22. H. Mayhew, *London Labour and the London Poor*, New York, 1968, vol. III, pp. 186–7.

23. Salter, *The Asiatic in England*, pp. 232–3.

24. *Ibid.*, p. 76.

25. Visram, *Ayahs, Lascars and Princes*, p. 56.

26. Mayhew, *London Labour and the London Poor*, p. 188.

27. D.A. Lorimer, *Colour, Class and the Victorians: English Attitudes to the Negro in the Mid-nineteenth Century*, Leicester, 1978, p. 41.

28. Anon., *Visits to the Wynds and Closes of Edinburgh by Day and Night*, Edinburgh, 1850, p. 7.

29. Fryer, *Staying Power*, p. 233.
26. Mayhew, *London Labour and the London Poor*, p. 188.
27. D.A. Lorimer, *Colour, Class and the Victorians: English Attitudes to the Negro in the Mid-nineteenth Century*, Leicester, 1978, p. 41.
28. Anon., *Visits to the Wynds and Closes of Edinburgh by Day and Night*, Edinburgh, 1850, p. 7.
29. Fryer, *Staying Power*, p. 233.
30. Salter, *The Asiatic in England*, pp. 22–3.
31. Mayhew, *London Labour and the London Poor*, pp. 188–9.
32. R. Visram, *Asians in Britain: 400 Years of History*, London, 2002, pp. 25–9, 55–6, 59.
33. Fryer, *Staying Power*, p. 262.
34. Salter, *The Asiatic in England*, pp. 296–8.
35. *Ibid.*, p. 290.
36. *Ibid.*, p. 24.
37. *Ibid.*, p. 43.
38. *Ibid.*, p. 254.
39. *Ibid.*, pp. 52, 57.
40. *Ibid.*, p. 45.
41. *Ibid.*, p. 55.
42. Wright, *The Persians Amongst the English*, pp. 124–5.
43. Salter, *The Asiatic in England*, pp. 203–4.
44. F. Halliday, 'The *Millet* of Manchester: Arab merchants and cotton trade', *British Journal of Middle Eastern Studies*, 19, 2, 1992, p. 163.
45. *Ibid.*, pp. 173–4.
46. Stewart, trans., *Travels of Mirza Abu Taleb Khan*, p. xv.
47. G.F.I. Graham, *The Life and Work of Sir Syed Ahmad Khan*, Karachi, 1974, p. 129.
48. *Ibid.*, p. 131.
49. Visram, *Ayahs, Lascars and Princes*, pp. 178–9.
50. H. Malik, *Sir Sayyid Ahmad Khan and Muslim Modernization in India and Pakistan*, New York, 1980, p. 99.
51. R. Visram, 'The First World War and the Indian soldiers', *Indo-British Review*, XVI, 2, June 1989, pp. 20–1.
52. Curzon to Hamilton, 27 August 1902, MSS EUR File 111/161, IOR.
53. K. Ballhatchet, *Race, Sex and Class under the Raj: Imperial Attitudes and Politics and their Critics, 1793–1905*, London, 1980, pp. 119–20.
54. M. Hobhouse, 'Further skeches by an Indian pen', *Indian Magazine and Review*, March 1890, pp. 144–5.
55. Visram, *Ayahs, Lascars and Princes*, p. 32; E. Longford, *Victoria R.I.*, London, 1964, pp. 535–42.
56. Quoted in Longford, *Victoria R.I.*, p. 540.

57. *Ibid.*, p. 542.
58. W.S. Blunt, *My Diaries: Being a Personal Narrative of Events, 1888–1914*, London, 1921, vol. II, p. 13.
59. N. Daniel, *Islam, Europe and Empire*, Edinburgh, 1966, p. 37.
60. C. Bennett, *Victorian Images of Islam*, London, 1992, p. 117.
61. Daniel, *Islam, Europe and Empire*, p. 398.
62. *Muslim Outlook*, 20 November 1919.
63. J. Salt, *Imperialism, Evangelism and the Ottoman Armenians, 1878–1896*, London, 1993, p. 124.
64. *Ibid.*, pp. 138–9.
65. 'Moslemism in Liverpool', *Liverpool Review*, 28 November 1891.
66. *Ibid.*
67. *The Crescent*, 23 October 1895, p. 267.
68. E. Finch, *Wilfrid Scawen Blunt, 1840–1922*, London, 1938, p. 181.
69. *Ibid.*, p. 189.
70. *Ibid.*, p. 207. Blunt's diaries provide an excellent insight into the thinking of some of these Muslim activists of the time.
71. See F. Robinson, *Separatism among Indian Muslims: the Politics of the United Provinces' Muslims, 1860–1923*, Delhi, 1993, pp. 152, 196, 236–7; S. Lahiri, *Indians in Britain: Anglo-Indian Encounters, Race and Identity, 1880–1939*, London, 2000, pp. 176–80.
72. M. Forward, 'Syed Ameer Ali: a bridge-builder?', *Islamic and Christian Muslim Relations*, 6, 1, 1995, pp. 50–1.
73. R. Ahmed, 'A Moslem's view of the pan-Islamic revival', *The Nineteenth Century*, vol. XLII, September 1897, p. 528.
74. These included Aubrey Herbert, a Conservative MP, son of a Colonial Secretary and a romantic 'Turcophile', and Lords Mowbray, Newton and Lamington. I. Duffield, 'Duse Mohamed Ali, Afro-Asian solidarity and Pan-Africanism in early twentieth-century London' in J.S. Gundara and I. Duffield, eds, *Essays on the History of Blacks in Britain: from Roman Times to Mid-twentieth Century*, Aldershot, 1992, pp. 130–1.
75. *Ibid.*, pp. 136–7.
76. *Ibid.*, p. 141.
77. *Muslim Outlook*, 6 November 1919 and 30 October 1919.

4. 'BEING MUSLIM' IN EARLY TWENTIETH-CENTURY BRITAIN

1. M. Sherwood, 'Racism and resistance: Cardiff in the 1930s and 1940s', *Llafur*, 5, 4, 1991, p. 57.
2. *Ibid.*
3. *Ibid.*
4. K. Little, *Negroes in Britain: a Study of Racial Relations in English Society*, 2nd edn, London, 1972, p. 104.

5. R. Lawless, *From Ta'izz to Tyneside: an Arab Community in the North-east of England during the Early Twentieth Century*, Exeter, 1995, pp. 77, 114, 120.

6. Quoted in Little, *Negroes in Britain*, p. 260.

7. Lawless, *From Ta'izz to Tyneside*, p. 190.

8. *Ibid.*, p. 186.

9. *Ibid.*, p. 75.

10. *Ibid.*

11. *Ibid.*, p. 81.

12. *The Times*, 18 June 1919, p. 8.

13. *Western Mail*, 13 June 1919.

14. N. Evans, 'Regulating the reserve army: Arabs, blacks and the local state in Cardiff, 1919–1945', *Immigrants and Minorities*, 4, 2, July 1985, p. 88.

15. Lawless, *From Ta'izz to Tyneside*, p. 181.

16. S.F. Collins, 'The social position of white and "half-caste" women in colored groupings in Britain', *American Sociological Review*, 16, 4, 1951, pp. 798–9; L. Tabili, *'We Ask for British Justice':Workers and Racial Justice in Late Imperial Britain*, London, 1994, pp. 144–7.

17. S. Collins, *Coloured Minorities in Britain: Studies in British Race Relations based on African,West Indian and Asiatic Immigrants*, London, 1957, p. 161.

18. F. Halliday, *Arabs in Exile:Yemeni Migrants in Urban Britain*, London, 1992, pp. 27–39, and Lawless, *From Ta'izz to Tyneside*, pp. 236–44.

19. Little, *Negroes in Britain*, p. 263.

20. M.A. Sherif, *Searching for Solace: a Biography of Abdullah Yusuf Ali, Interpreter of the Quran*, Kuala Lumpur, 1994.

21. *Ibid.*, p. 136.

22. *Ibid.*, p. 190.

23. Lawless, *From Ta'izz to Tyneside*, pp. 194–206; D. Byrne, 'Class, race and nation: the politics of the "Arab issue" in South Shields 1919–1939', *Immigrants and Minorities*, 13, 2–3, July/November 1994, pp. 100–1; Little, *Negroes in Britain*, pp. 62–70.

24. N. Evans, 'The South Wales race riots of 1919', *Llafur*, 3, 1, 1980, pp. 23–4; Little, *Negroes in Britain*, p. 129.

25. *Ibid.*, p. 128; Lawless, *From Ta'izz to Tyneside*, p. 189.

26. Evans, 'Regulating the reserve army', p. 87.

27. *Ibid.*, pp. 93–5; for South Shields see Lawless, *From Ta'izz to Tyneside*, pp. 87, 187–94.

28. *Shields Daily Gazette*, 17 June 1940.

29. Little, *Negroes in Britain*, p. 126.

30. Byrne, 'Class, race and nation', p. 100; Lawless, *From Ta'izz to Tyneside*, p. 203.

31. Evans, 'Regulating the reserve army', p. 97. In South Shields too, councillors stressed provision of 'specific accommodation' to prevent 'Arabs penetrating … into good class residential areas'; see also *Shields Daily Gazette*, 23 March 1935.

32. *Shields Daily Gazette*, 8 November 1937.

33. S.F. Collins, '"Moslem" and "negro" groupings on Tyneside: a comparative study of social integration in terms of intra-group and inter-group relations', unpubl. PhD thesis, University of Edinburgh, 1952, pp. 169–71.

34. 'The Somalis, in particular, have a strong reputation for gambling', Little, *Negroes in Britain*, p. 164; Collins, '"Moslem" and "negro" groupings on Tyneside', pp. 182–7.

35. Little, *Negroes in Britain*, p. 139; Collins, '"Moslem" and "negro" groupings on Tyneside', p. 194.

36. Lawless, *From Ta'izz to Tyneside*, pp. 78, 103–4, 113–21; Evans, 'Regulating the reserve army', p. 82, and *The Seaman*, 25 February 1931.

37. Sherwood, 'Racism and resistance', p. 56.

38. Evans, 'Regulating the reserve army', p. 83; Tabili, *'We Ask for British Justice'*, p. 142.

39. Evans, 'Regulating the reserve army', p. 99.

40. D. Byrne, 'The 1930 "Arab riot" in South Shields: a race riot that never was', *Race and Class*, 18, 3, 1977, p. 266.

41. Tabili, *'We Ask for British Justice'*, pp. 104–8.

42. Lawless, *From Ta'izz to Tyneside*, p. 169.

43. Tabili, *'We Ask for British Justice'*, p. 147.

44. Sherwood, 'Racism and resistance', p. 66.

45. R.I. Lawless, 'Religion and politics among Arab seafarers in Britain in the early twentieth century', *Islam and Christian–Muslim Relations*, 5, 1, 1994, pp. 37–41, 115–18, 132–3; Lawless, *From Ta'izz to Tyneside*, pp. 156–60.

46. Byrne, 'The 1930 "Arab riot" in South Shields', p. 274.

47. *Shields Daily Gazette*, 1 October 1930, p. 5.

48. *Ibid.*, 30 January 1931, p. 2.

49. Lawless, *From Ta'izz to Tyneside*, p. 170.

50. Sherwood, 'Racism and resistance', p. 53.

51. Tabili, *'We Ask for British Justice'*, pp. 162–6.

52. *Ibid.*, p. 127.

53. Sherwood, 'Racism and resistance', p. 53.

54. Tabili, *'We Ask for British Justice'*, p. 123.

55. *Ibid.*, pp. 127–8.

56. Indeed, hundreds of Arabs from South Shields and about 1,000 'coloured men', likely to be mostly Muslim, sailing out of Cardiff lost

their lives during the First World War. See *Shield Gazette*, 11 March 1919, p. 2; Evans, 'The South Wales race riots of 1919', p. 16; see also D. Byrne, 'The "Arab issue" in South Shields 1919–39', *Immigrants and Minorities*, 13, 2–3, July/November, 1994, p. 102.

57. Instances of this assimilation can be seen at the beginning of the twentieth century with Yemenis marrying local white women in church and not seeming to object to their children being brought up as Christians; see *Shield Gazette*, 16 May 1968, p. 12.

5. 'WEAVING THE CULTURAL STRANDS TOGETHER': INSTITUTIONALISING ISLAM IN EARLY TWENTIETH-CENTURY BRITAIN

1. *The Crescent*, July 1896.
2. *Ibid.*, June 1896.
3. *Ibid.*, 1899.
4. 'Men who are talked about: Abdullah Quilliam', *The Porcupine*, Liverpool, 21 November 1896.
5. *The Crescent*, September 1896.
6. *Ibid.*, June 1897.
7. *Ibid.*, January 1896.
8. *Ibid.*, July 1896.
9. *The Islamic World*, July 1896.
10. W.H. Quilliam, *Fanatics and Fanaticism: a Lecture*, Vernon Temperance Hall, Liverpool, 1890.
11. The most popular of these were 'My God, my Father, whilst I stray' and 'Abide with me'; see M.M. Ally, 'History of Muslims in Britain, 1850–1980', unpubl. MA dissertation, University of Birmingham, 1981, p. 58.
12. *Daily Sketch*, 13 November 1913
13. Cited in *The Crescent*, 9 December 1893.
14. By the beginning of the twentieth century the number of South Asian Muslims resident in Britain, especially students, had become quite significant. For example, in 1903, an Indian newspaper reported eighty-eight students from Aligarh alone: see *Al Bashir* (Etawah), 3 March 1903. They had been arriving in increasing numbers since 1885: see S. Lahiri, *Indians in Britain, Anglo-Indian Encounters, Race and Identity, 1880–1930*, London, 2000, p. 7.
15. See *The Central Islamic Society: Rules and Regulations*, London, 1916. The document setting out the Society's objects is in the author's possession.
16. See *Muslim Outlook* bulletins, published by the Islamic Information Bureau in London during 1919–20, under the editorship of Mushir Hussain Qidwai.

17. Foreign Office File, FO 371 3419, 1918, PRO.

18. R. Visram, *Asians in Britain: 400 Years of History*, London, 2002, p. 397, n. 69. *Islamic Review and Muslim India*, December 1914, pp. 532–3. The first burial in Britain of anIndian Muslim soldier who died on the Western Front, however, took place at Brookwood in November 1914, before this cemetery for troops was set up: *ibid.*, p. 534.

19. *The Islamic Review and Muslim India*, April 1917, p. 83.

20. *Ibid.*, January 1914, pp. 31–2.

21. *The Islamic Review*, September 1915, p. 447.

22. For Khalid Sheldrake's further details, see M. Everest-Phillips, 'The suburban King of Tartary', *Asian Affairs*, October 1990.

23. 'British Muslim Society: President's address', *Islamic Review and Muslim India*, January 1915, pp. 9–16.

24. P. Clarke, *Marmaduke Pickthall: British Muslim*, London, 1986, pp. 43–4.

25. *The Islamic Review*, April 1923, p. 128.

26. Lord Headley, 'Is our house in order?', *Islamic Review*, September 1928, pp. 328–9.

27. *The Islamic Review*, August 1937, inside front cover.

28. See Chapter 4.

29. R.I. Lawless, *From Ta'izz to Tyneside: an Arab Community in the North-East of England during the Early Twentieth Century*, Exeter, 1995, pp. 209, 212.

30. See Chapter 4.

31. Lawless, *From Ta'izz to Tyneside*, pp. 84, 215–16.

32. The Association for British Muslims, an organisation that largely provides a network for white British converts, claims that its origins go back to the Western Islamic Association, an organisation which Quilliam, it says, set up in the early 1920s on his return from Turkey. 'By 1927, it was located in London's Notting Hill and the Amir [President] was HE Khalid Sheldrake.' See 'A brief history of the ABM', the Association for British Muslims website, *http://members.tripod.com/~british_muslims_assn/briefhistory.html*, 3 November 2002. He established branches among Yemeni and Somali seamen in Cardiff and South Shields with the aim of looking after their economic, moral and religious welfare. When the tension rose between Arabs and their white counterparts with the decline of employment in shipping during the depression years, Sheldrake took up the cause of the Arab seamen at British ports, strongly criticised the National Union of Seamen and accompanied their representatives to the Home Office and House of Commons to urge their case. However, when it came to the crunch he supported the government's policy, which went against the interests of the Arab seamen. Being of the middle class, it is probable that he was more comfortable among upper- and middle-class Muslim

intellectuals and professionals of cosmopolitan London, and had some difficulty in fully understanding the experience, viewpoint, concerns and needs of poorer Muslims. Hence he was ultimately perceived by these working-class Muslim communities, for whom improvement in the material conditions of their lives was always a priority, as an outsider and was never fully recognised as their spokesman; no wonder that he lost interest in them and departed abroad. Sheldrake appears to have spent an adventurous life in India and the Far East in the 1930s, lecturing and fund-raising, and ended up working part-time for the British Council in Ankara between 1940 and 1943. There is some speculation that he may have been operating as a secret agent for the British. He returned to England in 1944 and died in 1947.

33. Lawless, *From Ta'izz to Tyneside* pp. 135–52, and F. Halliday, *Arabs in Exile:Yemeni Migrants in Urban Britain*, London, 1992, pp. 44–50.
34. Lawless, *From Ta'izz to Tyneside*, pp. 216–18.
35. *Ibid.*, pp. 218–20.
36. *Ibid.*, p. 225.
37. Halliday, *Arabs in Exile*, pp. 146–7.
38. *Shields Gazette and Shipping Telegraph*, 22 February 1937, p. 3.
39. K. Little, *Negroes in Britain: a Study of Racial Relations in English Society*, 2nd edn, London, 1972, p. 132.
40. *Ibid.*, p. 171.
41. *Ibid.*, pp. 116–17.
42. *Ibid.*, p. 134.
43. Lawless, *From Ta'izz to Tyneside*, p. 226.
44. Halliday, *Arabs in Exile*, pp. 31–9.

6. MUSLIM MIGRATION TO BRITAIN AFTER THE SECOND WORLD WAR

1. *The Economist*, 17 September 1988, p. 39.
2. N. Harris, *The New Untouchables: Immigration and the New World Worker*, London, 1995, p. 35
3. This trend is reflected in the ebb and flow of migration from South Asia, the biggest source of Muslim migration to Britain from the mid- to late twentieth century. For Pakistani and Bangladeshi Muslims the combined number, according to the consecutive censuses from 1951 to 1991, rose thus: from 5,000 in 1951 to 24,900 (1.2% British-born) in 1961; there was then an unprecedented sevenfold increase in this population between 1961 and 1971 to over 170,000 (23.5% British-born); it more than doubled in the next decade to 360,000 (37.5% British-born) by 1981 and then to 640,000 (47% British-born) by 1991. See

P. Lewis, *Islamic Britain: Religion, Politics and Identity among British Muslims*, London, 1994, p. 15.

4. M. Anwar, *The Myth of Return: Pakistanis in Britain*, London, 1979, p. 214.

5. For chain migration, see F. Alam, *Salience of Homeland: Societal Polarization within the Bangladeshi Population in Britain*, Research Paper no. 7, Centre for Research in Ethnic Relations (CRER), University of Warwick, Coventry, January 1988, p. 15; A. Shaw, *A Pakistani Community in Britain*, Oxford, 1988, p. 22; R. Oakley, 'Family, kinship and patronage: the Cypriot migration to Britain' in V.S. Khan, ed., *Minority Families in Britain: Support and Stress*, London, 1979, pp. 22–37. For Muslims in Manchester see P. Werbner, *The Migration Process: Capital, Gifts and Offerings among British Pakistanis*, Oxford, 1990.

6. G. Karmi, 'The health status and health beliefs of two London migrant communities', *International Migration*, vol. 29, no. 1, p. 8. *The Economist's* figure of '50,000 Moroccans working in Britain' seems implausible: see 'In a world of their own', *The Economist*, 17 September 1988, p. 39; for 1991 figures, see M. Anwar, *Muslims in Britain: 1991 Census and Other Statistical Sources*, CSIC Paper no. 9, Centre for the Study of Islam and Christian–Muslim Relations, Selly Oak Colleges, Birmingham, September 1993, p. 5.

7. See V. Robinson, 'Correlates of Asian immigration: 1959–1974', *New Community*, 8, 1–2, 1980.

8. Shaw, *A Pakistani Community in Britain*, p. 9.

9. *Ibid.* The per capita income in Pakistan in the mid-1960s was as low as £ 30 per annum. See E.J.B. Rose, *Colour and Citizenship: a Report on British Race Relations*, London, 1969, p. 59.

10 Peter Loizos, 'Aspects of pluralism in Cyprus', *New Community*, 1, 4, summer 1972, p. 301.

11. R. Patrick, 'Intercommunal conflict in Cyprus—some demographic and geopolitical consequences', *New Community*, 2, 2, spring 1973, p. 137.

12. F.M. Bhatti, *Turkish Cypriots in London*, Research Paper no. 11, Centre for the Study of Islam and Christian–Muslim Relations, Birmingham, September 1981, p. 2.

13. Oakley, 'Family, kinship and patronage', pp. 22–37.

14. See Robinson, 'Correlates of Asian immigration: 1959–1974', pp. 115–22.

15. C. Peach, 'Estimating the growth of the Bangladeshi population of Great Britain', *New Community*, 16, 4, July 1990, p. 490.

16. C. Peach, ed., *Ethnicity in the 1991 Census: the Ethnic Minority Populations of Great Britain*, 2, 1, London, 1996, pp. 9–10.

17. F. Halliday, *Arabs in Exile: Yemeni Migrants in Urban Britain*, London, 1992, pp. 56–8.

18. C. Searle and A. Shaif, '"Drinking from one pot": Yemeni unity, at home and overseas', *Race and Class*, 32, 4, 1991, pp. 65–81.

19. B. Dahya, 'Yemenis in Britain: an Arab migrant community', *Race*, 6, 3, January 1965, p. 177.

20. See Rose, *Colour and Citizenship*, p. 72, for a comparison of '[e]stimated immigrant population in England and Wales in 1951 and 1961'.

21. *Ibid.*, pp. 70–1.

22. R. Oakley, 'Cypriot migration and settlement in Britain', unpubl. DPhil thesis, University of Oxford, 1971, pp. 28, 88–91.

23. *Ibid.*, pp. 29–31.

24. See Rose, *Colour and Citizenship*, p. 83.

25. See C. Holmes, *A Tolerant Country? Immigrants, Refugees and Minorities in Britain*, London, 1991; P. Panayi, *Immigration, Ethnicity and Racism in Britain, 1815–1945*, Manchester, 1994.

26. While it would be accurate to suggest that Egyptians are one of the largest Arab groups if not the largest, in Britain, it remains extremely difficult to say what their precise number might be. See M. Al-Rasheed, 'The other-others: hidden Arabs?' in C. Peach, ed., *Ethnicity in the 1991 Census*, 2, 2, London, 1996, p. 207, which quoted a figure, based on the 1991 census, of 23,000 who gave Egypt as their place of birth; C.F. Elolh, 'Arab communities in Britain: cleavages and commonalities', *Islam and Christian–Muslim Relations*, 3, 2, December 1992, p. 239, suggested 70,000; *The Economist*, 17 September 1988, p. 39, put their number at between 90,000 and 120,000.

27. M. Al-Rasheed, 'Political migration and downward socio-economic mobility: the Iraqi community in London', *New Community*, 18, 4, July 1992, p. 537.

28. K. Siddiqi, 'Generating "power" without politics', speech delivered at conference on the Future of Muslims in Britain, Muslim Institute, London, 14 July 1990, pp. 4–6.

7. CONTOURS OF MUSLIM LIFE IN BRITAIN SINCE 1945

1. D. Owen, *Country of Birth: Settlement Patterns*, 1991 Census Statistical Paper no. 5, Centre for Research in Ethnic Relations (CRER), December 1993, p. 10.

2. T. Kucukcan, 'The politics of ethnicity, identity and religion among Turks in London', unpublished PhD thesis, University of Warwick, 1996, p. 89; on the other hand, a report in *Q-News*, November 1999, p. 11, estimated that around 300,000 (!) Turks lived in Britain. What

makes calculating community sizes difficult is that no distinction has ever been drawn between Greek and Turkish Cypriots in existing studies. The difficulties in separating the Greek and Turkish Cypriot populations in Britain have been explained by M. Storkey in her research, *Identifying the Cypriot Community from the 1991 Census*, London Research Centre, 1993. Of the estimated population of Cypriots in Britain, it is generally accepted that since the ratio of Turkish to Greek Cypriots in Cyprus in the 1960s and 1970s, when much of the migration took place, was 1: 4, Turkish Cypriots would also number a fifth of the Cypriot population in Britain. Thus it was estimated that by 1966, 75,000 Cypriots had entered Britain since the Second World War. According to the 1971 census, there were 72,270 persons born in Cyprus and, when taken with the children born to them since arrival, it was concluded that perhaps 100,000 Cypriots were settled in Britain. Since the 1970s the Turkish Cypriot population increase has been overwhelmingly through natural growth. It is difficult to arrive at accurate figures for Turkish Cypriots since they have had to be deduced from the data on the birthplace of the head of the household, and enumeration of third- and fourth-generation migrants is excluded. Based on the 1981 census figures, which gave a figure of 84,327 Cyprus-born persons in Britain, the estimates for Turkish Cypriots have ranged between 45,000 and 80,000 in the mid-1980s. See also Ann Bridgwood, 'Marriage, honour and property—Turkish Cypriots in North Cyprus', unpublished PhD thesis, University of London, 1986, pp. 34–5; R. Oakley, 'Cypriot migration and settlement in Britain', unpubl. DPhil thesis, University of Oxford, 1971, and R. Oakley, *Changing Patterns of Distribution of Cypriot Settlement*, Research Papers in Ethnic Relations No. 5, CRER, University of Warwick, 1987; M.J. Taylor, *Worlds Apart?*, London, 1988, pp. 3–8; S.R. Sonyel, *The Silent Minority: Turkish Muslim Children in British Schools*, Cambridge, 1988, pp. 16–17. By 1991 the number of Cyprus-born persons had gone down to 78,031, suggesting that the Cypriot population had stabilised, but the proportion of those born in Britain, including heads of household, has probably gone up and this no longer forms part of the calculations on migrant Cypriots since they would be included in the white ethnic category. See Owen, *Country of Birth: Settlement Patterns*, p. 10.

3. P. Lewis, *Islamic Britain: Religion, Politics and Identity among British Muslims*, London, 1994, p. 14.

4. *Ibid.*

5. J. Nielsen, *Muslims in Western Europe*, Edinburgh, 1992, p. 41.

6. 'In a world of their own', *The Economist*, 17 September 1988, p. 39. Al-Rasheed considered these figures to be 'over-inflated'; see Madawi

Al-Rasheed, 'Arab communities in Britain: a plea to go beyond numbers', paper given to the Second Arab Communities Conference, November 1993.

7. F. Halliday, *Arabs in Exile: Yemeni Migrants in Urban Britain*, London, 1992, p. 59.

8. C.F. El-Solh, 'Arab communities in Britain: cleavages and commonalities', *Islam and Christian–Muslim Relations*, 3, 2, December 1992, p. 239.

9. M. Al-Rasheed, 'The other-others: hidden Arabs?' in C. Peach, ed., *Ethnicity in the 1991 Census: The Ethnic Minority Populations of Great Britain*, 2, 2, London, 1996, p. 206.

10. M. Anwar, *Muslims in Britain: 1991 Census and other Statistical Sources*, CSIC Paper no. 9, Centre for the Study of Islam and Christian–Muslim Relations, Selly Oak Colleges, Birmingham, September 1993; C. Peach, 'Estimates of the 1991 Muslim population of Great Britain', paper given to the Exploratory Seminar on Statistics and the UK Religious Communities, University of Derby, 24–25 May 1994.

11. *Social Trends*, no. 30, London, 2000, p. 25.

12. A more definite estimate of the British Muslim population has emerged from the 2001 Census data, since the Census for the first time included a question on religious affiliation. According to the figures published by the Office for National Statistics (ONS) on 13 February 2003, the Muslim population of the UK (in April 2001) was 1.591 million. See 'The Big Picture Census 2001—benchmark for the 21st Century' on the ONS website *www.statistics.gov.uk/census2001*. However, the broad consensus considers two million as being more realistic since it is contended that a significant number of 'undocumented' and asylum-seeking Muslims probably remain unaccounted for.

13. See *Scottish Office Survey of Ethnic Minorities*, Edinburgh, Chapter 3, p. 15; see also B. Maan, *The New Scots: The Story of Asians in Scotland*, Edinburgh, 1992. The current estimates of Scotland's Muslim population are between 40,000 and 60,000. See *www.bbc.co.uk/scotland/webguide/religion* and the *Guardian*, 17 June 2002, pp. 6–7.

14. See the *Guardian*, 17 June 2002, pp. 6–7. See also G. Irwin and S. Dunn, *Ethnic Minorities in Northern Ireland*, Centre for the Study of Conflict, University of Ulster, Coleraine, 1997, p. 58; H. Donnan and M. O'Brien, '"Because you stick out, you stand out": perceptions of prejudice among Northern Ireland's Pakistanis' in P. Hainsworth, ed., *Divided Society: Ethnic Minorities and Racism in Northern Ireland*, London, 1998, p. 199.

15. Peach, ed., *Ethnicity in the 1991 Census*, 2, 2, London, pp. 157–8; P. Ratcliffe, ed., *Ethnicity in the 1991 Census*, vol. 3, London, 1996, p. 123.

16. D. Coleman and J. Salt, eds, *Ethnicity in the 1991 Census*, vol. 1, London, 1996, p. 91.

17. G.W. Kearsley and S.R. Srivastava, 'The spatial evolution of Glasgow's Asian community', *Scottish Geographical Magazine*, 90, 2, 1974, pp. 110–24; D. McEvoy, 'The segregation of Asian immigrants in Glasgow: a note', *Scottish Geographical Magazine*, 94, 3, 1978, pp. 180–2; J.M. Ritchie, 'A survey of the Muslim community of the City of Glasgow', 1972, typescript available at the Centre for Islam and Christian–Muslim Relations, Selly Oak Colleges, Birmingham; H.R. Hones and M. Davenport, 'The Pakistani community in Dundee: a study of its growth and demographic structure', *Scottish Geographical Magazine*, 88, 2, 1972, pp. 75–85; K. Little, *Negroes in Britain: A Study of Racial Relations in English Society*, 2nd edn, London, 1972, p. 18; S.F. Collins, *Coloured Minorities in Britain: Studies in British Race Relations based on African, West Indian and Asiatic Immigrants*, London, 1957, pp. 221, 224. South Asian Development Partnership, *UK–Asian Population Report* at *www.southasian.org.uk/research_popreport_app8.html*, based on the analysis of 1991 census data, states that, of the combined Pakistani and Bangladeshi population of 9,500 in Wales, 4,318 are resident in Cardiff; the Pakistani population of Glasgow is 11,269. Figures for Wales were taken from D. Owen, *Ethnic Minorities in Great Britain: Settlement Patterns*, 1991 Census Statistical Paper no. 1, CRER, University of Warwick, Coventry, November 1992, p. 17.

18. R. Oakley, 'The Cypriots in Britain', *Race Today*, 2, 1970, pp. 99–102. According to Kucukcan, 'The politics of ethnicity, identity and religion among Turks in London', p. 93, 'Almost all Turks live in Greater London.' See also Oakley, *Changing Patterns of Distribution of Cypriot Settlement*, pp. 5–6.

19. T. Modood *et al.*, *Ethnic Minorities in Britain: Diversity and Disadvantage*, London, 1997, p. 187.

20. Al-Rasheed, 'The other-others: hidden Arabs?', Tables 9.3 and 9.4; Modood *et al.*, *Ethnic Minorities in Britain*, p. 213. In 1994, Anwar put the figure for Moroccans at over 16,000 (adults and children); see M. Anwar, 'Census data and Muslims in Britain', paper presented at the Conference on Statistics and the UK Religious Communities, University of Derby, 24–25 May 1994, p. 5. The vast majority of Moroccans in Britain are resident in the North Kensington area of London; see G. Karmi, 'The health status and health beliefs of the London migrant communities', *International Migration*, 29, 1, 1990, pp. 5–12.

21. In the 1990s estimates varied a great deal, from 60,000 in Britain as a whole to between 10,000 and 15,000 in London's East End alone.

Given that between 1980 and 1991 7,141 Somalis applied for asylum in Britain and between 1993 and 2001 34,945 applied, it would be reasonable to say that over 42,000 Somalis entered between 1980 and 2001. Hence the estimates of the total Somali population in Britain appear to be fairly sound. H. Ditmar, 'Somalis in limbo—longing for home', *New African*, January 1995, pp. 8–9; D. Griffiths, 'Somali refugees in Tower Hamlets: clanship and new identities', *New Community*, 23, 1, January 1997, p. 9; C.F. El-Solh, 'Somalis in London's East End: a community striving for recognition', *New Community*, 17, 4, July 1991, p. 542; Peach, ed., *Ethnicity in the 1991 Census*, p. 48; T. Heath and R. Hill, *Asylum Statistics United Kingdom 2001*, London, 31 July 2002, Table 2.1.

22. J.M. Ritchie, 'Report on the Muslim community in South Shields', 1972. A typescript of this report is available at the Centre for Islam and Christian–Muslim Relations, Selly Oak Colleges, Birmingham.

23. B. Dahya, 'The nature of Pakistani ethnicity in urban cities' in A. Cohen, ed., *Urban Ethnicity*, London, 1974, p. 77; V. Robinson, *Transients, Settlers, and Refugees: Asians in Britain*, Oxford, 1986, p. 204.

24. N. Dokur-Gryskiewicz, 'A study of adaptation of Turkish migrant workers to living and working in the United Kingdom', unpubl. PhD thesis, University of London, 1979, p. 187.

25. R. Unsworth, 'First and second generation Pakistanis in Slough: social and spatial assimilation', unpubl. DPhil thesis, University of Cambridge, 1986, p. 260.

26. *Ibid.*, p. 229; P. Werbner, 'Avoiding the ghetto: Pakistani migrants and settlement shifts in Manchester', *New Community*, 7, 1979, pp. 376–89.

27. *Ibid.*, p. 378; see also P. Werbner, *The Migration Process: Capital, Gifts and Offerings among British Pakistanis*, Oxford, 1990, pp. 40–7.

28. See A. Kundnani, *From Oldham to Bradford: the Violence of the Violated*, London, 2001, p. 2.

29. In Manningham, Bradford, an inner-city area in which Pakistanis form 55% of the population, 45% of the young men were recorded as unemployed in a report in 1996; see *The Bradford Commission Report*, London, November 1996, p. 24.

30. Peach, ed., *Ethnicity in the 1991 Census*, Table 5.11, p. 142.

31. *Ibid.*, Table 5.12, p. 144.

32. *Ibid.*, pp. 156–7.

33. 'Bangladeshi housing crisis', *Race and Immigration: Runnymede Trust Bulletin*, 203, May 1987, pp. 4–5; Commission for Racial Equality, *Homelessness and Discrimination: Report of a Formal Investigation into the London Borough of Tower Hamlets*, London, July 1988, p. 55; *Begum v. Tower Hamlets LBC*, legal action, July 1998, p. 12.

34. For a comparison of amenities, see Peach, ed., *Ethnicity in the 1991 Census*, Tables 5.13 and 5.14, p. 145.

35. For a comparison of housing density, see *ibid.*, Table 5.14, p. 145.

36. See Modood *et al., Ethnic Minorities in Britain*, pp. 185–223.

37. *The Bradford Commission Report*, p. 126. However, while the census data suggested substantial housing stress, they did not necessarily provide the whole picture, since they also showed that a considerably larger proportion of Pakistanis and Bangladeshis lived in houses with six or more rooms (11.10% and 12.38%) than do whites (5.97%). See Peach, ed., *Ethnicity in the 1991 Census*, Tables 5.16 and 5.17, p. 146.

38. *Ibid.*, Table 9.9, p. 217.

39. Modood *et al., Ethnic Minorities in Britain*, pp. 207–12.

40. Computed from D. Owen, *Ethnic Minorities in Great Britain: Age and Gender Structure*, 1991 Census Statistical Paper no. 2, CRER, University of Warwick, Coventry, February 1993, Table 2, p. 3.

41. Peach, ed., *Ethnicity in the 1991 Censusn*, 2, 1, London, 1996, Table 5, p. 9.

42. Modood *et al., Ethnic Minorities in Britain*, pp. 40–1.

43. *Ibid.*, p. 21. The British-born proportion of the longer-established Turkish Cypriots is even greater. Kucukcan, 'The politics of ethnicity, identity and religion among Turks in London', and Storkey, *Identifying the Cypriot Community from the 1991 Census.*

44. See Peach, ed., *Ethnicity in the 1991 Census*, 2, 2, p. 128.

45. *The Bradford Commission Report*, p. 19.

46. See Peach, ed., *Ethnicity in the 1991 Census*, 2, 2, Table 9.5, p. 214.

47. *Ibid.*, Table 9.7, p. 216.

48. *Ibid.*, Table 9.6, p. 214.

49. For instance, an upper school head teacher estimated that up to 50% of pupils in the Bradford school system would benefit from English-language support; see *The Bradford Commission Report*, p. 141.

50. Modood *et al., Ethnic Minorities in Britain*, pp. 60–3.

51. *Ibid.*, p. 62.

52. *Ibid.*, p. 68.

53. T. Jones, *Britain's Ethnic Minorities: an Analysis of the Labour Force Survey*, London, 1993, pp. 38–9.

54. Modood *et al., Ethnic Minorities in Britain*, pp. 64–8.

55. Peach, ed., *Ethnicity in the 1991 Census*, 2, 2, p. 216; V. Karn, *Ethnicity in the 1991 Census: Employment, Education and Housing among the Ethnic Minority Populations of Great Britain*, vol. 4, London, 1996, pp. 5–10.

56. Peach, ed., *Ethnicity in the 1991 Census*, 2, 2, p. 216.

57. Modood *et al., Ethnic Minorities in Britain*, pp. 63–6; M.J. Taylor with S. Hegarty, *The Best of Both Worlds...? A Review of Research into the*

Education of Pupils of South Asian Origin, Windsor, 1985, pp. 354–7, 359–60, 549–50. By the end of the 1980s South Asian Muslim parents' views, challenged by the wider society and their children, had changed considerably, although the following opinion still tended to resonate with many: 'Our girls ultimately have to get married so they do not need any education.' S. Shaikh and A. Kelly, 'To mix or not to mix: Pakistani girls in British schools', *Educational Research*, 31, 1, February 1989, p. 14. See also H. Afshar, 'Gender roles and the "moral economy of kin" among Pakistani women in West Yorkshire', *New Community*, 15, 2, January 1989, pp. 211–25; H. Afshar, 'Education: hopes, expectations and achievements of Muslim women in West Yorkshire', *Gender and Education*, 1, 3, 1989, pp. 261–72; T.N. Basit, *Eastern Values; Western Milieu: Identities and Aspirations of Adolescent British Muslim Girls*, Aldershot, 1997.

58. M. Anwar, *British Pakistanis: Demographic, Social and Economic Position*, Coventry, 1996, pp. 47–8.
59. Modood *et al.*, *Ethnic Minorities in Britain*, p. 73.
60. *Ibid.*
61. See C. Peach, ed., *Ethnicity in the 1991 Census: Social Geography and Ethnicity in Britain; Geographical Spread, Spatial Concentration and Internal Migration*, vol. 3, London, 1996, pp. 17–21.
62. G. Lomas, 'Employment and economic activity—1972 census data', *New Community*, 7, 2, 1979, Table 2, p. 219.
63. Jones, *Britain's Ethnic Minorities*, p. 88.
64. *Ibid.*, p. 63.
65. 51% each according to the LFS 1988–90 analysis. *Ibid.*, p. 88.
66. Peach, ed., *Ethnicity in the 1991 Census*, 2, 2, p. 157.
67. Modood *et al.*, *Ethnic Minorities in Britain*, p. 87.
68. *Ibid.*, p. 87.
69. *Ibid.*, p. 217.
70. Anwar, *British Pakistanis*, p. 61.
71. *Ibid.*, p. 62.
72. See Peach, ed., *Ethnicity in the 1991 Census*, 2, 2, Table 5.1, p. 134.
73. 60% of Bangladeshi men, according to Modood *et al.*, *Ethnic Minorities in Britain*, pp. 108–9.
74. Peach, ed., *Ethnicity in the 1991 Census*, 2, 2, p. 218.
75. *Ibid.*, Table 5.2, p. 135.
76. Jones, *Britain's Ethnic Minorities*, p. 82.
77. *Ibid.*, p. 83.
78. See Peach, ed., *Ethnicity in the 1991 Census*, 2, 2, Table 6.3, p. 156.
79. Modood *et al.*, *Ethnic Minorities in Britain*, p. 110.
80. See Peach, ed., *Ethnicity in the 1991 Census*, 2, 2, Tables 6.3 and 6.4, pp. 156–7.

81. *Ibid.*, Table 5.5, p. 137.
82. *Ibid.*, p. 138.
83. *Ibid.*, Tables 5.6 and 5.7, pp. 138–9.
84. *Ibid.*, Table 5.8, p. 140.
85. *Ibid.*, Tables 5.9 and 5.10, p. 14.
86. 17% of Indians, 16.3% of Pakistanis and 12.2% of Bangladeshi were self-employed, compared with 11.5% of whites, 4.7% of Black Caribbean and 5.6% of Black African. See S.Y. Ho and J. Henderson, 'Locality and the variability of ethnic employment in Britain', *Journal of Ethnic and Migration Studies*, 25, 2, April 1999, p. 325.
87. *Ibid.*, p. 327.
88. *Ibid.*
89. Werbner, *The Migration Process*, pp. 50–78.
90. P. Werbner, 'From rags to riches: Manchester Pakistanis in the textile trade', *New Community*, 8, 1–2, 1980, pp. 84–7.
91. M. Rafiq, 'Ethnicity and enterprise: a comparison of Muslim and non-Muslim owned Asian businesses in Britain', *New Community*, 19, 1, 1992, p. 44.
92. P.I. Panayiotopoulos, 'Challenging orthodoxies: Cypriot entrepreneurs in the London garment industry', *New Community*, 22, 3, July 1996, p. 454.
93. A. Brah, '"Race" and "culture" in the gendering of labour markets: South Asian young Muslim women and the labour market', *New Community*, 19, 3, July 1993, p. 453.
94. H. Metcalf, T. Modood and S. Virdee, *Asian Self-employment: the Interaction of Culture and Economics in England*, London, 1996, p. 38.
95. *Ibid.*, pp. 40–1. Evidence in respect of other Muslim ethnic groups such as Bangladeshis and Turkish Cypriots confirms these patriarchal attitudes. For Turkish Cypriots see Taylor, *Worlds Apart?*, pp. 16–17; for Bangladeshis see N. Kabir, 'The structure of "revealed" preference: race, community and female labour supply in the London clothing industry', *Development and Change*, 25, 1994, pp. 307–31.
96. For instance, while two-thirds of the self-employed Pakistanis earned less than £193 per week, only a third of African Asians and Indians did so. On the other hand a comparatively much smaller proportion of Bangladeshis and Pakistanis were in the £500+ bracket. See Modood *et al., Ethnic Minorities in Britain*, p. 127.
97. Rafiq, 'Ethnicity and enterprise: a comparison of Muslim and non-Muslim owned Asian businesses in Britain', pp. 43–9.
98. *Ibid.*, pp. 54–5.
99. D. Owen, *Ethnic Minorities in Great Britain: Economic Characteristics*, 1991 Census Statistical Paper no. 3, CRER, University of Warwick, Coventry, March 1993, p. 7.

100. *Ibid.*

101. Modood *et al., Ethnic Minorities in Britain*, p. 89.

102. Owen, *Ethnic Minorities in Great Britain: Economic Characteristics*, p. 7.

103. Peach, ed., *Ethnicity in the 1991 Census*, 2, 2, Tables 9.11 and 9.12, p. 218.

104. Ho and Henderson, 'Locality and the variability of ethnic employment in Britain', p. 330.

105. Jones, *Britain's Ethnic Minorities*, Table 5.4, p. 127.

106. 'Hypercyclical' means that 'when unemployment rises among the general population, it rises much faster among minorities, to a higher peak; and as the national trend goes in reverse and jobs become plentiful, minority unemployment falls faster than among whites'. See P. Braham, A. Rattansi and R. Skellington, eds, *Racism and Antiracism: Inequalities, Opportunities and Policies*, London, 1992, p. 54.

107. Modood *et al., Ethnic Minorities in Britain*, pp. 83–4.

108. P. Weller, A. Feldman and K. Purdam, *Muslims and Religious Discrimination in England and Wales*, Home Office Research Study 220, London, 2001, p. 77.

109. *British Muslims Monthly Survey (BMMS)*, July 1998.

110. For instance, neighbours objected to Muslim presence in the locality, *BMMS*, July 1997, February 1999, December 1999, and resorted to harassment by hurling abuse such as 'Get back to f*****g Pakistan', *BMMS*, February 2000.

111. Traders successfully blocked a mosque scheme in Sheffield, *BMMS*, November 1998. Planning permission was refused to an Islamic teaching centre, *BMMS*, June 2000. There were mass protests against plans to create a Muslim burial site in Hainault in London, *BMMS*, July 1999. Other examples of discrimination included a Muslim woman wearing *hijab* awarded £2,000 damages after being prevented from viewing a house by an estate agent, *BMMS*, August 1997.

112. Dress codes and uniforms have emerged as a major area of potential conflict, for Muslim women in particular, *BMMS*, October 1997. Muslim women have been dismissed from jobs for wearing *hijab*, *BMMS*, March 1995, November 1996, November 1997, July 2000.

113. Muslim women have been reported to be on the receiving end of verbal abuse and, when it came to school or employment, this has resulted in their having to leave or to compromise their beliefs, *BMMS*, November 1999.

114. Two Muslim chefs were sacked from the Joseph's Restaurant Bar for a similar misdemeanour, *BMMS*, October 1993, August 1996, October 1998.

115. *BMMS*, April 1993, December 1993, January 1994, May 1995.

116. *BMMS*, published since 1993, has regularly reported on policies of different institutions on *halal* food. For the latest reporting of concerns on this subject see its 2002 issues.

117. Examples have included arson attacks on mosques and religious centres. *BMMS*, April 2000, May 2000, August 2000; pigs' heads being left on doorsteps, *BMMS*, November 1994, November 1997; and offensive graffiti, *BMMS*, July 2000.

118. *BMMS*, 1995, November 1996, October 1998, May 2000.

119. For instance, a reception of aid workers, attended by 450 people, which was organised by Buckingham Palace, failed to invite any representatives of Muslim charities, *BMMS*, December 1995.

120. For example PC Akhtar Aziz stressed in a Commission for Racial Equality report the problems Muslims face in regard to police culture. His colleagues 'could not understand' why he was not prepared to purchase alcohol. 'In a way,' he said, 'he had been treated differently' and had not been accepted. *BMMS*, March 1996.

121. *BMMS*, August 1994.

122. *BMMS*, March 1997.

123. *BMMS*, January and September 1998, December 2000.

124. The Runnymede Trust, *Islamophobia: A Challenge for Us All*, London, 1997.

125. Modood *et al.*, *Ethnic Minorities in Britain*, p. 343.

8. ASSIMILATION, INTEGRATION, ACCOMMODATION: ASPECTS OF MUSLIM ENGAGEMENT WITH BRITISH SOCIETY SINCE 1945

1. P. Lewis, *Islamic Britain: Religion, Politics and Identity among British Muslims*, London, 1994, p. 53.

2. *Ibid.*

3. *Ibid.*, p. 52.

4. B. Dahya, 'The nature of Pakistani ethnicity in industrial cities in Britain' in A. Cohen, ed., *Urban Ethnicity*, London, 1974, p. 94.

5. Lewis, *Islamic Britain*, p. 19; for aspects of institutional completeness in the Turkish Cypriot community see A. Bridgwood, 'Marriage, honour, property: Turkish Cypriots in North London', unpubl. PhD thesis, University of London, 1986, p. 136.

6. P. Werbner and M. Anwar, eds, *Black and Ethnic Leaderships in Britain: the Cultural Dimensions of Political Action*, London, 1991, p. 141.

7. M. Halstead, *Education, Justice and Cultural Diversity: an Examination*, Falmer, 1988, p. 114.

8. E.J.B. Rose, *Colour and Citizenship: a Report on Race Relations*, London, 1969, p. 24.

9. Speech given at a meeting of the Voluntary Liaison Committees on 23 May 1966, NCCI, London.

10. F.M. Bhatti, *Turkish Cypriots in London*, Research Paper no. 11, Centre for the Study of Islam and Christian–Muslim Relations, Selly Oak Colleges, Birmingham, September 1991, p. 9.

11. Bridgwood, 'Marriage', p. 18.

12. G. Karmi, 'Identity and sense of belonging', paper for the Second Arab Communities Conference, Imperial College, London, November 1993, p. 3; for an earlier study of an economic migrant Yemeni community detached from wider society, see B. Dahya, 'Yemenis in Britain: an Arab migrant community', *Race*, 6, 3, January 1965, pp. 177–90.

13. C. Nagel, 'Hidden minorities and the politics of "race": the case of British Arab activists in London', *Journal of Ethnic and Migration Studies*, 27, 3, July 2001, pp. 381–400.

14. T. Modood *et al., Ethnic Minorities in Britain: Diversity and Disadvantage*, London, 1997, pp. 354–5.

15. See T. Modood, S. Beishon and S. Virdee, *Changing Ethnic Identities*, London, 1994, pp. 68–80.

16. P. Ratcliffe, ed., *Ethnicity in the 1991 Census: Social Geography and ethnicity in Britain: Geographical Spread, Spatial Concentration and Internal Migration*, vol. 3, London, 1996, pp. 42–9.

17. T. Jones, *Britain's Ethnic Minorities*, London, 1993, pp. 17–19.

18. Ratcliffe, ed., *Ethnicity in the 1991 Census*, p. 49.

19. Modood *et al., Ethnic Minorities in Britain*, p. 188.

20. M. Anwar, *British Pakistanis: Demographic, Social and Economic Position*, Centre for Research in Ethnic Relations (CRER), University of Warwick, Coventry, 1996, p. 24; for concentration of Bangladeshis, see C. Peach, ed., *Ethnicity in the 1991 Census: the Ethnic Minority Populations*, vol. 2, part 1, London, 1996, p. 14.

21. *Ibid.*

22. A ghetto is a neighbourhood where a single ethnic or racial group forms the whole of the population of the residential district and all of that group is found in it. See Radcliffe, ed., *Ethnicity in the 1991 Census*, pp. 115–16.

23. *Ibid.*, p. 123.

24. Modood *et al., Ethnic Minorities in Britain*, p. 190.

25. Ratcliffe, ed., *Ethnicity in the 1991 Census*, p. 130.

26. The impact of socialisation on the religiosity of British Muslims has been the subject of considerable research. Recent surveys suggest that the young in every faith in Britain value religion less. Among Muslims, the data suggest that those who entered Britain at a young age are likely to be less religious than the older ones. Length of stay in Britain

was also relevant, with those who were born in Britain less likely to be religious than those who have spent only a proportion of their lives here. The length of stay in Britain appears to be directly correlated to religiosity. Thus, one survey revealed that, while 57% of Pakistanis and 50% of Bangladeshis born in Britain said, 'Religion is very important to how they live their lives', these figures rose to 88% and 86% of those who had spent a third or less of their lives in Britain. Similarly, while 69% of Pakistanis and 74% of Bangladeshis who had entered Britain before sixteen years of age agreed with the above statement, the figures rose to 83% and 81% for those who entered after the age of sixteen. Further, the figures were much higher for those over the age of thirty-five than for those below it. See Modood *et al., Ethnic Minorities in Britain*, pp. 305–8.

27. *Ibid.*, pp. 326–8.
28. R. Unsworth, 'First and second generation Pakistanis in Slough: social and spatial assimilation', unpubl. DPhil thesis, University of Cambridge, 1986, p. 203.
29. Modood *et al., Ethnic Minorities in Britain*, pp. 317–19.
30. Unsworth, 'First and second generation Pakistanis in Slough', p. 204.
31. Modood *et al., Ethnic Minorities in Britain*, pp. 314–15.
32. See D. Coleman and J. Salt, eds, *Ethnicity in the 1991 Census: Demographic Characteristics of the Ethnic Minority Populations*, vol. 1, London, 1996, table 7.10, pp. 200–1.
33. *Ibid.*, pp. 202–3.
34. See M. Anwar, *Between Two Cultures: A Study of Relationships Between Generations in the Asian Community of Britain*, London, 1981; A. Shaw, *A Pakistani Community in Britain*, Oxford, 1988, pp. 156–80; M.H. Siddiqi, 'Muslims in a non-Muslim society', *Brighton Islamic Centre Bulletin*, vol. 15, no. 3, July–September 1991, pp. 12–13; Lewis, *Islamic Britain*, p. 179; T. Kucukcan, 'Continuity and change: young Turks in London' in S. Vertovec and A. Rogers, eds, *Muslim European Youth: Reproducing Ethnicity, Religion, Culture*, Aldershot, 1998, pp. 107–13; C.E. Alexander, *The Asian Gang: Ethnicity, Identity, Masculinity*, Oxford, 2000. For evidence on incidence of forced marriages, see *The Bradford Commission Report*, London, November 1996, p. 21; for instances of violence against Muslim women perpetrated by their male relatives, see Southall Black Sisters, *Forced Marriage: an Abuse of Human Rights One Year After 'A Choice by Right'*, Interim Report, Southall, July 2001.
35. 'Corruption! Fanaticism! Old prejudices die hard when British Asians pursue politics or religion', *Observer*, 19 March 1995.
36. Birt, 'Drugs, criminality and Muslims', *Q-News*, October 2000, p. 17.

37. *Ibid.*
38. *Q-News*, May 1998, p. 5.
39. Lewis, *Islamic Britain*, p. 179.
40. *Guardian*, 26 March 1990.
41. Lewis, *Islamic Britain*, p. 177.
42. *Ibid.*, p. 181.
43. *Q-News*, April 1998, p. 25.
44. S. Sharma, J. Hutnyk and A. Sharma, eds, *Dis-Orienting Rhythms: the Politics of the New Asian Dance Music*, London, 1996, pp. 156–89.
45. Lewis, *Islamic Britain*, p. 180.
46. *Q-News*, September 1997, p. 22.
47. *Guardian*, 8 October 1994, p. 29.
48. In many cases this has come close to intimidation. B. Hugill, in an article in the *Observer*, reported the taunts to which a girl studying A-level art was subjected by a group of Muslim boys at a sixth-form college in East London, 'Do modern art and you'll burn in Hell', *Observer*, 5 February 1995, p. 3.
49. J.M. Halstead, 'Some musical reflections on the debate about music in Islam', *Muslim Educational Quarterly*, 12, 1, 1994, pp. 51–62.
50. See K. Azzam, 'Islamic Art and Architecture', *Muslim Educational Quarterly*, 12, 1, 1994, pp. 63–71.
51. Y. Alibhai-Brown, 'Sacred beauty', *Guardian Weekly*, 15 January 2000, pp. 33–8.
52. Motara, 'Centre of beauty and tradition', *Q-News*, August 2001, p. 11.
53. Alibhai-Brown, 'Sacred beauty', p. 33.
54. *Ibid.*, p. 36.
55. His play *East is East*, later turned into a film, received much praise from reviewers internationally.
56. 'Best of young British', *New Statesman*, 22 July 2002, p. 15.
57. See *Show Case Arts*, no. 7, June–September 2000, published by IMAN, an Islamic organisation based in London.
58. *Guardian Education Supplement*, 2 June 1998.
59. Even more surprising is his wife Aisha's testimony to having challenged him to a race and on one occasion indeed outpaced him! L. Sfeir, 'The status of Muslim women in sport: conflict between cultural tradition and modernization', *International Review for the Sociology of Sport*, 20, 4, 1985, p. 294.
60. There is a considerable literature on racism in British sport, which describes the exclusion of Muslims from access to sports opportunities and from participation at various levels. The following are offered as a sample: 'English cricket must bring Asians in from the cold', *Daily Telegraph*, 4 October 1997. I. McDonald and S. Ugra, *Anyone for*

Cricket?, Centre for Sport Development Research, Roehampton Institute, London, in association with the Centre for New Ethnicities Research, University of East London, 1998, show how exclusion of ethnic minorities takes place in cricket through both subtle and explicit forms of racism, locally and nationally; Commission for Racial Equality, 'Let's kick racism out of football', Commission for Racial Equality website, and J. Bains, *Asians Can't Play Football*, Midland Asian Sports Forum, 1995, explored the nature of racial exclusion in soccer, including the marginalisation of South Asians from many areas of the game. Likewise, the Commission for Racial Equality's *Tackle It! Racism in Rugby League*, London, 1999, investigated barriers to the participation of ethnic minorities in Rugby League.

61. S. Vertovec and A. Rogers, eds, *Muslim European Youth*, Aldershot, 1998, p. 96.

62. A. Khan, 'Welcome to the Quaid-I-Azam League' in *Hit Racism for Six: Race and Cricket in England Today*, London, 1996, pp. 12–15.

63. *Q-News*, August 1998, p. 31.

64. J.S. Nielsen, 'A Muslim agenda for Britain: some reflections', *New Community*, 17, 3, p. 469.

65. See *The Muslim Manifesto—a Strategy for Survival*, The Muslim Institute, London, 15 June 1990.

66. See Lewis, *Islamic Britain*, p. 53; Kalim Siddiqui even suggested 'symbolic breaking of the law', *ibid.*, p. 162.

67. Nielsen, 'A Muslim agenda for Britain', p. 471.

68. S.A. Pasha, 'Muslim family law in Britain', unpublished paper presented at the House of Commons, 20 January 1977.

69. J.L. Nielsen, *Emerging Claims of Muslim Populations in Matters of Family Law in Europe*, CSIC Papers no. 10, Centre for the Study of Islam and Christian–Muslim Relations, Selly Oak Colleges, Birmingham, November 1993, p. 3.

70. S. Poulter, 'The Muslim community and English law', *Islam and Christian–Muslim Relations*, 3, 2, December 1992, p. 266.

71. That said, when approached by the Union of Muslim Organisations in 1998, the then Home Secretary Jack Straw ruled out, on practical grounds, the possibility of integrating Islamic family law into legislation embracing the European Convention on Human Rights. However, he promised to raise the possibility of issuing a consultative document on Muslim family law with the Law Commission. Reported in *Q-News*, August 1998, p. 8.

72. D. Pearl, 'The family, the law and the ethnic minorities: a bibliographic essay', *Sage Race Relations Abstracts*, 5, 2, May 1980, pp. 3–8.

73. For more about how the Sharia Court functions see 'The Mosque', a programme shown on BBC 2, 14 August 2001.

74. See Lewis, *Islamic Britain*, pp. 118–22.

75. See *Q-News*, April 1997, p. 7.

76. Fleming's OASIS international equity fund was similarly designed; see *Q-News*, June 1997, p. 7.

77. A local radio poll in Bradford carried out in 1991 'suggested that 90% of Muslims were against the fatwa'; see Lewis, *Islamic Britain*, p. 170.

78. *Yorkshire Post*, 18 January 1989.

79. *Need for Reform: Muslims and the Law in Multi-faith Britain*, memorandum submitted by the UK Action Committee on Islamic Affairs, Autumn 1993, p. 8.

80. Lewis, *Islamic Britain*, p. 163.

81. *British Muslims Monthly Service (BMMS)* and Muslim periodicals such as *Q-News* and the *Muslim News* have regularly reported instances of continuing and specific discrimination and attacks against and exclusion and harassment of Muslims throughout the last decade.

82. J. Eade, 'Nationalism and the quest for authenticity: the Bangladeshis in Tower Hamlets', *New Community*, 16, 4, July 1990, pp. 493–503.

83. Research in 1964 suggested that less than half the Commonwealth settlers were registered. See N. Deakin, ed., *Colour and the British Electorate, 1964*, London, 1965. Anwar's research in Bradford and Rochdale suggested that fewer than half of the Pakistanis in these areas were on the electoral register in the 1950s. Anwar, *British Pakistanis*, p. 121.

84. See Anwar, *British Pakistanis*, p. 121.

85. Werbner and Anwar, eds, *Black and Ethnic Leadership in Britain*, p. 46.

86. B. Lewis and D. Schnapper, *Muslims in Europe*, London, 1994, p. 86.

87. See Anwar, *British Pakistanis*, p. 121.

88. Commission for Racial Equality, *Ethnic Minorities and Electoral Politics: Lessons of the 1997 General Elections*, London, September 1998, pp. 1–2.

89. *Ibid.*, p. 2.

90. Werbner and Anwar, eds, *Black and Ethnic Leadership in Britain*, pp. 48–9; see also Anwar, *British Pakistanis*, pp. 121–2, for statistical comparisons during the period 1974–87.

91. M. Lelohe, 'The Asian vote in a northern city' in H. Goulbourne, ed., *Black Politics in Britain*, Aldershot, 1990, p. 70; see also K. Purdam, 'The impacts of democracy on identity: Muslim councillors and their experiences of local politics in Britain', unpublished PhD thesis, University of Manchester, 1997, p. 37.

92. See S. Saggar and A. Geddes, 'Negative and positive racialisation: re-examining ethnic minority political representation in the UK', *Journal of Ethnic and Migration Studies*, vol. 26, no. 1, January 2000, pp. 34–6.

93. See *Runnymede Quarterly Bulletin*, June 2001, p. 16.

94. See the *Muslim News* website.
95. That religion does not trump all other factors for Muslims was also demonstrated in the 1992 general elections. When the Islamic Party of Britain (IPB) put up candidates in the Bradford constituencies hoping to capitalise on the Islamic sentiment, it was disappointed as the vast majority of Muslims voted for the mainstream political parties. All three IPB candidates lost their deposits despite Muslims forming a very substantial proportion of the Bradford West and Bradford North constituencies. In Bradford West, Daud Musa Pidcock, president of the IPB, won 471 votes out of an estimated 16,000 Muslim votes and Mustaqim Bleher, the general secretary, received 304 votes out of 7,000 Muslim votes. See Lewis, *Islamic Britain*, p. 235.
96. Purdam, 'The impacts of democracy on identity', p. 127; a survey carried out before the 1992 general election gave some indication of the scale of this support. It found that 8% of Pakistanis and 11% of Bangladeshis backed the Conservative Party, K. Amin and R. Richardson, *Politics for All*, Runnymede Trust, London, 1992, something corroborated by Anwar's 1999 data, which show that 82% of 'Asians' continued to support the Labour Party.
97. Anwar, *British Pakistanis*, p. 123.
98. As Saggar has explained, some Asians, as a result of 'economic and social embourgeoisement', may have adopted the conservative values of similarly classed white Britons and, in turn, shifted their support to the Conservatives, see *Runnymede Quarterly Bulletin*, no. 325, March 2001, p. 8.
99. *BMMS*, March 2001, p. 2.
100. Purdam, 'The impacts of democracy on identity', p. 125.
101. See Anwar, *British Pakistanis*, pp. 125–7.
102. '23 Muslim prospective parliamentary candidates were standing this year [1997]—up from only 11 in 1992', *Q-News*, 14 March 1997, p. 16.
103. See Operation Black Vote Website, *http://www.obv.uk/blackpolitician/peers.html*, 3 November 2002.
104. *Q-News*, February 2000, p. 18.
105. Purdam, 'The impacts of democracy on identity', graph, pp. 40.1, 41.
106. *Muslim News*, 25 May 2001.
107. Anwar, *British Pakistanis*, p. 127.
108. Purdam, 'The impacts of democracy on identity', p. 47.
109. Lewis, *Islamic Britain*, pp. 24, 61–2.
110. Anwar, *British Pakistanis*, p. 127.
111. Purdam, 'The impacts of democracy on identity', pp. 164–164.1.

112. *Ibid.*, p. 140.

113. See H. Chapman, 'Mahmood disproves detractors and becomes the second Muslim MP', *Muslim News*, 29 June 2001.

114. K. Purdam, 'The political identities of Muslim local councillors in Britain', *Local Government Studies*, 26, 1, spring 2000, pp. 47–64; for a more detailed discussion see Purdam, 'The impacts of democracy on identity', pp. 69–123.

115. *Ibid.*, pp. 99, 120.

116. Modood *et al., Ethnic Minorities in Britain*, p. 302.

117. See Operation Black Vote website.

118. See S. Saggar, 'The general election and beyond', *Connections*, Commission for Racial Equality, summer 2001, p. 11.

119. M. Anwar, 'Pakistani participation in the 1973 Rochdale local elections', *New Community*, 3, 1–2, 1974, pp. 67–72.

120. Lewis and Schnapper, eds, *Muslims in Europe*, p. 88; H. Goulbourne, ed., *Black Politics in Britain*, Aldershot, 1990, pp. 63–74.

121. *Q-News*, 14 March 1997, p. 16.

122. *Ibid.*, June 2001.

123. See the Institute of Contemporary Islamic Thought website.

124. *Q-News*, 14 March 1997, p. 27.

125. *Ibid.*, 12–19 August 1994, p. 9; see also Hizb-ut-Tahrir website.

126. *Common Sense*, No. 32, p. 8.

127. *Q-News*, April 2001, p. 13.

128. *Ibid.*, 14 March 1997, p. 26.

129. *Ibid.*, pp. 5, 16.

130. *Ibid.*, April 2001, p. 12.

131. See W.A.R. Shadid and P.S. van Koningsfeld, eds, *Political Participation and Identities of Muslims in Non-Muslim States*, Kampen, 1996, p. 106.

132. A. Andrews, 'Muslim attitudes towards political activity in the United Kingdom' in *ibid.*, pp. 124–6.

133. M.S. Raza, *Islam in Britain: Past, Present and Future*, 2nd edn, Leicester, 1993, p. 36.

134. M.J. Herskovits, 'Some Psychological Implications of Afro-American Studies' referred to in M. Mead, 'Socialization and enculturation', *Current Anthropology*, 4, 2, 1963, p. 184.

135. *Ibid.*

136. P. Weinreich, C.L. Luk and M.H. Bond, 'Ethnic Stereotyping and Identification in a multicultural context', *Psychology of Developing Societies* vol. 8, no. 1, 1996, p. 150.

137. N. Ali, 'Community and identity of the Kashmiri community: a case study of Luton', unpubl. PhD thesis, University of Luton, 1999, pp. 2–3, 29–30, 32.

9. MUSLIM WOMEN AND FAMILIES IN BRITAIN

1. See E.J.B. Rose, *Colour and Citizenship: a Report on British Race Relations*, London, 1969; M. Anwar, *The Myth of Return: Pakistanis in Britain*, London, 1979, p. 39.
2. Rose, *Colour and Citizenship*, p. 72.
3. A. Shaw, *A Pakistani Community in Britain*, Oxford, 1988, pp. 46–8.
4. Figures extracted from Rose, *Colour and Citizenship*; D.J. Smith, *Racial disadvantage in Britain: The PEP Report*, Harmondsworth, 1977; C. Brown, *Black and White Britain: the Third PSI Survey*, London, 1984; and Anwar, *The Myth of Return*.
5. J. Ellis, *Meeting Community Needs: A Study of Muslim Communities in Coventry*, Centre for Research in Ethnic Relations (CRER), University of Warwick, Coventry, September 1991, p. 46.
6. Shaw, *A Pakistani Community in Britain*, p. 82.
7. See R. Oakley, 'The Cypriot migration to Britain' in V.S. Khan, ed., *Minority Families in Britain: Support and Stress*, London, 1979, pp. 19, 22; S. Ladbury, 'The Turkish Cypriots: ethnic relations in London and Cyprus', in J.L. Watson, ed., *Between Two Cultures: Migrants and Minorities in Britain*, Oxford, 1977, pp. 301–31; F.M. Bhatti, *Turkish Cypriots In London*, Research Paper no. 11, Centre for the Study of Islam and Christian–Muslim Relations, Selly Oak Colleges, Birmingham, September 1981; A. Bridgwood, 'Marriage, honour and property—Turkish Cypriots in North London', unpubl. PhD thesis, University of London, 1986, pp. 47–61; M.J. Taylor, *Worlds Apart?: A Review of Research into the Education of Pupils of Cypriot, Italian, Ukranian and Vietnamese Origin, Liverpool Blacks and Gypsies*, Windsor, 1987, pp. 1–206.
8. C.F. El-Solh, 'Somalis in London's East End: a community striving for recognition', *New Community*, 17, 4, July 1991, pp. 544–6.
9. Ladbury, 'The Turkish Cypriots: ethnic relations in London and Cyprus', p. 308.
10. By 1966 the male Cypriot population was already only 52% of the total. See R. Oakley, 'Cypriot migration and settlement in Britain', unpubl. DPhil thesis, University of Oxford, 1971, pp. 54–7, for the changes in sex ratio between 1951 and 1966.
11. Oakley, 'The Cypriot migration to Britain', p. 18.
12. Bridgwood, 'Marriage, honour and property', p. 34.
13. *Ibid.*, p. 209.
14. M. Stopes-Roe and R. Cochrane, 'Marriage in two cultures', *British Journal of Social Psychology*, vol. 27, 1988, p. 166.
15. See V.S. Khan, 'Asian women in Britain: strategies of adjustment of

Indian and Pakistani migrants' in A. de Souza, ed., *Women in Contemporary India and South Asia*, New Delhi, 1980, pp. 276–81.

16. S.P. Rack, 'Diagnosing mental illness: Asians and the psychiatric services' in V.S. Khan, ed., *Minority Families in Britain: Support and Stress*, London, 1979, pp. 167–80; see S. Fenton and A. Sadiq, *The Sorrow in my Heart...*, London, 1993, especially pp. 5, 10, 19.

17. A. Wilson, 'A burning fever: the isolation of Asian women in Britain', *Race and Class*, 20, 2, 1978, p. 132.

18. N. Patel, 'Psychological disturbance and social support: a comparison between immigrant Asian women and indigenous population', unpubl. MSc thesis, University of Hull, 1989.

19. Wilson, 'A burning fever', pp. 135–6.

20. G. Karmi, 'The health status and health beliefs of two London migrant communities', *International Migration*, vol. 29, p. 8.

21. M. Al-Rasheed, 'The meaning of marriage and status in exile: the experience of Iraqi women', *Journal of Refugee Studies*, 6, 2, 1993, pp. 89–104.

22. M.H. Kahin, *Educating Somali Children in Britain*, Stoke on Trent, 1997.

23. B. Wade and P. Souter, *Continuing to Think: the British Asian Girl*, Clevedon, 1992; A. Osler, *Speaking Out: Black Girls in Britain*, London, 1989.

24. R.N. Rapoport, P.M. Fogarty and R. Rapoport, eds, *Families in Britain*, London, 1982, pp. 192–3.

25. See Shaw, *A Pakistani Community in Britain*, p. 5; P. Werbner, *The Migration Process: Capital, Gifts and Offerings among British Pakistanis*, Oxford, 1990, pp. 134–5.

26. The nature of the family in Britain has been undergoing rapid and radical change over the past four decades. See A.H. Halsey, 'Changes in the family', *Children and Society*, 7, 2, 1993, pp. 125–36. In the majority population until the early 1960s people entered into formal marriage partnerships relatively early and remained together, generally for life. Divorce was infrequent. In the following period, while marriage remained popular, the rate of divorce quickened, both men and women married later, had fewer children and hadextramarital sexual intercourse, and cohabitation and births outside marriage increased sharply. There has emerged undeniable evidence of a weakening of the norms of the traditional family, mounting multiple instability of marriage and increasingly fragile support for mothers and children outside wedlock since the 1960s. Between 1961 and 1989 the incidence of divorce rose from 2.1 to 12.7 per 1,000 married people. Births outside marriage rose from 5% in 1960 to 11% in 1979 to 28% in 1990 and a record 37% in 1997. Similarly, the number of lone-par-

ent families has been growing inexorably since the 1960s, from 600,000 in the early 1970s to 1.6 million in the late 1990s, with the burden of child care falling mainly on women. Indeed, the likelihood of being a single parent increased among mothers from less than 20% aged 30 to almost 50% among those aged 22. According to Patricia Morgan, 'What we are witnessing is not the formalisation of other "family structures" but the deregulation of the conjugal nuclear family which we have known for centuries.' These new trends in family formation 'may reflect', in J. Haskey's view, 'the growth of individualism or the increasing exercise of choice': *Guardian*, 17 January 1998, p. 9.

27. *British Monthly Muslim Survey* (henceforth *BMMS*), March, 1993.

28. T. Modood *et al.*, *Ethnic Minorities in Britain: Diversity and Disadvantage*, London, 1997, p. 42.

29. *Ibid.*, p. 44.

30. Oakley, 'Cypriot migration and Settlement in Britain', pp. 280, 287.

31. *Ibid.*, p. 287.

32. *Ibid.*, p. 285.

33. *Ibid.*, p. 286.

34. Taylor, *Worlds Apart?*, p. 12.

35. D. Owen, *Country of Birth: Settlement patterns: 1991*, Census Statistical Paper no. 5, CRER, University of Warwick, Coventry, December 1993, p. 18.

36. A. Berrington, 'Marriage patterns and inter-ethnic unions' in D. Coleman and J. Salt, eds, *Ethnicity in the 1991 Census: Demographic Characteristics of the Ethnic Minority Population*, vol. 1, London, 1996, p. 182.

37. Modood *et al.*, *Ethnic Minorities in Britain*, pp. 24–6.

38. A. Berrington, 'Marriage and family formation among the white and ethnic minority populations in Britain', *Ethnic and Racial Studies*, 17, 3, July 1994, p. 521.

39. Berrington, 'Marriage patterns and inter-ethnic unions', p. 185.

40. *Ibid.*, see table 7.3 on p. 185; also see pp. 188–9; Modood *et al.*, *Ethnic Minorities in Britain*, pp. 25, 29, 33.

41. D. Owen, *Ethnic Minorities in Great Britain: Housing and Family Characteristics: 1991*, Statistical Census Paper no. 4, CRER, University of Warwick, Coventry, April 1993, p. 4.

42. T. Jones, *Britain's Ethnic Minorities*, London, 1993, p. 20.

43. Modood *et al.*, *Ethnic Minorities in Britain*, p. 38.

44. Taylor, *Worlds Apart?*, p. 7.

45. The corresponding figures from a similar survey carried out in 1982 were 7% for whites and 2% for South Asians, see Brown, *Black and White Britain*, p. 50.

46. Berrington, 'Marriage patterns and inter-ethnic unions', pp. 211–12.
47. According to Smith, *Racial Disadvantage in Britain*, only 2% of South Asian women were married to a white man. In a similar survey in 1982 only 1% of South Asian women had white partners, Brown, *Black and White Britain*, p. 33.
48. Modood *et al., Ethnic Minorities in Britain*, p. 30.
49. Berrington, 'Marriage and family formation', p. 529. In 1982, 4% of South Asians were married to or cohabiting with a white partner, Brown, *Black and White Britain*, p. 33. In 1991, 11.2% of the 16–24 age-group and 9.9% of the 25–39 age-group of white women against 0.2% of the 16–24 age-group and 1.0% of the 25–39 age-group of Pakistani and Bangladeshi women were cohabiting, Berrington, 'Marriage patterns and inter-ethnic unions', p. 193.
50. Berrington, 'Marriage and family formation', p. 530.
51. The proportion of Pakistani and Bangladeshi women in the labour force doubled between 1979 and 1987–9, from 3% to 6%. See I. Bruegel, 'Labour market prospects for women from ethnic minorities' in R. Lindley, ed., *Labour Market Structures and Prospects for Women*, London, 1994, pp. 60–1.
52. Rose, *Colour and Citizenship*, pp. 157, 161.
53. *Ibid.*, p. 151.
54. Taylor, *Worlds Apart?*, p. 69.
55. Brown, *Black and White Britain*, p. 186.
56. According to Modood *et al., Ethnic Minorities in Britain*, p. 86, 'over 80% of Bangladeshi women were looking after home and family, as were 70% of Pakistani women'. Around a quarter of white and a third of Indians were in this position. The economic activity figures for white, Indian, Pakistani and Bangladeshi women according to the 1991 census data were: 68.3%, 47.6%, 28.3% and 22.2%, respectively. V. Karn, ed., *Ethnicity in the 1991 Census: Employment, Education and Housing among Ethnic Minority Populations of Britain*, London, 1996, p. 33.
57. Brown, *Black and White Britain*, p. 189.
58. J. West and S. Pilgrim, 'South Asian women in employment: the impact of migration, ethnic origin and the local economy', *New Community*, 21, 3, July 1995, p. 358.
59. Modood *et al., Ethnic Minorities in Britain*, p. 89.
60. Z. Dahya, 'Pakistani wives in Britain', *Race*, 6, 3, 1965, pp. 311–21, and V. S. Khan, 'Purdah in the British situation' in D.L. Barker and S. Allen, eds, *Dependence and Exploitation in Work and Marriage*, London, 1976, pp. 225–45.
61. A. Brah, '"Race" and "culture" in the gendering of labour markets:

South Asian young Muslim women and the labour market', *New Community*, 19, 3, April 1993, pp. 441–58.

62. Ellis, *Meeting Community Needs*, pp. 41, 50, 60–3.
63. S. Mitter, *Common Fate, Common Bond: Women in the Global Economy*, London, 1985, p. 130.
64. West and Pilgrim, 'South Asian women in employment', pp. 366, 375.
65. S. Mitter, 'Rise of a semi-proletariat: Bangladeshi female homeworkers in the London rag trade', *International Labour Studies Newsletter*, no. 12, April 1984, pp. 7–9.
66. See West and Pilgrim, 'South Asian women in employment', p. 358.
67. For example, a dressmaker was sacked after ten years' service for wearing 'a black scarf during working hours': *BMMS*, April 1995, p. 7. A 19-year-old woman was dismissed by her London consultancy firm for wearing the *hijab* as she no longer conformed to the company's 'unwritten' policy of wearing Western clothes: *BMMS*, February 1996, p. 7. Jaseem ul Haq, a worker at a Newcastle branch of an estate agents, lost her job after turning up for work wearing a headscarf during Ramadan: *Muslim News*, 25 October 1996. Farida Khanum, aged 21, an electrical engineer at the IBC (Vauxhall) car plant in Luton, was subjected to abuse and harassment and prevented from working on the shop floor after she began wearing the *hijab* on her return from Mecca: *Q-News*, 8 November 1996. Several employers in the retail sector, perhaps pandering to their customers' prejudices, have thrown Muslim women out of jobs on similar grounds. Amna Mehmood, 17, who worked for Body Shop in Hounslow, was dismissed six days after she started wearing the *hijab*: *Observer*, 31 January 1997. Shamma Ahmed was suspended at Safeways store in Chorlton for refusing to remove her headscarf, which the manager said did not fit in with the store's uniform policy. After the case was referred to the head office she was reinstated and allowed to return to work with her *hijab*: *Manchester Evening News*, 28 February 1997. N. Shahin, a part-time sales assistant at What Everyone Wants in Walsall, claimed she was dismissed for wearing the *hijab*: *Muslim News*, 23 May 1997.
68. Brown, *Black and White Britain*, p. 187.
69. Modood *et al.*, *Ethnic Minorities in Britain*, p. 88. However, it is possible that these figures underestimate Muslim women's economic participation as many of them are involved in 'homeworking', which has rarely been accounted for. See R. Ballard, 'The Pakistanis: stability and introspection', *Ethnicity in the 1991 Census*, 2, 2, 1996, p. 135, and A. Phizacklea and C. Wolkowitz, *Homeworking Women: Gender, Racism and Class*, London, 1995, p. 32.
70. P. Parmar, 'Gender, race and class: Asian women in resistance', in

Centre for Contemporary Cultural Studies, *The Empire Strikes Back: Race and Racism in 70s Britain*, London, 1982, p. 247; for figures for 1981, 1984, 1991, 1997 and LFS, see Brown, *Black and White Britain*, Jones, *Britain's Ethnic Minorities* and F.P. Bari, 'The effects of employment on the status of Pakistani immigrant women within the family in Britain', unpubl. PhD thesis, University of Sussex, 1991, p. 66.

71. *Ibid.*, p. 253.

72. In a study carried out in the late 1980s, while some women agreed that employment gave them some independence, 70% of the women had found that taking up waged work made little difference, primarily because they had no control over how their earnings were used. S. Guru, 'Struggle and resistance: Punjabi women in Birmingham', unpublished PhD thesis, University of Keele, 1987, pp. 343–4; K. Bhopal, *Gender, 'Race' and Patriarchy: a Study of South Asian Women*, Aldershot, 1997, pp. 126–8.

73. See Bari, 'The effects of employment on the status of Pakistani immigrant women within the family in Britain', and Bhopal, *Gender, 'Race' and Patriarchy*, p. 126.

74. *Ibid.*

75. Bridgwood, 'Marriage, honour and property', pp. 139–45; C.F. El-Solh, '"Be true to your culture": gender tensions among Somali Muslims in Britain', *Immigrants and Minorities*, 12, 1, March 1993, pp. 21–46; Bhopal, *Gender, 'Race' and Patriarchy*.

76. H. Summerfield, 'Patterns of adaptation: Somali and Bangladeshi women in Britain' in G. Buijs, ed., *Migrant Women: Crossing Boundaries and Changing Identities*, Oxford, 1993, pp. 83–98; El-Solh, '"Be true to your culture"'.

77. Summerfield, 'Patterns of adaptation', pp. 90–3.

78. *Ibid.*, p. 83.

79. J. Bowker, 'The nature of women and their status' in *Voices of Islam*, Oxford, 1995, pp. 119–22; see also M. Iqbal, 'Education and Islam in Britain—a Muslim view', *New Community*, 5, 4, 1977, p. 399.

80. J.A. Badawi, *The Status of Women in Islam*, Birmingham, n.d., p. 20.

81. H.H. Afshar, 'Gender roles and the "moral economy of kin" among Pakistani women in West Yorkshire', *New Community*, 15, 2, January 1989, p. 216.

82. A. Brah, 'Women of South Asian origin in Britain: issues and concerns' in P. Braham, A. Rattansi and R. Skellington, eds, *Racism and Antiracism: Inequalities, Opportunities and Policies*, London, 1992, p. 72.

83. T. Modood, S. Beishon and S. Virdee, *Changing Ethnic Identities*, London, 1994, p. 79.

84. *BMMS*, December 1994, p. 9.

85. Bhopal, *Gender, 'Race' and Patriarchy*, p. 75.

86. *Ibid.*, p. 77.

87. A. Shaw, 'The Pakistani community in Oxford' in R. Ballard, ed., *Desh Pardesh: The South Pardesh Asian Presence in Britain*, London, 1994, p. 55. For a more recent discussion see S.L. Evans and S. Bowlby, 'Crossing boundaries: racialised gendering and the labour market experiences of Pakistani migrant women in Britain', *Women's Studies International Forum* (Online), 23, 4, July–August 2000.

88. Bari, 'The effects of employment on the status of Pakistani immigrant women within the family in Britain', pp. 225–6.

89. Bridgwood, *Marriage, Honour and Property*, p. 209.

90. *Ibid.*, p. 210.

91. Modood, Beishon and Virdee, *Changing Ethnic Identities*, pp. 74, 77–8.

92. M. Anwar, *Young Asians Between Two Cultures*, London, 1986, p. 55.

93. Stopes-Roe and Cochrane, 'Marriage in two cultures', pp. 159–69.

94. *Ibid.*, p. 167.

95. The process has gone even further among Turkish Cypriots than it has among South Asian Muslims. Many marriages that are made by the couple themselves are often presented as arranged marriages, conceding their parents the formal right to discuss them; see Bridgwood, 'Marriage, honour and property', p. 209.

96. Modood, Beishon and Virdee, *Changing Ethnic Identities*, p. 80.

97. *BMMS*, March 1993.

98. Z. Muhsen with A. Croft, *Sold*, London, 1994.

99. *BMMS*, May 1996, p. 2.

100. *Independent*, 21 July 1998.

101. Modood, Beishon and Virdee, *Changing Ethnic Identities*, p. 76.

102. *Ibid.*, p. 80.

103. *Ibid.*, pp. 70, 72–3.

104. *Ibid.*, p. 80.

105. P. Lewis, *Islamic Britain: Religion, Politics and Identity among British Muslims*, London, 1994, pp. 183–9; R. Sharif, *Interviews with Young Muslim Women of Pakistani Origin*, Research Paper no. 27, Centre for the Study of Islam and Christian–Muslim Relations, Selly Oak Colleges, Birmingham, September 1985, and K. Mirza, *A Silent Cry: Second Generation Bradford Muslim Women Speak*, Research Paper no. 43, Centre for the Study of Islam and Christian–Muslim Relations, Selly Oak Colleges, Birmingham, September 1989; C. Butler, 'Religion and gender: young Muslim women in Britain', *Sociology Review*, vol. 4, no. 3 February 1995, pp. 18–22; T. Basit, *Eastern Values, Western Milieu: Identities and Aspirations of Adolescent British Muslim Girls*, Aldershot, 1997; Bhopal, *Gender, 'Race' and Patriarchy*; Bridgwood, 'Marriage, hon-

our and property'; T. Kucukcan, 'Continuity and change: young Turks in London' in S. Vertovec and A. Rogers, eds, *Muslim European Youth: Reproducing Ethnicity, Religion, Culture*, Aldershot, 1998, pp. 103–31.

106. Sharif, *Interviews with Young Muslim Women of Pakistani Origin*. In April 1993 the BBC television programme 'Panorama' threw some light on how some adolescent Muslim girls surreptitiously engaged in activities which their white counterparts did openly.

107. Ellis, *Meeting Community Needs*, p. 55.

108. Shaw, *A Pakistani Community in Britain*, pp. 167, 170–80.

109. Afshar, 'Gender roles and the "moral economy of kin" among Pakistani women in West Yorkshire', p. 212.

110. *Ibid.*, pp. 214–15.

111. *BMMS*, December 1994, p. 14.

112. *Daily Jang*, 21 September 1995.

113. *BMMS*, June 1998, p. 11.

114. H. Afshar, 'Education: hopes, expectations and achievements of Muslim women in West Yorkshire', *Gender and Education*, 1, 3, 1989, pp. 266–7.

115. As portrayed in a Channel 4 television documentary in the early 1990s called 'Black Bag'.

116. 'Inside Story', BBC 2, 3 February 1998.

117. See *BMMS*, November 1993.

118. See the *Independent*, 21 July 1998; also Sharif, *Interviews with Young Muslim Women of Pakistani Origin*, and A. Ali, 'Wife abuse in Asian marriages', unpubl. MSc dissertation, London School of Economic and Political Science, 1991.

119. *BMMS*, December 1993, p. 12; April 1994, p. 18; November 1996, p. 7; see also Ali, 'Wife abuse in Asian marriages'.

120. K. Bhopal, 'Driving passions', *Guardian*, 10 February 1998.

121. Basit, *Eastern Values, Western Milieu*, pp. 171–2.

122. Muslim Conservative Women's Association, Huddersfield; more than 100 women have joined. *BMMS*, October 1993.

123. *BMMS*, November 1993.

124. See S. Currah, 'Faith, family and future: religious belief and practice among young Pakistani Muslim women in Bradford', unpubl. MPhil thesis, University of Leeds, 1995, Chapter 4 and Conclusion.

125. Muslim Women's Helpline, *Annual Report*, 1994 and 1997.

126. *BMMS*, February 1995, p. 15.

127. *Ibid.*, January 1997, p. 13.

128. *Ibid.*, October 1997, p. 15.

129. *Ibid.*, January 1998, p. 11.

130. *Ibid.*, November 1996, p. 7.

131. *Ibid.*, July 1997, p. 12.

132. See S. Armstrong, 'Female circumcision: fighting a cruel tradition', *New Scientist*, 2 February 1991, p. 46.

133. See El-Solh, '"Be true to your culture"', p. 40.

134. Y. Alibhai-Brown, *Who Do We Think We Are? Imagining New Britain*, London, 2000, p. 216.

135. Shaw, *A Pakistani Community in Britain*, pp. 164–7; H. Hoodfar, 'The veil in their minds and in their heads', *Resources for Feminist Research*, 22, 3–4, 1993, p. 15.

136. Mirza, *A Silent Cry*, p. 15.

137. L.A. Odeh, 'Post-colonial feminism and the veil: thinking the difference', *Feminist Review*, no. 43, 1993, p. 33; see also P. Mule and D. Barthel, 'The return to the veil: individual autonomy vs. social esteem', *Sociological Forum*, vol. 7, June 1992, pp. 323–32.

138. C. Connolly, 'Washing our linen: one year of Women Against Fundamentalism', *Feminist Review*, no. 37, spring 1991, p. 69.

139. *Ibid.*, p. 72.

140. P. Patel, 'Alert for action', *Feminist Review*, no. 37, spring 1991, p. 100.

141. *Ibid.*, p. 71.

142. R. Kabbani, *Letter to Christendom*, London, 1989, chapter 3; H. Siddiqui, 'Winning freedoms', *Feminist Review*, no. 37, spring 1991, p. 81.

143. Odeh, 'Post-colonial feminism and the veil', p. 28.

144. Siddiqui, 'Winning Freedoms', p. 81.

145. S. Arebi, 'Gender anthropology in the Middle East: the politics of Muslim women's misrepresentation', *American Journal of Islamic Social Sciences*, vol. 8, no. 1, March 1991, p. 99; Hoodfar, 'The veil in their minds and in their heads', p. 15.

146. *BMMS*, November 1993.

147. *Ibid.*, June 1995, p. 22.

148. *Ibid.*, July 1994, p. 16.

149. *Chingford Guardian*, 17 October 1996.

150. *BMMS*, June 1994, p. 8.

151. *Ibid.*, April 1998, p. 12.

152. *Ibid.*, February 1994, p. 23.

153. For details see Z. Gifford, *The Golden Thread: Asian Experiences of Post-Raj Britain*, London, 1990.

154. Mirza, *A Silent Cry*, p. 24.

155. Alibhai-Brown, *Who Do We Think We Are?*, p. 122.

156. *Ibid.*, p. 118.

157. Rapoport, Fogarty and Rapoport, eds, *Families in Britain*, pp. 179–251; see also Modood, Beishon and Virdee, *Changing Ethnic Identities*, pp. 24–35.

158. M. Rafiq, 'A comparison of Muslim and non-Muslim owned Asian businesses in Britain', *New Community*, 19, 1, October 1992, pp. 49, 55–6.

159. Kucukcan, 'Continuity and change: young Turks in London', pp. 107–13; Bridgwood, 'Marriage, honour and property'; Shaw, *A Pakistani Community in Britain*, pp. 167–80; see Berrington, 'Marriage patterns and inter-ethnic unions', pp. 198–204, and Modood, Beishon and Virdee, *Changing Ethnic Identities*, pp. 77–8. For comparison with the early 1980s, see Brown, *Black and White Britain*, p. 33.

10. BRITISH MUSLIMS AND EDUCATION: ISSUES AND PROSPECTS

1. For details about the rising number of immigrant children in state-run schools in England and Wales in the 1960s, see J. McNeal, 'Education' in S. Abbott, ed., *The Prevention of Racial Discrimination in Britain*, London, 1971, Chapter 5.

2. See the Crowther Report, 15 to 18, London, 1960, and *the Newsom Report: Half our Future*, London, 1963; the Plowden Report of the Central Advisory Council for Education, London, published in 1967, recognised this disadvantage and recommended the adoption of 'education priority areas' into which extra resources needed to be injected; see Abbott, ed., *The Prevention of Racial Discrimination in Britain*, p. 120.

3. In Bradford, the vast majority of children of Pakistani and Bangladeshi background were gathered in just six out of 150 schools; similar concentrations were beginning to develop, for example, in some of the boroughs of London, and the industrial conurbations, cities and towns of the Midlands, Lancashire and Yorkshire; 50–70% of the pupils in some of the schools in the London Borough of Islington and Haringey came from a Turkish Cypriot background. See N. Hawkes, *Immigrant Children in British Schools*, London, 1966, pp. xvii, 111, 116.

4. Home Office, *Second Report of Commonwealth Immigrants Advisory Council* (CIAC), London, 1964.

5. The CIAC confirmed the government's thinking in its guidance; see R. Jeffcote, *Ethnic Minorities and Education*, Unit 13, Milton Keynes, 1982, p. 26.

6. C. Bagley, 'The education of immigrant children: a review of problems and policies in education', *Journal of Social Policy*, 2, 4, 1973, p. 304.

7. See Abbott, ed., *The Prevention of Racial Discrimination in Britain*, pp. 125–7; for the origins and rationale of the dispersal policy, see p. 123. The dispersal policy was further endorsed and generalised in 1965 in the Department of Education and Science Circular 7/65, *The Education of Immigrants*, in a section headed 'Spreading the Children', DES, London,

1965; it advocated limiting the proportion of immigrant pupils to about a third of a school or class. The policy was rushed in the autumn of 1963, when white parents protested sufficiently vigorously in Southall, a western suburb of London, to compel the local authority to keep the proportion of immigrant children down to 30% in the borough's schools.

8. H.E.R. Townsend and E.M. Brittan, *Organization in Multiracial Schools*, Windsor, 1972.

9. M.J. Taylor, *Worlds Apart?*, Windsor, 1988, p. 134.

10. *Ibid*. Similarly, J. Bhatnagar, *Immigrants at School*, London, 1970, p. 159, showed a clustering of Turkish Cypriots in the lower streams.

11. *Ibid*., p. 126.

12. M.J. Taylor and S. Hegarty, *The Best of Both Worlds ...? a review of Research into the Education of Pupils of South Asian Origin*, Windsor, 1985, p. 294.

13. *Ibid*., p. 319.

14. *Ibid*., pp. 118–24, 142.

15. M. Anwar, *The Myth of Return: Pakistanis in Britain*, London, 1979. That these conclusions had some validity was shown by research conducted by Essen and Ghodsian, which suggested that when allowance was made for social and home circumstances the difference in test scores was reduced: J. Essen and M. Ghodsian, 'The children of immigrants: school performance', *New Community*, winter 1979, p. 426. See also Taylor and Hegarty, *The Best of Both Worlds ...?*, p. 265. For the adverse effect of social background on the educational achievement of Turkish children in Britain, see S.R. Sonyel, *The Silent Minority: Turkish Muslim Children in British Schools*, Cambridge, 1988, pp. 39–41.

16. Taylor, *Worlds Apart?*, pp. 135–6.

17. *Ibid*., p. 136.

18. *New Statesman*, 13 May 1985.

19. G.K. Verma and B. Ashworth, *Ethnicity and Educational Achievement in British Schools*, London, 1986.

20. M. Swann, *Education For All: the Report of the Committee of Inquiry into the Education of Children from Ethnic Minority Groups*, London, 1985, p. 687.

21. F. Kysel, 'Ethnic background and examination results', *Educational Research*, 30, 2, June 1988, p. 87.

22. T. Jones, *Britain's Ethnic Minorities*, London, 1993.

23. See Taylor, *Worlds Apart?*, pp. 156–69; Taylor and Hegarty, *The Best of Both Worlds ...?*, pp. 354–5, 357, 359–60, 371–2, 376–7, 391–4, 400–1, 549–50; S. Shaikh and A. Kelly, '"To mix or not to mix": Pakistani girls in British schools', *Educational Research*, 31, 1, February 1989,

pp. 14–16; Sonyel, *The Silent Minority*, pp. 45, 48–9, 51, 57, 59; P. Lewis, *Islamic Britain: Religion, Politics and Identity among British Muslims: Bradford in the 1990s*, London, 1994, p. 187. For more recent parents' views on daughters education and careers see T. Basit, *Eastern Values, Western Milieu: Identities and Aspirations of Adolescent British Muslim Girls*, Aldershot, 1997, pp. 140–57. For young Muslim men's attitudes towards young Muslim women, see S. MacLoughlin, '"An underclass in purdah"? Discrepant representations of identity and the experiences of young British-Asian Muslim women', *Journal of the John Rylands University of Manchester Library*, 1998, pp. 95–7; S. Burlet and H. Reid, 'A gendered uprising: political representation and minority ethnic communities', *Ethnic and Racial Studies*, 21, 2, March 1998, pp. 279–82.

24. Runnymede Trust, *Islamophobia: a Challenge for Us All*, London, 1997, p. 44; M. Anwar, *British Pakistanis*, Coventry, 1996, p. 47. See also D. Gillborn and C. Gipps, *Recent Research on the Achievements of Ethnic Minority Pupils*, London, 1996, pp. 23–6. The academic achievements of Somali children, another Muslim group, have not compared at all favourably with those of their peers. A study in the mid-1990s revealed that less than 30% of Somali pupils entered for GSCE O-level examinations in 1995/6 achieved grades A–C in more than five subjects, compared with the national average of 43.3%. Apparently the results were even poorer in the inner-city London boroughs of Tower Hamlets and Hackney, see M.H. Kahin, *Educating Somali Children in Britain*, London, 1997, p. 79.

25. Although a television programme in 1993 still suggested that visits abroad continued to have a damaging effect on pupils' educational performance, see 'Underclass in Purdah', Panorama, BBC 1, 29 March 1993.

26. D.J. Smith and S. Tomlinson, *The School Effect: a Study of Multi-Racial Comprehensives*, London, 1989.

27. S. Tomlinson, 'Curriculum option choices in multi-ethnic schools' in B. Troyna, ed., *Racial Inequality in Education*, London, 1987, pp. 105–6.

28. *Ibid.*, p. 103. For illustrative material see J. Egglestone, J. Dunn, M. Anjali and C. Wright, *Education for Some*, Stoke on Trent, 1986; Cecile Wright, 'Early education: multiracial primary school classrooms', pp. 8–13, and M. Mac an Ghaill, 'Coming of age in 1980s England: reconceptualising black students' schooling experience' in D. Gill, B. Mayor and M. Blair, eds, *Racism and Education: Structures and Strategies*, London, 1992, pp. 50, 54–6; A. Rattansi, 'Changing the subject? Racism, culture and education' in J. Donald and A. Rattansi, eds, *'Race', Culture and Difference*, London, 1992, pp. 21–2, and H. Mirza,

Young, Female and Black, London, 1992, p. 55. For more recent research on teachers' perceptions of Muslim pupils, see Basit, *Eastern Values, Western Milieu*, pp. 114–64; Runnymede Trust, *Islamophobia*, p. 46, and J. Eade, *Routes and Beyond: Voices from Educationally Successful Bangladeshis*, London, 1994, pp. 18–20.

29. D. Gillborn, *'Race', Ethnicity and Education*, London, 1990, p. 10.
30. Shaikh and Kelly, "'To mix or not to mix'", p. 17; see also Sonyel, *The Silent Minority*, p. 59, for Turkish Cypriot parents' attitudes to girls' education.
31. The 1980 HM Inspectorate Report on the ILEA highlighted the impact of low teacher expectations. It stated that, while schools frequently blamed their pupils' backgrounds for the poor results, this was largely unjustifiable and the fault lay in teacher expectations. In regard to comparative abilities, the 1985 Swann Report found that teachers saw Turkish Cypriots as potential underachievers and disruptive elements. See Swann, *Education for All*, pp. 689–90; also Sonyel, *The Silent Minority*, pp. 34, 53.
32. Eade, *Routes and Beyond*, p. 19.
33. H.E.R. Townsend, *Immigrant Pupils in England: the IEA Response*, Slough, 1971, Chapter 6.
34. Townsend and Brittan, *Organization in Multiracial Schools*, pp. 57–77.
35. Donald and Rattansi, eds, *'Race', Culture and Difference*, pp. 12–13, 20–1; Runnymede Research Report, *Racism, Anti-racism and School: a Summary of the Burnage Report*, London, 1989, p. 15, and Eade, *Routes and Beyond*, p. 18.
36. Taylor and Hegarty, *The Best of Both Worlds...?*, pp. 485–6.
37. M. Halstead, *Education, Justice and Cultural Diversity: an Examination of the Honeyford Affair, 1984–5*, Lewes, 1988, pp. 61, 70.
38. R. Preiswerk and D. Perrot, *Ethnocentrism and History: Africa, Asia and Indian America in Western Textbooks*, London, 1978, p. 150.
39. *Ibid.*, pp. 83, 87, 183–6, 198–203; see also E. Said, *Orientalism*, London, 1985.
40. Swann, *Education for All*, p. 689.
41. S.A. Ashraf and S.S. Hussain, *Crisis in Muslim Education*, London, 1979, p. 3.
42. Leach, *The School in a Multicultural Society*, p. 182.
43. R. Grinter, 'Transferring the national curriculum developments in an anti-racist campaign', *Multicultural Teaching*, 8, 3, summer 1990, p. 26.
44. Townsend and Brittan, *Organization in Multiracial Schools*, pp. 107–8.
45. *Ibid.*, pp. 103–8.
46. Taylor and Hegarty, *The Best of Both Worlds...?*, p. 95.
47. Quoted in S. Patterson, *Immigration and Race Relations: 1960–1967*, London, 1969, p. 113.

48. D. Milner, *Children and Race*, London, 1975.

49. *A Language for Life*, London, 1975, p. 286.

50. G. Sarwar, *Muslims and Education in the UK*, Muslim Education Trust, Dept. of Education and Science, London, 1983, p. 26.

51. K. Young and N. Connelly, *Policy and Practice in the Multi-racial City*, London, 1981, p. 123.

52. Halstead, *Education, Justice and Cultural Diversity*, p. 232.

53. In 1975, Birmingham led the way by making the RE syllabus 'consistently multifaith in orientation at all age levels, and the religions included were to be studied for their own sakes, not through the perspectives set by any other religion', see J. Nielsen, 'Muslims in English schools', *Journal of the Institute of Muslim Minority Affairs*, 10, 1, January 1989, p. 229.

54. *Ibid.*

55. M. Parker-Jenkins, *Children of Islam: a Teacher's Guide to Meeting the Needs of Muslim Pupils*, Stoke-on-Trent, 1995, pp. 52–6.

56. See R. Jeffcote, *Ethnic Minorities and Education*, London, 1984, pp. 82–3.

57. Halstead, *Education, Justice and Cultural Diversity*, p. 233.

58. Parker-Jenkins, *Children of Islam*, p. 14.

59. M. Iqbal, *Islamic Education and Single-sex Schools*, Union of Muslim Organisations of UK and Eire, London, 1975.

60. Evidence of continuing support for single-sex schooling among many Muslims since the 1960s has been documented in Taylor and Hegarty, *The Best of Both Worlds...?*, pp. 376–7, and Taylor, *Worlds Apart?*, pp. 154–5.

61. Halstead, *Education, Justice and Cultural Diversity*, pp. 233–6.

62. See P. Gordon and F. Klug, *New Right, New Racism*, London, 1986; S. Randall, 'The New Right, racism and education in Thatcher's Britain', *Sage Race Relations Abstracts*, 13, 3, August 1988, pp. 3–17.

63. See F. Palmer, ed., *Anti-racism: An Assault on Education and Value*, London, 1986.

64. Swann, *Education for All*, p. 515.

65. See Parker-Jenkins, *Children of Islam*, pp. 37–82, and Halstead, *Education, Justice and Cultural Diversity*, pp. 203–30.

66. Lewis, *Islamic Britain*, pp. 69–72, 104, 147–53; Halstead, *Education, Justice and Cultural Diversity*, pp. 32–46; D. Joly, *Ethnic Minorities and Education in Britain: Interaction Between the Muslim Community and Birmingham Schools*, Research Paper no. 41, Centre for the Study of Islam and Christian–Muslim Relations, Birmingham, March 1989.

67. See *Race and Immigration: Runnymede Trust Bulletin*, no. 208, October 1987, pp. 1–2; no. 218, September 1988, pp. 1–2; and no. 251, December 1991, pp. 1–2.

68. See Swann, *Education for All*, pp. 512–20.
69. See Nielsen, 'Muslims in English schools', pp. 232–4; Parker-Jenkins, *Children of Islam*, p. 42.
70. Halstead, *Education, Justice and Cultural Diversity*, p. 60.
71. *Ibid.*, p. 205.
72. Runnymede Research Report, *Racism, Anti-racism and Schools*.
73. Donald and Rattansi, eds, *'Race', Culture and Difference*, p. 13.
74. Parker-Jenkins, *Children of Islam*, p. 52.
75. As one Muslim commentator said, 'What causes difficulty is the implication that the study of Christianity is more important and more relevant than the study of Islam ... that other religions are subordinate to Christianity. Indeed, it is very damaging for children to grow up believing that to be really British and contribute meaningfully to society, a Christian background is almost essential.' *Ibid.*, p. 62.
76. *The Times*, 24 January 1990, p. 1.
77. See various issues of the *British Muslim Monthly Survey* (*BMMS*) from the 1990s.
74. Parker-Jenkins, *Children of Islam*, p. 52.
75. As one Muslim commentator said, 'What causes difficulty is the implication that the study of Christianity is more important and more relevant than the study of Islam ... that other religions are subordinate to Christianity. Indeed, it is very damaging for children to grow up believing that to be really British and contribute meaningfully to society, a Christian background is almost essential.' *Ibid.*, p. 62.
76. *The Times*, 24 January 1990, p. 1.
77. See various issues of the *British Muslim Monthly Survey* (*BMMS*) from the 1990s.
78. Estimates vary; 80% of Muslim parents were in favour of Muslim schools according to the Muslim Educational Trust; 50% among South Asian Muslims in Shaikh and Kelly's research, '"To mix or not to mix"', in 1989, pp. 12–13, 16. Very few Turkish Cypriots supported Muslim schools; see Swann, *Education for All*, pp. 678–9; Sonyel, *The Silent Minority*, p. 57; Taylor, *Worlds Apart?*, pp. 154–5. It should nevertheless be noted that many Muslims who themselves do not favour separate Muslim schools maintain that the choice should be available to others.
79. *Guardian*, 31 January 1989.
80. Y. Zaki, 'The teaching of Islam in schools: a Muslim viewpoint', *British Journal of Religious Education*, 5, 1, autumn 1982, pp. 33–8.
81. According to current estimates of 25,000 schools, there are 6,973 state faith schools—6,384 are in the primary sector and 589 in the secondary sector. All but 40 of the faith schools are of Christian

denominations: of the 40, 32 are Jewish, 4 Muslim and 2 Sikh. P. Wintour, 'Religious schools "must integrate in the community"', *Guardian*, 14 November 2001. An earlier study in the 1990s estimated that there were 4,936 Church of England, 2,245 Roman Catholic, 31 Methodist and 21 Jewish schools in Britain. See Parker-Jenkins, *Children of Islam*, p. 11.

82. Joly, *Ethnic Minorities and Education in Britain*.

83. See C.T.R. Hewer, 'Introductory review', in *British Muslims and State Education*, St Catherine's Conference, Windsor, 23–25 November 1994, p. 3. Bradford's first Asian Lord Mayor, Ajeeb Khan, reflected this approach: 'I don't want separation in any form ... what we want is accommodation of our cultural needs, especially in the education system.' See Halstead, *Education, Justice and Cultural Diversity*, p. 52.

84. Lewis, *Islamic Britain*, p. 148.

85. *Ibid.*

86. C. Dwyer and A. Meyer, 'The institutionalisation of Islam in The Netherlands and in the UK: the case of Islamic schools', *New Community*, 21, 1, January 1995, pp. 45–7.

87. E. Masood, 'Supping with the devil', *Q-News*, 2, 4, 23–30 April 1993, p. 8; C. Dwyer, 'Constructions of Muslim identity and the contesting of power: the debate over Muslim schools in the UK', p. 14 (typescript in the author's possession).

88. Dwyer and Meyer, 'The institutionalisation of Islam', pp. 48–9.

89. *A Guide on Religious Education in a Multi-faith Community*, first published in 1974 and revised in 1983, reflected these policies; see Halstead, *Education, Justice and Cultural Diversity*, pp. 36–7.

90. The depth of their feeling can be gauged from the fact that 1,200 people signed the petition; see *Impact International*, 23 April 1987.

91. *Keighley News*, 7 April 1989.

92. Similarly in 1996 a Muslim girl withdrew from Altrincham Grammar School after she was refused a place in a girls-only school. *BMMS*, September 1998; March 1996; *Runnymede Bulletin*, October 1996, pp. 11–12.

93. For instance, Berkshire, Bradford, Sheffield, Lancashire, Blackburn and Brent. See J. Nielsen, *A Survey of British Local Authority Response to Muslim Needs*, Research Paper no. 30/31, Centre for the Study of Islam and Christian–Muslim Relations, Selly Oak Colleges, Birmingham, June/September 1986, p. 30.

94. In 1989 there were 15 Muslim schools, see Parker-Jenkins, *Children of Islam*, p. 12. Their number was 19 in 1993, *Muslim News*, 24 December 1993, and 32 in 1994; see *BMMS Review 1994*, p. 7. In 1996 there were estimated to be 45 Muslim schools in Britain, see

BMMS, March 1996, p. 11. See also *BMMS*, January 1997, p. 6. The number of Muslim schools in October 2002 stood at 77 according to the Association of Muslim Schools, of which 49 are members of the Association; see *http://www.amsoffice.fsnet. co.uk/ams.htm*, 25 October 2002.

95. For example, Small Heath Comprehensive School, Birmingham, see P. Cumper, 'Muslim schools: the implication of the Education Reform Act 1988', *New Community*, 16, 3, April 1990, p. 386, and Stratford School in East London, see *Runnymede Bulletin*, no. 256, June 1992, p. 6.

96. See *Race and Immigration*, no. 251, December 1991, pp. 12–13; *BMMS*, February 1994, pp. 2–4; *BMMS*, November 1995, p. 19; *BMMS*, July 1996, p. 12; *BMMS*, January 1997, p. 17. These campaigns finally bore fruit and two Muslim schools were granted state funding in January 1998; See *Runnymede Bulletin*, no. 309, February 1998, pp. 8–9.

97. *BMMS*, April 1996, p. 12. See also issues of the *BMMS* from January to May 1996 for the RE controversy in Batley, etc.

98. *Ibid.*

99. See issues of *BMMS* during 2001 for campaigns in Oxford and Manchester.

100. *BMMS*, August 1993, pp. 1–5; the government awarded grant-maintained status to Oakington Manor Primary School just two weeks after refusing state funding for the nearby Islamia Primary School, ostensibly because too many surplus places existed in the north-west of London. *The Runnymede Bulletin*, no. 269, October 1993, p. 9.

101. S. Akhtar, *White Paper on Muslim Education in Great Britain*, Muslim Parliament of Great Britain, London, March 1992, p. 29.

102. According to a 'white paper' produced by the Muslim Parliament for Muslims, no less than for other people living in Britain, the purpose of education was to prepare children for a fruitful life in a plural setting. But this would be achieved, in its view, through the inculcation of Muslim moral values. Muslim schools could indeed lead to greater integration with the passage of time: 'After being fully acquainted with their own faith and traditions, Muslim children could proceed to a tolerant exploration of other cultures and beliefs.' See Akhtar, *White Paper on Muslim Education in Great Britain*, pp. 28–9.

103. *Times Educational Supplement*, 4 January 1991, p. 3.

104. *The Times*, 5 July 1989.

105. Many Muslim scholars hold the view that music *per se* is forbidden by the Prophet except in the most strictly defined circumstances. See J.M. Halstead, 'Some reflections on the debate about music in Islam', *Muslim Education Quarterly*, 12, 1, 1994, pp. 51–61; see also *BMMS*,

December 1993, p. 12. Muslim parents who have accepted this interpretation have objected to their children taking part in musical activities. In Keighley, a girl refused to play the recorder on religious
grounds. Others disagree and contend that music is permitted as a
thing of beauty provided it does not promote immorality or encourage deviation from 'the straight path'; see *BMMS*, January 1994,
pp. 4–5. At another school in Keighley, Muslim pupils have taken
tabla and harmonium as their music subjects. In Birmingham, when
a Muslim teacher at a secondary school left children in tears after
accusing them of betraying their religion by singing Christmas car-
ols, he received little support from within the Muslim community,
and, although five pupils withdrew after his 'outburst', the concert
went ahead, with many Muslim boys and girls taking part; see *BMMS*,
December 1996, p. 2.

106. *BMMS*, September 1994, p. 12.
107. At Mulberry School in Tower Hamlets, with 98% of the pupils
     Muslim, children welcomed the opportunity to participate in a
     scheme exploring ancient dance routines; see *BMMS*, May 1995,
     p. 25.
108. When a 13-year-old boy at a school in Slough refused to participate
     in a mixed aerobic dance class, a 'modesty screen' was erected so
     that he could be 'shielded' from the girls. Most Muslim parents of
     the pupils at the school, however, neither objected to the dance pro-
     vision nor supported the pupil; see *BMMS*, April and May 1994.
109. MacLonghlin, "'An underclass in Purdah'".
110. D. Gillborn and C. Giffs, *Recent Research on the Achievements of Ethnic
     Minority Pupils*, London, 1996. See also G. Klein, 'Recent Research
     on the Achievements of Ethnic Minority Pupils', *Runnymede Bulletin*,
     no. 297, September 1996, pp. 2–3.
111. D. Drew and J. Gray, 'The black–white gap in examination results:
     a statistical critique of a decade's research', *New Community*, 17, 2,
     April 1991, p. 170.
112. There are indications that when Britain is involved in confrontation
     or violent conflict with the Muslim world Muslim pupils experience
     more Islamophobic harassment than before and continue to feel less
     comfortable and more vulnerable in schools and colleges after the
     conflict has ended. During the Gulf War in 1991, teachers at some
     schools apparently asked pupils whether they supported Saddam
     Hussein or not, and those who responded in the affirmative were
     told: 'You should be shot.' A number of parents complained that their
     children were distressed after teachers questioned them in public
     about which side they were on; see *Runnymede Bulletin*, no. 243, April
     1991, p. 2.

113. *BMMS*, August 1997, p. 6.

114. In 2001, Al-Furqan and Al-Hijrah were among several of the Muslim schools that produced impressive academic results. Al-Hijrah was listed among the top 20 schools in Birmingham while Islamia was seventh in Brent in 1999; see *BMMS*, September 2001, April 2001, January 2000, March 1999, November 1999, and so on.

115. Report no. 46, in *British Muslims and State Education*, St Catherine's Conference, Windsor, November 1994, pp. 6–10. That said, Muslims have continued to battle to have their demands met in cultural and curricular areas, see *BMMS*, 1994, 1–9, for ongoing campaigns in this respect. Despite the introduction of new sex and religious guidance with the support of Muslim schools, opposition is still occasionally expressed with regard to the teaching of the sex education syllabus, see *BMMS*, April 2001, September 1994, February 1995. Similar problems continue to plague religious education and school assemblies; see *BMMS*, February 1999, September and October 1994, December 1995, March, May and December 1996, September 1997, January 1999.

116. T. Modood *et al., Ethnic Minorities in Britain: Diversity and Disadvantage*, London, 1997, p. 73.

117. *Ibid.*, p. 74.

118. As in the 1970s, in 2001 Khalil Hussain, 12-year-old Ayesha's father, was to be found resisting, on religious grounds, pressure from the authorities to send her to a local mixed school in Manchester, even though he risked a fine or a jail sentence. She studied at home while the stand-off continued, see *BMMS*, June 2001, p. 13.

119. Akhtar, *White Paper on Muslim Education in Great Britain*, p. 34.

120. *Q-News*, January 1998, and *BMMS*, September 2001, p. 13.

121. *Ibid.*

122. *BMMS*, September 2001, pp. 12–13.

123. *Birmingham Sunday Mercury*, 9 September 2001.

124. T. McVeigh, 'Faith schools spark fears of "apartheid"', *Observer*, 30 September 2001, p. 8. In a poll by the *Observer*, when asked whether they supported the extension of single-faith schools-to include 'religions such as Islam and Judaism'—80% said that they did not. K. Ahmed, '80 percent are against new faith schools', *Observer*, 11 November 2001. A MORI poll for the *Times Educational Supplement* in November 2001 found that 43% opposed expansion of state-funded faith schools and 25% were in favour; 80% said that faith schools should be inclusive. W. Woodward, 'Faith in the system', *Guardian*, 12 December 2001. See also P. Toynbee, 'Keep God out of class', *Guardian*, 9 November 2001.

125. McVeigh, 'Faith schools spark fears of "apartheid"'. See also her earlier article 'Apartheid claim over Islam school', *Guardian*, 10 February 2001. For the views of former Education and current Home Secretary David Blunkett regarding faith schools, see *BMMS*, August 2001, pp. 8–9.

121. *Ibid*.

122. *BMMS*, September 2001, pp. 12–13.

123. *Birmingham Sunday Mercury*, 9 September 2001.

124. T. McVeigh, 'Faith schools spark fears of "apartheid"', *Observer*, 30 September 2001, p. 8. In a poll by the *Observer*, when asked whether they supported the extension of single-faith schools-to include 'religions such as Islam and Judaism'—80% said that they did not. K. Ahmed, '80 percent are against new faith schools', *Observer*, 11 November 2001. A MORI poll for the *Times Educational Supplement* in November 2001 found that 43% opposed expansion of state-funded faith schools and 25% were in favour; 80% said that faith schools should be inclusive. W. Woodward, 'Faith in the system', *Guardian*, 12 December 2001. See also P. Toynbee, 'Keep God out of class', *Guardian*, 9 November 2001.

125. McVeigh, 'Faith schools spark fears of "apartheid"'. See also her earlier article 'Apartheid claim over Islam school', *Guardian*, 10 February 2001. For the views of former Education and current Home Secretary David Blunkett regarding faith schools, see *BMMS*, August 2001, pp. 8–9.

11. THE EVOLUTION OF MUSLIM ORGANISATION IN BRITAIN SINCE THE SECOND WORLD WAR

1. See G. Marshall, *Oxford Dictionary of Sociology*, London, 1998, pp. 317–18, in which an institution is defined as 'a set of mores, folkways, and patterns of behavior that deals with major social interests: law, church, and the family for example. Thus a social institution consists of all the structural components of a society through which the main concerns and activities are organized, and social needs (such as those of order, belief and reproduction) are met'. In this sense, 'institutionalisation' encompasses more than physical institutions and markers of ethnic and religious identity. It is also about the complex sets of rules and myriad beliefs within the institution(s).

2. See the periodical *The Islamic Review*, published regularly from Woking between 1913 and 1970, for the kinds of activity in which the Woking Mosque was engaged during the period 1945–60.

3. See the Islamic Cultural Centre website.

4. S. Barton, *The Muslims of Bradford*, Research Paper no. 13, Centre for the Study of Islam and Christian–Muslim Relations (CSIC), Birmingham, March 1982, p. 12.

5. In particular Ritchie mentions the Yemenis (*Shafa'i*) and the Muslims from the subcontinent (*Hanafi*), see Revd J.M. Ritchie, *Report on the Muslim Community in South Shields*, October 1972, p. 8. Similarly, in Glasgow, where the Muslim community was overwhelmingly Pakistani, Richie found that Muslims belonging to the Shia sect prayed at the Sunni mosque, see Revd J.M. Ritchie, *A Survey of the Muslim Community of Glasgow*, September 1972, p. 11. Both these reports can be found at the Centre for the Study of Islam and Christian–Muslim Relations, Selly Oak Colleges, Birmingham. Scantlebury confirms this phenomenon in her research on Muslims in Manchester. She found that in the late 1940s a small group of Muslims (around 70) from Lebanon, Syria, Pakistan, Iraq, Egypt and India purchased a semi-detached house in Upper Park Road and converted it into a mosque, see E. Scantlebury, 'Muslims In Manchester: the depiction of a religious community', *New Community*, 21, 3, July 1995, p. 426.

6. Ritchie, *A Survey of the Muslim Community of Glasgow*, p. 6. The Twaqulia Islamic Society founded the Bengali mosque in Bradford in 1969, see S. Barton, *The Bengali Muslims in Bradford*, Leeds, 1986, p. 22. The institutions established by the Yemenis and Somalis in port cities and towns such as South Shields, Cardiff, Liverpool and Hull continued to function and grow after the Second World War.

7. See B. Dahya, 'Pakistani ethnicity in industrial cities in Britain' in A. Cohen, ed., *Urban Ethnicity*, London, 1974, p. 96. Ritchie mentions Arabs, Turks and Nigerians attending the same mosque as Pakistanis in Glasgow, see Ritchie, *A Survey of the Muslim Community of Glasgow*, p. 14. This 'fission and segmentation of the immigrant community' is analysed by Dahya in 'Pakistani ethnicity in industrial cities in Britain', pp. 87–8.

8. F. Halliday, *Arabs in Exile: Yemenis in Urban Britain*, London, 1992.

9. R. Geaves, *Sectarian Influences within Islam in Britain*, Leeds, 1996, p. 159.

10. P. Lewis, *Islamic Britain: Religion, Politics and Identity*, London, 1994, p. 81.

11. *Ibid.*, p. 57.

12. See P. Werbner, 'Factionalism and violence in the British Pakistani communal politics' in H. Donnan and P. Werbner, eds, *Economy and Culture in Pakistan: Migrants and Cities in a Muslim Society*, Basingstoke, 1991, pp. 188–215.

13. For a detailed account of the emergence of the *Tablighi Jamaat* in

Britain, see Yoginder S. Sikand, 'The origins and growth of the *Tablighi Jamaat* in Britain', *Islam and Christian–Muslim Relations*, 9, 2, 1998, pp. 171–92.

14. *Ibid.*, p. 174.

15. *Ibid.*, p. 177.

16. *Ibid.*, p. 180.

17. For instance, *Behishti Zewar* written by Ashraf Ali Thanwi in Urdu in 1906 is still considered a classic text and guide for Muslim women's social and personal conduct. See Lewis, *Islamic Britain*, pp. 101, 195–6, for an analysis of its contents on Muslim women.

18. Sikand, 'The origins and growth of the *Tablighi Jamaat* in Britain', pp. 182–3.

19. Lewis, *Islamic Britain*, p. 104.

20. The Union of Muslim Organisations of UK and Ireland also has a section to address issues regarding Muslim education. It set up the National Muslim Education Council of UK in 1978, and among its range of activities has been the provision of advice to state schools on religious education. See Union of Muslim Organisations of UK and Ireland, *A Record of 25 Years' Achievement*, London, 1995, p. 10.

21. See J. Nielsen, *Muslims in Western Europe*, Edinburgh, 1992, p. 45.

22. See S. Vertovec and C. Peach, eds, *Islam in Europe: Migration, Minorities and Citizenship*, London, 1997, p. 24.

23. T. Kucukcan, 'The politics of ethnicity, identity and religion among Turks in London', unpubl. PhD thesis, University of Warwick, 1996, p. 252.

24. *Ibid.*, p. 254.

25. *Ibid.*, p. 256.

26. See *ibid.*, Chapters 8–10. For instance the institutionalisation of Islamic education through the founding of an independent Turkish primary school, IKRA, in September 1994; the progress of the Suleymanci Jama'a's UK Turkish Islamic Cultural Centre Trust (TICCT) and the Valide Sultan Mosque (founded in 1982), with its different priorities and interpretation of religious traditions from those of UKTIA, most noticeable in the dress code (suits and ties and indifference to beards), as well as in its more political stance and its comparatively greater flexibility in addressing religious matters; the mystical approach of Sheikh Nazim's more ethnically mixed *Jama'a*. Among the religio-political organisations with origins in Turkey is the London Islamic Turkish Association (LITA) (established in the late 1970s), which argues for religious tolerance and religious music and art as part of Islamic education. While maintaining a close connection with the religious domain, National Vision operates with a remit that engages widely

with the secular world. It encourages political participation to secure minority rights, includes women in all its activities and, 'from a religious-philosophical point of view', sees 'no difficulty in … establishing closer ties with Europe for a Muslim believer'.

27. See *The Muslim Directory*, London, 2000, pp. 88, 93.

28. *Ibid.*, pp. 84–92.

29. R. Charlton and R. Kaye, 'The politics of religious slaughter: an ethnoreligious case study', *New Community*, 7, 3, winter 1985, pp. 490–503.

30. R. Kaye, 'The politics of religious slaughter of animals: strategies for ethno-religious political action', *New Community*, 19, 2, January 1993, p. 238.

31. In the end, the recommendation that religious slaughter be phased out over three years was eventually rejected, primarily, it appears, due to the efforts of the Jewish community, whose greater communal cohesion, more efficient use of organisational resources and strategic placing of personnel carried the day. Indeed, such was the sophistication of Jewish tactics in defence of religious slaughter that neither the farm animals welfare lobby, which had been so passionate in their denunciation of this practice, nor the politically powerful New Right were able to mount any serious attacks. *Ibid.*, pp. 235–50.

32. Union of Muslim Organisations of UK and Ireland (UMO) press release, May 1986.

33. The Halal Food Authority (HFA) is an independent non-profit-making organisation that monitors and authenticates the halal meat and poultry trade in Britain. It works closely with the Food Standards Agency and has engaged animal rights and welfare groups such as the Humane Slaughter Association and Compassion in World Farming in discussions. See the HFA website, *http://www.halalfoodauthority.com*.

34. S. Poulter, *Asian Traditions and English Law. A Handbook*, Stoke-on-Trent, 1990, p. 114.

35. Nielsen, *Muslims in Western Europe*, p. 51.

36. See 'A short biography of Hazrat Inayat Khan', at *www.om-guru.com/html/saints/khan.html*.

37. See Al-Murabitoun website and J. Nielsen, 'Muslims in Britain: searching for an identity?', *New Community*, 3, spring 1987, pp. 384–94.

38. R. Geaves, *The Sufis of Britain: An Exploration of Muslim Identity*, Cardiff, 2000, p. 71.

39. See Al-Murabitoun website.

40. A. Kose, *Conversion to Islam*, London, 1996, p. 163.

41. Lewis, *Islamic Britain*, p. 82.

42. Geaves, *The Sufis of Britain*, pp. 85–100.

43. See Union of Muslim Organisations of UK and Ireland, *A Record of 25 Years' Achievement*, London, 1995.

44. M. Swann, *Education for All: the Report of the Committee of Inquiry into the Education of Children from Ethnic Minority Groups*, London, 1985.

45. Zaki Badawi, a former Director of the Islamic Cultural Centre, is its Principal. This 'moderate' Muslim is a scholar of Al-Azhar University in Cairo.

46. *UKACIA Newsletter*, July 1989.

47. The analysis of the Muslim Parliament has drawn on material available on the Institute of Contemporary Islamic Thought (ICIT) website.

48. P. Werbner, 'Islamic radicalism and the Gulf War: lay preachers and political dissent among British Pakistanis' in B. Lewis and D. Schnapper, eds, *Muslims in Europe*, Lon don, 1994, p. 100.

49. S. Vertovec and C. Peach, eds, *Islam in Europe: The Politics of Religion and Community*, Basingstoke, 1997, p. 32.

50. For example, the survey commissioned by the National Interim Committee on Muslim Unity; see Muslim Council of Britain (MCB) website.

51. *Ibid.*

52. J. Waardenburg, 'Muslim associations and official bodies in some European countries' in W.A.R. Shadid and P.S. van Koningsveld, eds, *The Integration of Islam and Hinduism in Western Europe*, Kampen, 1991, p. 34.

53. See J.S. Nielsen, *A Survey of British Local Authority Response to Muslim Needs*, Re search Paper, no. 30/31, Centre for the Study of Islam and Muslim–Christian Relations, Birmingham, June/September 1986, pp. 19–21, 35–58.

54. See *Muslim Directory*, pp. 409–13.

55. *Ibid.*, pp. 378–84.

56. *Ibid.*, p. 128.

57. See S. Gilliat, 'Muslim youth organisations in Britain: a descriptive analysis', *American Journal of Islamic Social Sciences*, 14, 1, spring 1997, pp. 101–2.

58. See World Assembly of Muslim Youth website.

59. Lewis, *Islamic Britain*, p. 122.

60. *Ibid.*, p. 176.

61. *Ibid.*, p. 112.

62. *Jewish Chronicle*, 8 September 1995.

63. Q.N. Ahmed, 'Driving a wedge between Muslims', *Guardian*, 12 April 1994, p. 26.

64. A. Taher, 'Call to arms', *Guardian Education*, 6 May 2000, pp. 12–13.

65. 'The Islamic rule on hijacking aeroplanes', statement issued by Hizb-ut-Tahrir on 8 April 1988.

66. A.Y. Andrews, 'Muslim women in a Western European society:

Gujarati Muslim women in Leicester' in J. Fulton and P. Gee, eds, *Religion in Contemporary Europe*, Lampeter, 1994, p. 83.

67. F. Daftary, *The Ismailis: Their History and Doctrines*, Cambridge, 1990, p. 526.
68. T.N. Basit, *Eastern Values, Western Milieu: Identities and Aspirations of Adolescent British Muslim Girls*, Aldershot, 1998, p. 42.
69. S. Currah, 'Faith, family and future: religious belief and practice among young Pakistani Muslim women in Bradford', unpubl. MA thesis, University of Leeds, 1995, pp. 101, 126, 130.
70. *Ibid.*, pp. 13, 133.
71. Lewis, *Islamic Britain*, pp. 194–5.
72. See the Muslim Women's Helpline website.
73. P. Werbner, 'Political spaces, political voices: gender, feminism and aspects of British Muslim participation in the public sphere' in W.A.R. Shadid and P.S. van Koningsveld, eds, *Political Participation and Identities of Muslims in Non-Muslim States*, Kampen, 1996, p. 55.
74. Quoted in Lewis, *Islamic Britain*, p. 182.
75. P.B. Clarke, 'The Ismaili Khojas: a sociological study of an Islamic sect in London', unpubl. MPhil thesis, University of London, 1974, p. 24.
76. R.N.M. Hallam, 'The Shi'a Imami Ismailia community in Britain', unpubl. MPhil thesis, University of London, 1971, p. 133.
77. Clarke, 'The Ismaili Khojas', p. 131; by 1981 there were 74 *jamaat-khanas* catering for fewer than 10,000 Ismailis. Other institutions established in London were the Institute of Ismaili Studies and the Ismaili Centre.
78. Clarke, 'The Ismaili Khojas', p. 133.
79. Karim Aga Khan, 'Speech at the outreach dinner held at the Ismaili Centre', London, 9 August 1994, *http://ismaili.net/~heritage/speech/s940809.html*.
80. The Constitution of the Shi'i Imami Ismaili Muslims, 1986, *http://www.ismaili.net/~heritage/Source/extra.1.html*
81. *UK Ismaili*, Vol. 1, August 1981.
82. N. Yavari, 'The evolving nature of the Shari'a', supplement to *The Ismaili United Kingdom*, 1999, n.p.
83. A.M.V. Karim, 'Issues in teacher education in the contemporary Ismaili community', unpubl. MEd thesis, University of London, 1986, p. 55.
84. The curriculum is designed 'to educate the pupils in the faith, history and cultures of Muslim peoples and of the Ismaili Muslim community in particular. In this connection it seeks to promote self-development, learning, and a moral engagement with society', Institute of Ismaili Studies, *IIS Update*, London, January 2000.
85. Mission statement of the Institute of Ismaili Studies in R. Keshavjee,

Mysticism and the Plurality of Meaning: the Case of the Ismailis of Rural Iran, London, 1998, n.p.

86. *UK Ismaili*, 6, 3, December 1986, n.p.
87. The Constitution of the Shi'i Imami Ismaili Community.
88. See *http://www.ismaili.net/jk/europe/jkaddress.html1#j7*.
89. Nielsen states that the first recorded demand for the introduction of some form of Islamic law into the domestic legal structure for Muslims came from the Union of Muslim Organisations in the UK and Eire in 1975 in a petition to Parliament. See Nielsen, *Muslims in Western Europe*, p. 109.
90. For details about the Council and its functions, see *The Islamic Shari'a Council: an Introduction*, London, 1995.

12. CONCLUSION: BRITISH MUSLIM IDENTITIES

1. Speaking on BBC television in June 2001, BNP leader Nick Griffin stated that troubles in the area were 'not an Asian problem, but a Muslim one'. Islamic Human Rights Commission (IHRC), *The Oldham Riots: Discrimination, Deprivation and Communal Tension in the United Kingdom*, London, 2001, p. 12.
2. F. Halliday, 'Orientalism and its critics', in his *Islam and the Myth of Confrontation: Religion and Politics in the Middle East*, London, 1995, pp. 195–217.
3. Press coverage produced by *British Muslims Monthly Survey* (*BMMS*), September 2001, pp. 1–3, and 'Attacks in the UK', *Q News*, October 2001, p. 8.
4. 'Islam in Europe: a changing faith', *Time*, 24 December 2001, p. 51.
5. Runnymede Trust, *Islamophobia: a Challenge for Us All*, London, 1997, p. 5.
6. Norman Daniel, *Islam and the West: the Making of an Image*, 2nd edn, Oxford, 1993, p. 11.
7. *Ibid.*, p. 1.
8. Fred Halliday presents a critique of the Runnymede Trust report and other similar analyses, for example, D. Browning, *Building Bridges between Islam and the West*, Wilton Park Paper 138, Steyning, West Sussex, 1998, and B.S. Sayyid, *A Fundamental Fear: Eurocentrism and the Emergence of Islamism*, London, 1997, in his review article '"Islamophobia" reconsidered', *Ethnic and Racial Studies*, 22, 5, September 1999, pp. 892–901; see also F. Halliday, 'Anti-Muslimism and contemporary politics: one ideology or many?' in his *Islam and the Myth of Confrontation*, London, 1995, pp. 160–94.
9. B.S. Turner, *Orientalism, Postmodernism and Globalism*, London, 1994, p. 186.

10. See G.R. Bunt, *Virtually Islamic: Computer-mediated Communication and Cyber Islamic Environments*, Cardiff, 2000, pp. 5–6, who describes how 'the computer and modem have become a (or *the*) medium for analysing and discussing a wide range of Islam-related topics, transcending traditional barriers to communication'. He discusses the various forms that 'Cyber Islamic Environments', created by this technology, have taken in order 'to determine how they have integrated conventional paradigms of Muslim understanding with new patterns of behaviour'.

11. *Ibid.*, p. 7.

12. *Ibid.*, pp. 9, 11. The Muslim Hackers' Club provides guidance on this aspect on *http://www.ummah.net/mhc*

13. For instance, *http://catstevens.com/*, and *http://www.arches.uga.edu/~godlas/IslArt.html*

14. *http://www.angelfire.com/ca2/queermuslims* and *http://www.geocities.com/West Hollywood/Heights/8977/index.html*

15. See S.R. Ameli, *Globalization, Americanization and British Muslim Identity*, London, 2002, pp. 276–8.

16. *Ibid.*, pp. 182–3.

17. A. Ibrahim, 'The ummah and tomorrow's world', *Futures*, vol. 26, 1991, p. 306.

18. *Ibid.*, p. 309.

19. R. Gill, *Competing Convictions*, London, 1989, p. 23.

20. E. Gellner, *Postmodernism, Reason and Religion*, London, 1992, p. 75.

21. P. Mandaville, *Transnational Muslim Politics: Reimagining the Umma*, London, 2001, p. 181.

BIBLIOGRAPHY

PRIMARY SOURCES

Official records

The Central Islamic Society: Rules And Regulations
MSS EUR File 111/161, India Office Records. FO 371 3419, 1918, Public
   Records Office

SECONDARY SOURCES

Monographs, articles and unpublished works

A Language for Life, London, 1975.
C. Adams, *Across Seven Seas And Thirteen Rivers: Life Stories of the Pioneer Sylheti
   Settlers in Britain*, London, 1987.
H. Afshar, 'Gender roles and the "moral economy of kin" among Pakistani
   women in West Yorkshire', *New Community*, 15, 2, January 1989.
————, 'Education: Hopes, Expectations and Achievements of Muslim
   Women in West Yorkshire', *Gender and Education*, 1, 3, 1989.
R. Ahmed, 'A Moslem's View of the Pan-Islamic Revival', *Nineteenth Century*,
   vol. 42, September 1897.
S. Akhtar, *White Paper on Muslim Education in Great Britain*, The Muslim
   Parliament of Great Britain, London, March 1992.
————, 'Ex-defender of the faith', *Times Higher Education Supplement*,
   London, 22 August 1997.
F. Alam, 'Salience of Homeland: Societal Polarization within the Bangladeshi
   Population in Britain', Research Paper no. 7, Centre For Research In
   Ethnic Relations, University of Warwick (hereafter 'CRER'), Coventry,
   January 1988.
A. al-Azmeh, *Islams and Modernities*, London, 1993.

BIBLIOGRAPHY

C.E. Alexander, *The Asian Gang: Ethnicity, Identity, Masculinity*, Oxford, 2000.
A. Ali, 'Wife Abuse in
Asian Marriages', unpubl. M.Sc. thesis, London School of Economic and Political Science, 1991.

N. Ali, 'Community and Identity of the Kashmiri Community: a Case Study of Luton', unpubl. Ph.D. thesis, University of Luton, 1999.

Y. Alibhai Brown, *Who do we think we are? Imagining New Britain*, London, 2000.

————, 'Sacred Beauty', *The Guardian Weekly*, 15 January 2000.

M. Al-Rasheed, 'Invisible and Divided Communities: Arabs in Britain' in *Arabs in Britain: Concerns and Prospects*, London, 1991.

————, 'The Other-Others: hidden Arabs?' in C. Peach, ed., *Ethnicity in the 1991 Census*, vol. 2, part 2, London, 1996.

————, 'Political Migration and Downward Socio-economic Mobility: the Iraqi Community in London', *New Community*, 18, 4, July 1992.

————, 'The Meaning of Marriage and Status in Exile: the Experience of Iraqi Women', *Journal of Refugee Studies*, 6, 2, 1993.

————, 'Arab Communities in Britain: a Plea to go Beyond Numbers', paper given to the Second Arab Communities Conference, November 1993.

M.M. Ally, 'History of Muslims in Britain, 1850–1980', unpubl. M.A. thesis, University of Birmingham, 1981.

S.R. Ameli, *Globalization, Americanization and British Muslim Identity*, London, 2002.

K. Amin and R. Richardson, *Politics For All*, London, 1992.

A. Andrews, 'Muslim Attitudes Towards Political Activity in the United Kingdom' in W.A.R. Shadid and P.S. van Koningsveld, eds, *Political Participation and Identities of Muslims in Non-Muslim States*, Kampen, 1996.

A.Y. Andrews, 'Muslim Women in a Western European Society: Gujarati Muslim Women in Leicester' in J. Fulton and P. Gee, eds, *Religion in Contemporary Europe*, Lampeter, 1994.

M. Anwar, *The Myth of Return: Pakistanis in Britain*, London, 1979

————, 'Religious Identity in Plural Societies: the Case of Britain', *Journal of the Institute of Muslim Minority Affairs*, 2, 2–3, 1980.

————, *Young Muslims in a Multi-Cultural Society: Their Educational Needs and Policy Implications: the British Case*, Leicester, 1982.

————, *Young Asians Between Two Cultures*, London, 1986.

————, *Between Two Cultures: a Study of Relationships Between Generations in the Asian Community of Britain*, London, 1981.

————, *Muslims in Britain: 1991 Census And Other Statistical Sources*, CSIC Paper no. 9, Centre for the study of Islam and Christian–Muslim Relations, Selly Oak Colleges (hereafter 'CSIC'), Birmingham, September 1993.

BIBLIOGRAPHY

————, 'Census Data and Muslims in Britain', unpubl. paper presented at the Conference on Statistics and the UK Religious Communities, University of Derby, May 1994.

————, *British Pakistanis: Demographic, Social and Economic Position*, CRER, Coventry, 1996.

————, 'Pakistani participation in the 1973 Rochdale local elections', *New Community*, 3, 1–2, 1974.

Anon., *Visits to the Wynds and Closes of Edinburgh by Day and Night*, Edinburgh, 1850.

S. Arebi, 'Gender anthropology in the Middle East: the politics of Muslim women's misrepresentation', *American Journal of Islamic Social Sciences*, March 1991.

S. Armstrong, 'Female circumcision: Fighting a cruel tradition', *New Scientist*, 2 February 1991.

T. Asad, 'Multiculturalism and British Identity in the Wake of the Rushdie Affair', *Politics and Society*, 18, 4, 1990.

S.A. Ashraf and S.S. Hussain, *Crisis in Muslim Education*, London, 1979.

K. Azzam, 'Islamic Art And Architecture', *Muslim Educational Quarterly*, 12, 1, 1994.

J.A. Badawi, *The Status of Women in Islam*, Birmingham, n.d

C. Bagley, 'The Education of Immigrant Children: A Review of Problems and Policies in Education', *Journal of Social Policy*, 2, 4, 1973.

J. Bains, *Asians Can't Play Football*, Midland Asian Sports Forum, 1995.

R. Ballard, ed., *Desh Pardesh: the South Asian Presence in Britain*, London, 1994.

R. Ballard, 'The Pakistanis: stability and introspection' in C. Peach, ed., *Ethnicity in the 1991 Census: The ethnic minority populations of Great Britain*, vol. 2, part 2, London, 1996.

K. Ballhatchet, *Race, Sex and Class under the Raj: Imperial Attitudes and Politics and their Critics, 1793–1905*, London, 1980.

M. Banton, *The Coloured Quarter: Negro Immigrants in an English City*, London, 1955.

F.P. Bari, 'The Effects of Employment on the Status of Pakistani Immigrant Women within the family in Britain', unpubl. Ph.D. thesis, University of Sussex, 1991.

S. Barton, *The Muslims of Bradford*, Research Paper no. 13, CSIC, March 1982. Birmingham.

————, *The Bengali Muslims in Bradford*, Leeds, 1986.

T.N. Basit, *Eastern Values; Western Milieu: Identities and Aspirations of Adolescent British Muslims Girls*, Aldershot, 1997.

C. Bennett, *Victorian Images of Islam*, London 1992.

A. Berrington, 'Marriage patterns and inter-ethnic unions' in D. Coleman and J. Salt, eds, *Ethnicity in the 1991 Census: Demographic characteristics of the ethnic minority population*, vol. 1, London, 1996.

BIBLIOGRAPHY

A. Berrington, 'Marriage and family formation among the white and ethnic minority populations in Britain', *Ethnic and Racial Studies*, 17, 3, July 1994.

J. Bhatnagar, *Immigrants at School*, London, 1970.

F.M. Bhatti, *Turkish Cypriots In London*, Research Paper no. 11, CSIC, Birmingham, September 1981.

K. Bhopal, *Gender, 'Race' and Patriarchy: a Study of South Asian Women*, Aldershot, 1997.

J. Bowker, The Nature of Women and their Status' in *Voices Of Islam*, Oxford, 1995.

A. Brah, 'Women of South Asian Origin in Britain: Issues and Concerns' in P. Braham, A. Rattansi and R. Skellington, eds, *Racism And Antiracism: Inequalities, Opportunities And Policies*, London, 1992.

————, '"Race" and "culture" in the gendering of labour markets: South Asian young Muslim women and the labour market', *New Community*, 19, 3, April 1993.

P. Braham, A. Rattansi and R. Skellington, eds, *Racism and Antiracism: Inequalities, Opportunities and Policies*, London, 1992.

A. Bridgwood, 'Marriage, Honour And Property—Turkish Cypriots in North Cyprus', unpubl. Ph.D. thesis, University of London, 1986.

C. Brown, *Black and White Britain: the third PSI survey*, London, 1984.

J. Brown, *Modern India: the origins of an Asian democracy*, Oxford, 1994.

B. Browning, *Building Bridges between Islam and the West*, Wilton Park Paper 138, 1998.

I. Bruegel, 'Labour Market Prospects for Women from Ethnic Minorities' in R. Lindley, ed., *Labour Market Structures and Prospects for Women*, London, 1994.

W.S. Blunt, *My Diaries: being a personal narrative of events 1888–1914*, London, 1921.

G.R. Bunt, *Virtually Islamic: Computer-mediated Communication and Cyber Islamic Environments*, Cardiff, 2000.

S. Burlet and H. Reid, 'A Gendered Uprising: Political Representation and Minority Ethnic Communities', *Ethnic and Racial Studies*, 21, 2, March 1998.

C. Butler, 'Religion and gender: Young Muslim women in Britain', *Sociology Review*, February 1995.

D. Byrne, 'The 1930 'Arab riot' in South Shields: a race riot that never was', *Race and Class*, XVIII, 3, 1977.

————, 'The 'Arab Issue' in South Shields 1919–39', *Immigrants and Minorities*, 13, 2–3, July/November 1994.

J. de Candole, 'The Politics of Muslim Schooling', *Salisbury Review*, March 1991.

D. Caradog Jones, ed., *The Social Survey of Merseyside*, Liverpool, 1934.

BIBLIOGRAPHY

D. Cesarani, 'Anti-Alienism in England After the First World War', *Immigrants and Minorities*, 6, 1, March 1987.

R. Charlton and R. Kaye, 'The Politics of Religious Slaughter: an Ethno-Religious Case Study', *New Community*, 7, 3, winter 1985.

P. Clarke, *Marmaduke Pickthall: British Muslim*, London, 1986.

P.B. Clarke, 'The Ismaili Khojas: A Sociological Study of an Islamic Sect in London', unpubl. M. Phil. thesis, University of London, 1974.

A. Cohen, ed., *Urban Ethnicity*, London, 1974.

D. Coleman and J. Salt, eds, *Ethnicity in the 1991 Census*, London, 1996.

S.F. Collins, 'The Social Position of White and "Half-Caste" Women in Colored Groupings in Britain', *American Sociological Review*, 16, 4, 1951.

————, '"Moslem" and "Negro" Groupings on Tyneside: a Comparative Study of Social Integration in Terms of Intra-Group and Inter-Group Relations', unpubl. Ph.D. thesis, University of Edinburgh, 1952.

————, *Coloured Minorities in Britain: Studies in British Race Relatins based on African, West Indian and Asiatic Immigrants*, London, 1957.

Commission for Racial Equality, *Homelessness and Discrimination: Report of a formal investigation into the London Borough of Tower Hamlets*, London, 1988.

————, *Ethnic Minorities and Electoral Politics: Lessons of the 1997 General Elections*, London, 1998.

————, *Tackle It! Racism In Rugby League*, London, 1999.

Commission on British Muslims and Islamaphobia, *Islamaphobia: a Challenge for Us All*, London, 1997.

C. Connolly, 'Washing our Linen: One Year of Women Against Fundamentalism', *Feminist Review*, no. 37, spring 1991.

S. Constantine, *Unemplyment in Britain between the wars*, London, 1980.

————, *Social Conditions in Britain, 1918–1939*, London, 1983.

P. Cumper, 'Muslim schools: the implication of the Education Reform Act 1988', *New Community*, 16, 3, April 1990.

S. Currah, 'Faith, Family And Future: Religious Belief and Practice among Young Pakistani Muslim Women in Bradford', unpubl. M.Phil. thesis, University of Leeds, 1995.

F. Daftary, *The Ismailis: their history and doctrines*, Cambridge, 1990.

B. Dahya, 'Yemenis In Britain: an Arab Migrant Community', *Race*, 6, 3, January 1965.

B. Dahya, 'The nature of Pakistani Ethnicity in Urban cities' in A. Cohen, ed., *Urban Ethnicity*, London, 1974.

————, 'Pakistani Ethnicity in Industrial Cities in Britain' in A. Cohen, ed., *Urban Ethnicity*, London, 1974.

Z. Dahya, 'Pakistani Wives in Britain', *Race*, 6, 3, 1965.

N. Daniel, *Islam, Europe and Empire*, Edinburgh, 1966.

————, *Islam and the West: the Making of an Image*, 2nd edn, Oxford, 1993.

BIBLIOGRAPHY

Dean Mahomet, *The Travels of Dean Mahomet*, Cork, 1794.

N. Deakin, ed., *Colour and the British Electorate, 1964*, London, 1965.

H. Ditmar, 'Somalis in limbo—longing for home', *New African*, January 1995.

C. Dixon, 'Lascars: The Forgotten Seamen' in R. Ommer and G. Panting, eds, *Working Men Who Got Wet*, Proceedings of the Fourth Conference of the Atlantic Canada Shipping Project July 24–July 26, 1980, Newfoundland, 1980.

N. Doku-Gryskiewicz, 'A Study of Adaptation of Turkish Migrant Workers to Living and Working in the United Kingdom', unpubl. Ph.D. thesis, University of London, 1979.

J. Donald and A. Rattansi, eds, *'Race', Culture and Difference*, London, 1992.

H. Donnan and P. Werbner, eds, *Economy and culture in Pakistan: migrants and cities in a Muslim society*, Basingstoke, 1991.

H. Donnan and M. O'Brien, 'Because you stick out, you stand out': Perceptions of Prejudice among Northern Ireland's Pakistanis' in P. Hainsworth, ed., *Divided Society: Ethnic Minorities and Racism in Northern Ireland*, London, 1998.

D. Drew and J. Gray, 'The Black-White gap in examination results: a statistical critique of a decade's research', *New Community*, 17, 2, April 1991.

I. Duffield, 'Duse Mohamed Ali, Afro-Asian solidarity and Pan-Africanism in early twentieth-century London' in J.S, Gundara and I. Duffield, eds, *Essays on the History of Blacks in Britain: from Roman times to mid-twentieth century*, Aldershot, 1992.

A. Dunlop, 'Lascars and Labourers: Reactions to the Indian Presence in the West of Scotland during the 1920s and 1930s', *Scottish Labour History Society Journal*, no. 25, 1990.

C. Dwyer, 'Constructions of Muslim Identity and the Contesting of Power: the Debate over Muslim Schools in the UK' (typescript with the author).

————and A. Meyer, 'The institutionalisation of Islam in the Netherlands and in the UK: the case of Islamic schools, *New Community*, 21, 1, January 1995.

J. Eade, 'Identity, Nation And Religion: Educated Young Bangladeshi Muslims In London's "East End"', *International Sociology*, vol. 9.

————, 'Nationalism and the quest for authenticity: the Bangladeshis in Tower Hamlets', *New Community*, 16, 4, July 1990.

————, *Routes and Beyond: Voices from Educationally Successful Bangladeshis*, London, 1994.

J. Egglestone, J. Dunn, M. Anjali and C. Wright, *Education for Some*, Stoke on Trent, 1986.

C.C. Eldridge, *England's Mission: the Imperial Idea in the Age of Gladstone and Disraeli, 1868–1880*, London, 1973.

J. Ellis, *Meeting Community Needs: A Study of Muslim Communities in Coventry*, CRER, Coventry, September 1991.

BIBLIOGRAPHY

C.F. El-Solh, 'Somalis in London's East End: a community striving for recognition', *New Community*, 17, 4, July 1991.

———, 'Arab Communities in Britain: Cleavages and Commonalities', *Islam and Christian–Muslim Relations*, 3, 2, December 1992.

———, '"Be true to your culture": Gender Tensions among Somali Muslims in Britain', *Immigrants and Minorities*, 12, 1, March 1993.

J. Essen and M. Ghodsian, 'The children of immigrants: School performance', *New Community*, winter 1979.

N. Evans, 'The South Wales Race Riots of 1919', *LLafur*, 3, 1, 1980.

———, 'Regulating the Reserve Army: Arabs, Blacks and the Local State in Cardiff, 1919–1945', *Immigrants and Minorities*, 4, 2, July 1985.

S.L. Evans and S. Bowlby, 'Crossing boundaries: Racialised gendering and the labour market experiences of Pakistani migrant women in Britain', *Women's Studies International Forum* (Online), vol. 23, issue 4.

M. Everest-Phillips, 'The Suburban King of Tartary', *Asian Affairs*, October, 1990. S. Fenton and A. Sadiq, *The sorrow in my heart*, London, 1993.

A.G.B. Fisher and H.J. Fisher, *Slavery and Muslim Society in Africa: the institution in Saharan and Sudanic Africa, and the trans-Saharan trade*, London, 1970.

E. Finch, *Wilfrid Scawen Blunt 1840–1922*, London, 1938.

M. Forward, 'Syed Ameer Ali: a bridge-builder?', *Islamic and Christian Muslim Relations*, 6, 1, 1995.

J.B. Fraser, *Narrative of the Residence of the Persian Princes in London in 1835 and 1836*, London, 1838.

P. Fryer, *Staying Power: the History of Black People in Britain*, London, 1984.

J. Fulton and P. Gee, eds, *Religion in Contemporary Europe*, Lampeter, 1994.

K. Gardner and A. Shukur, 'I'm Bengali, I'm Asian and I'm Living Here: the Changing Identity of British Bengalis' in R. Ballard, ed., *Desh Pardesh: the South Asian Presence in Britain*, London, 1994.

E. Gellner, *Postmodernism, Reason and Religion*, London, 1992.

Z. Gifford, *The Golden Thread: Asian Experiences of Post-Raj Britain*, London, 1990.

R. Gill, *Competing Convictions*, London, 1989.

C. Gillborn and C. Gipps, *Recent Research on the Achievements of Ethnic Minority Pupils*, London, 1996.

D. Gillborn, *'Race', Ethnicity and Education*, London, 1990.

S. Gilliat, 'Muslim Youth Organisations in Britain: a Descriptive Analysis', *American Journal of Islamic Social Sciences*, 14, 1, spring 1997.

P. Gordon and F. Klug, *New Right, New Racism*, London, 1986.

H. Goulbourne, ed., *Black Politics in Britain*, Aldershot, 1990.

G.F.I. Graham, *The Life and Work of Sir Syed Ahmad Khan*, Karachi, 1974.

Greater London Council, *A History of the Black Presence in Britain*, London, 1986.

BIBLIOGRAPHY

R. Geaves, *Sectarian Influences within Islam in Britain*, Leeds, 1996.

————, *The Sufis of Britain: an Exploration of Muslim Identity*, Cardiff, 2000.

D. Griffiths, 'Somali refugees in Tower Hamlets: clanship and new identities', *New Community*, 23, 1, January 1997.

R. Grinter, 'Transferring the National Curriculum Developments in an anti-racist campaign', *Multicultural Teaching*, 8, 3, summer 1990.

S. Guru, 'Struggle and Resistance: Punjabi women in Birmingham', unpubl. Ph.D. thesis, University of Keele, 1987.

R.N.M. Hallam, 'The Shi'a Imami Ismailia Community in Britain', unpubl. M.Phil. thesis, University of London, 1971.

F. Halliday, *Arabs in Exile:Yemeni Migrants in Urban Britain*, London, 1992.

————, 'The *Millet* of Manchester: Arab Merchants and Cotton Trade', *British Journal of Middle Eastern Studies*, 19, 2, 1992.

————, *Islam and the Myth of Confrontation: Religion and Politics in the Middle East*, London, 1995.

————, 'Orientalism and its Critics' in *Islam and the Myth of Confrontation: Religion and Politics in the Middle East*, London, 1995.

————, '"Islamophobia" Reconsidered', *Ethnic and Racial Studies*, 22, 5, September 1999.

A.H. Halsey, 'Changes in the Family', *Children and Society*, 7, 2, 1993.

M. Halstead, *Education, Justice and Cultural Diversity: An Examination of the Honeyford Affair, 1984–5*, Falmer, 1988.

J.M. Halstead, 'Some Reflections on the Debate about Music in Islam', *Muslim Education Quarterly*, 12, 1, 1994.

N. Harris, *The New Untouchables: Immigration and the New World Worker*, London, 1995.

N. Hawkes, *Immigrant Children in British Schools*, London, 1966.

T. Heath and R. Hill, *Asylum Statistics United Kingdom 2001*, London, 31 July 2002.

C.T.R. Hewer, *British Muslims and State Education: Introductory Review*, St Catherine's Conference, Windsor, 23–25 November 1994.

D. Hiro, *Black British, White British: a History of Race Relation in Britain*, London, 1992.

S.Y. Ho and J. Henderson, 'Locality and the variability of ethnic employment in Britain', *Journal of Ethnic and Migration Studies*, 25, 2, April 1999.

E. Hobsbawm, *Age Of Extremes: the Short Twentieth Century, 1914–1991*, London, 1994.

C. Holmes, *John Bull's Island: Immigration and British Society, 1871–1971*, Basingstoke, 1988.

————, *A Tolerant Country?: Immigrants, refugees and minorities in Britain*, London, 1991.

H.R. Hones and M. Davenport, 'The Pakistani Community in Dundee: a

Study of its Growth and Demographic Structure', *Scottish Geographical Magazine*, 88, 2, 1972.

H. Hoodfar, 'The Veil in their Minds and in their Heads', *Resources for Feminist Research*, 22, 3–4, 1993.

K. Hunter, *History of Pakistanis in Britain*, Norwich, 1963.

A. Ibrahim, 'The ummah and tomorrows world', *Futures*, vol. 26, 1991.

M. Iqbal, *Islamic Education and Single-Sex Schools*, Union of Muslim Organisations of UK and Eire, London, 1975.

———, 'Education and Islam in Britain—a Muslim view', *New Community*, 5, 4, 1977.

G. Irwin and S. Dunn, *Ethnic Minorities in Northern Ireland*, Centre for the Study of Conflict, University of Ulster, Coleraine, 1997.

Islam and State Education, St Catherine's Conference Report no. 46, Cumberland Lodge, Windsor, November 1994.

Islamic Human Rights Commission (IHRC), *The Oldham Riots: discrimination, deprivation and communal tension in the United Kingdom*, London, 2001.

J. Jacobson, 'Religion and Ethnicity: Dual and Alternative Sources of Identity among young British Pakistanis', *Ethnic and Racial Studies*, 20, 2, April 1997.

R. Jeffcote, *Ethnic Minorities and Education*, Milton Keynes, 1982.

———, *Ethnic Minorities and Education*, London, 1984.

D. Joly, *Ethnic Minorities and Education in Britain: Interaction between the Muslim Community and Birmingham Schools*, Research Paper no. 41, CSIC, Birmingham, March 1989.

T. Jones, *Britain's Ethnic Minorities: an analysis of the Labour Force Survey*, London, 1993.

R. Kabbani, *Letter to Christendom*, London, 1989.

N. Kabir, 'The Structure of "Revealed" Preference: Race, Community and Female Labour Supply in the London Clothing Industry', *Development and Change*, vol. 25, 1994.

M.H. Kahin, *Educating Somali Children in Britain*, Stoke on Trent, 1997.

G. Karmi, 'The Health Status and Health Beliefs of the London Migrant Communities', *International Migration*, 29, 1, 1990.

———, 'Identity and Sense of Belonging', unpubl. paper given at Second Arab Communities Conference, Imperial College, London, November 1993.

V. Karn, ed., *Ethnicity in the 1991 Census: Employment, education and housing among ethnic minority populations of Britain*, London, 1996.

A.M.V. Karim, 'Issues in Teacher Education in the Contemporary Ismaili Community', unpubl. M.Ed. dissertation, University of London, 1986.

R. Kaye, 'The politics of religious slaughter of animals: Strategies for ethno-religious political action', *New Community*, 19, 2, January 1993.

BIBLIOGRAPHY

G.W. Kearsley and S.R. Srivastava, 'The Spatial Evolution of Glasgow's Asian Community', *Scottish Geographical Magazine*, 90, 2, 1974.

R. Keshavjee, *Mysticism and the Plurality of Meaning: the Case of the Ismailis of Rural Iran*, London, 1998.

A. Khan, 'Welcome to the Quaid-I-Azam League' in *Hit Racism for Six: Race and Cricket in England Today*, London, 1996.

V.S. Khan, 'Purdah in the British situation' in D.L. Barker and S. Allen, eds, *Dependence and Exploitation in Work and Marriage*, London, 1976.

————, ed., *Minority Families in Britain: Support and Stress*, London, 1979.

————, 'Asian Women in Britain: Strategies of Adjustment of Indian and Pakistani Migrants' in A. de Souza, ed., *Women in Contemporary India and South Asia*, New Delhi, 1980.

K. Knott and S. Khokher, 'Religious and Ethnic Identity among Young Muslim Women in Bradford', *New Community*, 19, 4, 1993.

A. Kose, 'Conversion to Islam: a Study of Native British Converts', unpubl. Ph.D. thesis, University of London, 1994.

————, *Conversion to Islam*, London, 1996.

T. Kucukcan, 'The Politics of Ethnicity, Identity and Religion among Turks in London', unpubl. Ph.D thesis, University of Warwick, 1996.

————, 'Continuity and Change: Young Turks in London' in S. Vertovec and A. Rogers, eds, *Muslim European Youth: Reproducing Ethnicity, Religion, and Culture*, Aldershot, 1998.

A. Kundnani, *From Oldham to Bradford: the violence of the violated*, London, 2001.

F. Kysel, 'Ethnic background and examination results', *Educational Research*, 30, 2, June 1988.

S. Ladbury, 'The Turkish Cypriots: Ethnic Relations in London and Cyprus' in J.L. Watson, ed., *Between Two Cultures: Migrants and Minorities in Britain*, Oxford, 1977.

S. Lahiri, *Indians in Britain: Anglo-Indian Encounters, Race and Identity, 1880–1939*, London, 2000.

R.I. Lawless, 'Religion and Politics among Arab Seafarers in Britain in the Early Twentieth Century', *Islam and Christian–Muslim Relations*, vol. 5, no. 1, 1994.

————, *From Ta'izz to Tyneside: an Arab Community in the North–East of England during the Early Twentieth Century*, Exeter, 1995.

M. Lelohe, 'The Asian vote in a northern city' in H. Goulbourne, ed., *Black Politics in Britain*, Aldershot, 1990.

B. Lewis and D. Schnapper, eds, *Muslims in Europe*, London, 1994.

P. Lewis, *Islamic Britain: Religion, Politics and Identity among British Muslims: Bradford in the 1990s*, London, 1994.

K. Little, *Negroes in Britain: a Study of Racial Relations in English Society*, 2nd edn, London, 1972.

BIBLIOGRAPHY

P. Loizos, 'Aspects of Pluralism in Cyprus', *New Community*, 1, 4, summer 1972.

G. Lomas, 'Employment and economic activity—1972 census data', *New Community*, 7, 2, 1979.

E. Longford, *Victoria R.I.*, London, 1964.

D.A. Lorimer, *Colour, class and the Victorians: English attitudes to the Negro in the mid-nineteenth century*, Leicester, 1978

M. Mac an Ghaill, 'Coming of age in 1980s England: reconceptualising black students' schooling experience' in D. Gill, B. Mayor and M. Blair, eds, *Racism and Education: Structures And Strategies*, London, 1992.

S. MacLoughlin, '"An Underclass in Purdah"? Discrepant Representations of Identity and the Experiences of Young-British-Asian-Muslim Women', *Journal of the John Rylands University of Manchester Library*, 1998.

B. Maan, *The New Scots: the Story of Asians in Scotland*, Edinburgh, 1992.

M. Macy, 'Class, Gender and Religious Influences on Changing Patterns of Pakistani Muslim Male Violence in Bradford', *Ethnic and Racial Studies*, 22, 5, September 1998.

H. Malik, *Sir Sayyid Ahmad Khan and Muslim Modernization in India and Pakistan*, New York, 1980.

P. Mandaville, *Transnational Muslim Politics: Reimagining the Umma*, London, 2001.

G. Marshall, *Oxford Dictionary of Sociology*, London, 1998.

N.I. Matar, 'Muslims in Seventeenth-Century England', *Journal of Islamic Studies*, 8, 1, 1997.

N. Matar, *Islam in Britain, 1558–1685*, Cambridge, 1998.

R. May and R. Cohen, 'The Interaction Between Race and Colonialism: a Case Study of the Liverpool Race Riots of 1919', *Race and Class*, XVI, 2, 1974.

H. Mayhew, *London Labour and the London Poor*, vols III and IV, New York, 1968.

I. McDonald and S. Ugra, *Anyone For Cricket?*, Centre for Sport Development Research, Roehampton Institute, London, in association with The Centre for New Ethnicities Research, University of East London, 1998.

C. McEvoy, 'The Segregation of Asian Immigrants in Glasgow: a Note', *Scottish Geographical Magazine*, 94, 3, 1978.

J. McNeal, 'Education' in S. Abbott, ed., *The Prevention of Racial Discrimination in Britain*, London, 1971.

M. Mead, 'Socialization and Enculturation', *Current Anthopology*, 4, 2, 1963.

H. Metcalf, T. Modood and S. Virdee, *Asian Self-Employment: the interaction of culture and economics in England*, London, 1996.

D. Milner, *Children and Race*, London, 1975.

H. Mirza, *Young, Female and Black*, London, 1992.

BIBLIOGRAPHY

K. Mirza, *A Silent Cry: Second Generation Bradford Muslim Women Speak*, Research Paper no. 43, CSIC, Birmingham, September 1989.

S. Mitter, 'Rise of a semi-proletariat: Bangladeshi female homeworkers in the London rag trade', *International Labour Studies Newsletter*, no. 12, April 1984.

————, *Common Fate, Common Bond: women in the global economy*, London, 1985.

T. Modood, *Not Easy Being British: Colour, Culture and Citizenship*, London, 1992.

————, *Muslim Identity: Real or Imagined? A discussion by John Rex and Tariq Modood*, CSIC Papers no. 12, Birmingham, November 1994.

————*et al., Ethnic Minorities In Britain: Diversity and Disadvantage*, London, 1997.

T. Modood, S. Beishon, and S. Virdee, *Changing Ethnic Identities*, London, 1994.

Z. Muhsen with A. Croft, *Sold*, London, 1994.

W. Muir, *Life of Mahomet*, London, 1858–61.

P. Mule and D. Barthel, 'The Return to the Veil: Individual Autonomy vs. Social Esteem', *Sociological Forum*, vol. 7, June 1992.

K. Murad, *Muslim Youth in the West, Towards a New Education Strategy*, Leicester, 1986.

C. Nagel, 'Hidden minorities and the politics of 'race': the case of British Arab activists in London', *Journal of Ethnic and Migration Studies*, 27, 3, July 2001.

Need for Reform: Muslims and the law in multi-faith Britain, Memorandum submitted by the UK Action Committee on Islamic Affairs, autumn 1993.

J.S. Nielsen, 'Muslim immigration and settlement in Britain', Research Papers: Muslims in Europe, no. 21, CSIC, Birmingham, 1984.

————, *A Survey of British Local Authority Response To Muslim Needs*, Research Paper no. 30/31, CSIC, Birmingham, June/September 1986.

————, 'Muslims in Britain: Searching for an Identity?', *New Community*, 13, 3, spring 1987.

————, 'Muslims in English Schools', *Journal of the Institute of Muslim Minority Affairs*, 10, 1, January 1989.

————, 'A Muslim Agenda for Britain: Some Reflections', *New Community*, 17, 3, April 1991.

————, *Muslims in Western Europe*, Edinburgh, 1992.

————, *Emerging Claims of Muslim Populations in Matters of Family Law in Europe*, CSIC Papers, no. 10, CSIC, Birmingham, November 1993.

G. Nonneman, T. Niblock and B. Szajkowski, eds, *Muslim Communities in the New Europe*, Reading, 1996.

R. Oakley, 'The Cypriots in Britain', *Race Today*, no. 2, 1970.

BIBLIOGRAPHY

————, 'Cypriot Migration and Settlement in Britain', unpubl. D.Phil. thesis, University of Oxford, 1971.

————, 'Family, Kinship and Patronage: The Cypriot Migration to Britain' in V.S. Khan, ed., *Minority Families in Britain: Support and Stress*, London, 1979.

————, *Changing Patterns of Distribution of Cypriot Settlement*, Research Papers in Ethnic Relations, no. 5, CRER, Coventry, 1987.

————, 'The Control of Cypriot Migration to Britain Between the Wars', *Immigrants and Minorities*, 6, 1, March 1987.

L.A. Odeh, 'Post-Colonial Feminism and the Veil: Thinking the Difference', *Feminist Review*, no. 43, 1993.

A. Osler, *Speaking Out: Black Girls in Britain*, London, 1989.

D. Owen, *Ethnic Minorities In Great Britain: Settlement Patterns*, 1991 Census Statistical Paper no. 1, CRER, Coventry, November 1992.

————, *Ethnic minorities in Great Britain: Age and gender structure*, 1991 Census Statistical Paper no. 2, CRER, Coventry, February 1993.

————, *Ethnic Minorities in Great Britain: Economic Characteristics*, 1991 Census Statistical Paper no. 3, CRER, Coventry, March 1993.

————, *Ethnic Minorities in Great Britain: Housing and family characteristics*, 1991 Census Statistical Paper no. 4, CRER, Coventry, April 1993.

————, *Country of Birth: Settlement patterns*, 1991 Census Statistical Paper no. 5, CRER, Coventry, December 1993.

F. Palmer, ed., *Anti-Racism: an Assault on Education and Value*, London, 1986.

P. Parmar, 'Gender, race and class: Asian women in resistance' in Centre for Contemporary Cultural Studies, *The Empire Strikes Back: Race and racism in 70s Britain*, London, 1982.

P. Panayi, *Immigration, ethnicity and racism in Britain, 1815–1945*, Manchester, 1994.

P. I. Panayiotopoulos, 'Challenging orthodoxies: Cypriot entrepreneurs in the London garment industry', *New Community*, 22, 3, July 1996.

M. Parker-Jenkins, *Children of Islam: a Teacher's Guide to Meeting the Needs of Muslim Pupils*, Stoke on Trent, 1995.

S.A. Pasha, 'Muslim family law in Britain', unpubl. paper presented at House of Commons, 20 January 1977.

N. Patel, 'Psychological disturbance and social support: a comparison between immigrant Asian women and indigenous population', unpubl. M.Sc thesis, University of Hull, 1989.

P. Patel, 'Alert for Action', *Feminist Review*, no. 37, spring 1991.

R. Patrick, 'Intercommunal conflict in Cyprus—some demographic and geopolitical consequences', *New Community*, 2, 2, spring 1973.

S. Patterson, *Immigration and Race Relations, 1960–1967*, London, 1969.

C. Peach, 'Estimating the growth of the Bangladeshi population of Great Britain', *New Community*, 16, 4, July 1990.

BIBLIOGRAPHY

————, 'Estimates of the 1991 Muslim Population of Great Britain', Paper given to the Exploratory Seminar on Statistics and the UK Religious Communities, University of Derby, 24–25 May, 1994.

————, ed., *Ethnicity in the 1991 Census: the ethnic minority populations of Great Britain*, London, 1996.

————, ed., *Ethnicity in the 1991 Census: Social geography and ethnicity in Britain—geographical spread, spatial concentration and internal migration*, London, 1996.

D. Pearl, 'The family, the law and the ethnic minorities: a bibliographic essay', *Sage Race Relations Abstracts*, vol. 5, no. 2, May 1980.

A. Phizacklea and C. Wolkowitz, *Homeworking Women: Gender, Racism and Class*, London, 1995.

S. Poulter, *Asian Traditions and English Law: a Handbook*, Stoke on Trent, 1990.

————, 'The Muslim Community and English Law', *Islam and Christian–Muslim Relations*, 3, 2, December 1992.

R. Preiswerk and D. Perrot, *Ethnocentrism and History: Africa, Asia and Indian America in Western Textbooks*, London, 1978.

K. Purdam, 'The Impacts of Democracy on Identity: Muslim Councillors and their Experiences of Local Politics In Britain', unpubl. Ph.D. thesis, University of Manchester, 1997.

————, 'The Political Identities of Muslim Local Councillors in Britain, *Local Government Studies*', 26, 1, spring 2000.

W.H. Quilliam, *Fanatics and Fanaticism: a Lecture*, Vernon Temperance Hall, Liverpool, 1890.

S.P. Rack, 'Diagnosing Mental Illness: Asians and the psychiatric services' in V.S. Khan, ed., *Minority Families In Britain: Support and Stress*, London, 1979.

M. Rafiq, 'Ethnicity and Enterprise: a comparison of Muslim and non-Muslim owned Asian businesses in Britain', *New Community*, 19, 1, 1992.

F. Rahman, *Islam*, Chicago, 1979.

R. Ramdin, *The Making of the Black Working Class in Britain*, London, 1987.

S. Randall, 'The New Right, Racism and Education in Thatcher's Britain', *Sage Race Relations Abstracts*, 13, 3, August 1988.

R.N. Rapoport, P.M. Fogarty and R. Rapoport, eds, *Families in Britain*, London, 1982.

P. Ratcliffe, ed., *Ethnicity in the 1991 Census: Social geography and ethnicity in Britain: Geographical spread, spatial concentration and internal migration*, vol. 3, London, 1996.

A. Rattansi, 'Changing the Subject? Racism, Culture And Education' in J. Donald and A. Rattansi, eds, *'Race', Culture and Difference*, London, 1992.

M.S. Raza, *Islam in Britain: Past, Present and Future*, 2nd edn, Leicester, 1993.

J. Rex and R. Moore, *Race, Community and Conflict*, London, 1967.

J.M. Ritchie, 'A Survey of the Muslim Community of Glasgow', September 1972, typescript available at CSIC, Birmingham.

BIBLIOGRAPHY

————, 'Report on the Muslim Community in South Shields', October 1972, typescript available at CSIC, Birmingham.

F. Robinson, *Separatism among Indian Muslims: the Politics of the United Provinces' Muslims 1860–1923*, Delhi, 1993.

V. Robinson, 'Correlates of Asian immigration: 1959–1974', *New Community*, 8, 1–2, 1980.

————, *Transients, Settlers, and Refugees: Asians in Britain*, Oxford, 1986.

M. Rodinson, *Europe and the Mystique of Islam*, London, 1991.

E.J.B. Rose, *Colour and Citizenship: a Report on British Race Relations*, London, 1969.

Runnymede Research Report, *Racism, Anti-Racism and School: a summary of the Burnage report*, London, 1989.

Runnymede Trust, *Islamophobia: a Challenge for us all*, London, 1997.

A. Saeed, N. Blain and D. Forbes, 'New Ethnic and National Questions in Scotland: post-British Identities among Glasgow Pakistani Teenagers', *Ethnic and Racial Studies*, 22, 5, September 1999.

S. Saggar, 'The General Election and Beyond', *Connections*, Commission for Racial Equality, summer 2001.

————and A. Geddes, 'Negative and positive racialisation: re-examining ethnic minority political representation in the UK', *Journal of Ethnic and Migration Studies*, 26, 1, January 2000.

E. Said, *Orientalism*, London, 1985.

J. Salt, *Imperialism, Evangelism and the Ottoman Armenians, 1878–1896*, London, 1993.

J. Salter, *The Asiatic in England: Sketches of Sixteen Years' Work among Orientals*, London, 1873.

Y. Samad, 'Imagining a British Muslim Identification' in Vertovec and Rogers, eds, *Muslim European Youth: Reproducing Ethnicity, Religion and Culture*, Aldershot, 1998.

Y. Samad and J. Eade, *Community Perceptions of Forced Marriage*, Foreign and Commonwealth Office, 2002.

G. Sarwar, *Muslims and Education in the UK*, Muslim Education Trust, 1983.

B.S. Sayyid, *A Fundamental Fear: Eurocentrism and the Emergence of Islamism*, London, 1997.

E. Scantlebury, 'Muslims In Manchester: the depiction of a religious community', *New Community*, 21, 3, July 1995.

C. Searle and A. Shaif, '"Drinking from one pot": Yemeni unity, at home and overseas', *Race and Class*, 32, 4, 1991.

L. Sfeir, 'The Status of Muslim Women in Sport: Conflict between Cultural Tradition and Modernization', *International Review for the Sociology of Sport*, 20, 4, 1985.

W.A.R. Shadid and P.S. van Koningsveld, eds, *The Integration of Islam and Hinduism in Western Europe*, Kampen, 1991.

BIBLIOGRAPHY

————, eds., *Political Participation and Identities of Muslims in Non-Muslim States*, Kampen, 1996.

S. Shaikh and A. Kelly, 'To mix or not to mix: Pakistani girls in British schools', *Educational Research*, 31, 1, February 1989.

R. Sharif, *Interviews with Young Muslim Women of Pakistani Origin*, Research Paper no. 27, CSIC, Birmingham, September, 1985.

S. Sharma, J. Hutnyk and A. Sharma, eds, *Dis-Orienting Rhythms: the Politics of the New Asian Dance Music*, London, 1996.

A. Shaw, *A Pakistani community in Britain*, Oxford, 1988.

————, 'The Pakistani Community in Oxford' in R. Ballard, ed., *Desh Pardesh: the South Asian Presence in Britain*, London, 1994.

M.A. Sherif, *Searching for Solace: a Biography of Abdullah Yusuf Ali, Interpreter of the Quran*, Kuala Lumpur, 1994.

M. Sherwood, 'Race, nationality and employment among Lascar seamen, 1660 to 1945', *New Community*, 17, 2, January 1991.

————, 'Racism And Resistance: Cardiff in the 1930s and 1940s', *Llafur*, 5, 4, 1991.

F.O. Shyllon, *Black People in Britain, 1555–1833*, London, 1977.

H. Siddiqui, 'Winning Freedoms', *Feminist Review*, no. 37, spring 1991.

————, 'Generating 'Power' Without Politics', Speech at Conference on the Future of Muslims in Britain, London, 14 July 1990.

M.H. Siddiqui, 'Muslims in a non-Muslim Society', *Brighton Islamic Centre Bulletin*, 15, 3, July–September, 1991.

Y.S. Sikand, 'The Origins and Growth of the *Tablighi Jamaat* in Britain', *Islam and Christian–Muslim Relations*, 9, 2, 1998.

A.K. Singh, *Indian Students in Britain: a survey of their adjustment and attitudes*, Bombay, *c.* 1963.

D.J. Smith, *Racial Disadvantage in Britain: The PEP Report*, Harmondsworth, 1977.

S.R. Sonyel, *The Silent Minority: Turkish Muslim Children In British Schools*, Cambridge, 1988.

C. Stewart, trans., *Travels of Mirza Abu Taleb Khan in Asia, Africa and Europe during the years 1797 to 1803*, London, 1814.

M. Stopes-Roe and R. Cochrane, 'Marriage in two cultures', *British Journal of Social Psychology*, vol. 27, 1988.

M. Storkey, *Identifying the Cypriot Community from the 1991 Census*, London, 1993.

Southall Black Sisters, *Forced Marriage: an abuse of human rights one year after 'A Choice by Right'*, Interim Report, Southall, July 2001.

S. Sulaimani, 'The Multiple and Changing Identities of Young Pakistani Women in Woking', Safer Surrey Partnership, Woking, 2000.

H. Summerfield, 'Patterns of Adaptation: Somali and Bangladeshi Women in

BIBLIOGRAPHY

Britain' in G. Buijs, ed., *Migrant Women: Crossing Boundaries and Changing Identities*, Oxford, 1993.

M. Swann, *Education For All: the report of the Committee of Inquiry into the education of children from Ethnic Minority Groups*, London, 1985.

L. Tabili, *'We Ask for British Justice':Workers and Racial Difference in Late Imperial Britain*, New York, 1994.

J.H. Taylor, *The half-way generation: a study of Asian youths in Newcastle upon Tyne*, Windsor, 1976.

M.J. Taylor with S. Hegarty, *The Best of Both Worlds...?: a Review of Research into the Education of Pupils of South Asian Origin*, Windsor, 1985.

M.J. Taylor, *Worlds Apart?: A Review of Research into the Education of Pupils of Cypriot, Italian, Ukranian and Vietnamese Origin, Liverpool Blacks and Gypsies*, Windsor, 1987.

W.M. Thackeray, *The Four Georges*, London, 1856.

The Bradford Commission Report, London, November, 1996.

The Home Office, *Second Report of Commonwealth Immigrants Advisory Council* [CIAC], London, 1964.

The Islamic Shari'a Council: an Introduction, London, 1995.

Muslim Directory, London, 2000.

The Muslim Manifesto—a strategy for survival, The Muslim Institute, London, 15 June 1990.

H. Tinker, *A new system of slavery: the export of Indian labour overseas, 1830–1920*, London, 1974.

S. Tomlinson, 'Curriculum option choices in multi-ethnic schools' in B. Troyna, ed., *Racial Inequality in Education*, London, 1987.

H.E.R. Townsend, *Immigrant Pupils in England: The LEA Response*, Windsor, 1971.

————and E.M. Brittan, *Organization in Multiracial Schools*, Windsor, 1972.

B.S. Turner, *Orientalism, Postmodernism and Globalism*, London, 1994.

F. Ulug, 'A study of Conflicting Cultural Pressures with Particular Attention to the Turkish Cypriot Community and a Small Group of Secondary School Turkish Girls now Living in North London', unpubl. B.Ed. dissertation, Middlesex Polytechnic, 1981.

Union of Muslim Organisations of UK and Ireland, *A record of 25 years achievement*, London, 1995.

R. Unsworth, 'First and Second Generation Pakistanis in Slough: Social and Spatial Assimilation', unpubl. D.Phil. thesis, University of Cambridge, 1986.

G.K. Verma and B. Ashworth, *Ethnicity and Educational Achievement in British Schools*, London, 1986.

S. Vertovec and C. Peach, eds, *Islam In Europe: Migration, Minorities and Citizenship*, London, 1997.

BIBLIOGRAPHY

————, eds, *Islam In Europe: the Politics of Religion and Community*, Basingstoke, 1997.

S. Vertovec and S. Rogers, eds, *Muslim European Youth: Reproducing Ethnicity, Religion, and Culture*, Aldershot, 1998.

R. Visram, *Ayahs, Lascars and Princes: the Story of Indians in Britain, 1700–1947*, London, 1986.

————, 'The First World War and the Indian Soldiers', *Indo-British Review*, 16, 2, June 1989.

————, *Asians in Britain: 400 Years of History*, London, 2002.

J. Waardenburg, 'Muslim Associations and Official Bodies in Some European Countries' in W.A.R. Shadid and P.S. van Koningsveld, eds, *The Integration of Islam and Hinduism in Western Europe*, Kampen, 1991.

B. Wade and P. Souter, *Continuing to Think: the British Asian Girl*, Clevedon, 1992.

D. Waines, *An Introduction to Islam*, Cambridge, 1995.

J. Walvin, *Black and White: the Negro and English Society, 1555–1945*, London, 1973.

W.M. Watt, *The influence of Islam on medieval Europe*, Islamic Surveys no. 9, Edinburgh, 1972.

P. Weller, A. Feldman and K. Purdam, *Religious Discrimination in England and Wales*, Home Office Research Study 220, London, 2001.

P. Werbner, 'Avoiding the ghetto: Pakistani migrants and settlement shifts in Manchester', *New Community*, vol. 7, 1979.

————, 'From rags to riches: Manchester Pakistanis in the textile trade', *New Community*, 8, 1–2, 1980.

————, *The Migration Process: Capital, Gifts and Offerings among British Pakistanis*, Oxford, 1990.

————, 'Factionalism and Violence in the British Pakistani Communal Politics' in H. Donnan and P. Werbner, eds, *Economy and culture in Pakistan: migrants and cities in a Muslim society*, Basingstoke, 1991.

————, 'Islamic Radicalism and the Gulf War: Lay Preachers and Political Dissent among British Pakistanis' in B. Lewis and D. Schnapper, eds, *Muslims in Europe*, London, 1994.

————, 'Political Spaces, Political Voices: Gender, Feminism and Aspects of British Muslim Participation in the Public Sphere' in W.A.R. Shadid and P.S. van Koningsveld, eds, *Political Participation and Identities of Muslims in Non-Muslim States*, Kampen, 1996.

————and M. Anwar, eds, *Black and Ethnic Leaderships in Britain: The Cultural Dimensions of Political Action*, London, 1991.

J. West and S. Pilgrim, 'South Asian women in employment: the impact of migration, ethnic origin and the local economy', *New Community*, 21, 3, July 1995.

BIBLIOGRAPHY

I. Wilkinson, *Muslim Beliefs and Practices in a Non-Muslim Country: a Study of Rochdale*, Research Papers, Muslims in Europe, no. 39, CSIC, Birminghan, September 1988.

A. Wilson, 'A burning fever: the isolation of Asian women in Britain', *Race and Class*, 20, 2, 1978.

C. Wright, 'Early education: multiracial primary school classrooms' in D. Gill, B. Mayor and M. Blair, eds, *Racism And Education: Structures And Strategies*, London, 1992.

D. Wright, *The Persians amongst the English: Episodes in Anglo-Persian History*, London, 1985.

N. Yavari, 'The Evolving Nature of the Shari'a', supplement to *The Ismaili United Kingdom*, 1999.

K. Young and N. Connelly, *Policy and Practice in the Multi-racial City*, London, 1981.

Y. Zaki, 'The Teaching of Islam in Schools: A Muslim Viewpoint', *British Journal of Religious Education*, 5, 1, autumn 1982.

Newspapers and journals

British Muslims Monthly Survey (*BMMS*), Birmingham
The Crescent, Liverpool
Dail Jang
Daily Sketch
Daily Telegraph
The Economist
The Guardian
Impact International, London
The Independent
Indian Magazine And Review
Islamic Review, Woking
Islamic Review and Muslim India, Woking
Islamic World, Liverpool
Jewish Chronicle
Keighley News
Liverpool Review
Muslim Directory
Muslim News, London
Muslim Outlook, London
New Statesman
Public Advertiser
Q-News
Race and Immigration: Runnymede Trust Bulletin
Shields Daily Gazette, South Shields

BIBLIOGRAPHY

Show Case Arts, London
Social Trends
South Wales Daily News, Cardiff
The Observer
The Porcupine, Liverpool
The Seaman
The Times
The Times Educational Supplement
UK Ismaili
Western Mail, Cardiff
Yorkshire Post

ACKNOWLEDGEMENTS

At Royal Holloway, University of London, my thanks go to June Jackson for her endless supply of positive support; Pene Corfiel for her helpful comments on the first draft of the book; Francis Robinson for his supportive interest in this whole project; and the College's library staff, whose help was invaluable in making source materials available. In addition, I would like to thank Duna Sabri, Fuad Nahdi and Shagufta Yaqub, and to all those in the Muslim communities around Britain, especially in Egham, Woking, Slough, Cardiff and London, for their hospitality, for giving their time to discuss British Muslim themes and issues, and for offering advice and suggestions. Many thanks also to Christopher Hurst and Michael Dwyer at Hurst & Co. for their time and effort in getting this book ready for publication.

My final thanks go to my sons Akbar and Zafar, who have kept me in good humour, and to Sarah, my wife, for her encouragement and all the help she has given me throughout the preparation of this book. Without her support it would most certainly not have seen the light of day.

INDEX

INDEX

INDEX

INDEX